Palgrave Studies in the History of Social Movements

Series Editors

Stefan Berger, Institute for Social Movements, Ruhr University Bochum, Bochum, Germany

Holger Nehring, Contemporary European History, University of Stirling, Stirling, UK

INSTITUT FÜR SOZIALE BEWEGUNGEN

Around the world, social movements have become legitimate, yet contested, actors in local, national and global politics and civil society, yet we still know relatively little about their longer histories and the trajectories of their development. This series seeks to promote innovative historical research on the history of social movements in the modern period since around 1750. We bring together conceptually-informed studies that analyse labour movements, new social movements and other forms of protest from early modernity to the present. We conceive of 'social movements' in the broadest possible sense, encompassing social formations that lie between formal organisations and mere protest events. We also offer a home for studies that systematically explore the political, social, economic and cultural conditions in which social movements can emerge. We are especially interested in transnational and global perspectives on the history of social movements, and in studies that engage critically and creatively with political, social and sociological theories in order to make historically grounded arguments about social movements. This new series seeks to offer innovative historical work on social movements, while also helping to historicise the concept of 'social movement'. It hopes to revitalise the conversation between historians and historical sociologists in analysing what Charles Tilly has called the 'dynamics of contention'.

Stefan Berger · Stefano Musso ·
Christian Wicke
Editors

Deindustrialisation in Twentieth-Century Europe

The Northwest of Italy and the Ruhr Region in Comparison

palgrave
macmillan

Editors
Stefan Berger
Institute for Social Movements
Ruhr University Bochum
Bochum, Germany

Stefano Musso
Department of Historical Studies
University of Turin
Turin, Italy

Christian Wicke
Department of History and Art History
Utrecht University
Utrecht, The Netherlands

ISSN 2634-6559 ISSN 2634-6567 (electronic)
Palgrave Studies in the History of Social Movements
ISBN 978-3-030-89630-0 ISBN 978-3-030-89631-7 (eBook)
https://doi.org/10.1007/978-3-030-89631-7

Cover image: Duisburg Landschaftspark © Christian Wicke

This Palgrave Macmillan imprint is published by the registered company Springer Nature Switzerland AG
The registered company address is: Gewerbestrasse 11, 6330 Cham, Switzerland

Series Editors' Preface

Around the world, social movements have become legitimate, yet contested, actors in local, national and global politics and civil society, yet we still know relatively little about their longer histories and the trajectories of their development. Our series reacts to what can be described as a recent boom in the history of social movements. We can observe a development from the crisis of labor history in the 1980s to the boom in research on social movements in the 2000s. The rise of historical interests in the development of civil society and the role of strong civil societies as well as non-governmental organizations in stabilizing democratically constituted polities has strengthened the interest in social movements as a constituent element of civil societies.

In different parts of the world, social movements continue to have a strong influence on contemporary politics. In Latin America, trade unions, labor parties and various left-of-center civil society organizations have succeeded in supporting left-of-center governments. In Europe, peace movements, ecological movements and alliances intent on campaigning against poverty and racial discrimination and discrimination on the basis of gender and sexual orientation have been able to set important political agendas for decades. In other parts of the world, including Africa, India and South East Asia, social movements have played a significant role in various forms of community building and community politics. The contemporary political relevance of social movements has undoubtedly contributed to a growing historical interest in the topic.

Contemporary historians are not only beginning to historicize these relatively recent political developments; they are also trying to relate them to a longer history of social movements, including traditional labor organizations, such as working-class parties and trade unions. In the longue durée, we recognize that social movements are by no means a recent phenomenon and are not even an exclusively modern phenomenon, although we realize that the onset of modernity emanating from Europe and North America across the wider world from the eighteenth century onward marks an important departure point for the development of civil societies and social movements.

In the nineteenth and twentieth centuries, the dominance of national history over all other forms of history writing led to a thorough nationalisation of the historical sciences. Hence, social movements have been examined traditionally within the framework of the nation state. Only during the last two decades have historians begun to question the validity of such methodological nationalism and to explore the development of social movements in comparative, connective and transnational perspective taking into account processes of transfer, reception and adaptation. While our book series does not preclude work that is still being carried out within national frameworks (for, clearly, there is a place for such studies, given the historical importance of the nation state in history), it hopes to encourage comparative and transnational histories on social movements.

At the same time as historians have begun to research the history of those movements, a range of social theorists, from Jürgen Habermas to Pierre Bourdieu and from Slavoj Žižek to Alain Badiou as well as Ernesto Laclau and Chantal Mouffe to Miguel Abensour, to name but a few, have attempted to provide philosophical-cum-theoretical frameworks in which to place and contextualize the development of social movements. History has arguably been the most empirical of all the social and human sciences, but it will be necessary for historians to explore further to what extent these social theories can be helpful in guiding and framing the empirical work of the historian in making sense of the historical development of social movements. Hence, the current series is also hoping to make a contribution to the ongoing dialogue between social theory and the history of social movements.

This series seeks to promote innovative historical research on the history of social movements in the modern period since around 1750. We bring together conceptually-informed studies that analyze labor movements, new social movements and other forms of protest from early modernity to the present. With this series, we seek to revive, within the context of historiographical developments since the 1970s, a conversation between historians on the one hand and sociologists, anthropologists and political scientists on the other.

Unlike most of the concepts and theories developed by social scientists, we do not see social movements as directly linked, a priori, to processes of social and cultural change and therefore do not adhere to a view that distinguishes between old (labor) and new (middle-class) social movements. Instead, we want to establish the concept "social movement" as a heuristic device that allows historians of the nineteenth and twentieth centuries to investigate social and political protests in novel settings. Our aim is to historicize notions of social and political activism in order to highlight different notions of political and social protest on both left and right.

Hence, we conceive of "social movements" in the broadest possible sense, encompassing social formations that lie between formal organizations and mere protest events. But we also include processes of social and cultural change more generally in our understanding of social movements: this goes back to nineteenth-century understandings of "social movement" as processes of social and cultural change more generally. We also offer a home for studies that systematically explore the political, social, economic and cultural conditions in which social movements can emerge. We are especially interested in transnational and global perspectives on the history of social movements, and in studies that engage critically and creatively with political, social and sociological theories in order to make historically grounded arguments about social movements. In short, this series seeks to offer innovative historical work on social movements, while also helping to historicize the concept of "social movement". It also hopes to revitalize the conversation between historians and historical sociologists in analyzing what Charles Tilly has called the "dynamics of contention".

The contributors to this edited collection by Stefan Berger, Stefano Musso and Christian Wicke provide a sustained comparison about the deindustrialization processes in two of Western Europe's most important industrial regions, the Ruhr region of Germany and the industrial triangle between Genoa, Milan and Turin in the North-West of Italy. Social movements, trade unions and political parties have played a major role in both regions in shaping the trajectories of deindustrialization from the 1960s to the present day.

The book is organized in thematic tandem chapters dealing with the same theme for the two regions that are being compared here. As the book is dealing with industrial regions, it is fitting to begin with chapters discussing to what extent one can compare the self-understanding of both regions as regions. Here, it emerges clearly that the understanding of the people living in the Ruhr region that they share a common geographical and mental space is far more developed than is the case in the North–West of Italy, despite the fact that also in the Ruhr the 53 cities and districts that make up the region have a strong separate identity that stands next to and often rivals forms of regional identity.

The next tandem of chapters deals with the mental scars that are left by processes of deindustrialization among the workers and their families affected by job losses and changes in their social and cultural environment. Making use of oral history approaches, the book discusses the experiences of the population in the Ruhr and the North–West of Italy with deindustrialization and highlights their resourcefulness in dealing with the changes and the resistance to them which often resulted in their mobilization in various social movements. The next two chapters turn the lens from the people to the political and economic elites who managed forms of deindustrialization in both regions highlighting how important political cultures were in determining to what extent the regional forms of governance intervened and attempted to cushion the social consequences of deindustrialization. Separate chapters tackle one of the most crucial actors among organizations reacting to deindustrialization: the trade unions who played a vital role in providing the framework for deindustrialization in the Ruhr, whereas they could not exert a similar influence in the North–West of Italy.

The urban landscapes in both regions changed significantly under the impact of deindustrialization, and the next tandem of chapters describes the ways in which the industrial past was integrated into those changing landscapes and to what extent that past was overruled and silenced in the construction of new cityscapes signaling a long goodbye from the industrial pasts of both regions. The greening of regions once famous for their industrial pollution has been a significant aspect of the remaking of urban industrial landscapes, and the next two chapters discuss to what extent narratives of ecological rejuvenation have contributed to a new self-understanding of both regions.

Finally, the last tandem of chapters discusses the diverse ways in which industrial work has been replaced by cultural work in both regions. Industrial heritage features prominently in both regions and is often combined with a thriving culture and leisure industry that produces a variety of different memories of industrial pasts that sustain visions of the future of both regions. They are invariably contested, and once again, social movements have been important actors in providing their own interpretations of the past as ground to stand on in the present and from which to develop visions of the future.

Overall, as the concluding chapter by one of the leading scholars of deindustrialization studies highlights, the book makes an important contribution to the transnational and comparative study of the transformations of former industrial regions and it looks at various aspects of deindustrialization that have, in sum, contributed to how those industrial regions have fared in their transition processes from dominant industrial landscapes to landscapes in which industry has rarely disappeared completely but in which it plays a far less prominent role. The book highlights throughout the role of social movements in shaping those transition processes of industrial regions.

Stefan Berger (Ruhr-Universität Bochum)
Holger Nehring (University of Stirling)

Contents

Notes on Contributors

Stefan Berger is Professor of Social History and Director of the Institute for Social Movements at Ruhr-Universität Bochum. He is also executive chair of the Foundation History of the Ruhr and an Honorary Professor at Cardiff University in the UK. He has published widely on the comparative history of labor movements, deindustrialization, industrial heritage, nationalism and national identity as well the history of historiography and historical theory and British–German relations. Among his most recent publication are *Constructing Industrial Pasts* (Berghahn Books, 2020) and *Making Sense of Mining History* (with Peter Alexander, Routledge, 2020).

Giorgio Bigatti teaches Economic History at Bocconi University in Milan. He is the Scientific Director of the Isec Foundation, Institute for the History of the Contemporary Age. He has published widely on the history of Milan and its industrialization. Among his recent publications are: *Story of a District. Milano-Bicocca: People, Places, Recollections*, with G. Nuvolati eds., 2018 and "Crisi e rigenerazione urbana nella Milano contemporanea", *CoSMo-Comparative Studies in Modernism*, n. 17 (2020).

Piero Bonavero is Professor of Economic and Political Geography at the University of Turin, Department of Territorial Sciences. His fields of study include the topic of the structure of the European urban system and the analysis of the evolution of the "Made in Italy" industrial districts, and, more recently, he has sought to bring a geographical perspective to the study of food systems at different territorial scales, and the food policies carried out at a local and urban scale: "Towards a Local Food Agenda in Turin. Mapping Practices and Processes Through Resilience", in R. Roggema (ed.), *Agriculture in an Urbanizing Society, Volume Two*, Cambridge, Cambridge Scholars Publishing, 2017, with Egidio Dansero, Giacomo Pettenati and Alessia Toldo. He teaches Political and Economic Geography and Development Geography.

Egidio Dansero is Full Professor of Economic and Political Geography at the University of Turin, Department of Culture Politics and Society. He has published widely on abandoned industrial areas and urban and environmental policies, territorial approach to sustainable development, megaevents and places, alternative food networks and urban food policies. Among his most recent publications is: *Alternative Food Networks. An Interdisciplinary Assessment* (with F. Barbera, A. Corsi, C. Peano; Palgrave, 2018).

Marco Doria is Full Professor of Economic History at the University of Genova. He is author of several studies on Italian economic history of the nineteenth and twentieth centuries, with specific focus on business history, on the industrial development and its social aspects. Among his works are *Ansaldo. L'imresa e lo Stato*, Milano 1989, and *L'imprenditoria industriale in Italia dall'Unità al "miracolo economico*, Torino 1998.

Pia Eiringhaus joined Martin Luther University Halle-Wittenberg in November 2018. She is working toward her doctorate in the context of the DFG-funded project "Precarious kinship. Negotiations about adoption and incest after 1945", which explores the post-1945 history of adoption in the Federal Republic of Germany. Before, she was a Researcher at the Institute for Social Movements in Bochum and she spent the autumn of 2018 as a Research Fellow at the University of Sao Paulo, Brazil. She completed her history and teaching degree at Ruhr-Universität Bochum in March 2017. Her research interests are contemporary German history, the history of education and the family, and cultures of history and memory around structural change and deindustrialization.

Roberta Garruccio is Assistant Professor of Economic History in the Department of Studies in Language Mediation and Intercultural Communication, University of Milan. Over the last decade, she has been practicing oral history, investigating firms, organizations and markets. She is a member of the Italian Oral History Association and has been collecting several oral archives. Since 2015, she has been working in the field of deindustrialization studies. Among her recent publications are: "Hardly a Cause for Tears", Job Insecurity and Occupational Psychology Culture in Italy. Oral Narratives from the Falck Steelworks in Sesto San Giovanni (Milan)', in S. Berger (ed.), *Constructing Industrial Pasts: Heritage, Culture and Identity in Regions Undergoing Structural Economic Transformation*, Oxford–New York, Berghahn Books, 2020.

Stefan Goch is a Political Scientist and Adjunct Professor at the Faculty of Social Science at the Ruhr University Bochum. He was Research Assistant (from 1990) and Head (2011–2018) of the Institute for Urban History in Gelsenkirchen. From 2018, he works at the state parliament of North Rhine-Westphalia in planning a house of history for North Rhine-Westphalia and a project on the biographies of parliamentarians. He published on the workers' movements and culture, on National Socialism, on the development of the Ruhr area, on political milieus as well as on structural change.

Steven High is a historian at the Centre for Oral History and Digital Storytelling at Concordia University in Montreal. He has been the director of the seven-year research project entitled 'Deindustrialization and the Politics of Our Time', funded by the Canadian Research Council (2021 – 2028). He has been the President of the Canadian Historical Association (2021 – 2023). He has published widely on deindustrialization and postindustrial transformations in North America and comparatively with other parts of the world.

Simone Mangili is currently Aide to the Mayor of Torino, Italy, responsible for managing strategic planning processes requiring cross-sector collaboration and developing policy and delivering projects to realize an ambitious sustainability agenda for the twenty-first century. Prior to joining the Mayor's team, he was Head of Projects and Operations at Torino Internazionale where he managed metropolitan strategic planning processes including development of the metropolitan area's third strategic plan: Torino Metropoli 2025. His international experience ranges from real estate consulting and development management to designing public engagement processes to building private-public partnerships for the development of green infrastructure. In addition to his professional experience, he has served as traveling faculty in World Learning's Cities in the twenty-first-century study abroad program, developed World Learning's Rethinking Food Security program and is an External Lecturer at the Polytechnic University of Turin in territorial and environmental planning. He holds a Bachelor degree in Community, Regional and Environmental Studies from Bard College and a Master in Regional Planning from Cornell University.

Stefan Moitra is a Researcher at Deutsches Bergbau-Museum Bochum and a Guest Researcher at the Foundation History of the Ruhr where he has co-led an oral-history project on experiences and memories of the German coal-mining industry. He has also worked on education and scientific knowledge in the mining industry, on visual cultures of labor and on the place of cinema in working-class cultures after 1945. Recent publications include a special issue on oral history and deindustrialization: *(Post-)Industrial Memories: Oral History and Structural Change* (Bios 31, 2018, ed. with Katarzyna Nogueira.

Anna Moro is a lecturer in the Dept. of Architecture and Urban Studies at the Politecnico di Milano. She has published widely on urban cultures and architectural landmarks in cities. Among her recent publications in English are Playtime: an Action Framework for Public Space in Fragile Urban Contexts, Maggioli: Santarcangelo di Romagna, 2020, and Bovisa: un Parco per la Ricarca e il Lavoro, Maggioli: Santarcangelo di Romagna, 2017.

Stefano Musso is Associate Professor of Contemporary History at University of Turin. Past President on the Italian Society for Labour History, he is member of the Coordinating Committee of the European Labour History Network. He has published on labor and social movements, economic and business history, industrial relations, labor market and vocational training. Among his recent publication, Storia del lavoro in Italia. Il Novecento (editor, 2 volumes, Catelvecchi, 2015); *Iren, protagonista della storia industriale italiana. Dal primo Novecento a oggi* (editor, Celid, 2019); *Le trasformazioni del lavoro nelle rivoluzioni industriali industriali*, in *Lavoro: la grande trasformazione* (ed. Enzo Mingione), Annals of the Feltrinelli Foundation, a. LIV, 2020.

Giacomo Pettenati is Assistant Professor of Economic and Political Geography in the Department of Cultures, Politics and Society of the University of Turin. He holds a Ph.D. in Spatial Planning and Local Development at the Polytechnic University of Turin. His main research topics are food geographies, rural areas spatial processes, landscapes as cultural heritage and participatory mapping. He teaches Political and Economic Geography; International Cooperation for Development and Gis for International Cooperation. He is participating in the H2020 project ProGIreg: Productive Green Infrastructure for post-industrial urban regeneration (2018–2023).

Christa Reicher is a Professor for Urban Design and Director of the Institute for Urban Design and European Urbanism at the Faculty of Architecture at the RWTH Aachen University since 2018. Her research focuses on urban qualification strategies and urban design tools as well as on the process of urban transformation. Several projects, conferences and publications in the research field "Transforming City Regions" deal with the potentials and challenges of the Ruhr Region. She established the European Master's program "Transforming City Regions", which started in the winter semester 2019/2020 at RWTH Aachen University and deals with the transformation of neighborhood, city and region.

Sergio Scamuzzi is Full Professor of Sociology at the University of Turin. He teaches Social Innovation in academic curricula dedicated to ICT and media. He published widely on modernizations theories, local development, the role of culture and sciences in the knowledge societies, the social and economic functions of Olympic games. Among his publications: *La modernizzazione e le sue immagini* (1998), *Apriti scienza* (2015), several essays on omero-urban.it and fondazionesantagata.it.

Manfred Wannöffel is Professor of Sociology and Director of the Center of Cooperation between Ruhr-Universität Bochum and IG Metall. He is also Guest Professor at Puebla University in Mexico. He has published widely on comparative studies of Industrial Relations in Europe and worldwide. Among his recent publications is the *Palgrave Handbook of Workers' Participation at Plant Level*. New York 2019: Palgrave Macmillan (with Stefan Berger and Ludger Pries).

Hans-Werner Wehling is Retired Professor for Regional Geography of old industrial regions at the University of Duisburg-Essen. His main research interests are urban systems in general and particularly the modeling of urban industrial development and the transformation of old industrial regions, in the Ruhr as well as in Britain.

Christian Wicke is Assistant Professor in Political History at Utrecht University. He is currently working on a history of urban movements in the long 1970s. Recently, he edited *Remembering Social Movements: Activism and Memory* (2021, with Stefan Berger and Sean Scalmer). Within the European Labour History Network, he has chaired the working group on “Memory and Deindustrialisation”.

Gilda Zazzara is Lecturer in Contemporary History at the Ca’ Foscari University of Venice where she teaches Labour History and Environmental History. She has published widely on the historiography of the workers’ movement, on the history of trade unions and on labor cultures in Italy; she also edited several autobiographies of workers and unionists. In recent years, she is focusing on deindustrialization processes in Italy, with particular regard to the area of Venice. Among her recent research products are the podcast series *Strade di Porto Marghera* (broadcasted by the national radio) and an essay on the intersections between deindustrialization and heritage studies (*Deindustrializzazione e Industrial Heritage. Approcci convergenti alla memoria del passato industriale*, «Italia contemporanea», 2020, n. 292).

List of Figures

List of Tables

CHAPTER 1

The Unmaking of Industrial Landscapes: The North-Western Italian Industrial Triangle and the Ruhr Region in Germany

Stefan Berger, Stefano Musso, and Christian Wicke

Across the globe, we find iconic industrial landscapes. In Europe, they often have a deep past stretching back to the beginnings of industrialization in the eighteenth and nineteenth centuries. This is also the case

S. Berger (✉)
Institute for Social Movements, Ruhr University Bochum, Bochum, Germany
e-mail: Stefan.Berger@ruhr-uni-bochum.de; stefan.berger@rub.de

S. Musso
Department of Historical Studies, University of Turin, Turin, Italy
e-mail: stefano.musso@unito.it

C. Wicke
Department of History and Art History, Utrecht University, Utrecht, The Netherlands
e-mail: c.wicke@uu.nl

S. Berger et al. (eds.), *Deindustrialisation in Twentieth-Century Europe*, Palgrave Studies in the History of Social Movements,
https://doi.org/10.1007/978-3-030-89631-7_1

for the two landscapes that are being compared in the present volume[1]: the industrial triangle in the North West of Italy and the Ruhr region in Germany. Both stand at the historical centers of industrialization processes in the two respective countries. Without the coal and steel industry of the Ruhr, Germany would not have advanced to become the most advanced industrial country in Europe just before the First World War. It would not have been capable of rising from the ashes twice, after two lost world wars in the first half of the twentieth century. Without the industrial powerhouse of the North West of Italy, the country would have remained, to a large extent, an agricultural country without much impact on the industrial map of Europe. Germany and Italy were both countries that were unified as nation states very late in the day, when compared with other West European nation states: 1871 and 1861, respectively. And for both nation states, the regions under discussion here were vital to their nation building.

Yet they occupy very different positions as regions in the imaginary landscapes of the two countries. As the contributions to this volume show, the North West of Italy always remained an analytical construction. Politicians, administrators, scholars and businessmen looked at the region and identified, above all, an industrial hub. But the people living in the region never really felt that they were living in a region that hung together as a region—they never imagined themselves as being from the North West. This was the case, despite the fact that there were strong economic links between the three key cities in the North West: coal from the port of Genoa served Turin and Milan, steel from Genoa and Sesto San Giovanni went to the engineering industry in Turin and Milan, big marine engines made in Turin went to the shipyards in Genoa, batteries and tires made in Milan went to the Turin car industry, and there were manifold financial ties between the three cities. But this would never constitute an imagined community, unlike the Ruhr region.

The imaginary landscape of the Ruhr region has been dominated by the coal and steel industries, regardless of the fact that it also was home to an important textile industry and that it was the birthplace of the idea

[1] The volume originates from a conference held at the German Historical Institute in Rome. For the report by Florian Meier in German see, Tagungsbericht: Deindustrialization: The Structural Transformation of Nord-Ovest and the Ruhr in Comparative Perspective, 18.04.2018–20.04.2018 Rom, in: H-Soz-Kult, 16.06.2018, www.hsozkult.de/conferencereport/id/tagungsberichte-7751.

of the 'discounter' in the world of retail. Around 1900 its skylines were dominated by mineshafts and chimney stacks. Hundreds of mines and steel factories attracted hundreds of thousands of workers who occupied industrial villages that grew to veritable city sizes around those places of work. Initially, until well into the interwar period, known as the Rhenish-Westphalian coal district, it only slowly developed an identity as a region. But since then, for a variety of reasons, a strong feeling of togetherness, one might even talk about a feeling of *Heimat*, developed in the region. These very different positions of the two regions under comparison here make the comparison a 'most different' one in some respects and the differences between them need to be considered strongly also when asking about the impact of deindustrialization on both regions.

Many of the iconic industrial landscapes of Europe, including the two under investigation here, have undergone processes of deindustrialization and economic restructuring from the 1970s onwards, and these will be the focus of our analysis here.[2] This introduction will, first of all, provide some overall context for the comparison of deindustrialization processes in the North West of Italy and the Ruhr by reviewing the broad lines that deindustrialization studies have taken since its beginnings in the 1970s. It will, of course, not be possible to do this comprehensively. The point here is rather to locate this volume in a literature that has been focusing on the impact of deindustrialization. We highlight its development from local case studies to more comparative perspectives—a development to which this current volume wishes to contribute. And we also stress the transdisciplinarity of the field[3] and situate the current volume in some of the theoretical and methodological concerns that have been important for the field. It is indeed characteristic for the field of deindustrialization studies that scholars from a wide range of disciplines, including sociology, political science, economics, history, anthropology, geography, literary studies, museum studies, memory studies and social movement studies, are active in this field, and the line-up of contributors to this volume reflects this too.

[2] Bert Altena and Marcel van der Linden (eds.), *De-industrialization: Social, Cultural and Political Aspects, IRSH Supplements* (Cambridge: Cambridge University Press, 2002).

[3] We use the term 'transdisciplinarity' here to emphasize that different disciplines have engaged with the phenomena associated with deindustrialization. Often there still is a lack of 'interdisciplinarity' in the sense of a sustained and constructive dialogue between the disciplines, although promising beginnings have no doubt been made.

In the second part of this chapter, we then aim to provide some specific comparative perspectives on deindustrialization processes of the North West and the Ruhr. Starting from the conceptualization of space in both regions, we aim to identify major milestones of development over time and analyze both differences and similarities between the attempts to restructure both regions economically, socially and culturally. Here, we will build on the insights provided by the chapters in this volume. We grouped the chapters into tandems that deal with the same theme for both regions, and the authors of the tandems have developed their respective chapters in collaboration with each other. Thereby, we aimed to make the chapters speak to each other in the hope that it would improve the comparative and transdisciplinary insights to be drawn from those chapters. As always, the proof of the pudding will be in the eating.

Deindustralization Studies—Developments, Agendas and Theoretical Perspectives in a Transdisciplinary Field of Studies

Global competition in the age of industrial capitalism has led to comprehensive transformations, especially in highly industrialized regions, which often had to deal with and make sense of their industrial legacies and pasts under new conditions. Deindustrialization in the global north was the flipside of industries moving to the global south and has become part of the master narrative on the alleged structural break following the post-war boom that ended in the 1970s. It had major effects on class structures, consumer cultures and more broadly the implementation of neoliberal ideology from the 1980s onwards.[4] This transition has been greatly affecting the work of scholars' imagination from various disciplines already during the beginnings of deindustrialization in the 1970s. Thus, for example, Daniel Bell in 1974 published an influential study where he argued that Western societies were moving from an industrial to a postindustrial age, a prophecy which did not materialize fully in many of the regions undergoing deindustrialization.[5] In many areas across the world,

[4] Lutz Raphael, *Jenseits von Kohle und Stahl. Eine Gesellschaftsgeschichte Westeuropas nach dem Boom* (Frankfurt: Suhrkamp, 2019).

[5] Daniel Bell, *The Coming of Post-Industrial Society* (New York: Basic Books, 1976).

processes of deindustrialization were accompanied with the rise of service-sector industries and with processes of reindustrialization in different areas of the economy. In 1980, showing the scales of changing employment figures in industrial countries around the world, economist Nigel Harris wrote: 'A spectre is haunting the treasuries of the advanced capitalist countries. It is not yet, regrettably, the spectre of proletarian revolution, but of the obsolescence of capitalism itself, or rather of its great productive engine, industry'.[6] This statement already indicates to what extent some of the literature on deindustrialization was influenced by Marxist perspectives in scholarship. Steven High's seminal and hugely impressive work on deindustrialization in North America is a good example of this influence of Marxism on the scholarship surrounding deindustrialization.[7]

Marxism's hostility to capitalism made Marxist scholars place special emphasis on the detrimental effects of deindustrialization on the industrial working class, thus opening perspectives of looking at deindustrialization 'from below', including effects on everyday life and emotions. Mass unemployment raised the specter of a society in which work would not be available for all anymore and in which unemployment and immiseration would spread.[8] The golden years of welfare capitalism seemed a passing and short phase in the development of capitalism, which was to give way to a new, more inhumane form that already characterized industrial capitalism from its birth to the period after the Second World War. The short

[6] Nigel Harris, *Selected Essays of Nigel Harris: From National Liberation to Globalisation* (Leiden: Brill, 2018), p. 238.

[7] Steven High, *Industrial Sunset: The Making of America'a Rust Belt* (Toronto: University of Toronto Press, 2003); see also idem and David W. Lewis, *Corporate Wasteland: The Landscape and Memory of Deindustrialization* (Toronto: Between the Lines, 2007); Steven High, Lachlan MacKinnon and Andrew Perchard (eds.), *The Deindustrialized World: Confronting Ruination in Postindustrial Places* (Vancouver: UBC Press, 2017); Steven High, *One Job Town: Work, Belonging and Betrayal in Northern Ontario* (Toronto: University of Toronto Press, 2018); Stefan Berger and Steven High (eds.), '(De-)Industrial Heritage, Special Issue of Labor', in *Studies in Working-Class History* 16:1 (2019), pp. 1–170.

[8] See, for example, Thor Berger and Carl B. Frey, 'Structural Transformation in the OECD: Digitalisation, Deindustrialisation and the Future of Work', in *OECD Social, Employment and Migration Working Papers* 193 (2016), OECD Publishing, Paris, https://doi.org/10.1787/5jlr068802f7-en. Much more bottom-up accounts, looking at what happened to working-class families under conditions of deindustrialization, is, for example, Christine J. Walley, *Exit 0: Family and Class in Postindustrial Chicago* (Chicago: University of Chicago Press, 2013).

decades from the 1950s to the 1970s with full employment, rising real wages for the industrial working class and the emergence of an affluent society in the global north now all seemed under threat.

Those less intent on indicting capitalism often found the deindustrialization and the accompanying structural changes contained a silver lining. It reduced work-related injuries[9] and it helped the environment by bringing down emission levels.[10] It allowed new and often 'cleaner' industries to thrive. Debates about 'work 4.0'[11] and the 'future of good work' discuss how team and network-based work forms can foster more democratization at the workplace and allow for greater empowerment of workers. New industries, for example in the realms of 'cyber physical systems', IT-security or in the health sector and knowledge-based economies, united with an ever-growing service sector. In fact, looking at 'smart product-service systems', we note that any division between production and service has become practically meaningless, as companies are offering solutions that integrate digital services.[12]

In this view, restructuring the economy has not only losers but also winners who can realize their dreams of a better life at a comparatively high level. Processes of requalification stand next to processes of dequalification just as processes of the renewal of old city quarters mean a better life for some, while for others, these processes of urban change amount to 'gentrification'. New forms of education, including education at work but also higher education in industrial areas that formerly had few universities, provide new opportunities for deindustrializing regions. Old sites of industries become cultural and knowledge hubs that help rejuvenate former industrial regions. They also are magnets for tourists wishing to

[9] Dana Loomis, David B. Richardson, and James F. Bena, 'Deindustrialisation and the Long Term Decline in Fatal Occupational Injuries', in *Occupational and Environmental Medicine* 61 (2004), pp. 616–621.

[10] The deindustrialization of the former GDR had an important impact of the image of reunified Germany as a green country due to large-scale reduction of emissions in the East, see, e.g., Benjamin Becker and Caspar Richter, 'Klimaschutz in Deutschland: Realitaet oder Rheotorik', in *Momentum Quarterly* 4:1 (2015), pp. 3–22.

[11] German Federal Ministry of Social Affairs, Re-Imagining Work. Green Paper Work 4.0, Berlin: BMAS, 2015, https://www.bmas.de/SharedDocs/Downloads/DE/PDF-Publikationen/arbeiten-4-0-green-paper.pdf;jsessionid=FD5D548A3D5C42D51FBB9C9B04DC9C27.delivery2-master?__blob=publicationFile&v=1 [accessed 8 October 2020].

[12] Bojan Lalic et al. (eds.), *Advances in Production Management Systems: Towards Smart and Digital Manufacturing*, 2 vols (Berlin: Springer, 2020).

get to know the icons of an industrial past.[13] Industrial heritage thus revives former industrial regions further and leads to new opportunities.[14] In this reading, deindustrialization undoubtedly provided a challenge to political, administrative and business elites but was one that could be handled, shaped and directed. Nowhere was this upbeat assessment of opportunities provided by deindustrialization more prevalent than in Germany, where the specific corporatism, often referred to as 'Rhenish capitalism', offered a framework in which to manage deindustrialization from above. The German term 'Strukturwandel', used much more frequently in Germany than 'deindustrialization', reflects this belief in the possibility of shaping deindustrialization processes in order to produce a better future for everyone involved in those processes.[15]

Whichever way one looked at it, deindustrialization certainly seemed a momentous process that very quickly was studied by many disciplines. Ever since the groundbreaking publications of *Deindustrialization* by Frank Blackby of 1978 and of *The Deindustrialization of America* by Barry Bluestone and Benett Harrison in 1982, deindustrialization studies have become an important field of research.[16] The incredible scale of the loss of industrial jobs in the Western world and the ruination of many of the former hubs of industrial production ensured that many scholars were attracted to this field. In the United States alone, roughly 2 million jobs in manufacturing industry were lost between 1973 and 2012. In Great Britain, between 1979 und 2010, that figure was a staggering 4.3 million.[17] Much of the ensuing research was, however, highly

[13] On Genoa, see, for example, Emanuela Guano, 'Touring the Hidden City: Walking Tour Guides in Deindustrializing Genoa', in *City and Society* 27:2 (2015), pp. 160–182.

[14] In this respect, Margaret Cowell's concept of 'adaptive resilience' is also interesting. See Margaret Cowell, *Dealing with Deindustrialization. Adaptive Resilience in American Midwestern Regions* (London: Routledge 2015).

[15] For a largely positive balance sheet of this management approach to deindustrialization in Germany's former key area of heavy industry, the Ruhr, see Stefan Goch, *Eine Region im Kampf mit dem Strukturwandel: Bewältigung von Strukturwandel und Strukturpolitik im Ruhrgebiet* (Essen: Klartext, 2002); see also his contribution in this volume.

[16] Frank Blackby (ed.), *Deindustrialization* (London: Heinemann, 1978); Barry Bluestone and Bennett Harrison, *The Deindustrialization of America* (New York: Basic Books, 1982).

[17] For details, see Steven High, Lachlan MacKinnon, and Andrew Perchard, 'Introduction', in eidem (eds.), *The Deindustrialized World*, pp. 3–24.

localized, asking about the impact of the closure of individual plants or the fate of individual cities undergoing deindustrialization. Many valuable case studies were produced over several decades highlighting in particular the plight of local people who were victims of such processes of deindustrialization.

A number of important themes have emerged from this research, of which we would like to highlight seven. Firstly, many studies focused on the economic, social, political and cultural processes connected with deindustrialization, investigating how different actors developed differing strategies of how to cope with changing economic circumstances.[18] Secondly, many scholars chose to concentrate their attention on those classical industrial workers who belong to the losers of deindustrialization.[19] The movement toward knowledge economies associated with the fourth industrial revolution brought forth the search for a different type of worker than the one that dominated fordist production modes during the third industrial revolution. Thirdly, much research has discussed changing identities of class, gender, ethnicity/race and religion but also changing spatial identities in cities and regions.[20] Thus, for example,

[18] We cannot provide here an extensive list of the literature that is available on each of the seven themes. Hence, we restrict ourselves to give some prominent examples for each theme. On the first theme compare: Dora Apel, *Beautiful Terrible Ruins. Detroit and the Anxiety of Decline* (New Brunswick: Rutgers University Press, 2015); Alexis S. Boutefeu-Moraitis, 'The Politics of Deindustrialization: The Experience of the Textiles and Clothing Sector (1974–1984)', in *French Politics* 16:1 (2018), pp. 38–63; Margaret Cowell, *Dealing with Deindustrialization. Adaptive Resilience in American Mid-Western Regions* (New York: Routledge, 2015).

[19] Kathryn Marie Dudley, *The End of the Line: Lost Jobs, New Lives in Postindustrial America* (Chicago: University of Chicago Press, 1994); Owen Jones, *Chavs: The Demonization of the Working Class* (London: Verso, 2011); Jackie Clarke, 'Closing Time: Deindustrialization and Nostalgia in Contemporary France', in *History Workshop Journal* 79:1 (2015), pp. 107–125.

[20] Christian Wicke, Stefan Berger and Jana Golombek (eds.), 'Special Issue: Deindustrialization, Heritage and Representations of Identity', in *The Public Historian* 39:4 (2017); James Rhodes, 'The "Trouble" with the "White Working-Class": Whiteness, Class and "Groupism"', in *Identities: Global Studies in Culture and Power* 19:4 (2012), pp. 485–492; Lex Heerma van Voss, and Marcel van der Linden (eds.), *Class and Other Identities: Gender, Religion and Ethnicity in the Writing of European Labor History* (Oxford: Berghahn Books, 2002).

we have a formidable literature on what is happening to 'shrinking cities'—often connected to processes of deindustrialization.[21]

Fourthly, an increasing amount of scholarship is highlighting how processes of structural change have been connected to developments in the realm of civil society. Here, a range of new and highly relevant actors have been playing a vital role in resisting and reshaping processes of deindustrialization.[22] Fifthly, we have many studies looking at social movements and their positioning toward processes of deindustrialization. In 2002, Johnson observed that '[o]ne of the great ironies of differential regional deindustrialization, which is the standard form of capitalist 'crisis', is that it hardly leads to revolution, but rather engenders quiescence, the internalization of despair'.[23] While it is true that structural change has nowhere led to revolution, there have been manifold attempts to resist and cushion the consequences of deindustrialization. Trade unions and social movements were often at the forefront of this resistance demanding greater social justice. Therefore, scholars have been re-assessing how reactions to structural change went beyond acquiescence and despair.[24]

Sixthly, environmental scholars in particular have been dealing with the ecological challenges posed by deindustrialization that are often

[21] Clemens Zimmermann (ed.), *Industrial Cities: History and Future* (Frankfurt/Main: Campus, 2013); Ronan Paddison and Tom Hutton (eds.), *Cities and Economic Change: Restructuring and Dislocation in the Global Metropolis* (London: Sage, 2014).

[22] Martin Baumeister, Bruno Bonomo and Dieter Schott (eds.), *Cities Contested: Urban Politics, Heritage and Social Movements in Italy and West Germany in the 1970s* (Frankfurt/Main: Campus, 2017); Marion Fontaine and Xavier Vigna (eds.), 'La Déindustrialisation: une histoire en cours', in *Revue d'Historique* 21/22 (2019).

[23] Christopher H. Johnson, *The Life and Death of Industrial Languedoc 1700–1920: The Politics of Deindustrialisation* (Oxford: Oxford University Press, 1995), p. 259; see also: idem, 'Introduction: De-industrialization and Globalization', in *International Review of Social History* 47 (2002), pp. 3–33.

[24] Jefferson Cowie and Joseph Heathcott, *Beyond the Ruins: The Meaning of Deindustrialization* (Ithaca, NY: Cornell University Press, 2003); Tim Strangleman and James T. Rhodes, 'The "New" Sociology of Deindustrialization? Understanding Industrial Change', in *Sociology Compass* 8:4 (2014), pp. 411–421; Michael Peter Smith and L. Owen Kirkpatrick (eds.), *Reinventing Detroit: The Politics of Possibility* (New York: Taylor & Francis, 2017); Steven P. Dandaneau, *A Town Abandoned: Flint, Michigan, Confronts Deindustrialization* (Albany: State University of New York Press, 1996).

massive and a legacy of industrialization and high industrial modernity.[25] Seventhly, processes of deindustrialization have gone hand in hand with the development of industrial heritage—as tourist destination, branding ploy and foil for postindustrial identities.[26] A strong media discourse on industrial heritage in novels, films, photography and art has led to a comprehensive historicization of industrial modernity that is tightly connected with diverse strategies for the future of formerly industrial regions.[27] Here, scholars have examined often in great detail the relationship between the people and their collective memories in deindustrializing landscapes.[28] Others have analyzed the effects on popular and alternative culture in processes of deindustrialization, such as music or writing in or about deindustrialized cities.[29]

[25] Mario Reimer and Karsten Rusche, 'Green Infrastructure under Pressure: A Global Narrative Between Regional Vision and Local Implementation', in *European Planning Studies* (2019). https://doi.org/10.1080/09654313.2019.1591346; Pia Eiringhaus, *Industrie und Natur: Postindustrielle Repräsentationen von Natur und Umwelt im Ruhrgebiet* (Bochum: SGR, 2018); Tim Edensor, 'The Ghosts of Industrial Ruins: Ordering and Disordering Memory in Excessive Space', in *Environment and Planning D: Society and Space*, 23:6 (2005), pp. 829–849.

[26] Christian Wicke, Stefan Berger and Jana Golombek (eds.), *Industrial Heritage and Regional Identities* (London: Routledge, 2018); Laurajane Smith, Paul Shackel, and Gary Campbell (eds.), *Heritage, Labour and the Working Classes* (London: Routledge, 2011); Philip Feifan Xie, *Industrial Heritage Tourism* (Bristol: Channel View Publications, 2015).

[27] Sherry Lee Linkon, *The Half-Life of Deindustrialization: Working-Class Writing About Economic Restructuring* (Ann Arbor: University of Michigan Press, 2018); Anna Trubek, *Voices from the Rust Belt* (New York: Picador, 2018); Tim Strangleman, '"Smokestack nostalgia", "ruin porn" or Working Class Obituary? The Role and Meaning of De-industrial Representation', in *International Labour and Working-Class History* 84 (2013), pp. 23–37.

[28] Anna Storm, *Post-industrial Landscape Scars* (London: Palgrave, 2014); George Jaramillo and Juliane Tomann, *Transcending the Nostalgic: Deindustrialised Landscapes Across Europe* (New York: Berghahn Books, 2021).

[29] Giacomo Bocca, *Deindustrialisation and Popular Music: Punk and 'Post-Punk' in Manchester, Düsseldorf, Torino and Tampere* (Lanham: Rowman & Littlefield, 2020); Keith Gildart and Stephen Catterall, *Keeping the Faith: A History of Northern Soul* (Manchester: Manchester University Press, 2020); Sherry Lee Linkon, 'Navigating Past and Present in the Deindustrial Landscape: Contemporary Writers on Detroit and Youngstown', in *International Labor and Working-Class History* 84 (2013), pp. 38–54.

The memory landscapes of deindustrialization have often been affected by sentiments of nostalgia.[30] Under conditions of a capitalist economy, the past is often used in industrial heritage initiatives to create surplus value for particular sites and locations, so that they can be marketed in more profitable ways.[31] Yet, scholars pursuing oral history research that has been critical of capitalist forms of deindustrialization and their impact on working-class communities have also created a densely populated canvass of experiential worlds that contain much nostalgia.[32] They show how nostalgic memories can be a resource in the struggle of working-class communities facing the consequences of deindustrialization. They can help create what Hayden White referred to as 'practical past'[33] that helps to forge a specific future.

Nostalgia thus can be the opposite of a purely antiquarian longing for what has been irredeemably lost and instead becomes a powerful means to establish future-oriented narratives. Sociological and cultural theory approaches to nostalgia have hinted at the power of nostalgia to forge futures in oppositional ways to capitalist logics.[34] It is no coincidence that radical democratic movements as early as the nineteenth century have made good use of nostalgia to further their radical democratic agendas.[35] Nostalgic sentiments under conditions of deindustrialization have often been intimately connected to what Raymond Williams had termed 'structure of feeling', i.e. values and ideals that had a lived and felt reality in the everyday existence of working-class communities attached to memories

[30] Stefan Berger, 'Vom Nutzen und Nachteil der Nostalgie. Das Kulturerbe der Deindustrialisierung im globalen Vergleich', in Zeithistorische Forschungen 2022 (forthcoming).

[31] Luc Boltanski andArnaud Esquerre, *Bereicherung. Eine Kritik der Ware*, Frankfurt a.M. 2018. On the role of nostalgia in the commodification of industrial pasts, see also Bella Dicks, *Heritage, Place and Community*, Cardiff 2000, und Laurajane Smith, *Uses of Heritage*, London 2006.

[32] Two recent examples are Lachlan MacKinnon, *Closing Sysco. Industrial Decline in Atlantic Canada's Steel City*, Toronto 2020; Steven High, *One Job Town. Work, Belonging and Betrayal in Northern Ontario*, Toronto 2018.

[33] Hayden White, *The Practical Past*, Evanston 2014.

[34] Fred Davis, *Yearning for Yesterday. A Sociology of Nostalgia*, New York 1979; Svetlana Boym, *The Future of Nostalgia*, New York 2001.

[35] Alastair Bonnett, *Left in the Past. Radicalism and the Politics of Nostalgia*, New York 2010, S. 5.

of both their workplaces and their neighborhoods.[36] These feelings and accompanying sentiments of nostalgia could be a source of resistance to changes brought about by deindustrialization. Where rapid change questioned established identities, nostalgia was a means of bolstering those threatened identities.[37] As Sherry Lee Linkon put it in her analysis of working-class literature rooted in experiences of deindustrialization: 'It involves both nostalgia and haunting, a longing for what has been lost and a reckoning with past injuries. Remembering the best qualities and effects of industrial labor can be productive and critical, in part because it provides a clear contrast that clarifies the problems of the present'.[38] Laurajane Smith and Gary Campbell concur when they speak about nostalgia's ability to mobilize powerful emotions in order to bring values and ideals of working-class communities from an industrial past into a postindustrial future.[39]

More recently, and the current volume sees itself very much in line with these developments, deindustrialization studies have moved to more transregional and comparative perspectives, sometimes attempting comparisons at European level and sometimes even going in the direction of a global typology of experiences with deindustrialization.[40] These can build on the manifold discussions surrounding the 'varieties of capitalism' debates.[41] Drawing attention to different institutional contexts in which capitalism was developing means being aware of a variety of different actors and their differing reactions to processes of deindustrialization. Regional and national distinctiveness can be explained through the varieties of institutional responses to deindustrialization. Coordinated

[36] Raymond Williams, *The Country and the City*, Oxford 1973.

[37] Tobias Becker, 'The Meanings of Nostalgia: Genealogy and Critique', in *History and Theory* 57 (2018), S. 234–250.

[38] Sherry Lee Linkon, *The Half-Life of Deindustrialization. Working-Class Writing About Economic Restructuring*, Ann Arbor 2018, S. 23.

[39] Laurajane Smith/Gary Campbell, '"Nostalgia for the Future": Memory, Nostalgia and the Politics of Class', in *International Journal of Heritage Studies* 23 (2017), S. 612–627.

[40] Stefan Berger (ed.), *Constructing Industrial Pasts: Heritage, Identities and Historical Cultures in Regions Undergoing Structural Economic Transformation* (New York: Berghahn, 2020); *Alice Mah, Industrial Ruination, Community and Place: Landscapes and Legacies of Urban Decline* (Toronto: University of Toronto Press, 2012).

[41] Peter A. Hall and David Soskice (eds.), *Varieties of Capitalism: The Institutional Foundations of Comparative Advantage* (Oxford: Oxford University Press, 2001).

market economies thus reacted fundamentally different to deindustrialization than radical market economies. The comparison that is being undertaken in the current volume is one within the type of the 'global north'; that is, we are not dealing here with post-colonial path trajectories that are so characteristic of deindustrialization processes in the global south.[42]

Within the global north, both regions belong to states, Germany and Italy, that knew relatively high levels of corporatism and state interventionism in the economic and social sphere; that is, we are not dealing with regions undergoing deindustrialization under conditions of a neoliberal states, as was the case in the United States and Britain. Both in Italy and in Germany, governments did not give up the idea of macroeconomic steering in the 1980s. In both cases, the state continued to intervene in economic and social processes, including the framing of specific programes to help alleviate the worst consequences of deindustrialization. Hence, the North West of Italy and the Ruhr in Germany share certain macro-systemic preconditions for the restructuring of both regions. Yet, as we shall see the end result was still very different—something that should serve as a timely reminder that typologies can only present a highly aggregated and abstract ordering of a multitude of different cases.

Both the rich vein of individual case studies[43] and the more recent comparative and transregional approaches have been building on a highly diverse body of methods and theories. Economic modeling and quantitative social science approaches stand next to studies connecting to memory history, oral history or heritage studies and social movement studies. Industrial relations approaches have been employed just as ideas surrounding 'governance'. Marxist and Weberian approaches stand next to the influence of practice theory, connected with Pierre Bourdieu and Anthony Giddens, and poststructuralist approaches, related to the work

[42] On the global south, see, for example, R. Hassink, X. Hu, D. H. Shin, S. Yamamura, and H. Gong, 'The Restructuring of Old Industrial Areas in East Asia', in *Area Development and Policy* 3:2 (2018), pp. 185–202; Katharine Frederick, 'Global and Local Forces in Deindustrialization: The Case of Cotton Cloth in East Africa's Lower Shire Valley', in *Journal of Eastern African Studies* 11:2 (2017), pp. 266–289; Chitra Joshi, *Lost Worlds: Indian Labour and Its Forgotten Histories* (New Delhi: Permanent Black, 2003).

[43] To cite just one recent among many wonderful examples, see Tim Strangleman, *Voices of Guinness: An Oral History of the Park Royal Brewery* (Oxford: Oxford University Press, 2019).

of Michel Foucault and Jacques Derrida. The field of deindustrialization studies has, overall, benefitted enormously from a happy eclecticism when it comes to theories and methods. Macro-sociological birds' eye perspectives stand next to anthropologically inspired micro-studies. The influence of neo-institutionalist approaches has been as noticeable as the strength of an actor-centered analysis of structural change. The fact that so many studies of deindustrialization have emphasized the social and human dimension of deindustrialization has encouraged many scholars to employ oral history and interviewing as techniques eminently suited to recording the personal, human and subjective sides of abstract economic and social changes.[44] Indeed, many studies have shown how deeply personal lives can be affected by deindustrialization, not only in terms of household incomes, but also, for example, with regard to individual identities and mental well-being.[45] In the current volume, we get a glimpse of this diversity of methodological and theoretical perspectives.

The historical comparison of two regions in Italy and Germany that we attempt here has the practical virtue that, through such studies, regions can learn from each other. In other words, they can find out about how deindustrialization has been managed or mismanaged in other regions, and how the resulting public memory or perhaps cultural trauma of deindustrialization can be managed. Comparison thus foremost assists us in understanding the particularities and similarities of the regions under conditions of deindustrialization, a complex process dependent on particular local conditions and with many unintended consequences ranging from social, cultural and political to environmental impact on the specific localities.[46] Using the region or city, rather than the nation, as a unit of

[44] Stefan Moitra and Katarzyna Nogueira (eds.), 'Industrial Memories. Oral History and Structural Change', in *BIOS. Zeitschrift für Biographieforschung*, (forthcoming).

[45] See, e.g., George Karl Ackers, 'Rethinking Deindustrialisation and Male Career Crisis', in *British Journal of Guidance & Counselling*, 42:5 (2009), pp. 500–510; Valerie Walkerdine and Luis Jimenez, *Gender, Work and Community after De-industrialisation: A Psychosocial Approach to Affect* (Basingstoke: Palgrave, 2012).

[46] See, e.g., Ron Martin and Bob Rowthorn (eds.), *The Geography of Deindustrialization* (Basingstoke: Palgrave MacMillan, 1986); W. F. Lever, 'Deindustrialisation and the Reality of the Post-Industrial City', in *Urban Studies* 28:6 (1991), pp. 983–999; Mark Allen Rhodes, William R. Price, Amy Walker (eds.), *Geographies of Post-Industrial Place, Memory and Heritage* (London: Taylor & Francis, 2020).

comparison is an acknowledgment of the fact that deindustrialization is best studied at the local and regional levels.[47]

Comparative Perspectives on Deindustrialization Process in the North West of Italy and the Ruhr Region in Germany[48]

What are the two regions that we are comparing here? The North West is not a region according to Italian administrative division, but a larger area of three administrative regions, Piedmont, Liguria and Lombardy. The North West's population is 16 million, 10 for Lombardy, 4.5 for Piedmont and 1.5 for Liguria. After decades of dramatic population increase, concentrated in the urban industrial areas, Milan, Turin and Genoa, in the last twenty years of the twentieth century there has since been a slow decrease due to deindustrialization. In the early twenty-first century, a very limited population growth started again, especially in Lombardy, because of immigration, mainly from abroad.

The Ruhr region of Germany, by contrast, is an administrative unit associated with the Regionalverband Ruhr (RVR) that has some influence on the region but is constantly having to negotiate its remit with the 53 individual municipalities comprising the Ruhr district, not to speak of the federal government of North Rhine-Westphalia and the national government in Berlin. The Ruhr's population is about 5.5. million declining from a high of almost seven million in the late 1950s to its current level—largely due to deindustrialization. The recent wave of one million refugees into Germany has seen only a small overall increase in the population of the Ruhr (Figs. 1.1, 1.2 and 1.3).

Industry shaped the historical economic development of both regions. The North West was the core of Italy's industrialization. The term 'North West' was not used until the end of the 1970s. Previously, economic history manuals used 'industrial triangle', referring to Milano, Turin, and Genoa as the vertices, and considering that most of the industrial plants were located in the capital cities and their larger metropolitan areas. The

[47] Pathbreaking for deindustrialization studies in this respect was Mah, Industrial Ruination, who compared Niagara Falls, Canada/USA, Newcastle-upon-Tyne, UK; and Ivanovo, Russia.

[48] What follows is drawing strongly from the chapters of this book, and therefore, we have not provided any referencing in the following section.

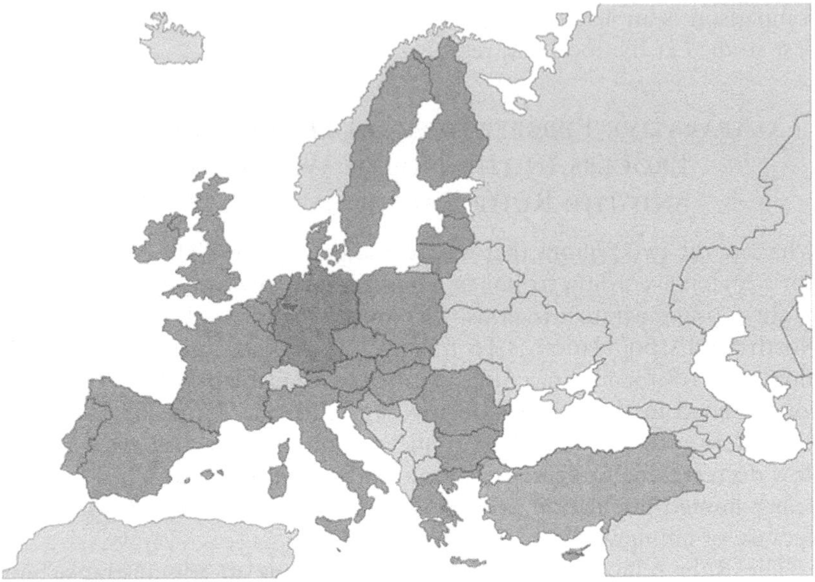

Fig. 1.1 Territory of the regional administrative body for the Ruhr region, the Regionalverband ruhr, on a map of Europe

growth of the urban population was due to immigration, mainly from the regional countryside until the Second World War, while in the post-war 'economic miracle', in the 1950s and 1960s, the largest migration streams came from the Italian South.

The Ruhr was similarly at the heart of German industrialization. The very name, Ruhr region (Ruhrgebiet), only began to be used more widely in the interwar period. This had much to do with political rather than economic developments, as the region was at the heart of the revolutionary conflicts in Germany between 1918 and 1920, and, later on, the focus of national attention during the so-called Ruhr struggle against French and Belgian occupation of the Ruhr region in 1923. From the second half of the nineteenth century, it witnessed massive in-migration, first from the surrounding regions, but increasingly from further afield, especially from the Polish-speaking regions of Imperial Germany. In the boom period of the 'economic miracle' after the Second World War, many

Fig. 1.2 Internal structure of the Regionalverband Ruhr consisting of many independent cities and districts

so-called guest workers migrated to the region, especially from southern Italy, Spain, Greece and Turkey.

The North West of Italy remained always more a term of analytical description than a lived reality. When, in the 1970s, big industrial companies started to decentralize their production, largely in response to the strike wave also known as 'Hot Autumn', the new outsourced networks of production were largely to be found in the North East and center of Italy. They amounted to a string of smaller-sized firms, often dependent on the bigger and more well-known companies in the North West. Scholars, studying those new networks, referred to a 'Third Italy'. From then on, the North West became the First Italy, the South the Second, and the North East and Centre (acronym NEC) the Third Italy. Such definitions, however, did not go beyond Italian scholarship and did not create new identities in the regions concerned. People rather continued to consider themselves as 'Northern' or 'Southern'. Identities remained linked to traditional regions, shaped by the history of the various states in pre-unification Italy. Regional identities continued to be mainly anchored

Fig. 1.3 Atlante generale metodico De Agostini, edited by Istituto Geografico De Agostini, Novara. No date

in regional dialects. There is, until this very day, no sense of belonging to the North West or to NEC.

This is one of the most striking differences to the Ruhr region of Germany, where gradually, from the second decade of the twentieth century onwards, a strong sense of regional identity developed among the population of the Ruhr. Of course, there were also manifold divisions, ideological, class, ethnic, religious and gender ones—to name just the most obvious. But regardless of an often acutely divided society, the notion of being from a particular region grew markedly. The process remains relatively poorly researched, but there is some evidence that a sense of regional belonging grew exponentially with the ongoing process of deindustrialization, when the more educated and better paid children of former miners and steelworkers felt the need to create a sense of *Heimat* for themselves. This would explain their often loving attention to sites of industrial heritage and memories of the industrial pasts more generally. Over the decades, the region also developed its own dialect, *Ruhrdeutsch*, which forms a strong part of the identity of the region, and many people living in the Ruhr refer to themselves as *Ruhris*—a term that is also used by outsiders, often to describe the inhabitants of the Ruhr in rather endearing ways.[49] The region developed its own myths—of hard work, of a multicultural and tolerant society, of a proletarian mindset that told it straight and hated formality, all things that need to be severely questioned but that nevertheless acquired a certain force as part and parcel of a regional identity.

To understand that major difference between the North West of Italy and the Ruhr in Germany, it is necessary to refer briefly to the very different histories of regionalism in both countries. Starting from Italy's unity in 1861, the new Italian State adopted a strongly centralized politics in order to overcome localized oppositions. Centralism continued under the Fascist regime. The new anti-Fascist constitution of 1948 provided for the creation of regional administrative governments that should lead to a de-centralization of power according to national laws. The traditional Napoleonic-style dualism between the State and the Provinces was to be overcome by a threefold structure: State, Regions and Provinces. But, the institution of the Regions was delayed until the 1970s, because the central government resisted delegating power. Regions in Italy are mainly in charge of providing functional services, such as job placements and labor intermediation, vocational training and medical services. They thus have never been able to develop a sense of deeply rooted historical identity.

In Germany, by contrast, the unification of the country only ten years after Italy was accompanied by a strong federalization, with the older constituent parts of the new Reich retaining a high degree of autonomy over political decisions, the army and other matters usually reserved for the sovereign state. The strong federal traditions of Germany continued into the Weimar Republic and the Federal Republic of Germany and the only times that were associated with processes of centralization of power were times of dictatorship, under National Socialism and under Communism in East Germany. Hence, the regions in Germany were not so much

[49] Achim Prossek, 'Sympathieträger der Region: Erinnerungsort Ruhri', in Stefan Berger, Ulrich Borsdorf, Ludger Classen, Heinrich Theodor Grütter and Dieter Nellen (eds.), *Zeit-Räume Ruhr: Erinnerungsorte des Ruhrgebiets* (Essen: Klartext, 2019), pp. 279–295.

seen as enemies of the nation but rather as building blocks of the nation. Regionalism and nationalism were not opposed to each other but went hand in hand. A sense of regional *Heimat* coincided and was the basis of a sense of national *Heimat*.[50] And this remains the case very much until today. Hence, it is also not very surprising that there is a long tradition of writing the history of particular regions in Germany. The phenomenon of Landesgeschichte goes back for many centuries and is tied to the idea of the different German states making up a larger unit, be it the Holy Roman Empire of the German Nation before 1805, the German Federation between 1815 and 1866, or the German Reich and its successor states after 1871.

The Ruhr region, however, was not a traditional historical region in Germany. In fact, the territory of the Ruhr region belonged to several older and more historical regions, in particular the Rhineland (the western parts of the Ruhr) and Westfalia (the eastern parts of the Ruhr). When the political regions of Germany were restructured after 1945, a new state, North Rhine-Westphalia (NRW), came into being, which had weak historical roots.[51] The historiography about the Ruhr, now arguably one of the most important regions within NRW, already began in the interwar period with some early industrial, technological, economic and business histories going even further back, but a most sustained interest in the region arguably only began from the 1950s onwards when a rich stream of literature appeared covering many aspects of the political, economic, social and cultural history of the region.

By contrast, the stronger tendencies toward centralization following Italian unity in 1861 meant that regional histories had to be rediscovered in connection with the institution of the administrative regions in the second half of the 1970s. This new historiographic interest in the regions arose as side effect of the prestigious multi-volume *Storia d'Italia* published by one of the main Italian publishing house, Giulio Einaudi Editore, starting from 1972. The same publishing house started, from 1977 onwards, a new series of regional monographs, covering the period

[50] On the concept of Heimat, see Jens Jäger, Heimat (english version), in *Docupedia-Zeitgeschichte*, first published 13 August 2018, https://docupedia.de/zg/Jaeger_heimat_v1_en_2018 [accessed 9 October 2020].

[51] Christoph Cornelissen, 'Der lange Weg zur historischen Identität. Geschichtspolitik in Nordrhein-Westfalen seit 1946', in Thomas Schlemmer and Hans Woller (eds.), *Politik und Kultur im föderativen Staat, 1949–1973* (Munich: Oldenbourg, 2004), pp. 411–484.

from Italian unity until the present day. In all of the diverse attempts since then to recover a regional dimension in Italian history, the North West was seldom considered a historical unit of analysis. The only exception was in studies on deindustrialization, where the region often figured prominently.

In other regards, e.g. in terms of landscapes, transport routes, agricultural and industrial structures, administrative and political traditions and historical and cultural capital, there is little sense of togetherness in the North West. While there are also territorial differentiations in the Ruhr, they play much less of a role in providing striking contrasts within the region. The various 'zones' comprising the Ruhr region are zones of industrialization, with the zone around the River Ruhr in the south being the oldest, and the zones then moving northwards, first to the River Emscher and later reaching the River Lippe. While the hills of the *Bergische Land* are still reaching the southern parts of the Ruhr, everything north of the Ruhr valley is flat land and any hills are likely to be former slagheaps. The four major cities in the region are old medieval Hanse towns, from east to west, Dortmund, Bochum, Essen and Duisburg. They are positioned in the Hellweg zone, which was a medieval pilgrim's path. To the north, we have only industrial villages which grew into towns exceeding 100,000 very quickly in the period of massive industrialization after the 1870s. There are clearly rivalries and local sentiments within the Ruhr attached to individual cities, or to being either a Rhinelander or a Westphalian, but none have been strong enough to seriously dent the existence of an overriding feeling of belonging to the Ruhr region that developed from the interwar period onwards.

From the above-sketched picture of the North West and the Ruhr, we can see that both areas were core industrial regions of Germany and Italy. Both were heavily affected by processes of deindustrialization. If we ask how these processes compare, we can identify a number of themes that reveal both major differences and similarities. We have structured this book into sections that follow these themes. Thus, we look, first, at the **industrial landscapes** themselves. Here, we can observe that it is far more difficult to analyze the landscape of the industrial North West of Italy due to its far greater heterogeneity. Nevertheless, both were part and parcel of the cycle of a move away from industrial capitalism in the global west from the 1970s onwards and both developed strong strategies of reindustrialization in the face of deindustrialization. In other words, in both regions, we have witnessed sustained attempts not to accept deindustrialization as a force of nature but develop interventions that would help to shape and guide the process, thereby ameliorating its consequences. These strategies involved a move to service and knowledge economies and attempts to re-use industrial sites and transform them into industrial heritage. It is also interesting to observe that in both industrial landscapes economic considerations always outweighed those concerned with urban development during the high time of industrialization and that it was only within an increasingly (albeit never entirely) postindustrial landscape that considerations about urban development began to prevail over economic issues. Finally, within the overall theme of the development of industrial landscapes, it is noticeable that it has been an uphill battle to redevelop former industrial areas and to find the investments necessary to do this.

Chapters by Hans-Werner Wehling and Stefano Musso provide a general picture of the Ruhr in Germany and the North West in Italy, starting from the historical process of economic development that shaped the industrial landscape of the two areas. The economic boom time in both regions lasted from the middle of the nineteenth century to the 1960s. Deindustrialization started earlier in the Ruhr, because of its specialization in mining and steel. In the North West of Italy, there was no mining. Starting from the end of the 1950s, the first branch undergoing deindustrialization was the textile industry. Yet, it was not so much perceived as a crisis, because it happened in a period of boom that helped overcome temporary employment difficulties, when the textile mills closed. Overall, it would appear as though the Ruhr has been more successful in devising a strategy to handle deindustrialization because it could mobilize more financial assets needed for economic and social transformation.

The second section of this book looks at the **life worlds of deindustrialization**. We note how in both regions industrial workers were the main victims of deindustrialization processes. Highlighting the plight of Sesto San Giovanni, Roberta Garrucio's chapter sheds light on an absence of attempts to create a transition from industrial to postindustrial spaces, leaving a non-man's land of despair, despite claims by Italian businessmen and politicians that 'no one was left behind' by the closure of the Falck works in Sesto. Both Garrucio's work on Sesto and Stefan Moitra's work on the Ruhr demonstrate the importance of oral history methods for a comprehensive understanding of the human dimension of the effects of deindustrialization.[52] Both interestingly take their cue from the work of the British cultural theorist Raymond Williams, and Garrucio's notion of a 'deindustrial structure of feeling' that can be recuperated in all of its ambiguities through oral history research also echoes through Moitra's chapter. Both chapters underline how oral history can be a window onto everyday experiences and interpretative practices of workers in disappeared mines and factories. These workers strongly identified with those places of work and the destruction of the economic order with which they grew up pulled the carpet from underneath their existences. In Sesto San Giovanni, it resulted, above all, in a deep mistrust in established politics that resulted in a seismic shift of the city from a bulwark of the left to a stronghold of the populist right. In the Ruhr, recent successes of the right-wing populist Alternative für Deutschland (AfD) point in a similar direction.

Yet, Moitra's chapter also underlines that the workers, in his case the miners, retained considerable agency through the creation of heritage and the construction of meanings of the past that contained feelings of loss and disappointment but also celebrated a pride in past achievements that are, in musealized memories, strongly associated with collective endeavors. Arguably, similar structures of feeling in Sesto San Giovanni have not had the possibility of finding enough outlets in which such memories could become part and parcel of a similar memorial landscape. The oral history work done by Garrucio and others would be a powerful base for making memory a battle site over the meaning of the town's industrial past that reaches out to wider audiences and underlines how collective forms of solidarity have achieved considerable advances for working people in the past—advances that were lost or are in the process of being lost under conditions of deindustrialization. In the Ruhr, similar

52 In the English-speaking world, there have been important centers for oral history that spearheaded the examination of diverse aspects of the history of deindustrialization. See, for example, the Scottish Oral History Centre at Strathclyde University in Glasgow, https://www.strath.ac.uk/humanities/schoolofhumanities/history/scottishoralhistorycentre/ [accessed 9 October 2020], and the Centre for Oral History and Digital Storytelling at Concordia University in Montreal, http://storytelling.concordia.ca/ [accessed 9 October 2020]. Oral history has also been important in investigating stories of deindustrialization in both Germany and Italy, even if both countries lack a distinct center and if, like in the Ruhr, the oral history sources are widely dispersed between different institutions. See also the classic: Alessandro Portelli, *They Say in Harlan County. An Oral History* (Oxford: Oxford University Press, 2011).

narrative patterns have been able, partly because of the generous financial support of politics, wider civil society and also business interests, to gain far more public exposure through a dense landscape of museums and industrial heritage sites speaking the language of collective solidarity.

There are other intriguing comparisons emerging from the chapters by Garrucio and Moitra. Thus, we see in Italy how the proximity of Sesto to Milan was a key strength for the town during its existence as an industrial town. Under conditions of deindustrialization, it has turned into a decisive disadvantage, as Sesto has become a kind of rust belt of the booming and cosmopolitan city of Milan. In the Ruhr, we can observe similar spatial differentiations, with the southern parts of the Ruhr, including the southern parts of the four main cities in the region, developing well economically and in terms of urban structures, and incorporating largely middle-class left-of-center populations, the northern parts of the Ruhr have become problem areas with much higher unemployment figures and forms of ruination also at times reminiscent of rust-belt charm. Here, we also find the strongholds of right-wing populism.

This section on the life worlds of deindustrialization in the Ruhr and in the North West of Italy also highlights the impact of moral economies of workers that influenced their reactions toward deindustrialization processes. The concept of 'moral economy' is, of course, connected to Edward Thompson's ideas about the reactions of English workers toward the industrial revolution in the eighteenth and early nineteenth centuries.[53] According to Thompson, they were often endowed with a clear moral compass that was calibrated to a pre-industrial world and often reacted negatively to the new values and ideals connected with industrialism. After 1945, diverse waves of deindustrialization and moves toward postindustrialism in the global north challenged the moral economy of industrial workers, who again reacted negatively to values and ideals that were undermining their own moral order and understanding of the world. In the history of emotions, Ute Frevert has pleaded to rediscover the value of Thompson's concept of 'moral economy' and to develop it further.[54] It seems that deindustrialization studies would also be well advised to think about 'moral economy' and its influence in

[53] Edward P. Thompson, 'The Moral Economy of the English Crowd in the Eighteenth Century', in *Past and Present* 50 (1971), pp. 76–136.

[54] Ute Frevert, 'Moral Economies: Present and Past. Social Practices and Intellectual Controversies', in: idem (ed.), Moral Economies, Göttingen, 2019, 13–44.

deindustrialization processes more intensely. Scholars, such as Tim Strangleman, have already started this, and it would appear that there is a lot to be gained from this concept if we are trying to understand the emotional response of industrial workers to deindustrialization.[55]

The third theme and section of this book looks in detail at political responses to deindustrialization. They have been of utmost importance in both regions, and it is impossible to understand deindustrialization without accounting for the political attempts to **manage economic decline**. Massive sectoral changes in the manufacturing sector and soaring unemployment rates were met by structural policies from the 1970s onwards that betrayed active state intervention which arguably was heavier and more coordinated in the Ruhr than it was in the North West of Italy. The different levels of federalism were again of vital importance here. While in the Ruhr local municipalities, the regional administrative bodies, the federal government and the national government often worked hand in hand to develop a range of specific programes to help the Ruhr region, nothing as concerted, coordinated and big as those programes existed in the North West of Italy. Here, the municipalities were much more left to their own devices to develop strategies for change and outline infrastructural programes as well as programes for urban renewal that could transform old industrial regions. The strong regional level of governance in the Ruhr was a key element of its relative success in comparison with other industrial regions, including the North West of Italy.

Marco Doria's and Stefan Goch's contributions deal with the ways of managing economic decline. It is characteristic of the missing regional response to the crisis in the North West of Italy that Doria's chapter just deals with one city, Genoa, while Goch's chapter can deal with the entire industrial region. Genoa's industrial fabric is partly similar to the Ruhr because of the importance of steel, produced, in the case of Genoa, by state-owned enterprises. Both in the Ruhr and in Genoa, local and national authorities tried to counteract decline with expensive rationalization programes, which delayed but did not stop deindustrialization. In Genoa, the lack of joint institutional governance was to a certain extent counterbalanced by state funding for state-owned companies. When privatization and the EU's prohibition of public help stopped state funding,

[55] Tim Strangleman, 'Deindustrialization and the Historical Sociological Imagination: Making Sense of Work and Industrial Change', in *Sociology* 51 (2017), pp. 466–482.

the difficulties for local administration grew. Entering into a competition for new industries with other cities, it had to deal also with the decline of smaller and medium-size companies in the city. Nevertheless, as Doria shows, local politics succeeded, in contrast to a mono-industrial city like Turin, to diversity Genoa's industrial base and through urban planning restructure the city into a postindustrial showcase. Reading Goch's chapter though, one cannot help wondering whether a more concerted regional response to deindustrialization would not have benefitted the entire region of the North West of Italy. While it did not entirely prevent competition of the cities in the Ruhr among each other, it provided the frame for a more cooperative and solidaristic mindset that we find in the region today.

The role of the trade unions in the governance of deindustrialization is the topic of the essays by Manfred Wannöffel and Gilda Zazzara that make up the fourth section of this book. The governance of deindustrialization in the Ruhr was strongly dependent on corporatist structures which saw the state work hand in hand with employers and unions in order to develop strategies that would allow the region as a whole to transition from industrial hub to a more diversified economic landscape. Powerful unions in the Ruhr played an influential role in this process. Although corporatism was less marked in the Italian case and although, unlike in Germany, the trade union movement was ideologically divided, labor relations also played an influential part in shaping the processes of deindustrialization in the North West of Italy. Hence, both Wannöffel's and Zazzara's chapters look in detail at **labor relations under conditions of deindustrialization.**

In comparative perspective, we note how a more united trade union response in the Ruhr was better able to defend the interests of the unions' members than the more divided one in the North West of Italy. Faced with processes of downsizing, all unions tried to avoid job losses. Yet, different union cultures reacted differently: the more radical CGIL demanded that employment levels should not decline at all, while CISL was more inclined to acknowledge the need of companies to enhance competitiveness through technological change that would involve job losses. Admittedly, the strategies of employers in the North West of Italy were far more aggressive than those of their Ruhr counterparts, from outsourcing, off-shoring and delocalization to the campaigning for the weakening of labor protection laws. It also did not help that the Italian state and its programes of privatization further weakened the union movement that, as Zazzara argues, was struggling to prevent the wholesale impoverishment and immiseration of working-class communities, giving them at least some protection. Still, while the state in the Ruhr was more of an arbiter between the interests of business and unions, in Italy it often sided more clearly with the interests of business. In particular, the tradition of co-determination in the coal and steel industries of the Ruhr provided a solid foundation from which deindustrialization was tackled, while in Italy the social dialogue between employers and unions, implemented through the wage integration fund, was a much weaker base from which to seek common solutions to the problems brought by deindustrialization. Hence, the structural transformation in the Ruhr has been more socially embedded than the one in the North West of Italy.

The fifth section of this book compares the specific **development of urban planning under conditions of deindustrialization** in both regions. Here, we can observe how the industrial development in the North West of Italy was leaving traces in a much older urban landscape that always remained the hallmark of places such as Turin or Milan, as the contributions by Giorgio Bigatti and Sergio Scamuzzi underline. Urbanity itself was not connected solely or predominantly with industrialization. By contrast, without the industrial development in the Ruhr, there would have been little urbanity in the region and it would have looked entirely different, as is shown in Christa Reicher's contribution. The major cities of the Ruhr had already been towns in medieval and early modern Germany, but they were completely reshaped by industrialization, which produced a polycentric urban space spanning the entire region and dividing it into 'cores' and 'strings', 'focal points' and 'fringes'. By contrast, in the North West of Italy, the older urban structures remained dominant and industrialization did not change them significantly—at least not in their inner centers. The fierce independence of Italian cities prevented them from merging into a larger regional development. Urban spaces remained distinct, and they contained important layers of non-industrial pasts, so that they could never be reduced to being only an industrial landscape.

Under conditions of deindustrialization, the redesigning of the Ruhr urban structures was accomplished largely as a result of the international building exhibition Emscher Park (IBA), on which all subsequent developments for urban renewal in the Ruhr could build. It instigated a new culture of regional planning that was aware of international developments and paid attention to new planning formats that referred in particular to the interlinking of spaces for work, living and leisure. In the North West of Italy, urban planning was not regional but local—with different planning histories for different parts of the region. The redesigning of the industrial parts of its ancient cities often paid much less attention to its industrial histories, simply because it had many other histories that it could build legacies on. Urban planners in Italy who sought to integrate the industrial past into the cityscape of postindustrial cities had a tough time being heard by local governments. The latter prioritized economic regeneration in tumultuous times over the preservation of disused industrial sites. Yet, their disregard for the abandoned spaces of an industrial past also had much to do with a severe shortage of funding. Altogether, while deindustrialization led to a major revival of urban planning on a regional scale in the Ruhr, it played a minor role in managing deindustrialization in the North West of Italy.

As Bigatti and Scamuzzi show for Milan and Turin, this is not to say that the transformation of these two cities over recent decades was unsuccessful. In many respects, both have undergone remarkable metamorphoses. Using private capital much more than public funds, local governments have successfully diversified the local economy, where in particular leisure and knowledge industries play a much bigger role. Yet, many of these private initiatives were far less conscious of the place of industrial heritage in the urban landscape than was the case for the public initiatives in the Ruhr. They, Reicher underlines, did not follow the logic of profit maximization, but carefully considered questions of social cohesion, historical culture and collective identity. A range of public–private partnerships in the redevelopment of urban structures under conditions of deindustrialization were also informed by such concerns.

Deindustrialization was not just a challenge for urban renewal, but also for **environmental renewal**, as industrialization led to massive pollution and the need for major clean-ups after factory closures. Both regions have seen impressive attempts to set new environmental standards and demonstrate how economic development and environmental concerns can go hand in hand. The greening of the Ruhr and the discourse of 'industrial nature', which are at the center of Pia Eiringhaus's contribution to this volume, are good examples of that commitment to a more environmentally sustainable future that, in the case of the Ruhr, also provides an important function for giving the region a new postindustrial identity.

It has been precisely the search for such new urban and regional identities that have had motivating effects on the greening of spaces and the re-definition of industrial heritage against the background of the increasingly important environmentalist discourse the world has been witnessing in recent years. Re-enforcing calls for higher environmental standards and stronger environmental politics, the concept of 'industrial nature' highlights attempts to stress the 'livability' of postindustrial urban landscapes, and it also contains traces of a proud and self-celebratory regionalism that combines commitment to an industrial past with engagement for more sustainable postindustrial futures.

As shown in the contribution by Egidio Dansero and his collaborators, in the North West of Italy very similar processes of combining urban renewal with greening strategies can be observed, albeit in a far more localized space. This confirms, once again, the relative absence of a regional mindscape for the North West. In their article, the authors focus specifically on three tributaries of the Po River in the city of Turin. They show how these once exploited, contaminated and buried rivers were part and parcel of processes of re-territorialization that made them foundational elements in the city's postindustrial landscape—in line with new environmental concerns that have been on the rise in Italy since the 1970s. Paying attention to new ecologies produced new landscapes in the city. The Dora Riparia River was unburied and became part of a vast industrial landscape park, the Dora Park that has become one of the most important green spaces in Turin and the backbone of a new and thriving neighborhood. The Stura River, completely contaminated and remolded under conditions of industrialization, has seen sustained attempts to restore its eco-systems—a major challenge still for the future of the city. Finally, the Sangone River has become central again to the inhabitants of one of the most iconic working-class neighborhoods in Turin, Mirafiori. Overall, the chapter by Dansero and his colleagues shows many parallels to the re-territorialization of key rivers in the Ruhr area, above all the renaturation of the Emscher River but also the remaking of the Ruhr River itself. These parallels are at least partly the consequences of a sustained dialogue across former industrial regions on how to regenerate those landscapes poisoned by industrial use. Industrial landscape parks in both regions were designed, in part, by the same people. Thus, Peter Latz was involved in both the construction of the Duisburg North Landscape Park in the Ruhr and the Dora Park in Turin. Ideas and concepts cross regional and national borders with relative ease in a Europeanized and globalized context.

In both, the North West of Italy and the Ruhr region processes of deindustrialization raised the issue of what to do with the often large areas that were formerly reserved for industrial complexes and that had been forbidden territory for everyone not working there. Once mines and factories had been closed, and machineries dismantled, the erstwhile cathedrals of industry became ghostly specters and as such the object of fascination for a whole range of people. They included those who wanted to explore those forbidden sites and traveled long distances to enter ruins, taking photographs and documenting the morbidity of decline. They also included artists who produced photographs, and paintings and writers who produced novels and poems about deindustrialization.

Comparing the **cultures of deindustrialization** in the North West of Italy and the Ruhr, we can, first of all, observe that the physical preservation of an entire industrial landscape in the Ruhr is pretty spectacular and testimony to the degree to which that industrial past has become the anchor of regional identity, as Stefan Berger's chapter underlines. By comparison, Anna Moro's chapter also showcases many impressive attempts of preserving industrial heritage in the North West of Italy, but these are far more isolated and dotted in an overall landscape where the previous industrial past is disappearing fast. Similar ideas appear in both regions—the idea of the landscape park, the idea of the industrial museum, the idea of the re-use of industrial buildings such as office buildings, art centers, housing and entertainment complexes as well as decoration for shopping malls. At least some of these re-uses of industrial heritage sites have suffered from an ahistorical approach, where the locations have become decontextualized and only serve commercial functions. While in both the Ruhr and the North West of Italy heritagization has worked best where public institutions joined forces with civil society and private companies, such public–private partnerships need to be aware of the complexity of the sites they are transforming into heritage. Attempts at touristification also occasionally suffer from the desire to present through the sites of industrial heritage a rather too nostalgic view of the industrial past. Future research on industrial heritage in both regions will have to pay greater attention to the many silences and omissions that we find about the industrial past.

Conclusion: The Future of Two Iconic Industrial Landscapes in Europe

For the past two decades, right-wing populisms across North America and Europe have been drawing support from a white working class directly affected by deindustrialization.[56] In the nineteenth and twentieth centuries, most industrial hubs across the Western world were strongholds of the political left—trade unionism and left-wing political parties tended to be strong. But under conditions of deindustrialization many former union members felt that their unions could no longer protect them and that the left-of-center political parties that they had voted for had no recipes for dealing with their plight.[57] Hence, sections of the working class have been moving to the populist right, even if, as a sustained comparison between the North West of Italy and the Ruhr region of Germany underlines, both regions have seen important and partially successful attempts to weather the storm of deindustrialization.

Nevertheless, in December 2016, a 72-year-old left-wing dominance on the city council of Genoa ended and a populist right-wing mayor came in on a programe of expelling migrants, blocking plans for a local mosque and putting white Italians first. In the northern parts of the Ruhr, the right-wing Alternative für Deutschland (AfD) achieved some of their best results in West Germany—getting more than 20% of the vote in some urban districts in the regional elections for the state diet of North Rhine-Westphalia in 2017. One of the party's election posters in the Ruhr showed a former Social Democratic town councilor in Essen and convinced trade unionist, Guido Reill, who had moved to the AfD. He was dressed in miners' clothing and the slogan on the poster read: 'At heart a Social Democrat, therefore AfD'. The AfD was claiming to be the heirs of a Social Democratic tradition which, thus the message of the election poster, had been abandoned by the Social Democrats. This idea of betrayal must have rung true to at least some of the former voters of

[56] See, e.g., Seth Schindler, http://blog.gdi.manchester.ac.uk/the-new-geography-of-deindustrialization-and-the-rise-of-the-right/ [accessed 9 October 2020], and Jim Tomlison, https://blogs.lse.ac.uk/brexit/2017/04/28/de-industrialisation-rather-than-globalisation-is-the-key-part-of-the-brexit-story/ [accessed 9 October 2020]; see, more generally, Fernando López-Alves and Diane E. Johnson (eds.), *Populist Nationalism in Europe and the Americas* (London: Routledge, 2018).

[57] W. Rand Smith, *The Left's Dirty Job: The Politics of Industrial Restructuring in France and Spain* (Toronto: University of Toronto Press, 1998).

the Social Democrats in the northern, most deprived parts of the Ruhr, at least judging by the election results.[58]

The two examples show clearly that what is currently at stake in deindustrialization processes in Italy, Germany and many other parts of the world is a political challenge: how to prevent the victims of deindustrialization, those who perceive themselves as having lost out, to move to the political right that is currently threatening democracies in many parts of the world. What answers democratic politicians, administrators, businessmen and trade unionists as well as social movements find to the challenges of deindustrialization will impact in a major way on our chances to defeat right-wing populisms.[59] In the Ruhr and in the North West of Italy, we can encounter several success stories of structural change but also some failures. As we are dealing with an ongoing process, the balance sheet of the overall process cannot yet be drawn up.

The futures of former industrial landscapes such as the ones in the North West of Italy and in the Ruhr will depend on whether governance processes manage to provide 'good work' for the vast majority of the people living in those regions, whether the growing precarity of work can be stopped, unemployment contained and whether the people see a future for themselves and for their children in those areas undergoing deindustrialization. Karl Polanyi in his seminal work *The Great Transformation* powerfully argued in favor of the social embeddedness of capitalism.[60] Neoliberal responses to deindustrialization have ignored that insight and instead left structural change to markets that turned everything into commodities. With such rapidly increasing processes of commodification, human relationships are destroyed, as societal cohesion

[58] It should be noted that the AfD also managed to mobilize many non-voters and that it draws support from diverse sections of the ideological spectrum, but in places like the Ruhr it undoubtedly also appeals to working-class voters who traditionally voted for parties on the left of the political spectrum. See Wolfgang Schroeder and Bernhard Weßels, *Smarte Spalter: die AfD zwischen Bewegung und Parlament* (Bonn: J.W.H. Dietz Nachf, 2019); Hambauer, Anja Mays Verena, 'Wer wählt die AfD? Ein Vergleich der Sozialstruktur, politischen Einstellungen und Einstellungen zu Flüchtlingen zwischen AfD WählerInnen und den WählerInnen anderer Parteien', in *Zeitschrift für vergleichende Politikwissenschaft* 12:1 (2018), pp. 133–154.

[59] Yascha Mounk, *The People vs. Democracy. Why Our Freedom Is in Danger and How to Save It* (Cambridge, MA: Harvard University Press, 2018).

[60] Karl Polanyi, *The Great Transformation: The Political and Economic Origins of Our Time* (Boston: Beacon Press, 2001) (first published in 1944).

is lost and values once underpinning industrial societies, such as solidarity, are forgotten. This process has been particularly marked in the United States and Britain, where neoliberal governments from the late 1970s onwards pioneered the marketization of everything.[61] Italy and Germany went different paths, and this comparison of deindustrialization of two former industrial hubs in Italy and Germany provides plenty of examples of why it is necessary for the state to intervene and limit the commodification brought about by markets. Where this has been done, it has led to a new social and environmental embedding of capitalism. However, both in the Ruhr and in the North West of Italy, the partially successful intervention in the logic of markets has not been able to prevent entirely feelings among working-class voters that they have lost out in processes of deindustrialization which is why we have also seen the rise of right-wing populism here. The politics of deindustrialization needs to be studied in greater depth and more comparatively in order to find answers to how the anti-democratic, nationalist populist right may be stopped.[62]

References

Ackers, George Karl, 'Rethinking Deindustrialisation and Male Career Crisis', in British Journal of Guidance & Counceling 42:5 (2009), pp. 500–510.

Alterna, Bert and van der Linden, Marcel (eds.), 'De-industrialization: Social, Cultural and Political Aspects', IRSH Supplements (Cambridge: Cambridge University Press, 2002).

Apel, Dora, Beautiful Terrible Ruins. Detroit and the Anxiety of Decline (New Brunswick: Rutgers University Press, 2015).

Baumeister, Martin, Bonomo, Bruno and Schott, Dieter (eds.), Cities Contested: Urban Politics, Heritage and Social Movements in Italy and West Germany in the 1970s (Frankfurt/Manin: Campus, 2017).

Becker, Tobias, 'The Meanings of Nostalgia: Genealogy and Critique', in History and Theory 57 (2018), S. 234–250.

[61] See, for example, David Byrne, 'Deindustrialization and Dispossession: An Examination of Social Division in the Industrial City', in *Sociology* 29:1 (1995), pp. 95–115.

[62] A consortium of scholars from North America and Europe, led by Steven High at Concordia University, Montreal, is doing precisely this in a seven-year project that started in 2020. See https://www.concordia.ca/news/stories/2020/06/03/sshrc-awards-2-5-m-to-concordia-led-collaborative-research-on-deindustrialization-and-the-rise-of-populism.html [accessed 12 October 2020].

Becker, Benjamin and Richter, Caspar, 'Klimaschutz in Deutschland: Realitaet oder Rhetorik', in Momentum Quarterly 4:1 (2015), pp. 3–22.

Bell, Daniel, The Coming of Post-industrial Society (New York: Basic Books, 1976).

Berger, Stefan (ed.), Constructing Industrial Pasts: Heritage, Identities and Historical Cultures in Regions Undergoing Structural Economic Transformation (New York: Berghahn, 2020).

Berger, Thor and Frey, Carl B., 'Structural Transformation in the OECD: Digitalisation, Deindustrialisation and the Future of Work', in OECD Social, Employment and Migration Working Papers 193 (2016), OECD Publishing, Paris, https://doi.org/10.1787/5jlr068802f7-en.

Berger, Stefan and High, Steven (eds.), '(De-)Industrial Heritage, Special Issue of Labor', in Studies in Working-Class History 16:1 (2019), pp. 1–170.

Blackby, Frank (ed.), Deindustrialization (London: Heinemann, 1978).

Bluestone, Barry and Harrison, Bennett, The Deindustrialization of America (New York: Basic Books, 1982).

Boltanski, Luc and Esquerre, Arnaud, Bereicherung. Eine Kritik der Waren (Frankfurt/Main: Suhrkamp, 2018).

Bonnett, Alastair, Left in the Past. Radicalism and the Politics of Nostalgia (New York: Bloomsbury Academic, 2010).

Boutefu-Moraitis, Alexis S., 'The Politics of Deindustrialisation: The Experience of the Textiles and Clothing Sector (1974-1984)', in French Politics 16:1 (2018), pp. 38–63.

Boym, Svetlana, The Future of Nostalgia (New York: Basic Books, 2001).

Byrne, David, 'Deindustrialization and Dispossession: An Examination of Social Division in the Industrial City', in Sociology 29:1 (1995), pp. 95–115.

Clarcke, Jackie, 'Closing Time: Deindustrialization and Nostalgia in Contemporary France', in History Workshop Journal 79:1 (2015), pp. 107–125.

Cornelissen, Christoph, 'Der lange Weg zur historischen Identität. Geschichtspolitik in Nordrhein-Westfalen seit 1946', in Thomas Schlemmer and Hans Woller (eds.), Politik und Kultur im föderativen Staat, 1949–1973 (Munich: Oldenbourg, 2005), pp. 411–484.

Cowell Margaret, Dealing with Deindustrialization. Adaptive Resilience in American Midwestern Regions (London: Routledge, 2015).

Cowie, Jefferson and Heathcott, Joseph, Beyond the Ruins: The Meaning of Deindustrialization (Ithaca, NY: Cornell University Press, 2003).

Dandaneau, Steven P., A Town Abandoned: Flint, Michigan, Confronts Deindustrialisation (Albany: University of New York Press, 1996).

Davis, Fred, Yearning for Yesterday. A Sociology of Nostalgia (New York: The Free Press, 1979).

Dicks, Bella, Heritage, Place and Comminity (Cardiff: University of Wales Press, 2000).

Dudley, Kathryn Marie, The End of the Line: Lost Jobs, New Lives in Postindustrial America (Chicago: University of Chicago Press, 1994).

Edensor, Tim, 'The Ghosts of Industrial Ruins: Ordering and Disordering Memory in Excessive Space', in Environment and Planning D: Society and Space 23:6 (2005), pp. 829–849.

Eiringhaus, Pia, Industrie und Natur: Postindustrielle Repräsentationen von Natur und Umwelt im Ruhrgebiet (Bochum: SGR, 2018).

Feifan Xie, Philip, Industiral Heritage Tourism (Bristol: Channel View Publications, 2015).

Fontaine, Marion and Vigna, Xavier (eds.), 'La Désindustrialisation: une histoire en cours', in Revue d'Historique 21/22 (2019), pp. 2–17.

Frederick, Katharine, 'Global and Local Forces in Deindustrialization: The Case of Cotton Cloth in East Africa's Lower Shire Valley', in Journal of Eastern African Studies 11:2 (2017), pp. 266–289.

Frevert, Ute, 'Moral Economics: Present and Past. Social Practices and Intellectual Controversies', in: idem (ed.), Moral Economies (Göttingen: Vandenhoeck and Ruprecht, 2019), pp. 13–44.

German Federal Ministry of Social Affairs, Re-Imagining Work. Green Paper Work 4.0 (Berlin: BMAS, 2015), https://www.bmas.de/SharedDocs/Downloads/DE/PDF-Publikationen/arbeiten-4-0-green-paper.pdf;jsessionid=FD5D548A3D5C42D51FBB9C9B04DC9C27.delivery2-master?__blob=publicationFile&v=1 [accessed 8 October 2020].

Goch, Stefan, Eine Region im Kampf mit dem Strukturwandel. Bewältigung von Strukturwandel und Strukturpolitik im Ruhrgebiet (Essen: Klartext, 2002).

Guano, Emanuela, 'Touring the Hidden City: Walking Tour Guides in Deindustrializing Genoa', in City and Society 27:2 (2015), pp. 160–182.

Hall, Peter A. and Skice, David (eds.), Varieties of Capitalism: The Institutional Foundations of Comparative Advantage (Oxford: Oxford University Press, 2001).

Harris, Nigel, Selected Essays of Nigel Harris: From National Liberation to Globalisation (Leiden: Brill, 2018).

Hassink, R., Hu, X., Shin, D.H., Yamamura, S., Gong, H., 'The Restructuring of Old Industrial Areas in East Asia', in Area Development and Policy 3:2 (2018), S. 185–202.

High, Steven, Industrial Sunset: The Making of Americ's Rust Belt (Toronto: University of Toronto Press, 2003).

High, Steven, MacKinnon, Lachlan and Perchard, Andrew (eds.), The Deindustrialized World: Confronting Ruination in Postindustrial Places (Vancouver: UBC Press, 2017).

High, Steven, One Job Town. Work, Belonging and Betrayal in Northern Ontario (Toronto: University of Toronto Press, 2018).

Jäger, Jens, Heimat in Docupedia-Zeitgeschichte, first published 13 August 2018, https://docupedia.de/zg/Jaeger_heimat_v1_en_2018 [accessed 9 October 2020].
Johnson, Christopher H., The Life and Death of Industrial Languedoc 1700-1920: The Politics of Deindustrialisation (Oxford: Oxford University Press, 1995), p. 259.
Johnson, Christopher H., 'Introduction: De-industrialization and Globalization', in International Review of Social History 47 (2002), pp. 3–33.
Jones, Owen, Chavs: The Demonization of the Working Class (London: Verso, 2011).
Joshi, Chitra, Lost Worlds: Indian Labour and Its Forgotten Histories (New Delhi: Permanent Black, 2003).
Lalic, Bojan et al. (eds.), Advances in Production Management Systems: Towards Smart and Digital Manufacturing, 2 vols (Berlin: Springer, 2020).
Lever, W.F., 'Deindustrialization and the Reality of the Post-industrial City', in Urban Studies 28:6 (1991), pp. 983–999.
Lewis, David W., Corporate Wasteland: The Landscape and Memory of Deindustrialization (Toronto: Between the Lines, 2007).
Linkon, Sherry Lee, The Half-Life of Deindustrialization. Working-Class Writing About Economic Restructuring (Ann Arbor: University of Michigan Press, 2018).
Loomis, Dana, Richardson, David B. and Bena, James F., 'Deindustrialisation and the Long Term Decline in Fatal Occupational Injuries', in: Occupational and Evironmental Medicine 61 (2004), pp. 616–621.
López-Alves, Fernando, and Johnson, Diane E. (eds.), Populist Nationalism in Europe and the Americas (London: Routledge, 2018).
MacKinnon, Lachlan, Closing Sysco. Industrial Decline in Atlantic Canada's Steel City (Toronto: University of Toronto Press, 2020).
Mah, Alice, Industrial Ruination, Community and Place: Landscapes and Legacies of Urban Decline (Toronto: University of Toronto Press, 2012).
Martin, Ron and Rowthorn, Bob (eds.), The Geography of Deindustrialization (Basingstoke: Palgrave, [1986] 2012).
Moitra, Stefan and Nogueira, Katarzyna (eds.), 'Industrial Memories. Oral History and Structural Change', in BIOS. Zeitschrift für Biographieforschung, (forthcoming).
Mounk, Yasha, The People vs. Democracy, Why Our Freedom Is in Danger and How to Save It (Cambridge, MA: Harvard University Press, 2018).
Paddison, Ronan and Hutton, Tom (eds.), Cities and Economic Change: Restructuring and Dislocation in the Global Metropolis (London: Sage, 2014).
Polanyi, Karl, The Great Transformation: The Political and Economic Origins of Our Time (Boston: Beacon Press, 2001) (first published in 1944).

Prossek, Achim, 'Symphatieträger der Region: Erinnerungsort Ruhr', in Berger, Stefan, Borsdorf, Ulrich, Classen, Ludger, Grütter, Heinrich Theodor, Nellen, Dieter (eds.), Zeit-räume Ruhr: Erinnerungsorte des Ruhrgebiets (Essen: Klartext, 2019), pp. 279–295.

Raphael, Lutz, Jenseits von Kohle und Stahl. Eine Gesellschaftsgeschichte Westeuropas nach dem Boom (Frankfurt: Suhrkamp, 2019).

Reimer, Mario and Rusche, Karsten, 'Green Infrastructure Under Pressure: A Global Narrative Between Regional Vision and Local Implementation', in European Planning Studies (2019), pp. 1542–1563, https://doi.org/10.1080/09654313.2019.1591346.

Rhodes, James, 'The "Trouble" with the "White Working-Class": Whiteness, Class and "Groupism"', in Identities: Global Studies in Culture and Power 19:4 (2012), pp. 485–492.

Rhodes, Mark Allen, Price, William R. and Walker, Amy (eds.), Geography of Post-industrial Place, Memory and Heritage (London: Taylor & Francis, 2020).

Schindler, Seth, http://blog.gdi.manchester.ac.uk/the-new-geography-of-deindustrialization-and-the-rise-of-the-right/ [accessed 9 October 2020].

Smith, W. Rand, The Left's Dirty Job: The Politics of Industrial Restructuring in France and Spain (Toronto: University of Toronto Press, 1998).

Smith, Laurajane, Use of Heritage (London: Routledge, 2006).

Smith, Laurajane and Campbell, Gary, '"Nostalgia for the Future": Memory, Nostalgia and the Politics of Class', in International Journal of Heritage Studies 23 (2017), S. 612–627.

Smith, Laurajane, Shackel, Paul and Campbell, Gary (eds.), Heritage, Labour and the Working Classes (London: Routledge, 2011).

Smith, Michael Peter and Kirkpatrick, L. Owen (eds.), Reinventing Detroit: The Politics of Possibility (New York: Taylor & Francis, 2017).

Strangleman, T. and Rhodes James T., 'The "New" Sociology of Deindustrialization? Understanding Industrial Change', in Sociology Compass 8:4 (2014), pp. 411–421.

Strangleman, T. 'Deindustrialization and the Historical Sociological Imagination: Making Sense of Work and Industrial Change', in Sociology 51 (2017), pp. 466–482.

Strangleman, Tim, Voices of Guinness: An Oral History of the Park Royal Brewery (Oxford: Oxford University Press, 2019).

Thompson, Edward P., 'The Moral Economy of the English Crowd in the Eighteenth Century', in Past and Present 50 (1971), pp. 76–136.

Tomlison, Jim, https://blogs.lse.ac.uk/brexit/2017/04/28/de-industrialisation-rather-than-globalisation-is-the-key-part-of-the-brexit-story/ [9 October 2020].

Van Voss, Lex Heerma and van der Linden, Marcel (eds.), Class and Other Identities: Gender Religion and Ethnicity in the Writing of European Labour History (Oxford: Berghahn Books, 2002).
Walkerdine, Valerie and Jimenez, Luis, Gender, Work and Community after De-industrialization: A Psychological Approach to Affect (Basingstoke: Palgrave, 2012).
Walley, Christine J., Exit 0: Family and Class in Postindustrial Chicago (Chicago: University of Chicago Press, 2013)
White, Hayden, The Practical Past (Evanston: Northwestern University Press, 2014).
Wicke, Christian, Berger, Stefan and Golombeck, Jana (eds.), 'Special Issue: Deindustrialization, Heritage and Representations of Identity', in The Public Historian 39:4 (2017).
Wicke, Christian, Berger, Stefan and Golombek, Jana (eds.), Industrial Heritage and Regional Identities (London. Routledge, 2018).
Williams, Raymond, The Country and the City (Oxford: Oxford University Press, 1973).
Zimmermann, Clemes (ed.), Industrial Cities: History and Future (Frankfurt/Main: Campus, 2013).

PART I

Introducing Industrial Landscapes

CHAPTER 2

The Industrial Cultural Landscape of the Ruhr: Its Structures and Perspectives

Hans-Werner Wehling

Introduction

The shaft building of the Zollverein XII mine has become the iconic monument of the Ruhr area since it has been included into the UNESCO World Heritage in 2001. It is the leading monument of the Route of Industrial Culture, which itself is the backbone of the regional tourism and contributes to the increasing post-industrial identity of its population. Due to the fact that the Ruhr area still comprises the largest amount of industrial monuments of the classical nineteenth-century industries in Europe, a new application process has been launched in order to have a larger set of high-rank industrial monuments and installations inscribed in the World Heritage list under the headline "Ruhrgebiet Industrial Cultural Landscape". This idea behind is to exhibit not only a collection

H.-W. Wehling (✉)
University of Duisburg-Essen, Essen, Germany
e-mail: hans-werner.wehling@uni-due.de

S. Berger et al. (eds.), *Deindustrialisation in Twentieth-Century Europe*, Palgrave Studies in the History of Social Movements,
https://doi.org/10.1007/978-3-030-89631-7_2

of monuments but also the fabric of the landscape that connects them and which has widely been shaped by various industrial impacts.[1]

The industrial and urban development of the Ruhr can be divided into various phases of industrial and urban development that include the construction and de-construction of elements (sites, lines and areas) of the industrial cultural landscape of the Ruhr. The region is thereby being divided in west-easterly (development) zones (Fig. 2.1) that are deduced from the phases of the northward movement of coal mining. It is one of the qualities of the industrial cultural landscape Ruhr that the present entirety still reveals the various stages of its industrial development.

The Spatial Development of the Cultural Industrial Landscape

Pre-industrial and Early Industrial Foundations

Up to the early nineteenth century, the natural conditions determined the modes of land use and the distribution and sizes of settlements. In the south, an intensive pre-industrial colonization had been impeded by extensive oak and beech forests on the Ruhr Heights, and to the north by the swamp forests in the valley of the meandering River Emscher. Between these forest zones, the slightly rolling Hellweg plain was nearly free of forests by 1800; here and on the terraces and peninsulas of the River Ruhr, the fertile loess soils had been cleared and used by farming since medieval times. The rivers Ruhr and Lippe and the medieval trading route of the Hellweg were the transport guidelines. Along these lines, small and medium-sized towns were the major settlement concentrations; villages and hamlets were the settlements of the rural landscapes alongside the River Ruhr and the Hellweg, scattered farmsteads dominated the Emscher lowland.

[1] Hans-Werner Wehling, *Zollverein and the Industrial Cultural Landscape Ruhr. Report on its Theoretical/Conceptional Foundation and its Spatial Operationalization* (Essen: Klartext, 2015); Ursula Mehrfeld and Marita Pfeiffer, 'Das Welterbe-Projekt „Industrielle Kulturlandschaft Ruhrgebiet"', in *Industrielle Kulturlandschaft, Forum Geschichtskultur Ruhr* 2 (2015), pp. 15–22; Stiftung Industriedenkmalpflege und Geschichtskultur (SIG)/Foundation for the Preservation of Industrial Monuments and Historical Culture, *Ruhrgebiet Industrial Cultural Landscape. Draft Statement of Outstanding Universal Value. Proposal for an Update of the German Tentative List for UNESCO World Heritage* (Dortmund: The Foundation for the Preservation of Industrial Monuments and Historical Culture (SIG), 2017).

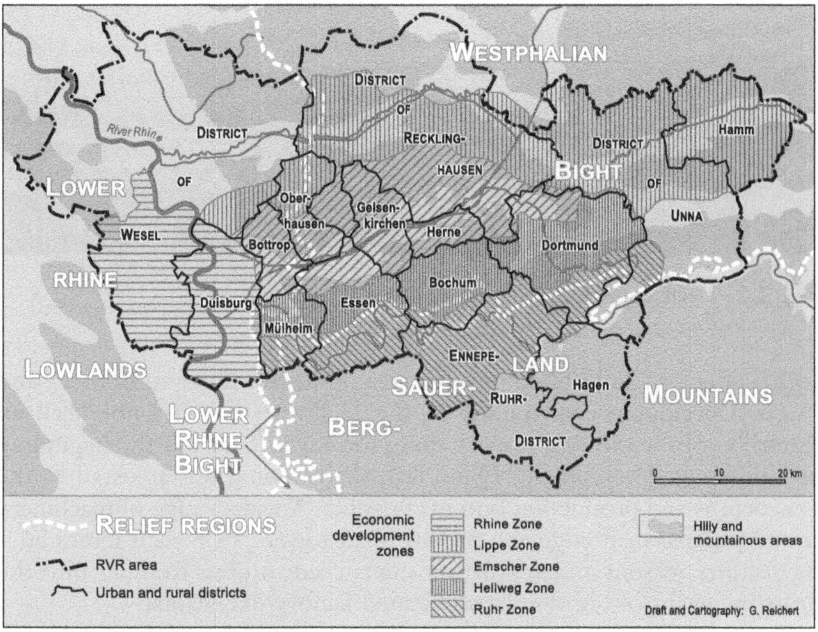

Fig. 2.1 Development zones, districts and relief regions

Before 1840, coal mining was restricted to the gallery mining in the Ruhr valley where the coal seams crop out. The lean and anthracite coals produced could be used in private households and in forges. The River Ruhr, stringed by some minor towns, was the transportation line for coal and kept this function until the late 1880s (Fig. 2.2). However, the technology of shaft mining had moved the center of coal mining to the north already in the 1860s. Altogether, the industrial impact on the Ruhr zone remained a restricted one, both spatially and in intensity, and has been the lowest in the whole region.

The Industrial Setup (1840–1869)

To its north, the Hellweg zone is the only zone with pre-industrial towns of some importance, lined along the medieval trading route of the Hellweg. The northward movement of coal mining into this zone started in 1837, and it was already in 1840 that the focus of the regional

Fig. 2.2 Coal shipping on the River Ruhr 1865

coal production had shifted into the area between Mülheim, Borbeck and Essen. Developing coal mining in the Hellweg zone has not been an extension of the old coal district along the River Ruhr but the beginning of a different development. Quite fast, shaft mining was adjusted to the new depths and production outputs possible. A wider range of machinery (water pumps, shaft engines), massive shaft towers, twin shaft mines built for security reasons and ventilation shafts used to press fresh air into the drifts by means of big ventilators created factory-like plants.

By spreading coal mining into the Hellweg zone, the geological knowledge was consolidated in so far that it became known that the coal seams sink underneath the rock cover which itself increases in thickness to the north. Still in 1826/1827, the Westfalia ironworks in Lünen as well as the smaller ironworks in the Sterkrade area used charcoal to smelt the local bog ores; the new availability of coking coal, however, was to substitute the charcoal in the smelting processes and a spatial symbiosis of coal mining and iron and steel industry, located on the coal deposits, came into being. From the mid-1860s to World War I, this zone became the main area of coal mining and of the iron and steel industries. An increasingly connected railway network was laid out and the population rose from 112,000 in 1852 to over one million in 1905. Mines and factories began to encircle the old Hellweg towns, which, however, widely failed to cope with this economic boom in both political and planning terms (Fig. 2.3). The entrepreneurs set the scene before the town councils could react, and by acquiring land, they exerted influence on the development and the structure of the landscape already in those early years. Both the industrialists and the national political authorities regarded the areas north of the River Ruhr as areas to be exploited for the benefit of the nation.

Fig. 2.3 City of Essen, seen from south-east, c. 1880

Any other spatial demands had to be subordinated under the industrial demands. Nevertheless, the Hellweg cities became the focal points of the overall development in the following decades and were able to steady this position particularly because they had to face no competitors from the northern areas.

The Industrial Expansion and the Setting of Early Urban Infrastructure (1870–1918)

The unification of the German Empire created a new sales market without any customs barriers, French reparations invigorated the capital market, and in Lorraine, new iron ore deposits came into reach. The developing German railway network became a major customer of the mining and the iron and steel industries. Increasing prices, revenues and stock prices caused a first period of promoterism from 1870 to 1875 and a second one from 1895 to 1913.

The Hellweg zone cities have only moderately been affected by the industrial expansion. Production and sales syndicates were founded, horizontal mergers of smaller mining companies ended up in big mining companies and the vertical concentration led to iron and steel companies of world-wide importance. Their headquarters and those of new regional organizations as well as the developing banking sector were allocated in the Hellweg cities, thus increasing their influence as central places. With respect to the production sites, however, the basic industries entered the areas on both sides of the River Emscher from 1870 onwards, and by 1900, coal mining crossed the River Lippe.

The areas alongside the River Emscher lacked pre-industrial towns, powerful local authorities and particularly a substantial number of population, and thus, they came under the comprehensive influence of the basic industries, in economic, social, political and spatial terms. Large coal mines with large mining claims and extensive properties as well as iron and steel works of vertically integrated companies were scattered all over the landscape, interrupted by badlands, moorlands and agricultural lands, intersected by the tracks of the regional and works railways as well as detracted from subsidence. Pre-industrial settlement cores were transformed, very often old villages shrunk to only some farm houses, and larger villages became encapsulated into new settlement patterns.

From 1871 to 1885, the population of the Ruhr increased by 50.0%, with the relative peak in the southern Emscher zone. The Hellweg cities took the highest absolute gains, even if their relative increase was only second to the Emscher zones. In the years of crises that followed until 1895 the highest relative increase moved into the southern Emscher zone, the northern Emscher zone was opened up. In the third boom phase from 1895 to 1905, the absolute population increase outstripped that of the previous phase. Never before the Ruhr had attracted so many people, nor did it ever after. This was due to the enormous demand for labor force that increased according to the spreading of big and integrated mines and of the large works of the iron and steel industries. But because this demand could no longer be satisfied in the neighboring West German regions, the mining and the iron and steel companies were forced to send out agents into the east provinces of Prussia, to Poland and to Austria and Hungary to recruit laborers.

Given this massive influx of migrants, the deficient settlement patterns and the non-existence of working local estate markets in the rural areas between the Hellweg cities and on both sides of the River Emscher, it was an economic precondition for the industrial companies to erect housing quarters for the workers at their own expenses. Considering the paramount housing shortage, there were no alternatives to these factory-own settlements and the workers' right to abode became a coercive of the companies. Interspersed into the countryside and often far away from any infrastructural facilities, the coalmines and the settlements of their miners—often referred to as "colonies"—formed symbiotic entities

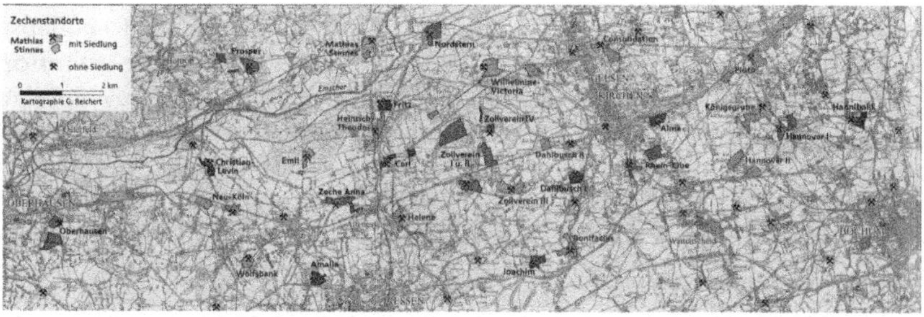

Fig. 2.4 Mines with and without settlements in the Emscher zone, 1894

which became constituent elements of the industrial cultural landscape of the Emscher zones (Fig. 2.4). Under prosperous economic conditions, these industrial villages would grow together with neighboring industrial villages, and if they exceeded a certain population threshold, they were declared cities; functional urban centers, however, did not develop here before the 1920/1930s.

On the other hand, the Hellweg cities increasingly gained influence as sites of the regional administrative bodies and as concentrations of retail units with regional hinterlands. Infrastructural facilities were systematically planned and erected in the 1890s. Among them were public gas lightning, water works, effective sewage systems, some intercommunal tramway networks and a variety of prestigious buildings. A stronger impact of local planning provided the framework of this development; thus, next to the structural development that was dominated by the demands of the basic industries, new objectives of urban development were pursued. Housing quarters on regular street grids were planned and built up as were prestigious quarters, which corresponded to the increasing social differentiation. Different forms of public greens were added to the urban structure as well. Tree lines along promenades or old city ramparts were among the first, as were city parks that met the recreation demands of the middle classes. By the end of the nineteenth century, urban parks, theaters, concert halls and meeting halls had become the basics of the urban infrastructure in the Hellweg and in some Emscher cities.

On the regional level, the Emschergenossenschaft was founded in 1899, the first German water management authority, which changed the River Emscher and its tributaries into an open sewer system and installed an overall water management. When the freshwater supply was to collapse in 1913, the water management authorities requested a water pollution control of the River Ruhr. The Ruhrverband was founded to operate purification plants, and the 1899 Ruhrtalsperrenverband was to build water reservoirs. Within the Emscher catchment area, one-third (330 qkms) has been effected by subsistence due to coal mining; consequently, a permanent drainage of the area has become an additional main task of the Emschergenossenschaft.

The Industrial Consolidation and the Beginning of Urban and Regional Planning (1919–1945)

After World War I, a period of economic recession, of restrained investments and of consolidating and concentrating companies, sites and processes began. Reparations, the Ruhr occupation as well as the inflation of the 1920s set the political and economic scene. Coal mining saw a sweeping process of rationalization, and due to technical innovations, the number of miners decreased from 507,000 (1923) to 355,000 (1929).[2] In the 1930s, however, the regional economy expanded further to the north and the west and achieved its point of culmination in terms of production technology as well as spatial and corporate complexity. The center of production had moved into the areas along the River Emscher and the Rhine-Herne canal along which extensive industrial sites and plants of increasing complexity had been allocated. Due to measures of rationalization that produced compound shaft mines like Zollverein XII in Essen and Gneisenau in Dortmund (Fig. 2.5), the regional coal mining reached its maximum production of 130.2 million tons in 1939.

As in coal mining, the overall economic recession caused processes of concentration and technical rationalization in the iron and steel industries as well. In the 1920s, by means of merging and by concentrating production processes, some 200 companies were absorbed by twelve big concerns; the most complex one of them was the 1925 founded Vereinigte Stahlwerke. Its production sites were arranged in a way that a region-wide division of labor could be achieved using the technical equipment of the works, the management expertise and the location. In the 1930s boom phase, the iron and steel industries expanded spatially and

[2] Paul Wiel, *Das Ruhrgebiet in Vergangenheit und Gegenwart* (Essen: Scharioth, 1963), p. 24.

Fig. 2.5 Zollverein XII mine, 1932

structurally, the production of the Ruhr exceeded that of Britain. Along the production line of coal, a comprehensive economic system of Europe-wide unchallenged efficiency had developed in the Ruhr region by the mid-1930s, comprising coal mines, iron and steel works, chemical works, any form of suppliers, powerful transport systems, etc.

As the basic industries ceased in reclaiming further production sites after having reached the peak of production, the way was open for urban and regional planning activities. The Essen and Dortmund city authorities drew up plans to develop their cities into major industrial cities; in the Emscher zone, new urban administrative units were formed out of structurally disaggregated industrial villages. Since the beginning of the 1920s, the local authorities acquired land, established housing companies on their own and supported housing cooperatives by providing building material and cheap building plots. Due to this official engagement, a wide range of compact housing quarters came into being in the interwar years. To ease the quantitative housing shortage, the communal housing companies tended to erect multiple-story residential buildings in the immediate vicinity of the city-centers, whereas building plots for two-story one-family dwellings were given to the housing cooperatives on the cheap fringes of the existing built-up areas. A semi-open design of the quarters was preferred thus following the principles of the garden city movement before World War I and those practiced in the companies' settlements since then. The rise of the cities became manifest in the city-centers and their fringes. In the Hellweg cities that had already experienced a phase of urban development before World War I, prestigious single buildings were built; in the new Emscher cities, local authority quarters were established as the new focal points of public life.

In addition to these local planning activities, the regional planning authority Siedlungsverband Ruhrkohlenbezirk was founded in 1920 in order to regulate the urban development, to work against further urban sprawl, to create open spaces for recreational purposes and to overcome the negative impacts of industrialization. Since its start, the Siedlungsverband has been developing and extending a regional system of open and green spaces that pervade the cities.

The Economic Reconstruction and Urban Reproduction (1947–c. 1960)

World War II brought multifold damages to the Ruhr area; particularly, the sites of the iron and steel industries were extensively bombarded. An even greater impact on the comprehensive economic system had the decartelization of the companies and the dismantlement of the production sites in the immediate post-war years. However, excluding the Krupp works in Essen, all basic industries had widely been reorganized by the mid-1950s, because the national reconstruction required an efficient industrial region, and both the politicians and the industrialists sought to achieve the pre-war status as soon as possible. Consequently, the land-use structures of the interwar years were widely reproduced in the 1950s and early 1960s. In addition, the Lippe zone in the north and the western Rhine area were completely integrated into the economic system. World War II bombardments and evacuations had halved the population, particularly in the Hellweg cities. With the return of the evacuees and an officially steered in-migration of refugees and displaced persons, the population of the Ruhr increased quickly again; in the Ruhr, the population grew quicker than in the rest of Germany. The regional population reached its peak of 5.67 million in 1961.

Since 1955, new technologies produced more efficient and bigger blast furnaces; the basic oxygen steelmaking technology and the production of electric steel allowed higher steel qualities and raised the crude steel capacities. In 1974, the production of crude iron and crude steel achieved the peak values of 25.5 million tons and 32.2 million tons, respectively. In coal mining, the number of miners reached its peak of 397,425 (1957) as well, but the pre-war productivity could never be achieved again due a long period of inadequate investment and great a number of inexperienced miners.

The Deindustrialization of the Coal Mining and Iron and Steel Industries (1957/1958–2018)

The 1957/1958 coal crisis started the deindustrialization of the Ruhr area. Continuously, the share of coal in the domestic market decreased. This development—at first regarded as cyclical crisis and only later as a structural one—was answered by waves of shutdowns, and in 1969, the Ruhrkohle AG was founded to organize a market-orientated reduction of the regional mining industry. Geographically, the closure of coal mines roughly followed the same south–north direction as did its expansion, and the last mine was shut down in 2018.

The iron and steel industries had seen job losses since 1960, and since 1973, the companies had to face an increasing competition from Japan and the threshold countries on the ordinary steel market. The classical export markets no longer could compensate the losses on the domestic market. Similar to coal mining, the iron and steel industries tried to improve the situation by closing down and concentration measures. Eventually, the iron and steel industries, and particularly its producing branches, have been concentrated along the Rhine front of Duisburg.

The Industrial Cultural Landscape of the Ruhr

With the deindustrialization increasing, the impact of the basic industries on the landscape dwindled away. So it can be assumed that in the late 1970s the formation of the industrial cultural landscape widely came to end. Accordingly, the industrial cultural landscape of the Ruhr is a historical one, and as such, it is embedded in the actual cultural landscape.

To determine this industrial cultural landscape conceptually, four dimensions can be defined—zones, axes, networks and systems. As stated above, the economic development of the Ruhr produced west-easterly zones that are deduced from the phases of the northward movement of coal mining. With the production focus of coal mining successively shifting to the north, industrial plants and technical/industrial relations of increasing complexity came into being and had different impacts on the landscape. The interaction of the pre-industrial potentials, of the intensity of industrial printing und overprinting, of different planning concepts and urbanistic visions, and of different stages of technology formed the spatial characteristics of the development zones. The Ruhr zone did not receive a lasting imprint in the phase of industrial expansion because the industrial importance of this zone decreased with the shift from gallery mining to deep shaft mining. From the second half of the nineteenth century onwards, the villas of the industrialists have been allocated in the Ruhr valley, and since the 1920s regional planning initiatives, the Ruhr zone became an area for housing and recreation purposes. The Hellweg zone exhibits the most intense pre-industrial imprint, whereas the imprint of the industrial expansion phase is limited; c. 1900 and in the interwar years, clusters of industrial and administrative services emerged and turned the Hellweg cities into regional centers.

The functional guideline of the southern Emscher zone is the Cologne-Minden railway track that gave birth to an industrial structure consisting of extended and efficient mining and iron and steel plants; the southern Emscher zone has been the core area of the industrial production for decades. With the northward movement of coal mining continuing, a second zone of industrial production developed north of the River Emscher and the Rhine-Herne canal; here, coal mining was the dominating industry. Its scattered sites and the pre-industrial village structure generated a settlement fabric, which is more disconnected than that of the southern Emscher zone.

The zonal division of the Ruhr is primarily a functional and economic one. For more than a century since 1840, however, the settlement structure of the Ruhr has followed the pre-industrial south–north-orientated regional roads. Thus, settlement axes developed that subdivide the economic zones into an alteration of built-up (maybe, urban) and less or not built-up ("interurban") areas. Considering the structural fabric of the landscape, it can thus be stated that each economic zone has widely been developed in the same period, but not equally in space (Fig. 2.6).

The linear character is intensified when the influence of both the railway lines and the Emscher sewage system is considered. Three big

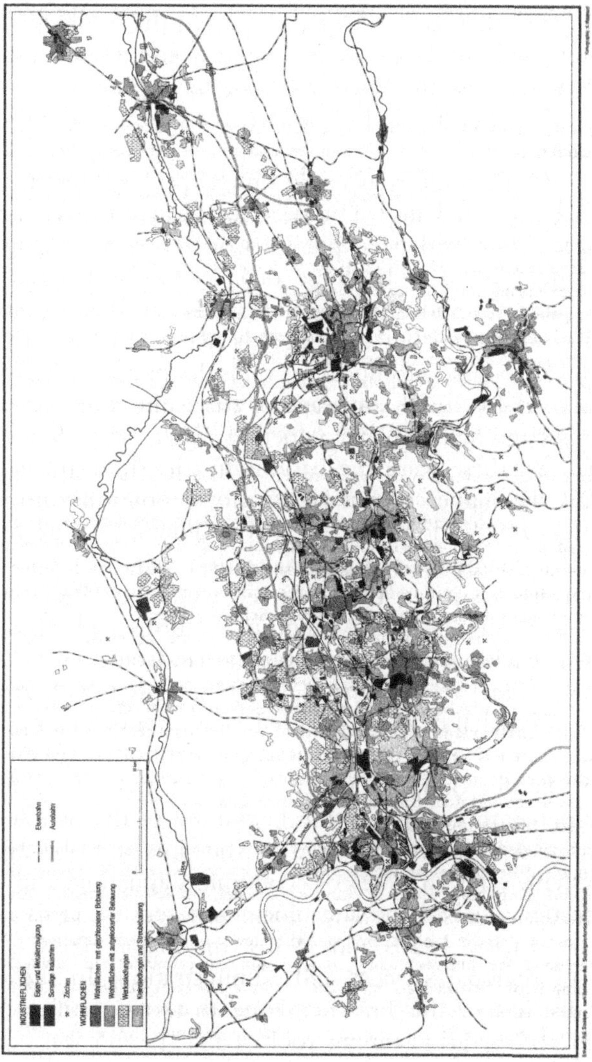

Fig. 2.6 Land uses and settlement axes, 1957

railway companies and some smaller ones have been operating in the region up to the 1880. Merged into one national company, the densest railway network of Europe had developed by 1900. Railway lines, constantly improved in their connectivity, connected the production sites and their customer areas but, at the same time, dissected the landscape in multiple ways. Particularly in the Emscher zone, railway stations were the only points of any functionality and so became the origin or the focus of some urban development (Fig. 2.7).

Coal mining and other industries could only enter the Emscher zone after the River Emscher and its tributaries had been canalized and an extensive drainage system had been put into operation to manage the effects of subsidence. So, it is by these determining spatial networks that across wide parts the industrial cultural landscape is not a continuously two-dimensional one, but also spreads like a network over the pre-industrial rural landscape causing cores, veins, loops and inner fringes.

Finally, the industrial cultural landscape of the Ruhr results from the time-spatial interests and demands of competing stakeholders. Sometimes operating in alliances, these were the basic industries/industrialists, the local councils and the higher regional or national political authorities. Resulting from this competition, two often contradicting spatial systems developed since the beginning of industrialization. The first one is the "economic organism"—as it has been referred to in the 1930s—which is mainly based on economic cause-symptom relations and which had sweeping effects of exclusive dominance on the landscape. Next to the economic system or under its dominance, an urban system with growing urban necessities and spatial demands evolved. Since the beginning, there has been a structural and particularly spatial competition between these two systems, the battleground of which has been the estate market. From the mid-nineteenth century to the beginning of the deindustrialization, the Ruhr area has been impacted by the aims and objectives of the economic system. Only in times of economic stagnation, the urban system took precedence, as in the late nineteenth century crisis and in the interwar years. In the 1920s and 1930s, the major Hellweg cities became centers of regional services and administration. In the newly founded urban districts of the Emscher zone that often still lacked a city-center, a state-of-the-art planning tool of that period was applied; to define a central point in the midst of the spatial "unurban" patterns, which had been caused by the economic system, a set of public buildings was installed to form a governmental/administrative quarter.

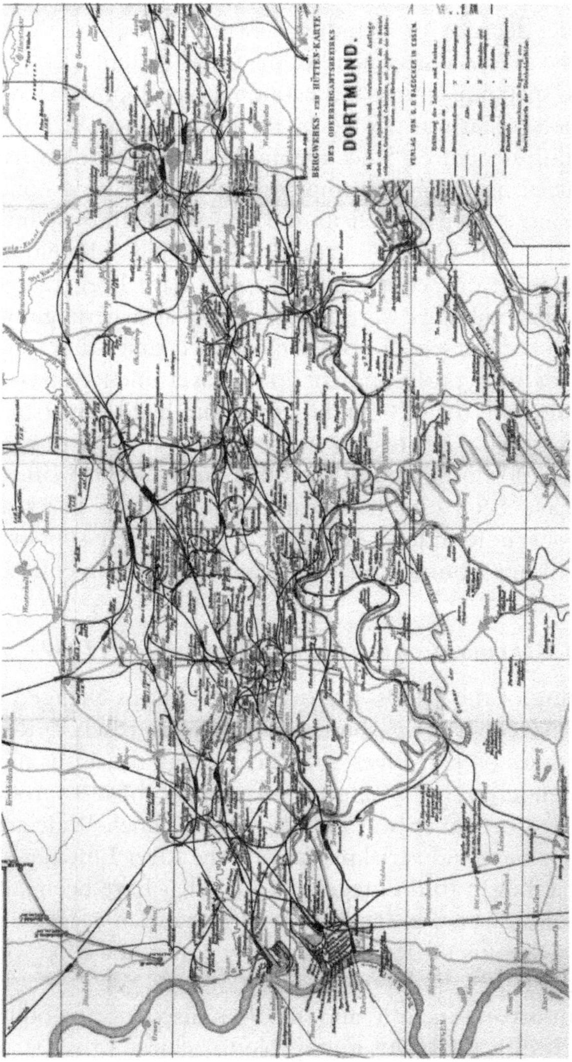

Fig. 2.7 Mines, ironworks and railway lines in the Ruhr, 1895

Structural Changes

Reducing Functional Deficits, Urban Repairs (c. 1965–...)

Consequently, the decades of deindustrialization have widely been a period in which the aims and objectives of the urban system were pursued. Up to the 1970s, spatial planning and economic development have been influenced by a policy that was guided by the idea to improve but also to preserve the existing structures. Since the mid-1960s, this policy has been supported by official programes to improve the bad housing conditions and to overcome infrastructural deficits and unwanted land-use mixtures. After old industrial sites had fallen vacant, the remaining old buildings had normally dismantled in due course and the sites have been reused ever since. Old industrial buildings were not regarded as a heritage; demolishing them was in the interest of both the old companies that wanted to sell the brownfields with profit and the local governments that saw the future only guaranteed if the old building structure had been abandoned.

In general, to develop an overall attractive urban structure and to achieve competitive positions among the other large German cities, technology centers have been established and new business parks and all universities have been founded. All changes have been supported by massive financial means from regional and national governmental bodies.

Urban and Regional Conversion and Innovation (1989–...)

Since the beginning of the 1980s, the overall conditions changed fundamentally, when the progressive shutdown of mines reached the large mines on both sides of the River Emscher, when the iron and steel industries had to undergo shrinking processes and mothballed production sites, and when the German railway company closed lines. Wide areas fell vacant, the broad zone of industrial plots along the River Emscher and the Rhine-Herne canal began to disintegrate. Cities that have been suffering from a shortage of industrial premises for more than ten years were now confronted with a surplus of derelict land they could not cope with due to limited local budgets.

The insufficient urban functions and the often disconnected built fabric made and makes it difficult, if not impossible to achieve urban structures similar to those in the Hellweg zone. Under these circumstances, the International Building Exhibition promoted new long-term planning aims based on the idea to discover the potentials that elements and components of the economic system might offer when being integrated into the urban system.

Thus, the Emscher sewage system is actually being converted into a system of natural water flows. This new system will be integrated into a new landscape park which itself will form the spatial framework of a modern urban development. Likewise, and in contrast to the structural changes in the Hellweg zone 20 years before, the built remains of the industrial past are no longer regarded as obstacles to a successful future but as testimonials of the industrial past and regional identity worth conserving and re-using. Numerous old production sites have at least been secured, some of them are being reused for cultural or commercial purposes. In total, the industrial cultural landscape comprises a plenty of industrial monuments that are unique in Europe. The most outstanding sites form the basis of the developing industrial. For this purpose, the RVR-run "Route of Industrial Culture" has been established that attracted some 5 million visitors in 2017.

The Industrial Cultural Landscape—Perspectives

With the process of change still going on, the industrial cultural landscape of the Ruhr shows two sides. Putting outstanding industrial monuments—coal mines, steel works, workers' settlements, ship-lifts or villas of industrialists—on the stage is to change the national image of the region and to strengthen the regional identity; "industrial cultural landscape" has become a positive term both inside the region and outside and has fostered the new application process to the UNESCO.

At the same time and particularly in the Emscher zone, "industrial cultural landscape" still means unoccupied areas and brownfields waiting for investment and change; it means settlement fabrics that are disconnected and far away from being urban as well as a landscape that is intersected by active and obsolete road tracks, railway lines and sewers, thus testifying that this region has once been Europe's largest industrial region.

References

Mehrfeld, Ursula and Pfeiffer, Marita, 'Das Welterbe-Projekt "Industrielle Kulturlandschaft Ruhrgebiet"', in Industrielle Kulturlandschaft, Forum Geschichtskultur Ruhr 2 (2015), pp. 15–22.

Stiftung Industriedenkmalpflege und Geschichtskultur (SIG)/Foundation for the Preservation of Industrial Moments and Historical Culture, Ruhrgebiet Industrial Cultural Landscape. Draft Statement of Outstanding Universal Value. Proposal for an Update of the German Tentative List for UNESCO Worlds Heritage (Dortmund: The Foundation for the Preservation of Industrial Monuments and Historical Culture (SIG), 2017).

Wehling, Hans-Werner, Zollverein and the Industrial Cultural Landscape Ruhr. Report on Its Theoretical/Conceptional Foundation and Its Spatial Operationalization (Essen: Klartext, 2015).

Wiel, Paul, Das Ruhrgebiet in Vergangenheit und Gegenwart (Essen: Scharioth, 1963).

CHAPTER 3

The North West of Italy

Stefano Musso

The North West was the core of the industrial revolution in Italy, starting from the second half of the nineteenth century. From then on, it has been hosting the most advanced components of Italian capitalism. The image of the so-called industrial triangle—Turin, Milan, Genoa—dominated the manuals of economic history. In a country characterized by deep territorial differences, the North West concentrated the bulk of the most important big companies up to the end of the 1970s, when sociologists and economic historians discovered the so-called Third Italy, characterized by business districts and flexible specialization carried on by small-size business, mainly in traditional goods manufacturing.[1] The discovery of the Third Italy, located in the North East and Center of the country, made more complex the traditional description of Italy as dominated by the dualism North–South, the North West being the First

[1] Arnaldo Bagnasco, *Tre Italie. La problematica territoriale dello svilupp italianio*, (Bologna: Il Mulino, 1978).

S. Musso (✉)
Department of Historical Studies, University of Turin, Turin, Italy
e-mail: stefano.musso@unito.it

S. Berger et al. (eds.), *Deindustrialisation in Twentieth-Century Europe*, Palgrave Studies in the History of Social Movements,
https://doi.org/10.1007/978-3-030-89631-7_3

Italy and the underdeveloped South the Second Italy. In the South, if we exclude the area of Napoli where industrial plants had a historical presence, there were just some "Cathedrals in the desert," i.e., big industrial plants for oil refinery and steel industry, which were established by State-owned enterprises in order to recover economically depressed areas. Such Cathedrals had no or little links with local economic fabric and were not able to give impulse to local autonomous economic development.[2]

According to census data, in 1911 the national average quota of the active population in industry was 23.6%. In Lombardy, it reached 35.6%, in Liguria 32.7% and in Piedmont, where agriculture still played a significant role, 26.4%. In 1981, the national average was 41.5%, in Lombardy 52.1%, in Piedmont 50.3 and in Liguria 33.3, due to the early development of the tertiary sector because of the trade activities linked to the ports of Genoa and La Spezia. In 1971, when industry was the first occupational sector in Italy and reached its maximum share of active population, equal to 44.4%, the North West exceeded by 15% the average national manufacture employment. The economic and social change occurred in the last 30 years of the twentieth century made the industrial fabric of the North West more similar to the rest of the country, so that in 2001 North West manufacture exceeded only by 5%.

The North West has thus shaped the Italian history of business culture, trade union cultures, and industrial relations for a long time. It is not by chance that the Socialist Party was born in Genoa in 1892, the General Confederation of Labor (CGDL) in Milan in 1906, and the Industrial Employers' association (Confindustria) in Turin in 1910.[3] Furthermore, the main initiative for the introduction of Taylorism in Italy began in Turin in 1927, when Fiat established the Italian Bedaux Company, which was chaired by the founder of Fiat Giovanni Agnelli with the establishment by Fiat, in 1927, of the Italian Bedaux Company, chaired by the founder of Fiat, Giovanni Agnelli.

In the second half of the 1930s, the Fascist government started some decentralized industrial initiatives in the North East and in the Center for

[2] Vera N. Zamagni, *Idustrialzzazione e squilibri regionali in Italia*, (Bologna: Il Mulino, 1978).

[3] Mario Abrate, *La lotta sindacale nell'industrializzazione in Italia, 1906–1926*, (Turin: Franco Angeli, 1968).

war preparation,[4] but the bulk of the productive apparatuses remained the prerogative of the North West, which reached even more economic weight in the post-war reconstruction and in the years of the Italian Golden Age between 1950 and 1970.

The two world wars accelerated the processes of concentration and formation of large enterprises, which exercised a leadership toward small and medium-sized companies, also through sub-supply links, not to say the political weight achieved under fascism by the few large entrepreneurial families linked to the leading sectors of the second industrial revolution: steel, mechanics, chemistry, and electric-power industry.[5]

In the first phase of Italian industrialization, during the second half of the nineteenth century, the leading sector was textile, which employed mainly female and child labor. It was located at the mouth of the Alpine valleys toward the plain of the Po Valley, to take advantage of cheap hydraulic power. In the second phase of Italian industrialization, throughout the twentieth century, large enterprises and the capital towns of the industrial triangle increased jointly. In the big industrial towns, a central working class grew. Predominantly male and concentrated in the large factories of the second industrial revolution, the central working class became protagonist of the arising labor movement.[6]

The economic, social, and political landscape of the North West's big towns was shaped by the dominance of large-sized companies. Notwithstanding this common framework, the economic development of the early twentieth century consolidated different characters for Genoa, Milan, and Turin. Genoa was the center of heavy industries, like steel, shipbuilding, and big mechanical products like turbines and large marine engines. These industries enjoyed strong State support, because of their importance for the productive autonomy of the country and its military endowments. The companies that operated with large plants requiring massive and risky

[4] Duccio Bigazzi, 'La fabbrica nella crisi del regime fascista', in: Angelo Ventura (ed.), *Sulla crisi del regime fascista 1938–1943. La società italiana dal "consenso" alla Resistenza*, (Venice: Marsilio, 1996).

[5] Roland Sarti, *Fascism and the Industrial Leadership in Italy. 1919–1940. A study in the expansion of private power under fascism*, (Berkeley, Los Angeles and London: University of California Press, 1971); Gianni Toniolo, *L'economia dell'Italia fascista*, (Rome-Bari: Laterza, 1980).

[6] Stephano Musso, 'Il lavoro e la città', in: Guiseppe Berta and Guido Alfani (eds.), *Torino Industria. Persone, lavoro, imprese*, (Turin: Archivio Storico della Città di Torino, 2008), pp. 109–166.

investments openly claimed the aid of the State for the national function they performed. Therefore, the Genoese capitalism can be considered a "political capitalism." The great Genoese entrepreneurial families reached its maximum development in Genoa at the beginning of the twentieth century, when the alliance between steel producers and universal banks asserted itself at the top of Italian economic power, of which the Genoese families were the main protagonists. In the aftermath of World War 1, the State rescued the biggest Genoese company Ansaldo, which underwent a deep crisis because of the end of war production. The great world crisis started in 1929 changed the tissue of economic power. In order to rescue from bankruptcy heavy industries and banks, the State assumed their ownership. In 1933, with the establishing of the Industrial Recovery Institute (IRI), the holding of State-owned companies and banks, the decision-making centers of the Genoese industry moved definitely to Rome, i.e., to the national government, which had already had relevant importance previously, given the role of State orders for steel and shipyards. In the interwar period, while in Genoa there was a move from political capitalism to State capitalism, in Italy a new axis of economic power was established, centered on the Milanese financiers and electricity industrialists.[7]

In Turin, Fiat emerged from the world crisis as the only center of economic power in the capital town of Piedmont. By the end of World War 1, Antonio Gramsci defined Turin as the industrial capital of Italy, thanks to the special modernity of its social structure. According to Gramsci, in Turin, class distinctions were clear. The biggest car company of the country created the most homogeneous and concentrated working class, who played a vanguard role for the Italian labor movement. This image of Turin was certainly over-simplified, but it evocated the early nature of Turin as a car town, destined to evolve into a mono-cultural economy: in the 1950s, 80% of Turin's industrial production depended on the automotive industry.[8]

Indeed, the true industrial capital of Italy was Milan, due to the big size of its production activities, in which all industrial branches were

[7] Franco Amatori and Andrea Colli, *Impresa e industria in Italia. Dall'Unità a oggi*, (Venice: Marsilio, 1999).

[8] Stephano Musso, 'La società industriale nel ventennio fascista', in: Nicola Tranfaglia (ed.), *Storia di Torino. 8. Dalla Grande guerra alla Liberazione,* (Turin: Einaudi, 1998), pp. 313–423.

largely present. But in Milan—as indeed in Genoa, thanks to the port—the economic and social fabric was more articulated than in Turin, due to the much greater diffusion of service, commercial, and financial activities. Therefore, the world of workers in Milan was more inhomogeneous than in Turin, due to the widespread presence of salaried workers in the service sector: in Milan, the industrial working class in the strict sense constituted a lower share of the total population than in Turin.[9]

As for the workers' movement, Milan was the capital of reformist socialism, but there was also a presence of anarcho-syndicalists. The latter were also active in Turin, but they lost consent after the defeat of the agitation they promoted in 1911–1912. Headed by Bruno Buozzi, the reformist-led Federation of metal workers (FIOM) was able to recover the leadership of workers, thanks to a more radical strategy and some significant conquests before the outbreak of the war.

In Genoa, the trade union scenario showed a sharp split between two Chambers of Labour. The reformist one, located in the town center, developed an imposing cooperative movement. On the other hand, the anarco-syndicalists led the Chamber of Labour of the surrounding village of Sestri Levante, which hosted the largest industrial plants of the town.[10]

Since the age of the "belle époque," the skilled workers and the employees of the big enterprises had become the most relevant social reference for socialism and the trade union movement. The extraordinary expansion of the industrial labor market during World War I led to a new mass dimension of unionism. The previous craft unions changed toward modern industrial unions, open to both skilled and unskilled workers. The change was so rapid to cause imbalances and uncertainties on strategies to adopt in the convulsions of the red biennium 1919–1920.

During World War 1, Confindustria and the reformist-led CGDL experienced a systematic mediation of collective labor disputes, in particular in the regional industrial mobilization committees of Piedmont, Lombardy

Ibidem., 'Il lungo miracolo economico. Industria, economia e società', in: Nicola Tranfaglia (ed.), *Storia di Torino. 9. Gli anni della Repubblica*, (Turin: Einaudi, 1999), pp. 49–100.

[9] Franco Della Peruta, *Milano. Lavoro e fabbrica. 1814–1915*, (Milan: Angeli, 1987); Gianfranco Petrillo, *La capitale del miracolo. Sviluppo potere lavoro a Milano 1953–1962*, (Milan: Angelo, 1992).

[10] Paolo Arvati and Paride Rugafiori, *Storia della Camera del lavoro di Genova. Dalla Resistenza al luglio'60*, (Rome: Editrice Sindacale Italiana, 1981).

and Liguria. At the end of the war, the two organizations continued a dialogue, trying to perform a joint management of post-war problems. In February 1919, in Milan, Confindustria and FIOM signed the first nation-wide agreement, which granted the historical claim of the eight hours of work without any single strike. Yet, the attempt to perform a corporatist compromise was destined to crumble under the blows of inflation, of political crisis and the breaking out of a sharp social conflict, which was not containable within the limits of a newly born and barely sketched out system of industrial relations.

Fascism stamped its authoritarian seal on labor relations, keeping the fascist union outside the workplace with the abolition of the previous system of worker's representatives within the factories, which was called "internal commissions." The former elective representatives of employees on trade union lists were only belatedly replaced by Fascist trustees, nominated from above, in October 1939. On the contrary, the regime guaranteed the organizational autonomy of Confindustria, even subjecting it to growing interferences.

In 1945, Confindustria was re-enacted under the guidance of the Genoese Catholic entrepreneur Angelo Costa, advocate of a conservative liberal-protectionist program, characterized by the dual demand for hands free for the enterprise, and State aid. On the labor front, the reborn free syndicalism experimented with a difficult unitary attempt with the foundation, in June 1944, of the Italian General Confederation of Labor (CGIL).

In the "unitary" CGIL, different union and political cultures flowed together. On the one side, the communist and socialist component linked by a unitary action pact between the reference parties, on the other side, the Christian-democratic one.

The short season of union unity and collaboration to economic reconstruction of the country would have broken in the cold war climate. The North West was the protagonist area of the clash between two different trade union cultures, the antagonism of the social-communist matrix embodied by the no longer unitary CGIL and the collaborative imprint of CISL and UIL.[11]

Union division weakened the contractual dynamics. Thanks to the union division, the industrialists started an autocratic management of the

[11] Guiseppe Acocella, Sergio Zaninelli, and Giuseppe Acocella (eds.), *Sessant'anni del "sindacato nuovo". La CISL fra storia e interpretazioni*, (Rome: Edizioni Lavoro, 2012).

workforce through the company hierarchy, without any union remedial role. In particular, employers refused to adhere to the CISL proposal to start a new industrial relation pattern based on the productivity drive of the Marshall Plan. Reacting to employer's refusal, CISL convinced the Christian Democratic-led government to detach State-owned companies (IRI and ENI) from Confindustria, in order to experiment with its new pattern of industrial relations with IRI and ENI.

At the dawn of the 1960s, thanks to the Italian economic miracle, the North West achieved full employment, which changed the balance of power between business and workers, in favor of the latter. Moreover, the entrepreneurial refusal to adhere to CISL proposal pushed the unions to unitary action that triggered a long cycle of conflict, which lasted until the late 1970s. The large workers' mobilizations of the 1970s had the North West as its core. Workers' struggle ended in the 1980s because of the progressive downsizing of employment in manufacturing.

Form the 1980s onward, business crisis changed union action from acquisitive to concession bargaining, in order to limit dismissals. In the deindustrialization era, the differences in North West resurfaced. Piedmont remained more anchored to the manufacturing activity and to the presence of large private enterprises. Lombardy instead developed a more diversified and dynamic economy progressively focused on the medium-size enterprise, while Liguria had a high weight of the tertiary sector alongside the permanencies of State-owned enterprises. From a political point of view, until the end of the1990s, Piedmont and Liguria maintained a labor movement tradition stronger than in Lombardy. Consequently, the regional administrative bodies in Piedmont and Liguria carried out a social dialogue with the social forces, which was higher in Piedmont and Liguria than in Lombardy. Also at national level, a new harsh crisis at the beginning of the 1990s and the goal to reach the Maastricht standards pushed CGIL, CISL, UIL, Confindustria, and Government to sign tripartite agreements in 1992 and 1993, in order to start an incomes policy.

The tripartite agreements meant a historical change in the Italian industrial relation system, from a century-long over-conflictive and over-politicized pattern, to a more cooperative one. From then on, there have been alternating periods of consultation and co-decision between social partners and center-left governments, and unilateral decisions by right-wing governments. In the years of the long-lasting international crisis started in 2008, also the last center-left government headed by Matteo

Renzi mostly refused social dialogue. Notwithstanding such refusal at national level, social dialogue persisted at local level to a certain extent in order to face deindustrialization and local development issues.

The advent of regional governments in the 1970s fostered local social dialogue, because of the rules for managing the European Social Fund and the European Regional Development Fund, requiring the participation of the social forces. The Italian social security system also fostered union action at local level. The Italian system of social insurance against unemployment has been extremely lacking, providing only meager roles to those who lost or could not find a job. The main historical redundancy scheme was a Wage Integration Fund (Cassa Integrazione Guadagni, CIG) that protected only the workforce of business of more than 15 employees and disregarded the rest of the labor market until 2014, when CIG extended allowances to small firms and to fix-term and "atypical" jobs. Rather than offering a system of insurance against unemployment, as in other European countries, the CIG provided a wage replacement allowance "integrating" employees' wages and salaries in the industrial sector for a temporary reduction or suspension of working time. The peculiar characteristics of the CIG stem from the fact that its system of wage integration was not initially designed to cater for unemployment welfare. The scheme firstly meant a device of industrial policy to allow firms the chance to finance temporary redundancies in cases of business cycle downturns. The Italian system of social security never developed a universal safety net against unemployment probably because of a historically highly segmented labor market accompanied by a long-lasting corporative tradition. When the entrepreneur submits an application to access the wage integration fund, he must consult the unions. Unions' opinion and agreement on company's application imply information rights. Therefore, the wage integration fund is a tool for unions in order to gain knowledge of market conditions and business reorganization strategies. Normally, unions intervene in the decision on the choice of which workers to put in layoffs. The union works to obtain rotation shifts involving all workers, in order to safeguard employment levels after recovering hopefully normal production standard. If the company is in serious difficulty or at full risk of closure, faced with the request for reduction of personnel or in dramatic cases of total dismissal, the union intervenes to contract early retirements for older workers and outplacement for the others.

Social dialogue is in deep crisis especially at national level, because governments tend always more often to refuse consulting intermediate bodies. Despite the governmental refuse of traditional neo-corporative arrangements, the difficult running of industrial dismissals fosters cooperation between local administrative bodies and unions in order to find solutions able to lessen social hardships.

Even if concession bargaining dampens the social consequences of business crisis, it cannot feed workers enthusiasm and propensity to union membership and militancy, since avoiding dismissals often triggers a worsening of working conditions, and/or differentiated solutions for involved workers, some of them not satisfactory. The privatization of State-owned enterprises, carried on under European Union pressures to foster market regulation, deprived unions of a strong point, because collective bargaining in State-owned enterprises allowed unions to gain improvements in working conditions, subsequently generalized to private companies. The outcome of all these phenomena has been curtailing union strength. Such difficulties for unions have been especially hard in North West, which was the stronghold of industrial workers' movement. North West was the realm of larger business, which underwent the most dramatic reduction of employment starting from the 1980s, due to the crisis of Fordism, the advent of new managerial strategies centered on downsizing, outsourcing, and so on.

In the last twenty years, small and medium-sized enterprises gained momentum in North West also, so that the differences in the North East and Emilia-Romagna significantly diminished. A sort of Po Valley megalopolis arose, fading the traditional borders.[12] Since the 1990s, the role of medium-sized enterprises grew, part of which can be characterized as "pocket multinationals," up to delineate the historical formation of a fourth capitalism, after the first—the large private enterprises of the North West; the second—the State-owned companies; and the third—the small-size business districts of the North East and Central Italy.[13] However, Lombardy is the cradle of the dynamic medium-sized enterprise, able to compete in international markets thanks to their specialized and niche products, while in Piedmont and Liguria the signs left by the traditional

[12] Giuseppe Berta, *Nord. Dal triangolo industriale alla megalopoli padana 1950–2000*, (Milan: Mondadori, 2008).

[13] Andrea Colli, *Il quarto capitalismo. Un profilo italiano*, (Venice: Masilio, 2002).

presence of the large private and public enterprise remain alive, though tempered by the new transformation trends.

Given the historical differences in the industrial fabric of Milan, Turin, and Genoa, the three deindustrialization processes developed differently, according to the weight of different branches. The first business suffering from developing countries competition was textile, which underwent downsizing starting from the late 1950s. Natural silk already almost disappeared in the interwar period. The textile deindustrialization was a common feature for the North West as a whole. Textile industry was not so much located in the big towns, but close to the mountain valleys. In Piedmont, there was an ancient wool area in Biellese and cotton in Valle Susa, in Liguria the Turchino Valley toward Piedmont, and in Lombardy the piedmont arch north of Milan.

In Genoa, investment for rearmament for World War II increased the number of plants and employees in the late 1930s, but post-war reconversion had severe occupational consequences, especially in metalworking and shipbuilding. Workers' mobilizations to defend employment resurfaced in successive waves of restructuring until the early 1960s. Excluding steel industry, there was a decline in employment in all industrial sectors. Genoa failed to take advantage of the Italian economic miracle, because its industry remained anchored to shipyard, big machinery and equipment production, and did not developed consumer goods businesses like motorcycles, cars, and home appliances, on which the unprecedented Italian growth was based. In the 1970s, difficulties hit the steel industry, while electro-mechanics, electronics, and big construction design showed a good dynamism. The internal and international crisis of the early 1980s, however, heavily affected the Genoese economy, also due to the start of the privatization processes of State-owned companies. The energy sector, which had held up in the 1970s, was particularly affected, while shipbuilding increasingly declined. Downsizing, transfers, mergers, and spin-offs were the result of attempts to redress the system with restructuring that heavily reduced employment. In Liguria, the crisis of the early eighties led to a fall in industrial workers from 70,000 in 1980 to 53,000 in 1985. One job in four disappeared, with a particularly heavy fall in the steel industry, which lost almost half of its employees. In total industry, blue-collar workers decreased by 30%, much more than white collars, whose number diminished by 10%. On the contrary, the number of managers increased by 14%. The move toward knowledge economy started. In just five years, industrial employment diminished by a percentage equal to half of the decrease that occurred in the previous thirty years, between 1951 and 1981. The adaptation of the labor market and of the entire society to these sudden changes inevitably generated difficulties and imbalances, which also affected local demography. Starting from 1965, the number of inhabitants in Genoa entered an irreversible decline and a much faster one than that suffered by the other large Italian towns. The result was an early and very high aging of the Genoese population. Already in 1985, young people under 14 were 11.9% of the total population, and people over 65 reached 18.3%. Genoa was the stronghold of the Communist Party, thanks to the large presence of skilled and relatively educated workers employed in non-standard metalworking.[14]

The recovery of the Turin industry after World War II was rapid thanks to the capacity of Fiat to obtain high shares of the aid of the Marshall Plan. In a short time, the automobile industry monopolized the local economy. By the mid-1950s, Fiat launched its mass-produced small cars, implementing a rigid Fordist system. The division and bitter polemics between the trade unions in the context of the Cold War prevented the continuation of the post-war struggles. The number of inhabitants and of industrial workers grew dramatically in the years of the Italian miracle, based on mass motorization. Turin population increased from 700,000 in 1950 to 1,200,000 in 1974. Adding the surrounding small towns, Turin's area scored one million and a half. Population growth stemmed from the arrival of thousands of migrants from rural areas and southern regions. Fiat employees in the local plants grew from 65,000 to 150,000. The special manufacturing vocation of Turin is evident in the share of industry in total active population, as high as 65% from the 1950s up to the 1970s. In Italy, the overtaking of the tertiary sector on the secondary in the share of the active population occurred in 1977. In Turin, the tertiary overtaking occurred only in the second half of the eighties, ten years after the nation as a whole. The share of employees in metalworking in total industry grew from 47% in 1951 to 53% in 1961, to 61% in 1971, and to 63% in 1981.

[14] Paolo Arvati, *Oltre la città divisas. Gli anni della ristrutturazione a Genova*, (Genoa: Sagep Editrice, 1988); Angelo Pichierri, *Strategie contro il declino in aree di antica industrializzazione*, (Turin: Rosenberg & Sellier, 1989); Fabrizio Loreto, *Il sindacato nella città ferita. Storia della Camera del lavoro di Genova negli anni sessanta e settanta*, (Rome: Ediesse, 2016).

Thanks to full employment and renewed union unitary action, by the end of the 1960s a long-lasting wave of worker mobilization started, that ended only in 1980, when Fiat succeeded in imposing the CIG for 23,000 workers. In the crisis of the early 1980s, a wave of restructuring started, reducing dramatically employment in large-size companies. The number of workers in large companies with over 500 employees, members of the local metalworking employers association (AMMA), dropped from 80% of the total in 1979 to 50% in 2011. The average number of employees per large company decreased from 3,050 to 1,260. This happened in the context of a dropping in the number of total employees from 261,000 in 1979 to 168,000 in 1987, to 86,000 in 2011.

While the advent of the service economy led to a fall in manufacturing employment, Turin's specialization in the transport sector continued to increase, although slightly, from a share in total industry rising from 30% in 1981 to 32% in 1991. In the 1980s, the mono-cultural character of the Turin industry still accentuated. Only in the crisis of the early 1990s and its aftermath, there was a decline in the share of transport construction, which, however, did not collapse, reducing to 27%. Since then, the reorganization of the supplying chain made component producers getting rid of an excessive dependence on Fiat and giving life to a great pole of components that remains an important asset of the local economy.

Turin's population, from its maximum in 1972 with 1,200 inhabitants, dropped in 2016 to 880,000, and, like in Genoa, increasingly aged, with over 65 reaching 25% in total population.

Fordism left today's Turin two negative inheritances. The mono-cultural elements have made its economy excessively sensitive to the car cycle, exposing it to the repercussions of the transition from a growing market to one of the most competitive globalized market. Another negative legacy lies in that the Fordist production methods created large layers of low-skilled and uneducated workers, massively employed in the assembly lines. During the years of the economic miracle and still in the 1970s, the low levels of schooling did not constitute a hindrance to stable and relatively well-paid work, so that the sons of those workers had a tendency to leave school prematurely, convinced that the labor market would continue to reproduce the pattern that had worked for their fathers.[15]

Turin economic situation was not that bad until the outbreak of the new crisis in 2008. From then on, economic recovery seems to meet serious hindrances. Fiat Group had in Turin 23,000 employees in 2008 and dropped nowadays to less than 15,000, with prospects less and less positive after the transformation of Fiat from a national champion into a multinational legally based in the Netherlands and with fiscal residence in England.

Milan adapted much better than Turin and Genoa to the advent to the service economy, thanks to its already diversified economic fabric. Also in Milan, after the dramatic population growth during the economic miracle—from 1,270,000 in 1951 to its peak in 1971, when it was 1,700,000—there was a decrease until the end of the century, mainly because of the re-use of building destined to be offices in downtown. At the same time, new migrant went to the surrounding belt of small towns, since the capital was already overcrowded. The same happened in Turin while in Genoa the population grew much less, because of the lack of space between see and mountains. Yet, in the last 25 years, unlike Turin, Milan population did not diminished at all. On the contrary, it increased a bit, from 1,335,000 in 1991 to 1,380,000 in 2017. In 2011, out of a total number of companies equal to 186,000, the number of industrial companies equaled only 10,000, 11,000 being the companies in building industry. All the rest, 165,000 were service enterprises. Commerce and transports equaled 40,000, hotel and restaurants 9,000, real estate 18,000, finance and insurance 6,000, rental, travel agencies, and business support services 10,000, information and communication services 9,000, and professional, scientific, and technical activities 48,000. Concerning employees, out of a total number of 770.000, manufacturing and power equals 70,000, building 35,000, commerce 125,000, and other services 540,000. Therefore, Milan has a very advanced economic fabric. Deindustrialization had less social uneasiness in Milan than in Turin and Genoa.

[15] Stephano Musso, 'Il lavoro e la città', in: Guiseppe Berta and Guido Alfani (eds.), *Torino Industria. Persone, lavoro, imprese*, (Turin: Archivio Storico della Città di Torino, 2008), pp. 109–166.

Even confronting the long-lasting crisis started in 2008, Lombardy reacted better than Liguria and Piedmont, which had the worst performance among the northern regions in cumulated added-value production between 2006 and 2017. All regional values were minus, yet the datum for Lombardy was minus 0.64, while for Piedmont it was minus 9.48 and for Liguria minus 11.91. Veneto with minus 5.50, Emilia-Romagna with minus 2.43, and Toscana with minus 4.30 did better.[16]

Considering North West as a whole, it was the crisis of large-size companies to make the quantitative outlook of North West more similar to the national framework. Between 1971 and 2001, the number of employees in North West manufacture decreased by 27%, while in the companies with more than 250 employees, it dropped by 66%.[17]

Such transformation hindered the trade unions' chance to keep up in terms of membership and bargaining power. In the Golden Age, in the big-sized firms, there was lifelong employment for large part of workers. Workers concentrated in big companies were the stronghold of the labor movement. In the globalization era, restructuring, outsourcing, downsizing, and offshoring contributed to growing job instability, and workers often underwent a sort of occupational blackmailing. Under employers' pressure, a new wave of policies involved reducing labor protection, in order to facilitate workforce adjustment by companies who had to face global competition. Facing de-regulation of labor market, the strategies of the unions diverged, at least partially, and long-lasting difference in union culture rose again.

In the history of Italian unionism after World War II, we can distinguish four phases linked to union unity or divergences. A first short period of unity linked to the anti-fascist common mobilization, followed by a split between free unions (CISL, UIL) and the communist/socialist union (CGIL) in the cold war context. Then a third period of united action from the 1960s to the early 1980s, a new phase of predominantly unity in the early 1990s. Afterward, facing the problems of globalization, renewed divergences emerged. Even if it is about complex issue, we can distinguish two strategies.

[16] Regional Observatory on Labour Market in Piedmont, 2018 report. www.ires.piemonte.it/index.php/relazione-annuale-2018 [accessed 5 May 2020].

[17] Consiglio Italiano per le Scienze Sociali, *Libro bianco per il Nord Ovest. Dall'economia della manifattura all'economia della conoscenza*, (Venice: Marsilio, 2007), pp. 55–57.

The first one is defending ancient worker rights against neo-liberal labor law and employers' attack and tackling deindustrialization processes through industrial policies initiatives. This is the strategy of CGIL, which launched a Job Plan (Piano del Lavoro) in 2013—recalling the historical Piano del lavoro launched in 1949—and 3 abrogative referendums in 2016, against the recent reform called Jobs act, accused of introducing further flexibility in the labor market. According to CGIL, State intervention through industrial policy should tackle unemployment, whose lessening should be the main goal of economic policy. CISL strategy is much more sympathetic to business competition pressures. Its proposal is an exchange between union collaboration to enhance productivity and economic rewards for workers, economic dynamism through productivity increases being the most effective way to lessen unemployment. Workers' and union participation is the main point of CISL strategy. The two different strategies have deep roots in traditional different union culture, which developed in the early 1950s. CISL was inclined to give priority to company-level bargaining, since linking wages to productivity implies measuring it in single companies. CGIL, on the contrary, defended the importance of national contracts.

Recently, in January 2016, the three main confederations, CGIL, CISL, and UIL, presented a joint proposal concerning a new pattern of industrial relations finalized to foster economic development through innovation, improved quality of work, and participation.[18] The unitary document seems to overcome traditional differences in unions' strategy. CGIL accepted participation, obtaining in exchange the confirmation of the importance of the national contract, alongside the company-level agreement. This document has been the base of a very recent agreement, signed in March 2018, between CGIL, CISL and UIL, with the organization of industrial employers (Confindustria) on a renewed system of collective bargaining, based on a system of measuring the representativeness of both unions and employers' association and stating norms for bargaining at national and company level. This agreement will have

[18] CGIL, CISL, UIL, *Un moderno sistema di relazioni industriali. Un modello di sviluppo fondato sulla qualità del lavoro e l'innovazione*. January 14, 2016. https://www.cisl.it/attachments/article/1352/Relazioni%20Industriali%2014.1.165%202.pdf [accessed 10 June 2020].

its effects in the near future. Unions hope that it will reinforce multi-employer bargaining, against contracts signed by "yellow" expedience unions.

Yet, the hardest issues for unions are facing the growing number of atypical fix-terms jobs, finding ways to represent and protect young workers in the dispersed jobs of the service sector. The main unions established special bodies to deal with precarious and self-employed workers. Yet, it is very difficult for unions, which were born and organized along Fordist lines, to gain balance bonds with young workers, who normally join the union only when their work contract is over and they have to start a legal dispute. In addition, unions are trying to launch the so-called inclusive bargaining, to extend collective bargaining to all kind of atypical workers operating for a firm, in order to include them in the company-level contracts. A second and even more important challenge is reforming the social security system, which was born in the years of stable employment and is now out of date, in the era of flexibility and high youth unemployment.

References

Abrate, Mario, La lotta sindacale nell'industrializzazione in Italia, 1906–1926, (Torino: Franco Angeli, 1968).

Acocella, Guiseppe; Zaninelli Sergio (eds.), Sessant'anni del "sindacato nuovo". La CISL fra storia e interpretazioni, (Roma: Edizioni Lavoro, 2012).

Amatori, Franco; Colli, Andrea, Impresa e industria in Italia. Dall'Unità a oggi, (Venezia: Marsilio, 1999).

Arnaldo Bagnasco, Tre Italie. La problematica territoriale dello svilupp italianio, (Bologna: Il Mulino, 1978).

Arvati, Paolo, Oltre la città divisas. Gli anni della ristrutturazione a Genova, (Genova: Sagep Editrice, 1988).

Arvati, Paolo; Rugafiori, Paride, Storia della Camera del lavoro di Genova. Dalla Resistenza al luglio '60, (Roma: Editrice Sindacale Italiana, 1981).

Berta, Giuseppe, Nord. Dal triangolo industriale alla megalopoli padana 1950–2000, (Milano: Mondadori, 2008).

Bertucelli, Lorenzo; Pepe Adolfo; Righi Maria L., Il sindacato nella società industriale, (Roma: Ediesse, 2008).

Bigazzi, "Duccio, La fabbrica nella crisi del regime fascista", in Angelo Ventura (ed.), Sulla crisi del regime fascista 1938–1943. La società italiana dal "consenso" alla Resistenza, (Venezia: Marsilio, 1996).

CGIL, CISL, UIL, Un moderno sistema di relazioni industriali. Un modello di sviluppo fondato sulla qualità del lavoro e l'innovazione. January 14, 2016. https://www.cisl.it/attachments/article/1352/Relazioni%20Industriali%2014.1.165%202.pdf.

Colli, Andrea, Il quarto capitalismo. Un profilo italiano, (Venezia: Masilio, 2002).

Consiglio Italiano per le Scienze Sociali, Libro bianco per il Nord Ovest. Dall'economia della manifattura all'economia della conoscenza, (Venezia: Marsilio, 2007).

Della Peruta, Franco, Milano. Lavoro e fabbrica. 1814–1915, (Milano: Angeli, 1987).

Loreto, Fabrizio, Il sindacato nella città ferita. Storia della Camera del lavoro di Genova negli anni sessanta e settanta, (Roma: Ediesse, 2016).

Musso, Stefano, "Gli operai, tra centro e periferia", in Musso S. (ed.), Operai, (Torino: Rosenberg & Sellier, 2006).

Musso, Stefano, "Il lavoro e la città", in Guiseppe Berta and Guido Alfani (eds.), Torino Industria. Persone, lavoro, imprese, (Torino: Archivio Storico della Città di Torino, 2008), pp. 109–166.

Musso, Stefano, "Il lungo miracolo economico. Industria, economia e società", in Nicola Tranfaglia (ed.), Storia di Torino. 9. Gli anni della Repubblica, (Torino: Einaudi, 1999), pp. 49–100.

Petrillo, Gianfranco, La capitale del miracolo. Sviluppo potere lavoro a Milano 1953–1962, (Milano: Angelo, 1992).

Pichierri, Angelo, Strategie contro il declino in aree di antica industrializzazione, (Torino: Rosenberg & Sellier, 1989).

Sarti, Roland, Fascism and the Industrial Leadership in Italy. 1919–1940. A study in the expansion of private power under fascism, (Berkeley-Los Angeles and London: University of California Press, 1971).

Toniolo, Gianni, L'economia dell'Italia fascista, (Roma-Bari: Laterza, 1980).

Zamagni, Vera N., Industrializzazione e squilibri regionali in Italia, (Bologna: Il Mulino, 1978).

PART II

Living Deindustrialization—Lifeworlds of Deindustrialization

CHAPTER 4

The People's Memories? Oral Histories of Industry in the Deindustrializing Ruhr

Stefan Moitra

The new permanent exhibition at Gelsenkirchen's Nordstern Mine, in many ways a symbol of the industrial as well as the post-industrial Ruhr, carries the title 'Wandel is' immer'—'Change is constant'.[1] Implicitly, this alludes to the German term *Strukturwandel*, structural change or structural transformation, usually employed when describing the Ruhr as a region struggling with deindustrialization. Semantically, *Strukturwandel* denotes a somewhat different notion of change than *deindustrialization*. Change and transformation of structures—economic as well as social—is a process that stretches over longer periods of time. In German public discourse, however, the term is frequently used from a hindsight perspective, focusing on the effects of change for post-industrial regions in

[1] https://www.nordsternturm.de/ausstellung.php [accessed 10 October 2020].

S. Moitra (✉)
Deutsches Bergbau-Museum Bochum, Bochum, Germany
e-mail: stefan.moitra@bergbaumuseum.de

S. Berger et al. (eds.), *Deindustrialisation in Twentieth-Century Europe*, Palgrave Studies in the History of Social Movements,
https://doi.org/10.1007/978-3-030-89631-7_4

distress or the fears of regions under threat.[2] This corresponds with recent debates that see a relatively sudden break-up of structures ('Strukturbruch') rather than an elongated change.[3] However, the Ruhr itself is a marked example for the long-term character of a structural transformation, with the decline of the coal mining industry effectively taking six decades, from the first signs of crisis in 1958 to the last coal mine closing its gates in 2018.[4]

Before this background, memories of deindustrialization and/or Strukturwandel are always also memories of a transition process in which industrial work was still distinctive for the region while at the same time the eroding of industrial structures was already visible. People's memories at a given point in time are shaped by both the experience of work and that of an industry vanished/vanishing. And even if speaking from a deindustrialized perspective, oral histories and life stories often address long-term experiences and narratives of an active working life rather than the mere post-industrial moment of the present. Such narratives certainly contain memories of tensions and struggles, in the context of both industrial labor and coming to terms with deindustrialization. Thus, the temporal imperative in 'Wandel is' immer', the slightly fatalistic recognition of a process unstoppable, finds its counterpart in a statement made by the former coal-mining trade unionist Klaus Südhofer in a recent life history interview: 'Einfach war dat nie'.—'It's never been easy'.[5]

Rather than looking at the actual struggles and strives of the structural transformation as such, this chapter will consider the ways in which memories, and in particular oral testimonies, from the deindustrializing

[2] See for instance 'Strukturwandel. Lausitzer Revier besucht. Erfolgreiche Rekultivierung als Beispiel für Elsdorf—Solidarität zwischen Lausitzer und Rheinischem Revier', in: *Rheinische Anzeigenblätter*, October 19, 2019, https://www.rheinische-anzeigenblaetter.de/mein-blatt/werbepost/elsdorf/strukturwandel-lausitzer-revier-besucht-33396100 [accessed 8 October 2020].

[3] Anselm Doering-Manteuffel and Lutz Raphael, *Nach dem Boom. Perspektiven auf die Zeitgeschichte nach 1970*, (Göttingen: Vandenhoeck und Ruprecht, 2008); Knut Andresen, Ursula Bitzegeio, and Jürgen Mittag (eds.), *"Nach dem Strukturbruch?" Kontinuität und Wandel von Arbeitsbeziehungen und Arbeitswelt(en) seit den 1970er-Jahren*, (Bonn: J.H.W. Dietz Nachf., 2011); Lutz Raphael, *Jenseits von Kohle und Stahl. Eine Gesellschaftsgeschichte Westeuropas nach dem Boom* (Frankfurt/Main: Suhrkamp, 2019).

[4] Stefan Goch, *Eine Region im Kampf mit dem Strukturwandel, Strukturpolitik und Bewältigung von Strukturwandel im Ruhrgebiet* (Essen: Klartext, 2002); Michael Farrenkopf et al. (eds.), *Die Stadt der Städte. Das Ruhrgebiet und seine Umbrüche* (Essen: Klartext, 2019).

[5] Interview with Klaus Südhofer, 17 March 2016, Archiv im Haus der Geschichte des Ruhrgebiets (AHGR), LINT 27.

Ruhr have been used to represent the region's history. This started at a time when the region was already in the midst of transition, in the late 1960s, and ends today, with an industrial heritage practice that covers academic research as much as heritage tourism.[6] From early on, it has been predominantly working-class memories which have come to be a central signifier of the regional experience in the works of journalists, cultural actors, academics and museum curators. However, while working-class culture was something to be recovered more explicitly in the earlier stages of transformation, as an "expedition to the people" as Franz-Josef Brüggemeier phrased it in 1983,[7] the Ruhr's current dominant discourse of industrial heritage rather uses images and memories gathered from the milieus of coal and steel as reference points for a broader regional identity based on nostalgia for the industrial past. Thus, how memories and stories are used, and to what ends, is always a matter of motivation on part of those staging them in the "theaters of memory".[8] The early turn toward oral history in the Ruhr entailed, for instance, both the desire to document and to some extent rescue, a working-class culture about to vanish and the urge to scrutinize a social and cultural milieu of workers from an academic point of view more narrowly. Oral history, the sharing of stories and memories, is at the same time fundamentally based on the interplay between the individual narrator and those who use such testimonies for the larger narratives of historical discourse and historical culture.[9] Matters of agency and the tensions of authority behind the historical narrative have therefore been a constant issue of

[6] Stefan Berger, 'Industriekultur und Strukturwandel in deutschen Bergbauregionen nach 1945', in: Dieter Ziegler (ed.), *Rohstoffgewinnung im Strukturwandel. Der deutsche Bergbau im 20. Jahrhundert. Geschichte des deutschen Bergbaus* 4 (2013), pp. 571–601; Stefan Berger, Jana Golombek, and Christian Wicke, 'A Post-Industrial Mindscape? The Mainstreaming and Touristification of Industrial Heritage in the Ruhr', in: Stefan Berger, Jana Golombek, and Christian Wicke (eds.), *Industrial Heritage and Regional Identities* (Abingdon and New York, NY: Routledge, 2018), pp. 74–94.

[7] 'Entdeckungsreise ins eigene Volk', Franz-Josef Brüggemeier, *Leben vor Ort. Ruhrbergleute und Ruhrbergbau 1889–1919* (Munich: C.H. Beck, 1983), p. 13.

[8] Raphael Samuel, *Theatres of Memory. Past and Present in Contemporary Culture* (London and New York, NY: Verso, 2012 [1994]).

[9] Jörn Rüsen, *Historische Orientierung. Über die Arbeit des Geschichtsbewußtseins, sich in der Zeit zurechtzufinden* (Köln: Böhlau, 1994); Aleida Assmann, *Geschichte im Gedächtnis. Von der individuellen Erfahrung zur öffentlichen Inszenierung* (München: C.H. Beck, 2007).

debate in oral-history writing.[10] In the context of the Ruhr, this leads to ask which stories were told by whom at which stage during the process of deindustrialization. Which kind of narratives have been represented in the region's historical culture and in which functions—as 'history from below', as academic source material or as broad reference points of regional identity? We will start with the early practices of oral history in the region, which to some extent had an initializing effect on German oral history more generally. The second section will consider the move of oral history into the Ruhr's industrial museums and the representational tensions arising from the success of the concept of 'industrial culture'. The final section will then look at more recent attempts to reshift the narrative and thematic perspective from the mainstreaming of industrial heritage to the re-emerging of a perspective 'from below'. At all these stages, the conditions of deindustrialization have formed a point of reference for the historical narrative, yet to varying degrees. Post-industrial memories, both individually and mediated through research or museums, seem to address that which has gone rather than the present. It is the differences in motives and themes, however, which will be dealt with in the following.

Cultural Activists And Oral Historians Encountering Change From The 1960s to 1980s

When historians in the Ruhr started to become interested in the collective memories of the local working-class communities in the late 1970s, there had already been a number of politically and culturally ambitious predecessors that had to some extent paved the way for them. And while the later historically oriented works mostly focused on the earlier phases of collective experience—from the beginning of the twentieth century through the Weimar Republic to National Socialism, usually ending with the wider post-war era and the re-building of West-German democracy—the largely journalistic and documentarist projects of the 1960s and 1970s

[10] Michael Frisch, *A Shared Authority: Essays on the Craft and Meaning of Oral and Public History* (New York: SUNY Press, 1990); special feature 'Shared Authority' in: *Oral History Review* 30, 1 (2003); Steven High, Sharing Authority. An Introduction, in: *Journal of Canadian Studies/Revue d'études canadiennes* 43 (2009), pp. 12–34.

employed a stronger interest in more contemporary issues.[11] Under the impression of the ongoing crisis of coal mining since 1958 and equipped with a left-leaning political as well as a sociological, even ethnographic interest, a young generation of filmmakers and writers, often from outside the Ruhr, turned to the region's industrial neighborhoods. Of particular impact was journalist Erika Runge's book 'Bottroper Protokolle', published in 1968.[12] Runge, who had before worked in theater and Television, went to the mining town of Bottrop, on the northern fringe of the Ruhr region, at the height of the coal crisis in the mid-1960s. Her work features selections from eight life-story interviews conducted with (mainly) working-class protagonists, such as a woman working as a cleaner on the mining compound, a veteran communist shop-steward, a singer in a beat band (actually an unemployed electrician), a housewife, but also a catholic priest. Additionally, she includes the minutes of an employees' meeting of the local Möller/Rheinbaben colliery, documenting the ensuing discussions when the workers hear of the decision to close the pit. While the threat of closure and fears of an unknown future are a point of reference for a number of interviewees, their narratives are significantly interlinked with both everyday details and the historical experience of living in the community. This includes the political tensions which the neighborhood had lived through over the years, but also experiences of severe poverty that feed into the present fears of mine closure. Maria B., the cleaner, for instance, interweaves her views of the present with memories of benefitting from the National Socialist welfare programes. (Though she also came to doubt the regime, so she says, after witnessing fascist violence against communists and Jews and hearing rumors about the genocide in the east.) B. is also at the center of a documentary film Runge made in 1968 under the title 'Warum ist Frau B. glücklich?' ('Why

[11] Katarzyna Nogueira, 'Geschichte und Geschichten. Zur Zeitzeugenschaft des Ruhrbergbaus', in: *Forum Geschichtskultur* 1 (2018), pp. 42–46.

[12] Erika Runge, *Bottroper Protokolle*, (Frankfurt/Main: Suhrkamp, 1968); Britta Caspers, 'Strategien einer "Regionalisierung der Region" am Beispiel der Bottroper Protokolle', in: Britta Caspers et al. (eds.), *Theorien, Modelle und Probleme regionaler Literaturgeschichtsschreibung* (Essen, Klartext, 2016), pp. 119–141.

is Frau B. happy?') which shows her in her everyday environment, both at home and at the hostel for unmarried miners where she cleans.[13]

A few years after Runge's work on Bottrop, a number of young filmmakers followed suit who were likewise interested in the current situation of the Ruhr's working-class communities, in their everyday lives and worldviews. Their approaches combined a somewhat ethnographic interest with a sense of solidarity in the struggles which many mining and steel communities were going through by the mid-1970s. Without explicitly applying the concept of 'oral history' as such, the films made in this context came along with a distinct 'from-below' perspective that sought to show 'a reality from the inside, the reality of a country, a region, its people', as the documentarist Christoph Hübner declared.[14] This included the stories of older miners and their wives about their upbringing during the Weimar Republic and National Socialism as much as the views of young people in the community about their lives and future expectations. The films largely followed a *cinema-verité* model and were meant to give the protagonists as much agency as possible to tell their own stories. This took on different forms. Students from DFFB film academy in Berlin made documentaries in support of tenants' campaigns to save their mining company houses from privatization and potential demolition. This was the case in the Duisburg Rheinpreußen neighborhood as well as at Flöz Dickebank in Gelsenkirchen.[15] A similar approach was used by the RuhrFilmZentrum, founded by Hübner and his partner Gabriele Voss, along with other collaborators in 1978.[16] Yet, in contrast

[13] Walter Delaber, 'Erika Runge's Bottroper Protokolle und ihr Fernsehfilm ‚Warum ist Frau B. glücklich?', in: Gertrude Cepl-Kaufmann and Jasmin Grande (eds.), *Schreibwelten—Erschriebene Welten. Zum 50. Geburtstag der Dortmunder Gruppe 61* (Essen, Klartext, 2011), pp. 224–229.

[14] Christoph Hübner, 'Filmarbeit vor Ort. RuhrFilmZentrum 1978–1982. Drei, bald vier Jahre Filmarbeit in einer Region', in: Bert Hogenkamp, *Bergarbeiter im Spielfilm*. Ed. by Westdeutsche Kurzfilmtage Oberhausen (1982), pp. 126–133, here p. 132.

[15] 'Flöz Dickebank. Wir sind mittlerweile wach geworden', directed by Johannes Flütsch, Klaus Helle, Marlis Kallweit., Deutsche Film- und Fernsehakademie Berlin 1975; 'Gegen Spekulanten', directed by Klaus Helle, Florence Kraak, Bernd Segin, (Deutsche Film- und Fernsehakademie Berlin 1978). 'Flöz Dickebank' is accessible online under https://dffb-archiv.de/dffb/floez-dickebank-wir-sind-mittlerweile-wachgeworden [accessed 5 October 2020].

[16] Christoph Hübner and Gabriele Voss, *Film/Arbeit. Texte, Dokumente und Arbeitsnotizen* (Berlin: Vorwerk 8, 2014).

to the more current campaign films, the RuhrFilmZentrum took on a long-term view. Like Runge, the filmmakers focused their work on the city of Bottrop, and particularly on the neighborhood of Bottrop-Ebel, with the Prosper colliery at its center. As the film crew actually moved to Ebel and became part of the neighborhood, what ensued in fact turned out to be a long-term cycle of films. Between 1979 and 1982, six films were made as part of 'Prosper/Ebel – Chronical of a Colliery and its Community' which were explicitly meant to present 'a cinematic history of the everyday'.[17] By looking at mine-work underground, at the situation of women as well as young people or by connecting the earlier with the newer, mainly Turkish migration histories of Ebel, all films approached everyday aspects of living in the community, intensively listening to and observing its protagonists. While such an approach allowed to view the long-term history of a mining community from the point of view and the experiences of its inhabitants, these early films did not yet allude to the threats of mine closure directly. There was a feeling, however, of an impending change. The 'idea of preserving something' that was bound to vanish was 'more important than the *Zeitgeist*', as Voss and Hübner say in a recent interview on their work.[18] This imminent shift was in full swing when the directors came back to Ebel for a seventh film in the mid-1990s. In 'Das Alte und das Neue' ('The Old and the New'), released in 1998, some of the old protagonists reflect on the changes over the last fifteen to twenty years. Some of the teenage apprentice miners from 'Die vierte Generation' (1980) are now adults, fearing for their jobs as the government threatens to substantially cut subsidies for the coal industry. Thus, one of the key sequences of the film depicts the ensuing protests in 1997 when the miners took to the streets, demonstrated in Bonn (still capital at the time) and 220,000 people participated in a human chain all through the coalfield.[19]

[17] Menschen, Orte, Alltag. Michael Girke im Gespräch mit Gabriele Voss und Christoph Hübner https://www.dokumentarfilminitiative.de/images/stories/pdfs/InterviewsRuhrgebietsfilm/interview_voss_hbner.pdf [accessed 7 October 2020].

[18] Ibid.

[19] Michael Farrenkopf, 'Wiederaufstieg und Niedergang des Bergbaus in der Bundesrepublik', in: Dieter Ziegler (ed.), *Rohstoffgewinnung im Strukturwandel. Der deutsche Bergbau im 20. Jahrhundert. Geschichte des deutschen Bergbaus* 4 (2013), pp. 183–302, here pp. 244–245.

In the meantime, filmic approaches such as Voss and Hübner's also had an impact, already in the late 1970s, on the research practice of a younger generation of historians in the region. This was particularly the case for another film by Hübner and Voss, released in 1978/79. 'Lebensgeschichte des Bergarbeiters Alphons S', almost solely consisted of a 22-h life history interview with Alphons Stiller, born into a mining family in Castrop-Rauxel in 1906. For some time a miner himself, Stiller's story comprises memories of unemployment, life as a tramp, as an agricultural worker, and living as a Marxist and anarchist in fascist Germany. With reference to Sergej Tretjakow, the filmmakers used the term 'bio-interview' for what they were doing rather than 'oral history'.[20] However, that was essentially what it was and directly fed into the first oral-history and history-from-below projects which were about to take root at the time.

Oral-history practice had been virtually absent from German historiography so far.[21] There had, however, been a recent upsurge in studies on social histories of the working class, on the labor movement and especially on forms of working-class opposition against fascism.[22] The stronger motivation to apply a perspective from below and focus more strongly on collective experiences of the working class quickly led to turning to the historical actors from below themselves. This was not least influenced in an international perspective by the British history-workshop movement and oral-history practice in both the UK and the US.[23] At this relatively

[20] Christoph Hübner and Gabriele Voss, 'Zu Konzeption, Produktion und Einsatz des Films [1980]', in: LWL-Medienzentrum für Westfalen (ed.), *Lebens-Geschichte des Bergarbeiters Alphons S. Ein Bio-Interview in acht Teilen von Alphons Stiller, Gabriele Voss, Christoph Hübner. Begleitheft zur DVD*, (Münster: LWL, 2018), pp. 9–13.

[21] Knut Andresen, Linde Apel, and Kirsten Heinson, 'Es gilt das gesprochene Wort. Oral History und Zeitgeschichte heute', in: Knut Andresen, Linde Apel, and Kirsten Heinson (eds.), *Es gilt das gesprochene Wort. Oral History und Zeitgeschichte heute* (Göttingen: Wallstein, 2015), pp. 7–22.

[22] Jürgen Reulecke (ed.), *Arbeiterbewegung an Rhein und Ruhr. Beiträge zur Geschichte der Arbeiterbewegung in Rheinland-Westfalen*, (Wuppertal: Hammer, 1974); Klaus Tenfelde, *Sozialgeschichte der Bergarbeiterschaft an der Ruhr im 19. Jahrhundert*. (Bonn: Neue Gesellschaft, 1977); Hans Mommsen and Ulrich Borsdorf (eds.), *Glück auf, Kameraden! Die Bergarbeiter und ihre Organisationen in Deutschland* (Cologne: Bund Verlag, 1979).

[23] Lutz Niethammer, 'Oral History in den USA. Zur Entwicklung und Problematik diachroner Befragungen', in: *Archiv für Sozialgeschichte* 18 (1978), pp. 457–501; Annette Leo and Franka Maubach, *Den Unterdrückten eine Stimme geben? Die International*

early stage, oral history was applied in a twofold manner: firstly, as a form of historical and political didactics to make communities reflect about themselves in a participatory manner and trigger historically informed debates about the past as well as the present; secondly, a more academic approach that sought to recover, through the oral narrative, forms of collective experience and their retrospective interpretation as a source for historiography. In both respects, projects in the Ruhr region were instrumental in opening up perspectives for oral-history practice elsewhere in Germany.[24]

With regard to community projects, the 'Hochlarmarker Lesebuch' (1981) proved to be pioneering. Part of the town of Recklinghausen, Hochlarmark was a close-nit mining community, with the two shafts of the Recklinghausen colliery at its center. In 1974, operation at the colliery ceased. Miners below the early retirement age of 50 were moved to collieries in adjacent Herten or wider afield. The number of inhabitants shrank in consequence and the population was aging. This situation formed the background for the idea to set up a project on the history of the community from the time of industrialization in the late nineteenth century to the problems of the present. This was primarily not meant to be a work of academic research. The municipality's secretary of culture, assisted by a historian and two graphic designers, offered a history workshop at the local community center in the course of which it was the Hochlarmarkers themselves who were supposed to be narrating and writing down their history. The participants' initial reluctance to see the significance of contributing their own individual memories was countered by watching parts of Voss und Hübner's recent film on Alphons Stiller which showed them 'that varying private memories nonetheless reflect common life worlds and can trigger interesting debates'.[25] Following on

Oral History Association zwischen politischer Bewegung und wissenschaftlichem Netzwerk (Göttingen: Wallstein, 2013).

[24] Franka Maubach, '"Mehr Geschichte wagen!" LUSIR und die ganze Geschichte der Arbeiter im Ruhrgebiet vor, während und nach dem Nationalsozialismus', in: *Sprache und Literatur* 47 (2018), pp. 29–57; Ulrike Jureit, 'Die Entdeckung des Zeitzeugen. Faschismus- und Nachkriegserfahrungen im Ruhrgebiet', in: Jürgen Danyel, Jan-Holger Kirsch, and Martin Sabrow (eds.), *50 Klassiker der Zeitgeschichte* (Göttingen: Vandenhoeck und Ruprecht, 2007), pp. 174–181.

[25] Margarethe Goldmann, Volker Hilgert, and Michael Zimmermann, 'Kohle war nicht alles. Projektbericht. Erfahrungen von 1978–1981', in: *HOCHLARMARKER Lesebuch* (1981), pp. 315–334, here p. 318.

from this starting point, the number of people involved in the workshop grew steadily. As a series of events for the wider public was organized, more and more interviews were conducted, historical photos and documents were gathered, all of which eventually led to the opening of an exhibition on the history of the community from the perspective of its inhabitants. The exhibition, supplemented by further interviews, was in turn developed into a book, the 'Hochlarmarker Lesebuch'.

While the main temporal focus again lay on the first half of the twentieth century into the post-war period, the book aimed to integrate the community's past with the present context. Before the background of the preceding historical reflections by interviewees and respondents, the final chapter, 'Hochlarmark Today', focused on the community's 'current situation' and 'the fears, hopes, expectations and activities' of its citizens.[26] Here, it was indeed a cross-section of perceived problematic developments in many Ruhr communities around 1980 which was addressed: the closing of the local pit and the consequential need for miners to commute to neighboring shafts, environmental issues stemming from mining and its connected industries, and the implications of privatizing former company-owned housing. Special emphasis was also given to the perspectives of women, young people and migrant workers. In all these aspects, the book was open to juxtaposing varying, potentially opposing views. The whole cycle of activities, from the first reflections about personal and collective histories to curating the exhibition and the eventual publishing of the book, was meant to trigger debate about the complex history of the community and ultimately to create a common discursive ground to tackle the community's problems in a changing environment. In this respect, the Hochlarmark project was not just an exercise in local history but had an imminent political and cultural impact. As such, it received a wide reception and developed a significant outreach, both inside and outside the Ruhr area.[27]

[26] HOCHLARMARKER Lesebuch, *Kohle war nicht alles. 100 Jahre Ruhrgebietsgeschichte. Bergarbeiter und ihre Frauen aus Recklinghausen-Hochlarmark haben in Zusammenarbeit mit dem kommunalen Staddtteilkulturreferat ihre Geschichte aufgeschrieben* (Oberhausen: Asso-Verlag, 1981), p. 278.

[27] Adolf Noll, Helmut Blumbach, and Margarethe Goldmann, *Wie man kleine Netze baut. Ein Handbuch stadtteilorientierter Kultur- und Bildungsarbeit* (Gelsenkirchen: Zwingmann, 1984). There was a negative reception as well, however, with conservative groups in the area accusing the project of misspending public funding for launching left-leaning worldviews and supporting a publisher who was assumed to have links to the

The project with the strongest academic impact overlapped with the Hochlarmark endeavor to some extent, but significantly broadened its geographic scope while at the same time focusing on a specific time frame. A group around Lutz Niethammer, professor of history at Essen University and later at Hagen University, embarked on the first systematic oral-history project in Germany, 'Life History and Social Culture in the Ruhr District, 1930–1960' (LUSIR). The core project was undertaken from 1980 to 1983 when the group members, mostly doctoral and post-doctoral researchers, conducted interviews with mine and steel workers, miners' wives, secretaries, shop stewards and trade unionists all over the Ruhr. One of the researchers, Michael Zimmermann, had also been part of the Hochlarmark project and now worked on a PhD thesis on Hochlarmark.[28] One of the group's main interests was to approach the everyday experience of fascism from the point of view of the working class. And focusing on the industrial realm of the Ruhr, with its industrial environment and deep-rooted labor movement traditions, provided them with a social–historical context in which it seemed likely to find traces of both opposition and assimilation. As it turned out, modes of adjusting to the regime were much more prevalent than stories of resistance in the narratives of LUSIR's interviewees.[29]

In its temporal focus, LUSIR understood the experience of National Socialism as a pre-history to the current West-German democracy which included the somewhat paradoxical question as to how the fascist dictatorship was followed by the strong Social Democratic hegemony that dominated most of the Ruhr in the decades after 1945 into the present

German Communist Party. See Britta Caspers et al., Ruhrgebietsliteratur seit 1960. Eine Geschichte nach Knotenpunkten (Stuttgart: J.B. Metzler, 2019).

28 Michael Zimmermann, *Schachtanlage und Zechenkolonie. Leben, Arbeit und Politik in einer Arbeitersiedlung 1880–1980* (Essen: Klartext, 1987).

29 Lutz Niethammer, 'Fragen—Antworten—Fragen. Methodische Erfahrungen und Erwägungen zur Oral History', in: Lutz Niethammer and Alexander von Plato (eds.), *"Wir kriegen jetzt andere Zeiten." Auf der Suche nach der Erfahrung des Volkes in nachfaschistischen Ländern. Lebensgeschichte und Sozialkultur im Ruhrgebiet*, Band 3, (Berlin and Bonn: J.H.W. Dietz Nachf., 1985), pp. 392–445; Franka Maubach, '"Mehr Geschichte wagen" "LUSIR und die ganze Geschichte der Arbeiter im Ruhrgebiet vor, während und nach dem Nationalsozialismus', in: *Sprache und Literatur* 47 (2018), pp. 29–57.

of the early 1980s.[30] What was not in the researchers' picture, however, at least not in their research outputs, were the current developments unfolding in the very context of pit closure and the beginning steel crisis. There were extensive discussions of trade unionists' pride in what they had achieved collectively as well as individually during the period of post-war reconstruction in their industrial environments and in terms of their communities' welfare.[31] Yet, whether such apparently strong positions continued to play a role, if at all, particularly in the ongoing process of pit closure was mostly left aside.[32]

Both LUSIR and the Hochlarmark project proofed influential. Hochlarmark inspired a range of local history groups in the Ruhr, in different forms and shapes, who collected memories, published brochures and books or put together exhibitions.[33] And, along with LUSIR, it

[30] Lutz Niethammer, 'Einleitung des Herausgebers', in: Lutz Niethammer (ed.), "*Die Jahre weiß man nicht, wo man die heute hinsetzen soll.*" *Faschismuserfahrungen im Ruhrgebiet. Lebensgeschichte und Sozialkultur im Ruhrgebiet*, Band 1 (Berlin and Bonn: J.H.W. Dietz Nachf., 1983), pp. 7–29.

[31] Alexander von Plato, "*Der Verlierer geht nicht leer aus.*" *Betriebsräte geben zu Protokoll*, (Berlin and Bonn: J.H.W. Dietz Nachf., 1984); Michael Zimmermann, "Geh zu Hermann, der macht dat schon" . Bergarbeiterinteressenvertretung im nördlichen Ruhrgebiet', in: Lutz Niethammer (ed.), *Hinterher weiß man, daß es richtig war, daß es schief gegangen ist. Nachkriegserfahrungen im Ruhrgebiet. Lebensgeschichte und Sozialkultur im Ruhrgebiet*, Band 2 (Berlin and Bonn: J.H.W. Dietz Nachf., 1983), pp. 277–310.

[32] The only contribution to LUSIR's core volumes to address industrial change was an article on shifting work identities in the Krupp steel concern: Ulrich Herbert, 'Vom Kruppianer zum Arbeitnehmer', in: Lutz Niethammer (ed.), *Hinterher weiß man, daß es richtig war, daß es schief gegangen ist. Nachkriegserfahrungen im Ruhrgebiet. Lebensgeschichte und Sozialkultur im Ruhrgebiet*, Band 2, (Berlin and Bonn: J.H.W. Dietz Nachf., 1983), pp. 233–276.

[33] IGBE-Bezirk Ruhr-Nord, *Jahre die wir nicht vergessen*, Recklinghausen 1980; IGBE, *Bergleute erzählen (Beiträge zur Geschichte der IGBE). Arbeitsmaterial der Industriegewerkschaft Bergbau und Energie X*, (Bochum: Berg-Verlag, 1982); Leben mit Gneisenau, *hundert Jahre… Eine Zeche zwischen Dortmund und Lünen. Begleitbuch zur Ausstellung der VHS Dortmund im Museum für Kunst- und Kulturgeschichte der Stadt Dortmund vom 12.0.-26.10.1986* (Essen: Klartext, 1986); Jutta de Jong (ed.), *Kinder, Küche, Kohle—und viel mehr! Bergarbeiterfrauen aus drei Generationen erinnern sich* (Essen: Klartext, 1991). Slightly parallel to this, Roland and Janne Günter, who were vocal actors in the campaign to save the Eisenheim neighborhood in Oberhausen from demolition, initiated local interview projects as well; see Janne Günter, Mündliche Geschichtsschreibung. Alte Menschen im Ruhrgebiet erzählen erlebte Geschichte, in: *Scheidewege. Vierteljahressschrift für skeptisches Denken* 11, 3 (1981), pp. 411–424; Janne Günter and Roland Günter, *Sprechende Straßen in Eisenheim. Konzepte und Texte sämtlicher Tafeln in der ältesten Siedlung (1846/1901) im Ruhrgebiet* (Essen: Klartext, 1999).

became an important part of the wider new history-from-below movement over the 1980s.[34] At this stage, however, a peculiar paradox remained. While historians, both lay and academic, sought to understand and potentially preserve older forms of working-class life from the perspective of a 'historiography of solidarity' (Niethammer, *Einleitung des Herausgebers*), the parallel vanishing of the communities' industrial core was addressed only in passing. In any case, as the visibility of many local history groups in the Ruhr remained limited on the long run, a new level of representing the industrial—and gradually also the deindustrial—history of the Ruhr was reached with the boom of industrial museums since at least the late 1980s. And while these predominantly centered on the old industrial sites of coal and steel, oral narratives started to play a key role in reconstructing the industrial life worlds of collieries, steel plants and forges as well as their respective communities. Gradually, such narratives started to address stories of coming to terms with closure more explicitly.

Industrial Heritage as Outlet for Collective Memory?

The museal representation of the coal mining and steel industries in the Ruhr has a relatively long history. Museums in Bochum, Essen and Gelsenkirchen opened in the 1920s and 1930s, mainly focusing on the technical and scientific aspects of mining and steel production but at the same time construing a specific spatial identity in relation to the region's formative trades.[35] In the meantime, today, the whole region seems to be covered by a vast network of industrial museums and heritage sites,

[34] Hubert C. Ehalt (ed.), *Geschichte von unten. Fragestellungen, Methoden und Projekte einer Geschichte des Alltags*, (Vienna/Cologne/Graz: Böhlau, 1984); Hannes Heer and Volker Ullrich (eds.), *Geschichte entdecken. Erfahrungen und Projekte der neun Geschichtsbewegung*, (Reinbek: Rowohlt, 1985); Manfred Scharrer, *Macht Geschichte von unten. Handbuch für gewerkschaftliche Geschichte vor Ort* (Cologne: Bund-Verlag, 1988).

[35] Olaf Hartung, *Museen des Industrialismus. Formen bürgerlicher Geschichtskultur am Beispiel des Bayerischen Verkehrsmuseums und des Deutschen Bergbaumuseums* (Cologne: Böhlau, 2007); Stefan Siemer, 'Industrie als Identitätsfaktor: Das Industriemuseum Heimaterde in Gelsenkirchen und sein Schaubergwerk (1928–1945)', in: *Der Anschnitt* 69 (2017), pp. 152–165; Frank Kerner, 'Der Bergbau im Museum. Erinnerungsort Grubenlampe und Arschleder', in: Stefan Berger et al. (eds.), *Zeit-Räume Ruhr. Erinnerungsorte des Ruhrgebiets* (Essen: Klartext, 2019), pp. 442–458.

which now, however, reflect the past 'industrial culture' (***Industriekultur***) from a hindsight perspective. The 'Foundation for the Preservation of Industrial Monuments and Historical Culture' alone comprises 15 former industrial sites, mostly related to coal mining. The two regional administrational authorities for the Rhenish, western, part of the Ruhr (LVR) and the Westphalian, eastern, part (LWL) have their own decentralized industrial museums where each includes a number of former mines, iron and steel works as well as a few further sites outside the Ruhr. And a further milestone of the Ruhr's heritagization process was the opening of the Ruhr Museum in 2010 onsite the former Zollverein colliery in Essen, itself recognized as world heritage site since 2001.[36]

As a main branch of the Ruhr's present historical culture, this museum landscape has facilitated a move of social history toward popular historical exhibitions rather than being a strict object of academic research. A major shift had taken place with the establishment of the LWL Industrial Museum in 1979. Its foundation as 'Westphalian Industrial Museum', run by the regional Westphalian administrational authority, signified a marked change of perspective that was drawn from similar motivations as the local history/history-from-below movement. In the first place, as a decentralized museum which brought a variety of former industrial sites under one organizational roof, the museum initiative was instrumental in providing new meaning to the industrial sites after they had been formally recognized as national monuments and listed buildings. At the same time, it was the museum's declared task to 'present the culture of the industrial age', the 'conditions of live and work' and the 'interconnections between the technical, legal and social developments concerned'.[37] This implied a deep historical look into the industrializing Ruhr since the nineteenth century. But at the same time, the views of the actual actors of the industrial surroundings were meant to play a role more actively. The systematic collection of life histories and memories of former workers and other

[36] Stefan Berger, 'Industriekultur und Strukturwandel in deutschen Bergbauregionen nach 1945', in: Dieter Ziegler (ed.), *Rohstoffgewinnung im Strukturwandel. Der deutsche Bergbau im 20. Jahrhundert. Geschichte des deutschen Bergbaus,* Band 4 (2013), pp. 571–601.

[37] Dagmar Kift, 'Heritage and history. Germany's industrial museums and the (re-)presentation of labour', in: *International Journal of Heritage Studies* 17 (2011), pp. 380–389, here 382.

members of local communities has been an integral part of the museum's work from the start. On the one hand, such narratives played a major role in reconstructing and presenting derelict sites as places of work, production and technology and provided the necessary inside knowledge to do so. Furthermore, this also showed mines and steel works as spaces of social interaction that included both the realm of production and the wider life worlds intermingled with these industries. On the other hand, such museal practice drew upon an outright participatory approach that aimed to give former workers a more active position in telling their own stories.[38]

While living up to the ideals of a 'shared authority'[39] and balance the power differences between 'lays' and 'professionals' can be difficult at times for museum curators, the memories and experiences articulated in life history interviews have certainly set the tone and themes of the LWL museum sites from the start, in both their permanent and temporary exhibitions. As much as the museums attraction relied on the sites' industrial aesthetics, the stories told in many exhibitions fundamentally drew on the memories of former workers and communities. Given the generations interviewed in the 1980s and 1990s, however, this again led to a temporal focus before the actual outbreak of industrial crisis. Thus, while the establishment of the new industrial museums was very much part of the shrinking of mining and steel, the narrative focus was overwhelmingly coined by the life worlds of an active industry, often focused on the experiences from the 1940s to 1970s. Both the curators' interests and the interviewees' narratives combined variances of social hardship with feelings of nostalgia for a lost sense of community that had the former sites of production at its core.

One of the earliest interview projects at the Zollern colliery in Dortmund set out the direction: between 1986 and 1989, photographer Martin Rosswog interviewed and portrayed miners and their family members from the Zollern community, all of whom belonged to the generations born between the turn of the century and the 1920s. Their

[38] Dagmar Kift and Olaf Schmidt-Rutsch, 'Tonband – Vitrine –Digitalisat. Das Erinnerungsarchiv des LWL-Industriemuseums', in: *Westfälische Forschungen* 65 (2015), pp. 283–292; Olaf Schmidt-Rutsch, 'Arbeit wie sie nicht im Buch steht. Das Erinnerungsarchiv des LWL-Industriemuseums', in: *Ferrum* 91 (2019), pp. 102–108.

[39] Michael Frisch, *A Shared Authority: Essays on the Craft and Meaning of Oral and Public History* (New York, NY: SUNY Press, 1990).

memories thus reflected the hunger period after the First World War as well as the crisis ridden 1920s, work under the National Socialist regime, experiencing the war both as miners and as soldiers and, finally, the years of post-war reconstruction.[40] Apart from such changing external, even though fundamental contexts, the interviewees' memories had a distinctly technical note and illustrated the ways in which work underground and above ground was structured and perceived. This was, in a slightly different vein, also reflected in a book/exhibition project on mining apprentices, 'Keine Herrenjahre', again at Zollern. While the interview sample included memories from the turn of the century, the main focus lay on the generations that started work after 1945, in the 1950s and 1960s. Largely on the basis of interviews, Olge Dommer and Dagmar Kift, who functioned as curators, interviewers and authors, sketched out a differentiated picture of mine training and life as an apprentice. This included a range of experiences in relation to working structures, skills and hierarchies as well as the—often mortal—dangers miners continued to face in this period.[41] At the same time, however, looking at teenagers and young adults also allowed for an easier identification and moments sof nostalgia when it came to stories of communal life in the 'apprentice villages', allotment farming, sports and leisure activities. Such narratives, on the one hand, hinted at the longevity of older forms of working-class life in the coalfield; on the other hand, they addressed the gradual ability of the Ruhr's population to adapt to the newly growing consumer society of the apparent 'economic miracle'.[42]

[40] Martin Rosswog, *Schichtaufnahmen. Erinnerungen an die Zeche Zollern II/IV* (Essen: Klartext, 1994).

[41] 'What put me off of mining a bit were the severe work accidents which used to happen frequently. Repeatedly, people you knew suffered a fatal accident. Something already happened in the first half-year of my apprenticeship. (…) Someone got his head between the coal tubs and died in front of our workshop. That was the first shock. Then there were severe accidents underground. The father of a guy I knew from my apprenticeship had a fatal accident underground while I was still learning. It happened time and time again in those years', see Olge Dommer and Dagmar Kift, *Keine Herrenjahre. Jugend im Bergbau 1898–1961. Das Beispiel Zeche Zollern II/IV* (Essen: Klartext, 1998), p. 119.

[42] Axel Schildt and Arnold Sywottek (eds.), *Modernisierung im Wiederaufbau. Die Westdeutsche Gesellschaft der 50er Jahre* (Bonn: J.H.W. Dietz Nachf., 1998); Axel Schildt, Detlef Siegfried, and Karl-Christian Lammers (eds.), *Dynamische Zeiten. Die Die 60er Jahre in den beiden deutschen Gesellschaften* (Hamburg: Christians, 2000).

As production at the Zollern mine had finally ceased in 1966, after it had already been merged with the neighboring Germania colliery in 1955, the image of underground work referred to here largely remained one preceding the major steps toward mechanization and automation since the 1970s. The period since has been addressed in a range of exhibitions addressing aspects crucial to the current shape of the region, most notably with respect to the Ruhr's migration history, and, gradually, also with regard to deindustrialization more directly.[43] An early attempt to represent the very moment of closure was an exhibition documenting the final months of Dortmund's last colliery, Minister Stein, which closed in 1987. Largely a photo exhibition, it intensely captured the atmosphere at the mining compound itself—both underground and aboveground, before and after production had stopped—as well as in the surrounding neighborhoods. Only two interview sections accompanied the photos, with groups of miners who reminisced about their working lives and on their views on the pit closing down. The ambiguous feelings articulated in these interviews somewhat stand exemplarily for the discourses on structural change in the 1980s and 1990s. A miner who had already witnessed five collieries closing during his career nonetheless insisted 'there is nothing to say against the welfare early retirement schemes, they were well planned'. But at the same time, as another interviewee maintains, 'Dortmund is dead. This was the last pit. The Ruhr region is dead. It has its name from coal. How can you destroy your own economy like this? What we built during the economic miracle in the 1950s, that's what's now being destroyed'.[44]

With some more temporal distance, the Ruhr's industrial museums provide a space in which it is possible to review such a bleak interpretation of the current moment of change. At the Henrichshütte Steel Works

[43] Anke Asfur and Dietmar Osses (eds.), *Neapel—Bochum—Rimini. Arbeiten in Deutschland. Urlaub in Italien. Katalog zur Ausstellung des Westfälischen Industriemuseums Zeche Hannover, Bochum, 12. Juli-26. Oktober 2003*, (Essen: Klartext, 2003); Jana Golombek (ed.), *Schichtwechsel. Von der Kohlekrise zum Strukturwandel. Katalog zur Ausstellung im LWL-Industriemuseum Zeche Hannover in Bochum, 3.7.-30.10.2011*, (Essen: Klartext, 2011); Dietmar Osses (ed.), *Nach Westen. Zuwanderung aus Osteuropa ins Ruhrgebiet. Katalog zur Ausstellung im Westfälischen Landesmuseum für Industriekultur, LWL-Industriemuseum, Zeche Hannover in Bochum 10.06.2012–28.10.2012* (Essen: Klartext, 2012).

[44] Minister Stein, *Dortmunds letzte Zeche. Bilder und Texte aus der Zeit der Stillegung* (Hagen: Linnepe, 1988), here pp. 24, 34f.

in Hattingen, as well part of the LWL Industrial Museum, this shift can be further exemplified. The closing of the plant in 1987, together with protests against the closure of the Krupp-Rheinhausen Steel works in 1987–1988, was at the time felt as epitomes of the Ruhr's industrial crisis. In both cases, the threats of closure and unemployment met with massive opposition which was not able to entirely stop the plans of closure or moving production elsewhere, but could at least facilitate similar early retirement schemes as in the mining industry. These protest movements also triggered a range of grassroots publications and exhibitions that reflected the anger and despair of workers and their families, yet at the same time conveyed strong feelings of community and solidarity, channelled by collective action.[45] Following closure and a period of restoration, the struggle with deindustrialization and structural change has become one of the main themes of the Henrichshütte as a museum site. The latest project took place between 2013 and 2016, when one hundred former Hattingen steel workers told about their lives with the plant from the time of post-war reconstruction to the end of production.[46] As a key moment for many turned out to be a human chain around the steel works in April 1987, a manifestation in which 5,000 people participated, the project resulted in photo portraits of all interviewees who virtually re-enacted the chain. The portrait chain is now surrounding the museum site (which consists of the last remaining blast furnace). Thus, while large parts of the stories told continue to be carried by feelings of loss and disappointment, the live-size photographic display puts the memories of collective action and solidarity in the past struggles into the public realm and becomes a vital part of Hattingen's industrial heritage practice.

[45] Waltraud Bierwirth and Otto König (eds.), *Schmelzpunkte. Stahl: Krise und Widerstand im Revier*, (Essen, Klartext, 1988); Ulrich Link (ed.), *Der Ofen ist aus. Stahlarbeiter erzählen ihre Geschichte*, (Iserlohn, Nolte, 1995); Otto König et al., *Das Ende der Stahlzeit. Die Stilllegung der Henrichshütte Hattingen* (Essen: Klartext 1997); Wolfgang Hindrichs et al., *Der lange Abschied vom Malocher. Sozialer Umbruch in der Stahlindustrie und die Rolle der Betriebsräte von 1960 bis in die neunziger Jahre* (Essen: Klartext, 2000).

[46] A selection of the interviews resulted in a film: Förderverein Industriemuseum Henrichshütte e.V., '100 Hüttenleben - Wie war es damals auf der Hütte?', https://www.youtube.com/watch?v=ig-6gKH6lmo [accessed 10 October 2020].

The 'Mainstreaming' of Industrial Heritage and the Return of a History from Below

As this and other examples show, the Ruhr's 'institutionalized' memory culture that is closely linked the realm of the museum has for a long time been shaped by attempts to provide space for voices and perspectives of those who were the very actors of the region's industrial settings. Yet, although the struggle with deindustrialization has been part of such representational practice, the key images still seem to focus on motives from the 'high time' of coal and steel, and in particular on the narratives from the 1950s and 1960s, before the coming of a more accelerated industrial decline. Patterns of male work underground or in the steel works, authoritarian work hierarchies which nonetheless combined with lived values of trust and solidarity amidst dangerous working conditions, but also the strengthened post-war position of the trade unions on the shop floor—all of these constitute aspects of a master narrative of the industrial Ruhr as told by curators and historians. In the wider realm of public discourse, however, many nuances of historical and curatorial reflection, let alone the multi-faceted character of memories from below tend to be overridden by the broad strokes of industrial heritage as a marketing construction. The preserved industrial architecture as well as the network of industrial museums creates a successful memory landscape that, at least potentially, entails the representation of a view from below, but all too often creates an image of nostalgia and easy identification lacking the social and political difficulties and hardships of the historical experience. Besides being a signifier for a lived historical experience among the Ruhr's working-class communities, industrial heritage has become a successful asset of marketing and touristification. In 2017, the number of visitors to the region has surpassed four million.[47] Noting this commercial interest is not to imply that historical differentiation is necessarily lost here. But it seems to overlap increasingly with images of the Ruhr's industrial past as a digestible commodity of nostalgia. This can also be seen in a range of television documentaries about the Ruhr, and in particular in the depiction of coal mining in the run up to the final

[47] https://presse.ruhr-tourismus.de/pressreleases/das-reiseziel-metropole-ruhr-erstmals-mehr-als-8-millionen-uebernachtungen-2424722 [accessed 5 June 2020].

closure of the last pits in 2018.[48] In their montage of bird-eye shots of the (post-)industrial landscape, historical black-and-white footage, interview snippets and musical dramatization, these films visualize a regional identity that draws heavily on construing an historical image, but at the same time blur many tensions and gaps. Interviewees are used as interchangeable talking heads who are supposed to illustrate a fixed narrative rather than providing new insights and interpretations.[49]

In contrast to such stylizations, we might look again at recent history and memory practices from below which partly play into the grand(er) narratives of museums and public discourse and partly articulate views from quite opposing angles to the established perspectives. Below the surface of the hegemonic heritage discourse, it is the grassroots initiatives who continue to claim shares in the broader histories. The historical practice of many 'traditional' miners' clubs is a case in point. Though it might well be argued that German mining tradition is, after all, an invention and has always been heavily entangled with political circumstances and in particular with the interests of the mining employers,[50] nonetheless the miners' clubs and associations play a most important role in articulating memory perspectives from below today. While the local 'Knappenvereine' all over the Ruhr region, the history of which goes back to the solidarity networks in mining at the beginning of industrialization,[51] function as everyday spaces for former mine workers to meet and interact with their pensioner colleagues, much of their activities can be described as historical activism. This combines a particular care for the material remains of the coal-mining heritage with diverse forms of storytelling. Campaigns to save local winding towers and other examples of industrial architecture as well as actively building mining collections and

[48] See in particular the films by the regional TV station WDR, for instance 'Der lange Abschied von der Kohle' (2018), 'Schicht im Schacht' (2016) or 'Das Ruhrgebiet von oben' (2013).

[49] Stefan Moitra, 'Nostalgie und dokumentarischer Blick. Vom Ende des Bergbaus im Film', in: *Forum Geschichtskultur Ruhr* 1 (2018), pp. 32–36.

[50] Dagmar Kift, 'Kultur, Kulturpolitik und Kulturgeschichte im Ruhrbergbau nach dem Zweiten Weltkrieg', in: Dagmar Kift et al. (eds.), *Bergbaukulturen in interdisziplinärer Perspektive. Diskurse und Imaginationen* (Essen: Klartext, 2018), pp. 31–43; Sebastian Felten, 'Mining culture, labour and the state in early modern Saxony', in: *Renaissance Studies* 34 (2019), pp. 119–148.

[51] Evelyn Kroker and Werner Kroker, *Solidarität aus Tradition. Die Knappenvereine im Ruhrgebiet* (Munich: C.H. Beck, 1988).

community museums signify the importance given to a shared history which they attempt to convey to the next generations.[52] This is the case at Zeche Hugo in Gelsenkirchen-Buer where a local miners' initiative succeeded in preventing the colliery tower from being taken down and which now functions as a cultural and community center. At the Nordstern-Stollen in Gelsenkirchen-Horst, the self-made visitors' mine attracts a wide audience, and readings of mainly local authors with a mining background are organized on a regular basis. Similarly, the Knappenverein of Kamp-Lintfort, on the western fringe of the region, where one of the last Ruhr collieries closed in 2012, managed to extend their older practice of collecting and archiving photos, documents and mining objects to converting the old surface 'training gallery' into a visitors' mine. Making such efforts and reaching out to broad audience groups—from local schools to heritage tourists from wider afield—largely aims at keeping the stories and agency of former industrial workers visible. As Manfred Reis, a miner from Kamp-Lintfort and active in the local miners' association, points out: 'I want the people who are new here, I want them to know: Those old bums in their [miners'] uniforms, those are the guys who shaped and built our town. And we won't forget them'.[53]

In addition to this vaster network of miners' associations, there are further attempts of historical activists from below who address issues of visibility in the wider public realm. This is particularly true with regard to the role of migrant communities in the Ruhr who have not simply left historical representation as a task for the 'professionals' in the museums in recent years, but have repeatedly been active to trigger new and different kinds of stories of the industrial context. This was true for instance in case of an exhibition at the German Mining Museum Bochum initiated by IFAK, an association for intercultural learning. In 'Glückauf und Ugur Ola' (2014/15), a title which combined both the German and Turkish forms of a special miners' greeting, it was specifically the history of skilled workers from the Turkish mining region of Zonguldak at the beginning of the 'guestworker' era which the exhibition focused on. While the public image of migrant workers is often associated with the unskilled who had

[52] For an overview on the mining collections including many of the Ruhr's Knappenvereine see https://bergbausammlungen.de/search/map [accessed 5 May 2020].

[53] Interview with Manfred Reis, 12 February 2015, AHGR, LINT 17; see also the testimonies regarding industrial heritage and miners' tradition collected here: https://menschen-im-bergbau.de/themen/?slide=7 [accessed 5 May 2020].

to come to the industrial metropole in order to get training and education, the (life-)stories of the Zonguldak workers gave Turkish migration a different angle.

More in line with the narrative of migrating from periphery to the center was 'Glückauf in Deutschland', an exhibition which nonetheless gave the conventional views a further twist.[54] Organized by an intercultural association, 'Verein für internationale Freundschaft' (ViF) in Dortmund, it followed the biographies of nine teenagers from Turkey who came to Germany in 1964, part of a group that totalled 76 future miners (some of whom were also from Zonguldak) and was split into four collieries in the Dortmund area. The nine protagonists basically contributed all material, photos and written documents, and, most importantly, shared their memories of making a living in the new environment. This includes stories of being welcomed into German host families and the local society more generally, but also experiences that were common to all miners of the generation: underground features, such as acquiring training and work skills, the adaption with technological change, as well as becoming an adult in the 1960s and 1970s. Some married women from German and some from Turkish families. What most of them had in common is that they did not stop qualifying and went on to become at least foremen ('Steiger') or climbed even higher up in the work hierarchy. All these biographical steps were entangled with the specific migrant perspective. 'As a Turk you always had to be better than the rest, you were not allowed to make mistakes and always had to proof you were skilled enough, even as a Steiger', Arif Sarıkaya remembers.[55] Notwithstanding such frankness in noting xenophobic tendencies in (post-war) German society, the overall message of the exhibition and its accompanying book conveys a much more positive note. It is a story of personal achievements and successful intercultural lives that revolved around the world of mining.

Another 'guestworker'-related exhibition based on personal histories was organized as a double presentation by VMDO, a roof organization for migrant cultural associations in Dortmund, and the Hoesch Museum, co-run by the city of Dortmund, which documents the history of labor

[54] https://vifdo.wordpress.com/glueckauf/ [accessed 3 September 2020].

[55] Viktoria Waltz and Verein für Internationale Freundschaften e.V. Dortmund (eds.), *Glückauf in Deutschland. Ein Projekt der lebendigen Erinnerung im Verein für Internationale Freundschaften e.V.* (Oberhausen: Asso-Verlag, 2015), p. 111.

at the former Hoesch Steel Works. As 'Onkel Hasan und die Generation der Enkel', it centered on the story of Hasan Koşan who came to work in the Hoesch Steel branch in Hagen in 1964 and moved to nearby Dortmund in 1977 when his family came to join him. While the exhibit in the museum focused on Koşan's generation and the conditions of work as a migrant in the Ruhr, a second part, based at the VMDO, juxtaposed these experiences with the views of the children's and grandchildren's generation. In doing so, the exhibition broadened the perspective in a number of ways. Firstly, it showed that—similar to the successful careers of the Turkish 'Steiger'—social mobility was not an uncommon occurrence. Thus, one of Koşan's sons studied engineering and remains in the steel industry, but as a skilled white-collar employee rather than blue-collar laborer. Secondly, the narrative opened the view to youngsters with a more diverse migration background than just the grandchildren of the 'guestworker' generation and in doing so gave reference to the real existing make-up of many places in the Ruhr today. Thirdly, this generational juxtaposition also entailed a transgression of the stricter conceptual borders of industrial heritage or industrial history. While the history of Uncle Hasan's generation was directly related to the industrial setting of the 1960s and the following decades (he retired in 1991), the grandchildren have grown up in a largely deindustrialized environment—at least one in which the old industries of coal and steel have vanished. Nonetheless, they still have to struggle with being positioned between cultures and, not least, being confronted with tendencies of old and new xenophobia.[56]

The sociologist Aladin El-Mafaalani has described the gradual integration and tendencies of upward social mobility of the second and third generations, the children and, by now, grandchildren of the 'guestworker' generation as the 'integration paradox'. The growing absorption and merging into the middle class of people with a migrant background signify a normalization process; but at the same time, the more articulate resonance of apparent 'migrant' voices in the wider society triggers increasing xenophobic affects in some parts of German society.[57] The higher visibility of migrant actors in the industrial/post-industrial narrative can be

[56] http://onkel-hasan.de; http://onkel-hasan.de/wp-content/uploads/2015/08/ECHO_der_Vielfalt_Onkel_web.pdf [accessed 6 October 2020].

[57] Aladin El-Mafaalani, *Das Integrationsparadox. Warum gelungene Integration zu mehr Konflikten führ* (Cologne: Kiepenheuer und Witsch, 2018).

understood as a further contribution to such an increasing recognition. Yet, unlike the integration paradox, all of the exhibitions mentioned above have over all received a very positive reception. Both 'Glückauf in Deutschland' and 'Onkel Hasan' have been traveling exhibitions and were shown way beyond the Ruhr region itself, including the Parliament of North-Rhine Westphalia. They are, in any case, good examples for the willingness of an important part of the Ruhr's former industrial workforce not just to be included in the grand narrative of the industrial past, but also to be heard with their own voices and their own experiences.

Conclusion: (De-)Industrial Memories then and Now

Although the beginning of oral history and of histories from below coincided with the height of deindustrialization in the Ruhr, both its heritage institutions and museums as well as academic research on the Ruhr's industrial experience have until recently been more concerned with memories of industry as an active center of community life rather than with the challenges of coming to terms with its vanishing. This has been mirrored to a great extent in oral histories collected in the various projects described above. It is only more recently that the deindustrialization process as such and its 'half-life' are addressed more explicitly.[58] This has been the case in Hattingen, where the steel workers' struggle against the closure of their plant is at the center of the LWL Industrial Museum's narrative for the local exhibition. And this is also reflected in more recent interviews with coal miners in view of the last colliery closures in 2018.[59] The ambiguities of being subjected to early retirement schemes, which were a key political feature to cope with the shrinking of the industry, are summed up by Jörg Uwe Trappmann, a former miner from Dortmund: 'Pension with 50 sounds great. But it was total crap. (…) Some get their pension with 50 or 49, and with 51 they're dead. Because they had nothing to do anymore'. At a later point in the interview, however,

[58] Sherry Lee Linkon, *The Half-Life of Deindustrialization. Working-Class Writing about Economic Restructuring* (Ann Arbor, MI: University of Michigan Press, 2018).

[59] Stefan Moitra, Katarzyna Nogueira, and Jens Adamski, 'Erfahrung, Erinnerung, Erzählung. Potenziale einer Oral History für die Bergbaugeschichte heute', in: *Der Anschnitt* 71 (2019), pp. 93–105; see also https://menschen-im-bergbau.de [accessed 10 October 2020].

Trappmann concedes that 'in any case, this slow transformation was, in my opinion, better than the abrupt change as they had it in England. Then everything would be dead here, there'd be nothing new, rather, everything would be in ruins, I guess. You've seen it in America, too, in the various steel towns. Whole cities have been destroyed. I think this socially coherent, responsible shrinking in the last 30, 40 years was a good thing. Whether it was financially okay, I don't know. But we have paid money for so much crap—I've found it a just investment into the Ruhr region. I think we have deserved it.[60]

While over time, it seems, a mainstreaming of industrial heritage has taken root, it may also be expected that more ambiguous notions about the political implications and social impact such as Trappmann's will be articulated more strongly in the future. Actors from below—former miners and steel workers—who were the very people affected by the shrinking of the old industrial sphere are already vocal in claiming their own histories. These claims are not necessarily opposed to the dominant narratives of industrial heritage—but they certainly aim at an acknowledgment of former workers in their role as historical actors. This is true in case of the local miners' associations as it is for the group exhibitions of former migrant workers. The latter also hint at a further potential of storytelling and memory work in this context. As much as the migrant perspective addresses issues of recognition and visibility, it also transgresses the frameworks of defining what is part of the Ruhr's industrial heritage discourse and what is not. The history of xenophobia and ethnic exclusion is certainly not restricted to the Ruhr region; but here it is closely entangled with its industrial history and the fallouts of experiencing deindustrialization. In this respect, the recurring waves of racist and neo-fascist violence in the region since at least the 1980s have to be understood before the background of the transformations the Ruhr's industrial communities went through. Current grassroots initiatives to review this history and bring repressed cases of racist violence into the public do not explicitly see themselves as part of the post-industrial discourse.[61] But they remind us that there are parts of the industrial context of the Ruhr and of the very

[60] Interview with Jörg-Uwe Trappmann, 19 July 2017, AHGR, LINT 68.

[61] Most notably see the 'Initiative DU 26. August 1984', http://www.inidu84.de [accessed 5 October 2020], who reconstruct the racist background and public neglect of an arson attack in Duisburg in which seven members of a family who hailed from Turkey were killed.

era of structural transformation, which have as yet not been highlighted as much as they probably have deserved.

Such a broadening of the scope opens the view, as well, to other aspects in the shift from the industrial to the post-industrial situation that have only found little recognition so far. Currently, the image of the region's past seems to stop with the end of the old industries. Yet while the struggles with structural change are frequently acknowledged in public discourse, the everyday experience of coping with high unemployment and destitution can be addressed much further and beyond mere statistics.[62] This could involve the simultaneity of potential social mobility for working-class children attending the Ruhr's universities since the late 1960s with the precarious life worlds in many parts of the region, shaped by the limits of education, unemployment and substance abuse. A cultural angle closely linked with this context is the many facets of youth culture and the extent to which particularly music cultures, from early Punk to the Ruhr as a center for the German Techno scene in the 1990s and early 2000s, interlinked with the deindustrializing process in the region.[63] Shifting the view away from the dominating grand narrative of coal and steel work might also allow to look more closely at predominantly female labor environments in the textile and retail industries which have become much more important over the years in terms of employment numbers but remain largely overlooked under the dominance of (male) heavy industry.[64] Turning to such issues would imply a stronger reference to the current life-worlds of the Ruhr. Its inhabitants today have a history that goes beyond the dominant focus of coal and steel.

References

ASSMANN Aleida (2007). Geschichte im Gedächtnis. Von der individuellen Erfahrung zur öffentlichen Inszenierung. München, C.H. Beck

[62] Michael Hüther/Jens Südekum and Michael Voigtländer, *Die Zukunft der Regionen in Deutschland. Zwischen Vielfalt und Gleichwertigkeit* (Köln: IW-Studien, 2019), pp. 99 and 124–127.

[63] Katarzyna Nogueira and Dietmar Osses (eds.), *Einfach anders! Jugendliche Subkulturen im Ruhrgebiet* (Essen: Klartext, 2014).

[64] Lutz Niethammer, Handel und Wandel im Pott. Wider „rostalgische“ Ruhrgebietsidentität, in: Werner Daum et al. (eds.), *Politische Bewegung und Symbolische Ordnung. Hagener Studien zur Politischen Kulturgeschichte. Festschrift für Peter Brandt* (Bonn: J.H.W. Dietz Nachf, 2014), pp. 243–260.

ANDRESEN Knut/BITZEGEIO Ursula/MITTAG Jürgen eds. (2011). "Nach dem Strukturbruch?" Kontinuität und Wandel von Arbeitsbeziehungen und Arbeitswelt(en) seit den 1970er-Jahren. Bonn, J.H.W. Dietz Nachf

ANDRESEN Knut/APEL Linde/HEINSON Kirsten eds. (2015). Es gilt das gesprochene Wort. Oral History und Zeitgeschichte heute. In ANDRESEN Knut/APEL Linde/HEINSON Kirsten eds. Es gilt das gesprochene Wort. Oral History und Zeitgeschichte heute. Göttingen, Wallstein, pp. 7–22

ASFUR Anke/OSSES Dietmar eds. (2003). Neapel—Bochum—Rimini. Arbeiten in Deutschland. Urlaub in Italien. Katalog zur Ausstellung des Westfälischen Industriemuseums Zeche Hannover, Bochum, 12. Juli-26. Oktober 2003. Essen, Klartext

ASSMANN Aleida (2007). Geschichte im Gedächtnis. Von der individuellen Erfahrung zur öffentlichen Inszenierung. München, C.H. Beck

BERGER Stefan (2013). Industriekultur und Strukturwandel in deutschen Bergbauregionen nach 1945. In ZIEGLER Dieter ed. Rohstoffgewinnung im Strukturwandel. Der deutsche Bergbau im 20. Jahrhundert. Geschichte des deutschen Bergbaus, Band 4. Münster, Aschen-dorff, pp. 571–601

BERGER Stefan/GOLOMBEK Jana/WICKE Christian (2018). A Post-Industrial Mindscape? The Mainstreaming and Touristification of Industrial Heritage in the Ruhr. In WICKE Christian/BERGER Stefan/GOLOMBEK Jana eds. Industrial Heritage and Regional Identities. Abingdon and New York, Routledge, pp. 74–94

BIERWIRTH Waltraud/KÖNIG Otto ed. (1988). Schmelzpunkte. Stahl: Krise und Widerstand im Revier. Essen, Klartext

BRÜGGEMEIER Franz-Josef (1983). Leben vor Ort. Ruhrbergleute und Ruhrbergbau 1889–1919. München, C.H. Beck

CASPERS Britta (2016). Strategien einer 'Regionalisierung der Region' am Beispiel der Bottroper Protokolle. In CASPERS Britta et al. eds. Theorien, Modelle und Probleme regionaler Literaturgeschichtsschreibung. Essen, Klartext, pp. 119–141

CASPERS Britta et al. (2019). Ruhrgebietsliteratur seit 1960. Eine Geschichte nach Knotenpunkten. Stuttgart, J.B. Metzler

DE JONG Jutta ed. (1991). Kinder, Küche, Kohle—und viel mehr! Bergarbeiterfrauen aus drei Generationen erinnern sich. Essen, Klartext

DELABER Walter (2011). Erika Runge's Bottroper Protokolle und ihr Fernsehfilm 'Warum ist Frau B. glücklich?'. In CEPLKAUFMANN Gertrude/GRANDE Jasmin eds. Schreibwel-ten—Erschriebene Welten. Zum 50. Geburtstag der Dortmunder Gruppe 61. Essen, Klartext, pp. 224–229

DOERING-MANTEUFFEL Anselm/RAPHAEL Lutz (2008). Nach dem Boom. Perspektiven auf die Zeitgeschichte nach 1970, Göttingen, Vandenhoeck und Ruprecht

DOMMER Olge/KIFT Dagmar (1998). Keine Herrenjahre. Jugend im Bergbau 1898–1961. Das Beispiel Zeche Zollern II/IV. Essen, Klartext
EHALT Hubert Ch. ed. (1984). Geschichte von unten. Fragestellungen, Methoden und Projekte einer Geschichte des Alltags. Wien/Köln/Graz, Böhlau
EL-MAFAALANI Aladin (2018). Das Integrationsparadox. Warum gelungene Integration zu mehr Konflikten führt. Köln, Kiepenheuer und Witsch
FARRENKOPF Michael (2013). Wiederaufstieg und Niedergang des Bergbaus in der Bundesrepublik. In ZIEGLER Dieter ed. Rohstoffgewinnung im Strukturwandel. Der deutsche Bergbau im 20. Jahrhundert. Geschichte des deutschen Bergbaus, Band 4. Münster, Aschendorff, pp. 183–302
FARRENKOPF Michael/GOCH Stefan/RASCH Manfred/WEHLING Hans-Werner eds. (2019). Die Stadt der Städte. Das Ruhrgebiet und seine Umbrüche. Essen, Klartext
FELTEN Sebastian (2019). Mining Culture, Labour and the State in Early Modern Saxony. In Renaissance Studies 34 (2019), pp. 119–148
FRISCH Michael (1990). A Shared Authority: Essays on the Craft and Meaning of Oral and Public History. New York, SUNY Press
GOCH Stefan (2002). Eine Region im Kampf mit dem Strukturwandel, Strukturpolitik und Bewältigung von Strukturwandel im Ruhrgebiet. Essen, Klartext
GOLDMANN Margarethe/HILGERT Volker/ZIMMERMANN Michael (1981). Kohle war nicht alles. Projektbericht. Erfahrungen von 1978–1981. In HOCHLARMARKER Lesebuch (1981), pp. 315–334
GOLOMBEK Jana ed. (2011). Schichtwechsel. Von der Kohlekrise zum Strukturwandel. Katalog zur Ausstellung im LWLIndustriemuseum Zeche Hannover in Bochum, 3.7.-30.10.2011. Essen, Klartext
GÜNTER Janne (1981). Mündliche Geschichtsschreibung. Alte Menschen im Ruhrgebiet erzählen erlebte Geschichte. In Scheidewege. Vierteljahressschrift für skeptisches Denken 11, 3 (1981), pp. 411–424
GÜNTER Janne and GÜNTER Roland (1999). Sprechende Straßen in Eisenheim. Konzepte und Texte sämtlicher Tafeln in der ältesten Siedlung (1846/1901) im Ruhrgebiet. Essen, Klartext
HARTUNG Olaf (2007). Museen des Industrialismus. Formen bürgerlicher Geschichtskultur am Beispiel des Bayerischen Verkehrsmuseums und des Deutschen Bergbaumuseums. Köln, Böhlau
HEER Hannes/ULLRICH Volker eds. (1985). Geschichte entdecken. Erfahrungen und Projekte der neun Geschichtsbewegung. Reinbek, Rowohlt
HERBERT Ulrich (1983). Vom Kruppianer zum Arbeitnehmer. In NIETHAMMER Lutz ed. Hinterher weiß man, daß es richtig war, daß es schief gegangen ist. Nachkriegserfahrungen im Ruhrgebiet. Lebensgeschichte und Sozialkultur im Ruhrgebiet, Band 2. Berlin and Bonn, J.H.W. Dietz Nachf., pp. 233–276.

HIGH Steven (2009). Sharing Authority. An Introduction. In Journal of Canadian Studies/Revue d'études canadiennes 43 (2009), pp. 12–34

HINDRICHS Wolfgang et al. (2000). Der lange Abschied vom Malocher. Sozialer Umbruch in der Stahlindustrie und die Rolle der Betriebsräte von 1960 bis in die neunziger Jahre. Essen, Klartext

HOCHLARMARKER Lesebuch (1981). Kohle war nicht alles. 100 Jahre Ruhrgebietsgeschichte. Bergarbeiter und ihre Frauen aus Recklinghausen-Hochlarmark haben in Zusammenarbeit mit dem kommunalen Staddtteilkulturreferat ihre Geschichte aufgeschrieben. Oberhausen, Asso-Verlag

HÜBNER Christoph (1982). Filmarbeit vor Ort. RuhrFilmZentrum 1978–1982. Drei, bald vier Jahre Filmarbeit in einer Region. In HOGENKAMP Bert. Bergarbeiter im Spielfilm. Ed. by Westdeutsche Kurzfilmtage Oberhausen, pp. 126–133

HÜBNER Christoph/VOSS Gabriele (2014). Film/Arbeit. Texte, Dokumente und Arbeitsnotizen. Berlin, Vorwerk 8

HÜBNER Christoph/VOSS Gabriele (2018). Zu Konzeption, Produktion und Einsatz des Films [1980]. In Lebens-Geschichte des Bergarbeiters Alphons S. Ein Bio-Interview in acht Teilen von Alphons Stiller, Gabriele Voss, Christoph Hübner. Begleitheft zur DVD. Ed. by LWL-Medienzentrum für Westfalen. Münster, LWL, pp. 9–13.

HÜTHER Michael/SÜDEKUM Jens and VOIGTLÄNDER Michael (2019). Die Zukunft der Regionen in Deutschland. Zwischen Vielfalt und Gleichwertigkeit. Köln, IW-Studien

IGBE-Bezirk Ruhr-Nord (1980). Jahre die wir nicht vergessen. Recklinghausen

IGBE (1982). Bergleute erzählen (Beiträge zur Geschichte der IGBE). Arbeitsmaterial der Industriegewerkschaft Bergbau und Energie X, Bochum, Berg-Verlag

JUREIT Ulrike (2007). Die Entdeckung des Zeitzeugen. Faschismus- und Nachkriegserfahrungen im Ruhrgebiet. In DANYEL Jürgen/KIRSCH Jan-Holger/SABROW Martin eds. 50 Klassiker der Zeitgeschichte. Göttingen, Vandenhoeck und Ruprecht, pp. 174–181

KERNER Frank (2019). Der Bergbau im Museum. Erinnerungsort Grubenlampe und Arsch-leder. In BERGER Stefan et al. eds. Zeit-Räume Ruhr. Erinnerungsorte des Ruhrgebiets. Essen, Klartext, pp. 442–458

KIFT Dagmar (2011). Heritage and history. Germany's industrial museums and the (re-)presentation of labour. In International Journal of Heritage Studies 17 (2011), pp. 380–389

KIFT Dagmar (2018). Kultur, Kulturpolitik und Kulturgeschichte im Ruhrbergbau nach dem Zweiten Weltkrieg. In KIFT Dagmar et al. eds. Bergbaukulturen in interdisziplinärer Perspektive. Diskurse und Imaginationen. Essen, Klartext, pp. 31–43

KIFT Dagmar/SCHMIDT-RUTSCH Olaf (2015). Tonband—Vitrine—Digitalisat. Das Erinnerungsarchiv des LWLIndustriemuseums. In Westfälische Forschungen 65 (2015), pp. 283–292

KÖNIG Otto et al. (1997). Das Ende der Stahlzeit. Die Stillegung der Henrichshütte Hattingen, Essen, Klartext

KROKER Evelyn/KROKER Werner (1988). Solidarität aus Tradition. Die Knappenvereine im Ruhrgebiet. München, C.H. Beck

Leben mit Gneisenau (1986). hundert Jahre... Eine Zeche zwischen Dortmund und Lünen. Begleitbuch zur Ausstellung der VHS Dortmund im Museum für Kunst- und Kulturgeschichte der Stadt Dortmund vom 12.9.-26.10.1986. Essen, Klartext

LEO Annette/MAUBACH Franka (2013). Den Unterdrückten eine Stimme geben? Die International Oral History Association zwischen politischer Bewegung und wissenschaftlichem Netzwerk. Göttingen, Wallstein

LINK Ulrich ed. (1995). Der Ofen ist aus. Stahlarbeiter erzählen ihre Geschichte. Iserlohn, Nolte

LINKON Sherry Lee (2018). The Half-Life of Deindustrialization. Working-Class Writing about Economic Restructuring. Ann Arbor, University of Michigan Press

MAUBACH Franka (2013). Gleichschwebende Aufmerksamkeit« und Plausibilitätsprüfung—Zur Ambivalenz der Interviewmethoden in der (west-) deutschen Oral History um 1980. In BIOS 26 (2013), pp. 28–52.

MAUBACH Franka (2018). "Mehr Geschichte wagen!" LUSIR und die ganze Geschichte der Arbeiter im Ruhrgebiet vor, während und nach dem Nationalsozialismus. In Sprache und Literatur 47 (2018), pp. 29–57

MINISTER STEIN (1988). Dortmunds letzte Zeche. Bilder und Texte aus der Zeit der Stille-gung. Hagen, Linnepe

MOITRA Stefan (2018). Nostalgie und dokumentarischer Blick. Vom Ende des Bergbaus im Film. In Forum Geschichtskultur Ruhr 1, pp. 32–36

MOITRA Stefan/NOGUEIRA Katarzyna/ADAMSKI Jens (2019). Erfahrung, Erinnerung, Erzählung. Potenziale einer Oral History für die Bergbaugeschichte heute. In Der Anschnitt 71, pp. 93–105

MOMMSEN Hans/BORSDORF Ulrich eds. (1979). Glück auf, Kameraden! Die Bergarbeiter und ihre Organisationen in Deutschland. Cologne, Bund Verlag

NIETHAMMER Lutz (1978). Oral History in den USA. Zur Entwicklung und Problematik diachroner Befragungen. In Archiv für Sozialgeschichte Vol. 18, pp. 457–501

NIETHAMMER Lutz (1983). Einleitung des Herausgebers. In NIETHAMMER Lutz ed. "Die Jahre weiß man nicht, wo man die heute hinsetzen soll." Faschismuserfahrungen im Ruhrgebiet. Lebensgeschichte und Sozialkultur im Ruhrgebiet, Band 1. Berlin and Bonn, J.H.W. Dietz Nachf., pp. 7–29

NIETHAMMER Lutz (1985). Fragen—Antworten—Fragen. Methodische Erfahrungen und Erwägungen zur Oral History. In NIETHAMMER Lutz/PLATO Alexander von eds. "Wir kriegen jetzt andere Zeiten." Auf der Suche nach der Erfahrung des Volkes in nachfaschistischen Ländern. Lebensgeschichte und Sozialkultur im Ruhrgebiet, Band 3. Berlin and Bonn, J.H.W. Dietz Nachf., pp. 392–445

NIETHAMMER Lutz (2014). Handel und Wandel im Pott. Wider "rostalgische" Ruhrgebietsidentität. In DAUM Werner et al. (eds.), Politische Bewegung und Symbolische Ordnung. Hagener Studien zur Politischen Kulturgeschichte. Festschrift für Peter Brandt, Bonn, J.H.W. Dietz Nachf., pp. 243–260

NOGUEIRA Katarzyna (2018). Geschichte und Geschichten. Zur Zeitzeugenschaft des Ruhrbergbaus. In Forum Geschichtskultur, Heft1, pp. 42–46.

NOGUEIRA Katarzyna and OSSES Dietmar eds. (2014). Einfach anders! Jugendliche Subkulturen im Ruhrgebiet. Essen, Klartext

NOLL Adolf/BLUMBACH Helmut/GOLDMANN Margarethe (1984). Wie man kleine Netze baut. Ein Handbuch stadtteilorientierter Kultur- und Bildungsarbeit. Gelsenkirchen, Zwing-mann

Oral History Review 30, 1 (2003). Special Feature: "Shared Authority"

OSSES Dietmar ed. (2012). Nach Westen. Zuwanderung aus Osteuropa ins Ruhrgebiet. Katalog zur Ausstellung im Westfälischen Landesmuseum für Industriekultur, LWL-Industriemuseum, Zeche Hannover in Bochum 10.06.2012–28.10.2012. Essen, Klartext

PLATO Alexander von (1984). "Der Verlierer geht nicht leer aus." Betriebsräte geben zu Protokoll. Berlin and Bonn, J.H.W. Dietz Nachf.

RAPHAEL Lutz (2019). Jenseits von Kohle und Stahl. Eine Gesellschaftsgeschichte Westeuropas nach dem Boom. Frankfurt am Main, Suhrkamp

REULECKE Jürgen ed. (1974). Arbeiterbewegung an Rhein und Ruhr. Beiträge zur Geschichte der Arbeiterbewegung in Rheinland-Westfalen. Wuppertal, Hammer

ROSSWOG Martin (1994). Schichtaufnahmen. Erinnerungen an die Zeche Zollern II/IV. Es-sen, Klartext

RUNGE Erika (1968). Bottroper Protokolle. Frankfurt am Main, Suhrkamp

RÜSEN Jörn (1994). Historische Orientierung. Über die Arbeit des Geschichtsbewußtseins, sich in der Zeit zurechtzufinden. Köln, Böhlau

SAMUEL Raphael (2012) [1994]. Theatres of Memory. Past and Present in Contemporary Culture. London and New York, Verso

SCHARRER Manfred (1988). Macht Geschichte von unten. Handbuch für gewerkschaftliche Geschichte vor Ort. Köln, Bund-Verlag

SCHILDT Axel/SYWOTTEK Arnold eds. (1998). Modernisierung im Wiederaufbau. Die Westdeutsche Gesellschaft der 50er Jahre. Bonn, J.H.W. Dietz Nachf.

SCHILDT Axel/SIEGFRIED Detlef/LAMMERS Karl-Christian eds. (2000). Dynamische Zeiten. Die Die 60er Jahre in den beiden deutschen Gesellschaften. Hamburg, Christians

SCHMIDT-RUTSCH Olaf (2019). Arbeit wie sie nicht im Buch steht. Das Erinnerungsarchiv des LWL-Industriemuseums. In Ferrum 91 (2019), pp. 102–108

SIEMER Stefan (2017). Industrie als Identitätsfaktor: Das Industriemuseum Heimaterde in Gelsenkirchen und sein Schaubergwerk (1928–1945). In Der Anschnitt 69 (2017), pp. 152–165

TENFELDE Klaus (1977). Sozialgeschichte der Bergarbeiterschaft an der Ruhr im 19. Jahrhundert. Bonn-Bad Godesberg

WALTZ Viktoria/Verein für Internationale Freundschaften e.V. Dortmund eds. (2015). Glückauf in Deutschland. Ein Projekt der lebendigen Erinnerung im Verein für Internationale Freundschaften e.V. Oberhausen, Asso-Verlag

ZIMMERMANN Michael (1983). "Geh zu Hermann, der macht dat schon". Bergarbeiterinteressenvertretung im nördlichen Ruhrgebiet. In NIETHAMMER Lutz ed. Hinterher weiß man, daß es richtig war, daß es schief gegangen ist. Nachkriegserfahrungen im Ruhrgebiet. Lebensgeschichte und Sozialkultur im Ruhrgebiet, Band 2. Berlin and Bonn, J.H.W. Dietz Nachf., pp. 277–310

ZIMMERMANN Michael (1987). Schachtanlage und Zechenkolonie. Leben, Arbeit und Politik in einer Arbeitersiedlung 1880–1980. Essen, Klartext.

CHAPTER 5

'The Master Director of All This is Time': An Oral History Project in Sesto San Giovanni

Roberta Garruccio

Introductory Remarks

This chapter describes a public oral history project which was conducted between 2013 and 2015 on the deindustrialization of Sesto San Giovanni. Sesto S.G. was formerly a center of heavy industry on the northern edge of Milan. From being a small village at the end of the nineteenth century, it mushroomed in the first decade of the twentieth century into a heavy engineering center supplying steel for the railway, automotive, aircraft and armaments industries, and merged into the urban sprawl of Milan. Its deindustrialization was meteoric: all four major firms that had embodied

[1] By 2020, even the office buildings of some of the largest companies that came later (Alitalia, Oracle, Wind, Epson, ABB, Alstom, Medtronic) have been gradually abandoned.

R. Garruccio (✉)
Università degli Studi di Milano, Milan, Italy
e-mail: roberta.garruccio@unimi.it

S. Berger et al. (eds.), *Deindustrialisation in Twentieth-Century Europe*, Palgrave Studies in the History of Social Movements,
https://doi.org/10.1007/978-3-030-89631-7_5

its manufacturing history closed down their plants over the 1980s and 1990s.[1]

In the following pages, I summarize the goals, starting assumptions, methodology, results of and insights from that project, but I think two initial considerations are important.

Firstly, the study of deindustrialization has been extensively enriched by new investigative directions and new publications since we designed our project at the beginning of the 2010s, and I have reconsidered our research and represented our findings here in the light of these contributions.

Secondly, since 2015, there have been seismic political developments at local, national and international level as a result of which at least two major events have projected Sesto San Giovanni into the international limelight and have changed the face of politics in the city. I will set out these events along a precise timeline and suggest their relevance to the subject matter of this book and to how scholarship is dealing with the long-term aftermaths—in the plural—of deindustrialization.

On 23 December 2016, Anis Amri, a Tunisian citizen believed to be responsible for the terrorist attack on a crowded Christmas market in Berlin a few days earlier when 12 people were murdered and 45 seriously injured, was shot and killed in Sesto San Giovanni by Italian police.[2] The official report said the policemen were carrying out a routine check when they came across Amri. The investigation that followed this shooting indicated that Anis Amri was familiar with Northern Italy, having arrived in Italy as one of tens of thousands of Tunisian migrants who entered the country after the Arab Spring protests broke out on the southern shore of the Mediterranean Sea in 2011. That may explain why Amri headed for Milan and then to Sesto, after the attack in Berlin where he drove a lorry into the crowd. Official statistics show that more than 650,000 migrants have reached Italian coasts since 2013—making Italy a major gateway into Europe—and that a majority of the arrivals by sea are Tunisian nationals.[3]

Countrywide anti-immigrant sentiment had been feeding on this influx, and the shooting of Anis Amri in front of the railway station is believed to have triggered a shift to the right among Sesto's electorate:

[2] Anis Amri, 'Berlin Attack Suspect, Shot Dead by Police in Milan', in *The Guardian*, 23 December 2016 (https://www.theguardian.com/world/2016/dec/23/anis-amri-berlin-attack-suspect-shot-dead-milan).

[3] https://data2.unhcr.org/en/situations/mediterranean/location/5205.

'Amri was heading for the street when he was shot dead. I believe he was going to one of those flats that rent out beds to migrants' the new mayor of Sesto San Giovanni Roberto Di Stefano declared to the newspapers in March 2018, when, during other investigative operations, a national criminal network—allegedly linked to Islamic State—was discovered to have had links to Anis Amri.[4]

In the June 2017 local elections in Sesto, a left-wing administration was defeated by the right-wing for the first time since the end of the Second World War. The new Mayor, Roberto Di Stefano, was a 40-year-old former worker in Pirelli, the son of Italian migrants from southern Italy, and was a member of a coalition between Silvio Berlusconi's center-right Forza Italia party and Lega Nord, the anti-migrant and Eurosceptic party. What made this result remarkable was that it ended 72 years of uninterrupted left-wing rule of the City Council, and that it happened in the town known as 'the Stalingrad of Italy' for its resistance to Fascism and Nazi occupation during the Second World War, for its strong labor-movement and working-class culture, for being a stronghold of the Italian Communist Party and for having a workforce unionized above 90% in the economic boom years. As one of our interviewees put it: 'Instead of Socialism in one country, we wanted Socialism in one town'.[5] It was not surprising, therefore, that RAI (the Italian national broadcasting company) dedicated a 60-minute prime-time special report in October 2017 to this political breakthrough and presented Sesto as a 'Political laboratory, and a blueprint for the country'.[6]

In March 2018, a few days before a general election that brought the Lega Nord (later rebranded as Lega for Salvini Premier) into Italian government, Sesto made further international headlines in the course of a political campaign inflamed by such critical issues and concerns as unemployment, social-programe funding, crime, diminishing purchasing power, government debt and deficit, social inequality, threats of terrorism and war, and above all, immigration. Reporters from 'The Washington

[4] 'Town That Banned Mosques Sets tone for Italian Elections', in *The Times*, 23 February 2018 (https://www.thetimes.co.uk/article/sesto-san-giovanni-town-that-banned-mosques-sets-tone-for-italian-election-w2z07f3t9).

[5] Giuseppe Vignati, interviewed by Roberta Garruccio, Sara Roncaglia and Sara Zanisi, Sesto San Giovanni, 21 March 2013.

[6] Fuori Roma, Sesto San Giovanni, 16 October 2017 (https://www.raiplay.it/video/2017/10/FuoriRoma-df7f2ed7-4e6d-4e45-a710-237cbefdc9d8.html).

Post', 'The Times', 'BBC' and 'Russia Today'—the global television network funded by the Russian government—interviewed the recently elected mayor.[7] Why this interest? The very first political act of the new administration in 2017 had been to block plans to build a mosque in Sesto which would have been the largest in Italy. In a comment for the media, Mayor Di Stefano said: 'Milan was hoping to unload its Muslims on us, and we would have become the Mecca of Italy! [but we stopped the Milan plan]'.[8] A few months later, and less than a week before elections in 2018, the new mayor announced that the town had successfully expelled nearly 200 migrants, a record for Italy. He declared: 'Sesto has become the model, the reference point for the nation. We are the first municipality in Italy – when it comes to expulsions. That shows you can rule and take action against urban-decay'.

In August 2020, the mayor formally switched parties definitively from Forza Italia to Lega. He described this change 'as the culmination of a move perfectly consistent with the policies of the municipal administration' and defined the Lega as 'a party with a strong tangible moderate component (and) the party which above all others would listen to citizens, understand their needs, and offer practical solutions to their problems [...] Sesto had become the most unsafe town in the hinterland of Milan, now the situation is reversed: robberies have been reduced by 36% and sexual assaults by 50%. We hold the Italian record for DASPO expulsions: over 700. [...] Sesto is for the Sestians!'.[9]

Proximity to Milan, a Double Edged Sword

The Economist, in a special report in April 2015 entitled 'Space and the City', emphasized 'if distance has died, location has not'.[10] This is also a feature of Sesto San Giovanni with respect to Milan. Proximity

[7] 'Town that Banned Mosques Sets Tone for Italian Elections', in *The Times*, 23 February 2018.

[8] Roberto Di Stefano, 'Io, nuovo sindaco di Sesto San Giovanni, cancello il passato che non tornerà più', in *La Repubblica*, 5 October 2017.

[9] 'Sesto San Giovanni. Il Sindaco spiega il suo ingresso nella Lega', in *NordMilano24.it*, 4 August 2020 (https://www.springer.com/it/book/9783319091792?utm_campaign=sl-buybox_bookPage_print&utm_medium=referral&utm_source=springerlink#otherversion=9783319091792).

[10] *The Economist*, 4 April 2015.

to Milan has long been important for Sesto. The industrial firms set up their factories and mills in Sesto at the beginning of 1900s because of the strategic location of the city: Breda (1903) manufacturing railway engines; Campari (1904) for industrial beverages; Ercole Marelli (1905) for power generating machinery; Falck (1906) for steelmaking; Magneti Marelli (1919) for magnetos and equipment for the automotive industry. On the crest of the wave of the second industrial revolution, Sesto San Giovanni developed as an industrial hub and became the fifth industrial center in Italy during the economic boom after the Second World War.[11]

Proximity to Milan (reinforced by the construction of the first underground line opened in 1964) is probably the single most important factor still influencing the city of Sesto, nowadays poised on a knife-edge between developing a new urban identity or becoming a Milanese rust belt or slum.

However, proximity to Milan is a double-edged sword for Sesto San Giovanni. On the one hand, Sesto is an integral part of the mega-municipality called 'Metropolitan City of Milan', where the per capita income is one of the highest in Europe and almost twice the Italian average, and where the unemployment rate is half the national average. On the other hand, Sesto has been diverging from the Milan city model as the latter has become ever more connected economically and culturally to outside world affairs. With soaring house prices and a cost of living that discourages newcomers, Milan is pulling away from its less well-off urban satellites.

Milan is among those cities in the Western world that have leaped ahead of other regions of their countries in terms of productivity and economic weight in recent decades. The global geographic divide between booming metropolis and broken city has now playing out in a new political divergence. If Sesto moved to the right in 2017, the Milan Municipality moved to the left in 2011 after 20 years of right-wing leadership. Since the 1990s, the gap (in terms of incomes, job growth and house prices) between Milan proper and its province has widened; a similar

[11] Valerio Varini, *L'opera Condivisa: La Città Delle Fabbriche, Sesto San Giovanni (1903–1952). L'industria*, (Milan: FrancoAngeli, 2006); Paolo Tedeschi and Luigi Trezzi, *L'opera Condivisa, La Città Delle Fabbriche. Sesto San Giovanni (1903–1952)*, (Milan: FrancoAngeli, 2007); Luigi Trezzi, *Sesto San Giovanni (1953–1973). Economia E Società. La Crescita*, (Milan: Skira, 2007); Luigi Trezzi, *Sesto San Giovanni Alla Fine Del XX Secolo (1974–1996)*, (Milan: FrancoAngeli, 2012).

gap has opened up in support for political parties. Many commentators consider the reciprocal dependence between metropolis and province has been brutally sundered in recent decades, together with the jettisoning of their shared identity.[12] Since the 1970s, Sesto has not only experienced economic setback, but has lost almost 20% of its population, now numbering eighty thousand residents according to the latest census of January 2015, of whom more than 17% are non-EU citizens. Compared to Milan, Sesto is experiencing a widening income gap, an increasingly diverse population and a rapidly aging native population (average age 45.5).

Before the end of the 2010s, much attention was being paid both to provincial urban areas and the inner regions of industrialized countries that have lost out in the globalization process of the last three decades, and to the complex interaction of globalization, deindustrialization, welfare and territorial policies, and demography during the new 'global chain revolution'.[13] Another report from The Economist in October 2017 stressed this same issue: the forces that drive growing spatial disparities are growing in strength, making it difficult for some places to resist them.[14] The lesson learned in Europe and US since 2016 is that the kind of political reaction which Sesto experienced in 2017 cannot be dismissed as localized or contingent. Places being left behind (or which feel as though they have been left in the lurch) protest in various ways: expressing increasing criticism of the European Union, showing low voter-turnout, opposing globalization and pro-global elites, fostering 'populist' sentiment and demanding more direct and immediate forms of democracy. This trend not only leads to political instability, but also deepens the critical fault-line mentioned above: a territorial division between prosperous globalized metropolitan areas and the small and medium-sized communities (often rural but sometimes urban, as is the case of Sesto) that have been removed from the main stream of growth and trade (or feel at risk of being removed therefrom). This split was

[12] Rodrigues Pose Andres, 'The Revenge of the Places That Don't Matter', in *Cambridge Journal of Regions, Economy and Society* 11 (1) (2017), pp. 189–201; Collier Paul, *The Future of Capitalism: Facing the New Anxieties*, (London: Penguin Random House, 2020).

[13] Richard Baldwin, *The Great Convergence: Information Technology and the New Globalization*, (Cambridge and London: MIT Press, 2016).

[14] *The Economist*, 21 October 2017.

widely confirmed in Italy during the latest round of elections (2019) and is increasingly influencing the political scene in Europe and North America where economic decay, declining opportunity, uncertain development prospects and a growing fear that some places have 'more past than future' are at the root of discontent in lagging/left-behind areas and have recently been expressed in the ballot box.[15]

What Has This to Do with Deindustrialization?

Whether Sesto is a left-behind place or by what parameters it should be so considered is debatable. In many respects it is not. What is certain is that the new city leaders have exploited this sentiment among voters who were being asked to spend money to support migrants when they themselves felt vulnerable after deindustrialization.

The factory closures in Sesto were concentrated into the 1980s and 1990s and unfolded under a large umbrella of social safety nets that were available at the time; nevertheless, one question remains unanswered: 'where have all the good jobs gone'? In other words, why have stable and decently-paid jobs for even the less-educated disappeared? This same question is widely asked in the oldest industrial countries.[16]

As mentioned above, new studies began to appear after 2015 when scholars and informed commentators increasingly suggested links between the powerful effects of the last wave of globalization, the main drivers of deindustrialization and the forces eroding long-established electoral bases of left-wing mainstream parties in Western countries. This indicates that a major task for analysts is a focus on trade-offs made in acute domestic transformations—to understand how people involved in such transformations account for these trade-offs—and how local democracies cope with the powerful and destabilizing effects of global dispersion. Deindustrialization is, among other things, also a way in which globalization goes local and creates long-term place-dependent effects. As Steven High, Lachlan MacKinnon and Andrew Perchard concluded in the *Afterword* of

[15] Martin Halla, Alexander Wagner and Josef Zweimüller, 'Immigration and Voting for the Far Right', in *Journal of the European Economic Association*, 15 (2017), pp. 1341–1385.

[16] David G. Blanchflower, *Not Working: Where Have All the Good Jobs Gone?* (Princeton: Princeton University Press, 2019).

a recently published book: 'Disillusionment with "establishment" politicians has led to the rise of new parties and new questions about old political projects [...]. Now more than ever, it is important for historians and other researchers to examine the socio-economic roots of this discontent and the spreading political fallout from the deindustrialization of what was once known as the "industrialized" world'.[17]

In positioning our research, we drew on the growing scholarship on deindustrialization. We worked in particular on the Jefferson Cowie and Joseph Heathcott suggestion that the central challenge in studying deindustrialization is to describe 'how a historical bound set of working conditions were experienced in terms of permanence in daily life, up to the plant closures; how - since then - people account for the destruction of an economic and social order that seemed so rooted and pervasive; in what sense the effects of deindustrialisation were more disorienting than overtly political, more elusive than tangible'.[18] In an analogous perspective, we were inspired by the social and cultural turn in historically informed studies of factory and mill closures.[19]

'Deindustrialization, moreover, was never only about economics', Sherry Linkon stated in her most recent book *The Half-life of Deindustrialization.* It was never only a matter of job loss. Social, psychological, environmental, gender and health effects of deindustrialization operated over time for decades. And continue—she argues—'across generations, affecting the world-views of younger people who never worked in steel mills'. Because long-term consequences of de-manufacturing also continue to ripple through culture and cultural representations, Linkon makes it clear that it is not a 'matter to get over', because memory shapes how people respond to present issues.[20] And we formulated our research questions on the basis of this kind of literature and on the consideration: how do people remember both industrial work and its loss, especially in

[17] Steven High, Lachlan Mackinnon and Andrew Perchard (eds.), *The Deindustrialized World: Confronting Ruination in Postindustrial Places*, (Vancouver: Ubc Press, 2017).

[18] Jefferson Cowie and Joseph Heathcott (eds.), *Beyond the Ruins: The Cultural Meaning of Deindustrialization*, (Ithaca: Cornell, 2003).

[19] Tim Strangleman, Sherry Linkon and Jameswere Rhodes, 'Crumbling Cultures. Deindustrialization, Class and Memory', in *International Labor and Working Class History Journal*, Special Issue, Fall (2013).

[20] Sherry Linkon, *The Half-life of Deindustrialization: Working-Class Writing About Economic Restructuring*, (Ann Arbor: University Of Michighan Press, 2018).

everyday life? How do they remember the aftermath of close-down? What strategies do people use to frame, make sense of, relate to and comment on the past? How do they use the history of the deindustrialization, and the fading claim of progress that went hand in hand with it, to understand the present and to think about the future?

If the usefulness and the pertinence of a source always depend upon the kind of knowledge a historian is looking for, oral history proved to be a suitable perspective for addressing such questions and issues. Where deindustrialization hit the hardest, oral histories engage feelings, attitudes and emotions. These mobilize the affective dimension of the experience: resentment and frustration, but also pride and resilience; consent but also resistance; a sense of risk and insecurity, but also attachment to a place that some people recognize as home; ambivalence between anxiety for losing a job and the release for new life opportunities. They also show how people exert 'agency' in coping with the tension and distress surrounding the closure of the industrial plants, when they 'saw it coming', and when they found themselves having to live with it.[21]

Our specific aim was therefore to study the memory in Sesto San Giovanni as a battleground over the meaning of the industrial past and deindustrialized present. This is why we chose an ethnographic focus and the qualitative research methodology of the in-depth interview, asking informants in Sesto to tell us how they experienced the deindustrialization process. For us, this meant studying not so much what happened in recent decades, but how the events have been remembered (or forgotten), interpreted and represented.

The Research Project

In a frequently quoted remark, Paul Thompson made a case for the transformative potential of oral history: 'Oral history is not necessarily an instrument for change [...]'. Nevertheless, oral history certainly can be a means for transforming both the content and the purpose of history. It can be used to change the focus of history itself and open up new areas of inquiry.[22]

[21] Trac E. K'Meyer and Joy L. Hart, *I Saw It Coming: Worker Narratives of Plant Closings and Job Loss*, (Basingstoke: Palgrave, 2009).

[22] Paul Thompson, *The Voice of The Past: Oral History*, (Oxford and New York: Oxford University Press, 1978), pp. 1–2.

I would like to use this note as a starting point to describe the public oral history project I had been engaged in with two independent scholars, Sara Roncaglia—an anthropologist—and Sara Zanisi—an oral and labor historian.[23]

Recognizing deindustrialization as a highly place-dependent phenomenon,[24] our project focused on a single emblematic place in a specific time period (the town of Sesto San Giovanni from the 1980s to the present), a place that can be seen as a community so long as that term implies some symbolic relationship to the local area.[25] While our original purpose had been to create an extensive oral history archive about the closing of the mills and factories and the aftermath of the industrial shutdowns in the city, it was actually progressively narrowed to the case of the Falck Steelworks, which shut down at the beginning of the 1990s.[26]

Supported by an independent association for ethnographic research (AVoce),[27] and by a historical foundation based in Sesto (Fondazione ISEC – Istituto per la storia dell'Età Contemporanea / Institute for the History of the Contemporary Age),[28] the first steps in the research

[23] Sara Zanisi and I are members of the Italian Oral History Association (AISO); Sara Roncaglia is a member of the Italian Association of Applied Anthropology (ANPIA). In realizing our project, we adhered to the best practice protocols issued in 2015 by AISO (http://aisoitalia.org/wp-content/uploads/2015/09/Good-Practices-in-Oral-History_EN.pdf) also discussed in ANPIA. The AISO best practice guidelines were updated in 2020 with respect to the 2018 GDPR: https://www.aisoitalia.org/risorse-2/; Affiliated to the International Oral History Association (IOHA), AISO was established in 2006 to facilitate communication among the many individuals, public and private entities, institutions and associations related to historical inquiry with oral sources promoted in Italy. All three of us participate in AISO training activity in the practice of oral history (both in the introduction of new scholars and researchers and in their ongoing training) and in developing awareness of the legal and ethical aspects peculiar to this methodology.

[24] Stefan Berger and Christian Wicke, 'Deindustrialization, Heritage, And Representation of Identitiy', in *The Public Historian*, Special Issue 39: (4) (2017), pp. 10–20.

[25] Dolores Hayden, *The Power of Place: Urban Landscapes as Public History*, (Cambridge, MA: MIT Press, 1996).

[26] I elaborated our project in Garruccio Roberta, 'Hardly a Cause for Tears', Job Insecurity and Occupational Psychology Culture in Italy. Oral Narratives from the Falck Steelworks in Sesto San Giovanni , (Milan)', in Stefan Berger (ed.), *Constructing Industrial Pasts: Heritage, Historical Culture and Identity in Regions Undergoing Structural Economic Transformation*, (Oxford-New York: Berghahn Books, 2019), pp. 160–183.

[27] http://www.avoce.eu/avoce/.

[28] https://www.fondazioneisec.it/.

project were taken in 2013, and the project had grown sufficiently to be financed by Regione Lombardia (the regional government authority) in the following year. In 2014, we replied to a Lombardy regional call for proposals, under the aegis of my university department, which is physically located in Sesto San Giovanni although it is actually part of the University of Milan. The call was concerned with the 'preservation of Lombard historical cultures' and the funding we obtained covered a year-long grant for Sara Roncaglia and Sara Zanisi, who were appointed to temporary research positions in the same department.

One of the main requirements of the call was the obligation to reach out to 'a wider than strictly-academic' audience. This is why we set up three main research projects outside written scholarship: an oral history archive about the aftermath of the industrial shutdowns in Sesto; a photographic project entrusted to an amateur photographer—Umberto Gillio—of the structural changes in Sesto to document the present deindustrialized landscape; and a 45-minute documentary film based on our interviews and including home-movies and archival footage produced with the help of a professional film-maker—Riccardo Apuzzo.[29]

The ability of oral history to alter the ways in which history is understood has often led scholars to open and explore new subjects of study, to ask new questions about the relationship between individual biography and collective memory, and to think up new ways of teaching history.[30] When we started our project, deindustrialization was a new area of enquiry in Italy—or at least a new catchword—but a term not much used in historical research.[31] I personally have to acknowledge a special

[29] The documentary is now accessible from ISEC Foundation YouTube channel, in Italian with English subtitles: https://www.youtube.com/watch?v=KcF1GY0DBlY&vl=en; Roberta Garruccio and Sara Zanisi, 'Il Polline e la ruggine: memoria, lavoro, deindustrializzazione a Sesto San Giovanni. Un documentario e un progetto di ricerca tra storia orale, storia pubblica ed etnografia', in *Clionet* (2018) (10 July 2018): https://Rivista.Clionet.It/Vol2/Societa-E-Cultura/Documentario/Garruccio-Zanisi-Il-Polline-E-La-Ruggine-Memoria-Lavoro-Deindustrializzazione-A-Sesto-San-Giovanni; Roberta Garruccio, 'Le rovine industriali. Note sulla storia lunga di una fascinazione culturale nuova', in *La Questione Romantica. Rivista interdiciplinare di studi romantici, Special Issue, 'L'arte Del Ricordo: Romanticismo E Cultural Memory'*, 12 (2020), pp. 213–234.

[30] Ronald J. Grele, 'Oral History as Evidence', in Thomas L. Carlton, Lois Myers and Rebecca Sharpless (eds.), *Handbook of Oral History*, (Walnut Creek, New York and Oxford: Altamira Press, 2006), p. 61.

[31] With a few exceptions: see Luigi Vergallo, *Una Nuova Era?: "Deindustrializzazione" E Nuovi Assetti Produttivi Nel Mondo (1945–2005)*, (Roma: Aracne, 2011).

debt to the four-day conference held in Montreal in May 2014, organized jointly by Concordia University's Center for Oral History and Digital Storytelling and the University of Strathclyde's Scottish Oral History Center, under the title 'Deindustrialization and (its) Aftermath: Class, Culture, and Resistance'. Attending this conference was extremely valuable for me; it revealed how intensely the transformative potential of public oral history had been deployed in deindustrialization studies of the North American Rust Belt. The many insights I brought back to Sesto proved essential in designing our research project long before the Montreal proceedings were published.[32]

Our interviewees were local trades-union leaders and delegates, residents and above all ex-workers (blue and white collar); they were mostly male ex-steelworkers, but we did manage to include a number of female workers. We also interviewed children of displaced workers, and we interviewed young people still at school, in training or employed in the new city businesses, because we were particularly interested in how deindustrialization is experienced by those who have never done any industrial work but have nonetheless been exposed to the process through the stories of their parents, or through urban landscape and industrial heritage. We interviewed middle and senior managers as well.

In the course of two years, we collected almost 50 audio- and videotaped interviews which were then transcribed. The interviews followed a life course model; each interview was 2 or 3 hours long on average. The complete collection resulted in more than 100 hours of recordings and is now stored at (and professionally maintained by) the ISEC Foundation which was founded in 1973 with the statutory mission of preserving the large archives of industrial concerns, labor movements and organizations related to the North Milan area: it is a large heritage of 5 km of archival records; 80,000 technical books; 200,000 photographs. My colleagues and I did all the interviewing, but we worked closely with several other professionals, including the archivists from the ISEC Foundation (searching historical corporate records and technical drawings).

Fifty interviews are certainly not a representative sample in any statistical sense, even though we were very careful to diversify the respondents. We could not escape the conclusion that our interviewees represented anything other than themselves. Oral history claims valid reasons for not

[32] Steven High, Lachlan Mackinnon and Andrew Perchard (eds.), *The Deindustrialized World: Confronting Ruination in Postindustrial Places*, (Vancouver: Ubc Press, 2017).

being restricted to the idea of large samples: even though our interviewees may not be representative, their stories may be so if we look for shared narrative patterns, structures and motifs, and if we search for revealing critical (or maximum variation) cases.[33]

In relation to this last point, the question of evidentiary value of oral sources and oral history requires an explanatory digression.

Oral History: Two Criticisms, a Necessary Digression

Oral history has long been confronted with two main criticisms. The first relates to the representativeness of the subjects interviewed; the second to the reliability (in the double connotation of consistency and validity) of oral sources. For oral historians, the answers to these two criticisms are intertwined.

Since the mid-1970s, Italian scholars have made both original and theoretically sound contributions to the discussion in Italy and established a fresh approach. In particular, the seminal studies of Luisa Passerini and Sandro Portelli were the first to concentrate on the role of working classes subjectivity.[34] They framed subjectivity as something that could be addressed with scientific procedures as well as the material condition of production, as something that must always be studied in its specific historical context and as a ground of political battle: subjectivity is not an attribute of the individual and is by no means intrinsically independent and antagonistic in itself. It is rather an area of symbolic activity that can express in multiple shades of acceptance and consent, but can also

[33] Alessandro Portelli, *The Death of Luigi Trastulli and Other Stories: Form and Meaning in Oral History*, (Albany: State University of New York Press, 1991), pp. 117–137.

[34] Luisa Passerini, 'Italian Working Class Culture Between The Wars. Consensus to Fascism and Work Ideology', in *International Journal of Oral History* 1 (1980), pp. 1–27; Luisa Passerini, *Fascism in Popular Memory: The Cultural Experience of Turin Working Class*, (Cambridge: Cambridge University Press, 1987); Luisa Passerini, *Storia e Soggettività: Le Fonti Orali, La Memoria*, (Firenze: La Nuova Italia, 1988); Alessandro Portelli, *The Death of Luigi Trastulli and Other Stories: Form and Meaning in Oral History*, (Albany: State University of New York Press, 1991); Alessandro Portelli, *The Battle of Valle Giulia: Oral History and the Art of Dialogue*, (University of Wisconsin Press, 1997); Alessandro Portelli, 'Oral History in Italy', in David K. Danaway and Willa Baum (eds.), *Oral History: An Interdisciplinary Anthology*, (Walnut Creek, New York and Oxford: Altamira Press, 1984), pp. 391–416.

be influenced by dominant stories. Finally, Passerini and Portelli were the first to analyze the narrative nature of orality in the interview, drawing on Gramsci and folklore theory. They looked at oral histories (in this connotation: ways in which people use stories to interpret the world) as representations (devices at the core of the production of meaning through language), in particular representations of subjectivity (produced from a specific standpoint and to be interpreted).

Because oral historians usually do not ask interviewees 'what happened?' but prefer to encourage them to tell the past from their perspective, accepting the partiality of this point of view (where partiality means both incompleteness and taking sides), oral histories can counteract hasty generalizations.

Because oral histories can reveal unknown events, unknown aspects of well-known events, or cast new light on unexplored areas of ordinary life, their epistemological content has a valuable potential for falsification and qualification of previous acquisitions.

Because interviews are narratives imbued not only with subjectivity, but also with inter-subjectivity (being multi vocal, influenced by the relationship between interviewee and interviewer), they involve relationships in which difference and equality are required to be respected at the same time and balanced.

As Lynn Abrams summarized, the idea was acquired that 'memories are reworked in the context of the respondent's own experience and politics. If one accepts this point, then the oral historian is obliged to think hard about how and why those memory stories are produced, about the cultural environment of memory (when the things happened) and of remembering (when the things are recalled)'.[35]

What is more, oral histories often include the role of chance in the narration: not necessarily what happened, but how things could have been otherwise: 'what people imagine or know might happen', the horizon of possibilities that 'defines the range of socially shared subjectivity [...], offers less a grid of standard experiences than a horizon of shared possibilities, real or imagined [...], indicates that each person entertains, in each

[35] Lynn Abrams, *Oral History Theory*, (London and New York: Routledge, 2010).

moment, multiple possible destinies, perceives different possibilities and makes different choices from others in the same situation'.[36]

Passerini and Portelli imported, discussed and further elaborated interdisciplinary theoretical impulses from UK and US that fed an entire range of new domestic research. Some of them found a comfortable milieu in literary studies and cultural studies, focusing not only on what has been represented in oral narratives solicited by the historians but on how the narrator gives meaning to things, 'makes sense of' the world, objects and events.

It goes without saying that subjectivity is not unique to oral history, but access to subjectivity through the dialogue between the narrator and the historian (in other words, through inter-subjectivity) is the value added to history by oral history. Within a decade, oral history had shifted the field from the search for information and a method of recovering the past, to reading interviews as texts. As Portelli stated, oral sources: 'tell us not just what people did, but what they wanted to do, what they believed they were doing, and what they now think they did'.[37]

Passerini and Portelli also scrutinized memory and forgetfulness about the past as an experience of the present, and oral sources as memory documents, subject to the strengths and weaknesses of memory itself. In doing so, they anticipated some of the results that were emerging from cognitive psychology and neuroscience from a different kind of evidence: individual memory does not function like a deposit or a sorted archive of lived experiences, but rather as an active, embodied and dynamic process of creation (and re-creation) of sense, revealed by narrative and linguistic forms.[38] This does not imply that oral history has no factual validity at all, adds Portelli, and oral sources can yield as much reliable factual information as other sources. It entrails instead that that oral sources are not taken by

[36] Alessandro Portelli, *The Battle of Valle Giulia. Oral History and the Art of Dialogue*, (University of Wisconsin Press, 1997), p. 88.

[37] Alessandro Portelli, *The Death of Luigi Trastulli and Other Stories. Form and Meaning in Oral History*, (Albany: State University of New York Press, 1991), p. 50.

[38] Joan Tumblety (ed.), *Memory and History: Understanding Memory as Source and Subject*, (London and New York: Routledge, 2013).

oral historians as data and information, but as means of accessing interpretations. 'The first thing that makes oral history different is that it tells us less about the events than about their meaning'.[39]

Including error, silence, inevitable selections and intentional concealment, involuntary disclosure, imagination, symbolism and desire, oral sources reveal not only the history of what happened, but the history of what it meant. The objective of finding meanings and interpretations is particularly served by the life course approach to the interview, the elicitation of a life story from interviews with ordinary people about their everyday life. After all, even if we, as historians, are interested in fixed events, and specific periods of time, the witness still narrates them as part of a dynamic process and introduces other elements, themes, connections and bundles of meaning, shuttling back and forth in time across the span of his/her lifetime, overthrowing our initial assumptions and priorities: 'because the events inside and outside the pool of light our spotlight casts are, for them, bound together. [...] This is one of the many reasons why oral history alters the epistemological base of historical enquiry: we find answers to questions we did not know existed'.[40] Even when the narrators are engaged in a sincere effort of truth-telling about facts and events, their life story still serves a different purpose: it makes sense of the past experiences and achieves coherence through the principles of causality and continuity. A life story is first of all a narrative device and a verbal artifact, a story that adheres to a chronological template, hangs related and unrelated—sometime even contradictory—experiences together and a story that takes shape from the listener's expectations.[41] As such, it is creative and fluid, and is the result of interpretations and reinterpretations; it is told and retold, and continually revised over time. It is up to the historian to base oral history firmly on research, keeping questions on track, in order not to loose the aim of the research in a fog of details.

[39] Alessandro Portelli, *The Death of Luigi Trastulli and Other Stories: Form and Meaning in Oral History*, (Albany: State University of New York Press, 1991), p. 50.

[40] Lindsey Dodd, 'Small Fish, Big Pond. Using a Single Oral History Narrative to Reveal Broader Social Change', in Joan Tumblety (ed.), *Memory and History: Understanding Memory as Source and Subject*, (London and New York: Routledge, 2013), pp. 34–49.

[41] Lynn Abrams, *Oral History Theory*, (London and New York: Routledge, 2010).

Public History: Three Ways of Being Public

The main point I want to underline in this paragraph is that we designed our investigation also as a public history endeavor, since we interpreted (and engaged) the term 'public' in three intertwined meanings.

Firstly, with reference to funding and partnership: we grounded our historical research in an academic department and in a cultural institution active in Sesto since the 1970s; our research is based on different collaborations at all stages of our project (creation, collection, management, preservation, dissemination of public history materials); as Steven High argued: 'it is no coincidence that the bulk of collaborative research is local. It takes time to build trusting relationships, and nothing beats face to face contacts'.[42] We had to be ever mindful that the project had been funded by Regione Lombardia, so we were working with a public body with public resources, which set at once the large framework of the research itself and the main constraints.

Secondly, the term public also referred to the audience: our research was designed to ensure communication and distribution of results to the general public outside the university ambit, and so had to address not only university scholars and students, but be accessible to a wider audience. To this end, starting from an initiative of the ISEC Foundation, we organized multiple public meetings in Sesto, Milan and the metropolitan city area beginning in 2015, and our documentary has also been regularly screened as a teaching aid at high school level.

Thirdly, from the beginning, we followed a participatory approach, and we found ourselves working not only for the public but also with the public. Therefore, we had to locate ourselves in relation to our multiple audiences, their assumptions, judgments and interpretations of their past. We involved the interviewees in the editing and in every public presentation of the documentary and welcomed documentary material that interviewees wanted to share with us (then deposited in ISEC). On this last point, for example, one of our interviewees, an important local trades-union official, gave us a copy of an extensive press release collection that he himself had collected between 1993 and 1995. This press review was related to the national newspapers that were covering the process of closing the Falck plants at that time. For us as researchers, it was a further

[42] Elisabeth Miller, Edward Little and Steven High, *Going Public: The Art of Participatory Practice*, (Vancouver: Ubc Press, 2017), p. 31.

valuable source, but not only this. It was also symbolic evidence of how workers also in Italy have increasingly been excluded from the media spotlight from that historical phase onwards, as being 'no longer newsworthy' and how the mainstream media have increasingly turned more and more away from to their working-class readers since the 1990s.[43]

Nevertheless, we remained invested in the ethics, the self-reflectivity and the time it took to build trust and relationships and discuss expectations with people involved. We also accepted responsibility for the fundamental choices made at every stage. We took the risk of doing so without the traditional protection of distance from the subjects under study, but we also committed ourselves to providing a critical analysis of the testimony we collected, and a broad sense of interpretation of their memories. We assumed that the public role of historian 'is not to hide behind the myth of equal validity for personal interpretations of the past' but to recognize 'the gap between the need to foster participatory construction of public history and the absence of any critical interpretation of the past'.[44]

'A Postponed Perception of the Present'

As I explained above, we addressed deindustrialization studies, but our oral history research in Sesto could not avoid interdisciplinary and intertemporal comparison with previous studies devoted to the city, and especially the use of oral sources promoted since the end of the 1970s.

An initial reference point was the work carried out by a group of researchers working with Franco Ferrarotti, within a qualitative sociology framework in turn influenced by the theoretical insights gained in the oral history field in that decade.[45] Ferrarotti was appointed to the first chair in Sociology in 1961 and is still Emeritus Professor at La Sapienza University in Rome, and is considered one of the fathers of this discipline in Italy.

[43] Christopher R. Martin, *No Longer Newsworthy: How the Mainstream Media Abandoned the Working Class*, (Ithaca: Cornell University Press, 2019).

[44] Thomas Cauvin, *Public History: A Textbook of Practice*, (London and New York: Routledge, 2016) p. 16.

[45] Franco Ferrarotti, 'Appunti Sul Metodo Biografico', in *La Critica Sociologica* 47 (1978); Pietro Crespi, 'La testimonianza orale tra storia e sociologia', in *Studi di sociologia* 2 (1978), pp. 155–168; Liliana Lanzardo (ed.), *Storia orale e storie di vita*, (Milano: FrancoAngeli, 1989).

But here, I refer in particular to the fieldwork conducted between 1977 and 1979 by one of his closest colleagues: Pietro Crespi, a sociologist at Pavia University during the 1970s and the 1980s. Crespi conducted 21 in-depth interviews in Sesto San Giovanni which each lasted many hours, sometimes over several days. His research was carried out under the aegis of the Istituto Milanese per la Storia della Resistenza e del Movimento Operaio (the Milan Institute for the History of the Resistance and Workers' Movement), the former name of ISEC Foundation. The ISEC archives now contain the recordings of these testimonies, and the full-length transcriptions were later published in *La Capitale Operaia*.[46] In a way that was innovative for its time, *La Capitale Operaia* investigated the 'then-present' and the 'then-past' of the city, from Fascism, through the Second World War, the labor struggles during the economic boom, down to the oil crisis. In his conclusions, Crespi underlines the persistence of a 'physiological connection to Milan' for which Sesto, with Labor as its driving force, represented the 'working class consciousness and engagement'; he did not draw generalizations but noted that the autobiographic accounts given by his respondents were often directed at demystifying the excessively monolithic and repetitive analyses given of the workers' situation in Sesto. He recognized the signs of a cultural crucible influenced by latent tensions, often unconscious, of contradictions, utopian and dystopian, of a growing need for independence and personal expression with respect to the traditional ideological models.[47]

The collective working-place culture that Crespi found in Sesto at the end of the 1970s had been summarily judged still 'untouched' by Franco Ferrarotti at the opening of the 1990s, when a part of those interviews was republished.[48]

This was a rush to judgment, at least in the light of the evidence uncovered by a further study published in 1992 which forms a second reference point for our analysis of the transformation of Sesto San Giovanni.

This study was carried out by two independent researchers, Lapo Berti and Claudio Donegà, who combined the tools of sociological analysis (new semi-structural interviews conducted with a panel of privileged

[46] Pietro Crespi, *Capitale Operaia: Stsrie di vita raccolte tra le fabbriche di Sesto San Giovanni*, (Milano: Jaca Book, 1979).

[47] Ibidem.

[48] Franco Ferrarotti, *La parola operaia: cento anni di vita operaia (1892–1992)*, (L'Aquila: Scuola Superiore Reiss Romoli, 1994), p. 113.

witnesses) with those of industrial economy, and applied them to the case of Sesto San Giovanni.[49] Berti and Donegà formulated a different thesis: they foresaw the break brought about by changes in the worker culture in Sesto and spoke of a 'postponed perception of the present'.[50] Postponed in a double sense. On the one hand, they recognized that the alignment of Sesto society was disintegrating from the end of the 1970s in line with the worldwide crisis in the steel industry and with the crisis of large firms in general. They underlined that this dynamic accelerated in the next decade; in the 1980s, the largest Sesto industries actually reduced the size of their workforces and their production plants with growing rapidity, while increasing the importance of the service sector and the fragmentation of the productive fabric.[51]

On the other hand, Berti and Donegà held that the persistence of the myth of the Italian Stalingrad had prevented the recognition of change which had begun in the 1960s, long before the cuts of the 1970s. The persistence of the idea of the city of workers and factories had distracted attention from two important phenomena. The first was the slow but steady reduction of the workforces of the industrial sectors that had created the economic identity of Sesto San Giovanni in the twentieth century (steel, mechanical and electro-mechanical engineering); between 1961 and 1971, the manufacturing sector in Sesto lost almost 30% of its labor force; another 25% were lost in the following decade.[52] The second phenomenon was the demographic dynamic: the ability of Sesto to attract population had begun to weaken already by the 1960s; the balance of migration had remained constantly negative since the end of the 1970s; the peak population (90,739) had been reached in 1978, and the mean aggregate age had begun to raise from the mid1980s; the reasons to live

49 Lapo Berti and Claudio Donega, *Sesto San Giovanni: gli scenari del cambiamento*, (Milan: FrancoAngeli, 1992).

50 Ibidem. pp. 36.

51 Small and medium-sized businesses, on the other hand, become even more important for the city. Even if they do not replace the historical and social role that had been played by large companies in the heavy industry sectors, they contributed to widening the articulation of Sesto's economic and social system, which became more complex but also more opaque (see SUFFIA 2015).

52 Ibidem. p. 76.

and work in Sesto began to decouple at the beginning of the 1990s, those who worked in Sesto didn't necessarily live there and those who lived there didn't necessarily work there. The focus of the population had shifted generally to 'la Grande Milano', the metropolitan area of the regional capital, Milan. This development led to the division of interests between the working and residential populations, which led in turn to the further dissolution of the cohesion and compactness of the city.[53]

A New 'Deindustrial' Structure of Feeling

The evidence that the research both of Crespi and of Berti and Donegà had collected was used to appeal to a public that was involved with social and urban renewal: local administrators and trade-union representatives, while it explained and illustrated such transformations. The research also helped to increase awareness of how the identity of city of Sesto was changing.

In our 2014–2015 research, many of our respondents began their submissions with a summary of the deindustrialization of Sesto since 1945: 'I think that the city of Sesto San Giovanni was involved in a continuous process of reorganization and restructuring from the end of the Second World War [...] in my opinion this was very important; the closure of the large factories involved the opening of centers of small and medium sized craft firms'.[54]

In our research, we did not intend the archival task of documenting deindustrialization in Sesto San Giovanni to be either exclusive or separate in any way from a social and cultural history perspective. On the contrary, we saw our project as an effort to contribute to historical knowledge more attuned to the present tensions and to the transformation of the economic and social order that we had seen in the last three decades, and to the cultural effects that the twilight of industrial citizenship produced locally in this span of time.

I have explained above how and when oral history shifted the field from a search for information and a method of recovering the past, to reading oral sources as representations (in so far as they represent the

[53] Ibidem.

[54] Canio Di Ruggiero, trade union leader FIOM-CGiL, interviewed by Sara Roncaglia and Zanisi, Sesto San Giovanni, 14 May 2013.

space of the lived). For us, that also meant actively opening a dialogue and an exchange with our interviewees as a search for understanding, accepting the lack of congruence and many conflicts that can surface in interviews,[55] taking seriously the inter-active and inter-subjective nature of oral history and accepting the responsibility of creating (and in some ways being included in) the very documentation that we would be called upon to interpret.[56]

Encompassing the deindustrialization process, the oral narratives we collected offered some early warnings of the onset of the 2017 political *volte face* in the tradition of city government and some insights into the deep roots of this caesura. I can now recognize that those narratives reveal many clues to historicize our current time. In this respect, one of our interviewee, a local union leader, gave a reckoning that I would like to quote at length:

> During the workers' struggles of the '70s and '80s, the perception of things was very different from that widespread today [even in Sesto]. The prevailing idea today is that it was politics that closed the factories. Politics has become one of many 'not-to-be trusted' institutions. Furthermore, in people's minds today politics is considered useless, which is even worse, in my opinion. [Back in the day, by doing politics through the union, we negotiated with the Ministry of Industry and obtained laws on early retirement and redundancy, the necessary social safety nets, but also the relocation to a new job for those workers who remained in the factory at the time of closure]. At that time, however, the workers of Sesto considered politics to be important in general because politics allowed them to think, to go beyond the factory with their minds. The workers of Falck and those of Breda attached great importance to laws that were passed by Parliament and decrees that were issued by the government and which concerned work, because those laws and decrees helped to solve their problems in the factory. Why do people of my generation keep voting for the left? Because we are linked to the Italian welfare system that we ourselves built with the struggles of the '70s and '80s and with the laws passed

55 Ronald J. Grele, 'Oral History as Evidence', in Thomas L. Carlton, Lois Myers and Rebecca Sharpless (eds.), *Handbook of Oral History*, (Walnut Creek, New York and Oxford: Altamira Press, 2006), pp. 46, 74.

56 Sara Zanisi, *Il Portello. Voci della Fabbrica, le Interviste di Duccio Bigazzi in Alfa Romeo* (Milano: Francoangeli, 2017).

afterwards. Yet what we claimed as rights then, is today often interpreted as privilege'.[57]

More generally, our oral history research offers an insight: that a new structure of feeling has been emerging in Sesto San Giovanni since the turn of the 1980s and the 1990s. Elaborated by Raymond Williams during the 1960s and the 1970s,[58] the concept of 'structure of feeling' foregrounds the everyday experiences and interpretative practices of ordinary men and women in a specific historical moment and refers to the different ways of thinking which are competing to stand out at any one time in history.

The structure of feeling has been refined as 'the agency of the subject in the transformation of cultural practices'.[59] By the same token, in the structure of feeling the subjective cannot be reduced to the individual. The structure of feeling is a 'structure', indeed, because the main idea of the term is that a shared set of ways of thinking and feeling demonstrates regular patterns and forms, which resonate with the driving forces and political struggles of the specific conjuncture. It is actually the sign of the historical conjuncture as it is. The structure of feeling is a 'feeling' nevertheless: Raymond Williams defines it as the never-ended comparison between the articulated and the lived: 'all that comes through as disturbance, tension, blockage, emotional trouble, seems to me precisely a major source of major changes in the relation between the signifier and the signified'.[60] In choosing this specific term, feeling, he then suggests a special and privileged link to the affective dimension of the experience. Moreover, what is at stake is not articulated in a fully worked-out form, but must instead be inferred by reading between the lines: 'It

[57] Canio Di Ruggiero, trade union leader FIOM-CGiL, interviewed by Sara Roncaglia and Zanisi, Sesto San Giovanni, 14 May 2013.

[58] Raymond Williams, *The Long Revolution*, (London: Chatto & Windus, 1961); Id., *Marxism and Literature*, (Oxford: Oxford University Press, 1977).

[59] Roman Horak and Monika Seidl, 'Raymond Williams—Towards A Cultural Materialism', in Monika Seidl, Roman Horak and Lawrence Grossberg (eds.), *About Raymond Williams*, (London and New York: Routledge, 2010), pp. 1–17: 9.

[60] Raymond Williams, *Politics and Letters: Interviews with* New Left Review, (London and New York: Verso), p. 168.

was a sensation. It was more of a sense that everything around you was decaying'.[61]

Not surprisingly, in deindustrialization literature the concept of 'structure of feeling' is being emphasized at the crossroad between oral history and cultural studies, where the distinction between structure and agency is conceived of as a fact of complementarity, not of opposition. It was Tim Strangleman in a recent contribution who first framed the idea of a deindustrial structure of feeling. He argued as well that individual and collective beliefs do not neatly fall into dichotomies of true and false, commenting that in oral history: 'the choice is not necessary'.[62] Strangleman has dedicated much reflection to understanding not only the role of 'Smokestack Nostalgia', but also the role of myth as embedded in experience, both growing from it and shaping its perception and both part of a structure of feeling related to deindustrialization. He evoked the publication edited by Raphael Samuel and Paul Thompson in 1990 as seminal for interpreting myth also as folklore. Formed in the face of contentious historical junctures, when human agency is crippled, myth is often articulated in narrations fraught with great failures.[63] And this is also a powerful insight for interpreting deindustrialization contexts.

The structure of feeling that we detected in our interviews is new in Sesto San Giovanni in the sense that a novel affective landscape, at some point, firstly filled the gap between official discussion of politics and policy and the response of ordinary people, and secondly dislodged previous cultural scripts and social expectations: 'If the mill dies because it has to die, that doesn't mean that we all have to die'.[64] Through some significant passages from the interviews we have collected, we can in fact capture scattered elements of a twentieth-century parable: 'Sesto today is no longer an industrial city'. Before, when you were asked 'where do you live?' you answered 'I live in Sesto, the city of factories'. Now you say 'I

[61] Silvana Rovelli, Falck employee, since 1960 to 1992, interviewed by Sara Roncaglia and Sara Zanisi, Sesto San Giovanni, 2 April 2015.

[62] Tim Strangleman, *Voices of Guinness: An Oral History of the Park Royal Brewery*, (Oxford and New York: Oxford University), p. 80.

[63] Ronald J. Grele, 'Oral History as Evidence', in Thomas L. Carlton, Lois Myers and Rebecca Sharpless (eds.), *Handbook of Oral History*, (Walnut Creek, New York and Oxford: Altamira Press, 2006), p. 88.

[64] Renato Falconati, employee in Falck since 1966 to 1996, interviewed by Roberta Garruccio, Sara Roncaglia, Sara Zanisi, Sesto San Giovanni, 1 October 2013.

live in Sesto, the city of abandoned plants and disused spaces'[65]; 'Seeing Sesto in the '60s was scary, because it was one huge smokestack: Breda, Falck, Magneti Marelli were all there. Today, for me, Sesto is no more than a dormitory city, because there's nothing left. It's better now only because you can breathe a little better'.[66]

It should be kept in mind that the concept of structure of feeling defines 'which experiences, behaviour, choices and emotions are possible or even obvious, and which are impossible and unimaginable'.[67]

> 'Falck is my story and the story of my family. The story of my grandfather, my father, eleven uncles, my sister [...]. In short, the story of a family that came from the valleys of the Province of Bergamo in the post-war period and that found employment for all its children in Sesto San Giovanni [...] They all came here and got a job, a house, and the chance for their children to study and get a job. [...] They could say proudly to their grandchildren 'Look, your grandparents, your father and your uncles all worked here!'[68]

As a company trainer put it: 'They – the Falck workers – spoke of the factory as if it was the continuation of their home [...] Falck meant everything for and to them. [...]. The retraining course [I taught in 1994–1995] was probably the one where I saw more suffering and more attachment to an idea. Il was like in the late '70s when, at some point, ideology collapsed. [In those workers] I saw the death of an idea. A self-constructed idea, but powerful nonetheless'.[69]

Going often against the grain of the linear and progressive narratives that usually inform life stories, oral histories are able to seize the very moment when, at the approach of the factory shutdowns, a paralyzing uncertainty, never known before, captured workers' imaginations: '[The

[65] Vittorio Riva, employee in Falck since 1974 to 1996, interviewed by Roberta Garruccio and Sara Zanisi, Sesto San Giovanni, 17 July 2013.

[66] Vittorio Tresoldi, former Falck worker, interviewed by Sara Roncaglia and Sara Zanisi, Sesto San Giovanni, 9 June 2015.

[67] Lawrence Grossberg, 'Making Culture Matter. Making Culture Political', in Cecile Sandten et al. (eds.), *Crisis Risks and New Regionalisms in Europe*, (Trier: Wvt, 2017), p. 40.

[68] Renato Falconati, employee in Falck since 1966 to 1996, interviewed by Roberta Garruccio, Sara Roncaglia, Sara Zanisi, Sesto San Giovanni, 1 October 2013.

[69] Maria Balena, independent company trainer, worked for Falck Observatory during the 1990s, interviewed by Sara Roncaglia, 5 May 2015.

thought of leaving the factory was not accompanied] by the question "what will I do tomorrow?" but by the fear of being frozen; I was afraid that I could not go forward or back. A bit like Italy today'.[70]

Oral histories are also able to seize the moment when the unthinkable actually takes place. I think the following interview extracts show what I mean: 'You couldn't even imagine a life outside [of the factory]'[71]; 'I never remotely saw myself saying 'I am leaving my job' […]. Until the very end I thought: 'This is simply not possible; they'll find some loophole''[72]; 'In 1992 it was clear that the plant for which I worked as a clerk would be closed soon; a new government decree was issued, I was 47 years of age, 32 years of contributions and I found myself able to retire: I was ashamed like crazy to be able to retire at just 47 years old'. Another passage from the same person's testimony is an even more intense example: 'I said to myself at the thought of it: 'Good Lord, how can you shut down such a big thing? […] I could not imagine they would close [everything]. I mean, you couldn't imagine it would be gone next year, it was unthinkable. But it happened…'.[73]

And if it was unthinkable to lose your job, it was equally unthinkable to also lose the house that Falck made available to its employees in the Falck Village:

> 'In 1988, the Falck executives said: Listen, our job is making steel, we are not real estate agents'.[74] The real estate was indeed a major cost factor for the company which had already decided to get rid of most of it. One of our interviewees recalled that when the Falck houses were actually put up for sale in 1995, many of his colleagues reacted this way: 'talking among themselves they said 'Hey, I've worked at Falck for 40 years, and they're trying to sell me my own flat! They should give it to me for free! After all

[70] Silvana Rovelli, Falck employee since 1960 to 1992, interviewed by Sara Roncaglia and Sara Zanisi, Sesto San Giovanni, 2 April 2015.

[71] Doriana Locatelli, Falck employee since 1976 to 1991, interviewed by Sara Roncaglia, Sesto San Giovanni, 20 February 2015.

[72] Fabiana Cestari, employee in Falck since 1988 to 1995, interviewed by Sara Roncaglia and Sara Zanisi, Sesto San Giovanni, 9 June 2015.

[73] Silvana Rovelli, Falck employee since 1960 to 1992, interviewed by Sara Roncaglia and Sara Zanisi, Sesto San Giovanni, 2 April 2015.

[74] Silvano Gianoli, Falck employee since 1959 to 1985, interviewed by Sara Roncaglia and Sara Zanisi, Sesto San Giovanni, 22 January 2015.

> I have done for the company!' Eventually all we could do was haggle over the price'.[75]

Oral histories are then also able to grasp the fact that at some point the *unthinkable* begins to be perceived or re-framed as *inevitable*: 'Tomorrow we are closing down. Nobody actually said it, until they actually did close it down'[76] one of our interviewees told us. And many recalled that when Falck came to the closure of the last foundry plant, on January 31, 1996, the workers organized a real funeral mass, complete with a coffin in the stalls, to underline this passage and to mitigate and share the shock on a symbolic level.

Over time, the very idea of 'transition'[77] has gradually left the meaning of a process of changing from one state or position to another, to take on the meaning of a simply unstoppable course: 'My trade-union life is divided into three different moments: the first ten years we built, we obtained something, we went on strikes to obtain something, we did our duty [as trades-unionists]; the second decade we worked to maintain what we had acquired, but only 'maintain'; the third decade [in the '90 s] we fought to lose as little as possible...'.[78]

> 'I had signed a letter of resignation but I didn't have a new job. I was 47, I had a high salary, a high position, a son at university, a daughter in high school, financial commitments, they were really tough times. [...] Now I realize that a heavy industry could no longer exist just a few short steps from Piazza del Duomo in Milan'....[79]

In our 2013–2015 project, we made no attempt to determine whether the heavy industry plants in Sesto San Giovanni should have been closed or not. Instead, we tried to address the predominant 'inevitability discourse'

[75] Ilio Dalla Frera, Falck worker since 1963 to 1991, interviewed by Roberta Garruccio and Sara Roncaglia, Sesto San Giovanni, 20 January 2015.

[76] Francesco Veronesi, plant manager in Falck since 1968 to 1995, interviewed by Roberta Garruccio and Sara Roncaglia, Sesto San Giovanni, 17 April 2015.

[77] Federico Falck, general manager in Falck steelworks since 1995 to 2003, interviewed by Roberta Garruccio, Milan, 7 July 2014.

[78] Vittorio Tresoldi, union activist and Falck worker since 1967 to 1991, interviewed by Sara Roncaglia and Sara Zanisi, Sesto San Giovanni, 9 June 2015.

[79] Francesco Ciampi, plant manager in Falck since 1967–1991, interviewed by Sara Roncaglia and Sara Zanisi, Sesto San Giovanni, 5 December 2014.

the idea that 'there was no policy alternative', an idea that even in Sesto took hold at some point in time, related to the shutting down of local industries.[80]

With this challenge in mind, we tried to understand how not only the workers but also the managers experienced the threat of job loss, if not actual job loss itself, because of advancing technology, globalization, erosion of rights and social and economic downshifting related to deindustrialization processes. Since in Falck the cuts hit managerial levels as well, we used the opportunity to examine not only the workers' reaction but also the managers' reaction to the shutdown. Changes in beliefs, affects, behaviour and the anticipation of job loss speak of a major breach of a psychological contract wherever the expectation of job continuity is a major component, as it was also for managers.

We met the Falck technical staff, industrial engineers and human resources executives who oversaw both the lay-offs and the social safety nets during the mill closures. Their narratives proved significant from two points of view: first because they represented a particular high-ranking perspective on the lay-offs and closures (conflicting with the memories coming from other oral sources, but by no means consistent with each other); secondly, because they showed cultures, expectations and aspirations other than those of the workers.[81] We then had the chance to explore a double assumption: as Geoff Eley underlined in a public presentation, there is no antinomy between 'history from below' and 'history from above' in studying capitalism[82]; as Stefan Berger and Christian Wicke recognized: 'it is high time that stories of deindustrialisation started talking about the middle classes'.[83]

[80] Barry Bluestone and Bennet Harrison, *The Deindustrialization of America. Plan Closings, Community Abandonment, and the Dismantling of Basic Industry*, (New York: Basic Books, 1982), p. 6.

[81] Roberta Garruccio, "'Hardly a Cause for Tears', Job Insecurity and Occupational Psychology Culture in Italy. Oral Narratives from the Falck Steelworks in Sesto San Giovanni (Milan)', in Stefan Berger (ed.), *Constructing Industrial Pasts: Heritage, Historical Culture and Identity in Regions Undergoing Structural Economic Transformation*, (Oxford and New York: Berghahn books, 2019), pp. 160–183.

[82] Geoff Eley, 'No Need to Choose: History from Above. History from Below', in *Viewpoint Magazine*, 27 June 2014 (https://Www.Viewpointmag.Com/2014/06/27/No-Need-To-Choose-History-From-Above-History-From-Below/).

[83] Stefan Berger and Christian Wicke, 'Deindustrialization, Heritage and Representation of Identity', in *The Public Historian*, Special Issue 39 (4) (2017), pp. 10–20, p. 15.

One of the main findings in our research has been that the most visible tension in the sense-making and memory of the abandonment of the steelworks was among executives. On the one side, managers with a long job tenures at Falck who had been made redundant in the 1990s; on the other side, the new cohort of executives appointed by the Human Resource Manager to deal with the closings down: these HR executives arrived in Falck at the beginning of the 1990s, and many came from large companies that had previously been restructured, so their reputation was that of being 'hatchet men'.

The managerial narrative was of a different experience of job insecurity, unlike the workers' experience, different from the union leaders' narratives and most of all 'at odds' with the strong 'inevitability' narrative expressed by the HR officials, who were proud of the Falck Observatory and its activity and who claimed that 'nobody in Falck was abandoned':

> 'When the issue of the mill closures first arose, about 1,000 people were still working there. Actually, when they began talking about restructuring there were more than that, but the early retirement and other standard schemes were already being implemented. So I had to address all specific situations that were not covered by law or by custom; my role was to deal specifically with the re-location of the personnel. [...] The re-location that the unions would accept – and did – was this: workers would move from one large company (Falck) to another large one and in all cases their jobs were guaranteed'[84]

Conclusion

I would like to conclude with one final comment. The post-industrial structure of feeling seems to involve a sort of temporal alienation. Our interviews contain several hints of a sense that time has become strange, the present does not feel present, and the relation of past, present and future has become unstable. The future itself has become a commodity which could be appropriated, consumed and exploited in advance:

'A girl attacked me during a public meeting, saying: 'Your generation has stolen my future!' I was astonished: 'But how did we steal your future? I don't feel as if I have stolen anyone's future; I was able to build my own

[84] Alberto Frizzi, Human Resources manager in Falck during the '90s, interviewed by Roberta Garruccio and Sara Roncaglia, Sesto San Giovanni, 7 July 2014.

future; certainly it was easier then, it was a collective endeavor. Now you have to find your own answer, not pin the whole thing on my generation but try to understand what's happening in the world today, why you don't have any opportunity. Why is it that in Italy today 30,000 out of 60,000 university graduates go abroad?' [85]

We had assumed that oral sources are sources of the present about the past and are 'documents of the here and now about the then and there'.[86] Because every oral source is a source of the present about the past in which the now and then are inextricably entangled, oral history challenges the classical notion of 'historical distance' as a condition for objectivity in historical work. It calls into question the claimed 'otherness of the past' or 'the past as a foreign country' and the presumption of an evident fracture between past, present and future.

As one of the most salient phenomena of recent decades, deindustrialization revolves 'around a growing conviction that, the once commonsense idea of a past automatically distancing itself from the present is fundamentally problematic and that the belief that the past is superseded by every new present has been more a wish than an experiential reality'.[87]

Nevertheless, referring to the fact that the economic change in Sesto San Giovanni can and should be interpreted along multiple chronologies, starting with the industrial restructuring of the 1950s, and contextualized with regard to the large array of social safety nets that were deployed between the 1980s and the 1990s, one of our trade-union interviewees concluded his testimony by saying, 'The master director of all this is time'.[88]

References

Abrams, Lynn, Oral History Theory (London and New York: Routledge, 2010).

[85] Canio Di Ruggiero, trade union leader FIOM-CGiL, interviewed by Sara Roncaglia and Sara Zanisi, Sesto San Giovanni, 14 May 2013.

[86] Ronald J. Grele, 'Oral History as Evidence', in Thomas L. Carlton, Lois Myers and Rebecca Sharpless (eds.), *Handbook of Oral History*, (Walnut Creek, New York and Oxford: Altamira Press, 2006), p. 58.

[87] Berber Bevernage and Chris Lorenz (eds.), *Breaking up Time: Negotiating the Borders Between Present, Past and Future*, (Goettingen: Vandenhoeck & Ruprecht, 2013), p. 16.

[88] Giampiero Umidi, trade union leader in Sesto San Giovanni, interviewed by Sara Roncaglia and Sara Zanisi, Sesto San Giovanni, 25 May 2015.

Alberto Frizzi, Human Resources Manager in Falck During the '90s, interviewed by Roberta Garrucio and Sara Roncaglia, Sesto San Giovanni, 7 July 2014.
Andres, Rodrigues Pose, 'The Revenge of the Places That Don't Matter', in Cambridge Journal of Regions, Economy and Society 11 (1) (2017), pp. 189–201.
Anis Amri, 'Berlin Attack Suspect, Shot Dead by Police in Milan', in The Guardian, 23 December 2016 (https://www.theguardian.com/world/2016/dec/23/anis-amri-berlin-attack-suspect-shot-dead-milan).
Baldwin, Richard, The Great Convergence: Information Technology and the New Globalization (Cambridge and London: MIT Press, 2016).
Berger, Stefan and Wicke, Christian, 'Deindustrialization, Heritage and Representation of Identity', in The Public Historian, Special Issue 39 (4) (2017), pp. 10–20.
Berti, Lapo and Donega, Claudio, Sesto San Giovanni: gli scenari del cambiamento (Milan: FrancoAngeli, 1992).
Bevernage, Berber and Lorenz, Chris (eds.), Breaking up Time: Negotiating the Borders Between Present, Past and Future (Goettingen: Vandenhoeck & Ruprecht, 2013).
Blanchflower, David G., Not Working: Where Have All the Good Jobs Gone? (Princeton: Princeton University Press, 2019).
Bluestone, Barry and Harrison, Bennet, The Deindustrialization of America. Plant Closings, Community Abandonment, and the Dismantling of Basic Industry (New York: Basic Books, 1982).
Cauvin, Thomas, Public History: A Textbook of Practice (London and New York: Routledge, 2016).
Cestari, Fabiana, Employee in Falck Since 1988 to 1995, interviewed by Sara Roncaglia and Sara Zanisi, Sesto San Giovanni, 9 June 2015.
Cowie, Jefferson and Heathcott, Joseph (eds.), Beyond the Ruins: The Cultural Meaning of Deindustrialization (Ithaca: Cornell, 2003).
Crespi, Pietro, 'La testimonianza orale tra storia e sociologica', in Studi di sociologia 2 (1978), pp. 155–168.
Crespi, Pietro, Capitale Operaia: Stsrie di vita raccolte tra le fabbriche di Sesto San Giovanni (Milano: Jaca Book, 1979).
Di Ruggiero, Canio, Trade Union Leader FIOM-CGiL, interviewed by Sara Roncaglia and Zanisi, Sesto San Giovanni, 14 May 2013.
Di Stefano, Roberto, 'Io, nuovo sindaco di Sesto San Giovanni, cancello il passato che non tornerà più', in La Republica, 5 October 2017.
Dodd, Lindsey, 'Small Fish, Big Pond. Using a Single Oral History Narrative to Reveal Broader Social Change', in Tumblety, Joan (ed.), Memory and History: Understanding Memory as Source and Subject (London and New York: Routledge, 2013), pp. 34–49.

Eley, Geoff, 'No Need to Choos: History from Above, History from Below', in Viewpoint Magazine, 27 June 2014 (https://www.viewpointmag.com/2014/06/27/No-Need-To-Choose-History-From-Above-History-From-Below/).

Federico, Falck, General manager in Falck Steelworks Since 1995 to 2003, interviewed by Roberta Garrucio, Milan, 7 July 2014.

Ferrarotti, Franco, 'Appunti Sul Metodo Biografico', in La Critica Sociologica 47 (1978), pp. 130–132.

Ferrarotti, Franco, La parola operaia: cento anni die cita operaia (1892–1992) (L'Aquila: Scuola Superiore Reiss Romoli, 1994).

Francesco, Veronesi, Plant Manager in Falck Since 1968 to 1995, interviewed by Roberta Garrucio and Sara Roncaglia Sesto San Giovanni, 17 April 2015.

Franceso, Ciampi, Plant Manager in Falck Since 1967–1991, interviewed by Sara Roncaglia and Sara Zanisi, Sesto San Giovanni, 5 December 2014.

Fuori, Roma, Sesto San Giovanni, 16 October 2017 (https://www.raiplay.it/video/2017/10/FuoriRoma-df7f2ed7–4e6d-4e45-a710–237cbefdc9d8.html).

Garuccio, Roberta, 'Hardly a Cause for Tears', Job insecurity and Occupational Psychology Culture in Italy. Oral Narratives form the Falck Steelworks in Sesto San Giovanni (Milan)', in Berger, Stefan (ed.), Constructing Industrial Pasts: Heritage, Historical Culture and Identity in Regions Undergoing Structural Economic Transformation (Oxford and New York: Berghahn Books, 2019), pp. 160–183.

Garruccio, Roberta, 'Le rovine industriali. Note sulla storia lunga di una fascinazione culturale nuova', in La Questione Romantica. Rivista interdiciplinare di studi romantici, Special Issue, 'L'arte Del Ricordo: Romanticismo E Cultural Memory', 12 (2020), pp. 213–234.

Garuccio, Roberta, and Zanisi, Sara, 'Il Polline e la ruggine: memoria, lavoro, deindustrializzazione a Sesto San Giovanni. Un documentario e un progetto di ricerca tra storia orale, storia pubblica ed etnografia', in Clionet (2018) 10 July 2018 (https://Rivista.Clionet.It/Vol2/Societa-E-Cultura/Documentario/Garruccio-Zanisi-Il-PollineE-La-Ruggine-Memoria-Lavoro-Deindustrializzazione-A-Sesto-San-Giovanni).

Giuseppe Vignati, Interviewed by Roberta Garruccio, Sara Roncaglia and Sara Zanisi, Sesto San Giovanni, 21 March 2013.

Grele, Ronald J., 'Oral History as Evidence', in Carlton, Thomas L., Myers, Lois and Sharpless, Rebecca (eds.), Handbook of Oral History (Walnut Creek, New York and Oxford: Altamira Press, 2006).

Grossberg, Lawrence, 'Making Culture Matter. Making Culture Political', in Cecile Sandten et al. (eds.), Crisis Risks and New Regionalisms in Europe (Trier: WvT, 2017), pp. 27–46.

Halla, Martin, Wagner, Alexander and Zweimüller, Josef, 'Immigration and Voting for the Far Right', in Journal of the European Economic Association, 15 (2017), pp. 1341–1385.

Hayden, Dolores, The Power of Place: Urban Landscapes as Public History (Cambridge, MA: MIT Press, 1996).

High, Steven, Mackinnon, Lachlan and Perchard, Andrew (eds.), The Deindustrialized World: Confronting Ruination in Postindustrial Places (Vancouver: Ubc Press, 2017).

Horak, Roman and Seidl, Monika, 'Raymond Williams – Towards A Cultural Materialism', in Seidl, Monika, Horak, Roman and Grossberg, Lawrence (eds.), About Raymond Williams (London and New York: Routledge, 2010), pp. 1–17.

Ilio Dalla Frera, Falck Worker Since 1963 to 1991, interviewed by Roberta Garruccio and Sara Roncaglia, Sesto San Giovanni, 20 January 2015.

Lanzardo, Liliano (ed.), Storia orale e storie di vita (Milano: FrancoAngeli, 1989).

Linkon, Sherry, The Half-Life of Deindustrializazion: Working_Class Writing About Economic Restructuring (Ann Arbor: University of Michigan Press, 2018).

Locatelli, Doriana, Falck Employee Since 1976 to 1991, interviewed by Sara Roncaglia, Sesto San Giovanni, 20 February 2015.

Maria, Balena, Independent Company Trainer, Worked for Falck Observatory During the 1990s, interviewed by Sara Roncaglia, 5 May 2015.

Martin, Christopher R., No Longer Newsworthy: How the Mainstream Media Abandoned the Working Class (Ithaca: Cornell University Press, 2019).

Meyer, Trac E. and Hart, Joy L., I Saw It Coming: Worker Narratives of Plant Closings and Job Loss (Basingstoke: Palgrave, 2009).

Miller, Elisabeth, Little, Edward, High, Steven, Going Public: The Art of Participatory Practice (Vancouver: Ubc Press, 2017).

Passerini, Luisa, 'Italian Working Class Culture Between The Wars. Consensus to Fascism and Work Ideology', in International Journal of Oral History 1 (1980), pp. 1–27.

Passerini, Luisa, Fascism in Popular Memory: The Cultural Experience of Turin Working Class (Cambridge: University Press, 1987).

Passerini, Luisa, Storia e Soggettività: Le Fonti Orali, La Memoria (Firenze: la Nuova Italia, 1989).

Paul, Collier, The Future of Capitalism: Facing the New Anxieties (London: Penguin Random House, 2020).

Portelli, Alessandro, 'Oral History in Italy', in Danaway, David K. and Baum, Willa (eds.), Oral History: An Interdisciplinary Anthology (Walnut Creek, New York and Oxford: Altamira Press, 1984), pp. 391–416.

Portelli, Alessandro, The Death of Luigi Trastulli and Other Stories: Form and Meaning in Oral History (Albany: State University of New York Press, 1991).
Portelli, Alessandro, The Battle of Valle Giulia: Oral History and the Art of Dialogue (University of Wisconsin Press, 1997).
Renato, Falconati, Employee in Falck Since 1966 to 1996, interviewed by Roberta Garruccio, Sara Roncaglia, Sara Zanisi, Sesto San Giovanni, 1 October 2013.
Rovelli, Silvana, Falck Employee, Since 1960 to 1992, interviewed by Sara Roncaglia and Sara Zanisi, Sesto San Giovanni, 2 April 2015.
'Sesto San Giovanni. Il Sindaco spiega il suo ingresso nella Lega', in Nord-Milano24.it, 4 August 2020 (https://www.springer.com/it/book/9783319091792?utm_campaign=slbuybox_bookPage_print&utm_medium=referral&utm_source=springerlink#otherversion=9783319091792).
Silvano, Gianoli, Falck Employee Since 1959 to 1985, interviewed by Sara Roncaglia and Sara Zanisi, Sesto San Gioanni, 22 January 2015.
Strangleman, Tim, Voices of Guiness: An Oral History of the Park Royal Brewery (Oxford and New York: Oxford University).
Strangleman, Tim, Linkon, Sherry and Rhodes, Jameswere, 'Introduction to Crumbling Cultures. Deindustrialization, Class and Memory', in International Labor and Working Class History Journal, Special Issue, Fall (2013), pp. 7–22.
The Economist, 4 April 2015.
The Economist, 21 October 2017.
Thompson, Paul, The Voice of The Past: Oral History (Oxford and New York: Oxford University Press, 1978), pp. 1–2.
'Town That Banned Mosques Sets Tone for Italian Elections', in The Times, 23 February 2018 (https://www.thetimes.co.uk/article/sesto-san-giovanni-town-that-banned-mosques-sets-tone-for-italian-election-w2z07f3t9).
Tedeschi, Paolo and Trezzi, Luigi, L'opera Condivisa, La Città Delle Fabbriche. Sesto San Giovanni (1903–1952) (Milan: FrancoAngeli, 2007).
Trezzi, Luigi, Sesto San Giovanni (1953–1973). Economia E Società. La Crescita (Milan: Skira, 2007).
Trezzi , Luigi, Sesto San Giovanni Alla Fine Del XX Secolo (1974–1996) (Milan: FrancoAngeli, 2012).
Tumblety, Joan (ed.), Memory and History: Understanding Memory as Source and Subject (London and New York: Routledge, 2013).
Umidi, Giampiero, Trade Union Leader in Sesto San Giocanni, interviewed by Sara Roncaglia nd Sara Zanisi, Sesto San Giovanni, 25 May 2015.
Varini, Valerio, L'opera Condivisa: La Città Delle Fabbriche, Sesto San Giovanni (1903–1952). L'industria (Milan: FrancoAngeli, 2006).
Vergallo, Luigi, Una Nuova Era? "Deindustrializzazione" E Nuovi Assetti Produttivi Nel Mondo (1945–2005) (Roma: Aracne, 2011).

Vittorio, Riva, Employee in Falck Since 1974 to 1996, interviewed by Roberta Garrucio and Sara Zanisi, Sesto San Giovanni, 17 July 2013.
Vittorio, Tresoldi, Former Falck Worker, interviews by Sara Roncaglia and Sara Zanisi, Sesto San Giovanni, 9 June 2015.
Williams, Raymond, The Long Revolution (London: Chatto & Windus, 1961).
Williams, Raymond, Marxism and Literature (Oxford: Oxford University Press, 1977).
Williams, Raymond, Politics and Letters: Interviews with New Left Review (London and New York: Verso).
Zanisi, Sara, Il Portello. Voci della Fabbrica, le Interviste di Duccio Bigazzi in Alfa Romeo (Milano: Francoangeli, 2017).

PART III

Managing Economic Decline

CHAPTER 6

Which Endogenous Potential and Which Exogenous Aids Promote the Management of Structural Change in the Region? Experiences from the Ruhr Area

Stefan Goch

Introduction

My contribution intends to use the example of the structural policy measures for the Ruhr region since the late 1950s to show that, in

[1] See my younger contributions: Stefan Goch, "Wandel ist immer, wir bemühen uns, haben es aber schwer". Erinnerungsort Strukturwandel', in Stefan Berger et al. (eds.), *Zeit-Räume Ruhr: Erinnerungsorte des Ruhrgebiets*, (Essen: Klartext, 2018), pp. 459–479 and Stefan Goch, '"Tief im Westen ist es besser als man glaubt"? Strukturpolitik und Strukturwandel im Ruhrgebiet', in Stefan Grüner and Sabine Mecking (eds.), *Wirtschaftsräume und Lebenschancen. Wahrnehmung und Steuerung von sozioökonomischem Wandel in Deutschland 1945–2000*, (Berlin: De Gruyter, 2017), pp. 93–115.

S. Goch (✉)
Ruhr-Universität Bochum, Bochum, Germany
e-mail: stefan.goch@rub.de

S. Berger et al. (eds.), *Deindustrialisation in Twentieth-Century Europe*, Palgrave Studies in the History of Social Movements,
https://doi.org/10.1007/978-3-030-89631-7_6

particular, processes of regional governance and corporate arrangements for regional revitalization are necessary in regions undergoing structural transformation.[1] However, despite the need for processes of negotiation, cooperation, compromise, and consensus, it is ultimately not possible to dispense with the ordering principles provided by public authorities.

History

The development of the Ruhr area is first of all a history of external control of exogenous influences. Thus, despite having a medieval history, the Ruhr area is primarily a product of the industrial age. It is a formerly sparsely populated area which developed its current form due to the occurrence of hard coal and, above all, through the help of foreign capital and know-how. The heavy industry and industries affiliated with it have shaped the region economically, socially, structurally, and culturally.[2]

Initial structural problems caused by the beginning mechanization of heavy industry in the 1920s had been masked by National Socialist autarchic policy and rearmament. After the liberation from National Socialism, the promotion of heavy industry for reconstruction again prevented structural adjustments in the Ruhr. Since the late 1940s, mining in the Ruhr area and the Ruhr area as a whole have been experiencing a new boom time.[3] Somewhat dramatically, one could say that perhaps a gentler structural change than this new boom was twice prevented from the outside by National Socialism and its consequences.

In the midst of the recovery boom, which was perceived as miraculous, the coal crisis broke out in February 1958, leading to cancelation of the first shifts. In addition to economic factors, extensive exogenous changes in the energy sector were responsible for the coal crisis. Hard coal mining reacted to overproduction in ways that were economically

[2] Michael Farrenkopf et al. (eds.), *Die Stadt der Städte: Das Ruhrgebiet und seine Umbrüche*, (Essen: Klartext, 2019).

[3] Stefan Goch, *Eine Region im Kampf mit dem Strukturwandel: Strukturpolitik und Bewältigung von Strukturwandel im Ruhrgebiet*, (Essen: Klartext, 2002), here pp. 128–134.

rational, including mechanization and increased productivity of labor. At the same time, production and workforce were reduced.[4]

Laissez-Faire Attitudes and Crisis Management in the Early Mining Crisis 1958–1966/7

Since the 1950s, the economic policy of the German Federal Republic had been marked by the liberal market program. Although, in fact, there were a number of public and corporate institutions by which economic policy activities were at least coordinated, initially a policy of non-interference in free economic life was propagated by the public sector. From this perspective, the coal crisis was a matter for the partners involved in collective bargaining. In part, at least under the moderation of political agents, voluntary commitments to slowing down the substitution process were more firmly proclaimed by producers of liquid fuels, but these proved to be ineffective.

In the so-called German Economic Miracle, however, the state could not remain quite idle regarding the issues of a central economic sector. A first law from 1965, later renewed or modified and extended, promoted the use of domestic hard coal in the power plant industry. Later, in 1967, substantial coking coal subsidies were also added to stabilize sales of coke from coal in the iron and steel industry. An expensive rationalization program, similar to that of the period of rebuilding after the Second World War, promoted investment into mining and ultimately ensured the productivity and profitability of the industry. But ultimately, in fact, this did not only promote closure of less profitable mines, it also channeled public funds into passive renovation.[5]

Above all, the protests of the concerned miners and the demand of the mining companies for relief from the social costs that resulted from

[4] Michael Farrenkopf et al. (eds.), *Glück auf! Ruhrgebiet - Der Steinkohlenbergbau nach 1945: Katalog der Ausstellung des Deutschen Bergbau-Museums Bochum vom 6. Dezember 2009 bis 2. Mai 2010*, (Bochum: DBM, 2009), here pp. 160–163.

[5] Karl Lauschke, *Schwarze Fahnen an der Ruhr. Die Politik der IG Bergbau und Energie während der Kohlekrise 1958–1968*, (Marburg: Arbeiterbewegung und Gesellschaftswissenschaften, 1984); Stefan Goch, *Eine Region im Kampf mit dem Strukturwandel: Strukturpolitik und Bewältigung von Strukturwandel im Ruhrgebiet*, (Essen: Klartext, 2002), here pp. 188–193.

the restructuring led the state to take measures to cushion the consequences of the crisis in the industry. At the end of the 1950s/beginning of the 1960s, the first social plans emerged. In negotiating on-site social measures, employers and workers benefited from the fact that the mining industry was an industry with experience of cooperation between the three key players—enterprises, workers' representatives, and the state. In the special situation of the early post-war period, the coal and steel industry had acquired a special form of industrial relations that developed into a specific participatory culture on a corporate, entrepreneurial, and regional level. For the peaceful and relatively conflict-free execution of endogenous measures of restructuring, *Montanmitbestimmung* (codetermination) was established as one of the cooperative forms of decision-making regarding structural transformations and their consequences. Since the second half of the 1960s, social plans have achieved a volume that, together with public policies, has secured the social status of workers affected by the restructuring of the heavy industry.[6]

Failure of Crisis Management and New Policies

The crisis management and the individual measures implemented were not suitable, however, for meaningful control of the crisis of overproduction in hard coal. The ideologically one-sided focus on market-based instruments of crisis management and thus the rejection of actively influencing the economy to correct market failure or politically undesirable consequences of the economic process became increasingly visible. The crisis that began in the late 1950s culminated in a "second coal crisis" in the mid-1960s. The expectations of all players in the coal industry were now directed toward the state in particular. The structural crisis had reached such proportions that the mining companies were forced to make social concessions and to cooperate more closely with the miners' union to ensure the smooth implementation of the measures designed to alleviate social consequences of the situation in the industry. The union was also cooperative toward them in turn by calming the workforce. Workers' representatives, understanding the necessity of shrinking Ruhr mining,

[6] Stefan Goch, '"Wandel ist immer, wir bemühen uns, haben es aber schwer". Erinnerungsort Strukturwandel', in Stefan Berger et al. (eds.), *Zeit-Räume Ruhr: Erinnerungsorte des Ruhrgebiets*, (Essen: Klartext, 2018), pp. 459–479, here p. 465.

in turn, had to rely on the measures for social cushioning of the consequences engendered by the reduction of hard coal production. It was hoped that the state would provide at least some of the necessary financial resources, which in turn was in line with the mining contractors' interest in avoiding their social responsibility. As far as the state was concerned, the structural crisis in the coal industry, in conjunction with the overarching economic crisis, reinforced the tendency to intervene in the economic process to ensure loyalty to the system. This was called into question by protests of those affected by the economic crisis. In accordance with their respective characteristics, the three main players in the coal industry depended on one another.[7]

The crisis of the coal industry and the inactivity of liberal economic policy contributed to changes of government in the Federal Republic and in the federal state of North Rhine-Westphalia (NRW). Subsequently, conditions emerged in the network of relationships within the coal industry that were favorable to a consensual solution for the Ruhr area. A corporatist pattern of crisis regulation was established, in which the social partners and the state coordinated their actions, extended and socially cushioned the adjustment of the coal industry.[8] Numerous plans for reorganization of the Ruhr mining industry were drafted and discussed. Finally, in 1968, a unitary society was created. This "Ruhrkohle AG"[9] comprised 94% of the Ruhr district's works (52 mines, 29 coking plants, 5 briquette factories, 20 coal-fired power plants for their own power supply and associated additional facilities with a total of about 183,000 employees) and 75% of German hard coal mining. Motives for the planning of the society did not only include technical ideas for rationalization, field cleansing, productivity increase, and forward-looking

[7] Stefan Goch, 'La politique prise entre deux feux et plus. Entreprises et pouvoirs publics et reconversion dans la Ruhr après 1945', Jean-François Eck and Michel-Pierre Chélini (eds.), *PME et grandes entreprises en Europe du Nord-Ouest XIXe – XXe siècle: Activités, stratégies, performances*, (Villeneuve d'Ascq: Presses Universitaires du Septention, 2012), pp. 267–284.

[8] Bernd Faulenbach, 'Mitbestimmung und politische Kultur im Ruhrgebiet', in Helmut Martens and Gerd Peter (eds.), *Mitbestimmung und Demokratisierung: Stand und Perspektiven der Forschung*, (Wiesbaden: Springer, 1989), pp. 216–228; Michael Zimmermann, 'Basisnahe Stellvertretung. Zur sozialdemokratischen Dominanz im Ruhrgebiet', in *Revierkultur* 2 (1987), H. 2, pp. 46–53.

[9] See on its predecessor, the "RAG Aktiengesellschaft" https://www.rag.de/ [accessed 18 September 2019].

Table 6.1 Development of the German coal industry[10]

Year	*Mines*	*Production Mio. t*	*Employees*	*Thereof Ruhr*
1957	173	149.4	607.349	485.847
1960	146	142.3	490.190	398.382
1970	69	111.3	252.742	201.808
1980	39	86.6	186.833	143.440
1990	27	69.3	130.255	98.675
2000	12	33.3	58.082	45.441
2010	6	12.9	24.207	18.563
2017	2	3.7	5.711	4.517

industry policy. It was also hoped that (in the long term) a limitation of subsidies for the coal industry could be achieved through the mobilization of rationalization reserves and synergetic effects.

With the reorganization of Ruhr mining in the form of the Ruhrkohle AG, the way for a continuous adjustment of hard coal production to economically determined developments in the energy sector was cleared. It was implemented through corporatist voting mechanisms. The state took over the financial risk and the trade union oft the employee interests. With a comprehensive social plan for those who were affected (Table 6.1) a social compensation was achieved,which should not be underestimated.

In the mid-1970s, the German iron and steel industry also went into crisis. This was approached by means of a rather conflicting asymmetric crisis regulation, which largely maintained structures of the private sector. But even there, *Montanmitbestimmung* (codetermination) proved effective for alleviating the consequences of reducing the core workforce.[11]

In consequence, there were huge job cuts in the entire mining industry complex of the Ruhr area. Despite all continuing economic problems, it can be said for the present that the structural transformation affecting the local mining industry has largely been completed; the Ruhr area has long ceased to be a mining region (Table 6.2).

[10] Information from https://kohlenstatistik.de/18-0-Steinkohle.html [accessed 18 September 2019].

[11] Manfred Rasch, 'Die Geschichte der Stahlindustrie im Ruhrgebiet', in Michael Farrenkopf et al. (eds.), *Die Stadt der Städte: Das Ruhrgebiet und seine Umbrüche*, (Essen: Klartext, 2019), pp. 127–142.

Table 6.2 Development of the economic sectors in % of the working population, September rates of the unemployed dependent labor force without soldiers (Regionalverband Ruhr [RVR], North Rhine-Westphalia [NRW], Federal Republic of Germany [FRG])[12]

	Agriculture and Forestry			*Industry/Manufacturing*			*Services*			*Unemployment rate*		
	RVR	*NRW*	*FRG*	*RVR*	*NRW*	*FRG*	*RVR*	*NRW*	*FRG*	*RVR*	*NRW*	*FRG*
1950	4.5	11.7	23.3	63.4	55.1	43.3	32.1	33.2	33.4		4.8	10.3
1961	2.4	6.4	13.6	61.3	56.4	47.7	36.3	37.2	38.8		0.4	0.5
1970	1.5	4.3	9.1	58.4	55.7	49.4	40.0	40.1	41.5	0.6	0.5	0.5
1980	1.4	2.5	5.3	51.7	48.4	45.3	47.0	49.2	49.4	5.3	4.4	3.5
1990	1.2	2.2	3.6	44.4	42.5	40.6	54.4	55.3	55.8	10.8	8.4	6.6
2000	1.2	1.7	2.5	33.3	33.5	33.5	65.4	64.9	64.0	12.2	9.5	10.0
2005	1.1	1.5	2.3	29.2	30.5	30.8	68.4	68.0	66.9	16.2	13.0	12.5
2010	1.1	1.5	2.3	27.8	29.5	29.7	71.1	69.0	68.0	12.1	9.2	8.1
2015	0.5	0.9	1.5	25.1	26.6	24.4	74.4	72.5	74.2	10.5	7.8	6.2
2018	0.4	0.7	1.4	23.3	25.4	24.1	76.3	73.9	74.5	8.9	6.6	5.0

In view of the massive job losses, the Ruhr area still has considerable, but probably lessening employment problems. However, the differences in development between the Ruhr area and the national and federal average originate from two simultaneously occurring trends that took effect on the region. The Ruhr area was not only faced with large but rapidly shrinking industries. Rather, the entire structure of industries, as it had grown over time, was undergoing structural change (Table 6.3).

The present sectoral structure of the region approximately corresponds to that of the general federal level. The Ruhr area is already rather under-industrialized and has development arrears, especially in the production-oriented and the highly specialized (advisory) services. With a relatively high unemployment rate, the Ruhr area has become an average agglomeration area in terms of economic structure. Significantly, however, as far as can presently be judged, new and promising industries have been successfully attracted to the region. Networks of new production lines, products, and processes have emerged around the "old" sectors of coal, iron and steel, chemicals, and energy. In the process of structural transformation, regional actors, over the last decades, have succeeded in

[12] Information from the "Regionalverband Ruhr".

Table 6.3 Employed persons by sector, annual average after the revision of 2014

	Agriculture and Forestry			*Industry/Manufacturing*			*Services*		
	RVR	*NRW*	*FRG*	*RVR*	*NRW*	*FRG*	*RVR*	*NRW*	*FRG*
2000	0.4	1.0	1.9	26.5	28.3	28.5	73.0	70.7	69.6
2005	0.4	1.0	1.7	22.8	24.9	25.7	76.7	74.1	72.6
2010	0.4	0.9	1.6	21.3	23.2	24.5	78.4	75.8	73.9
2013	0.4	0.9	1.5	21.2	23.3	24.7	78.5	75.8	73.8

repeatedly and successfully mobilizing external resources to cushion the consequences of structural change, so that this process has been relatively peaceful.[13]

During structural change, conflict of interests between employers and employees and their organizations, along with a shared interest in cushioning the consequences of the demise of the mining industry, had become less important. A regional policy model of social partnership ensured alleviation of the effects of the transformations. The crisis created a sense of unity, corporatist structures which were dominant in the search for consensus prevailed throughout regional political culture in the Ruhr area. The structural transformations also fostered the formation of a new region-wide self-image and identity, alongside marked distancing from external opposition against measures for socially acceptable and gradual structural change. The relative social homogeneity of the Ruhr area, the trade unions, the weakening of confessional barriers, enforcement of the *Montanmitbestimmung*, and tripartite industrial relations, as well as the experiences of National Socialism, were substantial preconditions for the overcoming of old social divisions in the Ruhr area. The developments in regional political culture, a need to counter criticism from outside the region, challenges presented by administrative fragmentation of the region, citizens' need to cope with ongoing changes economically, socially and also ecologically—these factors developed strong cohesive forces for

[13] Critically Jörg Bogumil et al. (eds.), *Viel erreicht - wenig gewonnen: Ein realistischer Blick auf das Ruhrgebiet*, (Essen: Klartext, 2012); differentiated overview Michael Farrenkopf et al. (eds.), *Die Stadt der Städte: Das Ruhrgebiet und seine Umbrüche*, (Essen: Klartext, 2019).

the entire region. Against the background of social struggles and tripartite industrial relations, confrontation with agents outside the region has given rise to specific sociopolitical notions, such as a well-publicized social conscience, and later also the "reconciliation" of economy and ecology and a self-image of a regional society of "small people".[14]

Until the end of 2018, the end of the German coal industry decelerated, but was controlled externally and influenced by the discussion about subsidization of mining. After the establishment of the Ruhrkohle AG, arrangements were finally made for a coordinated reduction of the coal industry, with the oil crisis of 1973 also appearing as a future prospect for hard coal. The sales of hard coal were secured by the coking coal subsidy, the electricity conversion laws and the so-called coal *Pfennig*. With the crisis of the iron and steel industry, at the latest, new difficulties for sales emerged. In the 1980s, for example, there were several "coal rounds" in which tripartite representatives of business, trade unions and politics agreed on further so-called adjustments, i.e., capacity reductions. In 1989, a coal commission drew up the "2005 coal concept" which, on the one hand, provided for the long-term preservation of the coal industry to ensure supply and, on the other hand, relied on subsidized sales of power stations and the iron and steel industry. Coal subsidies, however, remained a subject of public debate, while public support for other sectors was barely discussed. In 1994, a lawsuit against the price premium on electricity prices to co-finance coal-fired power generation was successful. Consequently, coal subsidies had to be paid solely from the state budgets of the federal government and those German federal states that had coal industries. By the end of the year 2000, the smelter contract for the sale of German hard coal in the iron and steel industry was due to expire. Thus, in 1997, in a renewed "coal round", a gradual reduction of subsidies for the coal industry was agreed upon. The envisioned timeframe was 2005, which forced the further reduction of production. From the beginning of the coal crisis up to that point in time, about 128 billion euros had been invested into subsidizing the coal industry. In 2003, due to the

[14] Bernd Faulenbach, 'Merkmale und Entwicklungslinien der politischen Kultur des Ruhrgebiets', in Rainer Bovermann, Stefan Goch and Heinz-Jürgen Priamus (eds.), *Das Ruhrgebiet - Ein starkes Stück Nordrhein-Westfalen: Politik in der Region 1946–1996*, (Essen: Klartext, 1996), pp. 365–377, pp. 373f; Stefan Goch, 'Die Selbstwahrnehmung des Ruhrgebiets in der Nachkriegszeit', in Klaus Tenfelde (ed.), *Raumbildung als mentaler Prozess: Schwerindustrielle Ballungsregionen im Vergleich*, (Essen: Klartext, 2008), pp. 21–47.

high costs, the future of hard coal mining had to be discussed, again. The long-term preservation of base mining had been decided upon by then, but by 2012, this necessitated a reduction in workforce and production in order to cut hard coal subsidies. After the formation of a "grand coalition" between CDU/CSU (Christian Democratic Union/Christian Social Union) and SPD (German Social Democratic Party) at the federal level in 2005, renewed negotiations over an overall concept of energy policy began. In 2007, an agreement for a socially compatible phasing out of subsidized hard coal mining in the Federal Republic of Germany by 2018 was reached. A revision clause was canceled in 2011, sealing the end of the German hard coal mining industry.[15]

Following the resolution of 2007, the RAG-Foundation was founded, which was to support the socially acceptable phase-out of mining and, from 2019, finance the "perpetual costs" (*Ewigkeitslasten*) of the German hard coal mining industry in the Ruhr and Saar areas. These perpetual costs are particularly centered around compensation for damages from former mining. The foundation generates the required funds through investment and investment income. The assets of the Foundation, which are ready for their tasks, are essentially the result of the resources that mining has itself created in the regions. Both Evonik Industries AG and Vivawest GmbH originate from mining and from the former RAG-Group.[16]

Efforts in Structural and Regional Policies Since the 1960s

The crisis, which at first was sectoral but then affected the entire heavily industrialized region, necessitated further efforts in structural and

[15] As overviews Michael Farrenkopf et al. (eds.), *Glück auf! Ruhrgebiet – Der Steinkohlenbergbau nach 1945: Katalog der Ausstellung des Deutschen Bergbau-Museums Bochum vom 6. Dezember 2009 bis 2. Mai 2010*, (Bochum: DBM, 2009), with Michael Farrenkopf (2009), pp. 93–109; older Stefan Goch, *Eine Region im Kampf mit dem Strukturwandel: Strukturpolitik und Bewältigung von Strukturwandel im Ruhrgebiet*, (Essen: Klartext, 2002).

[16] Perpetual burdens in the coal industry, in Michael Farrenkopf et al. (eds.), *Glück auf! Ruhrgebiet – Der Steinkohlenbergbau nach 1945: Katalog der Ausstellung des Deutschen Bergbau-Museums Bochum vom 6. Dezember 2009 bis 2. Mai 2010*, (Bochum: DBM, 2009), pp. 519–531; Lars Bluma, Michael Farrenkopf and Stefan Przigoda, *Geschichte des Bergbaus*, (Berlin: L&H, 2018), here pp. 250–255.

regional policy. In the long term, the challenges of structural transformation could be overcome. This could be achieved with active structural and regional policy on the different political levels (municipalities, regional actors, state, federal, EU). The state of North Rhine-Westphalia has a key role in this process. In a long process of learning, the economic and social problems of structural change have been addressed through regionalization designed to mobilize the endogenous potential of regional agents and through integrated measures in different areas of policy.

After the sectoral mining crisis had been addressed by means of the formation of a unitary society, the first major community programs of the federal and state governments resulted in the joint structural program "Improving the regional economic structure" *(Gemeinschaftsprogramm "Verbesserung der regionalen Wirtschaftsstruktur")* as an instrument of economic development and led to "cooperative federalism"[17] as a model of federal politics in Germany. This model was meant to support the expansion of infrastructure and to promote new settlements. At the same time, a nationwide expansion in research and technology policy began in the interest of modernizing the national economy.

Up to the present time, the planning committee of federal and state representatives, which is oriented toward reconciling interests and finding compromise, has not or only partially been able to concentrate limited funding on the areas that are particularly affected by structural change. In addition, the scope of support remained oriented toward unspecific new settlements or extensions of existing ones, which did not provide a means to predict the nature and pace of structural change in the assisted regions. It was only in the 1980s that regional policy regarding economic structures was transformed under pressure from strongly affected regions to better cope with the problems of old industrial areas. After the collapse of the GDR, the aid of the project "Improvement of the regional economic structure" was concentrated on the new federal states of Germany. This "politics after cardinal points" is criticized strongly, especially in West Germany.

[17] Fritz W. Scharpf, Bernd Reissert and Franz Schnabel (eds.), *Politikverflechtung: Theorie und Empirie des kooperativen Föderalismus in der Bundesrepublik*, (Kronberg/Ts: Scriptor, 1976).

Regional Structural Policy for the Ruhr Area in North Rhine-Westphalia: A Learning Process

In the state of North Rhine-Westphalia, coping with the regional crisis in the Ruhr area was a central problem. In a long cooperative communicative process, the agents in that federal country, networked with municipalities, trade unions, companies, and numerous initiatives, learned to deal with regional structural change and to develop prospects for Europe's largest mining region. The mining industry and the mining district benefited from the fact that corporatist or tripartist structures had had a long-standing tradition in the Ruhr mining industry were then consolidated through the *Montanmitbestimmung* (codetermination) and radiated into the region, making a cooperative policy for the Ruhr area possible.[18]

The federal country's regional and structural policies began in a climate of enthusiasm for planning at the end of the 1960s. Given the failure of the economy to mobilize its potential for self-control, one relied on political control and foresighted planning. Central structural policy measures that have continued over the decades include the nationwide expansion of universities, colleges, and schools. The Ruhr area received its first universities and numerous technical colleges or universities of applied sciences. In particular, with the comprehension of schools as high schools of the "small people", educational deficits of the working-class region could be compensated inter-generationally. In detail, structural policy measures for the region included improvement of transport infrastructure, first environmental measures, expansion of regional recreational facilities, urban renewal measures, and the mobilization of land in general and fallow land in particular for new settlements.[19]

To complement the sectoral energy and coal policy of the federal government, the NRW state government conceived of an integrated structural policy program, which would replace the often barely coordinated individual measures with new forms of regional structural policy. The "Development Program Ruhr" for the period from 1968 to 1973

[18] Stefan Goch, 'Politische Steuerung des Wandels', in Michael Farrenkopf et al. (eds.), *Die Stadt der Städte: Das Ruhrgebiet und seine Umbrüche*, (Essen: Klartext, 2019), pp. 275–280.

[19] Stefan Goch, '"Tief im Westen ist es besser als man glaubt"? Strukturpolitik und Strukturwandel im Ruhrgebiet', in Stefan Grüner and Sabine Mecking (eds.), *Wirtschaftsräume und Lebenschancen: Wahrnehmung und Steuerung von sozioökonomischem Wandel in Deutschland 1945–2000*, (Berlin: De Gruyter, 2017), pp. 93–115, pp. 100f.

was particularly effective and successful in eliminating infrastructural deficits of the Ruhr, improving (hard) conditions on site and also bringing about concrete improvements in the populations' living standards. Nonetheless, targeted diversification of the economic structure of the Ruhr, beyond the relatively nonspecific resettlement approach, was not yet pursued, or rather, it was left to the economy only.[20]

The "Development Program Ruhr" was included in the "North Rhine-Westphalia Program 1975" in March 1970 and thus extended to the whole country. For the Ruhr region, the North Rhine-Westphalia program expanded on the Ruhr development program using more detailed structural data. Due to disappointed hopes for new settlements, the promotion of new businesses was intensified. This was done by further promoting the conversion of already existing operations. A strategy that is being pursued up to the present is the establishment of large shopping centers. In these first structural policy programs, the integrative approach, which coordinated different sub-policies, proved to be particularly effective. The North Rhine-Westphalia program could also run smoothly, because overall economic growth was achieved and there were no major problems in the public budgets.[21]

Toward the mid-1970s, state structural policy developed a new series of differentiated measures. Based on the economic structure of the region, the existing companies were to be encouraged in their conversion so that they would again be able to meet the changing requirements. Products of this reindustrialization strategy for the Ruhr area were the "Technology Program Mining", the "Steel Technology Program", and the "Energy Technology Program". These programs were based on revitalization of the locally typical industries making them enhancements of previous functional specializations.[22]

[20] Landesregierung Nordrhein-Westfalen, *Entwicklungsprogramm Ruhr 1968–1973*, (Düsseldorf: Eigenverlag, 1968).

[21] Stefan Goch, '"Tief im Westen ist es besser als man glaubt"? Strukturpolitik und Strukturwandel im Ruhrgebiet', in Stefan Grüner and Sabine Mecking (eds.), *Wirtschaftsräume und Lebenschancen: Wahrnehmung und Steuerung von sozioökonomischem Wandel in Deutschland 1945–2000*, (Berlin: De Gruyter, 2017), pp. 93–115, p. 101.

[22] Rolf G. Heinze, Josef Hilbert and Helmut Voelzkow, 'Entwicklungen und Perspektiven industrieller Produktion in Nordrhein-Westfalen', in Rolf G. Heinze, Josef Hilbert and Helmut Voelzkow (eds.), *Strukturwandel und Strukturpolitik in Nordrhein-Westfalen: Entwicklungstrends und Forschungsperspektiven*, (Opladen: Springer, 1992), pp. 11–93.

The crisis on the labor market led to new structural policy activities at the end of the 1970s. Instead of reindustrialization, neo-industrialization was also being used. This meant a diversification of measures beyond the promotion of technology. The aim was to attract new industries to the crisis-ridden region. This was meant to enable the region to acquire new specializations through a process of spatial and structural transformation. These discussions in politics and concomitant science came at a time when the public took particular notice of the rise of new Asian industrialized nations, new technologies, and new regions, while on the "old continent" serious economic problems were attributed to a lack of innovation. In North Rhine-Westphalia and especially in the Ruhr region, in 1978, the "Technology Program Economy" ensured, which then also included other branches than the regionally traditionally important ones and in particular also addressed medium-sized companies. In addition to the project-related promotion of product and process innovations, it also supported institutions of knowledge and technology transfer and innovation consulting. In this context, numerous technology centers have emerged.[23]

The next program, the "Ruhr Action Program"[24] for the period 1980–1984, was mainly the result of increased pressure in the face of worrying unemployment figures. In the Ruhr Action Program, greater emphasis was placed on neo-industrialization, technological innovation and tertiarization. Developing the program took some time, because for the first time, a new approach was taken and a new style of politics was practiced. Even during the implementation process, the state government heeded criticism that had been expressed toward previous structural policy programs. It proved to be increasingly difficult for the planning authorities to develop and enforce partially differentiated and realistic programs. Individual residents, social groups, associations, and other organizations, including newly formed citizens' initiatives, staked their claims to participation in the planning processes. The state government hoped to be able

[23] Franz Josef Jelich, 'Strukturkonservatismus und Innovation, Neue Handlungsansätze der Strukturpolitik in den 1980er und 1990er Jahren', in Stefan Goch (ed.), *Strukturwandel und Strukturpolitik in Nordrhein-Westfalen*, (Münster: Aschendorff, 2004), pp. 200–216, pp. 201–206.

[24] Landesregierung Nordrhein-Westfalen, *Politik für das Ruhrgebiet: Aktionsprogramm Ruhr. Zwischenbericht*, (Düsseldorf: Eigenverlag, 1983); see Stefan Goch, *Eine Region im Kampf mit dem Strukturwandel Strukturpolitik und Bewältigung von Strukturwandel im Ruhrgebiet*, (Essen: Klartext, 2002), pp. 317–324.

to counteract such difficulties through a "policy of dialogue" and to be able to initiate a new beginning in the area with the help of participatory formats. Finally, the Ruhr Action Program was prepared on the basis of discussions at a Ruhr conference in May 1979. The basic objectives of the Ruhr Action Program were to

- reduce unemployment through labor market policy measures,
- expand vocational training,
- promote technology, innovation, and technology transfer in connection with a broadening of research potential in the Ruhr area,
- intensify urban renewal,
- find new land resources through the reuse of fallow land.

Furthermore, an expansion of environmental protection through modification of highly polluting facilities, promotion of more rational and environmentally friendly use of coal, strengthening of the financial and investment power of municipalities to improve infrastructure services and regional economic development, targeted expansion of cultural activities, recreational opportunities, and a targeted promotion of theaters, museums, and monuments were also among the aims of the program. This policy for improving the infrastructure of the Ruhr area cities yielded substantial and visible results. The numerous old and new measures of urban redevelopment and residential environmental improvement were slowly yielding results. As the mining companies received subsidies for their modernization, the Ruhr Action Program also pursued a strategy of reindustrialization. In addition to social cushioning as a classic means of improving infrastructure, it wanted to especially improve the location qualities of the region.

The advanced development of the neo-industrialization strategy was then represented by the "North Rhine-Westphalia Initiative for Future Technologies"[25] that was launched in July 1984 with a term from 1985 to 1988. It resulted from deliberations on the extension of means used

[25] Presse- und Informationsamt der Landesregierung NRW, *Nordrhein-Westfalen-Initiative Zukunftstechnologien*, (Düsseldorf: Eigenverlag, 1984); Stefan Goch, "Tief im Westen ist es besser als man glaubt"? Strukturpolitik und Strukturwandel im Ruhrgebiet', in Stefan Grüner and Sabine Mecking (eds.), *Wirtschaftsräume und Lebenschancen:*

in technology policy, their differentiated use, and the integration of different government policies to take greater account of social and environmental issues. The new name signaled that a stronger focus was to be placed on technologies that were considered promising. In addition to the ongoing programs designed to support older technologies, the Future Technologies initiative included a technology program called "Future Technologies", a program for socially responsible technology design ("People and Technology"), the intention to promote technology transfer and technologically oriented research funding. It focused on eight fields of work:

1. environmental technologies,
2. energy technologies,
3. microelectronics,
4. measurement and control technology,
5. information and communication technologies,
6. biotechnologies,
7. humanization technologies, and
8. materials technologies.

The state government supported the development of new products and processes, the use of existing technologies for new applications, and the investigation of economic potential. The structural policy program primarily promoted small and medium-sized enterprises, but could also be used by large companies for technologies that were desired by the state. The North Rhine-Westphalia Initiative "Future Technologies" was repeatedly renamed and reorganized after 1988. In addition to cross-industry technology programs and programs to promote innovation in the old industry, there are currently numerous technology initiatives in NRW for certain industries or technologies that are considered to be progressive and innovative.[26]

During the first half of the 1980s, it became increasingly clear in North Rhine-Westphalia that the disparities between the various regions of the federal country could not be addressed schematically with the same

Wahrnehmung und Steuerung von sozioökonomischem Wandel in Deutschland 1945–2000, (Berlin: De Gruyter, 2017), pp. 93–115, pp. 103f.

[26] Ibidem, p. 104.

strategies and instruments; the sub-regions of the country had different structural problems and each represented its own challenges, for which a central structural policy was considered unsuitable. In addition, it made sense to mobilize regional decision-makers and endogenous potential in order to gain new productive forces and use resources more sparingly. Structural policy, therefore, had to be (further) regionalized. Thus, NRW partook in a general trend toward decentralization, regionalization, federalization, and the strengthening of regional structures of decision-making. The core elements of a regionalized development strategy were the regional formulation of concepts for development based on regional strengths and the reduction of regional weaknesses with the help of cooperation between those relevant parties. Justification for endogenous development strategies was required in the context of the ongoing discussions about decentralization, debureaucratization, extension of participation, development aid, and regionally oriented management concepts, which were not only conducted in the context of citizen initiatives and alternative movements. In addition, the alternative to centralist strategies promised to mitigate the pressure of legitimacy and seemed to be able to mobilize new social and political-cultural resources in the regions, among the stakeholders and from the regional agents, while reducing financial leeway. Furthermore, the orientation of structural policy toward innovation necessarily led to an openness to different developments in the sub-regions of the Ruhr Area and the state of NRW.[27]

In a regionalized process of discussion in which numerous stakeholders participated, the forces of the municipalities, the federal state, the federal government, the EC, and the social partners were bundled into a structural policy program named "Zukunftsprogramm Montanregionen" (ZIM). A "Commission Montanregionen" conducted a detailed analysis of the situation, taking into consideration the practical experience of the local and regional actors. Thereby, the peculiarities of the sub-areas of the Ruhr area were also worked out more selectively/poignantly. The infrastructure program "Zukunftsinitiative Montanregionen" of 1987 explicitly

[27] Rainer Danielzyk and Gerald Wood, 'Innovative Strategien der politischen Regionalisierung in Nordrhein-Westfalen', in Heinz Heineberg and Klaus Temlitz (eds.), *Strukturwandel und Perspektiven der Emscher-Lippe-Region im Ruhrgebiet*, (Münster: Aschendorff, 2003), pp. 19–31; Rolf G. Heinze and Helmut Voelzkow (eds.), *Regionalisierung der Strukturpolitik in Nordrhein-Westfalen*, (Opladen: Springer, 1997); Arthur Benz et al. (eds.), *Regionalisierung: Theorie, Praxis, Perspektiven* (Opladen: Springer, 1999).

called for the use of local and regional potential for action and thus constituted an umbrella for the various support programs. It became less of a new program than a guideline for action regarding the modernization of existing programs and for coordination and cooperation between the agents in the region. Especially, regionalization of structural policy and consensual and social partnership strategies called for in the ZIM were perceived as procedural innovations. The region-specific formulation of concepts for renewal in "action programs" and their decentralized implementation were intended to lead to greater efficiency in structural policy. ZIM, thus, was a reformulation of the processes to be applied in structural policy transferring program development and implementation to regional agents, presupposing regional cooperation and consensus. Specifically, however, the state government provided the fields of action on which projects were to be developed. These were the promotion of innovation and technology, of future-oriented qualification of employees, development and modernization of infrastructure, and improvement of the environmental and energy situation. Consequently, the "Future Initiative" was not really a new program, even if additional funds were made available, but a bundling of existing programs according to new regionalized procedural rules.[28]

Given the "interest" of other parts of the country, from 1989 on, the "Future Initiative Montanregionen" was extended over the whole country of NRW under the name "Future Initiative for the Regions of North Rhine-Westphalia (ZIN)", as the "Development Program Ruhr" had been previously. Beyond the future initiative for the mining areas, the basic idea of ZIN was focused on insight into the necessity to regionalize structural policy in the face of competition from regional business locations in the context of European integration as a whole. This made the region the fundamental level for implementation of structural policy programs. In the end, ZIN again was a summary of existing programs and an application of the methods that had developed in the Ruhr area to other subspaces of NRW. Regional government demanded an analysis of the regional situation, qualitative assessment of future regional development, a draft of regional political models, "regional development concepts" and the presentation of suitably substantiated projects that

[28] Joachim Jens Hesse et al. (eds.), *Regionalisierte Wirtschaftspolitik: Das Beispiel "Zukunftsinitiative Montanregionen"*, (Baden-Baden: Nomos, 1991).

operationalized the ideas on these matters that had been gathered from relevant regional conferences and their participants.[29]

From 1997 on, the so-called Regionalen (regional ones) shaped the continuation of regionalized structural policy, which developed consensus models and projects and implemented them in cooperation with regional agents.[30]

Against the backdrop of further mine closures, the escalating steel crisis and the depressed mod in the area, the state government seized further initiative in addition to the "Future Initiatives". Building on the spirit of reform inherent in the 90-years of history of building exhibitions, the "International Building Exhibition Emscher Park" (Internationale Bauausstellung, IBA)[31] was to serve as a new structural political project for the economic and ecological renewal of the northern Emscher region—and not explicitly as an "architectural show". The focus on the Emscher-Lippe area was based on the realization that the inner-regional disparity in the Ruhr area was responsible for the disparity of the entire Ruhr area from other densely populated areas. The building exhibition was comprised of an integrated regional development program that went beyond previous building exhibitions. The "Structural Policy Program" for the Emscher region was to lead to a sustainable reorientation of local agents in numerous projects and circumvented systematic deficits in related planning process through its plurality. The concrete goals of this structural program were

- the removal of the locational disadvantages,
- ecological, urban, and social renewal,

[29] Uwe Kremer and Ralf Löckener, *ZIN am Scheideweg: Zwischenbilanz und Vorschläge zur Strukturpolitik in NRW. Eine Studie über die "Zukunftsinitiative für die Regionen Nordrhein-Westfalens"*, (Bochum: Eigenverlag, 1992).

[30] Ministerium für Bauen und Verkehr des Landes Nordrhein-Westfalen, *Institut für Landes- und Stadtentwicklungsforschung: Die Regionalen in Nordrhein-Westfalen, Impulse für den Strukturwandel*, (Dortmund: Eigenverlag, 2006).

[31] Karl Ganser, *IBA '99. Bilder einer neuen Landschaft*, (Dortmund: Harenberg, 1999); Heiderose Kilper, *Die Internationale Bauausstellung Emscher Park: Eine Studie zur Steuerungsproblematik komplexer Erneuerungsprozesse in einer alten Industrieregion*, (Opladen: Springer, 1999); also Stefan Goch, 'Sinnstiftung durch ein Strukturpolitikprogramm: Die Internationale Bauausstellung Emscher Park', in Gregor Betz, Ronald Hitzler and Michaela Pfadenhauer (eds.), *Urbane Events*, (Wiesbaden: Springer 2011), pp. 67–84.

- development of new possibilities for employment, culture, and housing,
- the long-term improvement of living conditions.

As a “regional structural program” of the state of North Rhine-Westphalia and the 17 cities on the Emscher region, the IBA especially served to improve the “soft” location factors, whereby local potential was to be mobilized through a maximum of opportunities for participation. In terms of content, the International Building Exhibition was based on key projects that enhanced already existent projects under the new names of “Emscher Landscape Park”, “Ecological Improvement of the Emscher System”, “Re-Use of Industrial Monuments”, “Work in the Park”, “Development of New Forms of Residential Development”, and “Strengthening of Cultural Activities”. For its flagship projects, the IBA defined quality standards in the tradition of building exhibitions and strove for a sensible culture of construction. The IBA structural policy program ultimately consisted of a number of projects implemented and supported by local promoters under recognition of the quality standards of an IBA planning society whose sway was limited to the country of NRW. With the help of projects, it was hoped to be able to reduce the complex tasks of mastering structural change and revitalization to manageable proportions. As a coordination office, the planning society was therefore primarily assigned the role of a moderator in all fields of politics.In the end, over 120 projects were implemented. By restoring industrial and technological monuments and putting them to new use, this structural policy project took up the historical and cultural identity of the Ruhr area. While the mobilization of new agents and potential through the IBA projects was quite successful in the social and cultural field, the implementation of quality standards and IBA philosophy in “tough” areas, which concerned the economic development of the northern Ruhr area, proved more difficult.

The experiences with the regionalization of structural policy were then taken up recently launched projects and can be understood as the beginning of a reflected development of regionalization. Experience so far suggests that industrial interconnectedness is central to regional development. Small and medium-sized enterprises, in particular, are increasingly faced with challenges that they can no longer cope with on their own, but only within the context of an innovative regional environment. The aim of the collaborative projects, therefore, is to strengthen innovation processes in the regions through inter-company networks and networks between companies, associations, research, development and qualification institutions, municipalities, and the state. The numerous collaborative projects, under keywords such as "clusters", "regional networks" and, for some time now, "competence fields", and "lead markets" are all about creating a regional profile and supporting its development.[32] This includes the systematic expansion of different regional competences from new technologies to strategies to knowledge and the qualification of skilled workers. Increasingly scarce resources for structural policy are thereby bundled strategically. Regional players from companies, politics and administration, trade unions and associations should therefore be networked in ways that allow their activities to be based on a common orientation to allow for their strategies to channel into a common mission statement. The desired benefit is that the interaction between the various actors creates a dynamic that contributes to making innovation in this region more common than in other regions. In addition, it is believed that in such a constellation, various informal processes, e.g., exchange of knowledge, take place, which are regionally unique and therefore difficult to imitate and transfer. Central fields of competence include:

- information and communication technologies,
- logistics,
- microstructure technology and microelectronics,
- new materials,
- medical technology and health economics,
- design,
- water and wastewater engineering,
- mechanical engineering,
- tourism and leisure,
- energy and new energy technologies,
- mining technology, and
- new chemistry.

[32] Dieter Rehfeld, 'Know how vor Ort, Die Regionalisierung der Strukturpolitik seit den 1980er Jahren', in Stefan Goch (ed.), *Strukturwandel und Strukturpolitik in Nordrhein-Westfalen*, (Münster: Aschendorff, 2004), pp. 217–241, pp. 227ff.; Matthias Kiese, *Regionale Clusterpolitik in Deutschland: Bestandsaufnahme und interregionaler Vergleich im Spannungsfeld von Theorie und Praxis*, (Marburg: Metropolis, 2012); Rolf G. Heinze, Josef Schmid and Rasmus C. Beck (eds.), *Strategische Wirtschaftsförderung und die Gestaltung von High-Tech-Clustern: Beiträge zu den Chancen und Restriktionen von Clusterpolitik*, (Baden-Baden: Nomos, 2009).

Policies regarding clusters or areas of competence depend on active contribution by all parties involved. These policies attempt to use the orientation of regional political culture toward (neo-)corporatism and compromise to accomplish structural change.

Integrated Measures in the Multi-Level System

The starting point of the newer strategies of structural policy for the revitalization of the Ruhr Area rely on already existing competences on the ground, the municipalities, thus lending local politics central importance. For the past decades of structural change in the Ruhr area, it can generally be said that local politicians of the region, within the framework of their options for action and under consideration of existing knowledge regarding control of processes of structural change, endeavored to provide prospects for their districts and cities. More recently, different programs have sought to integrate different policies into a holistic strategy of urban (partial) reconstruction, while dealing with the legacy of 150 years of mining in the region, and indeed with large areas of fallow land, as well as economic and social structures associated with that land.[33]

As part of a decentralized concept for the Ruhr, cities, counties, and the Regionalverband Ruhr (RVR) have been working together since 2007 to develop joint goals for sustainable urban and regional development, which are reviewed and updated annually. The jointly defined goals are implemented through a long-term project list. Its focus is on strategic approaches at the interfaces of the topics of "city", "education", and "climate". By bringing these areas together, municipalities and districts are taking into account the challenges of sustainable regional development, while at the same time adjusting to the framework of EU funding.

[33] Stefan Goch, Les dirigeants communaux sont-ils obtus? Politique municipale et reconversion dans le bassin de la Ruhr / Sind Kommunalpolitiker Betonköpfe? Handlungsspielräume der Kommunalpolitik im Strukturwandel des Ruhrgebiets, in Jean-François Eck, Peter Friedemann and Karl Lauschke (eds.), La *reconversion des bassins charbonniers, Une comparaison interrégionale entre la Ruhr et le Nord/Pas-de-Calais / Strukturwandel in altindustriellen Regionen, Nord/Pas-de-Calais und das Ruhrgebiet im Vergleich*, (Villeneuve-d'Ascq: Editions Revue du Nord, 2006), pp 107–124.

Just as regional structural policy in North Rhine-Westphalia depends on local agents', as well as economic and social players' capacity for action and cooperation, since the establishment of a European regional policy, the European level has also contributed to North Rhine-Westphalian policy for coping with the structural change and has therefore gained in importance in the Ruhr area. For example, the EU is helping regions that are experiencing problem with structural change. The state of North Rhine-Westphalia has coordinated many of the funding programs with the EU Commission and, in the meantime, a lot of money "from Europe" is flowing into North Rhine-Westphalian projects to promote innovation and social accommodation of structural change. Examples include the Community Initiatives for coal mining regions in the Ruhr area and the Aachen district (Rechar), for steel regions (Resider) or cross-border measures (Interreg) and measures for rural areas. From a "top-down" perspective, the European level has developed a strong consciousness of the issue of regionally differentiated development processes. Therefore, in the implementation of regional policy, it has considered regional knowledge about the problems of structural change on the ground at an early stage of program development. Regional action programs are drafted in coordination with local and regional agents.[34]

Regional Governance

Structural policy efforts for structural change in the Ruhr area are permeated by a process of learning. This process takes into account regional characteristics, traditions, particularities, and endogenous potential. It has led to a new policy model or supplemented existing forms of control. Forms of local and regional self-monitoring, of market and state control, despite their respective deficits, complement each other through cooperation and networking of various agents. This change in procedural forms ultimately represents a social and political innovation, especially through intermediate forms of action on the market that were found along the continuum of possible action or failure on part of either the state or the uncontrolled market. This also tapped into new resources in civil

[34] Stefan Goch, '"Tief im Westen ist es besser als man glaubt"? Strukturpolitik und Strukturwandel im Ruhrgebiet', in Stefan Grüner and Sabine Mecking (eds.), *Wirtschaftsräume und Lebenschancen: Wahrnehmung und Steuerung von sozioökonomischem Wandel in Deutschland 1945–2000*, (Berlin: De Gruyter, 2017), pp. 93–115, pp. 109f.

society and thus mobilized potential for self-help. For this (co-) control by different actors or the involvement of different actors, the concept of "governance" has become established as "government" beyond official state or government action, and as "regional governance" in the regional context. With the involvement of regional agents, special (soft) location factors for regional specializations must be taken into account beyond the (hard) factors of standard infrastructures.

"Regional governance" is a generic term for many very different, less structured systems of negotiation. The Ruhr area is just one example of its implementation. Modes of regulating structural and regional policy are generally in flux. A similar dynamic can be observed in the transformation of the Western European model of the welfare state. Similar procedures, simply put, albeit less participatory, have been carried out in the southern federal states of Germany. And in the European core zones of economic development, forms of regional governance have also been identified, with corresponding regional differences.

However, the example of the Ruhr region clearly shows that structural and economic change can only be achieved in a reasonable, socially justifiable, and ecological manner with the help of the public sector. Large sums of public money were used to cushion social consequences of transformations, socializing losses in the private sector and repairing the damage left behind in the region. Above all, the state of North Rhine-Westphalia and the municipalities overcame their limited options for action by arranging and organizing cooperation as quasi-immaterial resources. The political actors benefited from the fact that the mining industry was an economic sector that had experience in cooperation between the three key players, namely companies, workers' representatives, and the state. In the special situation of the early post-war period, the mining industry had acquired a particular form of industrial relations, namely the *Montanmitbestimmung* (codetermination), which evolved into a specific participatory culture on a corporate, entrepreneurial, and then regional level. Various forms of cooperative and corporatist policies constituted central procedural innovations and became resources for efforts in structural policy. These efforts involved many regional agents in the management of structural change. Here, social pacification was not the only thing achieved. Rather, to a limited extent, divergent interests were articulated and taken into account and joint solutions were reached.

Conclusion: Lessons Learned

Despite all persisting issues, the Ruhr region has managed to undergo the structural transformation from a region characterized by heavy industry to a diversified economic and quite social agglomeration area. Regional agents' gradually acquired endogenous capacity for cooperation and compromise and a prolonged process of learning to involve all relevant parties in the region in the effort of structural policy along with substantial external support have made this possible.

From the perspective of many years of experience with structural policy in the Ruhr region, central elements of exogenously supported endogenous strategies for the future of industrial regions that are affected by structural change are:

- Economic and ecological structural change is a never-ending story, especially if it is designed to be reasonably socially acceptable. Socially acceptable structural change takes a long time and causes high costs.
- Despite the need for negotiation processes, cooperation, compromise, and consensus, it is ultimately not possible to dispense with the regulatory mechanisms and powers of public authorities.
- The search for regionally adequate strategies of structural policy is not only a question of measures in different areas of policy, but also a problem of politics. It necessitates development of procedural forms that enable regional decision-making processes to achieve economic, ecological, and social management of structural change. The structure of regional governance varies, depending on the economic, political, and administrative conditions, as well as particular cultural and mental characteristics and traditions. However, functional equivalents of regional governance are necessary in any case. Beyond policy transfer, therefore, regionally adapted forms of politics have to be developed for each case individually.
- In terms of content of these envisioned changes, regions can search for new tasks in the sense of neo-industrialization or, in the sense of reindustrialization, build on existing potential and competences, the latter making development of innovations and of unique selling points particularly successful. In times of internationalized competition, specialization has to be competitive. If this applies to the formation of specific clusters, fields of competence or lead markets, this

is particularly profitable. After all, in the process of modernization, increasingly flexible specialization prevails over mass production. Monolithic structures must be replaced by a variety of structures.

In a modernizing and thus differentiating economy and society, the central promotion and control of regional self-development and specialization constitutes a promising strategy for structural policy—as does governing with the help of regional governance.

References

Benz, Arthur, Fürst, Dietrich, Kilper, Heiderose, Rehfeld, Dieter (eds.) (1999), Regionalisierung. Theorie, Praxis, Perspektiven, Opladen, Springer.

Berger, Stefan, Borsdorf, Ulrich, Claßen, Ludger, Grütter, Heinrich Theodor, Nellen, Dieter (eds.) (2018), Zeit-Räume Ruhr, Erinnerungsorte des Ruhrgebiets, Essen, Klartext.

Betz, Gregor, Hitzler, Ronald, Pfadenhauer, Michaela (eds.) (2011), "Urbane Events", Wiesbaden, Springer.

Bluma, Lars, Farrenkopf, Michael, Przigoda, Stefan (2018), Geschichte des Bergbaus, Berlin, L&H.

Bogumil, Jörg, Heinze, Rolf G., Lehner, Franz, Strohmeier, Klaus Peter (2012), Viel erreicht - wenig gewonnen, Ein realistischer Blick auf das Ruhrgebiet, Essen, Klartext.

Bovermann, Rainer, Goch, Stefan, Priamus, Heinz-Jürgen (eds.) (1996), Das Ruhrgebiet - Ein starkes Stück Nordrhein-Westfalen. Politik in der Region 1946–1996, Essen, Klartext.

Danielzyk, Rainer; Wood, Gerald (2003), Innovative Strategien der politischen Regionalisierung in Nordrhein-Westfalen, in: Heineberg, Temlitz (2003), pp. 19–31.

Eck, Jean-François, Chélini, Michel-Pierre (eds.) (2012), PME et grandes entreprises en Europe du Nord-Ouest XIXe – XXe siècle: Activités, stratégies, performances, Villeneuve d'Ascq, Presses Universitaires du Septention.

Farrenkopf, Michael (2019), Geschichte des Ruhrbergbaus, in: Farrenkopf, Goch, Rasch, Wehling (2019), pp. 93–109.

Farrenkopf, Michael, Ganzelewski, Michael, Przigoda, Stefan, Schnepel, Inga, Slotta, Rainer (eds.) (2009), Glück auf! Ruhrgebiet – Der Steinkohlenbergbau nach 1945, Katalog der Ausstellung des Deutschen Bergbau-Museums Bochum vom 6. Dezember 2009 bis 2. Mai 2010, Bochum DBM.

Farrenkopf, Michael, Goch, Stefan, Rasch, Manfred, Wehling, Hans-Werner (eds.) (2019), Die Stadt der Städte, Das Ruhrgebiet und seine Umbrüche, Essen, Klartext.

Faulenbach, Bernd (1989), Mitbestimmung und politische Kultur im Ruhrgebiet, in: Martens, Peter (1989), pp. 216–228.

Faulenbach, Bernd (1996), Merkmale und Entwicklungslinien der politischen Kultur des Ruhrgebiets, in: Bovermann, Goch, Priamus (1996), pp. 365–377.

Ganser, Karl (1999), IBA '99. Bilder einer neuen Landschaft, Dortmund, Harenberg.

Goch, Stefan (2002), Eine Region im Kampf mit dem Strukturwandel, Strukturpolitik und Bewältigung von Strukturwandel im Ruhrgebiet, Essen, Klartext.

Goch, Stefan (ed.) (2004), Strukturwandel und Strukturpolitik in Nordrhein-Westfalen, Münster Aschendorff.

Goch, Stefan (2008), Die Selbstwahrnehmung des Ruhrgebiets in der Nachkriegszeit, in: Tenfelde (2008), pp. 21–47.

Goch, Stefan (2011), Sinnstiftung durch ein Strukturpolitikprogramm: Die Internationale Bauausstellung Emscher Park, in: Betz, Hitzler, Pfadenhauer (2011), pp. 67–84.

Goch, Stefan (2012), La politique prise entre deux feux et plus. Entreprises et pouvoirs publics et reconversion dans la Ruhr après 1945, in: Eck, Chélini 2012), pp. 267–284.

Goch, Stefan (2017), '"Tief im Westen ist es besser als man glaubt"? Strukturpolitik und Strukturwandel im Ruhrgebiet', in: Grüner, Mecking (2017), pp. 93–115.

Goch, Stefan (2018) '"Wandel ist immer, wir bemühen uns, haben es aber schwer", Erinnerungsort Strukturwandel', in: Berger, Borsdorf, Claßen, Grütter, Nellen (2018), pp. 459–479

Goch, Stefan (2019), Politische Steuerung des Wandels, in: Farrenkopf, Goch, Rasch, Wehling (2019), pp. 275–280.

Grüner, Stefan, Mecking, Sabine (eds.) (2017), Wirtschaftsräume und Lebenschancen: Wahrnehmung und Steuerung von sozioökonomischem Wandel in Deutschland 1945-2000, Berlin, De Gruyter

Heineberg, Heinz, Temlitz, Klaus (eds.) (2003), Strukturwandel und Perspektiven der Emscher-Lippe-Region im Ruhrgebiet, Münster, Aschendorff

Heinze, Rolf G., Hilbert, Josef, Voelzkow, Helmut (eds.) (1992), Strukturwandel und Strukturpolitik in Nordrhein-Westfalen, Entwicklungstrends und Forschungsperspektiven, Opladen, Springer.

Heinze, Rolf G., Hilbert, Josef, Voelzkow, Helmut (1992), Entwicklungen und Perspektiven industrieller Produktion in Nordrhein-Westfalen, in: Heinze, Hilbert, Voelzkow, pp. 11–93.

Heinze, Rolf G., Schmid, Josef, Beck, Rasmus C. (eds.) (2009), Strategische Wirtschaftsförderung und die Gestaltung von High-Tech-Clustern, Beiträge zu den Chancen und Restriktionen von Clusterpolitik, Baden-Baden, Nomos.

Heinze, Rolf G., Voelzkow, Helmut (eds.) (1997), Regionalisierung der Strukturpolitik in Nordrhein-Westfalen, Opladen, Springer.

Hesse, Joachim Jens, Benz, Angelika, Benz, Arthur, Backhaus-Maul, Holger (1991), Regionalisierte Wirtschaftspolitik, Das Beispiel "Zukunftsinitiative Montanregionen", Baden-Baden, Nomos.

Jelich, Franz Josef (2004), Strukturkonservatismus und Innovation, Neue Handlungsansätze der Strukturpolitik in den 1980er und 1990er Jahren, in: Goch (2004), pp. 200–216.

Kiese, Matthias (2012), Regionale Clusterpolitik in Deutschland, Bestandsaufnahme und interregionaler Vergleich im Spannungsfeld von Theorie und Praxis, Marburg, Metropolis.

Kilper, Heiderose (1999), Die Internationale Bauausstellung Emscher Park: Eine Studie zur Steuerungsproblematik komplexer Erneuerungsprozesse in einer alten Industrieregion, Opladen, Springer.

Kremer, Uwe, Löckener, Ralf (1992), ZIN am Scheideweg, Zwischenbilanz und Vorschläge zur Strukturpolitik in NRW, Eine Studie über die "Zukunftsinitiative für die Regionen Nordrhein-Westfalens", Bochum, Eigenverlag.

Landesregierung Nordrhein-Westfalen (1968), Entwicklungsprogramm Ruhr 1968–1973, Düsseldorf, Eigenverlag.

Landesregierung Nordrhein-Westfalen (1983), Politik für das Ruhrgebiet, Aktionsprogramm Ruhr, Zwischenbericht, Düsseldorf, Eigenverlag.

Lauschke, Karl (1984), Schwarze Fahnen an der Ruhr, Die Politik der IG Bergbau und Energie während der Kohlekrise 1958–1968, Marburg, Arbeiterbewegung und Gesellschaftswissenschaften.

Martens, Helmut, Peter, Gerd (eds.) (1989), Mitbestimmung und Demokratisierung, Stand und Perspektiven der Forschung, Wiesbaden, Springer.

Ministerium für Bauen und Verkehr des Landes Nordrhein-Westfalen, Institut für Landes- und Stadtentwicklungsforschung (2006), Die Regionalen in Nordrhein-Westfalen, Impulse für den Strukturwandel, Dortmund, Eigenverlag.

Presse- und Informationsamt der Landesregierung NRW (1984), Nordrhein-Westfalen-Initiative Zukunftstechnologien, Düsseldorf, Eigenverlag.

Rasch, Manfred (2019), Die Geschichte der Stahlindustrie im Ruhrgebiet, in: Farrenkopf, Goch, Rasch, Wehling (2019), pp. 127–142.

Rehfeld, Dieter (2004), Know how vor Ort, Die Regionalisierung der Strukturpolitik seit den 1980er Jahren, in: Goch (2004), pp. 217–241.

Scharpf, Fritz W., Reissert Bernd, Schnabel, Franz (eds.) (1976), Politikverflechtung, Theorie und Empirie des kooperativen Föderalismus in der Bundesrepublik, Kronberg/Ts., Scriptor.

Tenfelde, Klaus (ed.) (2008), Raumbildung als mentaler Prozess: Schwerindustrielle Ballungsregionen im Vergleich, Essen, Klartext.

Zimmermann, Michael (1987), Basisnahe Stellvertretung, Zur sozialdemokratischen Dominanz im Ruhrgebiet, in: Revierkultur 2 (1987), H. 2, pp. 46–53.

CHAPTER 7

The Deindustrialization of Genoa: Resistance and the Search for a New Identity

Marco Doria

Features and Decline of an Industrial City

In 1963, Giorgio Bocca, a brilliant journalist and acute observer of Italy at a time of deep transformations, published a book where he described the situation in different Italian regions. Speaking of Genoa, he gave the following vivid image:

> Four hundred thousand people (...) live in Genoa's industrial area; it's a landscape instigating populist protest, worse than the black coal lands in Liege, worse than Essen or Dusseldorf. Not a single green breathing space, a densely built up area squeezed between the mountains and the sea, or crammed along the Valpolcevera, set clearly apart from middle class

M. Doria (✉)
Università degli Studi di Genova, Genova, Italy
e-mail: doria@economia.unige.it

S. Berger et al. (eds.), *Deindustrialisation in Twentieth-Century Europe*, Palgrave Studies in the History of Social Movements,
https://doi.org/10.1007/978-3-030-89631-7_7

> Genoa. (...) Two industrial giants, Italsider and Ansaldo, steelworks and shipyards. Then refineries. But few possibilities for the light industry; there is simply no room for that, and little hope for initiatives, improvement, and growth.[1]

Eighty years earlier, in 1884, the Swedish playwright August Strindberg, writing from Genoa to a friend, told him that, "the whole coast is so full of factories and shipyards that you can't even reach the beach! (...) Here nature is over! It's impossible to walk! The streets are full of dust! Really, a lot of dust".[2] In the eighties of the nineteenth century, a large swath of Genoese conurbation would already look like an industrial city. Industrialization had begun around the mid-nineteenth century and was practically completed by the turn of the century, when Genoa could actually be considered a sonecorner of the "industrial triangle" in Italy's North West.[3] The central role played by the steel and mechanical sectors—heavy industry focused on arms production—is the main feature of Genoese industry. During the long recurrent periods when the Italian government was pursuing policies of military expansion—namely, the decades between the nineteenth and twentieth centuries, the nineteen thirties and, obviously enough, during the two World Wars—all these plants were operating at full throttle and with increasing production capacity. But then, after the war, all these industries had inevitably to reckon with the subsequent crisis and the need to reconvert. A constant and close relationship between the entrepreneurial class, businesses, and the government was required by the very nature of Genoese industry.[4] For a long time, the Italian political class had placed significant strategic value on

[1] Giorgio Bocca, *La scoperta dell'Italia* (Bari: Laterza, 1963), pp. 301–303.

[2] Giuseppe Marcenaro (ed.), *Viaggio in Liguria* (Genova: Consiglio regionale della Liguria, 1973), p. 218.

[3] On economic transformations and industrialization of Genoa see Marco Doria, "Genova. Da polo del triangolo industriale a città in declino", in *Atti della Società Ligure di Storia Patria*, n.s. XXXVII, 2 (1997), pp. 367–408; Marco Doria, "Da un'economia di antico regime all'industrializzazione", in Giovanni Assereto and Marco Doria (eds.), *Storia della Liguria* (Roma and Bari: Laterza, 2007), pp. 211–228; Marco Doria, "'Economia mista' e deindustrializzazione", in *Storia della Liguria* (Roma and Bari: Laterza, 2007), pp. 266–283.

[4] It is one of the business models mentioned by Franco Amatori, "Big and Small Business in Italy's Industries History", in *Rivista di storia economica* 2 (2008), pp. 207–224.

these plants—large factories populated by communities of highly skilled male workers. This explains the rescue of struggling companies decided or encouraged by governments on several occasions, up to the more comprehensive operation carried out in 1933 by Mussolini's government. It featured the setting up of the Institute for Industrial Reconstruction (IRI), and aimed at bringing the most important companies and factories in the city back under public control. Genoa thus became the "capital of state-owned enterprises", keeping this title up to the privatization wave, which ended with the winding up of IRI in 2000.

As evidenced from various statistical surveys carried out during the twentieth century, the number of people working in industry in the municipality and province of Genoa shows that the secondary sector, together with the port, had been the cornerstone of the city's economy for a long time, and even in earlier periods compared to the rest of the Italian industrialization process (Table 7.1).

The importance of the secondary sector is further confirmed by industrial employment data that were regularly collected through censuses. On the eve of the Second World War, rearmament policies were exerting their effects. In the aftermath of the war, the physiological decrease in the number of workers was, on the whole, contained, for it was mostly offset by production expansion linked to and driven by an overall domestic

Table 7.1 Industry workers in the Province and Municipality of Genoa 1911–2011

	Province	*Municipality*	*Mechanical sector (Municipality of Genoa)*	*Steel sector (Municipality of Genoa)*
1911	90.694	77.373	29.492	29.492
1937–1940	117.280	95.833	45.260	9.497
1951	106.924	89.628	42.719	11.112
1961	106.353	88.163	39.604	15.214
1971	101.431	77.180	35.953	14.105
1981	93.291	69.821	34.760	15.071
1991	59.103	42.242	22.794	6.067
2001	46.623	31.818		
2011	38.717	25.945		

Source Marco Doria, "Genova: da polo del triangolo industriale a città in declino", Atti della Società Ligure di Storia Patria, n.s. XXXVII, 2 (1997), pp. 378, 380, 382–383; Comune di Genova, Annuario statistico (2016), Genova

economic growth. Stability was the dominant sign in the fifties and up to the early sixties. In the seventies, in spite of the difficult times the mechanical and steel sectors were going through, the number of workers did not change much. Any decrease in overall employment figures was rather due to the progressive weakening of other manufacturing sectors. This process further enhanced the "monocultural" character of the Genoese industry, as described by Giorgio Bocca for the previous decade. The economic decline became inexorable and precipitous from the 1980s onwards.

Demographic trends reflect and are largely explained by the above illustrated trends in the industry, which at first grew steadily and then declined. In 1861, there were 241,158 inhabitants in Genoa (within today's city borders). They reached 541,562 in 1921 and 848,121 in 1965, the highest number ever. After that year, population would keep declining constantly: in 1991, there were 678,771 inhabitants, in 2001, 610,000, and in 2011, 585,000. Genoa's population would then stabilize around this figure, with only a few minor decreases.[5]

Right in the mid-sixties, the first signs of difficulties faced by the Genoese industry became evident. In 1965, the owners of Ferriere Bruzzo, the main private steel mill in Genoa with 1,300 employees, announced several hundred redundancies. The plant had failed to keep up with technology developments. Despite having benefited from the country's economic boom, it was no longer able to remain competitive. A bitter trade union action began, with the occupation of the factory by the workers, to no avail. While workers would be guaranteed social protection by being hired by other local companies, through the use of the redundancy fund (*cassa integrazione*), and the so-called "dismissal indemnity" granted to iron and steel workers under ECSC agreements, the factory had to be closed.[6] This was followed by other plants closing business, as well as by some international oil companies—such as Esso and Mobil which had always been based in Genoa—moving their headquarters to Rome. The shipbuilding sector was also suffering a serious crisis, just like many other European companies having to fight off heavy Japanese competition. The state-owned shipbuilding sector controlled by

[5] Marco Doria, "Genova. Da polo del triangolo industriale a città in declino", in *Atti della Società Ligure di Storia Patria*, n.s. XXXVII, 2 (1997), p. 371.

[6] Fabrizio Loreto, *Il sindacato nella città ferita. Storia della Camera del lavoro di Genova negli anni sessanta e settanta*, (Roma: Ediesse, 2016), pp. 116–118; Salvatore Vento, 'Gli anni Sessanta', in *Classe*, XII, n. 19 (1981), pp. 179–211.

IRI was reorganized in 1966 with the setting up of Italcantieri. Despite the angry protests of Genoese politicians and trade unions, it was to be headquartered in Trieste. More troubled events involved the Piaggio group. Established and developed over time by an important family of Genoese businessmen, in the 1960s Piaggio controlled all leading private Italian shipyards.[7]In 1966, they were all merged into a single company, which, however, in 1970, failing an effective reorganization plan, filed for pre-bankruptcy. To prevent it from closing down, three special general managers(*commissari*) were appointed by IRI, which in 1973 acquired it and took over its large debt. During the same years, Piaggio's management sold two of its subsidiaries: Mira Lanza and Società italiana per l'industria degli zuccheri. The former was a chemical company whose operations had already been moved from Genoa to Latina in a new plant built using grants from the *Cassa per ilMezzogiorno*. Thus, a centuries-old history was brought to an end, proving the irreversible decline of some leading families of the Genoese industrial bourgeoisie.[8]

In the seventies, the shipbuilding industry had to face increasing difficulties, while the steel industry crisis worsened, with crippling effects in Italy as well as in the rest of Europe.Conditions of "manifest crisis" were invoked for the steel industry in 1981.The consequences were particularly devastating for IRI companies, especially Italsider, which had two major plants in Genoa.[9]

[7] Maria Canella and Germano Maifreda (eds.), *L'Italia dei Piaggio* (Milano: Nexo, 2012); Roberto Giulianelli, *I Piaggio: La parabola di un grande gruppo armatoriale e cantieristico italiano (1875–1972)* (Bologna: Il Mulino, 2012).

[8] On Piaggio and their industrial group see Maria Canella and Germano Maifreda (eds.), *L'Italia dei Piaggio* (Milano: Nexo, 2012) and Roberto Giulianelli, *I Piaggio: La parabola di un grande gruppo armatoriale e cantieristico italiano (1875–1972)* (Bologna: Il Mulino, 2012), on shipbuilding see Paolo Fragiacomo, *L'industria come continuazione della politica: La cantieristica italiana 1861–2011* (Milano: FrancoAngeli, 2012), on the decline of private entrepreneurship families see Paride Rugafiori, "Ascesa e declino di un sistema imprenditoriale", in Antonio Gibelli (ed), *Storia d'Italia: Le regioni dall'Unità a oggi. La Liguria* (Torino: Einaudi, 1994), pp. 255–333. On the general downsizing of Genoese industry in recent years in addition to the aforementioned Loreto (2016), also see Salvatore Vento,'Il nuovo ciclo di lotte: Cronaca del 1968–1969', in *Classe* XII, n. 19 (1981), pp. 213–242.

[9] Margherita Balconi, *La siderurgia italiana (1945–1990): Tra controllo pubblico e incentivi del mercato* (Bologna: Il Mulino, 1991); Ruggiero Ranieri and Salvatore Romeo, "La siderurgia IRI dal piano Sinigaglia alla privatizza-zione", in Franco Russolillo (ed.), *Storia*

In the 1980s, the "Chernobyl effect" hit an already worn out industrial fabric. Following the dramatic accident at this nuclear power plant in the Soviet Union, all construction plans for nuclear power stations in Italy came to a halt. Ansaldo, which had recently acquired leadership of the Italian thermo-electro-mechanical and nuclear industry, was largely dependent on it.[10]

Responding to the Crisis

After having briefly outlined the features and the crisis of an industrial city "model", we shall now look at the reactions by the various institutional, political, economic, and social players to these circumstances that had such a strong socioeconomic impact on Genoa. There were immediate talks of the city's industrial decline. This became a topical debate issue and a matter of controversy, since the second half of the sixties, when—as already mentioned—there was ever increasing evidence of the problems affecting the manufacturing industry. The Communist Party was strongly rooted in Genoa, in its factories, and working-class districts. Although it was the opposition party in both the city administration and in the national government, since the sixties it had polled the majority of votes in the city at both national and local elections.[11] The left-wing parties themselves—first and foremost the communist party—and the CGIL—the main trade union close to them—believed that the crisis was due, on the one hand, to the defeatist attitude of state-controlled companies, and, on the other, to a weak and inward-looking local class of entrepreneurs. Any structural difficulties faced by some industrial sectors on a European level—therefore not to be exclusively explained from a domestic point of view—were left out of the debate. The Left vehemently contended the vision suggested for Genoa by the city establishment, that it should become a "city of services", thus bound to a future of tertiarization.[12]

dell'IRI. 5: Un gruppo singolare. Settori, bilanci, presenza nell'economia italiana (Roma and Bari: Laterza, 2014), pp. 5–199.

[10] Vera Zamagni, *Finmeccanica: Competenze che vengono da lontano* (Bologna: Il Mulino, 2009).

[11] Paolo Arvati, "Classi e organizzazioni operaie", in *Storia d'Italia: Le regioni dall'Unità a oggi. La Liguria* (Torino: Einaudi, 1994), pp. 843–882.

[12] Lorenzo Caselli and Antonio Gozzi, "Un'economia in declino", in *Storia d'Italia: Le regioni dall'Unità a oggi. La Liguria* (Torino: Einaudi, 1994), pp. 883–914, pp. 885–887.

Neither side was obviously capable of finding adequate responses to the serious industrial decline.

The situation failed to improve in the 1970s. The Ligurian Institute for Economic and Social Research (Ilres) reported in its journal that the number of companies in critical situations—and particularly privately owned small and medium-sized enterprises—was multiplying. It was indeed very different from what was happening at national level: in the rest of Italy, SMEs, with their vitality, were indeed helping balance out the problems encountered by large sized companies. Conversely, in Genoa, smaller companies were negatively affected, on one hand, by their dependence on orders from large state-owned factories[13]; on the other hand, because they belonged to non-innovative sectors increasingly exposed to market competition. Yet, employment in the manufacturing sector as a whole was holding out quite well. The only exception was the building industry, hit by an acute crisis resulting from the phasing out of the intense construction driven by population growth which by then had also stopped. The number of employees in the metalworking sector was growing, while it was decreasing in the other sectors.[14] However, this figure is heavily influenced by a massive use of *Cassa Integrazione Guadagni* (CIG), a redundancy fund by which workers and employees remain employed with their companies, while part of the unworked hours are paid with public money.[15]

The showdown happened in the 1980s. In the first half of the decade, jobs were being persistently cut in all major industrial companies in the province. Between 1980 and 1984, they had dropped by 20%. Above all, blue-collar jobs were lost, while the number of white-collar jobs remained pretty stable, a clear effect of continuing industrial workforce shake-up, increasingly composed of white collars. However, significant pockets of "apparent employment" were hidden behind the total number

[13] Giancarlo Ferrero, "I rapporti di fornitura fra le piccole e medie imprese e le partecipazioni statali in Liguria", in *Ilres "Studi e notizie"*, XII, n. 3, luglio-settembre (1980).

[14] *Ilres "Studi e notizie"*, IX, n. 1–2, gennaio-aprile, "Alcuni riflessi della crisi sul tessuto industriale genovese" (1977).

[15] Fernando Marchitto, "Analisi dell'andamento della C.I.G. dal 1970 al 1979", in *Ilres "Studi e notizie"*, XII, n. 2, aprile-giugno (1980).

of employed people: these were mostly workers in long-term "*cassa integrazione*", namely those entitled to unemployment funds.[16]According to the analyses made in those years, the crisis was believed to be due to the strong impact on the industrial fabric of the so-called mature sectors (i.e., steel, shipbuilding, chemical industry).[17] This view was endorsed by the national government, then working to review the tasks and objectives of state-owned companies, and by IRI, led by Romano Prodi since 1982. During the first years of his mandate, he would focus on sectors deemed to be strategic, with more advanced technology, while downsizing companies in more mature sectors. At the same time, there was an, only partially successful, attempt at privatizing all those state-owned companies that were not regarded as IRI's core business, while concentrating on all the others that were.[18]

Right in Genoa, Prodi had the opportunity to illustrate IRI's strategic vision at a conference sponsored by the Communist Party entitled "Genoa: Frontier between Recession and Development".[19] This conference was held a few weeks after a major demonstration promoted by the trade unions to defend the city's industries. Prodi was a speaker together with Gianni De Michelis, then Minister of *Partecipazioni Statali* (i.e., in charge of state-owned companies). On that occasion, Prodi illustrated the objective of downsizing the state-owned steel industry, which was gobbling up enormous public financial resources to pay off Finsider's operating losses. Early retirement of 50-years old redundant workers was, among others, one of the proposed solutions. The continuing crisis affecting the shipyards was dealt with by corporate reorganization

[16] Mario Quochi, "L'occupazione industriale in Liguria nelle imprese con 200 addetti e oltre", in *Ilres "Studi e notizie"*, XVII, n. 1, gennaio-marzo (1985).

[17] See *Ilres "Studi e notizie"*, XIV, n. 2, aprile-giugno, "Liguria: società economia" (1982).

[18] Marco Doria, Roberto Tolaini, "Riposizionamento e ristrutturazione del gruppo negli anni Ottanta. Priorità e vincoli", in Silva Francesco (ed.), in *Storia dell'IRI. 3. I difficili anni'70 e i tentativi di rilancio negli anni'80* (Roma and Bari: Laterza, 2013), pp. 389–405.

[19] Federazione genovese del PCI (1984), in *La reindustrializzazione in Italia. Genova: frontiera tra recessione e sviluppo*,

Proceedings of the conference 11–12 November 1983. The debate that then develops as well as the social and economic transformations of the city are punctually analyzed by Paolo Arvati, *Oltre la città divisa: Gli anni della ristrutturazione a Genova* (Genova: Sagep, 1988).

aimed at streamlining Fincantieri's chains of command and operations. However, the underlying problem—lack of work-orders—persisted. The decision to focus on electronics and industrial plant engineering was quite clear. In these industrial branches in Genoa, there were big important IRI's factories with a long history. Apart from all statements and actual decisions made by the heads of government and IRI, the only real alternative was choosing between deindustrialization and reindustrialization. All managers of the Genoese companies—actually, mainly managers of state-owned enterprises—definitely opted for the second option. Under the umbrella of their own union, these executives took active part in the debate, proposing accurate conditions analyses of the various sectors and suggesting strategic guidelines aimed at reviving a rich heritage of industrial skills and competences, through its transformation,[20] In their contributions, they all pointed out that the difficulties faced by the city's industry were not specifically and exclusively ascribable to publicly owned enterprises, but were rather linked to the crisis of "mature sectors" equally hitting other Western European countries. This crisis could not be overcome simply by massively resorting to *Cassa Integrazione*. Irrespective of its actual contribution to significantly mitigating the crisis social costs, this redundancy fund failed to provide any solutions in terms of industrial reconversion and growth.[21] Faced with a drop in demand—or rather, greater difficulties finding market outlets due to tougher international

[20] Fabio Capocaccia and Raoul Prudente (eds.), *Città e industria. Contributo dei dirigenti industriali liguri sul "caso Genova"* (Genova: Sagep, 1984).

[21] For the steel industry, a comparison between the number of employees in the sector in the main European countries in the period 1974–1983 shows that only in Italy there has not been a contraction in employment. The data can be explained by the interdiction force (and rigidity) of the trade unions and must in any case be read by remembering the extension of the phenomenon of layoffs, which in any case postpones the adoption of net corporate restructuring choices (Capocaccia, Prudente 1984), p. 126.

Iron and Steel Industry'semployees in the main Western European countries.

	Italy	*Germany*	*France*	*Belgium*	*UK*
1974	95,700	232,000	157,800	63,700	194,400
1980	99,600	197,400	104,900	45,200	112,100
1984 (June)	91,700	168,100	92,400	40,400	67,400

competition—the government was called upon to adopt energy policies that could encourage the construction of power plants—including nuclear ones—an area in which the Ansaldo Group had specialized. As to shipbuilding, dependence on orders from the Italian Navy and the lack of competitiveness in the construction of merchant ships were pointed out. Conversely, no mention was made about the possibility of specializing in the building of large cruise ships, which, a few years later, would allow the rescue and revamping of Italian shipyards.

In this context with more shadows than lights, the electronic sector was a successful case. Elsag, specializing in factory automation and process control, remained IRI's rapidly growing company throughout the decade. After acquiring control of Bailey, a US company, Elsag became a leading international player.[22]

The 1990s were marked by IRI finally renouncing all its revitalization strategies and related attempts at Genoa's reindustrialization. Privatization policies prevailed, driven by pressures from the European Community on the Italian government, whose budget was burdened by high public debt and whose aid to companies was more and more rigorously monitored by Brussels.[23]

The first significant privatization of one "piece" of Genoese industry dates back to the 1980s. It involved the furnaces of the integral cycle steel plant in Cornigliano. Cogea (Genoese Steel Consortium) was set up, a joint public and private company that took over the management of the plant's blast furnaces and steelworks. In 1988, Cogea was wound up and its operations transferred to Acciaierie di Cornigliano controlled by the Riva group. In 1994, this group bought also Ilva (producing flat rolled products) from IRI, thus becoming the leading Italian steel manufacturer and acquiring full control of the Genoese plant.[24] In 1997–1998, Bailey

[22] Filippo Foschini, *Manager gentiluomo: Vita di Enrico Albareto* (Genova: Fondazione Ansaldo, 2008).

[23] It is dedicated to the privatization season: Roberto Artoni (ed.), *Storia dell'IRI. 4: Crisi e privatizzazione* (Roma and Bari: Laterza, 2013).

[24] Marco Doria and Roberto Tolaini, 'Riposizionamento e ristrutturazione del gruppo negli anni Ottanta. Priorità e vincoli', in Silva Francesco (ed.), *Storia dell'IRI. 3. I difficili anni'70 e i tentativi di rilancio negli anni'80* (Roma and Bari: Laterza, 2013), pp. 426–427; Ruggiero Ranieri and Salvatore Romeo, 'La siderurgia IRI dal piano Sinigaglia alla privatizzazione', in Franco Russolillo (ed.), *Storia dell'IRI. 5: Un gruppo singolare. Settori, bilanci, presenza nell'economia italiana* (Roma and Bari: Laterza, 2014), pp. 128–129, p. 137, pp. 168–172.

was sold. While without any direct effect on the Genoese production system as a whole, it did have an impact on the ambitious expansion plans nurtured in the electronics industry particularly in the 1980, which had to be scaled back. Finmeccanica, to which Ansaldo belongs, and Fincantieri, with a shipyard in Genoa Sestri Ponente, remained in public hands. More recently, in the second decade of the twenty-first century, Finmeccanica, still a state-owned company, sold Ansaldo Energia and Ansaldo STS to a Chinese company and to the Japanese company Hitachi, respectively. This double operation continued the long privatization process, while attesting to economic globalization also from the Genoese observatory. In Genoa too, as in the rest of Italy, privatizations have gone hand in hand with industrial decline and have failed to revitalize the manufacturing sector. Nor have they marked the emergence or strengthening of a national entrepreneurial class: the new groups which, at least in part, have taken the place of state-owned companies were called Siemens, Ericsson, Hitachi and were all headquartered far from Genoa.

How have these economic changes been experienced and addressed by the local community and in particular by the local political parties and trade unions? At first, in the 1960s and 1970s, trade unions constantly resorted to even bitter confrontation. There were frequent cases of occupation of factories by the workers, whenever layoffs or plant closures were threatened. Particularly significant was the case of Chicago Bridge, a US based company that controlled a factory located in Sestri Ponente, in Genoa's industrial zone, producing prefab aluminum products for fitting on LNG carriers. In 1968, its executives and managers, mostly from the United States, clashed with workers in very tough trade union disputes. In April 1969, the management announced their intention to lay off all the 678 employees, after fulfillment of all orders from the shipyard. An agreement was reached to protect the workers by resorting to *Cassa integrazione* and by having several more of them hired by other local companies.[25]. In 1970, Pettinatura Biella, a textile factory, was occupied by workers, mostly women, after the owners had announced their layoffs. In 1971, it was Paragon's turn, an English polygraph equipment manufacturer, which was occupied for five months by the workers. There was

[25] Fabrizio Loreto, *Il sindacato nella città ferita: Storia della Camera del lavoro di Genova negli anni sessanta e settanta* (Roma: Ediesse, 2016), pp. 170–172; Salvatore Vento, "Il nuovo ciclo di lotte: Cronaca del 1968–1969", in *Classe*, XII, n. 19 (1981), pp. 213–218.

strong solidarity with the workers. Among other things, two concerts were held inside the factory with the participation of composer Luigi Nono and pianist Maurizio Pollini. In March 1972, an agreement guaranteed by the municipal authorities was finalized. Under the agreement, *Cassa integrazione*, the redundancy fund, would be used and part of the staff would be reemployed with a new company. The same solution was adopted in another concurrent trade union dispute with CeramicaVaccari: after 18 months, an agreement was reached, under which social shock-absorbers (redundancy fund and early subsidized retirements) were adopted for some workers, while some others would be reemployed in a new company.[26] The fierce nature of these struggles, in defense of jobs and employment, is explained by the need to protect and safeguard workers at risk of losing their jobs and income, as well as by a season of vigorous workers' demands that involved not only Italy in those years.

In 1974, Pettinatura Biella got into financial crisis again, and all wages and salaries could no longer be paid. For over a year, the workers occupied the factory and managed to resist with considerable sacrifices, also supported by widespread community solidarity. In January 1975, the Municipality requisitioned the factory: the measure would remain in force until a new company would take over the factory and hire back all workers. The municipal administration took a similar action with Torrington, a subsidiary company of the American corporation Ingersoll Rand, which in June 1976 decided to wind up the company. The occupation of the factory by the workers—their average age was less than thirty years—took place just before the requisition of the plant by the Municipality. The regional administrative court granted the company suspension of the municipal measure. The occupation went on. At the same time, through political mobilization, the public entity *Gestione e Partecipazioni Industrali* (Gepi) stepped in to solve the issue. Established in 1971, Gepi's task was to rescue, restructure and—at least as a stated objective—subsequently sell private companies in dire straits. State intervention amounted to a real rescue, but could not spare the company the long ordeal of subsequent restructuring[27]. The city administration took active part in the whole process, alongside workers and the trade

[26] Fabrizio Loreto, *Il sindacato nella città ferita: Storia della Camera del lavoro di Genova negli anni sessanta e settanta,* (Roma: Ediesse, 2016), pp. 212–213.

[27] Fabrizio Loreto, *Il sindacato nella città ferita: Storia della Camera del lavoro di Genova negli anni sessanta e settanta* (Roma: Ediesse, 2016), pp. 294–307.

unions, which were to guide political parties' decisions. Since 1975, the communist party in particular had been playing a leading role in workers' struggles, through the action of its leaders and rank-and-file union members, as well as by governing the city, which would take side with the workers' struggles, ready to defend all industrial activities in the city to the bitter end. While in terms of protections granted to individual groups of workers the results achieved were not insignificant, no overall strategy of economic and industrial policy acknowledging the inevitability of restructuring (and closures) of factories was actually mapped out.

It should be pointed out that the above illustrated cases involved private companies. State-owned companies, despite often going through difficult times in the seventies, had kept the number of jobs unchanged. In some cases, they even increased them, since they would pursue "social stability" objectives, rather than "corporate" logics. When, in the following decade, downsizing became inevitable for them too, they did so in a much less confrontational way, thanks to a generalized use of social shock-absorbers—i.e., redundancy fund and early retirement—which weighed on public finances. The great general strike organized in September 1983, which the trade unions entitled "*Perchè Genova Viva*", (For Genoa's Survival), clearly had the big factories in mind. However, the imposing workers' demonstration ending in the city center was actually the swan song of a workers' movement strongly rooted in the city's industrial fabric: a movement that was actually staging its last great mass event without being able to counteract any of the adverse trends.[28]

The active role played by the municipal administration in the seventies at the time of the various corporate crises has already been mentioned. Urban planning was the tool the city government used to stand up to deindustrialization. In the second half of the 1970s, the new master plan for the city of Genoa was drawn up and enforced in 1980. This plan is to be credited for providing adequate urban services, especially in suburban areas that had previously grown in a disorderly manner and were lacking key public spaces It strictly kept all the industrial purposes in the areas where production activities were located, while introducing new stringent constraints on workers' employment rate requirements. This master plan (a vision for the city) had been designed with an economic and industrial

[28] Fabrizio Loreto, *Il sindacato nella città ferita: Storia della Camera del lavoro di Genova negli anni sessanta e settan-ta* (Roma: Ediesse, 2016), p. 368.

structure in mind, which, although it had deeply marked the history and the geography of Genoa, was beginning to face an irreversible crisis[29].

The master plan thus failed to achieve its objectives. In the 1980s, a neo-liberalist wave aimed, among other things, to challenge, or get rid of the very idea of urban planning. A so-called consensus-based urban planning approach became popular all over Italy: local public administrations accepted to agree the conditions from time to time with private investors in order to authorize their development projects, with subsequent amendments to the master plan. At the same time, the idea of reindustrialization and overcoming the marked contrast between the city's industrial and service sector vocation caught on. However, even this approach, which would rightly accept the inevitability of change, clashed with the lack of investors in new industrial enterprises. The authorized repurposing of areas by the local administration actually favored tertiarization. It led to the building of new large shopping centers, which inevitably contributed to weakening smaller traditional retailers, while yielding very limited results in terms of "reindustrialization" proper. With the turn of the century, the idea of using urban planning tools to guide industrial development as a whole was practically dismissed. However, some specific actions were still taken aimed at supporting individual and specific investment projects in the manufacturing sector.

On one single issue the city administration has shown—although at times a bit hesitantly—not to be ready to defend industries within the city borders: it's the case of polluting production processes and plants impairing the quality of the environment. The first important case concerns the ERG Group's oil refineries located in Valpolcevera, an industrial and working-class district. ERG operated at full throttle after the Second World War and drew up expansion plans in the 1960s, envisaging the use of abandoned steelmaking areas previously occupied by Bruzzo. In 1969, the Municipality, with the support of Cgil's Labour Council, rejected the company's plan, maintaining that those derelict industrial sites should be used for other types of industrial investments, rather than to further enlarge refineries, deemed to be a dangerous "tinderbox" right in the heart of the city. The decision by the city administration was also prompted by negligible job creation effects expected from a further extension of these plants. In 1973, the Municipality decided to move the

[29] Loredana Seassaro, "Riuso delle aree dismesse e decisioni di piano", in *Entropia: Crisi e trasformazione* 16 (1989), p. 19.

refineries to the province of Alessandria, on the other side of the Apennines, and signed an agreement with ERG in this regard. The deadline for the closure of all refinery operations in Genoa was set by 1980. A few years before the deadline, ERG asked to be granted a deadline postponement to 1990. At the end of difficult and lengthy negotiations, ERG request was met in exchange for the sale to the Municipality of areas intended for the establishment of small artisan businesses and wholesale markets, as well as ERG's commitment to resurrecting some ailing industries. When the refineries were finally shut down, the large surface area occupied by them was radically transformed based on a fully post-industrial approach. While environmental and urban improvements were clearly achieved, the overall operation outcome was not equally positive in terms of production growth and job creation.

The second case, which unfurled over a long period of time, concerns the large integral cycle steel plant in Cornigliano, built after the Second World War. This IRI's plant was the largest Italian steelworks until the construction of the Taranto plant. It immediately became a powerful driver of national industrial development. In Genoa, it was a major engine for job creation, but at the same time a main contributor to environmental pollution, caused in particular by coke oven and blast furnace operations. In the nineteen-seventies, there were more than 10,000 workers, including both directly employed workers and those working in the ancillary industries. Therefore, the benefits in terms of job creation had for long got the upper hand over the clear discomforts for the population living near the factory. Things changed in the 1980s, with the reduction in the number of workers and a growing awareness of environmental protection and citizen health issues. It was right then that a committee, mostly formed by women, was set up, with the involvement of CGIL's area managers as both attentive interlocutors and active members. The committee directly addressed the workers of the plant, in particular Cogea's ones, demanding to hold a debate to discuss the issue of the (very poor) quality of life in the neighborhood[30]. The broad-minded position

[30] "Cari lavoratori, da qualche tempo a questa parte vivere a Cornigliano è diventato molto difficile, in qualche caso impossibile. Il centro siderurgico continua a emettere rumori insopportabili, fumi e polvere...". Thus begins the text of a leaflet addressed to Cogea employees prepared by the Cornigliano health and environment defense committee (*Vivere a Ponente* [Milano: Vangelista, 1989], p.14).

taken by CGIL—the leading trade union in Genoa and in the factories—on citizens' environmental claims helped avoid open confrontation between workers and the population. Constant pressures were maintained until, years later, in 2005, an agreement was reached between the government, the company, the trade unions, and the local authorities. Under the agreement, the hot rolling mills had to be closed for good, and a large area was to be returned to the city following its proper clean up. In return for this, the State would extend its concession to the company of the areas occupied by the cold rolling mills.

Therefore, in Cornigliano, participatory attempts at designing and planning changes to the neighborhood were put to the test. This would be achieved by decreasing industrial activities, which in this case was a necessary precondition for urban and environmental regeneration. A search for new prospects for the city and the formulation of new development ideas—different from those that had characterized Genoa until then—had begun years before, as soon as the bitter controversy between the opposing sides of an "industrial" versus a "service" city had subsided. The idea took hold of reviving Genoa as a tourist city, starting from its unique historical and architectural heritage. The city still bears distinct traces from its glorious medieval and Renaissance past, starting from its medieval center still intact in its urban structure, despite several run-down areas. In 1980, the Municipality entrusted Ilres with producing a study report, which was presented the following year.[31] Their proposals were quite clear: revamping part of the old harbor for urban use and rebranding Genoa as a city of art and history, which had been put in the shade by more than a century of industrialization. In the immediately following years, little was done of what had been suggested, but a real change was in the making. The occasion was offered by the International Exhibition held in Genoa in 1992 in the old port area, duly revamped for the occasion according to a project designed by architect Renzo Piano, and then opened back to the city. Since then, the municipal administration has constantly committed to promoting Genoa as a city of art. Significant international recognition was obtained in 2004, when Genoa was chosen as the "European Capital of Culture". Therefore, by the beginning of the new millennium, the process of transformation of the city, its economic

[31] Comune di Genova, *Prime ipotesi per un rilancio turistico della città di genova. Studio effettuato dall'Ilres* (Comune di Genova: Ufficio del Piano, 1982).

structure, social stratification, and image can be deemed to have been largely completed.

Some Concluding Remarks

In Genoa, the process of deindustrialization began a little earlier than in the other major cities in North-West Italy. For some time, at least until the early nineteen-eighties, the various political and social players reacted to such process by opposing it, while rigidly defending the existing *status quo*. This is particularly true for the trade unions and left-wing parties, while moderate parties held much less antithetical positions. This course of action was inevitably bound to fail. Yet, it succeeded in providing sufficient protection to the workers involved, by mobilizing substantial public financial resources. Also, this attitude did not stand in the way of projects for the restructuring and repositioning of companies, especially state-owned ones, albeit in the context of a progressive drop in employment. At the same time, private industrial enterprises have shown very limited ability to rethink, reimagine, and revive themselves. The assumption of partial reindustrialization was at stake in the game played by all stakeholders of state-owned enterprises between the 1970s and 1980s. A game made more complicated by the defensive attitude of the workers' movement, often entrenched in defense of factories, its traditional strength. It would not be unreasonable to attribute some responsibility for the non-optimal use of public money to such attitude, which would often delay or make corporate restructuring efforts more difficult. As a matter of fact, public funds allotted to welfare and social purposes inevitably exceeded those used and available to foster new industrial growth opportunities. Hence, efforts made in favor of reindustrialization policies were partially undermined.

The local public administration has sided with the workers and trade unions without hesitation since the nineteen-seventies. During the last decades of the twentieth century, the role of the City Council was key. As illustrated above, the requisition of factories threatened with closure was in several occasions resorted to as a symbolic and political tool, rather than as an economically effective measure. Particular attention should be paid to urban policies adopted by the local authority. On closer look, the evolution of the underlying idea of a city can be discerned: the vision of a traditionally industrial city, progressively leaving room for a city with different activities, and finally developing the idea of a metropolitan area, where industry basically plays only a marginal role. Genoa, which escaped the social turmoil experienced by other "rust belt" cities worldwide, is now probably a more beautiful city, with undoubtedly improved environmental conditions, and better capitalizing on its artistic heritage. However, at the same time, it is an aging, and economically much less dynamic city. It is, therefore, a city in decline.

During this decades-long process, the memory and image of the old industrial city has not fully faded out. However, the "sentimental bond" between the community and the industry that had accompanied its history for so long has become more tenuous. For this bond not to erode completely, coordinated and conscious efforts are needed, which would certainly benefit from a serious and non-hagiographic reading of a more or less distant past.

References

Amatori Franco (2008), *Big and Small Business in Italy's Industries History*, "Rivista di storia economica", 2, agosto, pp. 207–224.

Artoni Roberto (ed.), *Storia dell'IRI. 4. Crisi e privatizzazione*, Roma-Bari, Laterza.

Arvati Paolo (1988), *Oltre la città divisa. Gli anni della ristrutturazione a Genova*, Genova, Sagep.

Arvati Paolo (1994), *Classi e organizzazioni operaie*, in *Storia d'Italia. Le regioni dall'Unità a oggi. La Liguria*, Torino, Einaudi, pp. 843–882.

Balconi Margherita (1991), *La siderurgia italiana (1945–1990). Tra controllo pubblico e incentivi del mercato*, Bologna, Il Mulino.

Bocca Giorgio (1963), *La scoperta dell'Italia*, Bari, Laterza.

Canella Maria, Maifreda Germano (eds.) (2012), *L'Italia dei Piaggio*, Nexo, *sl*.

Canepa Gabriella (1987), *Un nuovo impegno per lo sviluppo del capoluogo ligure: il turismo*, Ilres "Studi e notizie", XIX, n. 4, ottobre-dicembre, pp. 41–49.

Capocaccia Fabio, Prudente Raoul (eds.) (1984), *Città e industria. Contributo dei dirigenti industriali liguri sul "caso Genova"*, Genova, Sagep.

Caselli Lorenzo, Gozzi Antonio (1994), *Un'economia in declino*, in *Storia d'Italia. Le regioni dall'Unità a oggi. La Liguria*, Torino, Einaudi, pp. 883–914.

Comune di Genova (1982), *Prime ipotesi per un rilancio turistico della città di genova. Studio effettuato dall'Ilres*, Comune di Genova, Ufficio del Piano.

Comune di Genova (2016), *Annuario statistico 2016*, Genova.

De Maestri Sara, Tolaini Roberto (2011), *Storie e itinerari dell'industria ligure*, Genova, De Ferrari.

Doria Marco (1997), *Genova: da polo del triangolo industriale a città in declino*, in "Atti della Società Ligure di Storia Patria", n.s. XXXVII, 2, pp. 367–408.

Doria Marco (2007a), *Da un'economia di antico regime all'industrializzazione*, in Assereto Giovanni, Doria Marco (eds.), *Storia della Liguria*, Roma-Bari, Laterza, pp. 211–228.

Doria Marco (2007b), *"Economia mista" e deindustrializzazione*, in Assereto Giovanni, Doria Marco (eds.), *Storia della Liguria*, Roma-Bari, Laterza, pp. 266–283.

Doria Marco, Tolaini Roberto (2013), *Riposizionamento e ristrutturazione del gruppo negli anni Ottanta. Priorità e vincoli*, in Silva Francesco (ed.), *Storia dell'IRI. 3. I difficili anni '70 e i tentativi di rilancio negli anni '80*, Roma-Bari, Laterza, pp. 381–464.

Federazione genovese del PCI (1984), *La reindustrializzazione in Italia. Genova: frontiera tra recessione e sviluppo*, Atti del convegno 11–12 novembre 1983.

Ferrero Giancarlo (1980), *I rapporti di fornitura fra le piccole e medie imprese e le partecipazioni statali in Liguria*, Ilres "Studi e notizie", XII, n. 3, luglio-settembre.

Foschini Filippo (2008), *Manager gentiluomo. Vita di Enrico Albareto*, Genova, Fondazione Ansaldo.

Fragiacomo Paolo (2012), *L'industria come continuazione della politica. La cantieristica italiana 1861–2011*, Milano, FrancoAngeli.

Giulianelli Roberto (2012), *I Piaggio. La parabola di un grande gruppo armatoriale e cantieristico italiano (1875–1972)*, Bologna, Il Mulino.

Ilres (1977), "Studi e notizie", IX, n. 1–2, gennaio-aprile, "Alcuni riflessi della crisi sul tessuto industriale genovese".

Ilres (1982), "Studi e notizie", XIV, n. 2, aprile-giugno, "Liguria: società economia".

Loreto Fabrizio (2016), *Il sindacato nella città ferita. Storia della Camera del lavoro di Genova negli anni sessanta e settanta*, Roma, Ediesse.

Marcenaro Giuseppe (ed.) (1973), *Viaggio in Liguria*, Consiglio regionale della Liguria, Genova.

Marchitto Fernando (1980), *Analisi dell'andamento della C.I.G. dal 1970 al 1979*, Ilres "Studi e notizie", XII, n. 2, aprile-giugno.

Quochi Mario (1985), *L'occupazione industriale in Liguria nelle imprese con 200 addetti e oltre*, Ilres "Studi e notizie", XVII, n. 1, gennaio-marzo.

Ranieri Ruggiero, Romeo Salvatore (2014), *La siderurgia IRI dal piano Sinigaglia alla privatizzazione*, in Russolillo Franco (ed.), *Storia dell'IRI. 5. Un gruppo singolare. Settori, bilanci, presenza nell'economia italiana*, Roma-Bari, Laterza, pp. 5–199.

Rugafiori Paride (1994), *Ascesa e declino di un sistema imprenditoriale*, in *Storia d'Italia. Le regioni dall'Unità a oggi. La Liguria*, Torino, Einaudi, pp. 255–333.

Rugafiori Paride, Fasce Ferdinando (eds.) (2008), *Dal petrolio all'energia. ERG 1938–2008. Storia e cultura d'impresa*, Roma-Bari, Laterza.
Seassaro Loredana (1989), Riuso *delle aree dismesse e decisioni di piano*, in "Entropia. Crisi e trasformazione", 16, settembre 1989, pp. 16–46.
Vento Salvatore (1981), *Gli anni Sessanta*, in "Classe", XII, n. 19, pp. 179–211.
Vento Salvatore (1981), *Il nuovo ciclo di lotte. Cronaca del 1968-1969*, in "Classe", XII, n. 19, pp. 213–242.
Vivere a Ponente (1989), Milano, Vangelista.
Zamagni Vera (2009), *Finmeccanica. Competenze che vengono da lontano*, Bologna, Il Mulino.

PART IV

Labor Relations Under Conditions of Deindustrialization

CHAPTER 8

Forms of Glocalization: Economic Globalization and Political Regulation. The Role of Labor Relations in the Process of Economic Restructuring in the Ruhr Area

Manfred Wannöffel

For more than 60 years, economic restructuring in the Ruhr Valley is still an ongoing process of labor conflicts, search practices of conflict solution and political regulation. After World War II, this social process has built up a very specific system of labor relations which channels economic restructuring of regional industry partly until today.[1]

A current example is the collective agreement between ThyssenKrupp Steel Europe and Industrial Union of Metalworkers (IG Metall) from

[1] Stefan Berger, 'Ruhrgebiet: Bewundert von der ganzen Welt', in *DIE ZEIT*, 19 December 2018, p. 19.

M. Wannöffel (✉)
Ruhr-Universität Bochum, Bochum, Germany
e-mail: manfred.wannoeffel@rub.de

S. Berger et al. (eds.), *Deindustrialisation in Twentieth-Century Europe*, Palgrave Studies in the History of Social Movements,
https://doi.org/10.1007/978-3-030-89631-7_8

December 2017, which finally was not applied after the decision of the European Court of Justice refusing the merge in 2018. Against the economic background of massive competition from China and over-production on the world steel market, the two large enterprises of ThyssenKrupp Steel Europe (TKSE) from Germany and TATA Steel from India decided to merge. After two years of negotiation, the management of ThyssenKrupp and IG Metall agreed on a collective agreement, which underlines a typical social and political compromise typical of the Ruhr Valley. On the one hand, independently from possible site closures due to the merger, the agreement secures employment at all ThyssenKrupp plants in Germany until 2026. On the other hand, parity co-determination rights in the supervisory board of the merger will be reduced by resettling the new headquarter from the Ruhr Valley to the Netherlands. In sum, this social compromise follows the long tradition of political regulation of economic restructuring processes in the Ruhr Valley[2]: economic restructuring continues in the industrial sectors of the Ruhr Valley but is now channelled through the institutions of labor relations to finally avoid deep social crises.

The intention of this article is to explain the role of the institutions of labor relations for the process of economic restructuring in the Ruhr Valley. It will analyze the effects of these institutions on shaping the economic and social transformation processes in its interaction with the development of these social institutions themselves.

The article is divided into three parts. It starts with a short introduction of three theoretical approaches. The concepts of glocalization, labor relations and the main assumptions of the power resource theory are the theoretical framing of this article. In the second part, empirical findings of 60 years of processes mostly of economic restructuring of the coal sector in comparison with the automobile sector will be presented and explained. Finally, this article ends with conclusions and tries to give an outlook on future developments of economic restructuring and labor relations in the Ruhr Valley.

[2] Stefan Berger, 'Ruhrgebiet: Bewundert von der ganzen Welt', in *DIE ZEIT*, 19 December 2018, p. 19.

Theoretical Approaches: Globalization—Labor Relations—Power Resource Theory

The concept of glocalization was developed by the English sociologist Roland Robertson in the context of his main work 'Globalization: Social Theory and Global Culture'.[3] Glocalization refers to the interaction of the complex process of economic globalization and its local or regional modes of adaption and transformation. In this sense, glocalization characterizes multi-dimensional processes of economic globalization, regional impacts and specific processing modes. Enterprises and their business strategies are embedded structurally in national, regional and local social institutions. Social and political outcomes of economic restructuring processes differ because of national and regional path-dependencies regulating labor and social conflicts and political outcomes from other regions worldwide.[4] In the case of the Ruhr Valley, this becomes obvious in the crises of coal mine and heavy steel industry and the development to the most important university landscape of the European Union over the last 50 years. Labor relations are one of the most relevant social institutions in which global economic processes are embedded. The concept of labor relations refers to the institutionalized relationship between employers' and employees' organizations in the economic field, as well as political regulations on employment, working conditions and workers' participation. Berger et al. (2019) worked out recently that systems of workers' participation also differ extremely on global or even on European level through national path-dependencies since processes of industrialization had started during the nineteenth century.[5] Following the German sociologist Müller-Jentsch, the Ruhr Valley still embodies the laboratory of the Germany system of labor relations because of its economic and political importance during the twentieth century.[6] The German system is structured by five features:

First: Duality of labor regulation: Since World War I and with a short interruption of 12 years during the Nazi regime, the German

[3] Roland Robertson, *Globalization: Social Theory and Global Culture* (London, Thousand Oaks and New Delhi: Sage, 1992).

[4] Roland Robertson, 'Globalisation or Glocalisation?', in *The Journal of International Communication* 1: 1 (1994), pp. 33–52.

[5] Stefan Berger, Ludger Pries and Manfred Wannöffel (eds.), *The Palgrave Handbook of Workers' Participation at Plant Level* (New York: Springer Nature America, 2019).

[6] Walther Müller-Jentsch, *Strukturwandel der industriellen Beziehungen: ‚Industrial Citizenship' zwischen Markt und Regulierung*, 2. Ed. (Wiesbaden: Springer VS, 2017).

system has been characterized by a formal and functional differentiation of the processing of labor disputes in two separate arenas. The first arena consists of collective bargaining: at sector level, trade unions and employers' associations negotiate general employment relations and agree on frameworks for wages, working hours and holidays. That means that the central conflict concerning the value of labor and wage mediation takes place outside the workplace. The second arena consists of works constitution rights and the conditions of co-determination at plant level: Workers' representatives (works councils) and members of the management regulate the specific working conditions (work organization, qualification, health and safety). Duality of interest regulation means that unions and works councils—both representatives of employees—act formally independent from each other in different arenas.

Second: Intermediation between economic and social goals: Works councils link the conflict of interest between capital and labor as a border institution.[7] This term refers to the double function of works councils: representing the interests of employees (employment and working conditions) with explicit attention to economic objectives of the enterprise.

Third: Juridification by labor legislation: the German system is characterized by a high degree of legalization. The state, as the third actor of labor relations, establishes normative frameworks and procedures within which autonomous interests and goals of employer, unions and works councils can be pursued. Specific laws regulate the dual system: The Collective Agreement Act (1949) and the Works Constitution Act (1952). This juridification has led to legal limitations of industrial conflicts and labor disputes in the German economy.

Forth: Centralization of workers' voice: the system contains strong centralized features of the collective bargaining system by centralized and monopolistic organizations of employers and employees. The goal is the conclusion of collective agreements for large-scale industrial and economic sectors.

Fifth: Representation of interest: trade unions and works councils make their demands on behalf of the members' or the workforces' interest. However, they may assert these in relative independence without their

[7] Friedrich Fürstenberg, 'Der Betriebsrat: Strukturanalyse einer Grenzinstitution', *Kölner Zeitschrift für Soziologie and Sozialpsychologie* 10:3 (1958), pp. 418–429.

consent. Works councils are formally not bound by demands of its electorate but is obliged to its legal functions and the economic interests of the enterprise as well.[8]

While the concept of labor relations describes relevant structures of the German system, the power resource theory intents to explain the process how these institutions become powerful actors in the first place.[9] This theory comprehends the social consciousness and the political capacity of the working class not as a schematic outcome of economic developments and formal labor rights. Taking into account the specific economic and social situation, the political consciousness of employees are results of the distribution of power between social classes, their different interests and forms of conflict solution. The analysis focuses on the ability of employees to organize themselves and the capacity to balance the power between business strategies and workers' influence on these. The ways in which the conflicting interests are negotiated determine the evolution of various manifestations of policy models, particularly in the formation of West European welfare states after the end of World War II.[10] In the nation states of Western Europe, different features present the essential power resources of employees: the structural and organizational institutional power of the employees, their ability of conflict solution, the parliamentary presence and their participation in governments by allied parties as well as the extent of the protection mechanisms of the welfare state. The core thesis of the power resource theory is that the political influence of employees is well-developed if they are able to connect their primary structural power from the workplace at company level with secondary organizational power resources on the socio-political level outside the company. Primary rights are characterised by the position of the workforce in the production process. The workplace and the organization of work connect the employees by place, time and their experimental or tacit knowledge in the everyday working process. Labor, embedded in the work organization of factories, created the conditions

[8] Walther Müller-Jentsch, 'Auf dem Prüfstand. Das deutsche Modell der industriellen Beziehungen', in *Industrielle Beziehungen* 2:1 (1995), pp. 11–24.

[9] Walter Korpi, *The Working Class in Welfare Capitalism: Work, Unions and Politics in Sweden*, (London and Boston: Routledge & Kegan Paul, 1978); Gøsta Esping-Andersen, *The Three Worlds of Welfare Capitalism* (Princeton: Princeton University Press 1990).

[10] Gøsta Esping-Andersen, *The Three Worlds of Welfare Capitalism* (Princeton: Princeton University Press, 1990).

for solidary forms of cooperation and the formation of a similar social milieu between 'coal mine and community'.[11] Until the late twentieth century, the position of employees at the workplace in the coal mining and heavy steel industry or at the assembly lines in fordistic-tayloristic structures of mass production had been also the place of shared experiences of cooperation, lived solidarity and readiness of conflict solution and combat as well.[12] The secondary rights of the employees grew from below at the workplace as a social space of production. Trade unions, and in the context of German labor relations and especially in the Ruhr Valley, works councils at company level and labor directors as advisory board members of the mining and heavy steel industry, present collective workers' organizations as institutionalised results of everyday cooperation. These organizations have been the workers' voice of cooperation and have been able to organize certain solidarity among the employees, especially in large-scale companies of mine, steel and automobile industry. A minimum of experienced solidarity is a structural power resource that preconditions cooperation, union building processes and the conclusion of collective agreements. In order to anchor institutional collective labor rights outside a single company on sector and finally social level, however, political organizations are required that fulfil these objectives in the parliaments on regional, federal or even European level. As a result of social conflicts and negotiation processes concerning business strategies and economic outputs, the institutional power of the employees emerges. These are social rights which are relatively stable in terms of time, such as the formal rights of freedom of association and collective bargaining since the end of World War II. The Works Constitution Act (1952), the Collective Agreement Act (1949) and the development of the labor and social legislation of the Federal Republic of Germany mark the results of the relative sociopolitical power of the employees during the post-war period. This social power is characterized by the establishment of political and civil rights in the sphere of economy. These social rights arise from the structural and organizational power, with viable interrelations through allied political parties or social movements from below. Power resources promote the ability to intervene in social debates, to take political leadership

[11] Helmuth Croon and Kurt Utermann, *Zeche und Gemeinde: Untersuchungen über den Strukturwandel einer Zechengemeinde im nördlichen Ruhrgebiet* (Tübingen: Mohr, 1958).

[12] Richard Edwards, *Herrschaft im modernen Produktionsprozeß* (Frankfurt/Main and New York: Campus Verlag, 1981).

and finally to establish support structures for the realization of a certain social balance under capitalistic condition. These resources are based on a bottom-up principle. They start from a specific social milieu characterized by the close cooperation and solidarity of and between employees at the workplace. As a result workers' representatives at plant level were built. Finally, these works councils, labor directors, trade union organizations and political parties as the main social institutions channeled economic restructuring processes in the Ruhr Valley.

Strong Power Resources: The Regulation of the Coal Mining industry's Decline

In order to come to a deeper understanding of the interrelationship of primary and secondary power resources of employees, it is helpful to have a look at the history of industrial relations during the transition process from Nazi Germany to the Federal Republic of Germany. In October 1944, already eight months before the surrender of Nazi Germany in May 1945, first democratic elections took place at the coal mines in West German regions which had been liberated by the US Army.[13] During short-term phases of power vacuum at the coal mines, employees organized elections of their own representatives. In this transition period workers' committees took care of the employees, of the liberated forced workers from all over Europe, and of the population of the coal mining district. Under chaotic conditions, they played a central role in the field of local social policy. The committees cooperated with the military forces in identifying executives of the coal mines as collaborators of the Nazi regime. They took over crucial functions in the process of de-nazification in the management of German industries. Against this background, workers' representatives were indispensable actors for the militaries in shaping the transition from an authoritarian Nazi regime to a political democracy of the nascent Federal Republic. Furthermore, energy was essential for the German reconstruction process and thus, the fast recovery of the coal industry had highest priority. Under these economic and social conditions, the primary or structural power of the miners grew

[13] Werner Milert and Rudolf Tschirbs, *Die andere Demokratie: Betriebliche Interessenvertretung in Deutschland 1848 bis 2008* (Essen: Klartext-Verlag, 2012).

rapidly. Therefore, the formal recognition of work councils as legal workers' representatives by the British Military government in April 1946 was the logical consequence. The coverage rate of workers' representatives in the coal industry reached nearly 100 percent. In addition to the works councils the recognition of trade unions in the coal mine industry under the control of Military governments took place. The formation of Industrieverband Bergbau (IVB) with a high coverage of 320,000 members followed in December 1946. At the same time, the German Coal Distribution and formation of Deutsche Kohlenbergbau-Leitung (DKBL) was realized while the employers' organization Ruhrbergbau (UVR) followed six years later in 1952.[14] It has to be noted that during this transition period, both the structural and the organizational power resources of the miners had reached a very high degree. One year after the surrender of the authoritarian capitalistic regime of Nazi Germany, the reconstruction of the German dual system of labor relations of the former Weimar Republic was already completed.

Under the structural conditions of the West integration of the Federal Republic the political demands of works councils and trade unions for the socialization of the key industries of authoritarian capitalism could not be enforced. Additionally, the central union objective to realize a system of anti-capitalistic cooperative economy had failed. On the other hand, the Act on co-determination of employees in the supervisory boards of companies in the mining and iron and steel industry was reached in May 1951. This law on co-determination represents an important political compromise in the West German post-war period. It recognized the leaders of the coal mining and heavy steel industries as main actors of the authoritarian capitalism during the Nazi decade. As a political result it enabled an institutionalized social control of corporate strategies by works councils, labor directors and elected union members. Thus, it contains elementary economic-democratic rights. The economic recovery, growing exportations rates and technological modernization of coal mine and heavy steel industry in West Germany had been closely linked to the involvement of the US army in the Corean War from 1950 and 1953 and their needs of energy and raw material for the weapon production.

[14] Hans-Christoph Seidel, 'Arbeitsbeziehungen und Sozialpolitik im Bergbau. Vom Nationalsozialismus bis zum Ende der alten Bundesrepublik', in Dieter Ziegler (ed.), *Rohstoffgewinnung im Strukturwandel: Der deutsche Bergbau im 20. Jahrhundert* (Münster: Aschendorff, 2013), pp. 445–514.

Considering these historical facts, for works councils and unions this act on parity co-determination signified the key institutional power resources for the upcoming political regulation of the decline of coal mine industry from 1957 until 2018, when the last German coal mine shut down in the Ruhr. This act did not only guarantee a statutory parity between shareholders and workers' representatives in the supervisory boards of the companies. In addition, one neutral person as a labor director was institutionalized to avoid a stalemate. The peculiarity had been that individuals could only be chosen as labor directors when both sides—employer and employee organizations—agreed on them. That means that in decision-making processes concerning business strategies labor directors took over a crucial role. They were located between different economic and social interests, searching for social compromises. At the beginning of the coal crisis, approximately 150 labor directors were established in the companies of the coal mine and heavy steel industries and represented nearly one million employees.[15]

In addition to this act with some economic-democratic elements, the Works Constitution Act (WCA) of the year 1952 was the second important institutional power resource for the forthcoming bargaining processes in the context of industrial transition. This act guarantees basic rights and legitimates the range of actions of works councils in multiples processes of economic restructuring with two legislative adjustments in 1972 and 2001 until today. The lowest right is that on information (§80.2 and §111–113 WCA). It obliges the management to inform works councils previously as well as continuously about the economic situation of the company and business strategies in the context of global market challenges. The more developed right is that on consultation (§90.2 WCA). It demands deeper involvement of works councils in the development of business strategies. Works councils have to be informed in time about planned actions that can affect the workplaces of the employees. Here, works councils are involved as advisors in the process of economic restructuring. They have the right to develop alternative plans on workplace organization and qualification needs. These works councils' plans have to be considered in negotiations between members of the management.

[15] Walther Müller-Jentsch and Peter Ittermann, *Industrielle Beziehungen: Daten, Zeitreihen, Trends 1950–1999* (Frankfurt/M. and New York: Campus-Verlag, 2000), pp. 212f.

Fig. 8.1 The three steps of co-determination rights (*Source* Own chart)

The strongest right is that on co-determination and workers' participation (§87, 92–98 WCA). It covers all employment and social topics of a company. Issues of possible job cuts in the process of restructuring must be negotiated between management and works councils. Moreover, joint decisions must be found concerning the results of restructuring before they are implemented on the shop floor. That means that during the process of industrial restructuring all personal decisions could not be made only by the management without reaching an agreement with the works council. In the case of restructuring with employment reduction, the works council was able to establish social plans with the management to prevent dismissals or to present concepts for socially acceptable shutdowns of single mines in order to transfer employment to other coal mines (Fig. 8.1).

The interrelationship between the development of primary power at the workplace and secondary power of the employees underlines that the societal power of miners of the Ruhr Valley is finally a result of a long process of regulation of labor disputes and conflict solution from below. Social power of employees grew from the workplace based on everyday cooperation and lived solidarity, especially among the miners, strong works councils, labor directors and unions with a high degree of organization (Fig. 8.2).

In 1960, the coal mine union merged with the union of the chemical sector to IG Bergbau und Energie (Industrial Union of Mining and Energy). Both organizations saw a growing coverage rate from 85% (1955) to 98% (1968) (600,000 members) at the first height of the coal crisis.[16] Works councils and unions need to be recognized in the political arena in order to intervene in political debates, to exert political influence

[16] Hans-Christoph Seidel, 'Arbeitsbeziehungen und Sozialpolitik im Bergbau. Vom Nationalsozialismus bis zum Ende der alten Bundesrepublik', in Dieter Ziegler (ed.),

Fig. 8.2 Cooperation and lived solidarity at the workplace (*Source* Bundesarchiv)

on the regulation of industrial transition and finally to establish support structures in the society. They sent their representatives to the local, state and federal parliaments.[17] After the prohibition of the Communist Party in 1956 under the west integration, they came mostly from the Social Democratic Party (SPD). The political culture of the Ruhr Valley with the largest proportion of economic-democratic controlled companies was considered the 'Heart Chamber of Social Democracy' for more than 50 years. For decades, the SPD held the political majorities at local and state level and ensured that the decline of coal mine industry in the Ruhr Valley could be regulated socio-politically. The political regulation of the coal crisis over 60 years is considered to be a success story of economic transition in a global comparison.[18] The reduction of formerly more than

Rohstoffgewinnung im Strukturwandel: Der deutsche Bergbau im 20. Jahrhundert, (Münster: Aschendorff, 2013), pp. 445–514.

[17] Bernd Faulenbach, 'Montanindustrielle Struktur und politische Kultur im Ruhrgebiet. Zur neueren Diskussion ', in Werner Fricke et. al. (eds.), *Jahrbuch Arbeit und Technik Nordrhein-Westfalen 1987*, (Bonn: Neue Gesellschaft, 1987), pp. 411–422; Bernd Faulenbach, 'Mitbestimmung und politische Kultur im Ruhrgebiet', in Helmut Martens and Gerd Peter (eds.), *Mitbestimmung und Demokratisierung: Stand und Perspektiven der Forschung*, (Wiesbaden: Deutscher Universitäts-Verlag, 1989), pp. 216–228.

[18] Stefan Berger, 'Ruhrgebiet: Bewundert von der ganzen Welt', in *DIE ZEIT*, 19 December 2018, p. 19.

600,000 (1957) employees of 157 coal mines until the closure of the last German coal mine in December 2018 was handled without deep unemployment effects. The societal power resources of employees were made visible through a wide protest march to the former West German capital Bonn on 26 September 1959. IG Bergbau and 60,000 miners demonstrated in Bonn against planned mine closures. Their societal power enabled them to mobilize politicians of their allied parties in regional and federal parliaments to develop political regulations concerning the industrial transition in the Ruhr Valley. Until the year 2018, public subsidies of nearly 300 billion Euros were invested and made the German coal production relatively independent from the development of the world market prices.[19] The use of domestic coal especially in the coal-power plants and the regional heavy steel industry offered the companies and their employees planning security by special laws (e.g. Kohlepfennig & Verstromungsgesetz 1965, Hüttenvertrag 1969). Under the government of the great coalition of the Christian Democratic Union (CDU) and SPD (Economics and Finance Minister Schiller from SPD) and the implementation of Keynesian economic policy the Law for the Adaptation and Recovery of the German Coal Industry and the German Coalmining Areas was passed on 15 May 1968. This law was the basis for the foundation of Ruhrkohle AG (RAG) on 27 of November 1968 with the merger of the remaining 23 mining companies into one private–public enterprise.[20] Private companies and the Federal Republic of Germany joined the RAG as contracting parties. The state guaranteed the business organization of the RAG and took over the debt of the old companies. Since not all companies agreed with the parity co-determination structure in the advisory board of the new company initially some companies did not participate. But finally, the remaining mining companies joined the RAG AG in October 1969. In this economic and political context, the workers' representatives and the unionists from IG Bergbau and Energie secured a very significant political influence in the decision-making structures of the new enterprise. On the one hand, the RAG is subject to parity co-determination at the advisory board. On the other hand, the position of the labor director was installed not at only at enterprise level but also on

[19] Own estimation on: Deutscher Bundestag (2017): Dokumente – Kohlesubventionen, under: www.bundestag.de (5. 11. 2019).

[20] Werner Abelshauser, *Der Ruhrkohlenbergbau seit 1945: Wiederaufbau, Krise, Anpassung*, (München: Beck, 1984).

each single plant level. The peculiarity was that the right to determine the position of a labor director was the responsibility only of the union. The employees of the single mines became also employees of the Ruhrkohle AG at the same time. Thus, the structural condition was developed that in the case of expected further mine closures, the workforce did not have to be afraid of unemployment and social uncertainty. Ruhrkohle AG, as the owner of a closed mine, continued to operate. The younger workforce of closed mines was distributed to the other mines of the Ruhr Valley, while older employees received attractive offers of early retirement. The distribution happened while maintaining the current working and employment conditions. Any risk of unemployment and the fear of social decline were excluded formally until the shutdown of the last coal mine in the Ruhr Valley in December 2018.

This is the time for a first interim conclusion. The political regulation of the economic and social process concerning the termination of coal mining was enabled first by the strong relationship between primary or structural power resources of miners at their specific workplaces down in the mines, where daily cooperation and lived solidarity was practized necessarily. Additionally, the secondary or organizational power could emerge from below. In the dual system of German labor relations, the coverage rate of works councils at the 157 coal mines in the Ruhr Valley was nearly 100 percent and the union density reached 98 percent. Upon these power resources, specific laws were developed which channeled the actions of works councils, labor directors and unionists. The Law on Parity Co-determination of Employees in the Supervisory & Management Boards of Companies in the Coal, Iron & Steel Industry (1951) has been one of the key institutions to regulate the structural transformation of these sectors. The double function and border position of labor directors between management, works councils and unions played a crucial in the search for social compenzation. Furthermore, the Works Constitution Act (1952) has strengthened the role of the works councils legally by allowing them to participate in developing social plans. In order to anchor political regulation beyond a single coalmine, political organizations were required to fulfil the objectives of the employees in the parliaments on regional and federal level. Due to a close cooperation with the Social Democratic Party and the implementation of Keynesian economic policy, a very unique process of socially embedded economic transition of the energy sector in the Ruhr until today could be realized. This very special process of political regulation of economic restructuring cannot be found in any other economic sector in Germany.

Weak Power Resources: The Shut Down of the Automobile Plant in the Ruhr Valley

In 1962, at the first peak of the coal mining crisis, the first and only automobile plant of General Motors/Opel was opened in the Ruhr Valley. It was the second plant of GM/Opel in Germany beside the main plant in Rüsselsheim. Together with the foundation of a university in 1964—the Ruhr-University Bochum—and the opening of the largest shopping center in Europe at this time—the Ruhr-Park in Bochum, these facilities symbolized a structural change of this traditional industrial region between coal and steel. It meant the auto-mobilization of the whole region. At the beginning of 1960s, for the first time the Ruhr Valley experienced the introduction of mass production structures with a formerly unknown tayloristic-fordistic organization of work. The production of automobiles signified an important step to successfully overcome the coal crisis. Furthermore, the mass product—the car—itself mobilized the entire region. The plant started with 7000 workers at the assembly lines, most of them former miners or children of miner families. They earned high fordistic wages which enabled them to buy their own car, the legendary Opel Kadett.[21]

At the beginning of the 1990s—at the economic peak after the German unification—the GM/Opel plant employed more than 22,000 workers. They were organized up to 98 percent by the Industrial Union of Metalworkers (IG Metall), represented by generations of conflictive works councils who had experiences also with the labor relations of the coalmines. For nearly 30 years, the employees of the GM/Opel plant counted with strong primary structural and organizational power resources which also positively influenced the conclusion of collective agreements at plant level as well as for the complete metal sector of North Rhine-Westphalia. Thus, the plant was embedded socially in this traditional industrial region with its special labor and conflict culture (Fig. 8.3).

[21] Manfred Wannöffel, *Sachzwang Japan: Zum arbeitsorganisatorischen Umbruch in der internationalen Automobilindustrie* (Münster: Verlag Westfälisches Dampfboot, 1991); Manfred Wannöffel, '50 Jahre Opel-Werke in Bochum'/ 50 Years Opel Works in Bochum', in Schauspielhaus Bochum und Urbane Künste Ruhr (eds.), *Schichtwechsel. Das Detroit-Projekt: Ein Handbuch für Städte im Wandel / A Handbook for Changing Cities*, (Berlin: Theater der Zeit, 2015), pp. 27–30.

Werbeanzeige der Adam Opel AG 1962

Fig. 8.3 Young and agil: Opel Kadett overcomes the mining crisis (*Source* Opel archive Bochum)

The history of economic success could at first compensate the employment in the coal mine sector. However, that changed with the deep crisis of General Motors against the successful lean production system of Toyota (Toyotism) on global level and the heavy reductions of GM/Opel market share in Europe with the consequence of plant closures in Portugal, Sweden and Belgium during the first decade of 2000. First closure threats reached GM/Opel in the Ruhr in 2004.[22] Because of their structural and organizational power resources the workforce answered with a wildcat strike for seven days which the works councils finally called 'information days' according to the formal regulations of the Works Constitution Act. During the next ten years until the final shut down in December 2014, works council, experts from the workforce and the Industrial Union of Metalworkers developed numerous innovative concepts for maintaining the productions site and employment in the Ruhr Valley. The works council created publicity while regional networks with scientists from the surrounding universities developed technical innovations for the component manufacturing and initiated the development of an electric vehicle in cooperation with Bochum University of Applied Science. This prototype was manufactured using components from the GM/Opel plant until 2009–10. The results of these innovation strategies were presented to the GM/Opel management at the German headquarter in Rüsselsheim and also at employee meetings together with members of the regional government on several occasions—in the expectation of receiving political support for the diverse rescue initiatives.

Due to bankruptcy of General Motors in the USA in June 2009 and its reorganization strategies in Europe, the employees had to experience that the union and federal policies did not have enough political power to prevent the plant closures operated by an international corporation. Neither workplace innovation nor product innovation strategies of the works council led to an increase in societal power resources since there was no longer a close relationship between works councils, trade union and politics. A relationship that still characterized the political regulation of the coal crisis before. On the contrary, in 2013 a political event unique for the history of industrial relations in Germany and only understandable in the context of experienced labor conflicts in the Ruhr Valley happened.

[22] Antje Blöcker, Mark Esteban Palomo and Manfred Wannöffel, *Chancen und Grenzen nachhaltiger Standorte- und Beschäftigungssicherung: Das Beispiel der Opel-Standorte in Bochum* (Düsseldorf: Hans-Böckler-Stiftung, 2013).

In March 2013, the workforce of the GM/Opel plant rejected a collective bargaining agreement negotiated between the Industrial Union of Metalworkers and General Motors regarding the modalities of the planned closure of the Ruhr plant in December 2016 by a large majority of over 78 percent. The employees argued that this collective agreement only secured the survival of three other GM plants in Germany by the partial acquisition of the Bochum production. Due to the rejection of the collective agreement the workforce even accepted the premature closure two years earlier in December 2014. After ten years of developing innovative labor strategies and bargaining concession, the employees obviously were unable to sign and accept their own closure and their transition to unemployment as well as economic and social insecurity. One of the decisive reasons for the closure of GM/Opel plant in the Ruhr Valley was the lack of cooperation and solidarity between the workers of the other three Opel plants in Germany who finally subordinated themselves to the logic of market competition. The expectations of the employees and the works council to develop innovative labor policies on one hand and that unions and political representatives would have enough institutional and societal power to balance the interests of different production sites on the other hand had to be disappointed. Workforce surveys conducted in 2013 already indicated a major loss of confidence in the political agency of national unions and political parties in the face of increasing global competition.[23] Lack of experienced cooperation and lived solidarity but more competition among employees and disappointed expectations of the societal power resources of unions to intervene in political decision-making process—the decline of the automobile production in the Ruhr Valley stands for the deep loss of confidence of growing sections of employees regarding to political promise for social balance.

The results of accompanying research present innovative labor policies of local works council but also the reduced societal power of them as well as regional and national unions in the context of global competition, even if the primary and structural power of employees and their local representatives were well developed. Finally, the research analyzed

[23] Antje Blöcker, Mark Esteban Palomo and Manfred Wannöffel, *Chancen und Grenzen nachhaltiger Standorte- und Beschäftigungssicherung: Das Beispiel der Opel-Standorte in Bochum*, (Düsseldorf: Hans-Böckler-Stiftung, 2013).

collective agreements between unions and employer organizations which protected only a part of the workforce from the risks of unemployment and social uncertainty in the context of politics of market liberalization.[24]

Conclusions and a View into Future Developments

It must be stated that the political regulation of the mining crisis in the Ruhr Valley has been a unique case of a socially embedded economic restructuring process so far. Stefan Berger states that the Ruhr Valley is being 'admired by the whole world'.[25] This success story from 1957 until 2018 was based on the close linkage between the primary power resources of the miners with their secondary power through a high degree of union organization, and the institutional embedding of employment through co-determination at plant level by works councils and enterprise level (parity co-determination in the advisory boards) by labor directors and collective agreements. The relative societal power of the miners was reflected in the political electoral successes of parties that were close to the goals of social democracy based on social justice and balance, in particular according to the social performance of the miners in post-war period. Without the support of politicians of allied parties and economic-social policy of the state with a Keynesian welfare state orientation, this form of restructuring by effective laws and the founding of a private–public company by the state in 1968 would not have been possible. Reflecting the assumptions of the power resource theory, the interaction of these various levels of employees' power resources starting from below, the workplace, plant and enterprise level, via the union organization into the state and federal parliaments, has been of particular importance.

This is evident in the example of the closure of the Ruhr Valleys' first and only automobile factory in 2014 which in the beginning was a success story for overcoming the mining crisis. The accompanying research worked out a very strong primary power of employees and conflictive works councils during ten years of struggle processes of shut

[24] Antje Blöcker, Mark Esteban Palomo and Manfred Wannöffel, *Chancen und Grenzen nachhaltiger Standorte- und Beschäftigungssicherung: Das Beispiel der Opel-Standorte in Bochum* (Düsseldorf: Hans-Böckler-Stiftung, 2013).

[25] Stefan Berger, 'Ruhrgebiet: Bewundert von der ganzen Welt', in *DIE ZEIT*, 19 December 2018, p. 19.

down. Employees and their representatives were very active in developing innovation processes at plant level together with experts from regional universities (component manufacturing and electromobility) to maintain the production site in the Ruhr Valley. Due to the global crisis of General Motors in the USA they experienced that also results of their institutional power—collective agreements between the union and the employer organization—could turn against their interest under the condition of rough global market competition. Finally, workers' representatives of other German and European plants of GM/Opel have subordinated themselves to the logic of competition to maintain their production sites first. Cooperation and solidarity among the workers' representatives of the different plants did not take place any longer. The isolated resistance of the employees and their exercises of democracy at the workplace of the Ruhr Valley's automobile plant against the agreement of closure in 2013 will be part of the labor history of entire Germany.

But what does remain after the closure of the coal mines and of large mass production sites and the ongoing crisis of heavy steel industry in the Ruhr Valley? And what does this mean for future development of labor relations? Already today and in the future universities and universities of applied sciences, which themselves are the results of the mining crisis have assumed the role of structural policy actors. The intention is, on the one hand, to generate value added and employment from the knowledge of the universities by setting up new companies in the Ruhr Valley and, on the other hand, to attract and establish companies around the scientific cores. Knowledge will be the raw material of future economic and social development in the Ruhr Area. However, this new form of more academic employment and mainly belonging to science or service sectors are very different from the employment that was predominant in the coal, heavy steel and automobile sector (Fig. 8.4).

The slowly growing areas of a knowledge-based economy with a large proportion of scientific institutions, small companies and academically educated employees have not yet been characterized by establishments of works councils and a high level of trade union membership. Thus, the dynamic of economic structural change influences also a restructuring of labor relations in the Ruhr Valley. The collective agreement between Thyssenkrupp and the union from 2017 that was mentioned earlier could be achieved based on the organizational power resource of a trade union density of 98.3 percent and the institutional power of a labor director sent from the Metal union. The union membership in a newly settled

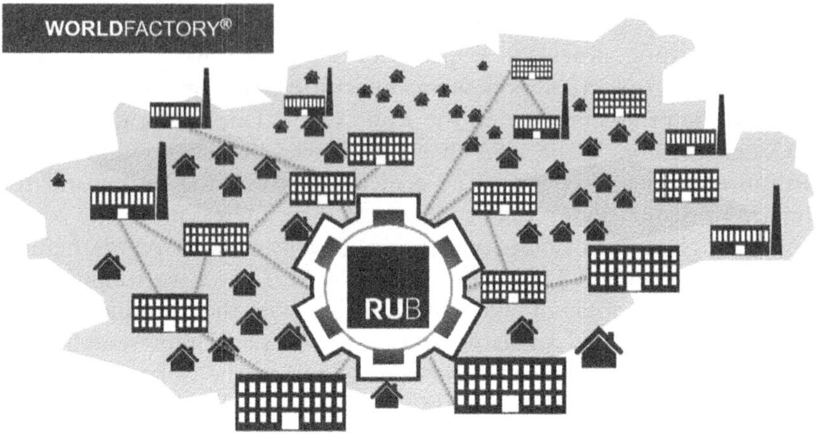

Fig. 8.4 Worldfactory: Universities as structural policy actors (*Source* Ruhr-University Bochum)

company of data processing, start-ups in the field of data security, and in the universities lies between 1.1% and 2.0%.

In order to influence the employment, working and participation conditions of the upcoming knowledge-based economy in the Ruhr Valley, it is therefore necessary to go beyond the traditional power resources of the employees.

The approach of social movement unionism opens channels to new allies from regional civil society who are jointly committed to shaping a socio-ecological and socially embedded economic change and, finally, to develop a liveable, colorful and cosmopolitan science and business metropole Ruhr.

References

W. Abelshauser (1984) *Der Ruhrkohlenbergbau seit 1945: Wiederaufbau, Krise, Anpassung* (München: Beck, 1984).

S. Berger (2018) 'Ruhrgebiet: Bewundert von der ganzen Welt', DIE ZEIT, 19 December, p. 19.

S. Berger (2019) 'Was ist das Ruhrgebiet? Eine historische Standortbestimmung', APuZ (I-III), pp. 4–11.

S. Berger, L. Pries and M. Wannöffel (eds) (2019) *The Palgrave Handbook of Workers' Par-ticipation at Plant Level* (New York: Springer Nature America).

A. Blöcker, M. Esteban Palomo and M. Wannöffel (2013) *Chancen und Grenzen nachhaltiger Standorte- und Beschäftigungssicherung: Das Beispiel der Opel-Standorte in Bochum* (Düs-seldorf: Hans-Böckler-Stiftung, 2013).

Bundesministerium der Justiz und für Verbraucherschutz: Bundesamt für Justiz (2018) Works Constitution Act, https://www.gesetze-im-internet.de/englisch_betrvg/englisch_betrvg.html#p0452, date accessed 4 November 2019.

H. Croon and K. Utermann (1958) *Zeche und Gemeinde: Untersuchungen über den Struktur-wandel einer Zechengemeinde im nördlichen Ruhrgebiet* (Tübingen: Mohr).

R. Edwards (1981) *Herrschaft im modernen Produktionsprozeß* (Frankfurt/Main and New York: Campus-Verlag).

G. Esping-Andersen (1990) *The Three Worlds of Welfare Capitalism* (Princeton: Princeton University Press). Gøsta

Faulenbach, B. (1987) 'Montanindustrielle Struktur und politische Kultur im Ruhrgebiet: Zur neueren Diskussion', in Werner Fricke et. al. (eds.), *Jahrbuch Arbeit und Technik Nordrhein-Westfalen 1987* (Bonn: Neue Gesellschaft, 1987), pp. 411–422.

Faulenbach, B. (1989) 'Mitbestimmung und politische Kultur im Ruhrgebiet', in Helmut Mar-tens and Gerd Peter (eds.), *Mitbestimmung und Demokratisierung: Stand und Perspektiven der Forschung* (Wiesbaden: Deutscher Universitäts-Verlag, 1989), pp. 216–228.

F. Fürstenberg (1958). 'Der Betriebsrat: Strukturanalyse einer Grenzinstitution', *Kölner Zeitschrift für Soziologie & Sozialpsychologie* 10 (1958), pp. 418–429.

W. Korpi (1978) *The Working Class in Welfare Capitalism: Work, Unions and Politics in Sweden* (London and Boston: Routledge & Kegan Paul, 1978).

W. Milert and R. Tschirbs (2012) *Die andere Demokratie: Betriebliche Interessenvertretung in Deutschland 1848 bis 2008* (Essen: Klartext-Verlag, 2012).

W. Müller-Jentsch (1995) 'Auf dem Prüfstand: Das deutsche Modell der industriellen Beziehungen', *Industrielle Beziehungen*, II (I), pp. 11–24.

W. Müller-Jentsch (2017) *Strukturwandel der industriellen Beziehungen: ‚Industrial Citizenship' zwischen Markt und Regulierung*, 2nd edn (Wiesbaden: Springer VS).

W. Müller-Jentsch and P. Ittermann (2000) *Industrielle Beziehungen: Daten, Zeitreihen, Trends 1950–1999* (Frankfurt/M. and New York: Campus-Verlag, 2000).

CHAPTER 9

The Role of Labor Relations in the Process of Deindustrialization in Italy's Northwest

Gilda Zazzara

Introduction

The role played by the trade unions in the dismantling of the large-scale industry in Italy has not become yet an object of historical research. There is a quite fair amount of literature about restructuring processes since the 1970s, issued either by the unions themselves or by labor relations' scholars, mostly as case studies. The reasons of the underestimation of economic and social history are manifold and complex: they lie in the overall fall of interest toward the union movement, in turn a consequence of the fading of its public role, as well as in the reluctance to recognize a proper process of deindustrialization in Italy. The stronger argumentation to the refusal of the concept of deindustrialization has been based for a long time on the successful performance of the small and medium enterprises of the suburban areas of the Northwest and the regions of the

G. Zazzara (✉)
Ca' Foscari University of Venice, Venice, Italy
e-mail: gilda.zazzara@unive.it

S. Berger et al. (eds.), *Deindustrialisation in Twentieth-Century Europe*, Palgrave Studies in the History of Social Movements,
https://doi.org/10.1007/978-3-030-89631-7_9

Northeast. This reasoning has weakened after 2008 crisis, as far as also those “alternative to mass production”, has proven its limits, and closures and relocations have hit the entire industrial apparatus.

Only from the beginning of the new century, by the way, Italian trade unions have begun to adopt the word “deindustrialization” in their current language, i.e. to recognize the accomplishment, in some areas, of an irreversible structural change. For the trade unions, however, deindustrialization keep being a negative phenomenon, for both the national economy and the workers. The shift to a service economy, in fact, resulted in a general precarization of working conditions. On the national scale, trade unions still consider deindustrialization as a danger to counter with policies of re-industrialization in high-tech and eco-compatible sectors.

In the following pages, I have tried to outline some points on the unions’ answers toward the challenge of industrial decline since the 1970s. When I say unions, I mean the main national confederations (CGIL, CISL and UIL), that until 1984 formally acted in a unified way. I could not take into due consideration neither the reasons of the end of unity, nor the different “cultures of change” within the single organizations. However, I believe that even after the breakdown of the “pact of unity”, a common approach prevailed in the “conflictual management” of deindustrialization.

At the beginning, I proposed a division of the Italian deindustrialization into three periods: from the oil crisis of 1973 to the decade 1980s, marked by the unions defeat at Turin Fiat plant in 1980; the 1990s, influenced by the European integration constraints and the increasing globalization of the markets; and the new century, that, in particular after the 2008 crisis, led to a further weakening of the national industry. I then argued that the first reaction of the unions to the metamorphosis of the large-scale industry of the “economic miracle” years was characterized by a strongly political interpretation: firstly, as a reaction of the capital against the “hot autumn” achievements, then as the sunset of the “working class centrality”: the idea that industrial working class was the keystone of work rights for all, and the pivot of democracy. These processes were particularly sharp in the “industrial triangle” and early in its capital cities: I therefore briefly outlined the main features of the industrial landscape of Milan, Genoa and Turin.

I then argued that throughout the 1980s the action against deindustrialization was conducted by claiming for new investments and innovations, but above all by protecting workers from the risk of redundancy, mainly with a specific welfare device: the “cassa integrazione guadagni”, a wage replacement allowance. The agreements providing it, accorded plant by plant, were always negotiated with the unions. I believe that the Italian trade unions have played a decisive role in delaying the dismantling of large industries and in protecting the income levels of displaced workers, thus avoiding a severe social crisis, but they have failed to influence industrial policies toward high-tech sectors and to safeguard the overall employment rate in the industry.

In the 1990s, the bankrupt and privatization of State-owned enterprises, that were the main interlocutor of a trade unionism with a strong vocation toward the public initiative, deprived the unions of their most important counterpart. With the broad “concertation” agreements and “pacts for work” of those years, the unions have accepted to moderate their claims on wages and to connect them to the recovery in productivity and competitiveness. This wasn’t enough to stop deindustrialization. In the new century, the unions have missed the chance of becoming structural policy actors in the processes of transition and regeneration of former industrial areas, and in the public debate on the social consequences of deindustrialization. For instance, in Italy a reflection on the link between deindustrialization and workers’ shift toward right-wing and xenophobic position has not developed.

In conclusion, I have assumed that also the courts are becoming a place where deindustrialization is being elaborated as an undergoing process under the global capitalism. Symbolically, I mentioned the trial against the managers of Thyssen Krupp, charged with murder in the death by fire of seven workers in Turin, in 2006. According to the public prosecutor and to the unions at the shop floor, the plant was working at full capacity, but due to the forthcoming dismantling safety measures were neglected.

The “Italian Way” Toward Deindustralization

Deindustrialization in Italy is part of a continuous process divided into three separate phases. The first phase began in the wake of the 1970s oil crisis and did not reveal the full extent of its ramifications until the following decade. This had a massive impact on the core industries most dependent upon imports of raw materials— the steel, chemical and shipbuilding industries above all. It emerged as a crisis affecting large groups and entire sectors of industry, which were forced to introduce “corporate readjustment” measures in order to restore profitability and efficiency, and make massive employment cuts.[1] For some idea of the scale involved: between 1982 and 1988, the number of workers employed by the steel division of the IRI group—Italy's largest State-owned enterprise—fell from 120,000 to 60,000[2]; between 1980 and 1983, the number of employees working for Italtel (formerly known as SIT-Siemens) dropped from 29,000 to 17,000[3]; and between 1980 and 1986 the Fiat Auto workforce went from 139,000 to 75,000 workers.[4]

The second phase began in the early 1990s. The signing of the Maastricht Treaty in 1992 required Italy to align its inflation rate with the European inflation rate as well as imposing strict limits on public expenditure with the aim of reducing debt, resulting in a major shift in industrial crisis management policies. With regard to the labor market, successive governments adopted deregulation and flexibilization measures.[5] Privatization followed by the winding-up of State-owned enterprises marked the end of the mixed economy model that had allowed Italy to be included in the category of countries with advanced economies.[6] The crisis of the large-scale enterprises was accompanied by the sustained development of the fabric of small and medium private enterprises, partly founded to meet "productive decentralization" needs, partly linked to independent dynamics of specialization in the light manufacturing sector. The regions in the Northeast became Italy's most dynamic industrial area.

The third phase took place between the late 1990s and the 2008 crisis. The fall in industrial value-added and in employment affected the

[1] Marino Regini and Charles F. Sabel (eds), *Strategie di riaggiustamento industriale*, (Bologna: il Mulino, 1989).

[2] Margherita Balconi, *La siderurgia italiana (1945–1990): Tra controllo pubblico e incentivi del mercato*, (Bologna, il Mulino, 1991), p. 404.

[3] Serafino Negrelli, "Il caso Italtel", in Marino Regini and Charles F. Sabel (eds), *Strategie di riaggiustamento industriale*, (Bologna: il Mulino, 1989), pp. 171–206, p. 171.

[4] Giuseppe Bonazzi, "Lasciare la fabbrica. Cassa integrazione e mobilità negli anni ottanta", in Arnaldo Bagnasco (ed.), *La città dopo Ford: Il caso Torino*, (Turin: Bollati Boringhieri, 1990), pp. 23–45, p. 30.

[5] Paolo Barbieri and Stefani Scherer, "Labor Market Flexibilization and its Consequences in Italy", in *European Sociological Review*, no. 6, (2009), pp. 677–692.

[6] Giuseppe Berta, *Che fine ha fatto il capitalismo italiano?*, (Bologna: il Mulino, 2016); Roberto Artoni (ed.), *Storia dell'IRI*, vol. IV, *Crisi e privatizzazione 1990–2002*, (Rome and Bari: Laterza, 2013).

entire country, reducing the traditional regional disparities and differences in scale. Small and medium enterprises adopted delocalization strategies moving production abroad and linked to the intensification of globalization and the opening of new markets. The presence of foreign shareholders rose while historic national entrepreneurial dynasties left the scene. Entire sectors were radically downsized and the attempt to bring about an industrial turnaround toward a production with a greater technological content failed, even in those areas where Italy was ahead of its competitors: that is, in the electronics, aeronautics, chemical and automotive sectors.[7] Although the country—political and economic actors and trade unionists included— continued to describe itself as "Europe's second largest manufacturing nation", it was impossible to ignore the deterioration and fragility of the productive fabric.

From 2008, the year of the international economic crisis, the term "deindustrialization" became a permanent part of the vocabulary of trade unions. In 2012, during a visit to the Maserati plant owned by the Fiat Chrysler Automobiles group, Maurizio Landini, general secretary of CGIL, stated that Turin "was no longer the city of Fiat and of work but was fast becoming the city of unemployment and deindustrialization".[8] After a protest staged in Milan by the struggling Lombard metalworking companies, Marco Bentivogli—general secretary of CISL, Italy's second largest trade union confederation—stressed that "the consequences of this crisis are familiar to us all. They are the triple curse of unemployment, deindustrialization and inequality".[9] Few months ago, again Landini referred to deindustrialization as a matter of fact, that has eroded workers' rights.[10]

Although it was not until very recently that trade unionists began to describe Italy as a country definitively experiencing a process of deindustrialization, the history of their response to the erosion of the importance of industry in the economy and of the working class in society is far longer. This "challenge to decline" began in Northwest Italy.

[7] Luciano Gallino, *La scomparsa dell'Italia industriale*, (Turin: Einaudi, 2003).

[8] Carlotta Rocci, "Landini. Torino non è più la città del lavoro", in *La Repubblica* (Turin edition), 13 December 2013 https://torino.repubblica.it/cronaca/2013/12/13/news/landini_torino_non_pi_la_citt_del_lavoro-73526480/ [accessed 2 September 2019].

[9] *"Il sistema-paese preferisce le rendite agli investimenti"*, interview given by Marco Bentivogli to Andrea Di Stefano, June 2015, https://www.fim-cisl.it/2015/06/24/bentivogli-il-sistema-paese-preferisce-le-rendite-agli-ivestimenti/ [accessed 2 September 2019].

[10] Roberto Mania, "Landini. Un'alleanza con governo e imprese per impedire che il Paese si sbricioli ", in *La Repubblica*, 8 December 2019.

Trade Unions in the Wake of Restructurings

Seen from the perspective of the Northwest, Italy, a relative latecomer to industrial modernity is also an early-comer to the post-industrial transition, one experiencing "premature deindustrialization".[11] Lombardy, Piedmont and Liguria, the three regions making up the so-called industrial triangle, went from being in the vanguard of nineteenth century industrialization to becoming forerunners of deindustrialization, already experiencing a decline in their production systems from the second half of the 1970s onwards. Considering that trade unionism in this area was hegemonic both in political terms and with regard to the size of these organizations, the experiences and responses developed in this part of the country have tended to steer the positions of the entire trade union movement, at least until recent years.

In Italy, the triggering of the processes that we now recognize as harbingers of the widespread deindustrialization that took place in the West—the 1973 oil crisis that was connected in turn to the emergence of new political and economic global actors—took place when the trade unions were at the height of their power, in a context of industrial relations that were still very conflictual and experiencing a strong tendency toward decentralization, and in a context of unity between the leading trade union confederations (CGIL, CISL and UIL).

The industrialist stamp of the Italian trade unions influenced the ways in which this decline was interpreted and negotiated as well as the timescales. For the men and women who had risen to become trade union leaders during the struggles of the conflictual cycle of the 1968–1972 period that were driven by the big factories apogee, recognizing that this development model might have entered a downward spiral was particularly difficult. In the words of Vittorio Foa, one of the key figures in Turinese trade unionism, even in the 1970s, when he looked at the huge steel-making plants he had the feeling that "this would continue to be the model of our modernity for another three hundred years at least".[12]

The Italian debate was distinguished by a highly political interpretation of structural change. There was a keen perception of the link between the decline of large factories and the weakening of the trade unions, on

[11] Aris Accornero, *Ancora il lavoro*, conversation with Patrizio Di Nicola, (Rome: Ediesse, 1995), pp. 115–116.

[12] Vittorio Foa, *Passaggi*, (Turin: Einaudi, 2000), p. 148.

the one hand, and between the "de-workerization" and the crisis of the political left, on the other.[13] Deindustrialization was initially experienced more as the decline of "working class centrality" in Italian society than as a structural change in the composition of subordinate work; more as a lacerating phenomenon of the unmaking of class than as a remaking of the foundations for consensus for workers organizations.[14] The sharp drop in the number of workers employed in industry was inevitably reflected in a fall in the numbers of union members who were blue-collars that was compensated for by pensioners and civil servants.[15]

Deindustrialization means that trade unions must cope with profound changes to their support and representation base, with consequences that are still uncertain. In a long poem on the narrative arc of the working class, the Lombard unionist Alberto Bellocchio expressed the difficulties intrinsic to this change: "Deindustrialization, advanced tertiary sector, new social classes: we searched for them, maybe rather aimlessly. It was easier to encounter them in books or magazines; in reality there was no way of contacting them. Without factories, we are not capable of doing so".[16] Bruno Trentin, another key figure in Italian trade union history, defined this condition as part of the mourning process for the "orphans of Fordism".[17]

The trade unions have reacted to the industrial crisis by developing various forms of "defensive bargaining" in the conviction that "a trade unionist knows that they have to do everything necessary, even drawing up exacting agreements, in order to keep the factory doors open".[18] In fact, the closure of a factory represents the "90th minute for a trade

[13] Sandro Antoniazzi, "Lettera alla classe operaia", in *Prospettiva sindacale*, no. 51, (1984), pp. 110–134; Aris Accornero and Nino Magna, "Il lavoro dopo la classe", in *Stato e mercato*, no. 17, (1986), pp. 253–270.

[14] Beverly J. Silver, Sahan Savas Karatasli, "Historical dynamics of capitalism and labor movements", in Donatella Della Porta and Mario Diani (eds), *The Oxford handbook of Social Movements*, (Oxford, NY: Oxford University Press, 2015), pp. 133–145.

[15] Mimmo Carrieri and Paolo Feltrin, *Al bivio: Lavoro, sindacato e rappresentanza nell'Italia d'oggi*, (Rome: Donzelli, 2016).

[16] Alberto Bellocchio, *Sirena operaia: Con una lettera di Vittorio Foa*, (Milan: Il Saggiatore, 2000).

[17] Bruno Trentin, *La città del lavoro: Sinistra e crisi del fordismo*, (Milan: Feltrinelli, 1997), p. 52.

[18] Marco Bentivogli, *Abbiamo rovinato l'Italia? Perché non si può fare a meno del sindacato*, (Rome: Castelvecchi, 2017), new revised and expanded edition, p. 72.

unionist, marking the end of the match".[19] Throughout the various stages of industrial decline, even as the balance of power between capital and labor gradually shifted, trade unionists have striven to keep the banner of resistance flying, to "never resign themselves to decline", vigorously opposing the complete closure of companies, even at the cost of accepting drastic downsizing.[20] At a social level, this position has taken the shape of providing income safeguards for workers who have been made redundant while at a political level it involved exerting constant pressure to convince the government currently in power to introduce public investment policies.

Northwest Metamorphosis

For some decades now, the capital cities of the regions in the industrial triangle have symbolized the Italy of "blue-collar workers" and the political and material cultures of factory workers.[21] Milan, along with adjoining municipality of Sesto San Giovanni—defined the "Italian Stalingrad" due to the importance of Communist culture-, offered the richest and most complex industrial fabric comprising everything from the car industry to electromechanics, from steel manufacturing to the chemical industry. Turin, on the other hand, was Italy's only Motor City thanks to the role of Fiat and its allied industries. In the post-war period, Genoa's identity as a port was overshadowed by what was to become the country's largest State-owned steel and ship-building industry.

Capitals of the "economic miracle", these cities are also palimpsests of the country's political history and the myth of the worker. In 1892, the Socialist party was founded in Genoa and in 1960 the city became the setting for the encounter between anti-fascism and the new working class that grew out of the post-war boom. In the 1920s, Turin was the capital of the factory councils movement and the cradle of the Italian Communist Party, and it was in its plants that Taylorist methods were first introduced to Italy. Milan was the seedbed for pioneering institutions of Socialist reformism: from the Società Umanitaria to the first "Chamber

[19] Ibid.

[20] Guglielmo Epifani and Carla Cantone, *Non rassegnarsi al declino: Politiche industriali per competitività e sviluppo*, (Rome: Ediesse, 2005).

[21] Andrea Sangiovanni, *Tute blu: La parabola operaia nell'Italia repubblicana*, (Rome: Donzelli, 2006).

of Labor". During Fascism, it was in the factories of these three cities that groups of brave political militants kept the flames of democracy lit, providing Nazi-occupied Europe with the heroic example of a strike for peace and justice in 1944. These class organization traditions nurtured the struggles of the 1960s, culminating in the "hot autumn" of 1969 and the attainment of extraordinary rights and powers for salaried workers and their organizations.[22]

Already by the mid-1970s the "industrial triangle" was experiencing a structural change. In the space of only thirty years—from 1971 to 2001—the percentage of workers employed in manufacturing industries fell from 56.7% to 37.4%.[23] If we consider only large factories, then the fall in the number of workers was 66%.[24] The number of industrial workers fell from 2.5 million to 1.8 million, which is exactly the number of service employees in 1971, which rose to 3 million thirty years later.[25]

The change was fastest and most evident in the regional capitals. The first city to transform itself was Milan, which took the first decisive steps to change from a workers' capital to a financial and fashion capital in the early 1980s. This shift was also noticed by the London *Times*, which dedicated a special report to the city and its new bosses including one Silvio Berlusconi, described as being at the head of one of Italy's most interesting post-industrial empires.[26]Turin, whose transformation was marked by the endless restructuring of Fiat and of its ubiquitous satellite industries, struggled to accept the decline of its industrial identity.[27] Genoa was the city most "afflicted" by the dismantlement of its production

[22] For an overview of the history of labor in Italy, see Stefano Musso, *Storia del lavoro in Italia dall'Unità ad oggi*, (Venice: Marsilio, 2002), revised edition 2011, p. 2.

[23] Giampaolo Vitali, "Gli indicatori della trasformazione", in Giuseppe Berta (ed.), *La questione settentrionale: Economia e società in trasformazione*, (Milan: Feltrinelli, 2007), pp. 143–173, p. 147.

[24] Consiglio italiano per le scienze sociali, *Libro bianco per il Nord Ovest: Dall'economia della manifattura all'economia della conoscenza*, (Venice: Marsilio, 2007), p. 56.

[25] Ibid., p. 59.

[26] Paolo Morando, *'80: L'inizio della barbarie*, (Rome and Bari: Laterza, 2016), p. 130.

[27] Marco Revelli, *Non ti riconosco: Un viaggio eretico nell'Italia che cambia*, (Turin: Einaudi, 2016), in particular Chapter 1, "Torino. La città promessa e la città perduta", pp. 21–70.

system.[28] Despite the sound industrial relations distinguishing this area with its publicly owned industries, there was a far greater negative impact in terms of urban and social decline that was more strongly perceived by the city's inhabitants.[29]

The response of the regional productive fabric was also very different. Milan's shift to the tertiary sector proceeded at the same pace as growth in the provincial areas: despite the structural changes in the size of businesses, Lombardy remained Italy's most industrialized region.[30] Turin's domination by a single sector meant that it struggled to introduce productive diversification to the region's economic system. In Liguria, on the other hand, the overwhelming weight of State industry hindered the development of a dynamic, autonomous network of smaller enterprises.[31]

Labor Relations in a Context of Industrial Decline

Italian trade unions reacted to the crisis and to the restructuring of large-scale industry by adopting similar positions and using similar words, even after the breach of their "pact of unity" in 1984, which had been one of the most important outcomes of the cycle of struggles that took place in the late 1960s. Before the 1973 oil crisis, the first signs of danger took the shape of "productive delocalization". Even the highest echelons of the union organizations saw the outsourcing of entire departments and processes to smaller companies as the "payback for workers' actions".[32] While undoubtedly justified, this political interpretation, in terms of "capitalist restructuring", led to the a priori defense of large

[28] Fabrizio Loreto, *Il sindacato nella città ferita: Storia della Camera del lavoro di Genova negli anni sessanta e settanta*, (Rome: Ediesse, 2016).

[29] Paolo Arvati, *Oltre la città divisa: Gli anni della ristrutturazione a Genova*, (Genova: Sagep, 1988); Paride Rugafiori, "Ascesa e declino di un sistema imprenditoriale", in Antonio Gibelli and Paride Rugafiori (eds), *La Liguria*, (Turin: Einaudi, 1994), pp. 255–333.

[30] Luigi Vergallo, "Deindustrializzazione e nuovi assetti produttivi: il caso lombardo (1971–2001)", in *Storia in Lombardia*, XXVI, no. 2, (2006), pp. 119–153.

[31] Marco Doria, "Economia mista e deindustrializzazione", in Giovanni Assereto and Marco Doria (eds), *Storia della Liguria*, (Rome and Bari: Laterza, 2007), pp. 266–283.

[32] Bruno Trentin, "Conclusioni", in Lucio Libertini and Bruno Trentin (eds), *L'industria italiana alla svolta: Sindacato, partiti e grande capitale di fronte alla crisi*, (Bari: De Donato, 1975), pp. 168–169.

factories that prevented trade unions—especially the militant leadership of Northwest Italy— from rising to the challenge of extending safeguards and representation in small and medium enterprises.[33]

However, the crisis also helped to extend the debate from the national conflict between capital and labor to wider scenarios of international division of labor. In 1976, while addressing a group of trade union executives during a conference on the crisis in Piedmont, Lucio Libertini, one of the leading exponents of political workerism (*operaismo*), stated that the driving sectors of the Italian post-war boom (domestic appliances and cars) would end up by moving to emerging countries. The only way to protect Italy from the risk of deindustrialization—although Libertini did not use this term—was to radically overhaul the production system and redirect it toward high-tech production areas like electronics and energy. He warned unionists that "it would not be the first time in history that a leading economic area began a decline from which there would be no return".[34]

In these years of crisis, calls for the development of a "new industrial policy" became the cornerstone of the trade unions. Such a process required considerable involvement of the State, especially with the aim of reducing the divide between North and South. The reform of State shareholding, sector by sector economic planning and loans for the turnaround of businesses became key aspects of union demands. They also requested the right to information and control of investments to be included in the first part of national and corporate employment contracts in order to involve workers in industrial strategies. In 1977, the trade unions supported a major bill for the public funding of enterprises experiencing difficulties. Almost ten years later, they recognized that only 5% of the funds disbursed had actually been allocated to advanced sectors like electronics and precision tool engineering. The bulk of the funding had gone to the North to combat the crisis in traditional manufacturing sectors.[35]

[33] Fabrizio Barca and Marco Magnani, *L'industria fra capitale e lavoro: Piccole e grandi imprese dall'autunno caldo alla ristrutturazione*, (Bologna: il Mulino, 1989).

[34] Lucio Libertini, "Introduzione", in Lucio Libertini and Bruno Trentin (eds), *L'industria italiana alla svolta: Sindacato, partiti e grande capitale di fronte alla crisi*, (Bari: De Donato, 1975), p. 9.

[35] *Transizione industriale e sindacato*, supplement to *Conquiste del lavoro*, no. 11, March 1985, p. 11; see also Graziella Fornengo, *Il problema della ristrutturazione industriale: la soluzione italiana*, (Milan: Franco Angeli, 1984).

For a long time, "job guarantee"—in other words, maintaining employment levels in the North and raising levels in the South—remained a non-negotiable pillar of the "new industrial policy" requested by the unions. In 1973, the Alfa Romeo works council unanimously opposed expanding the Milan plant and suggested relocating it to southern Italy. According to Pierre Carniti, the then leader of CISL— a native Lombard who learned his trade among the Milanese metal-workers—"the defence of existing jobs [...] is the only terrain that allows us to introduce an industrial turnaround programme".[36] Speaking with one voice, the Turinese trade union leaders underlined that they considered "the defence of the rigidity of employment and of salaries [...] a general political premise or condition to be able to impact upon industrial policies".[37] Unions sought to protect salaries as well as jobs from the effects of a crisis that had led to inflation in double figures in Italy.

These were the principles underpinning the bilateral agreements drawn up between unions and employers in 1975. The first agreement increased the effectiveness of the so-called "scala mobile", a mechanism automatically adjusting wages as the cost of living increased. The second agreement extended the possibility of making use of a redundancy fund ("cassa integrazione guadagni" or CIG) set up after the war to help companies return to the peacetime economy without mass layoffs. The CIG allowed companies to reduce workers' hours by integrating their earnings with funds disbursed by the National Social Security Institute (INPS). From 1968 onwards, this fund was also extended in order to support companies' restructurings. The bilateral agreement of 1975 extended the time limits, increased the percentage of salary covered and provided for the possibility of suspending workers completely ("zero hours" CIG). It also introduced compulsory consultation procedures with union representatives with the aim of protecting workers from discriminatory layoffs and of developing forms of "rotation" to guarantee the solidaristic obligation between employees in the same unit. The trade unions presented the

[36] Pierre Carniti, "Occupazione. Asse portante delle lotte per i contratti", in *Conquiste del lavoro*, no. 20, September 1975, p. 15.

[37] Contribution by Giovanni Avonto on behalf of Cgil-Cisl-Uil Torino, in Lucio Libertini, "Introduzione", in Lucio Libertini and Bruno Trentin (eds), *L'industria italiana alla svolta: Sindacato, partiti e grande capitale di fronte alla crisi*, (Bari: De Donato, 1975), p. 83.

CIG agreement, which was swiftly turned into law, as the historic attainment of the "guaranteed wage" and as a variable that was independent of the economic cycle and productivity performance. The 1975 agreement implemented numerous corporate agreements guaranteeing the salaries of suspended workers, inspired by the agreement signed the previous year with the State-owned automobile group Alfa Romeo, which employed 44,000 workers throughout Italy, in which CIG compensation was equal to 90% of a standard wage.[38]

The CIG proved to be something of a double-edged sword: on the one hand, in combination with the "scala mobile", it protected workers' living standards and kept the specter of collective layoffs at bay; on the other hand, its indiscriminate use turned it from a conjunctural device into a form of disguised unemployment benefit. In the large factories in particular, it ended up by aggravating relations between shop floor delegates and national unions. A few years after the agreement, there was a paradoxical situation at the Alfa Romeo plant in Milan where a number of workers who had been put in CIG with a trade union agreement went to court and were recognized as victims of a discriminatory provision agreed upon by their representatives.[39]

The lingering crisis caused polarization within the workers' movement: between the upper echelons who were increasingly inclined to adopt forms of concession bargaining and the grassroots, especially in more combative plants, which feared threats to recently acquired rights considered to be non-negotiable. Already in 1978, with the so-called turning point of EUR (after the neighborhood in Rome where the decision was made), the federation heads had steered the movement toward a more moderate position. Luciano Lama, the Communist General Secretary, announced the end of the concept of the "guaranteed wage", even suggesting that in a situation of crisis, companies had the right to sack workers.[40] In a political climate of "national solidarity"—the alliance between Communists and Christian-Democrats in a pro-labor

[38] Paola Rispoli, "Salario garantito. Vince, perché è una linea giusta", in *Conquiste del lavoro*, no. 13, April 1974, pp. 14–18.

[39] Giuseppe Medusa, *L'impresa tra produttività e consenso: Il caso Alfa Romeo*, (Milan: Etas Libri, 1983).

[40] "Lavoratori stringete la cinghia", in *La Repubblica*, 24 January 1978, now in Edmondo Montali, *Luciano Lama: Il riformatore unitario. Antologia di scritti*, (Rome: Ediesse, 2017), pp. 279–287.

government-, the trade unions chose an approach based on responsibility and sacrifices, agreeing to moderate their wage claims—in other words, conflictuality—and to reach agreements on surplus staff and intercorporate mobility. In 1984, a "protocol" was signed with the public group IRI that provided for close collaboration between companies and trade unions in managing restructurings.[41]

The restructurings that took place in the 1980s affected hundreds of thousands of workers, almost all in the Northwest. Unions failed to protect jobs while guaranteeing the material conditions of workers who had been made redundant. This outcome was not only made possible by CIG but also by another powerful instrument introducing early retirement at the age of 50 by means of ad hoc legislation applying to entire sectors and relieving industries and ports of almost 140,000 workers in the space of only a few years.[42]

Toward the end of the decade, industrial relations experts recognized that the restructuring of the leading factories in the Northwest had taken place by "pushing away the perspective of decline or of radical deindustrialization".[43] The large groups had become more streamlined, and productivity and profitability were on the increase, even in State-owned enterprises. Together with the boom of small and medium enterprises in the Northeastern regions—which attracted the attention of foreign experts keen to find out more about the winning strategy that had allowed Italy to leave behind Fordism while remaining a manufacturing country[44]—the restructuring of large groups seems to have made a positive contribution to the modern image of "the world's fifth economic power". The management of corporate crises also led to the marked centralization of industrial relations, in which the defense of employment guarantees had ended up by exhausting bargaining on the issues linked to

[41] Paolo Garonna and Elena Pisani, "Il sindacalismo italiano nella transizione. La crisi del sindacalismo politico", in Richard Edwards, Paolo Garonna and Elena Pisani (eds), *Il sindacato oltre la crisi*, (Milan: Franco Angeli, 1988), pp. 219–280, p. 254.

[42] Bruno Bertona, "I costi del non lavoro", in *Conquiste del lavoro*, no. 3, January 1985, p. 8.

[43] Ida Regalia, "L'area di Sesto S. Giovanni", in Marino Regini and Charles F. Sabel (eds), *Strategie di riaggiustamento industriale*, (Bologna: il Mulino, 1989), pp. 207–248, p. 246.

[44] Michael J. Piore and Charles F. Sabel, *The Second Industrial Divide: Possibilities for Prosperity*, (New York: Basic Books, 1984).

control of working conditions, which had been the signature feature of Italian trade unionism at the height of its power.[45]

The thorny question that put pay to the logic of political exchange was the issue of the cost of labor. In 1984, industrialists launched a direct attack on the institution of the "scala mobile" with the support of the newly installed government led by Socialist Bettino Craxi. The result was to shatter trade union unity, especially after the Communist Party organized a referendum to fight the decision, leading to a serious rift between the Socialist and Communist membership of the CGIL. The referendum ended with the victory of those in favor of the abolition of the "scala mobile", with a clear majority especially in the North of Italy. The signals coming from the workers' strongholds showed that the crisis and restructurings had already brought about profound changes in the individual conditions, expectations and strategies of workers.[46]

The "Industrial Triangle" in the 1980s

In 1980, there was a serious clash between the trade unions and the management at Fiat in Turin. In a situation of extreme conflictuality among workers and a sharp slowdown in demand in the automobile market, the company decided to carry out radical restructuring. The negotiations ended with 23,000 workers being made redundant. Among those were numerous workers held to be underproductive, serial absentees or "turbulents". The works council and Turinese trade unions responded by picketing the Mirafiori plant for over a month. The dispute only ended when white-collar workers staged a "counter-demonstration" to demand a return to work and acceptance of the company's conditions. Two years later, without any fanfare, the Lingotto, the historic Fiat plant inaugurated in 1922 and landmark of the city's industrial modernity, closed its doors forever. It was later converted into a shopping arcade by a world-renowned architects' studio.[47]

[45] Paolo Perulli and Bruno Trentin (eds), *Il sindacato nella recessione: Modelli e tendenze delle politiche contrattuali in Occidente*, (Bari: De Donato, 1983).

[46] Vittorio Rieser, *Fabbrica oggi: Lo strano caso del dottor Weber e di mister Marx*, (Siena: Sisifo, 1992).

[47] On the Turinese decommissionings of the 1980s, see Egidio Dansero, *Dentro ai vuoti: Dismissione industriale e trasformazioni urbane a Torino*, (Turin: Edizioni Libreria Cortina, 1993).

Following the 1980 Fiat-Mirafiori dispute, the CIG, previously regarded as an instrument protecting workers (despite criticisms of its political use as a "strike-prevention" tool),[48] went from being a temporary work suspension measure to becoming a structural method for the reduction of the workforce. Less than a quarter of the "suspended" Fiat workers returned to the shop floor, and then only from 1987 onwards, failing to comply with the commitments provided for under the agreement.[49] A report drawn up that same year described the "restructured" factory in which workers were responsible only for themselves, subjected to suffocating management controls and where strikes were few and far between.[50]

The Fiat-Mirafiori dispute has become a watershed in the Italian workers' movement: it marked the end of a period of ongoing conflict, the decline of "worker centrality", and caused numerous rifts within the trade unions: between moderates and radicals, between shop floor delegates and local representatives, between the grassroots and upper echelons of the organizations. But most importantly of all, it broke bonds of belonging and of class solidarity, revealing the differences in resources and social capital between workers. Some of the redundant workers found better jobs, others slid into illegal work, and yet others experienced mental health issues. Many workers agreed to hand in their notice in exchange for severance pay that would allow them to embark upon the path of self-employment.[51]

This case was unique both in terms of the bitter struggles of the trade unions and in the extent of the protection measures. As mentioned before, "Turin's redundant workers enjoyed levels of protection that were

[48] Andrea Graziosi, *La ristrutturazione nelle grandi fabbriche 1973–1976*, introduction by Andrea Ginzburg, (Milan: Feltrinelli, 1979).

[49] Ada Becchi Collidà and Serafino Negrelli, *La transizione nell'industria e nelle relazioni industriali: L'auto e il caso Fiat*, (Milan: Franco Angeli, 1986); Gabriele Polo, *Il mestiere di sopravvivere*, (Rome: Editori Riuniti, 2000).

[50] Gad Lerner, *Operai: Viaggio all'interno della Fiat. La vita, le case, le fabbriche di una classe che non c'è più*, (Milan: Feltrinelli, 1988).

[51] Giuseppe Bonazzi et al., *L'espulsione tutelata: Processi di riconversione socio-lavorativa degli ex dipendenti delle grandi fabbriche*, (Turin: Ires Piemonte, 1988).

not only inconceivable at the time of the crisis of the 1930s but incomparably superior to those provided [...] in other industrialized countries".[52] At the same time, this dispute can be considered as launching the process of "Italian deindustrialization" even though Fiat did not shut down or go bankrupt. Since then, the large factories in the Northwest have continued to hemorrhage workers and the working-class dream or hope of a "lifelong" job has long since fizzled out. The dispute was also a turning point for the trade unions, marking a "syndrome of defeat" as well as the start of a more collaborative approach to restructurings.[53]

The closure of Milan's historic Pirelli tire works in 1985 was far less traumatic. Opened in 1908 in Milan's Bicocca district, the factory became a symbol of Milanese working-class culture. Under the terms of the agreement four years would pass until the plant was fully decommissioned; the company was to open a new plant in the suburbs and consolidate production in the other plants owned by the Group. Local institutions—town council, provincial and regional government—were called upon to provide support through tax benefits and by taking responsibility for decommissioned sites. Around 1500 workers who were unlikely to find another job were guaranteed redundancy pay or early retirement. After being almost unanimously approved within the factory, the agreement was presented by the national secretary of chemists, Luciano De Gaspari, who described it as "one of the high points of the encounter on restructurings, even in the field of industrial relations".[54]

The Pirelli-Bicocca agreement is an example of "deindustrialization negotiations". Firstly, it satisfied the key principle of "compensation"—in this case, the exchange between "old" and "new" jobs (the latter were decentered jobs with a greater technological content). It spread out the impact of the complete closure over a long time period, with the inevitable corollary of "checks" necessary to confirm the commitments undertaken. Finally, it could count upon what was still considered the primary aim of trade unions: that no one would be fired.

[52] Giuseppe Bonazzi, "Lasciare la fabbrica. Cassa integrazione e mobilità negli anni ottanta", in Arnaldo Bagnasco (ed.), *La città dopo Ford: Il caso Torino*, (Turin: Bollati Boringhieri, 1990), pp. 23–45, p. 25.

[53] Pio Galli and Giancarlo Pertegato, *Fiat 1980. Sindrome della sconfitta*, with an essay by Bruno Trentin, (Rome: Ediesse, 1994).

[54] Simona Vettraino, "Il passato e il futuro", in *Rassegna sindacale*, no. 13, 29 March 1985, pp. 18–20, p. 18.

Although the involvement of local institutions in labor conflicts was no new thing, what was innovative was their role in the transition of these decommissioned industrial sites toward new uses. The subsequent memorandum of understanding between the company and institutions for the birth of "technological pole" or "technocity" for the quaternary sector based on the American model received the approval of the trade unions even though they were completely excluded from its development.[55] As with many other restructuring agreements, the spreading out of closures over time and the inclusion of inevitable checks ended up by eroding the bargaining power of the trade unions. In 1989, for example, the Pirelli group announced a further 2400 layoffs in addition to those agreed upon in 1985, this time in its plants in central and southern Italy.[56]

In Genoa, the Italsider steelworks were the epicenter of deindustrialization. This huge industrial plant symbolized Italian steelmaking in the post-war period. During the years of the "economic miracle", the local community agreed to pay the price of its devastating environmental impact. The crisis gave impetus to a movement that was largely guided by women who demanded that restructuring was carried out in line with environmental sustainability aims. The city's strong working-class tradition and the presence of a public counterparty helped drive an environmentalism that did not call for the definitive closure of the factory. However, in 1988, when Italsider was privatized, this equilibrium was permanently upset. The practice of collaborative industrial relations was brushed aside by the new owners who wasted no time in closing the more obsolete plant in Campi. The threat of decommissioning weakened the trade union's environmental demands while radicalizing those of local committees and had the dramatic consequence of splitting the united front of local citizens and workers, who had been previously united in their hopes for a sustainable form of production.[57]

[55] Carlo Bellavite Pellegrini, *Pirelli: Innovazione e passione.1872–2015*, (Bologna: il Mulino, 2015), pp. 179–180.

[56] Paola Rispoli, "Situazione grave alla Pirelli. Vuole tagliare l'occupazione", in *Conquiste del lavoro*, no. 126, May 1989, p. 6.

[57] Roberto Tolaini, "Il peso dell'acciaio. Siderurgia e ambiente a Genova. 1950–2005", in Salvatore Adorno and Simone Neri Serneri (eds), *Industria, ambiente e territorio: Per una storia ambientale delle aree industriali in Italia*, (Bologna: il Mulino, 2009), pp. 87–112.

A Blurred Transition

The 1990s saw the conclusion of the unmaking of the working class employed in large industry, the class described by trade unions and left-wing parties as playing a paramount role in the country's democratic structures and its progress. At the time, it was estimated that workers in factories with over 500 employees accounted for 6% of all workers, just over 3% of employees and 2% of total employment.[58] Manual work was concentrated in small enterprises, most of which were located outside of cities, often meeting with trade union apathy and sometimes even distinguished by right-wing political inclinations.

The trade unions lost both their main interlocutors and the tools used in previous years to prevent the crisis from leading to a decline. The State-owned enterprises system was dismantled; the redundancy fund was reformed and collective layoffs were reintroduced; the "scala mobile" was abolished under an agreement between trade unions, enterprises and government. The agreements of 1992–93 ushered in the season of "concertation", with unions undertaking to link their demands for higher wages to a productivity increase and to accept flexible forms of contracts and the reform of the pensions system.[59]

The series of "employment pacts" undersigned by successive governments with the aim of promoting growth, development, investment in training and research, and an increase in jobs were not capable of turning the tide of deindustrialization. A decade of restructurings was followed by an endless succession of permanent closures without any serious "productive compensations". And the image of a class struggling against decline and for a turnaround was replaced by that of a retreating army distinguished by tones of defeat, bitterness and "nostalgia for the future".

The 1992 law banning asbestos and granting early retirement to workers exposed to this mineral for a certain number of years drove thousands of workers from the shop floor and produced yet another corporate restructuring instrument. A train of court cases for cancer deaths made people aware of the heavy price that had been paid for the country's

[58] Emilio Reyneri, *Occupati e disoccupati in Italia*, (Bologna: il Mulino, 1997), p. 85.

[59] Giuseppe Sircana, "La transizione difficile. Il sindacato nella seconda Repubblica (1992–2008)", in Carlo Vallauri (ed.), *Storia dei sindacati nella società italiana*, (Rome: Ediesse, 2008), pp. 183–219; Salvo Leonardi, "Gli anni della concertazione. Un excursus storico-politico", in *Alternative per il Socialismo*, no. 25, (2013), pp. 1–14.

modernization by workers who had now become nothing more than useless, superfluous sick bodies.

1993 was marked by the closure of Milan's historic Innocenti steel tubing plant. In a contemporary reportage we read: "The workers leave the factory. Some of them wipe away tears. One is carrying a piece of sheet metal, others take bolts, an old poster of a Lambretta, someone else has a poster of a Mini". There were the usual positive reactions of the trade unions because the closure agreement included redundancy provisions for the last 800 workers, some of whom were to be re-deployed in the commercial structures replacing the factory.[60] These different narratives reveal the disconnect between the response of the workers and that of the trade union executives; in other words the difference between deindustrialization experienced at "grassroots" level and from "the top".

The following year saw Pirelli move from the tire sector to telecommunications. The success of the operation cost the closure of 28 production sites and the laying-off of over 100,000 employees over a three-year period.[61] The workers leaving the plants hoped that they would soon be able to return, hopes that were soon dashed: "You saw workers who had been made redundant tidying away their tools because that was where everyone worked and took care of their kit […] and then you saw the companies going there to demolish everything and throw everything away; it was mortifying".[62] In 1994, the Falck company in Sesto San Giovanni, Italy's largest private steelworks, switched off its furnaces. One by one all the businesses symbolizing the workers' Milan shut down, quietly, without making a fuss, in a climate of resignation and inevitability.

In Turin, the effects of Fiat's restructuring were starting to be felt by the employees and middle management whose loyalty had been the "Trojan Horse" that broke the unity of the workers' resistance in 1980. The Lancia and Ferriere plants ceased operations and Michelin was also shut down. The number of Fiat employees in the Turin area fell by 50%: by the end of the decade Mirafiori was still a large factory, the largest in

[60] Rinaldo Gianola, *Senza fabbrica*, (Milan: Baldini & Castoldi, 1993), p. 56. "Lambretta" and "Mini" were a motorbike and a car produced by Innocenti.

[61] Carlo Bellavite Pellegrini, *Pirelli: Innovazione e passione.1872–2015*, (Bologna: il Mulino, 2015), p. 258.

[62] Story provided by Mario Danieli in Luca Rimoldi, *Lavorare alla Pirelli-Bicocca: Antropologia delle memorie operaie*, (Bologna: Archetipolibri, 2017), p. 179.

Europe in terms of surface area, but its workforce of 20,000 had fallen to a third of that employed in the plant's heyday.[63]

For Genoa, the 1990s marked the beginning of an awareness of the lasting consequences of deindustrialization: demographic decline, an aging population, youth unemployment, environmental disruption and the decay of the old city center, repopulated by an immigrant population perceived as potentially dangerous outsiders.[64] The last trace of the past was the Cornigliano steel plant, whose threat to health and the environment had long been a proven fact. However, it was not until 2005 that institutional and social actors signed an Environmental Plan agreement to shut down the blast furnaces. Under the deal secured by the trade unions, the cold rolling mills were to continue operations and workers made redundant would either be offered early retirement, professional retraining or posts in the reclamation works.

In this final rundown of Italian deindustrialization, the concept of turnaround takes on a new meaning. It did not involve reshaping an industrial model but filling its empty spaces with alternative functions intended for other social groups. This was the season of major town-planning schemes outlining a future made of workerless cities, in which industrial archaeology became the setting of cultural spaces or metropolitan leisure activities, like the Hangar Bicocca that replaced the Pirelli plant or Turin's Parco Dora, often criticized for the lack of grassroots participation.[65] In other cases, industrial archaeology was merely used as a decorative backdrop or to promote new economic interests as in the case of steel press in a square in Genoa that was repainted in the colors of the adjoining retail chain.[66]

At the start of the new millennium, the Northwest was projecting a rather blurred although largely optimistic image of itself as an industrial macroregion in transition toward a services and knowledge economy. The changes that had taken place in Turin, Italy's own monotown,

[63] Gabriele Polo, *Il mestiere di sopravvivere*, (Rome: Editori Riuniti, 2000), p. 15.

[64] Rinaldo Gianola, *Senza fabbrica*, (Milan: Baldini & Castoldi, 1993), pp. 35–54.

[65] Emiliana Armano, Carlo Alberto Dondona and Fiorenzo Ferlaino (eds), *Postfordismo e trasformazione urbana: Casi di recupero dei vuoti industriali e indicazioni per le politiche nel territorio torinese*, (Turin: Ires Piemonte-Regione Piemonte, 2016); Luca Mocarelli, "Le aree dismesse milanesi o della cancellazione del patrimonio industriale: Il caso della Bicocca", in *Patrimonio industriale*, no. 7, (2011), pp. 69–75.

[66] Michela Bompiani, "Il giallo del verde", in *La Repubblica*, 15 April 2011.

were not remotely like Detroit's urban apocalypse. The "spectrum" of deindustrialization remained at arm's length when compared to other former industrial powers like Great Britain or the United States where the dismantling of the manufacturing industry was taking place on a very different scale. People were being encouraged to adopt a positive approach to the challenge of the "new economy" rather than defending the country's supposed "industrial vocation" to the bitter end.[67]

In the wake of the 2008 crisis, the outcome of the post-industrial transition has certainly not lived up to expectations, especially when compared to results obtained by Europe's other advanced industrial regions. A recent study carried out by the Bank of Italy shows that the Northwest is the region with the slowest levels of growth, where the leap toward manufacturing and services with a high knowledge content seems to have been least successful. Most importantly, this is the region whose labor market has suffered the greatest decline: it is less accessible to women and less fair to young people; there is more precarious work and a lower-quality human capital.[68]

Along with the workers who have been laid off and those coming to terms with precarious jobs with low levels of protection, the main losers in the trade-off between industry and services are the trade unions as a social organization, bargaining agent and political subject. Their role continues to be sound and clearly delineated in industry. However, this applies more in the context of ministerial roundtables on the crisis and relocations and of workers' councils all over Italy defending their factories from the threat of closure rather than in that of corporate discussions for the control of cycles and investments, negotiations concerning wages and workloads; more among the last strongholds of the "workers' aristocracy" than among the weaker categories of temps and contract workers (often immigrants).

In the wasteland of the large-scale industry of the "triangle", trade unions are often little more than custodians of the bitter-sweet memories of "worker centrality": of the key role played by workers in the democratization of Italian society but also of the price that they paid in terms

[67] Consiglio italiano per le scienze sociali, *Libro bianco per il Nord Ovest: Dall'economia della manifattura all'economia della conoscenza*, (Venice: Marsilio, 2007).

[68] Ibid., pp. 47–54.

of their lives and health.[69] High-profile criminal trials following deaths of workers due to exposure to dangerous substances or accidents at work—in other words, demands for justice for "deindustrialized bodies"—have become an important public arena for trade unions. The ThyssenKrupp fire that took place in Turin shortly before Christmas 2007 came to symbolize the most dramatic aspect of Italian deindustrialization. After passing from hand to hand, the former Fiat factory was taken over by this huge multinational group, which decided to dismantle it only a few years later: in 2007, seven workers spanning several generations were burnt to death in burning oil.[70] Although these "decommissioning workers" were a species in danger of extinction, they were not in a protected oasis. The initial charge brought against the company's executives was one of voluntary manslaughter (later changed to "omicidio colposo al secondo grado" or second-degree negligent homicide), motivated by the belief that the decommissioning programe had resulted both in accelerated work rhythms and the neglect of safety standards. In other words, the plant was working at full capacity in view of its imminent closure.

In 2017, Italy requested the extradition of the two German executives convicted, who had since returned to Essen in Germany, in the heart of the Ruhr district whose history closely mirrored that of North-west Italy. The plant never reopened after the fire, becoming a refuge for the homeless, stripped of copper by thieves as well as backdrop for thrill-seeking photographers.[71] Until the time comes for its redevelopment, this modern ruin will continue to remind us of the dark side of Italian deindustrialization. A selective, unfinished deindustrialization that was for long time negotiated by trade unions in exchange for safeguards and "productive compensations" and whose heritage may have included an increase in social inequalities and the impoverishment of work but has not yet led to devastating phenomena of pauperization or social exclusion.

[69] Marco Grasso, Marcello Zinola, *La strage silenziosa: Genova e i morti d'amianto, storia di una battaglia operaia*, (Soveria Mannelli: Rubbettino, 2018).

[70] Diego Novelli, *Thyssenkrupp. L'inferno della classe operaia*, (Milan: Sperling & Kupfer, 2008).

[71] Lodovico Poletto, "Dentro la Thyssen", in *La Stampa*, 22 November 2017, https://www.lastampa.it/torino/2017/11/22/news/dentro-la-thyssen-1.34389733 [accessed 2 September 2019].

Conclusion

Much has to be done on the role of the unions through the processes of deindustrialization, be they accomplished or underway. By now, the center of gravity of this change has shifted from the Northwest, were the post-industrial transition can be considered achieved (at least in the capital cities) to many other areas of Southern and Central Italy. The steelworks Arcelor-Mittal in Taranto and Thyssen Krupp in Terni, the mechanical Whirlpool in Naples and Bekaert in Florence are only some of tens of industrial crises affecting the country.

In these pages, I briefly tried to suggest some directions of research. I am convinced that the policies of negotiation and mitigation of closures should be observed in parallel with the social and cultural history of the unions, considering the ways post-industrial transition has been framed, and has affected the social composition of the unions members. Another area of research could be how the historical memory of workers' movement shaped unions reactions and proposals: there is no doubt that the "density" of historical memory in the Northwestern regions played a role in the strongly "industrialist" positions of the organizations, affecting their choices and interpretations.

Another important aspect, which I have not been able to take into account here, is that industrial relations in contexts of deindustrialization should be articulated according to the different cultures of the main organizations, and they also change as well as we change the scale of analysis. At the confederation level industrial policy prevail, at the federation or category level (mechanics, chemicals, textiles etc.) bargaining, at the shop floor the defense of job places. There is then an endless field of research on the feelings, experiences and memories of the "common" workers through the processes of industrial dismantling: on this topic too, Italy is much late in comparison with the nations of "first deindustrialization".

References

Accornero, Aris, Ancora il lavoro, conversation with Patrizio Di Nicola (Rome: Ediessee, 1995).

Accornero, Aris and Magna, Nino, "il lavoro dopo la classe", in Stato e mercato, no. 17 (1986), pp. 253–270.

Antoniazzi, Sandro, "Lettera alla classe operaia", in Prospettiva sindacale, no. 51 (1984), pp. 110–134.

Armano, Emiliana, Dondona, Carlo Alberto and Ferlaino, Fiorenzo (eds), Post-fordismo e trasformazione urbana: Casi di recupero der vuoti industriali e indicazioni per le politiche nel territorio torinese (Turin: Ires Piemonte-Regione Piemonte, 2016).

Artoni, Roberto (ed), Storie dell'IRI, vol. IV, Crisi e privatizzazione 1990–2002 (Rome and Bari: Laterza, 2013).

Arvati, Paolo, Oltre la città divisa: Gli anni della ristrutturazione a Genova (Genova: Sagep, 1998).

Balconi, Margherita, La siderurgia italiana (1945–1990): Tra controllo publico e incentive del mercato (Bologna: il Mulino, 1989).

Barbieri, Paolo and Scherer, Stefani, "Labour Market Flexibilization and its Consequences in Italy", in European Sociological Review, no. 6 (2009), pp. 677–692.

Barca, Fabrizio and Magnani, Marco, L'industria fra capitale e lavoro: Piccole e grandi imprese dall'autunnno caldo alla ristrutturazione (Bologna: il Mulino, 1989).

Bellocchio, Alberto, Sirena operaia: Con una lettera die Vittorio Foa (Milan: Il Saggiatore, 2000).

Bentivogli, Marco, Abbiamo rovinato l'Italia? Perché non si può fare a meno del sindacato (Rome: Castelvecchi, 2017), new revised and expanden edition.

Berta, Giuseppe, Che fine ha fatto il capitalism italiano? (Bologna: il Mulino, 2016).

Bertona, Bruno, "I costi del non lavoro", in Conquiste del lavoro, no. 3 (January 1985), p. 8.

Bompiani, Michela, Il giallo del verde, in Repubblica, 15 April 2011.

Bonazzi, Giuseppe, "Lasciare la fabbrica. Cassa integrazione e mobilità negli anni ottanta", in Bagnasco, Arnaldo (eds), La città dopo Ford: Il caso Torino (Turin: Bollati Boringhieri, 1990), pp. 23–45.

Bonazzi, Giuseppe et. al., L'espulsione tutelata: Processi di riconversione socio-lavorativa deglie ex dipenti delle grandi fabbriche (Turin: Ires Piemonte, 1988).

Carniti, Pierre, "Occupazione. Asse portante delle lotte per I contratti", in Conquiste del lavoro, no. 20 (September 1975).

Carrieri, Mimmo and Feltrin, Paolo, Al bivio: Lavoro, sindicato e rappresentanza nell'Italia d'oggi (Rome: Donzelli, 2016).

Collidà, Ada Becchi and Negrelli, Serafino, La transizione nell'industria e nelle relazioni industriali: L'auto e il caso Fiat (Milan: Franco Angeli, 1986).

Consiglio italiano per le scienze sociali, Libro bianco per il Nord Ovest: Dall'economia della manifattura all'ecnomie della conoscenza (Venice: Marsilio, 2007).

Dansero, Egidio, Dentro ai vuoti: Dismissione industriale e trasformazioni urbane a Torino (Turin: Edizioni Liberaria Cortina, 1993).

Doria, Marco, "Economia mista e deindustrializzazione", in Assereto, Giovanni and Doria, Marco (eds), Storia della Liguria (Rome and Bari: Laterza, 2007), pp. 266–283.

Epifani, Guglielmo and Cantone, Carla, Non rassegnarsi al decline: Politische industriali per competitive e sviluppo (Rome: Ediesse, 2005).

Foa, Vittorio, Passaggi (Turin: Einaudi, 2000).

Fornengo, Graziella, Il problema della ristrutturazione industriale: la soluzione italiana (Milan: Franco Angeli, 1984).

Galli, Pio and Pertegato, Giancarlo, Fiat 1980. Sindrome della sconfitta, with an essay by Bruno Trentin (Rome: Ediesse, 1994).

Gallino, Luciano, La scomparsa dell'Italia industrial (Turin: Einaudi, 2003).

Garonna, Paolo and Pisani, Elena, "Il sindicalismo italiano nella transizione. La crisi del sindicalismo politico", in Edwards, Richard, Garonna, Paolo and Pisani, Elena (eds), Il sindacato oltre la crisi (Milan: Francesco Angeli, 1988), pp. 219–280.

Gianola, Rinaldo, Senza fabbrica (Milan: Baldini & Castoldi, 1993).

Grasso, Marco and Zinola, Marcello, La strage silenziosa: Genova e I morti d'amianto. Storia di una battaglia operaia (Soveria Manelli; Rubbettino, 2018).

Graziosi, Andrea, La ristrutturazione nelle grandi fabbriche 1973–1976, introduction by Andrea Ginzburg (Milan: Feltrinelli, 1979).

"Il Sistema-paese preferisce le rendite agli investimenti", interview given by Marco Bentivogli to Andrea Di Stefano, June 2015, https://www.fim-cisl.it/2015/06/24/bentivogli-il-sistema-paese-preferisce-le-rendite-agli-ivesti menti/ [accessed 2 September 2019].

"Lavoratori stringete la cinghia", in La Repubblica, 24 January 1978, Now in Montali, Edmondo, Luciano Lama: Il riformatore unitario. Antologie di scritti (Rome: Ediesse, 2017), pp. 279–287.

Leonardi, Salvo, "Gli anni fella concertazione. Un excursus storico-politico", in Alternative per Socialismo, no. 25 (2013), pp. 1–14.

Lerner, Gad, Operari: Viaggio all'interno della Fiat. La vita, le case, le fabbriche di una classe che non c'è più (Milan: Feltrinelli, 1988).

Libertini, Lucio, "Introduzione", in Libertini, Lucio and Trenti, Bruno (eds), L'industria italiana alla svolta: Sindacato, partiti e grande capitale di fronte alla crisi (Bari: De Donato, 1975).

Libertini, Lucio and Trenti, Bruno (eds), L'industria italiana alla svolta: Sindacato, partiti e grande capitale di fronte alla crisi (Bari: De Donato, 1975).

Loreto, Fabrizio, Il sindacato nella città feritia: Storia della Camera del lavoro di Genova negli anni sessanta e settanta (Rome: Ediesse, 2016).

Mania, Roberto, "Landini. Un'alleanza con governo e imprese per imperdire che il Paese si sbriciolo", in La Republica, 8 December 2019.

Medusa, Giuseppe, L'impresa tra produttività e consenso: Il caso Alfa Romeo (Milan: Etas Libri, 1983).
Mocarelli, Luca, "Lee aree dismesse milanesi o della cancellazione del patrimonio industrial: Il caso della Bicocca", in Patrimonio industrial, no. 7 (2011), pp. 69–75.
Morando, Paolo, '80: L'inizio della barbarie (Rome and Bari: Laterza, 2016).
Musso, Stefano, Storia del lavoro in Italia dall'Unità ad oggi (Venice: Marsilio, 2002), revised edition 2011.
Negrelli, Serafino, "Ill caso Italtel", in Regino, Marino and Sabel, Charles F. (eds), Strategi die riaggiustamento inudstriale (Bologna: il Mulino, 1989), pp. 171–206.
Novelli, Diego, Thyssenkrupp. L'inferno della classe operaia (Milan: Sperling & Kupfer, 2008).
Pellegrini, Carlo Bellavite, Pirelli: Innovazione e passione 1872–2015 (Bologna: il Mulino, 2015), pp. 179–180.
Perulli, Paolo and Trentin, Bruno (eds), Il sindacato nella reccessione: Modelli e tendenze delle politiche contrattuali in Occidente (Bari: De Donato, 1983).
Piore, Michael J. and Sabel, Charles F., The Second Industrial Divide: Possibilities for Prosperity (New York: Basic Books, 1984).
Poletto, Lodovico, "Dentro la Thyssen", in La Stampa, 22 November 2017, https://www.lastampa.it/torino/2017/11/22/news/dentro-la-thyssen-1.34389733 [accessed 2 September 2019].
Polo, Gabriele, Il mestiere di sporavvivere (Rome: Editori Riunti, 2000).
Regalia, Ida, "L'area di Sesto S. Giovanni", in Regini, Marino and Sabel, Charles F. (eds), Stragie di riaggiustamento industrial (Bologna: il Mulino, 1989), pp. 207–248.
Regini, Marino and Sabel, Charles F. (eds), Strategi di riaggiutamento industrial (Bologna: il Mulino, 1989).
Revelli, Marco, Non ti riconosco: Un viaggio eretico nell'Italia che cambia (Turin: Einaudi, 2016).
Reyneri, Occupati e disoccupati in Italia (Bologna: il Mulino, 1997).
Rieser, Vittorio, Fabbrica oggi: Lo strano caso del dottor Weber I di mister Marx (Siene: Sisifo, 1992).
Rimoldi, Luca, Lavorare alla Pirelli-Bicocca: Antropologia delle memorie operaie (Bologna: Archetipolibri, 2017).
Rispoli, Paola, "Salario garantitio. Vince, perché è una linea giusta", in Conquiste del lavoro, no. 13 (13 April 1974), pp. 14–18.
Rispoli, Paola, "Situazione grave alla Pirelli. Vuole tagliare l'occupazione", in Conquiste del lavoro, no. 126 (May 1989), p. 6.
Rocci, Carlotta, "Landini. Torino non è più la città del lavoro", in La Republica (Turin edition), 13 December 2013, https://torino.repubblica.it/cronaca/

2013/12/13/news/landini_torino_non_pi_la_citt_del_lavoro-73526480/ [accessed 2 September 2019].

Rugafiori, Paride, "Ascesa e declino di un sistema imprenditoriale", in Gibelli, Antonio and Rugafiori, Paride (eds), La Liguria (Turin: Einaudi, 1994), pp. 255–333.

Sangiovanni, Andrea, Tute blu: La parabola operaia nell'Italia repubblicana (Rome: Donzelli, 2006).

Silver, Beverly J. and Karatasli, Sahan Savas, "Historical Dynamics of Capitalism and Labor Movements", in Della Porta, Donatella and Diani, Mario (eds), The Oxford handbook of nell'Italia D'oggi (Rome: Donzell, 2016), pp. 133–145.

Sircana, Giuseppe, "La transizione difficile. Il sindicato nella seconda Repubblica (1992–2008)", in Vallauri, Carlo (ed), Storia dei sindacati nella società italiana (Rome: Ediesse, 2008), pp. 183–219.

Tolaini, Roberto, "il peso dell'acciaio. Siderurgia e ambiente a Genova. 1950–2005", in Adorno, Salvatore and Serneri, Simone Neri (eds), Industria, ambiente e territorio: Per una storia ambientale delle aree industriali in Italia (Bologna: il Mulino, 2009), pp. 87–112.

Transizione industrial e sindacato, supplement to Conquiste del lavoro, no. 11, March 1985.

Trentin, Bruno, "Conclusioni", in Libertini, Lucio and Trentin, Bruno (eds), L'industria italiana alla svolta: Sindicato, partiti e grande capitale di fronte alla crisi (Bari: De Donato, 1975), pp. 168–169.

Trentin, Bruno, La città del lavoro: Sinistra e crisi del fordismo (Milan: Feltrinelli, 1997).

Vergallo, Luigi, "Deindustrializzazione e nuovi asseti produttivi: il caso lombardo (1971-2001)", in Storia in Lombardia, XXVI, no. 2 (2006), pp. 119–153.

Vettraino, Simona, "Il passato e il future", in Ressegna sindacale, no. 13 (29 March 1985), pp. 18–20.

Vitali, Giampaolo, "Gli indicatori della trasformazione", in Berta, Giuseppe (ed), La questione settentrionale: Economia e società in trasformazione (Milan: Feltrinelli, 2007), pp. 143–173.

PART V

Urban Developments Under Conditions of Deindustrialization

CHAPTER 10

Urban Development Under Conditions of Deindustrialization. Approaches from the Ruhr Region in Germany

Christa Reicher

Introduction

At the start of the twenty-first century, urbanization levels have reached 60–80% in virtually all European countries bar Lithuania.[1] One outcome of the increased rate of urbanization has been a merging of many

[1] *Eurostat 2017*, see Eurostat https://ec.europa.eu/eurostat/statistics-explai-ned/index.php/Statistics_on_rural_areas_in_the_EU#Population_distribution_by_degree_of_urbanisation.

[2] Example Angelika Krehl and Stefan Siedentop, 'Toward a Typology of Urban Centres and Subcenters. Evidence from German City Regions', in *Urban Geography* 40/1 (2019), pp. 58–82, https://doi.org/10.1080/02723638.2018.1500245.

C. Reicher (✉)
Institute for Urban Design and European Urbanism, Faculty of Architecture, RWTH Aachen University, Aachen, Germany
e-mail: reicher@staedtebau.rwth-aachen.de

S. Berger et al. (eds.), *Deindustrialisation in Twentieth-Century Europe*, Palgrave Studies in the History of Social Movements,
https://doi.org/10.1007/978-3-030-89631-7_10

small, medium and large cities into amorphous and contiguously developed urban agglomerations or city regions.[2] Differences at the level of spatial patterns of these agglomerations exist and scholars have characterized such city-regional structures as either monocentric (suburbanized regions), polynucleated regions and dispersed, or edgeless territories. From these, polycentric or polynucleated regions, which are comprised of a multitude of cities and municipalities rather than a single dominant city surrounded by suburbs or many smaller ones are quite common throughout Europe.[3] In fact, European city-regions frequently do not contain a single city with over a million residents but consist of multiple cities of similar size: the Dutch Randstad in the Netherlands, the Limmatal in the Zurich region (Switzerland), the Veneto (including Padua, Venice, Verona) in Italy, or the German Rhine-Main region around Frankfurt.

A classic example of a polycentric agglomeration is the Ruhr region in Germany; an urbanized area originally shaped during the nineteenth and twentieth century by the development of coal and steel industries. Following an extended period of urban growth and expansion, however, from the 1970s the region saw a significant decline of its heavy industry and subsequent re-organization of functional, economic and physical spatial patterns. As such, the Ruhr region has become a primary test bed for innovative urban development practices and approaches for areas transforming from industrial to post-industrial economies. A selection of these approaches will be examined and shared in this contribution.

Historical Context and Challenges of the Ruhr Region

Historical Developments

From the nineteenth century onward, the Ruhr region, bounded by the Rhine river on the west, the river Lippe to the north and the Ruhr in the south experienced immense transformational changes due to industrialization. The invention of the steam engine laid the base for the success of industrial mining in the region enabling access to rich deep lying seams of

[3] Martin J. Burger et al., 'Heterogeneous Development of Metropolitan Spatial Structure. Evidence from Commuting Patterns in English and Welsh City-Regions. 1981–2001', in *Cities* 28/2 (2011), pp. 160–170.

high-quality coal. The industrialization and associated urban development turned the medieval towns of Duisburg and Dortmund into industrial cities and former rural villages such as Bottrop into bustling towns of 50 000 residents and more. Several waves of (international) immigration led to significant population growth in the area as the buoyant economy offered comparatively well-paid employment and demanded an ever-growing workforce. By 1900, Germany was the third largest coal producer worldwide after the USA and Great Britain. Further expansion of coal mining in the first half of the twentieth century was accompanied by the establishment of additional industries such as chemical and defense industries, and electricity generation. These became the second mainstay of established steel manufacturers such as Thyssen, Krupp and Hoesch AG and marked the birth of large companies such as Degussa, RWE and Ruhrkohle AG.

Although the coal industry in the Ruhr region experienced its last heyday in 1956[4] when 494 000 employees worked in mining, the industry was doomed. The 1958 coal crisis triggered by an increasing replacement of coal with natural gas and oil, rang in the beginning of the post-mining era. It led to a first round of closures of mines and job cuts and "[b]y 1976 the number of mines had fallen from 148 to 35; production had halfed and the workforce had dropped to 150,000".[5] Initially, negative impacts on the regional economy and employment market were mitigated as the steel industry continued to grow due to the post WWII reconstruction boom in West Germany. The full extent of the crisis only hit following the world economic recession of 1974/1975, when the growing availability of cheaper steel from Asia and the increasing popularity of alternative materials (e.g. plastics) in certain manufacturing sectors led to job cuts in this sector as well. As a result, a ***sectoral decline and structural change***[6] in both, hard coal mining ***and*** the steel industry had begun in earnest. The Ruhr region, the former German industrial heartland began the arduous transition from an industrial to the service and ultimately knowledge economy with consequences for the demographic, urban and environmental development in the region.

[4] Wilfried Hoppe (ed.), *Das Ruhrgebiet im Strukturwandel*. Diercke Spezial, (Braunschweig: Westermann, Braunschweig, 2010).

[5] Ibidem, p. 28.

[6] Markus Eltges, 'Das Ruhrgebiet. Eine regionalwirtschaftliche Analyse', in *Informationen zur Raumentwicklung* 9/10 (2008), pp. 535–548, p. 535.

At the beginning of the twenty-first century, post deindustrialization, the Ruhr region is (still) one of the five largest agglomerations in Europe with 5 million residents, in a polycentric amorphous setting consisting of 53 cities and municipalities stretching over an area of roughly 4500 square kilometers. The region has no single dominant core city; rather, three of the region's largest cities have very similar population levels with Dortmund at around 600 000, Essen ca. 590 000 and Duisburg ca 500 000.

The diversity of demographic and socio-economic conditions on the ground is immense: "shrinking", "waiting" and "growing" represent some of the adjectives used to describe the mosaic of spaces of a region in which a vast variety of transformation processes can be detected. The region is dotted with numerous abandoned buildings telling tales of a flourishing past in a landscape upon which centuries of uninhibited industrial exploitation has inflicted severe environmental damage including rampant air and water pollution. The poor environmental conditions, in particular, have contributed to a very negative public image that beset the region for decades.

Planning Challenges and Opportunities

In terms of planning, the region's unique characteristics with a spatial structure defined by comparatively constant but relatively low-density urban development of adjoining city districts and neighborhoods interwoven by multifariously used open spaces create challenges but also interesting developmental opportunities. On one hand, there are no recognizable or distinct city boundaries that separate municipalities from each other. On the other hand, an abundance of internal edges exists were built up, residential areas about natural open spaces and provide access to leisure opportunities such as walking and cycling in semi-natural spaces. Residential areas adjacent to open spaces are considered attractive for development and living particularly for families with young children and offer thus potential for high-quality developments.

This raises the question of how these characteristics can be employed to shape development concepts for the future of the Ruhr agglomeration. While at the beginning of the twenty-first century, urban networks are empirical facts and in theory are seen as a promising model for contemporary and future urbanization processes—practical questions remain. How can such large-scale urban landscapes be re-designed, and according to which principles? What approaches and policies are needed to enable (urban) design at the regional scale?

The Ruhr region is predestined for these types of questions for several reasons. First, the revision of a regional plan by the Regional Association Ruhr (Regionalverband Ruhr) comes with the requirement of exploring new avenues for designing regional cityscapes.[7] This is essentially an invitation to test out new approaches. Second, the Ruhr region aspires to become a "metropolis" or a "metropolitan area" with the cooperation between the individual cities in the Ruhr region having reached a new quality. And, third, with numerous transformation processes ongoing, there is an increased chance for policy windows to test the viability of new visions for (urban) living in post-industrial regions and to develop them in a collaborative, participatory and democratic manner.

Approaches to Restructuring and Urban Redevelopment

As deindustrialization set in, a host of traditional economic, social and spatial intervention measures were used to guide and direct the transformation processes in the Ruhr region. In terms of spatial planning, the severity of the conditions—also brought to the fore different creative, and often informal planning instruments which were to shape the transformation of the region.

Economic Interventions, Education and Public Private Partnerships

The first phase of structural change (1958–1990) featured rationalizations (i.e. process optimization) by large companies and the closure of some mines and plants leading to a considerable rise in unemployment. To soften the impact and in view of the difficult situation of miners' families losing their livelihood, the government began to subsidize coal mining in 1974. Additionally, efforts were made to develop alternative employment opportunities especially for younger generations. In this vein, the region's first universities were established in 1965 as a structural policy

[7] Dietwald Gruehn, 'Regional Planning and Projects in the Ruhr Region (Germany)', in M. Yokohari et al. (eds.), *Science for Sustainable Societies: Sustainable Landscape Planning in Selected Urban Regions*, (Tokyo: Springer, 2017), pp. 215–225.

programe to promote the qualification of workforces for different sectors in conjunction with market-economic impulses.

After this initial phase, the decade between 1990 and 2000 was marked by "structuring and setting the course". *In the economic sphere*, at the end of the 1990s, the steel and coal sectors underwent further restructuring, to which companies responded with expanded product ranges and innovations, mergers and further site concentrations. As large companies invested in new products and locations, the job losses in the coal and steel industry were gradually offset by jobs in the service sector as well as in emerging industries such as logistics, microsystem technology, information technology and biomedicine. And although the new industries did not fully compensate for the job reductions in the mining and steel industry, "the services seem to have succeeded in catching up with the overall economic development".[8] Similarly, Hoppe[9] observed that at the beginning of the twenty-first century, "knowledge-based services and products are on the advance" in the region.

This economic transformation was to a large part a result of the new, close cooperation between universities, research institutions, public funding and investments of the established, indigenous big companies. Indeed, the public sector became a major driver of these changes as exemplified by the "Dortmund project". This project became a showcase for economic redevelopment and regeneration in the Ruhr region. Located on a brownfield sites of the former Phoenix steel works in the city of Dortmund the innovative private public partnership was derived from negotiations which started in 1997 between the state government, Krupp-Hoesch, Thyssen and the city of Dortmund. Its aim was to establish a high-tech cluster in Dortmund.[10] Ultimately, it led to the creation of a mixed-use development including a microsystem technology cluster

[8] Markus Eltges, 'Das Ruhrgebiet. Eine regionalwirtschaftliche Analyse', in *Informationen zur Raumentwicklung* 9/10 (2008), pp. 535–548, p. 543.

[9] Wilfried Hoppe (ed.), *Das Ruhrgebiet im Strukturwandel*. Diercke Spezial, (Braunschweig: Westermann, Braunschweig, 2010), p. 29.

[10] Marina Mihaila, 'Transforming the Built Landscapes. Initiatives on City Cultural Sustainability: Phoenix Project Dortmund', in *Proceedings Book ICAR 2105*, (Bukarest: EUIM Ion Mincu University Publishing House, 2015); Michael Jonas, 'The Dortmund Case. On the Enactment of an Urban Economic Imaginary', in *International Journal of Urban and Regional Research* 38 (2015), pp. 2123–2140.

consisting of 30+ companies. In addition, to supporting industry development, the project strengthened soft location factors for businesses and residential developments by upgrading open spaces and landscape.[11] To this effect, on the Eastern part of the site a lake affording recreational uses and amenities was created. Financially the project was supported by the Regional development agency, State and federal Government and EU funds as well as private sector investments.

Addressing Liveability, Environmental Quality and Image

Apart for this economic reorientation, the second phase of the post-mining transformation placed strategic emphasis *on a) increasing the environmental qualities,* and *b) enhancing liveability* in the Ruhr region. Both aspects had been severely impaired by neglecting environmental protection which led to—at times—unrestraint release of industrial waste into local rivers. To this end, the *International Building Exhibition (IBA) Emscher Park* was decisive. IBAs have become increasingly a strategic instrument in the toolbox of German planning practice. In the case of the Ruhr region, it was employed to drive, design and structure the process of spatial transformation in the region in a cooperative and flexible, yet integrated manner.

The IBA Emscher Park worked under the motto "Workshop for the future of old industrial regions" in an area which span—along the river Emscher between Duisburg and Bergkamen—with an east–west extension of about 70 km and a north–south extension of 15 km. Overall, the IBA saw itself as a means of "integrated regional development" in which the ecological and cultural renewal of the region was regarded as essential prerequisite for economic development.

Blast furnaces, machine halls, winding towers, collieries, gasometers and coking plants are among the most striking architectural features of the industrial era. With the onset of the mining crisis and the progressive structural change, these buildings lost their use and raised the question of how to deal with this industrial heritage. The goal of the IBA was to treat this industrial heritage respectfully and by creatively repurposing them with cultural uses to strengthen the regional character. IBA Emscher Park's strategy was to develop former industrial sites into catalysts for

[11] Lars Tata, 'Learning in Urban Regeneration. The Case of Phoenix in Dortmund', in *Conference Aalborg University Denmark*, 2005.

change in the Ruhr region by giving them new uses and meanings with an openness for contemporary trends. A prime example that drew worldwide attention includes the areal of the former Zeche Zollverein—which was awarded UNESCO World heritage status in 2001, fifteen years after the mine's closure. It is now a vibrant site for culture, food and art.[12] Another example is the Duisburg Landscape park which has become an ecological park with outdoor climbing, a diving center, meeting hall and a stage amidst the ruins of the former cookery. On weekend nights, a lightshow illuminates the buildings in an artful show.

Alongside over 100 projects focusing on industrial heritage and its re-use, there were many projects seeking to enhance the environmental quality. This included projects such as the ecological reconstruction of the Emscher system and the creation of the Emscher Landscape Park. In sum, with the International Building Exhibition (IBA) Emscher Park, the Emscher region and indeed the Ruhr region as a whole made significant advances toward a more sustainable development in the region and the transformation process has developed a worldwide media appeal especially with the above mentioned projects of industrial culture, art and ecological restoration. Thanks to the international building exhibition, which ran over a time period of ten years (1989–1999), the internal and external perception of the region has changed fundamentally. The region's negative image has been markedly improved and indeed the region now attracts international attention in the context of a new "Industrial Revolution" and tourism.

The long-term impact of the IBA Emscher Park includes follow-up project successes as in the designation of the European Capital of Culture RUHR 2010, an urban regional contract, the ruhrcities projects and the award of Green Capital of Europe 2017.

As such a transformation of the Metropolitan area of the Ruhr into a sustainable and polycentric organized urban region was well underway at the start of the new millennium but it was also clear that in order to continue this transformational work new impulses and ideas were needed to maintain the momentum of change.

[12] https://www.nrw-tourism.com/a-zollverein-coal-mine.

Beyond IBA Emscher Park: Emerging Planning Approaches Toward a Polycentric and Sustainable Region

Discussions regarding suitable future policies for spatial planning in the context of the next phase of structural change, i.e. structural change 2.0,[13] from the service economy to the knowledge economy with increasing percentages of employment situated in research and knowledge based institutions and companies have introduced a range of focal points or themes. In addition to facilitating this second structural change, future strategies for regional design and development need also to reflect that the formerly "shrinking" and stagnating region has "turned a corner". Since 2014, the region saw growth both for population and the economy which introduces challenges not experienced in decades as well as opportunities. In effect this means some policy themes from earlier transformation phases are being continued while new themes and territorial scales are introduced.

In terms of previous territorial-economic policies, the importance of supporting and developing new commercial-industrial uses remains. In 2016/2017 around 360 hectares of wasteland and open spaces in the Metropolitan region Ruhr were re-used for new commercial-industrial uses Metropole RUHR Business[14] for example. Such new commercial-industrial activities for example in the logistics or health care sectors have become vital employment generators that have made major contributions to the 35,000 new jobs that were created over the period of 2014/2015.[15] Likewise, ecological regeneration activities are being continued with projects such as the International Garden Exhibition IGA 2027. The goal of the IGA 2027 is to grow the Ruhr Region into the "greenest urban region in the world" with a clear focus on featuring nature-based solutions.

[13] See Matthias Kiese, 'Strukturwandel 2.0. Das Ruhrgebiet auf dem Weg zur Wissensökonomie', in *Standort. Zeitschrift für Angewandte Geografie* 43/2 (2019), pp. 69–75.

[14] Metropole RUHR Business, *Gewerbliches Flächenmanagement Ruhr: Phase IV. Zwischenbericht* (2018), p. 4.

[15] Matthias Kiese, 'Strukturwandel 2.0: Das Ruhrgebiet auf dem Weg zur Wissensökonomie', in *Standort. Zeitschrift für Angewandte Geografie* 43/2 (2019), pp. 69–75, p. 69.

As for new policy foci—there is still a need to

- Enhance liveability and attractiveness for knowledge workers in the region (regeneration of city centers, upgrading green and transport infrastructures; improving links between urban areas and university campuses)
- Enhance urban sustainability (upgrade energy efficiency/reduce carbon footprint of new and existing residential developments)
- Address social sustainability by reducing inequalities and deprivation

Spatial planning interventions at both the regional and the local (district or neighborhood) scale are undertaken and planned as means to promote this next stage of transformation. Regionally, transport and green/blue infrastructures need to be upgraded and extended. In parts transport infrastructure and green infrastructure can and ought to be considered jointly for example in respect to long distance bicycle paths. Other aspects such as enhancing energy efficiency or densification and diversification of urban centers require interventions at the district level. These are discussed in some greater detail below.

Strengthening the Regional Infrastructure

Connectivity and access are key to building a strong regional economy and strengthening the attractiveness of the Ruhr as business location (ref). This means, the cities, urban and suburban centers of the poly-centric region need to be effectively connected through a multimodal and efficient transport infrastructure that enhances sustainable mobility while also creating a parallel network of open green spaces, greenway to support eco-system services and ecological sustainability. Some of the green network structure was already conceptualized and implemented as part of the IBA Emscher Park, and additional projects were implemented under the auspices of the European City of Culture RUHR.2010 and the green capital of Europe projects. Naturally, extending and upgrading existing green spaces will also be a topic for the planned International Garden Exhibition (IGA Ruhr 2027).

These regional infrastructure planning activities are a classical task for spatial planning and regional design. However, traditional processes and approaches tend to treat both transport and open space networks as separate, linear and two-dimensional—failing to acknowledge their third dimension, potential multifunctionalities and synergies. Rather, a convincing and effective design of such network spaces should and indeed must strengthen the usability and user experience of such spaces. The typical Ruhr landscapes which are defined by the region 's history, geology, topography and hydrology should be strengthened to help form and support local identity, regional identification and improved quality of life for Ruhr residents.

To a large part, the ingredients to develop networks of attractive open spaces exist already. There is, however, a need to reframe the narrative of how open green spaces are presented and thus valued. It will be an important task for the future to interpret and contextualize landscape fragments as part of the urban landscape. Accessibility and creating meaningful (leisure) activities to enable residents to experience these spaces are key to ensure their value is recognized by larger segments of society. Only if citizens and residents derive personal benefits and recognize functionalities of these space beyond their mere contribution toward agriculture, habitat for protected species or water purification are they will they support their creation, enhancement, maintenance and long-term protection.

The aim to foster urban development with attractive and high-quality urban green space is well established not only as part of urban regeneration projects in the Ruhr region but in general. Additionally, creating attractive green space is a necessary strategy also for the internal city boundaries and borders in the fragmented settlement structure of the Ruhr region. Settlement areas along city edges are desirable due to their particular spatial qualities and affordances which include access to natural features such as creeks, orchards, forests and wetlands which typically cannot be found near districts in urban core areas. There is a need to design the near ubiquitous open spaces along the meandering urban-nature boundary with similar care and attention as the typical urban realm with its streets, squares and pocket parks in order to capitalize on the potential and opportunities of the typical spatial pattern in the region.

Aside from the green infrastructure network, the regional transport and mobility infrastructure requires further development. The Ruhr region at the start of the twenty-first century is still dominated by individual car mobility with a public transit offer that lacks viability. Bicycle and pedestrian pathways lack connectivity. With low urban residential densities and scattered employment mobility other than the private car is often not viable. A new approach to establish a connectivity corridor which links centers of different hierarchical levels particularly also in North–South direction in addition to the traditionally existing East–West corridors. An important building block is the bicycle highway RS1 which needs to be better integrated and amended by a N-S link to offer a real alternative to less-sustainable mobility.

Furthermore, the public transit system needs to be improved to enhance reliability, frequency and speed such that it can offer a viable (yet sensibly priced) alternative to using the private automobile. Modern functional transport systems are characterized by a good flow of information to its users with real-time arrival and departure data, details on route options and possible alternative, waiting times and so forth. Providing such a user-oriented system at the regional level would certainly enhance the quality of life in the region. Other features of a modern transit system are hierarchically structured options and mobility hubs where users can seamlessly and barrier-free switch between mobility modes (e.g. from the private vehicle to the regional train, or from the tram to the bicycle or footpaths). Mobility nodes that connect busses, trains, bicycle and carsharing services, and taxis, etc. are being tested and refined at present; they can serve as network points in space but also can offer additional functionalities in terms of services and retail. The hubs can even double up as meeting places and centers for neighborhoods and districts.

Finally, the projects associated with the development of the regional transit and green/blue infrastructure might also help to counteract regional segregation processes which are worsening and becoming increasingly visible. Examples are here the projects of the association "Neues Emschertal" (New Emscher Valley)[16]—expressed in the Masterplan Emscher Zukunft (Emscher Future)[17] which builds on the renaturalization of the river and continues work of the concepts developed for the Emscher Landscape park. New higher quality open and green spaces increase the attractiveness of the Emscher valley through for instance the Emscher Island (with its intermittent open air art exhibitions and installations) are offering valuable leisure spaces and opportunities to the adjacent residential developments. These enhancements create alternative

[16] http://ag-emschertal.metropoleruhr.de/neues-emschertal.html.

[17] http://www.emscherplayer.de/media/content/publication/000/025/000025417.pdf.

high-quality settlement spaces that can overcome the traditional lack of amenity spaces along the Emscher compared to the Ruhr valley.

Densification of Urban and Suburban Centers

The polycentric urban structure in the region enables and supports the development of urban vitality at a dense spatial scale. This means outside of the traditional and historical cities of the region, regional urban and suburban centers but also (transit) network nodes could be densified. The latter are areas which are suitable and offer opportunities for urban growth and expansion, i.e. urbanization as well as re-urbanization. The development of further higher density centers and subcenters will help to support the aspiration of the region to grow into a vital and functional city-region. In fact, this densification is a precondition to make the city-region visible as an urbanized metropolitan space. In this vein it is of note that practically no urban center in the Ruhr region is without vacant or underused land. Even in the few major cities such as Dortmund or Essen there are amble opportunities to increase densities and enhance urban vitality. This densification of the region however requires a considered approach which should diversify functions across the city-region. In other words, node, subcenters or urban cores should functionally diversity and enrich their entertainment, retail, tourism or services functions.

Districts as Innovation Hubs

In addition to enhancing the quality and functional mix in subcenters and urban cores, it will be important to improve quality of life in residential areas. The district or neighborhood has over time become a spatial unit within which residents feel connected socially and where (local) actors can effectively communicate and initiate transformations and change. Neighborhood networks are effective communication channels. There is evidence that local economic and entrepreneurial activity can be stimulated at this level (ref). Beyond that it is far easier than at the city level to maintain, enhance and even create local spatial character and identity at neighborhood and district level. Detailed knowledge and familiarity with the local situation are useful to engage districts' residents in participatory co-creation of future scenarios and enable the development of tailormade urban concepts and plans. At the regional scale, then, different neighborhoods and districts can be perceived as a mosaic of territories—each with different characteristics, qualities and innovation potential. It will be the task of planning to explore and develop these in the future.

One example, where districts became innovations hub for the implementation of renewable energies and energetic transformation in the Ruhr region from coal to clean energies has been in the city of Bottrop. As a result of winning a competition that funded "futureproofing projects", the city of Bottrop (population ca. 115,000) was selected as a model city for the Innovation City Ruhr (2010–2020) campaign (Urban Transitions Alliance 2018). Goal of the project is to reduce CO_2 emissions in selected city/districts by 50% over a period of only 10 years. A masterplan ensures a wholistic approach that goes beyond mere technological innovation implementation. This means renovation and energetic renewal of existing buildings is paired with novel mobility concepts and broad-based citizens participation and engagement. According to the assessment of the Urban Transition Alliance,[18] one of the success factors of the project has been the district level engagement via six service centers that provide free and non-binding consultations on how to improve households' energy efficiency. These consultations were much appreciated by property owners considering various measures and are seen as key to raise the modernization rate to 3% annually which is higher that the national average of 1% in districts with similar socio-economic make-up. In addition, due to the interest in relevant technologies over 30 companies now specialize in energetic modernization of buildings creating new employment opportunities.

Another set of potential innovation districts are formed by the areas around the Ruhr regions' institutions of higher education. *Many of these institutions are comparatively young. The* higher education landscape, which emerged with the opening of the Ruhr-Universität Bochum in 1965 and is an enormous economic factor with its more than 270,000 students and 27 universities at 38 locations (RVR 2017), yet the potential of the Ruhr area as a knowledge and science region has not yet been sufficiently exploited. To ensure long-term economic prosperity and the further transformation of the region into a knowledge and science-based society, it is important to entice graduates to remain in the Ruhr region

[18] Urban Transition Alliance, *InnovationCity Ruhr: Model City Bottrop A Blueprint for a Futureproof City. Case study by WBCSD and ICM*, November 2018. Available Online: https://urbantransitions.org/wp-content/uploads/2017/01/InnovationCity-Ruhr_20181127.pdf (accessed 5 December 2018).

by creating attractive environmental conditions, both in regard to exciting employment opportunities as well as high-quality living spaces.

As many universities in the Ruhr region were developed in the 1960s and 1970s as purpose-built facilities or campuses outside traditional settlement areas, they feature a mostly monofunctional character. At best one can find are some close-by residential neighborhoods as for example in Bochum. The technology and science "parks", which consist of clusters of research facilities and incubation centers and which were developed since the 1980s to promote the transfer of research into marketable products feature similar drab surroundings. A densification, and functional diversification or in other words—urbanization—of such singular focused innovation and knowledge hubs into lively university and science districts requisite with social, medical, entertainment and public transit infrastructure may be catalysts for future development and innovation of the regional structure.

Urban Planning for Social Justice and Cohesion

While much has been changed for the better since the 1990s in respect to quality of life in the Ruhr area, especially in the cities along the heavily polluted Emscher River there are also things that have not changed at all. Infact conditions might have worsened. Certain cities and city districts in the Ruhr region still exhibit unemployment figures above the State and national average.[19] There are also high levels of poverty among the population as many—even if not unemployed—work in part-time and unskilled posts with low salaries. Segregation into neighborhoods in which a majority of residents have foreign heritage, migration backgrounds and better of neighborhoods that gentrify are increasingly an issue. Municipalities and cities often lack the means and capacity to counter these developments, particularly not with traditional planning instruments.[20]

New, informal planning instruments and approaches however are more and more used to overcome social segregation particularly at the neighborhood level. One exemplary pilot—supported and initiated by two

[19] Matthias Kiese, 'Strukturwandel 2.0. Das Ruhrgebiet auf dem Weg zur Wissensökonomie', in *Standort. Zeitschrift für Angewandte Geografie* 43/2 (2019), pp. 69–75.

[20] Reicher, Aufwertung, 2013.

private partners RAG Montan Immobilien und Vivawest Pilotprojekte wie "Glückauf Nachbarn – Modellquartier Integration", illustrate the viability of such new measures. The explicit aim of this project was to develop ideas for how integration at neighborhood level could practically promoted. Integration was conceived broadly looking at social and cultural aspects. This meant not only looking at the integration of refugees in the local community but also making spaces accessible for all ages including disabled citizens and religious groupings. Conceptually and spatially, the project sought to integrate working, housing and living. Following idea and future workshops in 2017/2018—detailed interventions were developed for a sustainable urban renewal which will be implemented in the districts of Duisburg Vierlinden and the former mining area Kamp-Lintfort Friedrich-Heinrich.[21] Learning and experiences from these projects need to be extended to the sustainable and socially just renewal of other deprived areas in the Ruhr.

Space for Experiments

There is much uncertainty in regard to future development and in turn suitable responses, policies and solutions are also unknown and must still be developed. How can degrowth be structured or used to transform territories into something that adds value to the metropolitan area in its entirety. Where should new and emerging population growth be focused and channelled to support a sustainable development pattern of the overall region? Which subcenters should be enhanced to support the development of a better transit network? The spatial openness of the regions offers here greater opportunities than other regions with higher densities.

In this sense, the Ruhr region with its many vacant and underused spaces is predestined to serve a playground for pioneers. From a planning perspective, it will thus be important to reserve territories that can function as test beds where new models of ownership, uses or infrastructure technologies can be tested, evaluated and examined. At the same time, it is likely that new instruments and processes are needed to facilitate such experimentation. The experience from the IBA Emscher Park shows that important innovations can emerge from such experiments. And while

[21] https://www.glueckauf-zukunft.de/projekte/glueckauf-nachbarn/daten-und-fakten/.

there is a risk of failure in any such experiment, on the whole it is well worth to pursue them.

Experimental areas in the city region can be used to develop a new language for urban design and new forms and morphologies for settlements. There is a broad spectrum of possible functions. For example, former commercial and industrial areas which are currently vacant could be offered on a temporary basis cheaply and free from function usage prescription for cultural activities or start-ups. This would allow local actors to take ownership or assume responsibility or stewardship for abandoned areas or buildings.

One overarching regional policy to support the implementation of experimental territories could be an obligation that for all larger projects within the region 2% of the area or building floor ratio is reserved for "experimental use". In practice, this would mean that a small proportion of land or a building would be giving to pioneering users and uses such as non-profits with cultural or entrepreneurial aims. A similar policy was used to implement art installations as part of building and development projects ("Kunst am Bau"). Within these spaces reserved for experimentations new forms of living, producing, working or entertainment and cultural practices could be tested. A clear strategy to distribute these experimental territories in space will ensure that such innovative practices will not be relegated to special creative quarters but become part of day-to-day planning and life. Projects could be selected competitively and potentially be time-limited to establish the viability of new concepts without long-term commitments.

Summary and Conclusions

The structural change in the Ruhr area is a blueprint for many regions in Europe and worldwide. Despite the successful urban and regional development formats such as the International Building Exhibition IBA Emscher Park and remarkable large-scale projects such as the conversion of the Emscher sewer into an attractive river, more work is needed as the region transforms from an industrial power house to a service and knowledge based sustainable city region. At present a range of different ideas about future (economic) development paths exist oscillating between re-industrialization and science region. At times they appear to be in conflict and competing—yet, following (ref) it seems a mutually re-enforcing co-existence may be possible if not necessary.

What is perhaps more relevant is to focus on the spatial qualities of the region and to ensure that sustainable urban development patterns are developed that enable the development of a modern transport and green infrastructure network at the regional scale within which urban vitality and high-quality living quarters support a metropolitan life style appropriate for the twenty-first century.

References

Burger, M. J., de Goei, B., van der Laan, L., and Huisman, F. J. M. (2011): Heterogeneous Development of Metropolitan Spatial Structure: Evidence from Commuting Patterns in English and Welsh City-Regions, 1981-2001. *Cities* 28 (2): 160–170.

Eltges, M. (2008): Das Ruhrgebiet – eine regionalwirtschaftliche Analyse. *Informationen zur Raumentwicklung* 9 (10): 535–548.

Eurostat https://ec.europa.eu/eurostat/statistics-explai-ned/index.php/Statistics_on_rural_areas_in_the_EU#Population_distribution_by_degree_of_urbanisation.

Gruehn, D. (2017): Regional Planning and Projects in the Ruhr Region (Germany). In: Yoko-hari, M., Murakami, A., Hara, Y., Tsuchiya, K. (eds.) *Sustainable Landscape Planning in Selected Urban Regions*, pp. 215–225. Science for Sustainable Societies. Springer, Tokyo.

Hoppe, W. (2010): *Das Ruhrgebiet im Strukturwandel. Diercke spezial.* Verlag Westermann, Braunschweig.

Jonas, M. (2014): The Dortmund Case - On the Enactment of an Urban Economic Imaginary. *International Journal of Urban and Regional Research* 38: 2123–2140.

Kiese, M. (2019): Strukturwandel 2.0: Das Ruhrgebiet auf dem Weg zur Wissensökonomie. In: *Standort. Zeitschrift für Angewandte Geografie.* Heft 2, 43. Jahrgang, pp. 69–75.

Krehl, Angelika, and Siedentop, S. (2019): Toward a Typology of Urban Centres and Subcenters – Evidence from German City Regions. *Urban Geography* 40 (1): 58–82. https://doi.org/https://doi.org/10.1080/02723638.2018.1500245.

Metropole RUHR Business (2018): *Gewerbliches Flächenmanagement Ruhr.* Phase IV, Zwischenbericht.

Mihaila, M. (2015): *Transforming the Built Landscapes – Initiatives on City Cultural Sustain-ability: Phoenix Project Dortmund. Proceedings Book ICAR 2105.* Bukarest: EUIM Ion Mincu University Publishing House.

Polivka, J., Reicher, C., and Zöpel, C. (2017): Zukunftswege der Agglomeration Ruhr. In: *Raum-strategien Ruhr 2035+*, ss. 227–261. Ketteler Verlag, Dortmund.

Reicher, C., Kunzmann, K., Polívka, J., Roost, F., Utku, Y., and Wegener, M. (Hsg.) (2011): Schichten einer Region – Kartenstücke zur räumlichen Struktur des Ruhrgebiets, 248 S, Berlin.

RVR (Regionalverband Ruhr) (2017): Regionalstatistik Ruhr: Hochschulen 2017.

Tata, L. (2005): Learning in Urban Regeneration. The Case of Phoenix in Dortmund. *Confer-ence Aalborg University Denmark.*

Urban Transition Alliance (2018): *InnovationCity Ruhr | Model City Bottrop a Blueprint for a Futureproof City –Case study by WBCSD and ICM*—November 2018. Available Online: https://urbantransitions.org/wp-content/uploads/2017/01/InnovationCity-Ruhr_20181127.pdf (accessed 5 December 2018).

CHAPTER 11

Milan, the Story of an Urban Metamorphosis

Giorgio Bigatti

Introduction

Starting in the mid-1970s, it became increasingly apparent that the problems afflicting large industry in Milan were structural in nature, not just a cyclical downturn or management's reaction to the particularly acute social conflict in those years. The various crises faced by companies, though each one had its own causes and characteristics, were part of a widespread process, which gave rise to talk of deindustrialization.[1]

The currency tensions created by the end of dollar-to-gold convertibility (1971) and the first oil crisis (1973) had brought an unprecedented thirty-year period of growth to a halt. All the economies were faced with a situation of instability, marked by a sharp surge in inflation, driven by the rise in the price of oil and the cost of labor. While the digital revolution

[1] Roberta Garruccio, 'Chiedi alla ruggine. Studi e storiografia della deindustrializzazione', in *Meridiana* 85 (2016).

G. Bigatti (✉)
Università Commerciale Luigi Bocconi, Milan, Italy
e-mail: giorgio.bigatti@unibocconi.it

S. Berger et al. (eds.), *Deindustrialisation in Twentieth-Century Europe*, Palgrave Studies in the History of Social Movements,
https://doi.org/10.1007/978-3-030-89631-7_11

offered a glimpse of new production combinations, the companies reacted to the crisis of the Fordist model, put to the test by the worker struggles,[2] by reorganizing production, downsizing the workforces, and outsourcing numerous functions, and, increasingly often, by transferring production to areas where the labor was less costly and subject to regulation.

The desolation of the American Rust Belt and the smoldering heaps of rubbish in Detroit's working-class neighborhoods, the industrial desertification of northern England, the sense of abandonment common to many mining districts, the decline of many company towns all represent a reality of social despair and bleakness. Also, although Milan's recent metamorphosis should be seen within the context of the widespread process of the deindustrialization of cities and their outskirts, Milan has little in common with these scenarios of decline, despite its dramatic transformation.

The first to grasp the scope of the change was probably a photographer named Gabriele Basilico. In 1978, he published a volume simply entitled *Ritratti di fabbrica* (Factory Portraits), giving us a first classification of those "big machines laid down in the suburbs, about to disappear, and today completely gone".[3] Today, forty years later, Milan seems to be experiencing a boom, a phenomenon in sharp contrast with much of the rest of the country.

In these pages, I do not tell of the eclipse of the industrial city—about which I describe just a few features—but instead I try to highlight the elements of that story that made it possible for the city to weather the crisis better than the other industrial capitals of the Northwest, Turin, and Genoa; thus Milan was one of the few "former manufacturing giants" that managed a relatively smooth transition into the "post-industrial age".[4]

[2] Pietro Causurano, 'La fabbrica fordista e il conflitto industriale', in Stefano Musso (ed.), *Storia del lavoro in Italia: Il Novecento 1945–2000. La ricostruzione e il miracolo economico, la globalizzazione*, (Rome: Castelvecchi, 2015), pp. 59–101; Ferruccio Ricciardi, 'Il lavoro industriale nella crisi del fordismo. Scenari di declino e di trasformazione', in Stefano Musso (ed.), *Storia del lavoro in Italia: Il Novecento 1945–2000. La ricostruzione e il miracolo economico, la globalizzazione*, (Rome: Castelvecchi, 2015), pp. 599–630.

[3] Stefano Boeri, 'Elegia di una dismissione', in Gabriele Basilico (ed.), *Ritratti di fabbriche*, (Milan: Federico Motta, 2009), p. 16.

[4] Edward Glaeser, *Triumph of the City*, (New York, NY: Penguin Books, 2011).

The Eclipse of Industrial Milan

In the mid-seventies, Milan perceived the first warning signs of a crisis destined to change its economic profile. One after another, all the most important factories, which strongly contributed to the identity of the city, closed down or were dramatically downsized. It started with emblematic companies such as Alfa Romeo, Motta, Alemagna, symbolic city landmarks, and then Borletti, Face Standard, Sit-Siemens, Telettra, Ercole Marelli, Riva Calzoni, CGE, Brown Boveri, Innocenti, OM, Breda, Falck, Radealli, in the metalworking sector; Montedison, Farmitalia, Carlo Erba in the chemical sector; Richard Ginori, Lagomarsino, Lesa, Geloso—companies that differed in size and in business sphere, giving an idea of the richness and variety of the city's productive fabric.

Milan industrialized early on and was characterized by a great variety of sectors and a diverse business mix in terms of structure, dimensions, and capitalization. Even when the first large mechanical and chemical plants appeared at the close of the nineteenth century, Milan did not become a factory town, just as it would never become a "Fordist city" like Turin, nor did it have a similar productive focus. It was a city of industries. But it was also a city of trades. This is one aspect of its history that reaches far back in time. Milan became industrialized without betraying its agricultural and commercial origins, conserving its historical function as a gateway between different economic areas and markets, both within the regional territory and with respect to the international markets. Trade and industrial enterprises were in turn sustained by a financial milieu. There was a mix of functions, the relative weight of which changed over time. In the mid-nineteen hundreds, it was the industrial backdrop that dominated the city's narrative and its self-image. Milan was Italy's economic engine and its first financial center.

Starting at the end of the Seventies, the fabric of a new economy completely based on the service sector began to gain in strength. It was like a molecular exchange that, not by any plan, silently replaced the old industrial texture of the city. We are not looking at an industrial decline, but rather the disappearance of industry from the urban fabric. What is stunning is not only the size of the phenomenon, but also the rapidity of the process, which in little more than a decade (1981–1991) literally razed to the ground a century of industrial history. It was an authentic social upheaval.

Let's take a look at the numbers. Just a few figures suffice to understand the extent of the phenomenon. From 1971 to 1991, industrial workers in the city dropped from 392,325 to 186,131. The hemorrhage continued into the following decade, at which point the process of the regional capital's deindustrialization was apparent to everyone. At the start of the new millennium, industrial workers numbered little more than 90 thousand. At that time workers in the public and private service sectors had instead reached all of 732,395 employees. These data, though summary, tell us that in thirty years of Milanese industry, about 300 thousand jobs were lost.[5]

The closedown of the factories brought with it the loss of the community spirit that bound families and people to the places: a solidarity nourished by the shared class identity, by meetings and discussions in the neighborhood cafés, in the associations and the local branches of the leftist parties, or in the parishes, depending on one's political leanings. This was the atmosphere that was breathed in the working-class districts of the industrial outskirts of town. So, to dismantle a factory is equivalent to "making a clean slate of an entire neighborhood, it means canceling a worker component of the city, leading to the death of a part of the city's working culture".[6]

A New and Different Milan

Today, it is hard even to imagine that until a few decades ago the city was one of the vertices of the industrial triangle and its days were cadenced by the sound of the factory sirens. Little lingers on from that situation. Even in terms of memory, it is like a chapter that has been repressed and forgotten. The model, "centered around the great cathedrals of production," was forced out "by the emergence of more flexible alternatives".[7] Milan managed to put the industrial era behind by hitching its economic center of gravity to services instead of manufacturing, even though there

[5] Marco Martini, 'I mutamenti strutturali del sistema produttivo a Milano e alla Bicocca', in Nicolò Leotta (ed.), *La nascita di una università nuova: Milano-Bicocca. Dal lavoro di fabbrica alla fabbrica del sapere*, (Milan: Skira, 2002), pp. 131–146.

[6] Cesare Sommariva, *Le due morali: Scelte imprenditoriali, lotte operaie e intervento culturale alla Redaelli Sidas di Rogoredo (1979–1984)*, (Rome: Edizioni Lavoro, 1986).

[7] Dario Di Vico, 'Donne, competenze, stili di vita. A Milano metamorfosi vincenti', in *Corriere della Sera* 1 (2017).

are multiple points of juncture that render insignificant the traditional distinctions between the various business sectors.

Milan is "a city that changed its skin, that is different from the one we knew, not only for how it is, for who passes through, for who frequents it".[8] The lead players on the economic stage are also no longer the same. Finance and real estate have taken the place of the old factory, while fashion, design, neo-artisanal production, communications, and media are the motors of a new economy of culture and knowledge. The Assolombarda-City of Milan observatory on urban areas in Europe notes that Milan is one of the top five in the sectors of the life sciences (a sphere affected by the redevelopment projects of the Expo site and the ex-Falck areas, with significant public contributions), food farming, art, culture and design, and industry 4.0.[9] Several indicators confirm the growing appeal of a metropolis that attracts people and financial investments from every part of the world. The presence of over three thousand "foreign companies" and some forty branches of foreign banks[10] is a clear indication of the city's new international vocation. But perhaps what best represents the city's vitality is the galaxy of companies in the advanced service sector, ranging from business services to the new technologies.[11] Sometimes these are volatile activities and not always meant to last, but they are indicative of a trend typical of the most vibrant urban realities. It is a world in which work is done freelance, where it is not easy to distinguish the fine line between self-employed professionals and the precariat, who are not covered by traditional forms of labor protection. It is a social phenomenon that has gathered momentum, if it is true that a fifth of the Milanese population are self-employed, and freelancers working under the VAT regime number nearly 100 thousand.[12] These data, and their

[8] Pino Landonio, *Modello Milano: I vent'anni che hanno cambiato la città*, (Milan: Laurana, 2018), p. 225.

[9] Antonello Boatti, Valentina Brambilla and Francesco Samorè (eds.), *Aree produttive abbandonate: Ricerca sulle aree produttive abbandonate, sulle trasformazioni indotte, sui riflessi nei livelli occupazionali*, (Milan: CGIL-Politecnico di Milano, 2018), p. 96.

[10] Giuseppe Sala, *Milano e il secolo delle città*, (Milan: La nave di Teseo, 2018), p. 203.

[11] Ibid., p. 204.

[12] Aldo Bonomi, 'Comunità, prossimità, simultaneità', in Aldo Bonomi, Alberto Magnaghi and Marco Revelli (eds.), *Il vento di Adriano: La comunità concreta di Olivetti tra non più e non ancora*, (Rome: DeriveApprodi, 2015), p. 84.

fragmentary nature, offer an eloquent picture of the changes in the occupational structure of a city where, not too long ago, blue-collar workers were the mainstay of the labor market.

Situated at the heart of an economic region whose borders coincide only in part with the administrative ones, Milan continues to be, as in the past (if not more so), a vital center for the country. It is here where the business services with the highest added value cluster, while the metropolitan city, according to the Chamber of Commerce estimates, produces nearly one-tenth of the gross domestic product (GDP). In 2017, the city's GDP exceeded the 2008 level by three percentage points, while the rest of Italy remained a good 4 points below the pre-crisis period.[13]

The income data also confirm that the city overcame the difficulties that instead plague the other two vertices of what was once the industrial triangle. Genoa and Turin are still grappling with the heavy legacy of an industrial past that has not yet found viable alternatives to the crisis of large public industry and the biggest Italian private company. Turin suffered the consequences of the "industrial monoculture" and its dependency on a monocratic center of power.[14] Milan, on the other hand, pluralist and diversified, was able to adapt more swiftly to the end of this industrial era.

And yet, there is something that does not add up in these linear accounts. "Not because the structural data [of the shift] is not true," but because the "ideological narrative" masking it, that of a modernity without adjectives, neutral, is false.[15] To say it in Basilio Rizzo's class-conscious terms: "The truth is that today, Milan's narrative is made up by the rich".[16]

The city's ancient manufacturing and business vocation has not disappeared, but it has changed shape, and what remains of it has been spread

[13] Antonello Boatti, Valentina Brambilla and Francesco Samorè (eds.), *Aree produttive abbandonate. Ricerca sulle aree produttive abbandonate, sulle trasformazioni indotte, sui riflessi nei livelli occupazionali*, (Milan: CGIL-Politecnico di Milano, 2018).

[14] Silvano Belligni and Stefania Ravazzi, *La politica e la città: Regime urbano e classe dirigente a Torino*, (Bologna: Il Mulino, 2012).

[15] Mario Tronti and Andrea Bianchi, *Il popolo perduto: Per una critica della sinistra*, (Rome: Nutrimenti, 2019), p. 19.

[16] Pino Landonio, *Modello Milano: I vent'anni che hanno cambiato la città*, (Milan: Laurana, 2018), p. 227.

out over the larger container of the city-region, redefining the historical conditions of the relationship between Milan and its territory.[17] The working class has clearly disappeared, but not the workers. In the narrative of the urban transformation, there is a tendency to leave in the background the universe of poor workers, which represents the other side of the new economy. Seen from the bottom of the social pyramid, globalization means a new supply of unskilled and unregulated labor for the sectors of mass market retailers, logistics,[18] and cleaning and personal care services. The rose-tinged narrative of a smoothly occurring urban metamorphosis is thus challenged by interpretations focusing on the negative aspects of the process. Various studies render an image of a city that has lost its sense of community and its capacity for being inclusive, once one of its distinguishing traits.[19]

In recent years, inequality has been on the rise in Milan, and today the city appears more polarized both socially[20] and on a territorial level. The poverty in some of the old working-class quarters contrasts with colossal real estate investments[21] and widespread gentrification along lines that no longer follow the classic center/periphery dichotomy.[22] In short, according to these interpretations, the end of industry, powerful driving force behind conflict as well as integration, threatened the stability of the city's social equilibrium.

[17] Giancarlo Consonni and Graziella Tonon, 'La terra degli ossimori. Caratteri del territorio e del paesaggio della Lombardia contemporanea', in Duccio Bigazzi and Marco Meriggi (eds.), *Storia d'Italia: Le regioni dall'Unità a oggi. La Lombardia*, (Turin: Einaudi, 2001).

[18] Sergio Bologna, Per un breve panorama della logistica dagli anni 70 ad oggi (http://www.intotheblackbox.com).

[19] Costanzo Ranci and Rossana Torri, *Milano tra coesione sociale e sviluppo: Rapporto su Milano sociale*, (Milan: B. Mondadori, 2007).

[20] Marianna d'Ovidio, 'I redditi dei milanesi: aumento della ricchezza o polarizzazione?', in *impresa e Stato* 186, (2009), pp. 36–43; Luigi Vergallo, *La città che sa cambiare: Indagine su economia e società a Milano*, (Milan: Guerini e Associati, 2012).

[21] Maria Cristina Gibelli, 'Milano. A metropoli fordista a mecca del real estate', in *Meridiana* 85 (2016); Paola Dezza, 'Il Rinascimento di Milano. Piani d'investimento per 10 miliardi', *Il Sole 24 Ore*, 6 March 2019.

[22] Francesca Zajczyk and Silvia Mugnano (eds.), *Milano: Città poliedrica tra innovazione e sostenibilità*, (Soveria Mannelli: Rubbettino, 2019).

Factory Shutdowns and Urban Renewal

The spatial consequences of deindustrialization are no less relevant. "The demolition of the brick walls, reinforced floor slabs, smoke stacks, ethernet coverage of large areas, and suspended walkways represents the spatial side of the anthropological demolition of tens of thousands of life trajectories".[23]

The factory closings left millions of square meters to the city, to be reclaimed and repurposed. They involve areas extending radially around the city, with concentrations along the historical axes of industrialization. But there is not one city district that has not had to cope with the industrial legacy. The past may have been removed, but there often remain its bulky reminders, awaiting a new destination.

There is no overall assessment of the area impacted by the factory closures. The data vary, depending on whether they refer to the city territory or include the metropolitan area, industrial structures only or other areas as well (former railway yards, farmsteads...). Then, consideration must be given to the fact that these are processes spread out over the years, so that censuses carried out at different times yield different results, sometimes because during the intervals between one survey and another, a part of the abandoned areas may already have been built back up. In any case, they represent significant portions of the city, a total of six million square meters, corresponding, according to a 2009 assessment, to 13% of Milan's entire urban territory, the consequence of the shutdown of 168 "big industrial areas".[24] To these should be added the Breda, Marelli, and Falck areas (3.5 million square meter in Sesto San Giovanni and that of the former Agip refinery (1.5 million square meter) in Rho-Pero, where the new trade fair complex was to be built.

There is another point that is worth emphasizing. The widespread presence of industry in the urban territory and the different sizes of the plants have facilitated the redesign of the city through the adoption of targeted urban planning tools. In recent years, the city's urban planning policy has undergone a radical change in direction. The idea of a master plan with binding rules about building expansion and land use has made way for a strategy that limits public input to the definition of infrastructures

[23] Stefano Boeri, 'Elegia di una dismissione', in Gabriele Basilico (ed.), *Ritratti di fabbriche*, (Milan: Federico Motta, 2009), p. 16.

[24] Ibidem.

and services needed, then delegating the design and implementation of the individual projects to private initiative. The aim was to "unleash the market forces, orienting them towards the public interest and to deploy resources that the local authority was no longer able to muster".[25] This was scenario in which the great moneymaking deal of the factory closings played out. The key year was 1985 when Pirelli signed a nonbinding agreement with the local authorities for the creation of a large Technology Park in an area of more than 700,000 square meters, surrounded by research facilities, offices, and residential building on the land occupied by the old Bicocca plant. The closing of Bicocca was not intended as the liquidation of an historic industry founded in 1872, but rather as its adaptation to modern times. A factory that was no longer economically and environmentally sustainable was closing down, but the aim was to maintain strong links with production and working cultures. In reality, between the drawing up of the plans and the launch of the work, the project lost some of its defining features. The idea of a large Technology Center was replaced by the university, created from the splitting up of Milan's venerable Università degli Studi. Meanwhile, subsequent city and regional resolutions authorized an increase in the area designated for residences (150,000 square meters compared to 66,000 in the first project), and higher buildability indices than those previously established.[26]

Opinions are mixed about the design and, especially, the implementation of the project. For some, like Lodovico Meneghetti, the procedure opened the way to a policy "of urban expansion beyond any plan or even of an idea of the city". Regardless of the "general interests of the inhabitants and the daily visitors", the design was born of the "encounter between the overwhelming power" of the Pirelli "and the relative weakness of a city council lacking a high vision of what a public project should be, and therefore inclined to take a back-seat position".[27]

[25] Matteo Bolocan, *Geografie milanesi*, (Santarcangelo di Romagna: Maggioli, 2009), p. 32.

[26] Luca Mocarelli, 'Le aree dismesse milanesi o della cancellazione del patrimonio industriale. Il caso della Bicocca', in *Il patrimonio industriale*, 5/7 (2011), pp. 69–75; Giorgio Bigatti and Giampaolo Nuvolati (eds), *Story of a District: Milano-Bicocca. People, Places, Recollections*, (Milan: Scalpendi, 2019).

[27] Lodovico Meneghetti, 'Le nuove Milano estranee. L'architettura servile', 30 October 2004, in www.eddyburg.it.

Others, instead, feel that faced with a rapidly evolving reality, it is not the task of the public administration to impose rigid rules, as was done between 1976 and 1980 with the modified masterplan, but to adopt flexible tools of intervention, leaving the definition of the "building content up to the necessary encounter between public and private".[28] According to architect Stefano Boeri, "Milan's strength" lies in the fact that "politics does not presume to impose its vision", limiting itself "to coordinating, facilitating, promoting the energies that are present in the city".[29]

With adaptations and corrections, this has been the urban planning approach of the various councils governing the city (from 1997, center right: Mayors Albertini and Moratti; from 2011, center left: Pisapia and Sala). This is the context in which ambitious projects that changed the face of the city were carried out, such as the Garibaldi-Repubblica area and City Life, with its tall towers on the former Fiera Campionaria grounds. But there is not a city quarter where the old industrial fabric has not been replaced by new buildings—buildings that sometimes have kept the exterior appearance of their predecessors, as occurred with the Breda hangar, today an exhibition space (Hangar Bicocca). Or, along the axis of Via Tortona with the CGE-Ansaldo complex, which today houses service facilities of Teatro della Scala and a space called Base, where culture and work intertwine, complemented by the nearby Museo delle Culture (Mudec). Again, in the same district, there is the Riva Calzoni factory, a company renowned for its production of hydraulic turbines and pumps, today the headquarters of the Ermenegildo Zegna luxury fashion house. Another example of the repurposing of an industrial site as an exhibition center is Fondazione Prada, behind the Porta Romana freight yard.

In other cases, the old buildings were demolished and in their place shopping malls and mixed-use office-residential buildings were erected, as in the former OM grounds, not far from Pt. Romana railway station, in the Adriano quarter, site of the Ercole Marelli plant near Sesto San Giovanni, or in Santa Giulia, the fanciful name of the quarter designed for the Montedison acreage in Rogoredo in the extreme south-east outskirt of Milan.

[28] Pino Landonio, *Modello Milano: I vent'anni che hanno cambiato la città*, (Milan: Laurana, 2018), p. 123.

[29] Ibid., p. 136.

However meager this exemplification, it seems obvious how the territorial dispersion of the industrial areas and the decision to trust in the marketplace, possibly incentivized by substantial funding, as in the case of the major projects underway in the ex-Falck area or on the Expo 2015 site, promoted the quick assimilation of the city's industrial past, not always with satisfactory results. Suffice it to recall the projects left unfinished, or hastily cobbled together: the Innocenti grounds in Lambrate or the makeover of Bovisa, "Little Manchester". The transfer there of a section of the Politecnico university should have acted as a stimulus for an urban metamorphosis, still today incomplete.

Provisional Closing Remarks

I would like to conclude these notes by pointing out what seems to me an important aspect for understanding the city's metamorphosis and its recent success, which, "to tell the truth, nobody had foreseen".[30]

In the course of the twentieth century, Milan's narrative and its reality were that of the city of industry and labor. It is a fitting image, but an oversimplification. The city has always been many other things: a center of trade, finances, and services. But it was above all a meeting place between industry and culture, as demonstrated by the richness and intricacy of the ties between large industry, publishing companies, graphic studios, and advertising agencies. In 1881, between daily newspapers, entertainment magazines, technical reviews, and various other types of periodical, over two hundred mastheads were in publication.[31] It was the tip of an iceberg, around which rotated a universe of trades: photographers, graphic designers, advertisers, publicists found a market here that was absent elsewhere, fueled by the city's dynamic industrial fabric.

The capital of book publishing, Milan also became, between the two wars, the capital of advertising and business communication, as evidenced by the presence of firms like the one established by Antonio Boggeri, a bridge with the best European graphics culture, influenced by the Bauhaus,[32] or the publication of reviews such as *L'Ufficio moderno*, which

[30] Dario Di Vico, "Il paradosso della città che si avvicina all' Europa e distacca (ancora) l'Italia", in *Corriere della Sera*, 11 October 2016.

[31] Dario Papa, 'Giornali e giornalisti', in *Mediolanum*, (Milan: Vallardi, 1881).

[32] Giorgio Fioravanti, 'Grafica e pubblicità', in *Storia di Milano, vol. XVIII, Il Novecento, tomo III*, (Rome: Istituto dell'Enciclopedia italiana, 1996), pp. 605–625.

promoted the automation of office work, marketing, and advertising, contributing to the formation of a new generation of business consultants and communications experts. These are signs of an environment that was curious about modernity and open to its developments, which would come to full expression after 1945, in the climate of the return to democracy.[33]

In 1936, Leonardo Sinisgalli, an engineer and poet convinced of the need to merge humanistic and industrial culture, settled in Milan to take over the management of Olivetti's Advertising Office. He did not stay long, but his years there were rich in encounters and experiences. Years later, recalling mentors and friends from his early life in Milan (Vittorini, Quasimodo, Gatto, Sereni, and others), Sinisgalli made a consideration that to me seems decisive: "Our daring, our enthusiasm, my fanaticism of that time could find no justification and cannot be understood, if they weren't played out against the backdrop of a city like Milan".[34] We are not in Ivrea where the company was the center around which everything revolved, a place that bore the stamp of Adriano Olivetti, becoming it a pole of attraction and experiments whose light would continue to shine even after the company had ceased to exist.[35] In Milan, the city itself was the engine of change, the center of virtuous networking between the worlds of business, the professions, and culture. This would become apparent in the economic miracle years, when Milan was the Pirelli company and its "industrial humanism," and its plants in Bicocca would end up being a plastic interpretation of the city's transformation and its path from manufacturing to the knowledge economy; it was the Comit (Banca Commerciale Italiana) of Raffaele Mattioli, an extraordinary man of banking and culture[36]; it was the city of the Assolombarda industrialist association perched in defense of the electrical monopoly and of a diocese

[33] Raimonda Riccini, 'Progettare in prospettiva democratica. L'arredo popolare e altri temi del disegno industriale', in Luigi Ganapini (ed.), *L'Italia alla metà del XX secolo: Conflitto sociale, Resistenza, costruzione di una democrazia*, (Milan: Guerini e associati, 2005), pp. 293–304.

[34] Leonardo Sinisgalli, 'Le mie stagioni milanesi', in *Civiltà delle macchine* (1955), p. 23; Giuseppe Lupo, 'Sinisgalli e le industrie milanesi 1934–1973', in Giuseppe Lupo (ed.), *Sinisgalli a Milano: Poesia, pittura, architettura e industria dagli anni trenta agli anni sessanta*, (Interlinea: Novara, 2002).

[35] Paolo Bricco, *Olivetti, prima e dopo Adriano. Industria, cultura, estetica*, (Naples: l'Ancora del Mediterraneo, 2005).

[36] Sandro Gerbi, Raffaele Mattioli e il filosofo domato, (Turin: Einaudi, 2002).

capable of opening up, not without contrasts, to dialogue with modernity. It was the city of the large publishing groups and private publishers the likes of Giangiacomo Feltrinelli and Alberto Mondadori with Il Saggiatore, of the pragmatism of engineers and of the philosophical school of Antonio Banfi and his students, of Gio Ponti, the link between the world of the architects and that of the furniture craftsmen, forerunner of that breakthrough phenomenon that starting from the Sixties was design[37]; it was the realm of the seamstresses and the stylists.[38] And, finally, it was the city of *Rocco and His Brothers*, the city to which thousands of peasants from the South arrived in hope of carving themselves out a better life. Milan is all these things now and much more, a sort of continuously changing kaleidoscope.

It is this boundless mixture of genres, cultures, creativity, and styles of work that represents the city's uniqueness and fuels its capacity for generating design and intellectual endeavors that developed in relation to and in function of the impulses of a variegated and dynamic industrial fabric.

Herein lies, in my opinion, one of the deep-rooted reasons for Milan's vitality and the capacity for rebirth of a city that in recent decades has managed to disperse and immense capital of industrial history without, for all that, losing the art of generating wealth.

"The ancient doctrines are like snakeskins that, to shed the old one, all it takes is to have the new one underneath": this affirmation of Cattaneo's seems to me a salient metaphor for what has happened in Milan in the last few years. While the old blue-collar bloc started to crumble after the downsizing and eventual closure of the factories, as early as the 1930s the seeds of a new economy oriented toward the tertiary sector had already started to take hold. This was the foundation for the city's renewal after the collapse of industry.

[37] Raimonda Riccini, 'Disegno industriale in Lombardia. Un modello per il made in Italy', in Duccio Bigazzi and Marco Meriggi (eds.), *Storia d'Italia: Le regioni dall'Unità a oggi. La Lombardia*, (Turin: Einaudi, 2001), pp. 1161–1193.

[38] Elisabetta Merlo and Francesca Polese, 'Turning Fashion into Business. The Eemergence as an international Fashion Hub', in *Business History Review* 80 (2006), pp. 415–447.

References

Aldo Bonomi, Comunità, prossimità, simultaneità, in Aldo Bonomi, Alberto Magnaghi, Marco Revelli, Il vento di Adriano. La comunità concreta di Olivetti tra non più e non ancora, Roma, DeriveApprodi, 2015

Aree produttive abbandonate. Ricerca sulle aree produttive abbandonate, sulle trasformazioni indotte, sui riflessi nei livelli occupazionali, a cura di Antonello Boatti, Valentina Brambilla, Francesco Samorè, Milano, CGIL-Politecnico di Milano, 2018 (forthcoming)

Cesare Sommariva, Le due morali. Scelte imprenditoriali, lotte operaie e intervento culturale alla Redaelli Sidas di Rogoredo (1979–1984), Roma, Edizioni Lavoro, 1986

Chiedi alla ruggine. Studi e storiografia della deindustrializzazione, in "Meridiana", n. 85, 2016

Costanzo Ranci, Rossana Torri. Milano tra coesione sociale e sviluppo. Rapporto su Milano sociale, Milano, B. Mondadori, 2007

Dario Di Vico, Il paradosso della città che si avvicina all'Europa e distacca (ancora) l'Italia, in "Corriere della Sera", 11 ottobre 2016

Dario Di Vico, Donne, competenze, stili di vita: a Milano metamorfosi vincenti, in "Corriere della Sera", 1 ottobre 2017

Dario Papa, Giornali e giornalisti, in Mediolanum, Milano, Vallardi, 1881, vol. 1

Edward Glaeser, Triumph of the City, New York, Penguin Books, 2011

Elisabetta Merlo, Francesca Polese, Turning Fashion into Business. The Eemergence as an international Fashion Hub, in "Business History Review", autunno 2006, n. 80, pp. 415–447

Ferruccio Ricciardi, Il lavoro industriale nella crisi del fordismo: scenari di declino e di tra-sformazione, in Storia del lavoro in Italia. Il Novecento 1945–2000. La ricostruzione e il mira-colo economico, la globalizzazione, a cura di Stefano Musso, Roma, Castelvecchi, 2015, pp. 599–630

Giancarlo Consonni, Graziella Tonon, La terra degli ossimori. Caratteri del territorio e del paesaggio della Lombardia contemporanea, in Storia d'Italia. Le regioni dall'Unità a oggi. La Lombardia, a cura di Duccio Bigazzi e Marco Meriggi, Torino, Einaudi, 2001, pp.

Giorgio Bigatti, Giampaolo Nuvolati (eds), Story of a District. Milano-Bicocca. People, Pla-ces, Recollections, Milano, Scalpendi, 2019

Giorgio Fioravanti, Grafica e pubblicità, in Storia di Milano, vol. XVIII, Il Novecento, tomo III, Roma, Istituto dell'Enciclopedia italiana, 605–625

Giuseppe Lupo, Sinisgalli e le industrie milanesi 1934–1973, in Sinisgalli a Milano. Poesia, pit-tura, architettura e industria dagli anni trenta agli anni sessanta, a cura di G. Lupo, Interlinea, Novara 2002

Giuseppe Sala, Milano e il secolo delle città, Milano, La nave di Teseo, 2018

Leonardo Sinisgalli, Le mie stagioni milanesi, in "Civiltà delle macchine", a. III, n. 5, settem-bre-ottobre 1955

Luigi Vergallo, La città che sa cambiare. Indagine su economia e società a Milano, Milano, Guerini e Associati, 2012
Lodovico Meneghetti, Le nuove Milano estranee. L'architettura servile, 30 ottobre 2004, in www.eddyburg.it
Luca Mocarelli, Le aree dismesse milanesi o della cancellazione del patrimonio industriale: il caso della Bicocca, in "Il patrimonio industriale", V (2011), n. 7, pp. 69–75
Marco Martini, I mutamenti strutturali del sistema produttivo a Milano e alla Bicocca, in La nascita di una università nuova: Milano-Bicocca. Dal lavoro di fabbrica alla fabbrica del sa-pere, a cura di Nicolò Leotta, Milano, Skira, 2002, pp. 131–146
Maria Cristina Gibelli, Milano: da metropoli fordista a mecca del real estate, in "Meridiana", n. 85, 2016
Marianna d'Ovidio, I redditi dei milanesi: aumento della ricchezza o polarizzazione?, in "Im-presa e Stato", n. 186, 2009, pp. 36–43
Mario Tronti, con A. Bianchi, Il popolo perduto. Per una critica della sinistra, Roma, Nutri-menti, 2019
Matteo Bolocan, Geografie milanesi, Santarcangelo di Romagna, Maggioli, 2009
Milano. Città poliedrica tra innovazione e sostenibilità, a cura di F. Zajczyk e S. Mugnano, Soveria Mannelli, Rubbettino, 2019
Paola Dezza, Il Rinascimento di Milano: piani d'investimento per 10 miliardi, "Il Sole 24 Ore", 6 marzo 2019
Paolo Bricco, Olivetti, prima e dopo Adriano. Industria, cultura, estetica, Napoli, l'Ancora del Mediterraneo, 2005
Pietro Causurano, La fabbrica fordista e il conflitto industriale, in Storia del lavoro in Italia. Il Novecento 1945–2000. La ricostruzione e il miracolo economico, la globalizzazione, a cura di Stefano Musso, Roma, Castelvecchi, 2015, pp. 59–101
Pino Landonio, Modello Milano. I vent'anni che hanno cambiato la città, Milano, Laurana, 2018
Raimonda Riccini, Disegno industriale in Lombardia: un modello per il made in Italy, in in Storia d'Italia. Le regioni dall'Unità a oggi. La Lombardia, a cura di Duccio Bigazzi e Marco Meriggi, Torino, Einaudi, 2001, pp. 1161–1193
Raimonda Riccini, Progettare in prospettiva democratica: l'arredo popolare e altri temi del di-segno industriale, in L'Italia alla metà del XX secolo. Conflitto sociale, Resistenza, costruzione di una democrazia, a cura di Luigi Ganapini, Milano, Guerini e associati, 2005, pp. 293–304
Sandro Gerbi, Raffaele Mattioli e il filosofo domato, Torino, Einaudi, 2002
Sergio Bologna, Per un breve panorama della logistica dagli anni 70 ad oggi (http://www.intotheblackbox.com)
Silvano Belligni, Stefania Ravazzi, La politica e la città. Regime urbano e classe dirigente a Torino, Bologna, il Mulino, 2012
Stefano Boeri, Elegia di una dismissione, in Gabriele Basilico, Ritratti di fabbriche, Milano, Federico Motta, 2009

CHAPTER 12

Deindustrialization in Turin and the Role of Local Government for Economic and Urban Change

Sergio Scamuzzi

Introduction

Turin is a nearly ideal case of deindustrialization in a monocultural city. Both the government itself and their governance over the decline in industrial manufacturing were characterized by a historical defeat of working-class movement, a policy of local welfare that early left room to electoral changes and plans for innovation. The recovery from decline developed in a perspective of international competition and with the means of an inner social pact in the city. Public shared knowledge and policies of culture had also a significant role, a representation both for the self and the others (the stakeholder of the city). The essay cites major

S. Scamuzzi (✉)
Università Degli Studi Di Torino, Turin, Italy
e-mail: sergio.scamuzzi@unito.it

S. Berger et al. (eds.), *Deindustrialisation in Twentieth-Century Europe*, Palgrave Studies in the History of Social Movements,
https://doi.org/10.1007/978-3-030-89631-7_12

facts of local history and sociological processes that gave shape to the transformation in the economy and the urban structures.

The aimed direction of the transformation was a variant of the EU knowledge economy model with path dependent activities in the automotive sector, Ict and economy of culture (an arts and events city for tourism). But 2008 world financial crisis and its long-time effects on such a weak economy as the Italian one restrained the change. A second part of the essay is dedicated to this less successful history of more recent years, when a new radical change of local government happened after a long continuity. The dismissal of the social pact lessened the quality and impact of local policies. But also a fall of disposable income for local public expenses due to the national public debt policy added difficulties to the new government that confronts the challenges of a shrinking city.

In the concluding remarks, the thesis is exposed that the future of Turin is highly uncertain but can be better seen in a balance sheet of 'green and/or development 'perspectives that is helped by hints from comparisons with Genoa, Milan and the Ruhr region.

The Most Fordist Town of Italy, the Industrial Decline and its Administration

Turin used to be one of the most Fordist towns of Italy thanks to the Fabbrica Italiana di Automobili Torino, the Fiat of the Agnelli family, protagonist of the Italian industrialization, born in 1899, and that since the 20s put into operation the first large mass production factories (Lingotto of the origins and then Mirafiori, Rivalta in the Turin area and others throughout Italy), with a founder who was a friend of Henry Ford, since 1906 explicitly animated by the objective of "doing like Ford" in his company. Suppliers of Fiat and of the families of workers and employees that worked for it, their homes and neighborhoods, are the economic drive of the city, and the magnet of a massive immigration in the fifties and sixties, years of monopolistic growth of the company and the "monocultural" growth of the city. A trade union movement and an employers' movement, not as strong as elsewhere in numbers, were however pioneeristic, and in the sixties and seventies incisive and significant for the policy of the entire labor movement and for the country. In the seventies, the local administration went through the alternation of the liberal and Catholic right with the communist left and a success of the Catholic left, with a strong conditioning of Fiat resulting from the social impact of business choices that had certainly not been negotiated. Also its strong culture of the elite of national value through important publishing houses and the first Radio and public television headquarters is a reference for this Fordist modernity. Turin is undoubtedly an ideal type of Fordism.

The *industrial decline* of the city, centered on the decline of the Fiat, which used to be the major drive of the Turinese economy, was shrewdly administered for at least a decade. During this time the layoff of employees was gradual, with a high use of social shock absorbers, addressed by the city's welfare approach, a long-time historical continuity but reaffirmed by the authoritative and popular mayor Diego Novelli (mandates 1975–1985). Fiat's corporate authority was strengthened, despite the company's crisis, by a "heroic defeat" of the labor movement and the mobilization of the staff, the "march of forty thousand" of 1980. A first phase of conflict was followed by forms of collaboration with the city, necessarily in search of countervailing sources for its development, with the Castellani administration. The closing of numerous plants of the Fiat group operating in the city, of the companies that worked for the Fiat, of other important textile companies (the Rivetti Gruppo Finanziario Tessile) and mechanic companies, together with companies in other sectors, give rise to as many as 128 abandoned areas.[1] The problem arises of how to fill them, how to redeploy and train the workforce that remains valid, how to boost the development of the city through new ways, and this is the beginning of a season of commitment of the Turinese intellectuals and professional elite toward new solutions. The political, economic and cultural elite are renewed in their roles, while maintaining a high degree of continuity with their past. For example, high industrial executives become managers of public utilities, intellectuals become political administrators during the period of response to the crisis and to the de-legitimization of the political class consequent to the national corruption trials.

The demographic challenge of urban deindustrialization can be summed up in these figures: % employed in industry in Turin 1961 = 60%, 1981 = 50%, 2001 = 30%, 2011 = 25%. The working class, latently

[1] A detailed picture of the urban transformations in Emiliana Armano, Carlo A. Dondona and Fiorenzo Ferlaino (eds.), *Postfordismo e trasformazione urbana: Casi di recupero dei vuoti industriali e politiche nel territorio torinese*, (Turin: Ires Piemonte, 2016).

designed, declines from 57% in 1971 to 34% of the active population in 2001. The population of the city is gradually reduced from 1.200.000 in the 70 s to about 885.000 in recent years, but is compensated by the metropolitan area of the 14 neighboring municipalities, which reaches 1.295.000 inhabitants approximately, for a total of 2.180.000 people (data of 2017). According to an estimation, in 2014 10% of the apartments in Turin are empty, as a result of the decrease of the families. The city's population is reduced, also partly due to relocations into neighboring areas, and is maintained thanks to foreign immigration (Romanians and Arab communities being the most numerous). The larger metropolitan area which it belongs to has stabilized over roughly the last ten years. The decline of the population is not associated with a decline in per-capita income and in other economic indicators that rather see a stagnation in the twenty-first century with a modest yearly percentage oscillations of more or less 0% and a very modest growth in recent years. Also in more recent years, the reduction of industrial weight does not give rise to a strong tertiary sector: The added value of industry drops from 17.000 to 15.000 from 2007 to 2013 while the total rises very slightly from 49.787 to 59.750. The only value in net growth is the tourist influx.

Since the years of decline the city has activated a strong reflexivity not only on the social aspects of the decline, such as the massive recourse to the redundancy fund and the management of the exit from active life of thousands of workers, but also the company itself, the problems of the city, the end of a long historical cycle and national role of the city (a thesis to which precisely the changes added empirical evidence according to G. Berta, S. Musso and N. Tranfaglia) but ever more intensely on future prospects. A. Bagnasco publishes in 1986 an interpretation of the city of Turin as an organized society and "simple" society, which needs a governed market and greater complexity that has had very good luck: reflections and debates in the elite in preparation of the change have a meeting place at "Confronti a Torino" in casa Aurora, headquarters of the Textile Group GFT, then still in activity (it apparently closed in 2003) and some results are published. The Fondazione G.Agnelli of those days is also a very active center of reflection and propositions on the urban and regional planning, it advances the ideas of Turin Technocity and of networking in the North West macroregion, which will be successes. A meeting of the Chamber of Commerce of 1994 develops the idea of marketing places as a challenge for local development.[2]

The Recovery from Decline and the Perspective of a New Internationally Competitive City

The *response* to the challenge takes its cue from the new regime of direct election of mayors, in a climate of de-legitimization of the national political class with a few trawls on the local one, which allows a center-left coalition to split the Novelli's ex-Communist electorate and that of the right wing (little attracted by a weak candidate), with the candidacy of Valentino Castellani, former Vice Rector of the Politecnico and Professor of Electronic Engineering, a Catholic left-wing militant. The new phase in the history of the city is thus born in 1993 from a break with the past in some way consequent to other events that had marked the end of the post-war industrialization cycle and drastically reduced the role of the labor movement in one of its national strongholds, with its historical defeat at Fiat.

The breakage of the Castellani administration lies in members of the local government, partly newcomers in the political profession, and is unprecedented in a context such as the Italian one marked by politics as a profession; a type of alliance and approach marked by "development and solidarity", which will then be that of Romano Prodi and the Ulivo in

[2] The end of the parable: Giuseppe Berta, "Mobilitazione operaia e politiche manageriali alla Fiat 1969–1979", in Stefano Musso (ed.), *Tra fabbrica e società. Mondi operai nell'Italia del novecento. Annali della Fondazione Giangiacomo Feltrinelli XXX 1997*, (Milan: Feltrinelli, 1999); Nicola Tranfaglia and Brunello Mantelli, "Apogeo e collasso della 'città fabbrica' Torino dall'autunno caldo alla sconfitta del 1980", in Nicola Tranfaglia (ed.), *Storia di Torino: vol.IX- Gli anni della repubblica*, (Turin: Einaudi, 1999). The turning point: Vittorio Ravizza, *Turin style. Technocity and its province*, (Turin: Editurist, 1990); Giuseppina De Sanctis and Giuseppe Russo (eds.), *Un'alternativa al declino: 18 idee per lo sviluppo di Torino negli anni novanta*, (Turin: Torino Incontra, 1992); Gastone Ave and Franco Corsico (eds.), *Marketing urbano in Europa*, (Turin: Edizioni Torino Incontra, 1994). Arnaldo Bagnasco, *Torino. Un profilo sociologico*, (Turin: Einaudi, 1986) is the "founding" text for the new representation of the city for its decision-makers. A bibliography of studies on Turin for the period covered by this article, here not shown for reasons of space but used, includes as many as 75 titles: this is also a data on the strong reflectivity that accompanies the whole change of Turin.

the Italian and then European government; a clear objective to promote a diversified development of the city, starting from the economy of culture and of high training; an international opening, thanks to relationships activated in various European networks of cities and in particular with Barcelona; a policy of welcoming and conciliation with foreign immigration that aroused conflicts and nourished the right (a laboratory was the district of San Salvario, today regenerated); collaboration but with independence with Fiat (after a conflictual beginning wanted by Fiat) and with the Catholic world and that of religions in general, also for the purposes of social integration; a new master plan produced the first year of work and the first subway line; a plan for the suburbs.

The Strategic Plan of the City: International City Marketing and a Social Pact

The reflection already previously launched in intellectual and high industrial leadership circles is embodied in a *Strategic plan of the city launched in 2001*, but prepared since 1998, that presents strategic lines of internationalization, metropolitan and not only city government, promotion of training and research, promotion of new forms of entrepreneurship, a city of culture, tourism, commerce and sport, a better quality of life. This will encounter many successes and a few non-compliances. Before and during the first and the second strategic plan, frequent attention will be given to monitoring activities of acts and events by private foundations and university research groups, great attention from the media and public opinion. The association created to formulate strategies and manage round tables of the specific actions includes as many as 121 private and public shareholders and is called "Torino Internazionale": it is the voluntary governance structure, a most remarkable institutional innovation, which makes room for civil society. It is a case of "urban contract", a widespread phenomenon in many Western towns at that time, with local variations.[3]

A remarkable administrative continuity is ensured from 1993 to 2011 by the two mandates of Valentino Castellani (1993–2001) and by the two mandates of the next mayor Sergio Chiamparino (2001–2011), a professional politician with a long career in local administration in the Italian

[3] Paolo Perulli, *The Urban Contract: Community, governance and capitalism*, (London: Routledge, 2016), see Chapter 2.

and European parliaments, that share the same vision. Chiamparino follows up *in 2005 a Second strategic plan*, launched in 2006, also born from an analysis of what the previous one had not realized, with many directions of intervention: education, creativity, industrial transformation, work, health, urban transformations, mobility and logistics, urban and cultural regeneration, heritage of the Olympic Games. The unifying theme that emerges increasingly over the years is the vision of the economy and society of knowledge and culture.

Two new subjects that cannot be neglected on the scene are the banking foundations CRT and Compagnia di Sanpaolo—a very Italian type of institution created by the Amato government in 1990 to administer the assets of the banks by donating their profits to public purposes of social and cultural utility and leave banks for commercial purposes—with political appointment of leaders. Throughout the period of the strategic planning, they will support economically the significant actions of the local authority and the association for planning, also exerting a notable cultural influence on the agenda.

The *apex* of success as regards the public visibility of the transformation is constituted by the *Olympic Winter Games* in 2006. The main planned expectations are reached, starting from a significant tilting of the notoriety and the international image of the city, no longer tied to Fiat and in decline but to innovation and culture. A pride for the candidacy won, strong consensus and identification of the population with the games and confidence in the positive repercussions for the city diffused in public opinion, with success of participation in competitions and cultural events during the games. In the aftermaths, legacy of urban works was largely reused, albeit with a few delays and problems, and of know-how. The final expenditure for the event balanced with the revenue upon closure of the budget of the Organising Committee of the event, with reasonable prospect of retraction of the debt of the local budget for infrastructures, thanks to the planning of their reuse.

A Self-Representation of Success and the Role of an Economy of Culture and of Urbanism

The investment in public and political communication of the city is important both for its strategic planning and in the competition between the territories to which the local politics are called, turned inwards as well as outwards at international level. Some of the most significant and successful claims: "Turin always on the move" appears in the communication as opposed to traditional "bogia nen" (don't move, which moreover is reread as "hold your position" ordered by the officers to the Savoy infantry); another historical event is often proudly evoked for the present aim: when Torino lost its role a political capital city of Italy and its liberal elite "decided" to promote itself as an industrial capital after 1864; "Passion lives here" fills the 2006 Olympics and becomes a leitmotiv that is valid for the whole of the city and its transformation; "Turin surprises you" because it shows itself to tourists and guests differently from their expectation of greyness. For this activity, as for other government and urban management activities, throughout the period of the first and second strategic plan the administration implements practices of public comparison and of learning from foreign success cases, activating exchanges with Barcelona, Stockholm, Glasgow, Bilbao and other cities, and comparisons with Detroit, as a true "learning city".[4]

The same studies that support the planning and supply the public opinion in the various components of the local elites and in relation to the national ones become more numerous. It must be emphazised that these studies suggest keywords and concepts for the new vision of the city that were so far unknown: to those already born to counteract the decline, such as competition between territories and urban marketing, restoring the balance between the market and organization, are added overbearingly innovation, "strategic plan", large events, urban planning as "giving public value to the center" in contrast with the approach until then prevailing, based on criticism of the urban income and the suburbs and significant interventions of regeneration.[5]

The result is a strong narrative of the city, which acts *on the transformation* and contributes to the cohesion of the elite and to the proud sharing of the change by the population that sees tangible signs and benefits

[4] Anna Martina, *Comunicare la città. Il caso di Torino olimpica*, (Milan: Bruno Mondadori, 2006) and Tim Campbell, *Beyond smart city: how cities network, develop and innovate*, (London: Routledge, 2012) offer empirical evidence on communication and learning, which are often underestimated.

[5] On the Olympics and big events: Luigi Bobbio e Chito Guala (eds.), *Verso Torino 2006*, (Rome: Carocci, 2002). On planning: Mario Calderini and Giuseppe Scellato, *Interpretare l'innovazione*, (Turin: Edizioni Fondazione G. Agnelli, 2003), HYPERLINK "sps:urlprefix::http" www.torinostrategica.it contains documentation of the plans of Turin, part of European season well reconstructed by Paolo Perulli, *Piani strategici. Governare le città europee*, (Milan: Angeli, 2004).

also in construction and in the pedestrianization of the baroque historical center. The innovation also allows for the emergence of new skills and talents in management and in urban expertise.

A reuse of a series of *spaces* left vacant is implemented: the beginning in style is the conversion of the Lingotto factory into a shopping center inaugurated in 2004, followed by the restoration and reuse of the Officine Grandi Motori, previously owned by the State Railways, for a doubling of the Politecnico and as the venue for exhibitions and concerts begun with the celebrations of Italy's 150th anniversary on national union in 2011, by Fiat Skf (Parco Dora and industrial archaeology, venues for concerts and mass events, such as the closing ceremony of the Ramadan), from the previous Expo 1961 (Palazzo a Vela reconverted for sport and for events), railways that crossed the city to connect the establishments to the national network are abandoned or covered and used for new settlements ("Spine") and the renovated stations (Porta Susa, Porta Dora, Airport), also in view of high speed international connections (Tav Turin-Lyon, however then delayed and contrasted by a social movement rooted in Val di Susa). The list of successes and failures could continue at length. These operations and the others related to the Olympic Games are permitted by the new regulatory plan launched in 1991 with the Castellani administration and some international stars of architecture such as Gae Aulenti, Norman Foster, Massimiliano Fuksas, Arata Isozaki, Renzo Piano are the authors of important projects. But the essential and founding operation is a redrawing of the city from its "central backbone", the railway section that splits in two the west of the city from the east, that is buried and replaced with a large road and real estate operation of high architectural quality from north to south of the city.

Large abandoned cultural goods are restored (Palazzina di Caccia di Stupinigi and especially the large investment of the Reggia di Venaria), the baroque old town is pedestrianized and repainted, the Museo Egizio renewed in its form of management (Foundation) and in its staging, with extension of the spaces and the new Museum of Cinema created by previous collections, a whole system of galleries and events of contemporary art is born, intended for long duration (mainly the Artissima fair). These cultural goods become large attractors of foreign, national, local tourism and for the residents themselves, their success grows and then continues, also thanks to a policy of exhibitions. They are systemized by policies and constituted specific mixed (private–public) entities and are referred to as baroque system, contemporary art system, museum system, cultural system, the latter also for the search for sponsors. A hinterland of public structures such as municipal library networks and private cultural associations plays an effective internal function.

The city is diversified by reconverting itself in part toward *leisure*, and tourism begins to grow, services to people spread. Classical and pop music, art and cinema, municipal culture and books, food and gastronomy, neighborhoods and premises for the movida of young people, are the major themes of the cultural offer in Turin and the aspects of a new vital city. Also the production of culture receives a strong stimulus from this climate and from specific measures, with positive outcomes in some areas, such as a Film Commission that is a model in Italy, opportunities for young artists with the enhancement of creativity for the economy (not only in art markets), libraries and cultural associations, a lot of public and promotional communication of the city, but a major setback in public investment is the multimedia field: Lumiq and Virtual Reality Multimediapark, then closed in 2013 after substantial but unsuccessful investments.

In all the transformations remembered so far, the main lever of the local policy and its private partners remains public expenditure. Some of its entries such as culture are for a long time among the highest in Italy. The challenge more frequently evoked is the international competition between territories. A reader may wonder about what led to the above described high-level reflexivity and communication: we can guess that one reason was just a necessity of legitimation of this public expenses on voices of the public balance sheet so different from the past both for the local public opinion and for EU founding policies and foreign private investors, by a partly new political elite of academic origin that was also acquainted to applied research to prepare decisions and to international exchange of ideas and knowledge. An intellectual tradition of the city was still alive and made the rest: the three political doctrines of liberalism, communism and social catholicism that have roots in Turin (Einaudi, Gramsci, Gioberti) have in common the idea that politics and policies are a matter of thought, a shared thought, and not only of action.

The Path Dependent Innovation of the Local Economy Versus the Knowledge Economy Model of UE

Turin city of culture is only part of the story, because even the city of industry, albeit with reduced dimensions, is being renewed. Part of the innovation is path dependent: the "polytechnic" city, main national concentration of research and development for industry is confirmed and develops also internationally. The infrastructures receive new impetus in the perspective of a "multicentric" city. In the *business world* it is the moment of great relocations from abroad: Motorola for some time, General Motors more stably. Areas left empty by factories of the Fiat group and other companies are made available to new firms, without much success. But many local businesses move autonomously, starting from Fiat that becomes globalized in FCA and delocates its productions, leaving in Turin its high range and Headquarters. The automotive industry develops in a competitive manner, selectively converting a part of the old firms of the Fiat turnover and outsources into an international industry of components. Some medium ICT and High Tech companies generally assert themselves, foreign direct investments arrive, foreign companies incoming, and research and development activities at leader levels in Italy. Some companies linked to food and its distribution (Eataly, Lavazza, Leone and others) are established.

A composition effect of the private strategies is important for the development of this productive world; what instead remains significant is the public contribution to the allocation of Motorola and then of General Motors, directly through financing and discharge of urban charges and indirectly through the doubling of the Politecnico. The reciprocal is important: the commitment in the public field of figures and agencies of the private sector: determinant for the formation of a new culture of local government, before that for the support given to some of its shares through banks and banking foundations (Intesa, Unicredit, Compagnia di Sanpaolo, Fondazione CRT), the Chamber of Commerce and its agencies such as Torino Incontra, via its Presidents such as Enrico Salza, businessman, and Alessandro Barberis, some former Fiat executives with him and from other companies "recruited" to guide public utilities and large public service agencies.

Names like these provide the visible sign of a strong continuity in time and of homogeneity, movement and interaction in the Turinese elite between economic, political and cultural functions at the basis of a "Turin system" that ensures propensity to cooperation on large projects of the ruling class but will later be criticized politically.[6]

The Crisis of 2008 and Its Aftermaths: The Limits of Local Resilience

The financial crisis and the economic stagnation in the 2008–15 period descend upon the second strategic plan, already subject to some wear, and contribute to make it unfinished in some parts. They then hinder the birth of the *Third strategic plan* which undergoes a long gestation period. The new mayor Piero Fassino (in his 2011–2016 mandate), he too an experienced professional politician, from the Turinese militancy of his youth dedicated to the Pci and factory ratio, to that of parliamentarian and party secretary, shares the vision of the past strategic plans, moreover compliant with his experience in international politics. But he must handle them with much fewer resources for public expenditure, on which Monti's technical government (2011–12) has intervened with heavy cuts, intended to last to preserve sovereignty in favor of the UE and of the IMF, and consequent greater dependence on the central government and the European Union (with which he relates furthermore, as did Chiamparino and Castellani, from authoritative positions and international alliance among mayors), in the presence of struggling private companies and a population discouraged by the long crisis and stagnation which gradually limits its consumption: the cultural and formative consumption, free of charge or at a low price, hold on better than the others but over the years starts private health expenditure begins to decrease. Inequality of income in the urban population grows, as do social problems of poverty, unemployment and illegal immigration.

The new challenge is very difficult. The consequences of the previous policies remain strong but the new conditions of their sustainability are much more stringent. The narrative of the city by its leaders does not change but appears forced by the rhetoric of opposition of successes to difficulties, of opportunities for development to unmet needs. The investment in public communication and territorial advertising decreases, it seems more difficult in the case of events, it passes into the hands of the

[6] Sergio Scamuzzi et al., *Élites e reti in una città in trasformazione. Il caso Torino*, (Milan: Angeli, 2005), Silvano Belligni and Stefania Ravazzi, *La politica e la città: Regime urbano e classe dirigente a Torino*, (Bologna: Il Mulino, 2013).

mayor's political communication and, for the *pars destruens* of the difficulties, to the political and social opposition who develop a narrative of crisis and poverty. The communication of the opposition systematically digs into the depths of social media and perpetuate reasons of dissent, such as the costs of the not reused Olympic works, of the "useless" Tav and of the events, the "neglected suburbs" and the transformation elite (the "Turin system" is assimilated to the "national caste").

The poverty of the middle class created by the crisis and the stagnation, by the dualism of the development of the driving sectors and of their very limited size, means that the real challenge is a change of paradigm of development and of the local government of the city, and consequently also of the analytical concepts, but for a few years the old one declines while the new one does not appear. There is no analytical and especially proactive and shared reflection comparable to that which accompanied the previous step in the production of new concepts, the Lisbon strategy of the EU, through its industrial and urban policies inspired by an innovation that can make the development and solidarity synergetic. It becomes one of the few economic and cultural resources for the Regions and local Authorities but breaks on the difficulties of the economy to emerge from the crisis and the idea and the narrative of a decline returns to interpret the many negative indicators. Meanwhile the actors fail in their commitments or redefine their roles or change, and the strategic plan weakens its relevance. The political initiative of the Municipality and of its Board is strengthened. This initiative however depends for its realization of events and more innovative policies on the banking foundations which are reinforced as projectual actors, the only subjects of public commitment remained with sufficient resources and expertise and versatile in economic, social and cultural issues.

Regarding private economy, the crisis for Italy is partly financial part but partly due to a historical lack of innovation and consequent low labor productivity. The Italian banks—the two partly Turinese ones (Intesa San Paolo, Unicredit) are among the main in the country—face the first one well. There is a selection among the manufacturing enterprises and service in the Turin area: the companies that survive are those that best adapt to the decrease in consumption, such as the great mass distribution at the expense of shops or on the contrary small retailers linked to the new post-modern leisure; there is a development of true innovators in their product and outlet market, as suppliers of other companies, often foreign.

The building sector on the other hand remains stationary and experiences important failures.

The *new strategic plan, the third*, must have a different method of work and planning with respect to the past: more research of *grassroots* i.e. detection, enhancement for an implementation of existing plans of urban, entrepreneurial and especially social character, during the preparation phase that lasted from 2012 to 2014. It is more limited and oriented to social objectives, launched in 2015: sustainability, social inclusion, smart innovation and with a different philosophy: private–public partnership (no longer only public lever), territorial leadership (sought primarily in firms and universities) to free the energies for growth, metropolitan territory (in 2014 the Metropolitan Area provided by the new law is finally constituted). The actions proposed by the third plan are aggregated in large projects aimed at promoting social innovation, new business, dissemination of technologies, international mobility and logistics, administrative simplification. Also the name of the governance association that manages it changes to "strategic Turin", while internationalization remains a relevant objective.

Change of Local Government, Lack of Public Expenses, Dismissal of the Urban Contract

The long-term effects of the crisis and the slowness of the Italian recovery compared to other countries urge and prevent the city from being among the most dynamic in the country Italy. The city is also suffering from the effects of the restriction on public expenditure, basis of the existing planning model, and of the restrictions imposed on welfare by the national austerity policies. The indebtedness of the city to build its infrastructure is no longer rewarded by tax and indirect revenue, as it was in the previous development expectations, now proved wrong by an economy in stagnation or low growth, which squeezes consumption and also sees a reduction of the active population. It thus becomes an electoral campaign weapon and is represented as a waste.

The weakening of politics, the lever of the previous development, brings back to light the limits of the economy and of the local society that the strategic plans and local policies had not been able to overcome. The city thus anticipates a confidence crisis of one part of the electorate, in general toward the institutions and the center-left parties members of the national and local government, causing with the new local elections of 2016 a change of majority in favor of the M5S which has shrewdly cultivated this distrust, together with a proposal for the populist government, generically localist and environmentalist and toward the extreme right which fully exploits for electoral purposes the problems of immigration, indeed discharged by many governments in the UE onto Italy (with a few exceptions such as Germany): the effect of the elections is a change in the majority and local leadership. The breakage sign is immediately given by the new M5S mayor, Chiara Appendino, with the dissolution of the association in charge of the drafting of the strategic plan and the round tables and a return of planning in the institutions and in the political movement M5S, however, weak and controversial with the base of the movement itself that does not always provide the expected responses to the populist promises mobilized it, such as the participatory municipal budget, the veto to new supermarkets. It reflects pragmatic oscillations about the major events and large infrastructures, initially the object of veto principles. It supports urban ecology measures, however perceiving their individual costs and being faced in some cases with the disagreement of traders and residents. In others, it receives consent in exchange of listening, like with the anti-movida movement. What also weighs in the narration is the revolt against the "Turin system", to which applies a local translation of the national rhetoric of "caste" while it was previously, and was seen positively as, a method of cohesion of the elite on major objectives and a cooperation between the regional and local levels even if of a different political sign.

The elite of civil society that could be the protagonist of a new strategic planning, in part different from the previous decade in its economic component, at first waits pragmatically for the planning of the new local political elite—partly composed of exponents of the movement but partly recruited from administrative, commercial, university environments, a real paretian élite circulation—but then begins to mobilize in some of its components (construction and its professionals, printing, trade and finally industrials) to speak out against the disappearance of a vision of the city and of large shared objectives, or acts directly on the territory with its own investments, often to fulfil past choices (reuse of Officine Grandi Riparazioni, urban regeneration around the museum Ettore Fico and at the Lavazza headquarters, new venues of the universities). The agenda also includes numerous projects financed by the Piedmont Region and the EU on health, scientific research, the transition to Industry 4.0, smart city variants; the Chamber of Commerce launches a candidacy for new Winter

Olympic Games; there are many activities for the promotion and training of new youth entrepreneurship and social innovation. Comparison and general and comprehensive coordination round tables prefer agreements on individual issues and projects. The crises and difficulties of many asset of the past are weighing, first of all culture, and the competition of the territory with the neighboring Milano, in full recovery from the crisis—there is significant contention for a great historical event for Turin such as the Salone del libro (won) and for new Winter Olympics (lost)—and with foreign countries. The public communication of the city is limited to service communication, and the advertising investment on the territory and cultural events is modest and selective. The prevailing political communication comes from the mayor, but is mostly directed in social media to the movement that supports it. There is a strong representation of the local chronicle by the main daily newspaper, La Stampa, which enhances its action.

Studies and social reporting on the cities go on, but there is no more a strict connection with policies and aren't asked for by the new elite. This fall of reflexivity is a major rupture from the past, also due to the vanishing of intellectual traditions and to a realignment of the new political majority—a social group partly disembedded from past civic society and parties, partly coming from some issue movements—to the general trend of populistic politics, for which politics and policies are a matter of action and communication, not a matter of thought.

On the balance sheet of this latest phase of local development we can see, in sum, largely exogenous factor for the failure—comparatively seen to the past phase—but the local government and private governance 's response to this challenge by the new local èlite has not been performative enough, in spite of successful performances of single actors. Maybe because the local elite has not acted as a team and the successful actors were too few: a local social pact was missing.

Uncertain Perspectives of a New Model: The Search for Postgrowth After Deindustrialization

A composition effect is configured regarding private market strategies and public degrowth policies administered in its value of environmental sustainability, faced by a stagnant or low development rate economy, according to the periods. In one way the answer is positive. The administration promotes of its own accord—in 2014—an "*Action plan Turin*

2030 Sustainability and resilience", comprising classic "green" strategies, inclusion interventions characterized by social innovation logics (e.g. territorial low-cost dwelling networks) which serve the shortage of public funds, events for the interculturality and the youth, forms of participation and information sharing facilitated by new technologies (ICTs, big data, digitization of services to the citizen etc.), a "regulation of common goods", the revision of the regulatory plan as an important lever. Conceptually in line with the UE philosophy and policies, these measures however encounter contrasts and strong implementation difficulties, the action plan itself being more a summary communication of single projects.

Summarizing the recent years, thanks to competitiveness policies activated by various actors, especially by the regional authorities and by various companies and professional groups, with a very limited role of the city and consultations confined to the implementation of individual projects, the new Turin becomes an emerging effect, if there ever will be, of the composition of these actions without or with a weak political mission. The EU business innovation financing policies are however increasingly important, some with the participation of two Universities of the city. Their prominence also depends on the disappearance of the other actors present previously, so that the political agenda of the local government and civil society is thus a consequence of the EU policies. In addition to the usual automotive, companies and innovative sectors are emerging, such as aerospace, new materials and nanotechnologies, generation 4.0 ICTs applied mostly in factories of instrumental or intermediate goods, the agrifood sector, retail. Among the companies, FCA delocates its headquarters to Holland and only maintains its connection with the territory with high range cars. A group of medium-sized multinational companies, of "intelligent factories" and small long-lasting businesses is consolidated. The role of the two universities and of university health becomes more significant and is the levers of an economy of knowledge and consumption of a university city, as well as the subject of important urban interventions and economic development projects.

This leads to the appearance of an archipelago of economic, technological and in some cases social innovation projects, of medium and small scale, local but global in their origin and significance, of public engagement attempts, with an often residual role of the local government which becomes the city "maintenance worker". The competitiveness of the territory prospectively becomes a side effect of the competitiveness of its companies, and of other individual subjects, in contrast to the previous setting. The fundamental demographic constraint itself, the population decline, is strengthened by the confinement of politics to the city, in the difficulty of a comparison with the metropolitan area that instead would compensate for its decline, difficulties for a collaboration between the institutions due to both political and institutional reasons: the first dictated by the national political conflict to the different majorities in the municipalities, the second by a law that imposes a geographically senseless design of the area.

But if on the other hand we want to reread these more recent years from a point of view that is more attentive to the criticality and contradictions, taking advantage also of international comparisons with other similar areas, the city appears "between two fires", figuratively represented in public events opposing pro- and anti-TAV in 2018–19. From the analytical point of view it appears between two models that properly express responses to a challenge that the international literature identifies with the term "*shrinking cities*", referring to a phenomenology that is widespread in various cities of the United States and Europe with varying intensity (indeed not high for Turin) that dates back to the first wave of deindustrialization but was reintroduced by the recession of 2008 which weakened cities[7]: between a response of acceptance and use of the decline—postgrowth—and a response of contrast to the decline—newgrowth—which both take as a central theme resiliency as a declination of the environmental and economic sustainability.

The strength of the *postgrowth* model consists in the singular "adaptation" that allows the resizing of the city population, its economic decline, the relative poverty of part of the population, the extreme lack of public funds, and in being legitimized and rationalized by visions of more or less happy degrowth, in harmony with the mobilization of ideological minorities, in this case Italian and Turinese. The strength of the *newgrowth* model lies in its path dependence aspects and in the alignment of its postgrowth promise to strong areas of Europe, to the EU policies which express it, to subjects who participate in it and benefit from it and in

[7] Russel Weaver et al., *Shrinking cities: Understanding urban decline in the United States*, (London: Routledge, 2017) and Harry W. Richardson and Chang Woon Nam (eds.), *Shrinking cities. A global perspective*, (London: Routledge, 2014), of special interest for this essay are the contributions by Gert-Jan Hospers on European cities and by Georg Galster on Detroit.

the case of Turin in the fact that the whole industry globally "holds", together with other sectors of the economy, and tourism grows. The weakness of both lies in dealing with social inequality, since the first has for the moment privileged symbolic responses and the second a promise of social and territorial deployment that has not been kept so far. Also in this case the severity of the inequality, the diminished of income of most, and poverty problems in the decline of the city allow us to resize the seriousness of this challenge in Turin.[8] We can force a fragmented and heterogeneous reality toward two ideal types for analytical purposes, not without noting that their compresence can create contradiction and conflict in some cases, and in others be the reason for "pragmatic" choices.

Conclusion—Hints for a Comparison with Milano, Genova, Ruhr: Lessons from and for Torino

The development of the city of Turin has been reconstructed in these pages by selecting its events and its aspects more suitable to build guidance ideal types that make it comparable to or comparable with other western cities and their own development paths from the 1970s to today. This modeling thus allows us to sketch a synthetic and conceptual vision (Table 12.1).

We can conclude, by stressing some of the original characters of the Turin case, in part already previously mentioned, that are highlighted by the comparison with other cases studied in this volume: institution for the regulation of local economy, territorial scale, social mobilization are the issues at stake.

The role of politics and of organization prevails at length on the market and when the latter establishes itself it is still weak, if we compare the story of Turin with that of Milan. The rigidities inherited from Fordism are the origin of weaknesses for the Post-Fordist development of the city (industrial manpower that is less qualified and difficult to recycle, low

[8] IRES Piemonte, *Relazione annuale 2019: Verso un Piemonte sostenibile*, (Turin: IRES Piemonte, 2019), cap.1 for the loss of income, Urban Center Turin, *Atlante metropolitano* and Comitato Giorgio Rota's yearly reports on Torino since 2000 are the main sources of data on the city (all on line).

Table 12.1 Turin's three phases across eight dimensions

Turin *3 phases by 8 dimensions*	*Managed industrial decline* *1975–1992*	*Recovery and strategic plans (first 2001, second 2006, third 2015)* *1993–2016*	*New phase: coping with low growth and stagnation* *after 2016*
Main urban government actors	Local administration Fiat or individual economic actors	Mayor and administration coalition + civil society actors	Effect of the composition of economic actors + pro-environment actions of mayor and administration
Main challenges considered	Social cohesion	Competition between territories to attract/keep resources social cohesion	Climate change inclusion pure competition firms and markets and foreign social dumping
Economic sectors of recovery/development	Historical path in decline (cars)	Path dependent innovation (e.g. automotive) culture, heritage, tourism	Global and local individual innovators or archipelago (and FCA global player) ICT reindustrialization—oriented capital goods

Turin *3 phases by 8 dimensions*	*Managed industrial decline* *1975–1992*	*Recovery and strategic plans (first 2001, second 2006, third 2015)* *1993–2016*	*New phase: coping with low growth and stagnation* *after 2016*
Characterizing policies	Social	Economic urban cultural and communication	Environmental ICT diffusion and inclusion measures with UE support
Facilitators and constraints for an urban strategy	High public spending capacity legitimacy crisis of national political elite with local effects	High, then reduced public spending capacity national administrative decentralization legitimization of strong political and economic elite and consent collaboration between institutions of different political color	Low public spending capacity national administrative decentralization distrust of previous elite, elite change/circulation primacy of political competition
Narration and reflectivity	Administrative decline strong shared reflection	Transformation strong shared reflection	Managed decline or decrease unshared weak reflection
Population and development	Urban population decline industrial decline	Population decline alternation stagnation/recovery of local GDP and effects of 2008 crisis	City population decline, metropolitan area growth alternation stagnation/modest recovery local GDP

(continued)

Table 12.1 (continued)

Turin *3 phases by 8 dimensions*	*Managed industrial decline 1975–1992*	*Recovery and strategic plans (first 2001, second 2006, third 2015) 1993–2016*	*New phase: coping with low growth and stagnation after 2016*
Periodizing events	Mandate of mayor Diego Novelli 1975–85 and directly elected mayors 1993 industrial decline and Post-Fordism march of the of 40,000 and heroic defeat of the syndicate in 1980 beginning of world automobile crisis 1980 and of Fiat cars: Romiti's era 1976–98 EU Lisbon Strategy 2000 and Maastricht Treaty 2002	Mandates of the mayors Valentino Castellani 1993–2001, Sergio Chiamparino 2001–11, Piero Fassino 2011–16 International financial crisis 2008–16 Marchionne Ceo Fiat 2004–18 EU Lisbon Treaty 2007	Mandate of the mayor Chiara Appendino 2016–2022 slow Italian recovery, slower in Piedmont foundation of the Crysler Fiat Automobile, FCA Group, with Marchionne CEO 2014–2018 EU 2014 Program Horizon 2020 and Europe 2030

tertiary sector, industrial and political culture more inclined to planning than to negotiating) that innovators have had to face and overcome at the price of significant breakages. Pure monocultural Fordism has costs that the plural Fordisms of Milan have not paid and the Milanese transition to Post-Fordism appears instead more fluid. Also the entry into international competition was more difficult. Moreover, turning now to intermediate goods the diffusive effect and the "need" of tertiary has been lower, limited mostly to the business and university Research & Development function, and to the financial function.

The rapid loss of weight and influence of the labor movement in the face of the long resistance in Genoa has facilitated innovators who have however paid a price for their participation from below and for consensus, leaving space to antagonist movements and to a lack of confidence in the institutions. The transformation of Genoa has otherwise followed classical paths, from high tech to cultural tourism and other path dependent vocations, with the originality of a strong public role, consequent to the Iri membership of some companies, which brings out by contrast the exposure to the international market of Fiat, then FCA, and of the Turinese industry and the market logic in which they move, with effects on the local administration: the policy alternative, whether or not to support competition, delegating it to individuals, has made a difference in the Turinese Post-Fordist transition.

As regards the territorial scale, the city of Turin has gradually been isolated in the last step of its change without development from its metropolitan area, thus abandoning the advantages of the vast area, so present in a region city, as evidenced by the virtuous example of the Ruhr that has redesigned in the dimensions of a metropolitan region its conversion to a variety of sectors of the knowledge economy (ICT, health, high training, cultural tourism and environment, transport) and has carried out a profound green conversion by also using industrial construction itself. The projection of Milan on a large metropolitan area, even more than the one recognized by law, and the advantages gained are a further proof. Piedmont even experienced the creation of antagonisms at regional level between the regional capital and the rest of the territories. A history of Fordism but which was multisectorial and with many different investments which have occurred over time in the Ruhr has led to a radical transition process, allowed by a strong lever of public spending and policies, along with private investments, which were instead lacking in Turin after the Olympics, slowing down transformation and allowing the maturation of large disagreement areas in the population.

Finally, if we look at the local mobilization, the community engagement still seems weak but even Turin is seeing the appearance of social innovation experiences, that are more accentuated in Milan, and characteristic of the new phase of low development and resilience challenge of the cities that present various foreign experiences. The political role of the organized civil society in stronger than in the past, in addition to that of the civic action, which however requires a public administration that is more ready to stimulate it and use it than to attribute to it a sort of delegation. The future is therefore uncertain, but very interesting.

References

Armano, Emiliana, Dondona, Carlo A. and Ferlaino, Fiorenzo (eds.), *Post-fordismo e transformazione urbana: Casi di recupero dei vuoti industriali e politiche nel territorio torinese* (Turin: Ires Piemonte, 2016).

Ave, Gastone and Corsico, Franco (eds.), *Marketing urbano in Europa* (Turin: Edizioni Torino Incontra, 1994).

Bagnasco, Arnaldo, *Torino. Un profile sociologico* (Turin: Einaudi, 1986).

Belligni, Silvano and Ravazzi, Stefania, *La politica e la città: Regime urbano e classe dirigente a Troino* (Bologna: Il Mulino, 2013).

Berta, Guiseppe, Mobilitazione operaia e politiche manageriali alla Fiat 1969–1979, in Musso, Stefano (ed.), *Tra fabbrica e società. Mondi operei nell'Italia del Novecento. Annali della Fondazione Giangiacomo Feltrinelli XXX 1997* (Milan: Feltrinelli, 1999).

Bobbio, Luigi and Guala, Chito (eds.), *Verso Torino 2006* (Rome: Corocci, 2002).

Calderini, Mario and Scellato, Guiseppe, *Interpretare l'innovazione* (Turin: Edizioni Fondazione G. Agnelli, 2003).

Campbell, Tim, *Beyond Smart City: How Cties Network, Develop and Innovate* (London: Routledge, 2012).

IRES Piemonte, *Relazione annuale 2019: Verso un Piemonte sostenibile* (Turin: IRES Piemonte, 2019).

Mantelli, Brunello and Tranfaglia, Nicoal, Apogeo e collasso della 'città fabbrica' Torino dall'autunno caldo sconfitta del 1980, in Tranfaglia, Nicola (ed.), *Storia di Torino: vol. IX – Gli anni della republica* (Turin: Einaudi, 1999), pp. 829–862.

Martina, Anna, *Comunicare la città. Il caso di Torino olimpica* (Milan: Bruno Mondadori, 2006).

Perulli, Paolo, *Piani stragici. Governare le città europee* (Milan: Angeli, 2004).

Perulli, Paolo, *The Urban Contract: Community, Governance and Capitalism* (London: Routledge, 2016).

Ravizza, Vittorio, *Turin Style. Technocity and It's Province* (Turin: Editurist, 1990).

Richardson, Harry W. and Chang, Woon Nam (eds.), *Shrinking Cities. A Global Perspective* (London: Routlegde, 2014).

Russo, Guiseppe and De Sanctis, Giuseppina (eds.), *Un'alternativa al decline: 18 idee per lo sviluppo di Torino negli anno novanta* (Turin: Torino Incontra, 1992).

Scamuzzii, Sergio et al., *Élites e reti in una città in trasfomazione. Il caso Torino* (Milan: Angeli, 2005).

Weaver, Russel et al., *Shrinking Cities: Understanding Urban Decline in the United States* (London: Routledge, 2017).

PART VI

Environmental Developments Under Conditions of Deindustrialization

CHAPTER 13

Layers of New Green: Postindustrial Landscapes and Identity Formation in the Ruhr Valley, Germany

Pia Eiringhaus

Introduction: Landscape and Regional Identities

Visiting the Ruhr Valley today, it is hard to imagine that there were times when local people would not hang their laundry to dry in the open air due to air pollution, clouds of exhaust gases and smog. During the last decades, the image of the Ruhr as West Germany's black, dirty region has changed. It has transformed materially and symbolically. Industrial landscapes have become popular recreational areas, internationally representative park complexes and carriers of ecological model projects. The Ruhr is represented as innovatively natural space, characterized by ecological rehabilitation, new biodiversity and new aesthetics of nature. The success of this transformation can be seen in the city of Essen, the

[1] Essen, Grüne Hauptstadt Europas, *Grüne Hauptstadt Europas - Essen 2017 ist voller Erfolg*, (Essen: Klartext, 2018).

P. Eiringhaus (✉)
Berlin Wall Foundation, Berlin, Germany
e-mail: eiringhaus@stiftung-berliner-mauer.de

S. Berger et al. (eds.), *Deindustrialisation in Twentieth-Century Europe*, Palgrave Studies in the History of Social Movements,
https://doi.org/10.1007/978-3-030-89631-7_13

central and second largest city of the Ruhr, which, in 2017, was voted the European Green Capital, a prelude to a Ruhr Regional Association program called the Green Decade 2017–2027.[1] Only recently, the interactive promotion program "Climate Challenge Ruhr" was completed, a part of the long-term program "Klimametropole Ruhr 2022" aiming to create awareness for global climate change and to take action on a local level.[2] With the developments of the last decades, most recently various regional projects, the image of the "Green Metropolis" emerged, a marketing label created to advertise the region's remarkable ecological transformation, the shift from "black" to "green".

Ecological renewal is mirrored in the many endeavors of rebuilding and reinterpreting the Ruhr landscapes, formerly desolate and depressing landscapes, dominantly markers of environmental damage and the decline of the heavy industries. Such processes of landscape transformation correspond to what the Swiss geographer Claude Raffestin refers to as social space production.[3] He defines space as given natural ecosystem of which societies are an integral part of. Accordingly, people are interrelated and in constant interaction with the environment, and they thereby transform spaces into territory.[4]

During the 1980s, the Ruhr has intensified efforts to rework the given spaces, most prominent and effective in form of the Internationale Architecture Exhibition Emscher Park (*Internationale Bauausstellung Emscher Park*, IBA), a program for structural changes running from 1989 to 1999.[5] Such endeavors can be defined as processes of reterritorialization,[6] covering both the material rebuilding of spaces and the mental transformation, namely *how* spaces were represented and mediated, eventually reinterpreted and relabelled. The latter aspect, precisely the symbolic

[2] Regionalverband Ruhr, *Klimametropole Ruhr 2022* (2019), https://www.ruhr2022.de/.

[3] Claude Raffestin, 'Space, territory and territoriality', in *Environment and Planning D: Society and Space* 30 (2012), pp. 121–141.

[4] Ibidem, p. 122.

[5] Most influential program for structural changes in the German Ruhr region from 1989 to 1999 with the goal to ecologically and economically renew the most difficult parts of the Ruhr region.

[6] A process Raffestin has called TDR: territorialization, deterritorialization, reterritorilization, see Claude Raffestin, 'Space, territory and territoriality', in *Environment and Planning D: Society and Space* 30 (2012), pp. 121–141, p. 129.

dimension of producing space, becomes manifest in the concept of landscape. Following Raffestin, landscapes are layered, or leafed, ("*feuilleté*"), which means "at the same time to model and to browse: to model images and browse through representations of this reality".[7] The various IBA work groups had to "browse" the given landscapes in their material and symbolical structure to remodel what was there and create something new. The outcome of this first impetus of changing material and mind in the Ruhr was not foreseeable, and even after the end of the huge project, landscapes kept changing, being further remodeled and reinterpreted. Landscapes do not stand still, but their construction, deconstruction and reconstruction are constantly ongoing processes. Every time a landscape is remodeled, new layers are created that transform, replace or reproduce the old.[8] Today, we find a postindustrial landscape with manifold, heterogeneous layers, bridging the past and the present through the rearrangement of topoi, imageries and narratives.

With a cultural historical approach, I aim to analyze these layers of the Ruhr landscapes by deciphering their semantics, imageries and narratives to shed light on how new meaning was assigned to formerly desolated spaces. Taking a look at the present-day scenery, landscape narratives evolve around ideas of reconquering nature, industrial heritage and smokestack nostalgia, new nature aesthetics and romanticized imagery, and finally greening as an ecological and economic promise of successful structural change.[9] In this way, a postindustrial greening narrative emerged that has established a new, harmonious relationship between region and environment, accordingly a sustainable mode of coping with an ecological transformation.[10] In this process, the meaning of regional landscapes has changed as well, were they formerly perceived as visible result of industrial deformation, and now play a role to form and shape regional identification. Focusing on the particular link between landscape and regional identity formation, I argue that, despite their materially individual and heterogeneous realization, the layers of new green mainly form around the four themes of harmonization, identification, ecology

[7] Claude Raffestin, 'Space, territory, and territoriality', in *Environment and Planning D: Society and Space* 30 (2012), pp. 121–141, p. 122.

[8] Ibidem, p. 122.

[9] Pia Eiringhaus, *Industrie wird Natur: Postindustrielle Repräsentationen von Region und Umwelt im Ruhrgebiet*, (Bochum: Klartext, 2018).

[10] Ibidem.

and aesthetics.[11] This particular mode of reterritorializing the Ruhr landscapes made a substantial contribution to reinvent the Ruhr Valley as future-proof Green Metropolis and has significantly reinforced regional identification. Vice versa has the strong collective regional identity, mainly shaped by the rise and fall of the Ruhr industries, influenced the ways in which industrial landscapes were redesigned, thus territory was reproduced. In the following, I draw on material from two exemplary park complexes, the Duisburg North Landscape Park and the Zollverein Park in Essen, to identify and contextualize the layers of new green in these spaces and relate back landscape design to societal changes in the light of deindustrialization. This approach combines industrial heritage research and landscape theory to open new perspectives on a region facing the challenge of deindustrialization. In present-day memory culture, the extreme development from ecological crisis to environmental heritage is narrated as success story from black to green, which is part of the general tendency of nostalgically celebrating the region's successful restructuring into the present-day "Metropolis of Culture, Knowledge and Nature".[12] Instead, the goal here is to create awareness for ambivalences and contradictions, visible in the Ruhr landscapes and characteristic for a heavy industrial region in transition.

Industrial Nature and the Production of Postindustrial Landscapes

To understand the overarching landscape concepts of both park complexes, we first need to take a look at the concept of industrial nature, the ecological counterpart of industrial heritage and core of postindustrial landscape design in the Ruhr. Few studies have examined greening

[11] Ibidem.

[12] Stefan Berger, 'Industrial Heritage and the Ambiguities of Nostalgia for an Industrial Past in the Ruhr Valley, Germany', in *Labor Studies in Working-Class History of the Americas* 16/1 (2019), pp. 37–64; Pia Eiringhaus and Jan Kellershohn, ‚Und wer zahlt die Zeche?‘, *Frankfurter Allgemeine Zeitung* (18 August 2018).

in the postindustrial Ruhr and the importance of how nature is imagined and constructed for those who live and work in the Ruhr Valley.[13] Research on industrial heritage is primarily concerned with structural changes in social and economic perspective, as well as the historical localization of industrial heritage.[14] Current international and comparative works have broadened this research focus, developing critical perspectives on regional history culture.[15] One avenue of such research is the work of environmental historians who have examined the Ruhr Valley's ecological history and transformation,[16] however, these works have not investigated

[13] Hillary Angelo, *How Green Became Good: Urban Greening as Social Improvement in Germany's Ruhr Valley*, (New York: The University of Chicago Press, 2015); Pia Eiringhaus, *Industrie wird Natur: Postindustrielle Repräsentationen von Region und Umwelt im Ruhrgebiet*, (Bochum: Klartext, 2018).

[14] Berthold Bartel, ‚Das Unbehagen in der Industriekultur. Ein Zentralbegriff im Diffusen – ein Kurzinventar', in *Forum Industriedenkmalpflege und Geschichtskultur* 1 (2008), pp. 73–79; Hans Heinrich Blotevogel, ‚Die Region Ruhrgebiet zwischen Konstruktion und Dekonstruktion', in *Westfälische Forschungen* 52 (2002), pp. 453–488; Ulrich Borsdorf, ‚Industriekultur versus Geschichte?', in Land Nordrhein-Westfalen (ed.), *Industriekultur 2020: Positionen und Visionen für Nordrhein-Westfalen*, (Essen: Klartext, 2014), pp. 90–94; Stefan Goch, *Eine Region im Kampf mit dem Strukturwandel: Bewältigung von Strukturwandel und Strukturpolitik im Ruhrgebiet*, (Essen: Klartext 2002); Hans-Werner Wehling, ‚Annäherungen an die Industrielle Kulturlandschaft Ruhrgebiet. Prozesse und Strukturen – Zonen, Achsen und Systeme', in *ICOMOS: Hefte Des Deutschen Nationalkomitees* 62 (2016), pp. 88–102.

[15] Stefan Berger, 'Industrial Heritage and the Ambiguities of Nostalgia for an Industrial Past in the Ruhr Valley, Germany', in *Labor Studies in Working-Class History of the Americas* 16/1 (2019), pp. 37–64; Stefan Berger and Christian Wicke, 'Introduction: Deindustrialization, Heritage, and Representations of Identity', in *The Public Historian* 39/4 (2017), pp. 10–20; Stefan Berger, Christian Wicke and Jan Golombeck, ‚Erinnerung, Bewegung, Identität: Industriekultur als Welterbe im 21. Jahrhundert', in *Forum Industriedenkmalpflege Und Geschichtskultur* 2 (2015), pp. 15–23; Stefan Berger, Christian Wicke and Jan Golombeck, ‚Burdens of Eternity?: Heritage, Identity, and the "Great Transition" in the Ruhr', in *The Public Historian* 39/4 (2017), pp. 21–43; Lars Bluma, ‚Funktionen von Repräsentationen des Arbeiterkörpers: Objektivierende und idealisierende Darstellungen im industriellen Steinkohlenbergbau', in Knut Andresen et al. (eds.), *Repräsentationen der Arbeit: Bilder – Erzählungen – Darstellungen*,, (Bonn: J. H. W. Dietz Nachf., 2018), pp. 23–40; Jan Kellershohn, ‚Mobility and the crisis of intelligence. Mining industry and the negotiation of knowledge under "deindustrialisation"', in Torsten Meyer (ed.), *Boom – Crisis – Heritage: King Coal and the energy revolutions after 1945*, (forthcoming); Stiftung Bibliothek des Ruhrgebiets and Deutschen Bergbau-Museum Bochum, *Digitaler Gedächtnisspeicher: Menschen im Bergbau*, (2014, 2017), https://menschen-im-bergbau.de/impressum/.

[16] Franz-Josef Brüggemeier, *Blauer Himmel über der Ruhr: Geschichte der Umwelt im Ruhrgebiet: 1840 – 1990*, (Essen: Klartext, 1992); Franz-Josef Brüggemeier, *Schranken der*

greening the postindustrial region in the context of cultural history or memory studies. Despite the cultural impact of industrial nature is ubiquitous, it receives only little attention in current historical culture debates. However, it plays a vital role in what is understood, communicated and advertised as Green Metropolis Ruhr.

Industrial nature is an ecological term, originally used to describe the new vegetation on industrial production areas.[17] The term itself and its main symbolism, however, were coined and shaped by the International Architecture Exhibition Emscher Park and have lost none of its symbolic importance until today. A quotation from the exhibition "Other places are beautiful as well", conceptualized and realized by the *Landschaftsverband Rheinland* in 1999, sheds light on the associations and diverse symbolic meanings ascribed to the concept.

Every erosion, also the industrial one, has its wonders going beyond birch trees and old brickwork, bushes and dried grasses. The IBA would not be the inventive IBA, if they did not locate also this phenomenon and found a way to derive benefit from it: They call it "industrial nature".[18]

The reference to "industrial wonders" beyond old brickwork suggests that the location and characterization of the "phenomenon" are enough to harmonize the damaged history of the Ruhr Valley and its environment. The description that "industrial erosion" can be wonderful, hints at the narrative twist used to write a positive meaning into environmental destruction to make destructed landscapes attractive. Here we see what I have captured as regional greening narrative of harmonization: the IBA had to work with what was given, and the concept of industrial nature helped to bring together existing associations with new perspectives.

With the IBA, industrial nature, or the new green in the Ruhr Valley, emerged as essential element of landscape design and representation.

Natur: Umwelt, Gesellschaft, Experimente 1750 bis heute, (Essen: Klartext, 2014); Wolfram Siemann Nils Freytag (eds.), *Umweltgeschichte: Themen und Perspektiven*, (München: C.H.Beck, 2003); Frank Uekötter (ed.), *Ökologische Erinnerungsorte*, (Göttingen: Vandenhoeck & Ruprecht, 2014).

[17] Rainer Oligmüller, ‚Natur und Landschaft im Wandel. Potenziale, Inwertsetzung, Belastung', in Heinz Heineberg et al. (eds.), *Die Emscher-Lippe-Region: Der Kreis Recklinghausen, die Stadt Bottrop, die Stadt Gelsenkirchen (Städte- und Gemeinden in Westfalen)*, (Münster: Aschendorff, 2002); pp. 9–33; Anna Storm, *Postindustrial Landscape Scars*, (New York: Palgrave Macmillan, 2014).

[18] Landschaftsverband Rheinland, *Katalog zur Ausstellung „Schön ist es auch anderswo…"*„ (1999), p. 10.

During this process, existing landscapes did not disappear, but maintained as structural backbone for landscape transformation. This double-layering becomes evident when looking at the IBA project called *Route Industrial Nature*, which was made up of a network of various parks, as well as greening and recreation areas in the Ruhr Valley.[19] Exemplary points of this project include landmarks such as the Duisburg Nord Landscape Park or the Zollverein Park, Essen. The project was conceptualized as part of the Route Industrial Heritage, covering 13 guided tours with names including, *The desert alive*, *After us, the jungle*, or *From the beach to spoil heaps*. The route is supposed to show the Valley's most beautiful spaces and mediate the special experience of Ruhr nature to visitors. After the end of the International Architecture Exhibition, the route was made permanent with 19 guided tours with the Ruhr Regional Association its leading actor.[20] Looking at the titles of the guided tours, we see that former landscape perceptions were not neglected, but adapted and reinterpreted. *The desert alive*, for instance, implies that the Ruhr ("desert") is capable of ecological renewal ("alive").[21] Old landscape imageries were overlaid with a new, positive meaning and regional harmonization was mediated using well-known nature imageries. Semantics and imagery link the ecologically damaged past with the promise of ecological renewal and future transformation. At the same time, industrial nature only works together with industrial heritage. It is precisely the interplay between both, landscape as industrial nature and history as industrial heritage that allows reinventing the Ruhr Valley as both ecologically and culturally sustainable. Accordingly, industrial nature has gone beyond its solely

[19] Internationale Bauausstellung (1998). Entwurf Route der Industrienatur, Vorlage für den IBA Lenkungsausschuss am 20.4.1998 (AfsB IBA 1178 A; pp. 1–5). Archiv für Soziale Bewegungen; Kommunalverband Ruhr, *Eröffnungsveranstaltung Route Industrienatur im Rahmen der Duisburger Radfahrtage am 13.6.1999 im Landschaftspark Duisburg Nord*, press release, 6 June 1999; Kommunalverband Ruhr, *Themenflyer zur Route Industrienatur*, (2001).

[20] Jörg Dettmar, *Exkursionsführer zum Fachsymposium Neue Natur auf Industrieflächen, eine Veranstaltung der Internationalen Bauausstellung Emscher Park* (1991); Karl Ganser, *Liebe auf den zweiten Blick: Internationale Bauausstellung Emscher Park*, (Dortmund: Harenberg, 1999); Karl Ganser and Jörg Dettmar, *IndustrieNatur: Ökologie und Gartenkunst im Emscher Park*, (Stuttgart: Ulmer, 1999); Regionalverband Ruhr (ed.), *Unter freiem Himmel: Emscher Landschaftspark, Under the Open Sky: Emscher Landscape Park*, (Essen: Birkhäuser, 2010).

[21] Regionalverband Ruhr, *Regionalverband Ruhr: Broschüre Natur erleben 2016: Exkursionen und Aktionen, Touren und Seminare* (2016).

ecological meaning. Its cultural symbolisms function as a basis for what I identify as an industrial nature discourse, in which regional memory and desired future developments are negotiated.

Duisburg North Landscape Park—A Landscape Between Industrial Heritage, Nature and Light Display

The Duisburg North Landscape Park is a flagship project for the ecological transformation of the Ruhr. It is one of the most prominent industrial heritage sites as well as representative event area for manifold cultural, artist and music festivities. The space covers a total of 180 hectares with the former steel works *Duisburg Meiderich* at its heart, counting about more than one million visitors a year. The beginnings of today's park complex can be traced back to the IG Nordpark citizens' initiative, who advocated for preserving the area after the shutdown in 1985. Already in 1989, the city of Duisburg registered the former steel works and its surrounding areas as project for the IBA. The total costs amounted to 100 million DM, including land acquisition and resources for contaminated site management. As flagship project for the ecological and cultural renewal of the Ruhr valley, the planning and creation of the Landscape Park were funded and realized by the IBA, accordingly financed by the City of Duisburg, the state of North Rhine-Westphalia, the *LEG Landesentwicklungsgesellschaft NRW GmbH*, a German property company, and the German Federal Republic. An international planning competition had to decide what to do with the space, how to redesign and reinterpret the industrial wasteland, how to give new meaning to the spaces.[22] The landscape architect Peter Latz developed a design concept titled "Networks of industrial infrastructure and remains of a production plant becomes landscape".[23] He succeeded and was made responsible for the architectural and landscape-related re-conception. The works began

[22] Karl Ganser and Jörg Dettmar, *IndustrieNatur: Ökologie und Gartenkunst im Emscher Park*, (Stuttgart: Ulmer, 1999); Ralf Winkels and Günter Zieling, *Landschaftspark Duisburg-Nord: From Ironworks to Theme Park*, (Duisburg: Mercator, 2010).

[23] Peter Latz (ed.), *Rost Rot: Der Landschaftspark Duisburg-Nord*, (Munich: Hirmer, 2016).

in 1991 and already three years later, the park was opened.[24] Today, there are 350 people working at the Landscape Park, among them around 22 responsible for the park administration. Maintenance and operation are estimated around 6 million Euros a year, which is funded by the City of Duisburg, the state of North Rhine-Westphalia and the income from the park's touristic use and use as an event area. While there is no entrance fee for visitors to discover the areal, exercise or spend their leisure time, it is not unusual to spend high admission fees for special events like concerts, food markets or music festivals. Accordingly, the Landscape Park, referred to as figurehead for Duisburg, represents a cultural-creative space with historical significance, but still requires state and public funding to operate. To browse the layers of new green in the redesigned park complex, I consider topographical design as well as textual and visual representations. While the narrative theme of harmonization shapes all artistic and representational elements, the themes of aesthetics and identification are as site-specific layers of new green in the postindustrial park complex.

Harmonizing Region and Environment

Visiting the former steel works at the heart of the landscape park evokes the impression that industry and nature not only exist *next* to each other, but *with* each other. Plants and bushes are growing unregulated in the middle of industrial relicts, both are not separated, but visibly arranged together. In the entrance area, several fruit trees were planted directly in front of the blast furnace, each of them fixed with sectional steel. The architect explains, "the trees share their naturalness, while the steel works shares its technical existence".[25] In the area behind the former steel works, an "eco-friendly playground" was built, allowing children to

[24] Jörg Dettmar, ‚Landschaftspark Duisburg-Nord: Vorbild für den Wandel der Industrielandschaft', in Wilfried Hoppe and Stefan Kronsbein (eds.), *Landschaftspark Duisburg-Nord*, (Duisburg: Mercator 1999), pp. 9–19; Tanja Hasselberg, *Parks und Gärten auf Brachen Umnutzung industrieller Flächen im Ruhrgebiet*,, (Worms: Wernersche Verlagsgesellschaft, 2011); Sarah Hemmings and Martin Kagel, 'Memory Gardens: Aesthetic Education and Political Emancipation in the Landschaftspark Duisburg-Nord', in *German Studies Review* 33 (2010), pp. 243–261.

[25] Peter Latz (ed.), *Rost Rot: Der Landschaftspark Duisburg-Nord*, (Munich: Hirmer, 2016), here p. 17.

spend their leisure time while learning about local plant species, environment protection and global water supply. Past landscape layers of industrialization were merged with present layers of ecological awareness, environmental education and nature adventure, all together culminating in the park concept of "ecotainment". This special link is further reflected in the educational farm "Ingenhammshof", also built during the IBA. The agriculturally used farm was preserved and integrated into the park's broader design concept as spot for ecological teaching and learning, fully responding to the political issue of children's alienation from nature.[26] Arranging the farm and the steel works in a coherent way not only harmonizes industry and "natural nature", but also the damaged relation between pre-industrial landscapes and industrialization. With view to the Ruhr as region in transition, this specific modeling corresponds to the self-image of the Green Metropolis as cultural reinvention and significant link between past, present and future.

Harmonization is not only the core of topographical design, but also the foundation for textual and symbolic representation. In official information and press material on the Landscape Park, the catching phrase of "nature reconquering formerly naturalness areas" keeps reappearing. Until today, this phrase has become quite prominent, used in almost all advertisements and information material on the Ruhr's new industrial nature.[27] This idea of "recapturing nature" is present in Landscape Park flyers and visitor boards, emphasizing the new symbiosis between nature and industrial agglomeration, formerly "incompatible elements".[28] The bilingual publication "From Ironworks to Theme Park" even refers to the "amazement of the unyielding strength of nature", staging that "the age-old cycle of nature is repeated: growth, decay and

[26] Birgit Mühlhans and Marion Raffelsieper, 'Ganzheitliche Umweltbildung auf dem Ingenhammshof: Bilder einer vielschichtigen Kooperation im landschaftspark Duisburg Nord', in Wilfried Hoppe and Stefan Kronsbein (eds.), *Landschaftspark Duisburg-Nord*, (Duisburg: Mercator 1999), pp. 82–94.

[27] Karl Ganser and Jörg Dettmar, *IndustrieNatur: Ökologie und Gartenkunst im Emscher Park*, (Stuttgart: Ulmer, 1999); Kommunalverband Ruhr, *Eröffnungsveranstaltung Route Industrienatur im Rahmen der Duisburger Radfahrtage am 13.6.1999 im Landschaftspark Duisburg Nord*, press release, 6 June 1999; Kommunalverband Ruhr, *Themenflyer zur Route Industrienatur*, (2001); Regionalverband Ruhr (ed.), *Unter freiem Himmel. Emscher Landschaftspark, Under the Open Sky. Emscher Landscape Park*, (Essen: Birkhäuser, 2010).

[28] Landschaftspark Duisburg Nord, *Einer für alles – alles für Sie!* (2011).

new growth".[29] Semantics of reconquer evoke the imagery of a powerful, almost divine nature. Accordingly, social space production in the Landscape Park is characterized by the invention of completely new links, but, at the same time, draws on well-established, romanticized imageries of nature. Accordingly, the mediation of the new, innovative Ruhr landscape *requires* well-known imageries and associations that comply with well-established viewing habits, and simultaneously open up new perspectives. This ambivalence of old and new, aimed at promoting artificial nature in harmony with industrial relicts, demonstrates that the park's design concept is not completed, but an ongoing process. At the same time, it makes evident the strong link between landscape design and regional transformation. While new landscape ideals are still establishing, the old still remain meaningful, reflecting back on how the area is reterritorialized materially and symbolically. This renegotiation of the relation between region and environment, in broader sense between past and present, is symptomatic for the transition processes of the Ruhr Valley facing deindustrialization.

What does this ambivalent layering of industrial nature say about sociocultural realities and orientation needs? Harmonizing design concepts contribute to reinventing the Green Metropolis on two levels: *first*, industrial nature is advertised as hybrid nature and marker for the improvement of the region's ecological quality. *Second*, as self-declared artificial nature, the new green enhances the demarcation from classical "natural nature", serving to depict the Ruhr as innovative, avant-garde thinking region. This is mirrored in the semantics of the park catalogue published by the Regional Ruhr Association, which uses superlative adjectives, describing industrial nature as "most diverse composition" and "most remarkable example of nature growth".[30] The former deficit has become an optimized condition, perceptible in the postindustrial park complex. As pioneer for a new type of urban nature, industrial landscapes were made *capable* to identify with, thus responded to the sociocultural need to give the closed-down steel works, marker of economic decline and fear of unemployment, a new, positive meaning. The new Ruhr nature, emerged as result of mining industries, is not presented as equivalent to classical

[29] Ralf Winkels and Günter Zieling, *Landschaftspark Duisburg-Nord: From Ironworks to Theme Park*, (Duisburg: Mercator, 2010), p. 52.

[30] Karl Ganser and Jörg Dettmar, *IndustrieNatur: Ökologie und Gartenkunst im Emscher Park*, (Stuttgart: Ulmer, 1999), here p. 30.

nature, but as superior. This remarkable mixture of sense making and marketing necessity resulted in what I have referred to as success narrative from ecological crisis to environmental renewal.

Aestheticizing the New Green

While the theme of harmonization bridges past and present in the Landscape Park, the creation of new aesthetics is of crucial importance to make harmonization perceptible. Reinterpreting industrial wastelands requires dismissing, but at least aestheticizing well-established associations. This means not only changing landscapes, but also social viewing habits. To reinterpret perceptions of "ugly" and "beautiful", of "desolate" and "attractive", new aesthetic compositions needed to be invented, rearranging existing landscape-forming elements of industry, nature and art. Accordingly, the creation and mediation of new aesthetic designs play a major role for reterritorialization processes in the Ruhr. The IBA provided the initial impetus to refrain from classical beautiful landscapes, trying to redefine relevant categories of nature and landscape aesthetics. In the Duisburg Landscape Park, new nature aesthetics are a site-specific layer of the new green, and a particular mode of contradictory-innovative aesthetics emerged that allows mediating the park complex as strangely attractive industrial-natural space.

The relevance of new aesthetics becomes evident when looking at representations of the Landscape Park in advertisements and information material, in which semantics of peculiarity are dominating. For instance, the Tour de Ruhr, an important regional tourist agency, depicts the industrial-natural-interplay as "expression of unconventional, individualistic aesthetics".[31] Identical choice of words can be found in other regional publications, for instance in the various editions published by the Ruhr Regional Association, where the park is presented as "park of characteristic peculiarity" or as "place of surreal impression".[32] In a similar manner, the guided tour "Hüttenwerk Total" promotes industrial nature with the "particular beauty of the new, yet peculiar link

[31] Tour de Ruhr. Landschaftspark Duisburg-Nord: Führungen, (2015), p. 11.

[32] Regionalverband Ruhr (ed.), *Unter freiem Himmel: Emscher Landschaftspark, Under the Open Sky: Emscher Landscape Park*, (Essen: Birkhäuser, 2010), here p. 60.

between industrial relict and nature".[33] Contradictory elements are integrated, becoming the basis for the new postindustrial landscape. These semantics and imageries work with contrasting symbolisms and attributions, as a consciously antagonistic design trope, pairing the unusual link between relict and nature, or the "sharp contrast between 'young vegetation' and 'old iron'".[34] This design corresponds to postmodern concepts of radical plurality and multiple coding,[35] which does not neglect frictions, but artistically emphasizes their qualities. Accordingly, the site-specific layer of aesthetics is not shaped by the creation of new elements, but rather by skilfully staging alternating modes of accent and neglect. A harmonic scenery of contradictory heterogeneity was created, aestheticizing damaged landscapes, and altering well-established viewing habits. In this way, formerly dominant nature-culture-dichotomies were increasingly unravelled and transferred into one last relevant opposition: innovative vs. non-innovative. These new criteria of distinguishing were significantly promoted, if not even invented, during the IBA, a program that aimed at differentiating the region from old-established industrial structures.[36]

Regional identification in the Ruhr is firmly anchored in the emergence, flourishing and decrease of mining industries.[37] Accordingly, the theme of regional identification is of vital importance for the endeavors of redesigning the Ruhr landscapes. Already in the IBA-led ecological program from 1992, the Duisburg Landscape Park was announced as flagship project and "first experiment to transform an industrial district

[33] Tour de Ruhr. Landschaftspark Duisburg-Nord: Führungen, (2015).

[34] Karl Ganser, *Liebe auf den zweiten Blick: Internationale Bauausstellung Emscher Park*, (Dortmund: Harenberg, 1999); Johannes Middendorf and Michael Hamann, ‚Die Route Industrienatur', in *Forum Industriedenkmalpflege Und Geschichtskultur* 1 (1999), pp. 43–47.

[35] Olaf Kühne, *Landschaft in der Postmoderne: Das Beispiel des Saarlandes*, (Wiesbaden: Springer, 2006), p. 8.

[36] Stefan Goch, ‚Sinnstiftung durch ein Strukturpolitikprogramm: Die Internationale Bauausstellung Emscher Park', in Gregor Betz, Ronald Hitzler and Michaela Pfadenhauer (eds.), *Urbane Events*, (Wiesbaden: Springer, 2011), pp. 67–84; Christa Reichert, Lars Niemann and Angela Uttke (eds.), *Internationale Bauausstellung Emscher Park: Impulse: Lokal, Regional, National, International*, (Essen: Klartext, 2010).

[37] Stefan Berger, Christian Wicke and Jan Golombeck, ‚Erinnerung, Bewegung, Identität. Industriekultur als Welterbe im 21. Jahrhundert', in *Forum Industriedenkmalpflege und Geschichtskultur* 2 (2015), pp. 15–23.

into a landscape that uses both industrial past and industrial vegetation as means of design".[38] Likewise, in the assessment report from 1997, it is pointed out that the park complex was regarded a "significant means to reinforce the regional identification of the local population".[39] Accordingly, the strong linkage between industrial past, new nature, ecological awareness and regional identification can be traced back to the early planning phase of the park complex. The very same connections are still dominating present-day representations. Advertisements of the various guided tours integrate the historical relevance of the steel works with the opportunity to experience the new, region-specific nature. The locally unique industrial nature is presented as characteristic of a globally unique cultural landscape, which allows identification with both the historical and promising future developments of the Ruhr Valley.

Zollverein Park and World Heritage Zeche zollverein—"The Gateway to the Ruhr Valley"

Like the Duisburg North Landscape Park, the Zollverein Park in Essen is one of the most prominent sites of the Route Industrial Nature. The park covers a space of 70 hectares and is part of the Zollverein Coal Mine Industrial Complex, UNESCO World Heritage Sites since December 14, 2001 and anchor point of the European Route of Industrial Heritage.[40] After the colliery was closed down in 1986, a complete demolition of the facilities was considered, although the building ensemble of Shaft XII had been declared as historical monument in the very same year. The whole industrial complex was bought by the state of North Rhine-Westphalia. A demolition was no longer an option, but on the contrary, more and more pioneering design and art projects established at the Zollverein areal and a

[38] Karl Ganser, Schreiben von Karl Ganser an Dr. Wolfgang Roters und Thomas Neiß: Ökologieprogramm Emscher-Lippe, 27. August 1992 (AfSB IBA 408 B), p. 2.

[39] Landschaftspark Duisburg Nord, Ökologieprogramm Emscher-Lippe-Raum: Zuwendungsbescheid Nr. 216 vom 24.02.1997, Sachstandsbericht zu den einzelnen Maßnahmen (AfSB IBA 1178 A) (1997), p. 5.

[40] In 1986, Zollverein was closed down, and already in the same year, it was put under monument protection. In 1989, Zollverein became the lead project of the IBA and the restoration of buildings, landscapes and infrastructures began.

growing economic environment was created.[41] In 1998, the foundation Zollverein was established by the city of Essen and the State of North Rhine-Westphalia, donor is the Landschaftsverband Rheinland. The foundation has been responsible for the conservation and sustainable use of the Zollverein industrial complex. During the transitional period of the 1990s, regional planners began discussing possible concepts for the park's future use and design, but specific plans how to refine ideas were only realized in the beginning of the 2000s.[42] In 2003, the landscaping office "Agence Ter" won the call for tender for the construction of a new park concept. They conceptualized a masterplan titled "Industrial Landscape Zollverein".[43] As a result of an open space design competition, the local planning group "Planergruppe Oberhausen" was finally made responsible for the project and started reworking the industrial complex together with creative groups and individual artists.[44] In line with the spirit of the IBA, Zollverein and its surroundings became an IBA lead project, supposed to emphasize the value of the industrial complex and its surrounding landscapes as place of art where culture and nature engage in completely new ways. Accordingly, state and public funding was of vital importance for the conservation and redesign of the Zollverein Park, which again emphasizes the significant role of state and public subsidies to buffer the negative impacts of structural change and reinforce regional renewal.

Browsing the layers of industrial nature in the Zollverein Park, the theme of harmonization is no less significant for the landscape design, which becomes visible in park topography, as well as visual and textual

[41] The Design Centre NRW located in the former boiler house, the Casino restaurant in the former low-pressure compressor house, the exhibition "Sun, Moon and Stars" for the IBA Final in the former mixing plant, and the "Kunstschacht" in the former machine hall of the shaft 1/2/8.

[42] Manfred Prisching, ‚Die Kulturhauptstadt als Groß-Event', in Gregor Betz, Ronald Hitzler and Michaela Pfadenhauer (eds.), *Urbane Events*, (Wiesbaden: Springer, 2011), pp. 85–104; Oliver Scheytt, Christine Domgörgen and Gisela Geilert, ‚Kulturpolitik – Eventpolitik – Regional Governance: Zur Regionalen Aushandlung von Events am Beispiel der Kulturhauptstadt Europas RUHR.2010', in Gregor Betz, Ronald Hitzler and Michaela Pfadenhauer (eds.), *Urbane Events*, (Wiesbaden: Springer, 2011), pp. 297–318.

[43] Agence Ter, *Industrielandschaft Zollverein: Freiraum Masterplan, im Auftrag der Entwicklungsgesellschaft Zollverein*, (2003).

[44] Planergruppe Oberhausen, *Planergruppe Oberhausen: Der Zollverein Park. Ein Park entsteht. Freianlagen des UNESCO Welterbes Zollverein in Essen. Der Zollverein Park. Ein Park Entsteht*, (2019).

representation. However, the themes of aesthetics and identification manifest in a quite different manner. In Essen, aesthetization plays the same fundamental role for making the formerly industrial area attractive again, but instead of romantically integrating industrial decline and wild nature, the Zollverein landscape planners used the visual arts to create an innovatively creative space. Nature is artistically brought together with high cultural compositions, and attractiveness is created by integrating industry, nature, design and postmodern arts. Accordingly, space production at the Zollverein Park follows the same overarching logics of harmonizing region and environment through aesthetization, but manifests in a site-specific, individual manner.

Harmonizing Region and Environment at Zollverein

Visiting the Zollverein Complex today, visitors are looking at well-organized, clean spaces with the impressive, yet almost sacral Coal Washery at its heart, surrounded by event locations, administration buildings, rail tracks and neatly arranged gardens. Unlike the Duisburg Landscape Park, the industrial buildings at Zollverein are neither overgrown with vegetation nor located in the middle of reconquering wild nature. Instead, "fine, well-tended lawns are paired with the brown–red architecture",[45] and the contrast between industrial architecture and nature remains clearly visible. Compared to the Landscape Park, the whole scenery appears much neater and tidier, almost artificial. Also is the Zollverein Park, on the first glance, located more hidden, linking the Coal Washery and the Coking Plant.

Despite this different mode of harmonizing region and environment, the well-established phrase of "nature reconquering industrial spaces" dominates the textual representation of the Zollverein Park. For instance, the Zollverein Foundation, established in 1998, promotes the park complex in their walking map with the message that "nature has reclaimed its place".[46] In a similar manner, the Regional Ruhr Association describes Zollverein saying that "first and foremost, colourful nature has returned

[45] Regionalverband Ruhr (ed.), *Unter freiem Himmel. Emscher Landschaftspark, Under the Open Sky. Emscher Landscape Park*, (Essen: Birkhäuser, 2010), here p. 90.

[46] Stiftung Zollverein, *Die Halde lebt! Neue Wanderkarte „Natur auf Zollverein" erschienen, Pressemitteilung zur Veröffentlichung des Wanderführers „Natur auf Zollverein"*, 2015, https://www.essen.de/meldungen/pressemeldung_928909.de.html;

to the area".[47] Again, the downfall of the mining industries becomes the starting point for the new harmonization of region and environment, since "various flora and fauna have settled" and "a significant habitat for many species has developed". The industrial past is presented as necessary condition for new growth, characterizing the "special features of nature at the Zollverein World Heritage Site" (Stiftung Zollverein, 2016c). Both park design and representation correspond to the familiar imageries assigned to the new green by the early IBA work, drawing on the same symbolisms of ecological renewal, smokestack nostalgia, new nature aesthetics and romanticized nature imagery.

While these representations correspond to the landscape design at the Duisburg North Landscape Park, the theme of harmonization manifests in an individual variety. It is shaped by the international relevance of the World Heritage Zeche Zollverein, and—in connection with this—the particular role of the industrial past for promoting the Zollverein landscape. The Zollverein Foundation puts an accent on the visible contrast between the past "former city within the city" and todays "attractive recreational space and popular tourist destination".[48] Likewise, the architectural planning group from Oberhausen emphasizes the strong contrast between the "the former no man's land" and the "present-day open, accessible, and perceptible industrial-natural space".[49] It is emphasized that particularly visitors from abroad were "constantly astonished by the new green of the Ruhr Valley and the area".[50] This topos of the "surprisingly new green" hints at the local myth of the Ruhr as "misjudged region", constantly trying to assert itself against false perceptions by outsiders. At the Zollverein landscapes, this old myth was transferred into a new one, namely that against the common prejudices, the Ruhr *indeed* has become green again. This strong focus on distinguishing present and future developments from past stereotypes is a site-specific manifestation

Stiftung Zollverein, *Wanderkarte Natur auf Zollverein. Ruhr Museum/NABU im Ruhrgebiet: Veranstaltungskalender Natur auf Zollverein*: 2. Halbjahr 2016, 2016d.

[47] Regionalverband Ruhr (ed.), *Unter freiem Himmel: Emscher Landschaftspark, Under the Open Sky: Emscher Landscape Park*, (Essen: Birkhäuser, 2010), here p. 84.

[48] Stiftung Zollverein, *Basis Presseinformation UNESO Weltkulturerbe „Grün"*, 2016a.

[49] Planergruppe Oberhausen, *Planergruppe Oberhausen: Der Zollverein Park. Ein Park entsteht. Freianlagen des UNESCO Welterbes Zollverein in Essen. Der Zollverein Park. Ein Park Entsteht*, (2019), here p. 4.

[50] Ibidem.

of space production at the Zollverein Heritage Complex. Owing to the international representative standing of the World Heritage Site, the play with internal and external perceptions of the Ruhr plays a stronger role, in both material and symbolical landscape design. As part of the World Heritage Site, industrial nature becomes the supporting "green backbone" of the area, relevant to provide an ecologically conscious setting for the manifold events like motor shows, concerts, theater and fairs. Integrating the new green at Zollverein with the economically and culturally attractive activities clearly helps to promote the image of new Ruhr Valley as region successfully facing structural changes on both cultural and ecological level. At Zollverein, the new layer of green is closely entangled with the future vision to promote the Ruhr Valley as attractive location for creative industries, art and design, thus provide collective identification with a region that has found a new path after the decline of its heavy industrial heart.

This particular mode or reterritorilizing Zollverein keeps the distance between old and new, accordingly past and present, as big as possible. Interestingly, in instituionalized regional memory culture the industrial past is a nostalgically played tool to stage region-specific identification points, as solidarity, openness, simple directness or integration capacity. The very same past, or rather the negative aspects of this past, fade into the background when it comes to environmental damage or severe problematics like the huge underground cavities and elevation.[51] This strong focus on distinguishing present developments from past stereotypes is a site-specific manifestation of space production at the Zollverein Heritage Complex. The layers of new green in the Ruhr Valley, and at Zollverein in particular, rather help to show how the region has successfully transformed into a future-oriented and creatively-working region with ecological quality label.

Postmodern Art and the New Green

Aesthetics and aesthetization are fundamental themes shaping the layers of new green in both the Duisburg North Landscape Park and the Zollverein Park. Landscape architects at Zollverein Park were facing not only the challenge to redesign landscapes materially, but to change the

[51] Bernd Dörries, Markus Karl-Heinz Balser, & Büschemann, ‚Folgen des Kohlebergbaus: Löcher im Revier', *Süddeutsche Zeitung*, 26 November 2013.

well-established viewing habits of the local people. Their solution was to bring postmodern art to the area to create a new symbiosis between industrial relicts, industrial nature and high culture. For instance, in 1999, various plastic art installations were built within the Zollverein park complex, and monumental granite blocks, designed by the German artist Ulrich Rückriem, were set as highlights in the industrial forest to open up the desolated areas artistically and make it attractive for visitors.[52] Karl Ganser, IBA visionary and director, emphasized that "artists are welcome, even needed to create awareness for the new beauty in the Ruhr Valley".[53] The idea of the sculpture park within the industrial forest was already discussed in the early 1990s. The IBA policy paper titled "Involving Artists" stated that artists were of crucial importance to "open the spaces, create awareness, and establish a positive image". Art installations should help to "reinterpret the peculiar Ruhr Valley" to allow new identification for the local population with the "yet underestimated region".[54]

Artistic settings have not lost significance, as the landscape architect Sascha Wienecke points out in our interview. "Even from today's perspective", he argues, "the sculpture park plays a major role for the overarching development of Zollverein Park. It was the starting point for everything that has happened in this area".[55] The scenery of granite blocks within the industrial forest has created a form of postindustrial art that made both the industrial complex and the new green in the Ruhr Valley attractive. As in Duisburg, formerly oppositional elements, as industrial relicts, high culture and nature, were explicitly integrated, accordingly reconciled aesthetically. In a similar but still individual manner, contradicting accentuations gave rise to new understandings of landscape variety and appeal, also at the Zollverein Park: creative differences were not neglected, but confidently staged as visual enrichment. This particular park design fully

[52] Planergruppe Oberhausen, *Planergruppe Oberhausen: Der Zollverein Park. Ein Park entsteht. Freianlagen des UNESCO Welterbes Zollverein in Essen. Der Zollverein Park. Ein Park Entsteht*, (2019), here p. 4.

[53] Karl Ganser, *Liebe auf den zweiten Blick: Internationale Bauausstellung Emscher Park*, (Dortmund: Harenberg, 1999), p. 18.

[54] Gesellschaft Internationale Bauausstellung Emscher Park, Internationale Bauausstellung Emscher Park und die Einbeziehung von Künstlern: Bestimmung einer Position (AfSB IBA 110 A; pp. 1–4), 1991.

[55] Sascha Wienecke, Industrienatur auf Zollverein [Personal communication], 2016, November 10.

responds to the general significance of art and design as economic basis of the Zollverein complex, as the multitude of artistic uses points out.[56]

With view to a collective regional identity, the Zollverein Park as part of the Zollverein World Heritage Site, presents a remarkable space. The site is both representative flagship for successful structural change, and main promoter of promising future images of the Ruhr Valley. It is internationally advertised as "most beautiful coal mine in the world" and "gateway to the Ruhr Valley".[57] The landmark's international representativeness is mirrored in its landscape design. Political and social buzz words like multiculturalism and internationality significantly shape the layering of the new green on the site. Phrases like the "new vegetative multicultural mix" dominate the local descriptions of the new nature, and it is advertised that "diverse multicultural flora and fauna" and "exotic species from all over the world" are reunited at the Zollverein World Heritage.[58] This imagery of region-specific botanical multiculturalism merges ecological argument, as new biodiversity and red list species, with relevant political categories. When the "new botanical Ruhr Valley" is even promoted as the "new home for foreign flora from North America, China and Peru",[59] we feel reminded of the region-specific topoi of the Ruhr as international melting pot. This imagery of the successful integration of migrating flora and fauna clearly demonstrates that the new nature is firmly anchored in the existing set of regional identification points, here particularly its image as exceptional, and historically proven place of integration. Again, the reciprocal relation between landscape design and regional identity discourses becomes visible. The landmark demonstrates, like no other site, how the Ruhr Valley sees its future, namely as innovative metropolis of knowledge, culture and nature that keeps pace with the times without forgetting its industrial history.

[56] Stiftung Zollverein, *Kunst auf Zollverein. Zeitgenössische Künstler und ihre Werke*, 2016b.

[57] Stiftung Zollverein, *Glückauf Zollverein. Die schönste Zeche der Welt für Ihr Event*, 2018.

[58] Stiftung Zollverein. *Wanderkarte Natur auf Zollverein. Ruhr Museum/NABU im Ruhrgebiet: Veranstaltungskalender Natur auf Zollverein*: 2. Halbjahr 2016, 2016d.

[59] Stiftung Zollverein, *Basis Presseinformation UNESO Weltkulturerbe „Grün"*„ (2016a, p. 4).

Conclusions

By considering what I have defined as the new layers of green, I have analyzed postindustrial landscape design at two exemplary park complexes in the Ruhr Valley with particular focus on the relation between landscape and regional identity formation. With view to both park complexes, we see that the harmonization of region and environment through the pairing of contradictory design elements is an essential instrument for postindustrial space production in the Ruhr Valley. Looking at both park complex today, this form of social space production succeeded, and regional identification with the region, particularly their landscapes, was strengthened. Accordingly, harmonization as dominant element layering the new green in the Ruhr Valley allows to successfully embed industrial nature into a set of future-oriented regional characteristics. Thereby, the confusing attractiveness of prospering vegetation in front of industrial settings has become a positive feature of the Ruhr landscapes, helped to make the unattractive old "black" become the attractive new "green". Accordingly, creating new aesthetics is a central instrument for producing social spaces in the Ruhr, and the strong link between cultural transformation, landscape design and cultural transformation becomes evident. Despite the specific modes of aestheticizing industrial landscapes differ at both landmarks, they reflect back on the same sociocultural process: how to make the Ruhr landscapes capable for regional identification, and to create new territory that materially embodies successful structural change without neglecting the industrial past as significant cultural backbone of collective regional identity. Both park complexes were developed and established within the IBA, thus were "equipped" with the IBA philosophy of advancing regional renewal through reinterpreting existing infrastructures, buildings, complexes, and last but not least landscapes.

The impact of the IBA philosophy has been tremendous, and even the Ruhr River—a "natural" landscape diametrically opposed to former imageries of the grey and dirty Ruhr Valley—is now promoted with the narrative of the extreme development from ecological crisis to environmental heritage.[60] Accordingly, symbolic and material reinterpretations of the postindustrial Ruhr landscapes were extended even to those spaces not

[60] Pia Eiringhaus: Industriekultur und Industrienatur an der Ruhr, in Bodo Hombach, Brost Stiftung (eds.), *Die Ruhr und ihr Gebiet: Leben am und mit dem Fluss*, (Münster: Aschendorff, 2020), pp. 347–363.

necessarily in need of being reinterpreted in the first place. On a broader level, postindustrial greening is but one example for the general reinforcement of collective regional identity that has grown and prospered particularly *after* the decline of the mining industries. In other words: never has regional identification based on a nostalgically romanitcized past been as strong as today when this past has ceased. Based on the reciprocal relations between landscape design and sociocultural transformation, this study has related back regional identity to the environmental dimension of deindustrialization. When the Landscape Park is referred to as model example of how a region based on coal and steel has transformed into a multitude of cultures and economics,[61] this strong focus on integrating past and present time spheres is symptomatic for the Ruhr as formerly industrial region in transition, eventually even for modern to postmodern societies in general. Postindustrial landscapes are exemplary social spaces that allow identification for an unsettled society facing fundamental sociocultural and economic challenges. With their multi-layered design, they provide orientation and bridge the gap between industrial and postindustrial times. However, compared to other formally industrial regions, the transition of the Ruhr turned out to be successful in many ways, as the establishment of the Duisburg North Landscape Park and the Zollverein Park have demonstrated. In this context, one must keep in mind the significance of state and public funding, since both spaces, as well as many other flagship projects of the Ruhr's industrial heritage landscape, could have developed quite differently without government subsidies. Despite or maybe even because of this (from today's perspective) success story, the future question the Ruhr Valley has to face at some point, is, however, what happens, when the industrial past is desubjectified, fully converted in cultural heritage and individual (nostalgic) memory is not the reference point of history culture anymore? At the moment, the nostalgic celebration of the region's industrial past and its successful restructuring into the present-day "Metropolis of Culture, Knowledge and Nature" is celebrated as a dominant narrative of transformation. The question remains who is the target group here, and how viable are these interpretative frameworks in the long term, particularly with view to inevitable generational change? Maybe the Ruhr Valley has

[61] Andreas Rossmann, ‚Es gibt ein zweites Leben: Auferstanden als Ruine, Das Hüttenwerk Duisburg-Nord', *Frankfurter Allgemeine Zeitung*, 5 June 1999.

grown to the point that institutionalized memory culture and communicative memories are increasingly disintegrated, or, in other words, the point that the well-established nostalgization of the industrial past has fallen apart from the realities and orientation needs of the younger generations that simply do not share this very past as subjectively experienced history.

Future-oriented research requires not only greater reflexivity, but above all fresh perspectives on the regional developments of the last decades, allowing deeper interrogation of the production of the Ruhr Valley's memory landscapes which took place during the last decades. Although well-established research remains reluctant,[62] recent contributions have already moved into this direction; they call attention to a more critical engagement with regional historical culture and concepts of identity,[63] they contrast the image of the "Knowledge Metropolis Ruhr" with the history of education and knowledge,[64] and make visible histories beyond that associated with coal and steel.[65] These works are important approaches to develop new perspectives on the Ruhr Valley in times of deindustrialization.

[62] Heinrich Theodor Grütter, ‚Erinnerungskultur im Ruhrgebiet', in Michael Farrenkopf et al. (eds.), *Stadt der Städte. Das Ruhrgebiet und seine Umbrüche*, (Essen: Klartext, 2019), pp. 507–514.

[63] Stefan Berger, 'Industrial Heritage and the Ambiguities of Nostalgia for an Industrial Past in the Ruhr Valley, Germany', in *Labor Studies in Working-Class History of the Americas* 16/1 (2019), pp. 37–64; Stefan Berger, Christian Wicke and Jan Golombeck, ‚Burdens of Eternity? Heritage, Identity, and the "Great Transition" in the Ruhr', in *The Public Historian* 39/4 (2017), pp. 21–43; Pia Eiringhaus, ‚Zukünfte in der Metropole Ruhr. Überlegungen zur Problematik erinnerungs-kultureller Homogenität', in Stefan Goch et al. (eds.), *Stadt der Städte. Das Ruhrgebiet und seine Umbrüche*, (Essen: Klartext, 2019), pp. 526–530; Pia Eiringhaus and Jan Kellershohn, ‚Und wer zahlt die Zeche?', *Frankfurter Allgemeine Zeitung* (18 August 2018).

[64] Jan Kellershohn, Dissertation, *Der Wille zur Umstellung. Strukturwandel, Wissenspolitik und die Anthropologie der Arbeit (1953–1979)*, June 2020.

[65] Janosch Steuwer, *Jenseits von Kohle und Stahl. Ein altes Buch lädt ein, das Ruhrgebiet neu zu entdecken. Geschichte Der Gegenwart*, 26 August 2018, https://geschichtedergegenwart.ch/jenseits-von-kohle-und-stahl-ein-altes-buch-laedt-ein-das-ruhrgebiet-neu-zu-entdecken/.s.

References

Agence Ter. (2003). Industrielandschaft Zollverein: Freiraum Masterplan, im Auftrag der Entwicklungsgesellschaft Zollverein.

Angelo, H. (2015). How Green Became Good: Urban Greening as Social Improvement in Germany's Ruhr Valley.

Bartel, B. (2008). Das Unbehagen in der Industriekultur. Ein Zentralbegriff im Diffusen – ein Kurzinventar. *Forum Industriedenkmalpflege Und Geschichtskultur*, 1, 73–79.

Berger, S. (2019). Industrial Heritage and the Ambiguities of Nostalgia for an Industrial Past in the Ruhr Valley, Germany. *Labor Studies in Working-Class History of the Americas*, 16(1), 37–64.

Berger, S., & Wicke, C. (2017). Introduction Deindustrialization, Heritage, and Representations of Identity Stefan Berger. *The Public Historian*, 39(4), 10–20.

Berger, S., Wicke, C., & Golombeck, J. (2015). Erinnerung, Bewegung, Identität: Industriekultur als Welterbe im 21. Jahrhundert. *Forum Industriedenkmalpflege Und Geschichtskultur*, 2, 15–23.

Berger, S., Wicke, C., & Golombeck, J. (2017). Burdens of Eternity?: Heritage, Identity, and the "Great Transition" in the Ruhr. *The Public Historian*, 39(4), 21–43.

Blotevogel, H. (2002). Die Region Ruhrgebiet zwischen Konstruktion und Dekonstruktion. *Westfälische Forschungen*, 52, 453–488.

Blotevogel, H., Prossek, A., & Reulecke, J. (2009). Das Ruhrgebiet und seine Identität. *Forum Industriedenkmalpflege Und Geschichtskultur*, 2, 11–17.

Bluma, L. (2018). Funktionen von Repräsentationen des Arbeiterkörpers: Objektivierende und idealisierende Darstellungen im industriellen Steinkohlenbergbau. In K. Andresen, M. Kuhnhenne, J. Mittag, & S. Müller (Eds.), *Repräsentationen der Arbeit. Bilder – Erzählungen – Darstellungen* (pp. 23–40). Dietz.

Borsdorf, U. (2014). Industriekultur versus Geschichte? In Land Nordrhein-Westfalen (Ed.), *Industriekultur 2020: Positionen und Visionen für Nordrhein-Westfalen* (pp. 90–94). Klartext.

Brüggemeier, F.-J. (1992). *Blauer Himmel über der Ruhr: Geschichte der Umwelt im Ruhrgebiet: 1840 – 1990*. Klartext.

Brüggemeier, F.-J. (2014). *Brüggemeier, Franz-Josef: Schranken der Natur: Umwelt, Gesellschaft, Experimente 1750 bis heute*. Klartext.

Dettmar, J. (1991). *Exkursionsführer zum Fachsymposium Neue Natur auf Industrieflächen, eine Veranstaltung der Internationalen Bauausstellung Emscher Park.*

Dettmar, J. (1999). Landschaftspark Duisburg-Nord: Vorbild für den Wandel der Industrielandschaft. In W. Hoppe & S. Kronsbein (Eds.), *Landschaftspark Duisburg-Nord* (pp. 9–19). Mercator.

Eiringhaus, P. (2018). *Industrie wird Natur. Postindustrielle Repräsentationen von Region und Umwelt im Ruhrgebiet*. Klartext.

Eiringhaus, P. (2019). Zukünfte in der Metropole Ruhr. Überlegungen zur Problematik erinnerungskultureller Homogenität. In S. Goch, M. Farrenkopf, M. Rasch, & H.-W. Wehling (Eds.), *Stadt der Städte. Das Ruhrgebiet und seine Umbrüche* (pp. 526–530). Klartext.

Eiringhaus, P., & Kellershohn, J. (2018, August 18). *Und wer zahlt die Zeche? Frankfurter Allgemeine Zeitung*.

Ganser, K. (1992). Schreiben von Karl Ganser an Dr. Wolfgang Roters und Thomas Neiß: Ökologieprogramm Emscher-Lippe, 27. August 1992 (AfSB IBA 408 B).

Ganser, K. (1999). *Liebe auf den zweiten Blick: Internationale Bauausstellung Emscher Park*. Harenberg.

Ganser, K., & Dettmar, J. (1999). *IndustrieNatur: Ökologie und Gartenkunst im Emscher Park*.

Gesellschaft Internationale Bauausstellung Emscher Park. (1991). Internationale Bauausstellung Emscher Park und die Einbeziehung von Künstlern: Bestimmung einer Position (AfSB IBA 110 A; pp. 1–4).

Goch, S. (2002). *Eine Region im Kampf mit dem Strukturwandel: Bewältigung von Strukturwandel und Strukturpolitik im Ruhrgebiet*. Klartext.

Goch, S. (2011). Sinnstiftung durch ein Strukturpolitikprogramm: Die Internationale Bauausstellung Emscher Park. In G. Betz, R. Hitzler, & M. Pfadenhauer (Eds.), *Urbane Events* (pp. 67–84). Springer.

Grüne Hauptstadt Europas, E. (2018). *Press Release: Grüne Hauptstadt Europas - Essen 2017 ist voller Erfolg*.

Grütter, H. T. (2019). Erinnerungskultur im Ruhrgebiet. In M. Farrenkopf, S. Goch, M. Rasch, & H.-W. Wehling (Eds.), *Stadt der Städte. Das Ruhrgebiet und seine Umbrüche* (pp. 507–514). Klartext.

Hasselberg, T. (2011). *Parks und Gärten auf Brachen Umnutzung industrieller Flächen im Ruhrgebiet*. Wernersche Verlagsgesellschaft.

Hemmings, S., & Kagel, M. (2010). Memory Gardens: Aesthetic Education and Political Emancipation in the Landschaftspark Duisburg-Nord. *German Studies Review*, 33, 243–261.

Internationale Bauausstellung. (1998). Entwurf Route der Industrienatur, Vorlage für den IBA Lenkungsausschuss am 20.4.1998 (AfsB IBA 1178 A; pp. 1–5). Archiv für Soziale Bewegungen.

Kellershohn, J. (forthcoming). Mobility and the Crisis of Intelligence. Mining Industry and the Negotiation of Knowledge Under "Deindustrialisation". In T. Meyer (Ed.), *Boom – Crisis – Heritage. King Coal and the Energy Revolutions After 1945*.

Kommunalverband Ruhr. (1999). Eröffnungsveranstaltung Route Industrienatur im Rahmen der Duisburger Radfahrtage am 13.6.1999 im Landschaftspark Duisburg Nord, press release, 6 June 1999.

Kommunalverband Ruhr. (2001). *Themenflyer zur Route Industrienatur.*

Kühne, O. (2006). *Landschaft in der Postmoderne: Das Beispiel des Saarlandes.* Springer.

Landschaftspark Duisburg Nord. (1997). Ökologieprogramm Emscher-Lippe-Raum: Zuwendungsbescheid Nr. 216 vom 24.02.1997, Sachstandsbericht zu den einzelnen Maßnahmen (AfSB IBA 1178 A).

Landschaftspark Duisburg Nord. (2011). *Einer für alles – alles für Sie!*

Landschaftsverband Rheinland. (1999). *Katalog zur Ausstellung „Schön ist es auch anderswo…".*

Latz, P. (Ed.). (2016). *Rost Rot: Der Landschaftspark Duisburg-Nord.* Hirmer.

Middendorf, J., & Hamann, M. (1999). Die Route Industrienatur. *Forum Industriedenkmalpflege Und Geschichtskultur*, 1, 43–47.

Mühlhans, B., & Raffelsieper, M. (1999). Ganzheitliche Umweltbildung auf dem Ingenhammshof: Bilder einer vielschichtigen Kooperation im landschaftspark Duisburg Nord. In W. Hoppe & S. Kronsbein (Eds.), *Landschaftspark Duisburg-Nord* (pp. 82–94).

Oligmüller, R. (2002). Natur und Landschaft im Wandel. Potenziale, Inwertsetzung, Belastung. In H. Heineberg, A. Mayr, W. Seidel, & K. Temlitz (Eds.), *Die Emscher-Lippe-Region: Der Kreis Recklinghausen, die Stadt Bottrop, die Stadt Gelsenkirchen (Städte- und Gemeinden in Westfalen)* (pp. 9–33). Aschendorff.

Planergruppe Oberhausen. (2019). *Planergruppe Oberhausen: Der Zollverein Park. Ein Park entsteht. Freianlagen des UNESCO Welterbes Zollverein in Essen. Der Zollverein Park. Ein Park Entsteht.*

Prisching, M. (2011). Die Kulturhauptstadt als Groß-Event. In G. Betz, R. Hitzler, & M. Pfadenhauer (Eds.), *Urbane Events* (pp. 85–104).

Raffestin, C. (2012). Space, Territory, and Territoriality. *Environment and Planning D: Society and Space*, 30, 121–141.

Regionalverband Ruhr (Ed.). (2010). *Unter freiem Himmel. Emscher Landschaftspark, Under the Open Sky. Emscher Landscape Park.* Birkhäuser.

Regionalverband Ruhr. (2016). *Regionalverband Ruhr: Broschüre Natur erleben 2016: Exkursionen und Aktionen, Touren und Seminare.*

Regionalverband Ruhr. (2019). *Klimametropole Ruhr 2022.* https://www.ruhr2022.de/.

Reichert, C., Niemann, L., & Uttke, A. (Eds.). (2010). *Internationale Bauausstellung Emscher Park: Impulse: Lokal, Regional, National, International.* Klartext.

Rossmann, A. (1999, June 5). *Es gibt ein zweites Leben: Auferstanden als Ruine, Das Hüttenwerk Duisburg-Nord. Frankfurter Allgemeine Zeitung.*

Ruhr Regional Association. (2019). *Metropole Ruhr*. https://www.metropole.ruhr/.

Scheytt, O., Domgörgen, C., & Geilert, G. (2011). Kulturpolitik – Eventpolitik – Regional Governance: Zur Regionalen Aushandlung von Events am Beispiel der Kulturhauptstadt Europas RUHR.2010. In G. Betz, R. Hitzler, & M. Pfadenhauer (Eds.), *Urbane Events* (pp. 297–318).

Siemann, W., & Freytag, N. (Eds.). (2003). *Umweltgeschichte: Themen und Perspektiven*. C.H.Beck.

Steuwer, J. (2018, August 26). *Jenseits von Kohle und Stahl. Ein altes Buch lädt ein, das Ruhrgebiet neu zu entdecken. Geschichte Der Gegenwart*. https://geschichtedergegenwart.ch/jenseits-von-kohle-und-stahl-ein-altes-buch-laedt-ein-das-ruhrgebiet-neu-zu-entdecken/.

Stiftung Bibliothek des Ruhrgebiets, & Deutschen Bergbau-Museum Bochum. (2014, 2017). *Digitaler Gedächtnisspeicher: Menschen im Bergbau*. https://menschen-im-bergbau.de/impressum/.

Stiftung Zollverein. (2015). *Stiftung Zollverein: Die Halde lebt! Neue Wanderkarte „Natur auf Zollverein" erschienen, Pressemitteilung zur Veröffentlichung des Wanderführers „Natur auf Zollverein"*. https://www.essen.de/meldungen/pressemeldung_928909.de.html.

Stiftung Zollverein. (2016a). *Basis Presseinformation UNESO Weltkulturerbe „Grün"*.

Stiftung Zollverein. (2016b). *Kunst auf Zollverein. Zeitgenössische Künstler und ihre Werke*.

Stiftung Zollverein. (2016c). Stiftung Zollverein: Wanderkarte Natur auf Zollverein: Ein einzigartiger Lebensraum: Frösche, Flechten, Fliederspeer.

Stiftung Zollverein. (2016d). *Wanderkarte Natur auf Zollverein. Ruhr Museum/NABU im Ruhrgebiet: Veranstaltungskalender Natur auf Zollverein*: 2. Halbjahr 2016.

Stiftung Zollverein. (2018). *Glückauf Zollverein. Die schönste Zeche der Welt für Ihr Event*.

Storm, A. (2014). *Postindustrial Landscape Scars*. Palgrave Macmillan.

Tour de Ruhr. (2015). Landschaftspark Duisburg-Nord: Führungen.

Uekötter, F. (Ed.). (2014). *Ökologische Erinnerungsorte*. Vandenhoeck & Ruprecht.

Wehling, H.-W. (2016). Annäherungen an die Industrielle Kulturlandschaft Ruhrgebiet : Prozesse und Strukturen – Zonen, Achsen und Systeme. *ICOMOS: Hefte Des Deutschen Nationalkomitees*, 62, 88–102.

Wienecke, S. (2016, November 10). Industrienatur auf Zollverein [Personal communication].

Winkels, R., & Zieling, G. (2010). *Landschaftspark Duisburg-Nord: From Ironworks to Theme Park*. Mercator.

CHAPTER 14

Πάντα ῥεῖ (Panta Rhei, Everything Flows): Greening Industry's Rivers and the Making of New Landscapes in Turin

Egidio Dansero, Giacomo Pettenati, Simone Mangili, and Piero Bonavero

Introduction

Since its early developments, industrialization led to the birth of new (industrial) landscapes, through the *mise en paysage*[1] of morphological

[1] Claude Raffestin, *Dalla nostalgia del territorio al desiderio di paesaggio*, (Firenze: Alinea, 2005).

E. Dansero (✉) · G. Pettenati
Department of Culture Politics and Society, University of Turin, Turin, Italy
e-mail: egidio.dansero@unito.it

S. Mangili
Turin, Italy

P. Bonavero
Department of Territorial Sciences, University of Turin, Turin, Italy

S. Berger et al. (eds.), *Deindustrialisation in Twentieth-Century Europe*, Palgrave Studies in the History of Social Movements,
https://doi.org/10.1007/978-3-030-89631-7_14

elements, functions and values of industry. In recent decades, deindustrialization has led to morphological, functional and symbolic transformations of formerly industrialized areas, that very recently have been the subject of a new process of *mise en paysage* that shaped contemporary post-industrial landscapes. Such new landscapes in some cases are founded on the heritization of the industrial legacy, in other cases on new meaning that is (re-)attributed to the environment, as the main physical and symbolic dimension of the re-territorialization of post-industrial spaces.

More specifically, in this paper we will focus on how rivers, primary environmental and ecological components that industrial land uses exploited, buried and contaminated, return to be a (potentially) foundational element of post-industrial landscapes. We will present three case studies from the city of Turin in which the river emerges as a potentially structuring element in the rethinking of places deeply marked by deindustrialization and in the imagining and building of a new landscape.

The Industrial Region: Representations and Simplifications

As highlighted by other contributions in this volume, the comparison between the Italian Northwest and the Ruhr, however suggestive, requires some qualifications. We are in fact trying to compare two industrial regions that have actually been defined on the basis of very different parameters. The Ruhr has been identified as a homogeneous industrial region, for which the presence of a coal basin in an eco-region defined by the Ruhr and Emscher river basins has meant a complex intertwining of environmental and social components. Mirroring Angelo Turco's suggestion that identity formation for regions can involve denominations, the region is named after its main river, the Ruhr.[2] This same river has also played a relevant role in the post-industrial transition of the region and in the search for relationships between industry, society and environment, through the redesigning and reshaping of formerly industrial areas.

In comparison, the industrial region defined as the Italian Northwest is much larger and more diverse and is probably more precisely described by the metaphor of the "industrial triangle" (*Triangolo Industriale*), whose vertices are the urban areas of Milan, Turin and Genoa, where most of

[2] Angelo Turco, *Verso una teoria geografica della complessità,* (Milan: Unicopli, 1988).

the industrial activity has been concentrated. The industrial landscape of this area, in fact, can be defined as a combination of heavy industry and great urban concentration. The denominations of the region (Northwest or Industrial Triangle) are much more abstract and generic than that of the Ruhr, oscillating between the generically referential (Northwest) and the symbolic. The abstract triangle geometrically rationalizes the territorial complexity, reducing it to a few ordering and converging segments. Both expressions are, in any case, two strong rhetorical devices, which have guided the interpretation of industrial development in Italy and the related policies to promote it and to reduce territorial inequalities. These were interpreted as anomalies and quite different from the Northwest, which served as a model of territorial development,[3] with a questionable linear and evolutionary understanding of development.

The binomy of "great industry-great cities" that characterized the symbolic construction of the Northwest during the industrial decades concealed the internal diversity of this macro-region, of the place-specific characteristics of the different industrial sites and of the three main urban poles of the triangle (Turin, Milan and Genoa). Deindustrialization has contributed to revealing the diversity of industrial activity in the three poles (and in other areas within the triangle). The same is true of different strategies that cities and regions have adopted to deal with the problems and opportunities of industrial dismantling and of its legacy in terms of abandoned or underutilized industrial heritage (material and immaterial). Deindustrialization and the formation of the post-industrial landscape appear to have enforced the Ruhr's identity, while the idea of the Italian Northwest as one regional unit seems to have been weakened by the decreasing role of industrial production in the area. Why did this happen?

One hypothesis is that deindustrialization progressed very differently in the Ruhr and in the Italian Northwest, notably from the point of view of environmental discourse. The natural base of the Ruhr area, the two rivers Ruhr and Emscher, emerge as structural elements, shaping the material and symbolic transformation of this area from black heart to

[3] Giuseppe Dematteis, 'Le trasformazioni territoriali e ambientali', in Francesco Barbagallo (ed.) *Storia dell'Italia repubblicana* 2, (Turin: Einaudi, 1995), pp. 661–709.

green heart of Europe, as a Green Metropolis.[4] In the Northwest, the Po river basin touches only two of the poles of the industrial triangle (Turin and Milan), and the role of the Po itself was not as relevant, for the industrial history of the area, as that of other rivers. A case in point is one of its main tributaries running through Turin, the Dora Riparia. At the scale of the Italian Northwest or of the industrial triangle, there is no strategic reflection or project to meet the twofold crisis that links deindustrialization with the environmental question. There was no comparable thinking about and planning of a post-industrial region, as in the case of the Ruhr which takes rivers as a point of departure, as structuring elements, along with green infrastructures, nature-based solutions, rediscovering their values and their role in the ecosystem and moving beyond the techno-centric perspective that had been functional during the past industrial development. Even within a common, however generic, discourse on deindustrialization processes, on problems and opportunities related to disused industrial areas, on the urgent need for environmental remediation and on the need for an ecological restructuring of industrial activities, the Northwest is constituted of a plurality of situations. These are linked to the specificity of each place, to different industrial development and to different perspectives on regeneration and reuse of post-industrial areas.

We have to change the scale of analysis to find more comparable situations and discourses about deindustrialization. Especially from the perspective of environmental preservation, one needs to look at the larger picture. In the Milan area, for example, three minor rivers (Lambro, Seveso and Olona) have shaped urban and industrial history, and are now playing a new role in the reshaping of the contemporary metropolis.

[4] Stefan Berger, 'Industrial Heritage and the Ambiguities of Nostalgia for an Industrial Past in the Ruhr Valley, Germany', in *Labor Studies in Working-Class History of the Americas*, XVI, 1 (2019), pp. 37–64; Pia Eiringhaus, *Industrie wird Natur. Postindustrielle Repräsentationen von Region und Umwelt im Ruhrgebiet,* (Essen: Klartext, 2018).

The industrial area that extended across the basin of these three rivers[5] might allow for a comparison between the Northwest (at least a part of it) and the Ruhr. Such comparison would notably be regarding the environmental crisis linked to industrial production. It would also touch on the, only partially successful, attempts to counter this crisis with a comprehensive project of regional scale, as undertaken in the Ruhr area. In this contribution, however, we have opted for a more radical jump of scale and we will focus on the role of rivers in shaping the post-industrial landscapes at the urban scale of the city of Turin, one of the three urban vertices of the industrial triangle.

[5] The area of the Lambro, Seveso and Olona rivers' water basins (that we will call LSO) has been defined by the Ministry of the Environment as being "at high risk of environmental crisis". It is a very large area, with 381 municipalities divided into 4 provinces (Como, Milan, Pavia and Varese), for a region measuring 3340 km^2 and a population of almost 5 million. The LSO area has undergone a first restructuring plan, based on a functionalist approach and mitigation interventions, without questioning the structural causes of degradation. In response to the dissatisfaction associated with the first recovery plan, the Lombardy Region reconsidered profoundly in the early 1990s. It initiated a research program for an "integrated territorial and environmental remediation and enhancement project" of the area. See Giorgio Ferraresi and Alberto Magnaghi, 'La Valle del Lambro, Seveso e Olona: da area ad alto rischio a progetto integrato di valorizzazione territoriale', in Alberto Magnaghi and Raffaele Paloscia R. (eds.), *Per una trasformazione ecologica degli insediamenti,* (Milan: FrancoAngeli, 1992); Alberto Magnaghi A. (eds.), 'Bonifica, riconversione, valorizzazione ambientale del fiume Lambro-Seveso-Olona', *Urbanistica Quaderni* 2 (1995). Even if the LSO Project, as the first attempt in Italy to tackle the environmental degradation at the regional scale, in an integrated and structured manner, has not had an immediately operational follow-up, as a whole, it has played an inspiring role in the change of perspectives on the larger scale. Planning on the level of the water basin in Italy and in particular in the Milan area changed, inspiring the so-called "river contracts" (Maria Laura Scaduto, *River Contracts and Integrated Water Management in Europe,* [Berlin: Springer, 2016]) and neo-ruralist approaches (Mariella Borasio and Marco Prusicki, 'Milan rural metropolis. A project for the enhancement of waters towards the neo-ruralisation of territorial system in Milan', in *Scienze del Territorio* 2 [2014], pp. 135–146). This happened in Milan, a city which, after the Expo 2015, started to play a global leading role in rethinking local food policies and the integration between city and countryside (Andrea Calori et al., 'Urban Food Planning in Italian Cities: A Comparative Analysis of the Cases of Milan and Turin', in *Agroecology and Sustainable Food Systems,* XLI, 8 (2017), pp. 1026–1046).

From Industrial to Post-Industrial Landscape

Industrial development, between the different stages of territorialization, has certainly impressed increasingly heavy traces onto the environment and the territory. The need for environmental restoration, which concerns many former industrial areas, clearly demonstrates that bringing sites where industrial production (notably petro-chemical, iron and steel, mining, etc.) took place back to minimum levels of environmental and territorial quality requires a very long time and enormous financial resources. What we want to stress here is that the observation and interpretation of economic and territorial transformations from a sustainability perspective requires us to acknowledge long-term de-territorialization that has been perceived and represented as an "environmental/territorial crisis" in processes of production, consumption and settlement. The shift to sustainable development requires planning a profound re-territorialization that activates "complex settlement processes (housing, production, environmental and social) based on rules of territorial 'production and reproduction', capable in the medium and long term to reverse the tendencies towards degradation and death of the territory".[6]

The so-called Italian territorialist school interprets territory as a material, symbolic and organizational construction, not existing in nature, shaped by the actions, strategies and symbolic projections of the agents. Territorialization—i.e. the process of shaping territories—is considered, in this approach, as cyclical. It consists of a phase of strict territorialization, one of de-territorialization, due to change in or end of the forces that had determined a specific territoriality, and of a phase of a third phase of re-territorialization, in which new strategies and actions shape new territories. Drawing from the reflections of Deleuze and Guattari, the concept of the three phases cycle (territorialization/de-territorialization/re-territorialization) has been developed over time by

[6] Alberto Magnaghi, 'Bonifica, risanamento e valorizzazione del territorio', in Alberto Magnaghi and Raffaele Paloscia (eds.), *Per una trasformazione ecologica degli insediamenti,* (Milan: FrancoAngeli, 1992), p. 24.

authors such as Raffestin,[7] Turco[8] and Magnaghi.[9] The signs of the incessant cycle of territorialization can be detected at different levels: from the micro-spatial and temporal scale of ordinary everyday geographies, to scales greater in size and complexity, connected to the wider structural transformations of society and economy.

This is the case with Fordist processes of industrialization and subsequent deindustrialization of regions such as the Italian Northwest, which has seen the production of specific territories and landscapes which were subsequently replaced by new territories and new post-industrial, fluid and heterogeneous territorialities. The transition from one phase of territorialization to another entails redefining the ways in which a region is used and organized. The more marked this transition, the greater the elements of fracture and discontinuity in social, economic and territorial organization.

From this perspective, the widespread presence of industrial and non-industrial abandoned areas in most of the large urban-industrial areas in which Fordist industrial development took place, can be read as a strong and evident sign of discontinuity and of the inertia with which the territory dialectically adjusts its organization to the transformations of the economy, taking time in reabsorbing the "waste" (in terms of buildings, areas and structures) of the previous production systems. From proto-industry to the crisis of Fordism, each sub-phase of the process of industrial territorialization has produced its abandoned areas, its "voids", and has gradually filled them with new contents and meanings. Each re-territorialization prior to the industrial phase has produced innovation, while preserving, relying on previous sediments, selecting them, renaming them, recycling them, on the basis of new guiding values and available technologies.[10]

[7] Claude Raffestin, 'Territorializzazione, deterritorializzazione, riterritorializzazione e informazione', in Angelo Turco (ed.), *Regione e regionalizzazione,* (Milan: Franco Angeli, 1984), pp. 69–82; Claude Raffestin, 'Space, territory, and territoriality', in *Environment and Planning D: Society and Space* 30 (2012), pp. 121–141.

[8] Angelo Turco, *Verso una teoria geografica della complessità* (Milan: Unicopli, 1988).

[9] Alberto Magnaghi, *The Urban Village. A Charter for Democracy and Local Self-Sustainable Development,* (London: Zed Books, 2005).

[10] Claude Raffestin, 'Space, Territory, and Territoriality', in *Environment and Planning D: Society and Space* 30 (2012), pp. 121–141; Alberto Magnaghi, *The Urban Village. A Charter for Democracy and Local Self-Sustainable Development,* (London: Zed Books, 2005).

The idea of an "industrial landscape" is the result of the process of *mise en paysage* of morphological elements, of the functions and values of industrial production and spaces,[11] which significantly decreased through the process of deindustrialization that began in the 1980s. The industrial reticular landscape, expression of the widespread but not homogeneously distributed industrialization of the Northwest, has been juxtaposed—and often replaced—with a landscape of deindustrialization, characterized by new material components and above all by the loss of functions, meanings and values of the elements of industrial territoriality.[12] This transformation has paved the way for new perspectives of re-construction, re-functionalization and re-signification of places or, in other words, re-territorialization.[13] Deindustrialization has entailed the consideration of former industrial spaces by territorial actors as stakes, meeting places of different interests. Each of these groups has a different understanding of the strategies that can be imagined and of the territorial representations[14] that can be implemented and supported.

The scientific and technical debate on the material and symbolic production of post-industrial landscapes identifies different approaches, temporally and geographically differentiated, that can be clustered into three main groups.[15] The first is the almost complete deletion of the previous industrial landscape. This takes place through the economic valorization of brownfields as real-estate areas or new infrastructures,

[11] Egidio Dansero and Alberto Vanolo (eds.), *Geografia dei paesaggi industriali in Italia,* (Milan: FrancoAngeli, 2006).

[12] Egidio Dansero and Cristina Scarpocchi, 'Patrimoni industriali e sviluppo locale: un approccio geografico', in Augusto Ciuffetti and Roberto Parisi (eds.), *L'archeologia industriale in Italia. Storie e storiografia (1978–2008),* (Milan: FrancoAngeli, 2012), pp. 353–366.

[13] Angelo Turco, *Verso una teoria geografica della complessità,* (Milan: Unicopli, 1988).

[14] Marcella Arca Petrucci, 'Le rappresentazioni dei vuoti industriali' in Egidio Dansero, Carolina Giaimo and Agata Spaziante (eds.), *Se i vuoti si riempiono,* (Firenze: Alinea, 2001), pp. 211–224; Egidio Dansero and Agata Spaziante, 'Scoprire i vuoti industriali: analisi e riflessioni a partire da censimenti e mappature di aree industriali dismesse a Torino', in Emiliana Armano, Carlo Alberto Dondona and Fiorenzo Ferlaino (eds.), *Post-fordismo e trasformazione urbana. Casi di recupero di vuoti industriale e indicazioni per le politiche nel territorio torinese,* (Turin: Ires Piemonte, 2016), pp. 45–106.

[15] Wolfram Höfer and Vera Vicenzotti, 'Post-industrial landscapes. Evolving concepts', in Peter Howard, Ian Thompson and Emma Waterton (eds.), *The Routledge Companion to Landscape Studies,* (London: Routledge, 2019), pp. 499–510.

especially in the urban context,[16] or through the abandonment and the spontaneous re-naturalization of unused industrial spaces[17] which are "reclaimed by the natural world".[18] Not infrequently, however, the material marks of the industrial past, in the form of environmental contamination, prevent the immediate reuse of the areas. This necessitates the land to lie fallow for a long time or otherwise the implementation of extensive decontamination.[19] The second approach links a certain idealization of the industrial past with the heritization of its traces in the landscape. This happens through processes and interventions of different complexity, ranging from the conservation of some architectural elements in projects of transformation to more complex dynamics of shared construction. In the latter case, there are common values that are ascribed to the post-industrial landscape: examples include the valorization of museums (also with open-air museum projects on a larger scale), or even the recognition of some post-industrial landscapes as a World Heritage Site by UNESCO.[20] The third group of approaches focuses on the explicit recognition of the specificities and potential values of the post-industrial landscapes and ecologies. These are considered resources for trajectories of local development[21]; as a chance to experiment with

[16] Egidio Dansero and Cristina Scarpocchi, 'Patrimoni industriali e sviluppo locale: un approccio geografico', in Augusto Ciuffetti and Roberto Parisi (eds.), L'archeologia industriale in Italia. Storie e storiografia (1978–2008), (Milan: FrancoAngeli, 2012), pp. 353–366; Egidio Dansero, Cesare Emanuel and Francesca Governa (eds.), *I patrimoni industriali. Una geografia per lo sviluppo locale,* (Milan: FrancoAngeli, 2003).

[17] Alice Giulia Dal Borgo, Emanuele Garda and Andrea Marini, *Sguardi tra i residui. I luoghi dell'abbandono tra rovine, utopie ed eterotopie*, (Milano and Udine: Mimesis, 2016).

[18] Nate Millington, 'Post-Industrial Imaginaries: Nature, Representation and Ruin in Detroit, Michigan', in *International Journal of Urban and Regional Research* XXXVII, 1 (2013), pp. 279–296, p. 280.

[19] Meltem Erdem and Joan Iverson Nassauer, 'Design of brownfield landscapes under different contaminant remediation policies in Europe and the United States', in *Landscape Journal*, XXXII, 2 (2013), pp. 277–292.

[20] Calvin Jones and Maxim Munday, 'Blaenavon and United Nations World Heritage Site status. Is conservation of industrial heritage a road to local economic development?', in *Regional Studies*, XXXV, 6 (2001), pp. 585–590; James Douet, *Industrial heritage re-tooled: The TICCIH guide to industrial heritage conservation,* (London: Routledge, 2016).

[21] Egidio Dansero, Cesare Emanuel and Francesca Governa (eds.), *I patrimoni industriali: Una geografia per lo sviluppo locale,* (Milan: FrancoAngeli, 2003).

innovative ways of thinking, planning and experiencing urban spaces,[22] as a context of specific territorial and environmental processes, generated by specific relationships between human society and environmental components.[23]

The next chapter explores the process of material, social and cultural production of deindustrialized landscapes or post-industrial landscapes in the Italian Northwest. It focuses on the unequal geographies of process of deindustrialization (which correspond to the heterogeneous spatial distribution of industrial production) and on some structural components (urban voids, environmental pollution) from which the material production and the representation of new post-industrial landscapes are described in the case studies analyzed.

Industrial Crisis, Territorial Crisis

In the three main regions of the Italian Northwest (Piedmont, Liguria and Lombardy) the proportion of industry in the total economy already began to decline in the 1970s (from 48.2% in 1970 to 45.4 in 1980). This was different from developments that took place during the same period in the Northeast, where the percentage of the industrial sector in the economy has grown.[24] In the following decade, the deindustrialization process of the area intensified and was greater than in the Italian Northeast and in the other most strongly industrialized regions of Europe. In particular, between 1980 and 1990, in the Northwest, the share of industry-added value decreased by more than 7 percentage points. Correspondingly, the relative importance of the tertiary sector in the Northwest rose more rapidly, from 51.4 to 59.6%.

The structural transformation of the economy of large parts of the most economically advanced regions of the country led to a transition in the industrial landscape that had developed in the previous decades.

[22] Pierre Donadieu, 'Landscape Urbanism in Europe: From Brownfields to Sustainable Urban Development', in *Journal of landscape architecture* I,2 (2006), pp. 36–45.

[23] John Box, 'Nature Conservation and Post-industrial Landscapes', in *Industrial Archaeology Review*, XXI, 2 (1999), pp. 137–146; Matthew Gandy, 'From Urban Ecology to Ecological Urbanism: An Ambiguous Trajectory', in *Area*, LXII, 2 (2015), pp. 150–154.

[24] Antonio Accetturo et al., 'Deindustrializzazione e terziarizzazione: trasformazioni strutturali nelle regioni del Nord Ovest', in *Questioni di economia e finanza* 282 (2015).

The trend was toward a "non-landscape", which only later and only in places was perceived, thought of and planned as a post-industrial landscape. A symbolic element of this transition is the fact that, in the Italian debate, the spaces of deindustrialization have been defined, especially in urban contexts, as "voids" (*vuoti*): hybrid, undetermined and sometimes disturbing spaces, waiting to be filled again with new forms, functions and meanings.[25] The phenomenon is particularly evident in the large cities of the Northwest (Milan, Turin, Genoa, Brescia). Here, the importance of the former industrial, now abandoned, areas compared to the total surface area is considerable, and has opened up important possibilities for reuse and rethinking of significant portions of urban space.

One of the characteristics of industrial landscape is the reduction of the environment and of nature to residual, exploited, hidden, erased elements, impacted by production processes and by their material and socio-cultural infrastructures.

The Forgotten Environment

The Discovery of Risk and Environmental Crisis

The environmental issue began to emerge clearly during the 1960s. The first major international conference on the environment was held in the early 1970s in Stockholm. During the same period, the—still ongoing—debate of the limits of growth and development became animated. Part of this was the report (The Limits of Growth) commissioned to MIT by the Club of Rome, led by the Turinese Aurelio Peccei (to whom the city of Turin has significantly dedicated a new park built on the large abandoned industrial area of the Fiat Iveco Telai, in 2015). If, in its first stages, the debate on the relationship between industrial development and preservation of the environment, was marked by issues like pollution and resource management, soon, other topics, such as industrial and technological risks, emerged as relevant. The first political interventions in the environmental realm occurred in Italy in the mid-70s, well before the

25 Alberto Clementi, 'La rigenerazione dei paesaggi italiani', in Eugenio Turri et al. (eds.), *Il paesaggio italiano. Idee, contributi, immagini,* (Milan: Touring Club Italiano, 2000); Egidio Dansero, Cesare Emanuel and Francesca Governa (eds.), I patrimoni industriali. Una geografia per lo sviluppo locale (Milan: FrancoAngeli, 2003); Anna Maria Frallicciardi and Marcello D'Anna, 'Teoria e prassi dei vuoti urbani', in *Territorio della ricerca su insediamenti e ambiente*, VIII, 1 (2015), pp. 23–44.

signs of industrial crisis and the processes of deindustrialization began to emerge. In 1976, the so-called "Merli" law (n. 391/76) came into force in Italy to regulate pollution of surface water bodies (it was the second environmental law in Italy, after the 1974 anti-smog legislation in urban centers). It was a national regulation, which, although its implementation was strongly dependent on the individual cases, later played a big role in initiating a process of ecological restructuring for industrial activities in Italy and in particular in the Northwest. Initially, such processes were founded on a "business as usual" logic, but they gradually transitioned from a passive ecology (the environment as a cost factor for the company) to an active ecology (the environment as a constraint and opportunity).

A turning point in the management of industrial risk is marked by the ICMESA (Industrie Chimiche Meda Società Azionaria) accident in Seveso (in the Brianza region, north of Milan)[26] which lead to the approval of the "Seveso Directive 82/501 / CEE". The accident had a strong impact on the Italian and European environmental debate. Ten years later, in 1986, the Ministry of the Environment was set up in Italy and soon it had to face the environmental crisis, largely linked to previous industrial (and agro-industrial) development that had been substantially based on a linear vision of economic-environmental relations. These were simultaneously considered as a mine and landfill, both with inexhaustible capacities.

One of the first measures of the new Ministry was the recognition of the so-called "areas at risk of environmental crisis", with the identification, in the first instance, of 15 areas throughout the Italian territory. Two of these areas were located in the Northwest: the Lambro-Seveso-Olona area (around Milan) and the Val Bormida (on the border between Liguria and Piedmont). The status of the second area was linked to the presence of a chemical plant (the Acna in the Municipality of Cengio, Liguria, in the Upper Bormida Valley), which was located far out due to its potential significance in a situation of war. The area of Lambro-Seveso-Olona encompasses one of the three poles of the industrial triangle, as we already mentioned.

[26] On July 10, 1976 at 12.37, an explosion blew up the safety valve of the chemical reactor of the ICMESA plant. As a consequence of the accident, a cloud of highly toxic gas, containing about 10–12 kilos of dioxin, was released into the atmosphere and affected 158 workers, 37,000 inhabitants of the area, animals, and seriously polluted the soil. There also was an impact on the genetic heritage of the affected people and of the local population.

Black Holes of Industrial Legacy: The Contaminated Sites

The end of productive functions often coincides with a re-emergence of the environmental dimension of former industrial areas. This often plays a decisive role in the processes of transformation of such spaces and in building post-industrial landscapes and ecologies.[27] Initially, the environmental dimension often re-emerges in a predominantly negative manner, through the discovery of the pollution and contamination that the industrial past has left behind. The list of officially recognized contaminated post-industrial sites of national interest shows the environmental impact that the industrial past has had on many areas in the Italian Northwest[28]: of the 171,268 hectares of land to which contaminated sites amount, 113,930 are in Lombardy, Liguria, Piedmont and Valle d'Aosta (Table 14.1) with an incidence of 66.52% of the national total.

Similarly, the geography of plants that are still operational and at risk of major accidents (RIR—*Rischio di Incidente Rilevante*), according to the so-called Seveso II Directive (D.Lgs 238/05) shows how current industrial risks in Italy are concentrated in the Northwest, where there are 430 risk sites, equal to 37% of the national total, distributed across Lombardy (287), Piedmont (103), Liguria (34) and Valle d'Aosta (6). The decontamination of pollutants can be seen as the starting point of the anthropic production of new post-industrial ecologies,[29] which overcomes the almost complete negation of the environment manifest in industrial structures. The mitigation of the main environmental damages generated by decades of industrial production also has a strong symbolic value.

On the one hand, decontamination restores the former industrial spaces to the daily geographies of local populations; on the other hand, in trying to address them, it reveals the strong impacts that industry has

[27] Liviu Chelcea, 'Postindustrial Ecologies: Industrial Rubble, Nature and the Limits of Representation', in *Parcours anthropologiques*, 10 (2015), pp. 186–201.

[28] The Siti Contaminati di Interesse Nazionale (Contaminated Sites of National Interest), or SIN, are identified by the Ministry for Environment, according to the Legislative Decrees 22/97 and 152/2006. They represent large polluted areas that are considered dangerous to the environment and public health and whose decontamination is considered a national priority. Currently, there are 41 SIN across Italy which cover more than 1600 km^2 of land and 1300 km^2 of sea.

[29] Liviu Chelcea, 'Postindustrial Ecologies: Industrial Rubble, Nature and the Limits of Representation', in Parcours anthropologiques, 10 (2015), pp. 186–201.

Table 14.1 Officially recognized contaminated post-industrial sites of national interest (*Source* Italian Ministry for Environment, 2019)

N	*Sites name*	*Area (ha)*	*Province/metropolitan city (NUTS3)*
1	Casale Monferrato	73.895	Alessandria
2	Balangero	314	Torino
3	Pieve Vergonte	15,687	VCO
4	Serravalle Scrivia	74	Alessandria
5	Emarese	23	Aosta
6	Sesto San Giovanni	255	Milano
7	Pioltello - Rodano	85	Milano
8	Brescia-Caffaro	262	Brescia
9	Laghi di Mantova - Polo chimico	1027	Mantova
10	Broni	14	Pavia
11	Cengio e Saliceto	22,249	Savona/Cuneo
12	Cogoleto - Stoppani	45 (land surface) + 167 (water surface)	Genova

had on the environment and on people's health. The process of deindustrialization often changes industrial structures from an element of work landscapes into a dramatic component of a landscape of illness and death. This happened in the emblematic cases of the Eternit factory in Casale Monferrato,[30] where the link between work and disease clearly emerged in the public debate, most strongly so when industrial production ended. The production of these post-industrial ecologies has developed far beyond decontamination. It also encompasses the design and creation of new ecosystems in abandoned industrial areas—sometimes used as nature-based solutions for environmental requalification[31]—or the rediscovery

[30] The production site of the Eternit company in Casale Monferrato (closed in 1986) extended over an area of approximately 94,000 square meters of which approximately 50,000 were covered (with fiber cement slabs). At the end of the '70s, there emerged the possible links between the Eternit production activities (whose main component was asbestos) and the dramatic incidence of pulmonary pathologies in the Casale Monferrato area, which was much higher than in the surrounding areas.

[31] Lawrence Kitchen, Terry Marsden, and Paul Milbourne, 'Community Forests and Regeneration in Post-industrial Landscapes', in *Geoforum*, XXXVII, 5 (2006), pp. 831–843.

and physical reappropriation of natural elements hidden by factories, primarily rivers or the sea.

A well-known example of the first case, in the Italian Northwest, is the previously mentioned Bosco delle Querce, between Seveso and Meda (Brianza), which was planned and created with the aim of speeding up the decontamination of land contaminated by the ICMESA chemical factory industrial accident in 1976, a turning point for environmental policies throughout Europe (Ferrari, 2004). There are interesting projects that rediscovered or re-disclosed previously hidden natural treasures. Among these projects is the Parco Dora, in Turin (see following paragraphs) which concerned the area once occupied by Fiat and Michelin plants. Also, there is the new La Spezia waterfront, which has given citizens access to the sea, who had been barred from the docks of the port and the military arsenal for a long time.[32]

The mentioned projects concern the transformation and reuse of single abandoned industrial areas, often included in urban structures and landscapes. In other cases, larger areas acquire new functions and new forms. The material and symbolic construction of new ecologies and new landscapes concerns entire industrial systems, similarly to what happened in the Ruhr area. A notably interesting example is the middle Valle Olona (in the province of Varese), where the river banks, long occupied by industrial plants (cotton mills and paper mills) and today the backbone of a deindustrialized landscape, are the subject of a project of large-scale redevelopment, mostly based on bicycle touring (Governa and Santangelo, 2006; Gennari and Sportaro, 2016).

The Industrial City Turns Green: Rehabilitated Post-Industrial Landscapes in Turin

In this paragraph, we try to change the scale at which we read the environmental and territorial rehabilitation processes and we propose a reinterpretation of the industrial landscape, choosing three case studies in Turin. These are linked by the potential or effective centrality of a natural structural component: a river or, more precisely, three rivers: the Dora, Sangone and Stura di Lanzo. The river actually also re-emerges strongly

[32] Oriana Giovinazzi, 'Città portuali e waterfront urbani: costruire scenari di trasformazione in contesti di conflitto', in *Méditerranée. Revue géographique des pays méditerranéens/Journal of Mediterranean geography* 111 (2008), pp. 69–74.

in the construction of the industrial landscape of the other two poles of the former industrial triangle, as we have already seen in Milan and Genoa, too. In the case of Genoa, the relationship with the rivers is even more problematic and dramatic due to the urban particularities and the dynamics of industrial location and urbanization that have led to a techno-centric engineering approach that is oriented toward controlling rivers. These rivers are often channelled and covered but regularly resurface dramatically during catastrophic events related to floods and hydrogeological instabilities. A completely different approach to the management of a resilient city sitting between mountains and the sea is therefore necessary.

The selected case studies (Fig. 14.1) describe important transformations of the city, all strictly related to the material and immaterial management of a problematic industrial past:

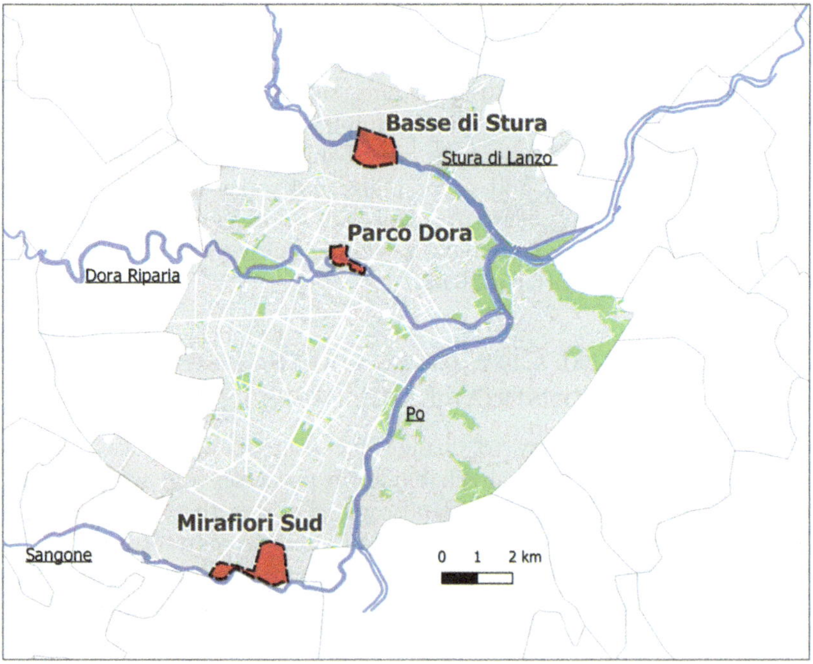

Fig. 14.1 Map of the case studies in Turin (Giacomo Pettenati, 2020)

- The case of Dora Park is part of a wider transformation of the city based on the reuse of abandoned industrial areas and railroads/yards. It is achieved through the redevelopment of the city's "backbone" (called Spina Centrale). Parco Dora is part of the Spina 3 redevelopment area, which has undergone several phases of transformation. These have not been fully completed, yet. This development combines the significance of the Spina and the potential centrality of the rivers.
- The Stura Lowlands, a heavily polluted area on the physical and symbolic margins of the city is the largest brownfield within the City of Turin. Notwithstanding widespread contamination, the area still supports significant ecological functions. Restoring the centrality of the river and rehabilitating the riparian habitat, prioritizing ecological function above human interests, the area stands to become the crowning piece of a metropolitan ecological corridor, providing ecosystem services critical to the health of the entire city and region.
- The last case is the Mirafiori Sud district, where industrial production still exists, albeit with an uncertain future. This used to be the iconic industrial neighborhood of the city and it is now an area of deep transformation, with different projects that combine bottom-up activism and top-down plans, policies and funding. This funding often comes from the context of European projects that focus on green infrastructures and nature-based solutions in rethinking, re-planning and reshaping the territory. The centrality of the river, the Sangone in this case, has not been established yet, but it is addressed in a dialogue with the neighboring municipalities (Moncalieri and Nichelino).

The Dora Park and the Iron Valley

The Parco Dora is one of the first urban parks created on former industrial areas in Italy, strongly inspired by the experiences of environmental and landscape redevelopment of the Ruhr. It is no coincidence that one of the professionals who signed the Dora Park project is the landscape architect Peter Latz, who has left his mark in the design of the Duisburg North Landscape Park and on other landscape works in the Ruhr.

The Parco Dora extends over an area of more than 45 hectares and covers almost half of the surface of the area of urban transformation called Spina 3 (about 100 ha). Spina 3 is one of the four parts of the largest linear structure called Spina Centrale (central backbone), identified by the urban masterplan that was launched in 1995 (designed by Gregotti and Cagnardi).[33] The masterplan seized the historical opportunity of the Passante Ferroviario, a project that included the establishment of the underground that runs underneath the city. This track used to divide the city into two parts and constituted a fundamental industrial location factor, along which most of the industrial areas in Turin were located. With the Spina Centrale, located above the Passante Ferroviario (currently nearing completion), a sort of new central line has been created that is adjacent to the historic center and connects the city in a North–South direction. This is probably the most important area of transformation in that part of the city. It is close to the railway toward Milan and runs along the Dora Riparia river, in whose surroundings, thanks to numerous derivation channels, mills for textile processing had already been installed since 1700. They used water that simultaneously was the driving force and fundamental component in many phases of processing. From the second half of the nineteenth century, large heavy industries were located around the Dora. These included the steel industry, the chemical and mechanical sectors (Ferriere Fiat, Michelin with the first industrial plant outside France, Savigliano and others) and, by the 1970s, more than 25.000 workers were employed in the area. The downsizing of steel production, decided at European level, with the choice of Italy to progressively close large factories in the north in favor of those in southern Italy, and the restructuring of other industrial sectors, led to the gradual closure of almost all the industrial plants in Spina 3 between the 1980s and the 1990s. The transformation of Spina 3 has been conceived in a unitary design, coordinated by the architect Jean Pierre Buffi, who was selected after 2000 through a public participatory process. In 2004, the international competition for the design and construction of the Parco Dora was launched on the basis of Buffi's and Andreas Kipar's master plan. It was won by a group of professionals including the aforementioned Peter Latz.

The Parco Dora is connected to the history of the site and to its industrial character. It was developed around the Dora Riparia River. The different areas of transformation into which Spina 3 is divided were

[33] Agata Spaziante, 'Recycling Cities, Recycling Turin: Problems and Opportunities', in Roberto D'Arienzo and Chris Younes (eds.), *Recycler l'Urbain: Pour une écologie des milieux habités* (Geneve: Metis Presses, 2014), pp. 309–360.

named after the previously existing industrial plants. In each area, an integration between the natural environment, along the river, and the re-functionalized pre-existing industrial structures is realized. Some of them have become important "landmarks" in the area, such as the Michelin cooling tower and the large covered structure of the stripping of the Fiat steelworks. The Dora Riparia River is the core of the project. Its banks have been redeveloped to make them accessible again. The river was already central in the previous pre-industrial and industrial territorialization, but only for its role in supporting industrial and energy production. Such a functional perspective led to part of the river being covered, between the 1950s and 1960s, to ensure wider spaces at the Ferriere Fiat plant. The resurfacing of the Dora, completed in 2017, has an important functional and symbolic value for the redevelopment of this part of the city and it allowed the completion of the Dora Park project that had been started in the second half of 2019 with the re-naturalization and re-functionalization of the Dora riverbanks. The last step of the transformation is represented by the project of an open-air cultural museum called "Iron Valley". It will provide new places for socializing and new itineraries across the new post-industrial neighborhood to tourists and local population (provided with augmented reality tools) (Photos 14.1, 14. 2, 14.3, 14.4).

The Spina 3 area was initially marked by the mere presence of industrial plants with residential areas all around them. These were mainly occupied by workers. Now, it is a new urban district, with over 7,500 new inhabitants and a new park at whose center the river Dora runs. It is an area still in search of an identity, between the attraction of the neighborhoods located around it and the attempt, also carried out thanks to the Parco Dora Committee,[34] to build an identity for new place. The denomination of the place is still in progress. It is situated between elements from the industrial past (ex Michelin, ex Teksid or steelworks), commercial names (Parco Dora is also the name of the new shopping mall built in the area), other possible names deriving from general and generic urban planning

[34] The Parco Dora Committee (Comitato Parco Dora) was established in 2006, with an agreement between the City of Turin, sub-municipalities 4 and 5 (two of the 8 into which the city is divided), private developers, the Metropolitan Bishopric (Curia Metropolitana) and citizens' representatives. It operated until 2015 as a strategic tool for the management of the process of transformation of the Parco Dora and Spina 3 area. The Committee worked to promote and support local development initiatives and to link the new parts of neighborhood with the pre-existing ones, strengthening the sense of local community.

Photo 14.1 The Dora river and the Parco Dora (*Source* Giacomo Pettenati, 2020)

designs (Spina 3, EuroTorino) and the new denomination Parco Dora, which is progressively establishing itself both at local, neighborhood and city level.

The requalification of the river, within the Torino Città d'Acque (Turin Water City) strategic project, the park, which has become one of the most important green spaces of the city, the re-naturation with which the industrial past is read, seems to gradually acquire a fundamental centrality for an important part of Turin. The Spina 3 operation, and in particular the Parco Dora, are now widely considered exemplary cases of redevelopment and capitalization operations of industrial areas and of the design of a new green and smart city.[35]

[35] Dormidontova V. and Belkin A. 'The Use of Post-Industrial Areas in the Formation of the Recreational Environment of the City', in *IOP Conf. Series: Materials Science and Engineering* 463 (2018); Beatriz Fernández Agueda, 'Urban Restructuring in Former Industrial Cities: Urban Planning Strategies', in *Territoire en mouvement. Revue de géographie et aménagement* 23–24 (2014).

Photo 14.2 The Dora river, the Parco Dora and the Michelin cooling tower (*Source* Giacomo Pettenati, 2020)

Stura Lowlands

The name of the area known today as Basse di Stura, or literally "The Stura River Lowlands" highlights the environmental and ecological dimensions of the site. While these characteristics formed the historic identity of the area, for the past century or so, the ecological value of the area has been largely compromised by the industrial interests that occupied the area. With industrial activity all but ceased, the Stura Lowlands have seen some remediation and re-naturalization of the abandoned areas, while large swaths still bear testament to the scars of that past. A unique opportunity exists to restore the ecological value of a vast portion of the area and to materialize its potential as an important source of ecosystem services for the city and the greater city region. The Stura River Lowlands comprise approximately 500 hectares along roughly 3 kms of the Stura River that form the natural flood lands of the Stura in this urban tract of its course just before the confluence with the Po River. Along much of the left bank, rising on a bluff just above the riverbed, an area of approximately 85 hectares was designated

Photo 14.3 The Parco Dora and the Michelin cooling tower (*Source* Giacomo Pettenati, 2020)

Photo 14.4 The Parco Dora and the structure of the stripping of the ex-Fiat steelworks (*Source* Egidio Dansero, 2013)

in 1947 as the site of the city's landfill. The Basse di Stura landfill was operated continuously until its ultimate closure in 2009, after which it was secured with an impervious cap and a methane recovery system.[36] The area extending to the south along the right bank of the Stura River is characterized by former industrial production, quarry operations and agricultural lands, creating a highly complex landscape with competing and often incompatible uses. The industrial uses, with origins in the early part of the last century, included metallurgic and smelting plants, power distribution plants, chemical manufacturing and industrial waste treatment and incineration. These activities are responsible for the extensive contamination of both soils and the water table, primarily from the storage of industrial waste laden with heavy metals directly on these sites, as well as the deposit of airborne contaminants produced in industrial processes. The contamination of many of these sites is so extensive as to make it impracticable to remove the waste material and contaminated soils for treatment elsewhere. The most traditional and often cost-effective remediation approach to ensure compliance with applicable regional and national regulations is, therefore, to permanently entomb contaminated areas underneath an either permeable or impermeable cap, and to backfill over the cap with clean soil to try and reconstitute a green surface capable of generating ecosystem services. The fragmented ownership of the sites adds additional complexity. One privately owned former industrial site has already been capped while a second, under different ownership, is in the process of being treated likewise. Over the years, the city has come into ownership of four sites, two of which have almost completed the certification process for a remediated site while a third is undergoing the process and the fourth, perhaps the most problematic of all, is still in feasibility analysis.

In addition to the industrial uses present on the right bank, quarry activity in the area generated artificial cavities (quarry ponds), some of which have been filled with industrial waste while two are still present. One of these, the so-called Bechis Lake, has benefited from spontaneous re-naturalization processes and is now a significant landscape feature of

[36] In order to recover minimal ecosystem services from this site, a vegetative layer of clean soil was placed over the entire surface of the site upon which grass could grow, thereby limiting the heat island effect generated by the impervious cap. The green surface area over the site helps preserve landscape continuity with the surrounding agricultural areas, as well.

the area, which supports aquatic and avian communities notwithstanding the proximity to contaminated industrial sites. The other, the so-called Martini Lake, is smaller in size and is in the process of being partially filled with excavation materials but will eventually constitute a shallow wetland area. The natural gas distribution facilities located just downstream along a significant stretch of the right bank of the Stura River are still operational but in and of themselves are not a source of contamination. However, contamination from surrounding industrial operations still requires remediation efforts prior to any future use. The area has been undergoing a spontaneous re-naturalization process. In particular, the areas closest to the riverbank have seen strong ecological growth over the past decade. This site likely does not require impervious capping but does require a previous cap of clean soil in order to eliminate the possibility of future users being exposed to any underlying contamination. Finally, there are agricultural uses adjacent to the gas distribution facility, under at least two different owners, which have seen evidence of contamination from the upstream plots. Agricultural production has been almost completely abandoned and some remediation efforts have been carried out in order to restore productivity. Unfortunately, these remediation efforts have themselves had an adverse impact on agricultural productivity because of the poor quality of the soils that were introduced as a previous cap. Smaller industrial uses persist along the furthest stretches of land downstream and the environmental status of these is not yet fully documented, as they are still in active use (Photos 14.5, 14.6, 14.7, 14.8).

Today, Basse di Stura represents an area in transition from industrial wasteland to a new future. Given the extent of environmental and ecological devastation, a full recovery to a former ecological function is not currently imaginable. Impervious capping over much of the former industrial sites will neither permit a restoration of the original hydrology of the area, nor of the carbon sequestration and other functions of the original soils. The original landscape is also permanently altered, with new water bodies and new elevations, as in some places mounding reaches 20 m in elevation. The former landfill is in a state of constant monitoring and is subject to methane capture operations. The areas most prone to re-naturalization processes are the former gas storage facility and agricultural areas. The industrialization of the vast majority of the area has clearly had irreversible impacts on the integrity of the natural systems of the area and their future potential. However, the true vocation of the area remains quite evident based on its unique geographical position along the city's

Photo 14.5 Lake Bechis (*Source* Egidio Dansero, 2007)

primary ecological corridor connecting the Po River and Hills environment to the pre-alpine ecosystem of the Stura di Lanzo valleys to the west, and with major natural reserves in-between. This vital ecological corridor, so intentionally compromised over decades, is slowly and spontaneously regenerating itself wherever possible in the Stura River Lowlands. Its role as an overflow area for the Stura River is still largely intact to this day.

Over the past two decades, the city administration's perspective on the future of this area has shifted significantly from an initial focus on the area's potential as a traditional urban park to an emphasis on the ecosystem and environmental value for the entire metropolitan area.[37]

[37] In 2000, public and private local and regional bodies signed a memorandum of understanding to carry out the Transmitting Sustainable City initiative, through which an international workshop was organized, with the task of developing strategies and projects to regenerate the Basse di Stura site. The vision of the future of the area was based on leisure, with a big park, and production, with agriculture and green industrial activities (Alessandro Giangrande, 'Un approccio partecipativo dinamico per la riqualificazione e la

Photo 14.6 Industrial landfill area (*Source* Città di Torino)

The current administration's vision for the site appears to be clear: the area represents a unique opportunity to right the environmental injustice of the past by supporting in every way possible a transition from industrial wasteland to ecological basin. In addition to performing vital hydrological functions as an overflow area for the Stura River, the area has significant biodiversity potential still. In particular, it still has the potential to host an important variety of bird and wildlife along riparian woodlands. This function must be supported through scientifically based reforestation efforts to promote a return to the indigenous vegetative environment. As such re-naturalization efforts take hold, the imported soils which will form a cap over much of the vast area will begin an enrichment process that will boost additional ecosystem functions, including carbon sequestration and nutrient cycling. As the vegetation matures, both along the

valorizzazione fluviale nei Contratti di Fiume. Il caso di Basse di Stura', in *SIU Conference Proceedings* [Rome: SIU, 2010]).

Photo 14.7 Industrial landfill area (*Source* Città di Torino)

riparian corridor and further from it on the higher elevations, the green surface area can be expected to play a role in capturing particulate matter, thereby assisting in mitigating poor air-quality. The mature vegetation will also play an important role in mitigating the city's carbon emissions, through the absorption of CO2 and the emission of oxygen into the atmosphere. Through the process of eco-transpiration, the foliage will have a cooling effect on the broader area, reducing the urban heat island phenomenon in the northern part of the city. Finally, while it will not be feasible to restore the permeability of large areas, given the impermeable capping required, the overall grading of the area can be engineered to favor initial percolation of stormwater through the clean soils above the impermeable layers, slowing drainage directly into the Stura River basin. Landscaping should also provide opportunities for limited use of the site for passive recreation, primarily in the form of pathways intended to maximize viewsheds created by raised elevations and the existing bodies of water.

Photo 14.8 Remediated plot with capped terracing and drainage infrastructure (*Source* Città di Torino, 2020)

Mirafiori Sud and the Sangone River

Mirafiori Sud (the southern part of Mirafiori district) is the place where the historical identification between Turin and its main factory—Fiat—has had its maximum expression. In 1939, Fiat moved its main plant here (previously, it had been located in the nearby Lingotto district), transforming a rural area outside urban structures into a symbolic space for Fordist industrialization on a national and international scale. In 1956, the expansion of the factories further increased the presence of industrial production in the neighborhood, where, at that time, more than 60,000 people worked in a production area of over 300 hectares. In parallel, the arrival of workers from all over Italy had a huge impact on the population of the neighborhood, which grew from 3,000 to 40,000 inhabitants in the period 1951–1971, and on its urban development. Between 1949 and 1971, 78 new buildings were built for a total of 1,681 housing units, which represent 75% of the total number of residences built during the same years throughout the whole city.[38] There has also been a radical transformation in the relationship between the neighborhood and its environmental context: the fertile countryside at the confluence of the Sangone and the Po Rivers almost disappeared, mostly because it was covered by industrial plants and residential buildings, and the neighborhood and its inhabitants progressively were identified (and identify themselves) almost exclusively with the factory and industrial life.[39]

The deindustrialization process started in the 1990s with the decrease in production in the Fiat plants (which went from more than 500,000 cars produced in 1997 to less than 200,000 in 2003). This meant a progressive transformation and loss of functions in the neighborhoods, also in the socio-economic and cultural realm. Regarding the urban fabric, though, deindustrialization is less visible in Mirafiori Sud than in other post-industrial neighborhoods. This is due to the inertial presence of productive and residential spaces that still characterize the neighborhood, even if they are underutilized.[40] Although less than 20,000 workers are employed in the Fiat plant (now FCA), industrial buildings still occupy 44.8% of the total space devoted to non-residential buildings in the neighborhood. Similarly, the tall residential towers, built between the 1950s and 1980s to house workers who came from all over Italy, still characterize the skyline of Mirafiori Sud, even if the density of the population living there has decreased. More than from a material point of view, deindustrialization has transformed the neighborhood from a socio-economic and symbolic perspective (Planet Idea, 2018). The decrease in the number of jobs in the car factory has in fact led to a slight loss of population in the neighborhood, an increase in unemployment (today at 21.7% against 9.8% of the national average), and above all the creation of a separation between the reality of the neighborhood, which is becoming less and less industrial, and its representation, as well as the representation of its population, in the public debate and collective image of Mirafiori.

[38] Francesca De Filippi and Ianira Vassallo 'Mirafiori sud: la città fordista oltre la Fabbrica. Scenari e progetti per (la costruzione di) una nuova identità', in *Rivista. Ricerche per la progettazione del paesaggio* 2 (2016), pp. 88–99.

[39] Erika Anna Savio and Federico Guiati, *Mirafiori Sud, vita e storia oltre la fabbrica* (Turin: Edizioni Graphot Spoon River, 2014).

[40] Francesca De Filippi and Ianira Vassallo 'Mirafiori sud: la città fordista oltre la Fabbrica. Scenari e progetti per (la costruzione di) una nuova identità', in *Rivista. Ricerche per la progettazione del paesaggio* 2 (2016), pp. 88–99.

The difficulty of imagining and implementing new transformation trajectories for Mirafiori Sud is well described by De Filippi and Vassallo,[41] who define this difficulty as "imprisonment of the factory" which preserves the identity of the neighborhood, not allowing a new narrative to form. From a spatial point of view, moreover, the loss of relevance of the factory as a workplace and social hub has deprived the neighborhood of an important central feature, increasing its "peripherality" with respect to the city center, to which Mirafiori inhabitants started to commute daily to be able to work.

The functional and symbolic re-signification (re-territorialization) process of the district developed along two different, but converging, paths. The first is the institutional one of urban regeneration projects, starting from the Periphery Project (*Progetto Periferie*) launched by the Municipality of Turin in the 1990s. The second is the bottom-up impulse from the dense and solid network of associations active in the neighborhood. For years, these have been promoting and implementing projects of social inclusion and community building. Since 2008, they have found an important reference point in the Fondazione di Comunità Mirafiori onlus. These processes and projects led to the development of different representations and discourses related to the future of the neighborhood. These were based on different potential levers of development, for example a light and innovative new industrialization or academic research (with new buildings of the Polytechnic and of the University of Turin). In recent years, institutional and civil society discourses and projects seem to converge on a re-territorialization of the neighborhood which is radically moving beyond the industrial past: that of Mirafiori as a "green" neighborhood, which paradoxically is based on some key characteristics of this part of the city. Despite almost 60 years as an industrial neighborhood, in fact, Mirafiori is characterized by large public green areas (11% of the total area), by inclusion of some of the main agricultural areas of the city, by a massive presence of urban gardens (formal and informal) and the presence of a natural ecosystem, landscape and natural elements of symbolic relevance, such as the Sangone River.

The process toward the production of new images (Photo 14.9) and new functions for the Mirafiori Sud district has been shaped by milestones,

[41] Ibidem, pp. 91.

Photo 14.9 Mirafiori after the Myth © Andrea Borgarello per Progetto "Mirafiori dopo il Mito"—Fondazione di Comunità Mirafiori Onlus

such as the action-research project Miraorti. This project aimed at participatory planning of a green area along the Sangone riverbanks, which are characterized by informal vegetable gardens and were targeted by an important urban transformation project. The project, only partially implemented in its original form, was a milestone in the physical transformation of some green areas of the neighborhood and above all in the production of a new way of thinking about this part of the city, based on environment and agriculture.[42] In 2012, the neighborhood's green potential was used by Turin Polytechnic as a field of research and experimentation, through the international competition "Tur(i)ntogreen - Farms in a Town", which was organized in collaboration with UN-Habitat and involved over 800 students from all over the world. They proposed projects focused on transforming parts of the neighborhood based on

[42] Maria Bottiglieri et al. (eds.), *Toward the Turin Food Policy: Good practices and visions* (Milan: Franco-Angeli, 2016); Francesca De Filippi and Ianira Vassallo 'Mirafiori sud: la città fordista oltre la Fabbrica. Scenari e progetti per (la costruzione di) una nuova identità', in *Rivista. Ricerche per la progettazione del paesaggio* 2 (2016), pp. 88–99.

the principles of resilience, sustainability and inclusion, mainly centered on urban agriculture.[43] In 2015, the Compagnia di San Paolo bank foundation funded the Mirafiori Social Green project, with the aim of supporting networking among the many associations and groups of citizens active in the neighborhood. It was concerned with projects focusing on two themes: the environment and food.[44] The apex in the growth of public discourse on Mirafiori Sud's green development probably is the Horizon 2020 project proGIreg (productive Green Infrastructure for post-industrial urban regeneration[45]). It is based on the implementation of nature-based solutions and wants to test their potential to address technical, social and economic challenges and their ability to make urban transformation work with and for citizens in post-industrial neighborhoods of four front-runner cities (Turin, Zagreb, Dortmund and the Chinese city of Ningbo). The project financed the realization of various nature-based solutions, such as hydroponic production, new soil production, pollinators attractor green areas, new riverbanks, green accessible spaces, roof and wall gardens, community gardens. The most interesting example of this last category is the Orti Generali project, previously known as the Miraorti project, which has created a new community space for urban agriculture, leisure and social interaction. It reconnects the neighborhood with the Sangone riverbanks—the most important natural resource in the area—and it probably represents the iconic significance of Mirafiori Sud as a "green neighborhood". The rediscovery of the Sangone River as a structural element of the Mirafiori Sud landscape and of its inhabitants' social life is rooted in the habits of the migrants—mostly from southern Italy—that contributed to the neighborhood's demographic boom, in the 1960s and 1970s. Despite the fact that working in the industrial plants was the main occupation of the Mirafiori population, and probably the main element of their social identity, they developed a strong link with the local environment, mostly through the cultivation of informal vegetable gardens along the Sangone riverbanks.

[43] Ibidem.

[44] Food is another important discursive resource used in the district's re-signification and re-territorialization processes, as the establishment of the first urban "food community" of Mirafiori in Mirafiori Sud shows.

[45] Project funded by the European Union's Horizon 2020 innovation action program under grant agreement no. 776528 (Source: https://progireg.eu/).

Final Remarks

On the one hand, the reflections presented in this chapter further highlighted the limits of a comparison between the Italian Northwest and the Ruhr. On the other hand, though, they highlighted the strong links between the two areas, which both were affected by processes and projects of reinterpretation of the industrial past and by the design of a new landscape, proposing a new hybrid relationship between nature and culture, as the concept of "industrial nature" seems to suggest.[46] The presented case studies also highlight the role of rivers as structural invariants,[47] green infrastructures for the redesign of the city in dialogue with its industrial past and its possible futures. Notably, the passage from a macro-territorial scale (the Northwest), to a geographically smaller scale, as that of the presented case studies, allows a more pertinent comparison with the case studies in the parallel paper by Pia Eiringhaus. This defines an ensemble of territorial projects that can be considered as a "learning environment" for research on the re-naturalization and ecological conversion of the areas affected by deindustrialization processes in the Italian Northwest.

The three Turin cases are examples of a more general approach, linking urban transformation with green infrastructures, nature-based solutions, as well as a new role for nature in the city and in formerly industrial areas—e.g. industrial nature.[48] These three cases also show potentials and ambiguities of such a perspective, which are widely discussed in scientific and political debate.[49]

Rivers play different roles in each of the three cases. The Dora Riparia is again brought to light, after having been covered by industries for decades and it is becoming the central backbone of the newly built neighborhood.

[46] See Pia Eiringhaus, "Layers of new Green – Postindustrial Landscapes and Identity Formation in the Ruhr Valley, Germany" (contribution in this volume).

[47] Alberto Magnaghi, *The Urban Village. A Charter for Democracy and Local Self-Sustainable Development,* (London: Zed Books, 2005).

[48] Caterina Gallizioli, 'Unveiling City Identity through Water', in *Erau 2014 - COMPOSITE CITIES* (2014), pp. 111:1–10; Mariella Borasio and Marco Prusicki, 'Milan Rural Metropolis. A Project for the Enhancement of Waters Towards the Neo-ruralisation of Territorial System in Milan', in *Scienze del Territorio* 2 (2014), pp. 135–146.

[49] Lucilla Barchetta, 'Green Is Not Always Perfectly Green: Temporality, Decay and Open Spaces in Riverside Turin (Italy)', in Gillian Evans (ed.), *Post-Industrial Precarity: New Ethnographies of Urban Lives in Uncertain Times* (Malaga: Vernon Press, 2020), pp. 175–198.

The river is also contributing to a renaming of the whole area, that is now commonly called "Parco Dora", instead of Spina 3, a generic and abstract toponymy. The Stura di Lanzo, currently already characterizing the Basse area, is the object of a project that aims at supporting the natural ecological restoration processes, beyond the human presence in the area. The Sangone, despite its being situated at the periphery of the city, is now at the center of a strategic project for the area. This concerns the connection between Turin and the neighboring towns of Nichelino and Moncalieri. Even if requalification projects initially paid poor attention to it as a local resource, its role in the new plans and functions of the district is growing.

References

Accetturo et al. (2015) 'Deindustrializzazione e terziarizzazione: trasformazioni strutturali nelle regioni del Nord Ovest', *Questioni di economia e finanza*, 282.

Agueda B.F. (2014) 'Urban Restructuring in Former Industrial Cities: Urban Planning Strategies', *Territoire en mouvement. Revue de géographie et aménagement*, 23–24.

Arca Petrucci M. (2001) 'Le rappresentazioni dei vuoti industriali', in Dansero E., Giaimo C. and Spaziante A. (eds.) *Se i vuoti si riempiono* (Firenze: Alinea), pp. 211–224.

Barchetta L. (2020) 'Green Is Not Always Perfectly Green: Temporality, Decay and Open Spaces in Riverside Turin (Italy)', in Evans G., (ed.) *Post-Industrial Precarity: New Ethnographies of Urban Lives in Uncertain Times* (Malaga: Vernon Press), pp. 175–198.

Berger, S. (2019) 'Industrial Heritage and the Ambiguities of Nostalgia for an Industrial Past in the Ruhr Valley, Germany', *Labor Studies in Working-Class History of the Americas*, XVI, 1, 37–64.

Borasio M. and Prusicki M. (2014) 'Milan Rural Metropolis. A Project for the Enhancement of Waters Towards the Neo-ruralisation of Territorial System in Milan', *Scienze del Territorio*, 2, 135–146.

Bottiglieri M., Pettenati G. and Toldo A. (eds.) (2016) *Toward the Turin Food Policy. Good practices and visions* (Milano: FrancoAngeli).

Box, J. (1999) 'Nature Conservation and Post-industrial Landscapes', *Industrial archaeology review*, XXI, 2, 137–146.

Calori A., Dansero E., Pettenati G., Toldo A., (2017) 'Urban Food Planning in Italian Cities: A Comparative Analysis of the Cases of Milan and Turin', *Agroecology and Sustainable Food Systems*, XLI, 8, 1026–1046.

Chelcea, L. (2015) 'Postindustrial Ecologies: Industrial Rubble, Nature and the Limits of Representation' *Parcours anthropologiques*, 10, 186–201.

Clementi A. (2000) 'La rigenerazione dei paesaggi italiani', in Turri E. et al. (eds.) *Il paesaggio italiano. Idee, contributi, immagini* (Milano: Touring Club Italiano).

Dal Borgo A.G., Garda E. and Marini A., (2016), *Sguardi tra i residui. I luoghi dell'abbandono tra rovine, utopie ed eterotopie* (Milano-Udine: Mimesis).

Dansero E. and Vanolo A. (eds) (2006), *Geografia dei paesaggi industriali in Italia* (Milano: FrancoAngeli).

Dansero E., Emanuel C. and Governa F. (eds) (2003) *I patrimoni industriali. Una geografia per lo sviluppo locale* (Milano: FrancoAngeli).

Dansero E. and Scarpocchi C. (2012) 'Patrimoni industriali e sviluppo locale: un approccio geografico', in Ciuffetti A. and Parisi R. (eds.) *L'archeologia industriale in Italia. Storie e storiografia (1978–2008)* (Milano: FrancoAngeli), pp. 353–366.

Dansero E. and Spaziante A. (2016) 'Scoprire i vuoti industriali: analisi e riflessioni a partire da censimenti e mappature di aree industriali dismesse a Torino', in Armano E., Dondona C.A. and Ferlaino F. (eds.) *Postfordismo e trasformazione urbana. Casi di recupero di vuoti industriale e indicazioni per le politiche nel territorio torinese* (Torino: Ires Piemonte), pp. 45–106.

De Filippi F. and Vassallo I. (2016) 'Mirafiori sud: la città fordista oltre la Fabbrica. Scenari e progetti per (la costruzione di) una nuova identità', *Ri-vista. Ricerche per la progettazione del paesaggio*, 2, 88–99.

De Finetti, G., Cislaghi, G., De Benedetti, M. and Marabelli, P. (2002) *Milano: costruzione di una città* (Milano: Hoepli).

Dematteis G. (1995) 'Le trasformazioni territoriali e ambientali', in F. Barbagallo (ed.) *Storia dell'Italia repubblicana, vol. II* (Torino: Einaudi), pp. 661–709.

Dematteis, G. and Governa, F. (eds.) (2005) *Territorialità, sviluppo locale, sostenibilità: il modello SLOT* (Milano: FrancoAngeli).

Donadieu P. (2006) 'Landscape Urbanism in Europe: From Brownfields to Sustainable Urban Development', *Journal of Landscape Architecture*, I, 2, 36–45.

Dormidontova V. and Belkin A. (2018) 'The Use of Post-Industrial Areas in the Formation of the Recreational Environment of the City', *IOP Conf. Series: Materials Science and Engineering*, 463.

Douet, J. (2016) *Industrial Heritage Re-tooled: The TICCIH Guide to Industrial Heritage Conservation* (London: Routledge).

Eiringhaus, P. (2018) *Industrie wird Natur. Postindustrielle Repräsentationen von Region und Umwelt im Ruhrgebiet* (Essen: Klartext).

Erdem, M. and Nassauer, J. I. (2013) 'Design of Brownfield Landscapes Under Different Contaminant Remediation Policies in Europe and the United States', *Landscape Journal*, XXXII, 2, 277–292.

Ferraresi G., Magnaghi A. (1992) 'La Valle del Lambro, Seveso e Olona: da area ad alto rischio a progetto integrato di valorizzazione territoriale', in Magnaghi A. and Paloscia R. (eds.) *Per una trasformazione ecologica degli insediamenti* (Milano: FrancoAngeli).

Ferrari L. (2004) 'La bonifica di un sito inquinato quale impulso alla progettazione dello spazio aperto: il Bosco delle Querce di Seveso e Meda', in Rizzo G. and Valentini A. (eds.), *Luoghi e paesaggi in Italia* (Firenze: Firenze University Press), pp. 135–148.

Frallicciardi A. M. and D'Anna M. (2015), 'Teoria e prassi dei vuoti urbani', *Territorio della ricerca su insediamenti e ambiente*, VIII, 1, 23–44.

Gallizioli C. (2014) 'Unveiling City Identity through Water', in Erau 2014 - COMPOSITE CITIES, pp. 111:1–10.

Gandy, M. (2015) 'From Urban Ecology to Ecological Urbanism: An Ambiguous Trajectory', *Area*, LXII, 2, 150–154.

Gennari I. and Sportaro E. (2016) 'Racconto di un paesaggio complesso. Percorso attraverso gli ambienti della Valle Olona, da Castelseprio al Parco Pineta', Master thesis in Landscape Architecture, Politecnico di Milano.

Giangrande A. (2010) 'Un approccio partecipativo dinamico per la riqualificazione e la valorizzazione fluviale nei Contratti di Fiume. Il caso di Basse di Stura', in *SIU Conference Proceedings* (Rome: SIU).

Giovinazzi, O. (2008) 'Città portuali e waterfront urbani: costruire scenari di trasformazione in contesti di conflitto', *Méditerranée. Revue géographique des pays méditerranéens/Journal of Mediterranean Geography*, 111, 69–74.

Governa F. and Santangelo M. (2006) 'Tra l'industria e il fiume. Il paesaggio del Medio Olona', in Dansero E. and Vanolo A. (eds.), *Geografia dei paesaggi industriali in Italia* (Milano: FrancoAngeli), pp. 201–222.

Höfer W. and Vicenzotti V. (2019) 'Post-industrial Landscapes. Evolving Concepts', in Howard P., Thompson I., Waterton E., Atha M. (eds.) *The Routledge Companion to Landscape Studies* (London: Routledge), pp. 499–510.

Jones, C. and Munday, M. (2001) 'Blaenavon and United Nations World Heritage Site status: Is Conservation of Industrial Heritage a Road to Local Economic Development?' *Regional Studies*, XXXV, 6, 585–590.

Kitchen, L., Marsden, T., and Milbourne, P. (2006) 'Community Forests and Regeneration in Post-industrial Landscapes', *Geoforum*, XXXVII, 5, 831–843.

Magnaghi A. (1992) 'Bonifica, risanamento e valorizzazione del territorio', in Magnaghi A. and Paloscia R. (eds.), *Per una trasformazione ecologica degli insediamenti* (Milano: FrancoAngeli).

Magnaghi A. (eds) (1995) 'Bonifica, riconversione, valorizzazione ambientale del fiume Lambro-Seveso-Olona', *Urbanistica Quaderni*, 2.

Magnaghi A. (2005) 'The Urban Village. A Charter for Democracy and Local Self-Sustainable Development' (London: Zed Books).

Millington N. (2013) 'Post-Industrial Imaginaries: Nature, Representation and Ruin in Detroit, Michigan', *International Journal of Urban and Regional Research*, XXXVII, 1, 279–296.

Planet Idea (2018), *Mirafiori Sud in numeri* (Torino: Planet Idea).

Prat A. and Mangili S. (2016) 'Turin Case Study', in Carter D. (ed.) *Remaking Post-Industrial Cities: Lessons from North America and Europe* (London: Routledge), pp. 210–229.

Raffestin C. (1984) 'Territorializzazione, Deterritorializzazione, Riterritorializzazione e informazione', in Turco A. (ed.), *Regione e Regionalizzazione* (Milano: Franco Angeli), pp. 69–82.

Raffestin C. (2005) *Dalla nostalgia del territorio al desiderio di paesaggio* (Firenze: Alinea).

Raffestin, C. (2012) 'Space, Territory, and Territoriality', *Environment and Planning D: Society and Space*, 30, 121–141.

Saccomani S. (1998) 'PRG di Torino: la variante per la Spina centrale', *Urbanistica Informazioni*, 162, 5–6.

Savio E. and Guiati F. (2014) *Mirafiori Sud, vita e storia oltre la fabbrica* (Torino: Edizioni Graphot Spoon River).

Scaduto M. L. (2016) *River Contracts and Integrated Water Management in Europe* (Berlin: Springer).

Spaziante A. (2014), 'Recycling Cities, Recycling Turin: Problems and Opportunities', in D'Arienzo R. and Younes C. (eds.), *Recycler l'Urbain. Pour une écologie des milieux habités* (Geneve: Metis Presses), pp. 309–360.

Turco A. (1988) *Verso una teoria geografica della complessità (*Milano: Unicopli).

PART VII

Cultures of Deindustrialization

CHAPTER 15

Re-using Industrial Sites in the Ruhr: Agendas and Developments

Stefan Berger

Introduction

Industrial sites, in particular those, on which coalmines and steelworks were located, became increasingly available in the Ruhr area from the 1960s onwards. Although the modernization of mining in the post-Second World War era had led to ever bigger mines and the closure of unproductive smaller ones, it had not produced major debates surrounding heritagization. These only began when it dawned on actors that the coal crisis, which had begun in the late 1950s, was not a cyclical crisis but a permanent and terminal one. In the course of the 1960s mining was re-organized. All of the mines came together under the roof of a new company, the Ruhrkohle AG, founded in November 1968 in order to coordinate the gradual decline of the coal industry in the Ruhr region. The mine owners, the mining trade union and the state had

S. Berger (✉)
Institute for Social Movements, Ruhr University Bochum, Bochum, Germany
e-mail: Stefan.Berger@ruhr-uni-bochum.de; stefan.berger@rub.de

S. Berger et al. (eds.), *Deindustrialisation in Twentieth-Century Europe*, Palgrave Studies in the History of Social Movements,
https://doi.org/10.1007/978-3-030-89631-7_15

agreed terms which effectively led to a long term managed decline of the industry over a period of 60 years. The last mine in the Ruhr closed in 2018. The corporatist arrangement, typical of the Rhenish capitalist model, provided modest subsidies to the RAG, so that the latter could sell coal to German power stations at world market prizes. At the same time, the company and the unions agreed redundancy schemes for hundreds of thousands of miners over decades that included retraining and reskilling schemes and generous redundancy packages. No one was supposed to end up socially deprived and economically poor by the winding down of one of the two industries that had defined the Ruhr since the middle of the nineteenth century.[1]

In the 1970s the other of the two key industries of the region, steel, entered a prolonged crisis that also, in all likelihood, will see the disappearance of the industry from the region within the next ten years or so. Although Duisburg in 2019 still boasts the biggest steelworks in Europe, the writing for the industry has been on the wall for some time. The arrangements for the winding down of the steel industry in the Ruhr have been very different from the one for coal. By the 1970s, there was no political will to work with tax-funded subsidies, and the unions had to undertake some iconic strike action, such as the ones in Hattingen in 1986 and in Rheinhausen in 1987 to achieve not the retention of the works but generous social plans and retraining schemes for the steel workers. Strong unions and a working corporatist arrangement with employers and the state once again managed to avoid social deprivation as a side result of economic decline.[2]

The relative success of the structural transformation of the Ruhr from a region of heavy industry to a region of knowledge formation, trade, and a diverse range of industries, including IT and high-tech industries, chemical industries and (for a while) car industries also meant that the Ruhr did not become the rust belt of Germany. Although it has its share

[1] Michael Farrenkopf, 'Wiederaufstieg und Niedergang des Bergbaus in der Bundesrepublik', in Dieter Ziegler (ed.), *Geschichte des deutschen Bergbaus*, Vol. 4: Rohstoffgewinnung im Strukturwandel: der deutsche Bergbau im 20. Jahrhundert (Essen: Klartext, 2013), pp. 183–280; Christoph Nonn, *Die Ruhrbergbaukrise: Entindustrialisierung und Politik. 1958–1969* (Göttingen: Vandenhoeck & Ruprecht, 2001).

[2] Josef Esser and Werner Väth, 'Overcoming the Steel Crisis in the Federal Republic of Germany. 1975–1983', in Yves Mény and Vincent Wright (eds.), *The Politics of Steel: Western Europe and the Steel Industry in the Crisis Years (1978–1984)* (Berlin: de Gruyter, 1987), pp. 623–691.

of economic and social problems and is no longer the economic powerhouse of the nation, its decline, if compared with other regions of heavy industry, has not been as dramatic and catastrophic. Such relative success also had a major impact on how the region was to deal with its industrial heritage related to the coal and steel industries.[3]

The Beginnings of Heritagization and the Formation of Heritage Actors

That industrial heritage was worthwhile preserving was not a view widely held during the first decade of intensive deindustrialization in the 1960s. Unions were struggling to keep jobs rather than putting those jobs into the museum. Employers and politicians sought to attract new industries to the empty spaces left by closed-down coal mines. When the car manufacturer Opel came to Bochum in the early 1960s it could use sites of former coal mines to build its factory. Mine buildings were often torn down, shafts closed, the earth was detoxed and the search for new industrial uses could begin.[4] Yet things began to change during the second half of the 1960s. Plans to demolish Zeche Zollern II/4 in Dortmund-Bövinghausen met with vociferous opposition. Many of its buildings resembled more a small castle than a functional mine building, and its machine hall was a jewel of pure art deco (Figs. 15.1 and 15.2).

It was not surprising that art historians and artists were among the protesters in the Ruhr, who did much to establish the aesthetics of industrial heritage, and who were among those imploring politicians to preserve the mine and especially its machine hall. In 1969 the latter became the first industrial building in Germany to be placed under a preservation order.[5] Eventually, the mine would become one of the key sites of the industrial museum of the Landschaftsverband Westfalen-Lippe (LWL),

[3] Stefan Berger, 'Das Ruhrgebiet im internationalen Vergleich', in Michael Farrenkopf, Stefan Goch and Manfred Rasch (eds.), *Die Stadt der Städte: das Ruhrgebiet und seine Umbrüche* (Essen: Klartext, 2019), pp. 571–576.

[4] Stefan Goch, *Eine Region im Kampf mit dem Strukturwandel: Bewältigung von Strukturwandel und Strukturpolitik im Ruhrgebiet* (Essen: Klartext, 2002), p. 332ff.

[5] Thomas Parent, *Das Ruhrgebiet: vom ‚goldenen ‘ Mittelalter zur Industriekultur* (Cologne: Dumont, 2000), pp. 197–202.

Fig. 15.1 The headgear of Zeche Zollern

Fig. 15.2 The entrance to the machine hall of Zeche Zollern

a peculiar administrative organization that stretches back to eighteenth-century Prussia and which today belongs to the champions of industrial heritage in the Ruhr.

In the rescue of Zeche Zollern artists and art historians had joined forces with academics from the newly established (in 1965) Ruhr University in Bochum and a range of intellectuals as well as a nascent history workshop movement, in which school teachers, trade unionists and workers sought to explore the history of the Ruhr region and preserve the remnants of what once defined the region: heavy industry. From the late 1960s an alliance of intellectuals and workers, in which the preservationist and Professor from Bielefeld university, Roland Günter, played a key role, formed, in order to prevent the authorities from demolishing a mid-nineteenth-century working-class housing estate, Eisenheim, and replace it with modern concrete high-rise buildings. It was a long struggle but the initiative eventually managed to convince the authorities to drop their demolition plans and instead modernize the old working-class housing

Fig. 15.3 Siedlung Eisenheim

estate, which is today a prime example of sought-after living space in a post-industrial Ruhr—complete with its own little museum telling the story of the estate and the struggle to preserve it[6] (Fig. 15.3).

Industrial heritage in the Ruhr was an initiative that started from below. During the 1970s and 1980s, it was, however, picked up from above in a major way. The Social-Democrat-led governments that ruled the Land of North-Rhine Westphalia continuously between 1966 and 2005, often in alliance with Social-Democrat-led municipalities that dominated the Ruhr region during this period sought to link industrial heritage to its core constituency, the workers in heavy industry. Their attempts to bring about a structural transformation of the region that did not harm the workers and that would protect their standards of living could make use of industrial heritage as a form of cultural repertoire that spoke to the ordinary workers in the region. It was a Social Democratic buildings minister,

[6] Janne Günther and Roland Günther, *‚Sprechende Strassen in Eisenheim: Konzepte und Texte sämtlicher Tafeln in der ältesten Siedlung (1846/1901) im Ruhrgebiet* (Essen: Klartext, 1999).

Christoph Zöpel, who declared another mine in Essen, Zeche Zollverein, today an UNESCO world heritage site, a protected monument after the mine closed in 1986. And Johannes Rau, the long-term Social Democrat minister president of North-Rhine Westphalia and later president of the republic, linked the idea of working for the ordinary working-class men and women with the preservation of industrial sites associated with those men (more than women).[7]

With financial support from North-Rhine Westphalia and many of the communities in the Ruhr, a ten-year long International Building Exhibition Emscher Park (IBA) was launched in 1989 which sought to help in particular the northern parts of the Ruhr, most affected by intensive deindustrialization, to make the structural transformation to a region no longer predominantly dependent on coal and steel. Under the spirited leadership of Karl Ganser, dozens of projects were launched that saw the transformation of former sites of industry into industrial heritage. Many of the icons of today's landscape of industrial heritage in the Ruhr, the Gasometer in Oberhausen, the Jahrhunderthalle in Bochum, the Landschaftspark Nord in Duisburg, the 'U' cultural center in Dortmund, and many more were created in this decade.[8] The Regionalverband Ruhr (RVR), an administrative body with some planning authority over aspects of regional development in the Ruhr that goes back to 1920, in alliance with the Land NRW built up the Route of Industrial Heritage which connected dozens of sites of industrial heritage on 400 kms of road and 700 kilometries of cycling paths. Many of the former coal trams in the region were transformed into these cycling paths.[9] The idea became so popular that its key architects were able to launch a European route of industrial heritage that today spans 29 European countries and is one of the most encompassing cultural routes of the EU underlining to

[7] Christoph Cornelissen, 'Der lange Weg zur historischen Identität: Geschichtspolitik in Nordrhein-Westfalen seit 1946', in Thomas Schlemmer and Hans Woller (eds.), *Bayern im Bund 3: Politik und Kultur im föderativen Staat, 1949–1973* (Munich: Oldenbourg, 2004), pp. 411–484.

[8] Heiderose Kilper, *Die Internationale Bauausstellung Emscher Park: eine Studie zur Steuerungsproblematik komplexer Erneuerungsprozesse in einer alten Industrieregion* (Wiesbaden: Springer, 1999).

[9] http://www.route-industriekultur.ruhr/route-industriekultur.html [accessed 28 August 2019].

what extent industry forms a common denominator across the European Union.[10]

During the years of the IBA, the industrialists and the trade unionists also became ardent supporters of industrial heritage. Before, they belonged to the camp of the skeptics: industrialists feared the costs of preserving industrial shells with no function. But once the Land NRW, in the 1970s, had paved the way of acquiring industrial land cheaply in return for allowing the industrialists to get rid of their responsibility for the sites, the latter looked more favorably onto industrial heritage projects. And with industrial heritage becoming so hip in the 1990s, the RAG's daughter company, RAG Montanimmobilien, founded in the 1970s, made a considerable profit from developing closed mining sites for a wide variety of post-mining usage, from housing estates, to public administrative buildings, to museums and new office spaces.[11] And the RAG, together with the Land NRW, also put its weight behind a multimillion Euro foundation that looks after some of the most important mining heritage sites in the region, the Foundation for the Preservation of Industrial Monuments and Historical Culture[12] (Fig. 15.4).

Trade unionists had long held out against heritage enthusiasts. Their job was to protect the jobs of miners and steelworkers. But with their success of managing the slow decline of the coal industry and achieving a good deal for those affected by the closing down of the steel works came a willingness to endorse the culture of industrial heritage which also gave their clientele and themselves a prominent place in historical remembrance. The industry and those who led the companies as well as its workers and those who represented them, the unions, were part and parcel of a proud story of the successful transformation of one of the foremost regions of heavy industry in Europe to a lively, multi-cultural and exciting new space, with many new industries, with leading universities and with cultural icons, including high culture such as four opera houses, four concert halls and more than a dozen of nationally renown theaters

[10] https://www.erih.net/ [accessed 28 August 2019].

[11] https://www.rag-montan-immobilien.de/ [accessed 28 August 2019].

[12] https://www.industriedenkmal-stiftung.de/en/ [accessed 28 August 2019].

Fig. 15.4 Kokerei Hansa, home of the Foundation for the Preservation of Industrial Monuments and Historical Culture

as well as hundreds of venues for music festivals that is unprecedented anywhere else in Germany.[13]

After the turn of the millennium, the region increasingly began to market itself on its success—relative economic success at structural transformation, social success in doing so with producing the kind of social deprivation that other regions of heavy industry suffered across the developed western world, cultural success in creating a world-wide unique industrial heritage landscape that served as proud reminder of the Ruhr's industrial past. Politicians from all political parties, not just the Social

[13] https://www.ruhr-tourismus.de/de/themen/kultur.html [accessed 28 August 2019].

Democrats, now identified with and championed industrial heritage that became the key marker for regional identity and its realms of memory.[14]

In 2010 Essen (as representative of the entire Ruhr region) became capital of culture, fending off strong opposition from other, more traditional cultural centers in Germany. Its motto was 'Change through Culture – Culture Because of Change' ('Wandel durch Kultur – Kultur durch Wandel') indicating the symbiotic relationship that had developed between images of industry and images of culture in the region. Many of the initiatives during 2010 celebrated the new cultural hub of the Ruhr and reminded the millions of visitors of its industrial past.[15] The year began with the opening of the newly designed Ruhr regional museum that now occupied the site of the coal washery at the UNESCO world heritage site Zollverein. Its founding director Ulrich Borsdorf and his team had created a daring and innovative design of state-of-the art regional cultural and natural history museum in the bowels of a former machine central to the working of the coal mine. |Its symbolism was breath-taking and its execution world-leading. It remains today one of the most impressive regional history museums that I am aware of[16] (Fig. 15.5).

Yet 2010 also showed up some cracks in the united front of industrial heritage aficionados in the Ruhr. Some critics of the cultural capital of Europe design argued that industrial heritage had been sidelined and was not central enough to its conceptualization. Other critics argued that industrial heritage had become a mere marketing toy. Its touristification had allegedly led to forms of aestheticization that were contrary to its origins in working-class culture. The blood, sweat and tears connected to that heritage, the grime, noise and unpleasantness disappeared behind the

[14] Stefan Berger, Jana Golombek and Christian Wicke, 'A Post-industrial Mindscape? The Mainstreaming and Touristification of Industrial Heritage in the Ruhr', in Christian Wicke, Stefan Berger and Jana Golombek (eds.), *Industrial Heritage and Regional Identity* (London: Routledge, 2018), Chapter 4; see also Stefan Berger, Ulrich Borsdorf, Heinrich Theodor Grütter and Dieter Nellen (eds.), *Zeit – Räume – Ruhr: die Erinnerungsorte des Ruhrgebiets* (Essen: Klartext, 2019).

[15] Jürgen Mittag and Kathrin Oerters, 'Kreativwirtschaft und Kulturhauptstadt: Katalysatoren urbaner Entwicklung in altindustriellen Ballungsregionen', in Gudrun Quenzel (ed.), *Entwicklungsfaktor Kultur: Studien zum kulturellen und ökonomischen Potential der europäischen Stadt* (Bielefeld: Transcript, 2009), pp. 61–94.

[16] Ulrich Borsdorf and Heinrich Theodor Grütter (eds.), *Ruhr Museum. Natur – Kultur – Geschichte* (Essen: Klartext, 2010).

Fig. 15.5 The Ruhrmuseum at Zeche Zollverein

rose-tinted spectacles of heritage. Next to the critics who wanted more and/or different forms of industrial heritage were those who criticized an overkill of industrial heritage tout court. They argued that the region's rootedness to its industrial past prevented it from looking ahead to its post-industrial future.[17] In recent years the right-wing populist Alternative für Deutschland (AfD) has been celebrating considerable successes in some of the most deprived areas of the northern Ruhr putting into question whether all segments of the population feel that they are part of the success story that is connected to the industrial heritage narrative in the Ruhr. The AfD appeals to the working-class population of the northern Ruhr by alleging that it is the true heir of the region's social democratic tradition which has been betrayed by the Social Democrats (Fig. 15.6).

[17] Christina Pachaly, *Kulturhauptstadt Europas Ruhr 2010: ein Festival als Instrument der Stadtentwicklung* (Berlin: Universitätsverlag der TU Berlin, 2010).

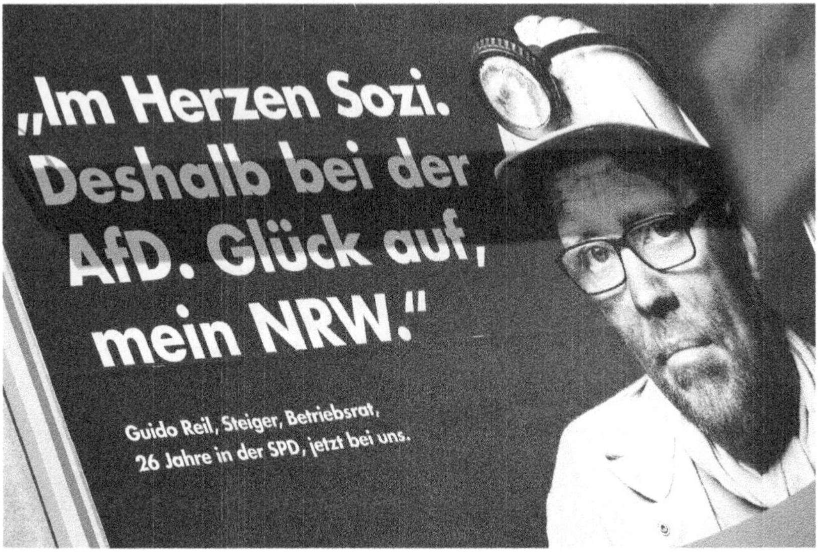

Fig. 15.6 AfD election poster showing one of their local councilors who defected from the SPD in miners' clothes with the slogan 'at heart a Social Democrat, therefore AfD' ©Marcel Doliwa

If cracks have begun to appear around issues of industrial heritage, the united front of those heritage actors in support of industrial heritage in the region is still truly impressive. As I have argued here, it has grown continuously over the last 60 years and spans all political parties, regional governments, regional administrative bodies such as the RVR and the LWL (which has its equivalent in the Rhineland in the Landschaftsverband Rheinland, LVR), municipalities, leading employers in the regions, the trade unions, and a rich bottom-up history culture that is today focused on the Association History Culture at Ruhr and Emscher with its state-of-the-art history journal, *Geschichtskultur an Ruhr und Emscher*.[18] In fact, as I have argued elsewhere, without this powerful alliance of heritage actors, it would be impossible to have achieved so much in the Ruhr over the past half-century. Today the region is a world superpower when it comes to industrial heritage. But that status also comes at a price.

[18] https://www.geschichtskultur-ruhr.de/ [accessed 28 August 2019].

Its unitary mindscape, its homogeneous narrativization of the industrial past that is linked to a project of ongoing modernization is producing a range of silences and is increasingly unable to engage those who are dissatisfied with the processes of deindustrialization and who feel left behind and voiceless in a region that has still many social and economic problems.[19]

However, in this chapter, I am focusing on the re-use of former industrial sites, and I will demonstrate the diversity of such re-uses by giving three distinct examples: the first two come from the decade of the IBA Emscher Park, the gasometer in Oberhausen and the landscape park in Duisburg, with the third example being the icon of industrial heritage in the Ruhr, the Zollverein mining site. It is, to some extent, an arbitrary choice, as I could have easily picked from dozens of other impressive sites in the Ruhr, but my choice has been led by the thought that I could show different things with those three sites that we can, of course, reproduce with more examples from different sites but that we cannot substantially add to or contradict.

Re-using Industrial Space: The Gasometer in Oberhausen

When the construction of the gasometer in Oberhausen, right next to the Rhein Herne canal, was finished in 1927, it was the biggest gasometer in Europe—117 m high and 67 m in diameter (Fig. 15.7).[20]

Badly damaged by bombing in the Second World War and by fire in 1946, it was reconstructed in 1949. When the cokery in Oberhausen was closed and gas increasingly came via long-distance pipelines, it became superfluous and was finally decommissioned in 1988. Like with many other icons of industrial heritage in the Ruhr today, the initial plan had been to destroy it as quickly as possible. It was only the high initial costs of getting rid of it that prevented its destruction before the advent of the IBA. The Oberhausen city council decided to buy the building in 1992. Transforming the gasometer, as one of the iconic cathedrals of industry

[19] Stefan Berger, 'Industrial Heritage and the Ambiguities of Nostalgia for an Industrial Past in the Ruhr Valley in Germany', in *Labor: Studies in Working-Class History* 16:1 (2019), pp. 37–64.

[20] https://www.gasometer.de/de/der-gasometer/industriekultur [accessed 28 August 2019].

Fig. 15.7 The Gasometer in Oberhausen

in the Ruhr, into a space for exhibitions was one of the projects of the IBA in the 1990s. During 1993/1994 its transformation cost 16 million Deutschmarks. Since then it has become a key symbol of the city of Oberhausen and its exhibitions have been remarkably successful, beating visitor records for more than two decades. 1.35 million visitors came to its 'wonders of nature' exhibition in 2017.[21]

It is located right next to one of the biggest shopping malls in the Ruhr, in Germany and in Europe, the so-called WESTFIELD CENTRO in Oberhausen.[22]

We do not know whether there is much overlap between those visiting the 'Centro' and those visiting the gasometer, but both have undoubtedly become key symbols of the structural transformation of the Ruhr area. Standing on top of the gasometer visitors have a wonderful view over Oberhausen and the Western Ruhr. They can appreciate how green it has become—a remarkable transformation from the greyish hell-hole of smoke and coaldust that it once was. Is it therefore a prime example of the commodification of industrial heritage that some critics of the industrial heritage discourse bemoan? The site itself is well contextualized and historicized. Various informative tablets, outside, inside and on top of the site inform the visitor what the gasometer was—with plenty of technical details, its history and its transformation into industrial heritage.[23] The message for the visitors is clear: this is a place that the visitors, if they come from the Ruhr, can be proud of—it stands for a great industrial past. Its transformation into heritage is also a story full of superlatives—no one entering the vast hollow inside of the building can fail to be impressed by this space. The most successful exhibitions that have been staged here since the 1990s have been using this space with great effect in creating hugely impressive simulacra—of the night sky, of alpine panoramas, of diverse spectacles of nature. The exhibitions staged at the gasometer, however, have rarely anything to do with its industrial past. Hence, the exhibitions themselves decontextualize the gasometer. It becomes a mere

[21] 1,350,000 Besucher bei Wunder der Natur Ausstellung im Gasometer, Westdeutsche Allgemeine Zeitung, 4 December 2017, https://www.waz.de/kultur/1-350-000-besucher-bei-wunder-der-natur-im-gasometer-id212734273.html [accessed 28 August 2019].

[22] https://www.centro.de/centre [accessed 28 August 2019].

[23] Stefan Rahner and Peter Schmidtmann, *Gasometer Oberhausen: Geschichte – Technik – Arbeit* (Essen: Klartext, 2007).

backdrop for a range of exhibitions on nature and culture that could be held at any venue and are definitely not venue-specific.

The gasometer in Oberhausen is in this respect and in others also a showcase for some of the key problems facing many industrial heritage sites in the region: industrial buildings were usually not made to last. They were functional buildings that had a specific industrial purpose for a limited amount of time. Hence, they are prone to more rapid deterioration than palaces, castles, gentry homes and more traditional forms of built heritage. Corrosion at the gasometer is so bad already 20 years after its initial transformation that it is in need of a complete overhaul costing another 14 million Euro, half of which is coming from the national government with the other half funded by the RVR and the Land NRW. In 2020 the gasometer will be closed for one year while it undergoes restoration. The costs for preserving the industrial heritage landscape of the Ruhr in the medium term will be enormous. Therfore, an increasing number of voices inside the Ruhr, including this author, have been calling for the creation of a national foundation, analogues to the National Foundation Preussischer Kulturbesitz, looking after the cultural heritage of Prussia. A National Foundation Industrial Heritage which will not just look after the heritage in the Ruhr but after all forms of industrial heritage in the Federal Republic would be a stark symbol of the recognition of the importance of industry for the development and success of Germany from the nineteenth century to the present day. Without such a foundation it is highly unlikely that the abundant wealth of industrial heritage in the Ruhr can be maintained already in the medium term.[24]

Re-using Industrial Space: The Landscape Park in Duisburg

These are also problems visible in the Industrial Landscape Park Duisburg-North—which has been created at the site of a former ironworks in Duisburg-Meiderich[25] (Fig. 15.8).

The blast furnaces and much of the pipework and buildings associated with them are not built to last and are crumbling fast. Repairing

[24] Stefan Berger, Uli Borsdorf and Dieter Nellen, 'Eine nationale Aufgabe. Das indusrielle Erbe an Rhein und Ruhr', in *Politik und Kultur* 4 (2015), p. 18.

[25] https://www.landschaftspark.de/ [accessed 28 August 2019].

Fig. 15.8 Detail of the landscape park Duisburg-North

and maintaining the structures at the heart of the landscape park is a very expensive affair, and the visitor might find that certain parts of the structure are no longer accessible, as they have become too unsafe to visit. Here, as elsewhere, the costs for maintaining this kind of heritage are easily spiraling out of control and a solution to this will have to be found before too long, if the impressive landscape of industrial heritage is to be preserved at the Ruhr.

The ironworks on site was founded in 1901 and in 84 years of its existence, its five blast furnaces have produced 37 million tons of raw iron, largely to be used in other steelworks that belonged to the same company that also owned the ironworks in Meiderich, the Thyssen concern. When the site closed in 1985, it languished for a number of years before it also became a key project of the IBA. A professional architectural bureau transformed the park between 1990 and 1999, and already from 1994 the park was open to the public. The idea of the architects was to retain many of the original buildings of the ironworks and transform them, so that they would be accessible to visitors and could be used in a variety of different ways. Different parks were created, like a water park or a railway park, and viewpoints were installed on top of the remaining furnaces.[26]

The flora and fauna that developed on site is incredibly rich and varied. In the Ruhr area a new term was coined for the kind of nature that developed on and around previous industrial sites: 'industrial nature' ('Industrienatur'). Pia Eiringhaus has recently analyzed the discursive construction of 'industrial nature' in the Ruhr, arguing that it fits in well with the modernizing agenda of the industrial heritage discourse as it has emerged over the last sixty years.[27] In a self-reflexive and self-critical manner, the devastation that industry wreaked on the natural landscape throughout much of the nineteenth and twentieth centuries is recognized and criticized in this discourse. The experience itself becomes part and parcel of a moral lesson: industrial development needs to be sustainable and in line with nature, not working against it. The sins of the past need to be transformed into a better, greener future. Industrial heritage plays its part in it, as on its sites, a new and richer and more diverse flora and fauna grows than the one that existed in the Ruhr before industrialization.

[26] Ralf Winkels and Günter Zieling, *Landschaftspark Duisburg-Nord: vom Eisenkochtopf zum Erlebnispark* (Dusiburg: Mercator-Verlag, 2009).

[27] Pia Eiringhaus, *Industrie wird Natur – postindustrielle Repräsentationen von Region und Umwelt im Ruhrgebiet* (Bochum: Institut für soziale Bewegungen, 2018).

Hence, what emerges in the post-industrial Ruhr is better than what was before. And the big projects of the future that are being thought of in the Ruhr today are entirely in line with the greener and more sustainable future. Thus, the city of Essen, for example, has become the green capital of Europe, reacting to the intensifying climate change debate globally.[28] Bottrop has become a city which is working toward being self-supporting in terms of energy efficiency.[29] Overall, the modernization discourse is sustained by the narratives of industrial nature that are such a prominent part of the landscape park in Duisburg-Meiderich.

The park has won many prizes and the *Guardian* newspaper in 2015 counted it among the top 10 landscape parks of the world, alongside the Highline in New York, the Parc Güell in Barcelona, Hampstead Heath in London, and the Buttes-Chaumont in Paris.[30] It is a prime example of the accessibility of industrial heritage to ordinary people in the Ruhr who can make use of the park in a variety of different ways. For a start, using the park is free of charge all year round. Everyone can walk it or cycle it or use it as a green space. Furthermore, the park offers a range of popular leisure facilities that range from climbing walls to a diving tank, a climbing path within the casting house of one of the furnaces, an open-air cinema and the former machine hall has been transformed into a multi-functional hall for concerts and theater performances. It is regularly used by music and theater festivals in the Ruhr region, such as the Piano Festival Ruhr and the Ruhrtriennale.[31] There is also a conference venue on site. A viewing platform on yet another furnace in the park allows

[28] See the extensive documention One Year European Green Capital—Essen 2017, https://media.essen.de/media/wwwessende/aemter/0115_1/gruene_hauptstadt_5/180803_GHE_0336_Dokumentation_22x27_96dpi.pdf [accessed 28 August 2019] which shows the full breadth and depth of the initiatives.

[29] Endbericht Technical Tour Smart Cities Amsterdam – Bottrop – Hamburg, published by the Bundesministerium für Verkehr, Innovation und Technologie, 3 December 2015, https://nachhaltigwirtschaften.at/resources/hdz_pdf/events/20150831_staedtebauliche_exkursion_am_alm-_bot_ham_endbericht.pdf?m=1469661506 [accessed 28 August 2019].

[30] Rowan Moore, 'The Ten Best Parks', in *The Guardian*, 7 August 2015, https://www.theguardian.com/culture/2015/aug/07/10-best-parks-urban-green-spaces-high-line-new-york-hampstead-london-park-guell-barcelona [accessed 28 August 2019].

[31] About the piano festival Ruhr see https://www.klavierfestival.de/index.php?id=69 [accessed 28 August 2019]; on the Ruhrtrienale compare https://www.ruhrtriennale.de/en/ruhrtriennale/History_of_the_festival [accessed 28 August 2019].

the visitors to enjoy panoramic views of Duisburg and the western Ruhr area. Millions of people make use of the park every year and visit it from near and far. There are multiple guided tours offered through the park all year round, some focusing more on industrial heritage, some on industrial nature.

Every evening, when it gets dark, until around 1 am in the morning, much of the industrial buildings are illuminated by light art created by artist Jonathan Park. It is the only of his light installations that are permanent. Park's intention is to transform the park into a 'magical space'.[32] Hilary Orange, who has researched the use of artificial light and light-based technologies at industrial heritage sites in the Ruhr region, understands the 'widespread and strategic use of light in the Ruhr' as representing 'a distincitive historically and culturally bound practice'.[33] Lighting industrial heritage venues contributes to making industrial heritage an aesthetically pleasing site that can further strengthen the identification of the people who live in the Ruhr region with their industrial past and contribute to feelings of pride and ownership in a collective past on which a future can be built. In this way, industrial heritage becomes a practical past in the Ruhr, which seeks to establish, through memory, an ethical discourse about the past which has meaning in the present.[34] Memorialization of the past becomes a political project that seeks to shape the future of the region. It is multi-directional, as the meanings of such memorializations are not fixed and can be interpreted in different ways.[35] Much depends on perspectives and interests. As I have argued above: at present the staging of industrial heritage in the Ruhr is tightly linked to narratives of ongoing modernization which is re-assuring the inhabitants and possible investors about the future of the

[32] Interview with Jonathan Park in Westdeutsche Allgemeine Zeitung, 4 May 2010, see: https://www.waz.de/staedte/duisburg/nord/strahlender-farbenfroher-id3500184.html [accessed 2 December 2018].

[33] Quote taken from Hilary Orange, Lighting the Ruhr website, see: https://hilaryorange.wordpress.com/2017/02/15/lighting-the-ruhr/ [accessed 2 December 2018].

[34] I borrow the idea of the practical past from Hayden White, *The Practical Past* (Evanston and Illinois: Northwestern Press, 2014), who has argued that history writing should contribute to an ethical understanding of the past that has meaning for the present. A similar argument can be made for memory.

[35] Michael Rothberg, *Multi-directional Memory: Remembering the Holocaust in the Age of Decolonization* (Stanford: Stanford University Press, 2009).

Ruhr. However, memorializations can also be about a criticism of capitalism, about alternatives to the neoliberal present, about celebrations of solidarity and struggle of the many to achieve a fuller and happier life. How we infuse the industrial heritage sites and the memorializations they convey with meaning is largely contingent on those actors engaged in shaping the collective memories of the region.

Re-using Industrial Space: The Zollverein Mining Site

Arguably the biggest memory machine of all in the Ruhr is the UNESCO world heritage site of Zeche Zollverein in Essen. This mine, with its twelve shafts, was the biggest and most modern in interwar Europe. The onsite former cokery of the mine, built between 1957 and 1961 and completely preserved, is also part of the world heritage site (Fig. 15.9).

Fig. 15.9 The cokery at the Zollverein site

Fig. 15.10 Ehrenhof at Zollverein

Going back to the middle of the nineteenth century, the name of the mine itself was programmatic: at a time when a German nation state did not yet exist, it was named after the German Customs Union of 1832 that many perceived as an important stepping stone on the road to national unity. After the First World War was lost, the comprehensive modernization of Zollverein in the interwar period can also be seen as a programmatic statement that the economic elites of the country were intent on making Germany the greatest economic nation in Europe again. The buildings surrounding the newly built shaft XII have been compared to an industrial Versailles[36] (Fig. 15.10).

The symmetry of the buildings surrounding the honor court, from where the gaze goes to the mighty Doppelbockfoerdertum of the shaft, makes the visitor humble, and the red-brick functionalism of the Bauhaus

[36] Wolfgang Ebert, *Kathedralen der Arbeit: historische Industriearchitektur in Deutschland* (Berlin: Wasmuth, 1996), p. 143.

design, built by architects Fritz Schupp and Martin Kremmer adds a magic of its own to the experience of the visitor.[37]

When the mine closed in 1986, it was declared an industrial monument and it became one of the lead projects of the IBA in 1989. Its transformation followed the principle of preservation through re-use of the buildings of the mine. Thus, the Compressor Hall was transformed into a restaurant, the Kasino, in 1996. Also in 1996 a former engine house became home to the Phaenomania which seeks to familiarize visitors with the world of the sciences.[38] The former boiler house that had been transformed by British architect Norman Foster has housed the Design Centre NRW (Red Dot Design Museum) after 1997.[39] The former pithead baths have been transformed into the Performing Arts Centre NRW (PACT Zollverein), which opened its doors in 2002.[40] In 1999 Zollverein became the central anchor point of the Route of Industrial Heritage. The cokery that had closed in 1993 was quickly integrated into the ensemble. The exhibition 'Sonne, Mond und Sterne' (Sun, Moon and Stars') curated by Ulrich Borsdorf made the cokery accessible to the public for the first time. The exhibition was part and parcel of the presentation of the final results of the IBA in 1999/2000 and it was seen by more than 300,000 visitors. It was an exhibition about energy and like the Ruhr museum itself it focused on the natural history and the cultural history of energy. It already worked with light installations, in this case a light installation of artist Peter Erskine.[41] It was the first of a long series of temporary exhibitions by the Ruhr museum staging the past of the region in hugely impressive ways. The museum has thus been shaping the mindscape of the region to a considerable extent. Zollverein also became a regular venue for concerts. In winter it offers an ice-skating rink the length of the entire cokery and in summer it offers an outdoor swimming pool (Figs. 15.11 and 15.12).

[37] Angela Schwarz, *Industriekultur, Image, Identität: die Zeche Zollverein und der Wandel in den Köpfen* (Essen: Klartext, 2008).

[38] https://www.erfahrungsfeld.de/ [accessed 28 August 2019].

[39] https://www.red-dot-design-museum.org/ [accessed 28 August 2019].

[40] https://www.pact-zollverein.de/ [accessed 29 August 2019].

[41] See the review of the exhibition: https://www.hsozkult.de/exhibitionreview/id/rezausstellungen-79 [accessed 2 December 2018].

Fig. 15.11 The ice-skating rink at the Zollverein site ©Stiftung Zollverein

Fig. 15.12 The swimming pool at the Zollverein site ©Stiftung Zollverein

The Zollverein site has been declared an UNESCO world heritage site in 2001. On 100 hectares, the visitors, like in the Landschaftspark Duisburg-Nord, experience a lot of industrial nature. It is not surprising that in 2017 Zollverein was one of the three major sites in Essen hosting the 'Green Capital of Europe – Essen 2017' project. The Ruhr museum at Zollverein is home of the Portal of Industrial Heritage—showcasing the development and depth as well as breadth of the industrial heritage landscape of the Ruhr. There is a monument trail at Zollverein, for which there are a range of guided tours available all year round, on which the visitor is introduced to the different parts of the mine that are still standing as well as to those monuments that have been added since the mine closed in 1986. Thus, for example, the sculptor Ulrich Rückriem had his workshop at Zollverein between 1992 and 1997. During the document 9 in 1992 he showed his works on site and left some of his sculptures that can today be visited, including his monumental 'Castell' sculpture (Fig. 15.13).

Fig. 15.13 Night of Industrial Heritage ©Ulrich von Born, Funke Foto Services

Zollverein is one of the key sites of the annual Night of Industrial Heritage, celebrated across the Ruhr region at many industrial heritage sites and attracting hundreds of thousands of visitors every year.[42] The Foundation Zollverein promotes 12 event locations at the Zollverein site on 18,000 square meters that can be hired for anything, ranging from academic conferences to private parties and business celebrations. In 2017 Zollverein was awarded the Event Location Award 2017 which, since 2010, awards its prize to the best event locations in Germany.

After it had been declared a world heritage site in 2001, Dutch architect Rem Koolhaas began developing the site according to a master plan that was to transform the 100 hectares into a lively location for culture and for new businesses. Between 2011 and 2017 around 1.5 million tourists visited Zollverein every year.[43] Around two-thirds of the visitors come from outside of the Ruhr region. The site has been attracting major investments, such as a 50 million Euro investment by the entrepreneur Reinhard Müller, who is, starting in 2018, building a business incubator for start-up companies on site—the idea would provide 2000 new jobs in the region—largely for highly qualified academics coming from the major universities in the area, which today already count around 300,000 students.[44] One of the many projects that are looking to be realized here is the transformation of one of the cooling towers at Zollverein into the world's biggest algae bio-reactor producing algae needed in the food, cosmetics, pharmaceutical and animal feed industries.[45] It chimes well with the 'Gründerfonds Ruhr', which is also going to be located at the Zollverein site.[46] Initiated by a conglomerate of powerful industrialists in the region, the Initiativkreis Ruhr,[47] it is meant to support new

[42] https://www.extraschicht.de/home/ [accessed 29 August 2019].

[43] Stiftung Zollverein, 'Das UNESCO-Welterbe Zollverein', press report, May 2018, https://www.zollverein.de/app/uploads/2018/05/180504_Basis_PM_lang_deutsch.pdf [accessed 29 August 2019].

[44] 'Investor will 2000 neue Jobs auf Zollverein schaffen', in *Westdeutsche Allgemeine Zeitung*, 10 October 2018, https://www.waz.de/staedte/essen/berliner-investor-kuendigt-2000-neue-jobs-auf-zollverein-an-id215527627.html [accessed 29 August 2019].

[45] https://www.stiftungen.org/aktuelles/blog-beitraege/symbol-fuer-den-wandel.html [accessed 29 August 2019].

[46] https://gruenderfonds-ruhr.com/ [accessed 29 August 2019].

[47] https://i-r.de/ [accessed 29 August 2019].

business ventures in the Ruhr. The major mining company that has overseen the winding down of the coal industry in the Ruhr, the RAG, has moved to the Zollverein site in 2018, as has the RAG-Foundation. The latter is responsible for looking after the so-called eternal costs ('Ewigkeitskosten') of mining, i.e. the costs associated with the aftermath of mining, such as continuously pumping water and managing water underground as well as looking after ongoing mining-related subsidence damages. Its budget at present is so big that it can also afford to finance generously various projects to do with the heritage of coal in the region.[48] The RAG Montanimmobilien, referred to above, has been at the Zollverein site for some time and will, in the years to come, continue its mission of preparing former mining sites for re-use in a way that is both profitable and takes care of preserving the mining heritage in the region. The Foundation Zollverein, founded in 1998 by the city of Essen and the Land NRW, has the central task of developing and promoting the UNESCO world heritage site.[49]

Conclusion

Zollverein is frequently described as 'jewel', 'crown' or 'cathedral' of industrial heritage in the Ruhr. Yet this spectacularly successful example of the re-use of 100 hectares of a former mine and cokery is only the tip of a huge iceberg of industrial heritage in the Ruhr with hundreds of locations of various sizes and forms. Zollverein is also a good example of how industrial heritage in the Ruhr has been contributing to the structural transformation of one of the foremost regions of heavy industry. Today, the site employs around 10,000 people—when the mine closed in 1986, it employed 6000.[50] The figures speak of successful transformation in terms of employment, but the kind of work has changed beyond recognition. Most of the 10,000 people who know work on the Zollverein site are university-trained or/and have jobs in office work and in the cultural sector. But the value of industrial heritage does ultimately not

[48] https://www.rag-stiftung.de/ [accessed 29 August 2019].

[49] https://www.zollverein.de/ueber-zollverein/stiftung-zollverein/ [accessed 2 December 2018].

[50] Guido M. Hartmann, 'Ein Weltkulturerbe als Jobmotor', in *Die Welt*, 11 June 2018, https://www.welt.de/regionales/nrw/article177206390/Das-Weltkulturerbe-Zollverein-in-Essen-schafft-Jobs.html [accessed 29 August 2019].

lie in the new jobs it creates. Here new industries that have moved to the Ruhr, other sectors, such as the chemical industry, as well as the booming university sector have been far more important. The true value of industrial heritage is two-fold: first of all it has become a magnet for tourists. Millions of them visit the Ruhr every year meaning that the tourism industry is becoming increasingly important for the region.[51]

Next to tourism, industrial heritage is also providing the region with a recognizable brand that does not only attract outside visitors but also provides internal cohesion. The region as a region only emerged with the onset of heavy industry around coal and steel. With the disappearance of coal in 2018 and the likely disappearance of steel within the foreseeable future, what is to prevent the disappearance of the entire region. The Western part of the Ruhr is part of the Rhineland while the eastern part is part of Westfalia, two regions of Germany with much deeper roots in history than the Ruhr. In the northern parts of the Ruhr one is looking toward the Münsterland, and in the southern parts one feels almost part of the Bergische Land. What keeps the region together after coal and steel is the memorialization of its industrial past and a sense that the region has been shaped in its mentality and its outlook by the phase in history between roughly the middle of the nineteenth and the end of the twentieth century. The impressive landscapes of industrial heritage are powerful reminders of a historically grown region. But what precisely is going to be remembered and how is this memory shaping the programe for the future? These are intensely political questions which are worthwhile fighting over—among democrats and using democratic processes and structures. I personally would favor a memorial landscape that is a reminder of the permanent need to embed capitalism in a morally responsible framework that benefits not the few but the many; a memorial landscape that celebrates the solidarity and fighting spirit of ordinary people who fought, often against the odds, for a more self-determined future; a memorial landscape that has learnt the lessons of sustainability and living in harmony with nature rather than pursuing a self-destructive race for profit; a memorial landscape that celebrates a multi-cultural region that was formed by successive waves of migration and struggled

[51] Frank Preuβ, '8 Millionen Übernachtungen: Revier wird Touristenmagnet', in *Westdeutsche Allgemeine Zeitung*, 29 January 2019, https://www.waz.de/region/rhein-und-ruhr/immer-mehr-touristen-kommen-ins-ruhrgebiet-id216313599.html [accessed 29 August 2019].

(and continues to struggle) to find ways of cohabiting and coalescing; a memorial landscape that is highly self-reflexive and open-ended in its discussions of what meanings it generates and what future it intends to build on which construction of the past. This is a vision that will not be shared by everyone in the Ruhr. Hence, it is a vision that will have to struggle to win political support among a majority of the people living in the Ruhr.

References

Berger, Stefan, Das Ruhrgebiet im internationalen Vergleich, in Farrenkopf, Michael, Goch, Stefan and Rasch, Manfred (eds.), Die Stadt der Städte: Das Ruhrgebiet und seine Umbrüche (Essen: Klartext, 2019), pp. 571–576.

Berger, Stefan, Industrial Heritage and the Ambiguities of Nostalgia for an Industrial Past in the Ruhr Valley in Germany, in Labor: Studies in Working-Class History 16:1 (2019), pp. 37–64.

Berger, Stefan, Borsdorf, Uli and Nellen, Dieter, Eine nationale Aufgabe. Das industrielle Erbe an Rhein und Ruhr, in Politik und Kultur 4 (2015), 34–36.

Berger, Stefan, Borsdorf, Ulrich, Grütter, Heinrich Theodor and Nellen, Dieter (eds.), Zeit – Räume – Ruhr: die Erinnerungsorte des Ruhrgebiets (Essen: Klartext, 2019).

Berger, Stefan, Golombek, Jana and Wicke, Christian, A Post-industrial Mindscape? The Mainstreaming and Touristification of Industrial Heritage in the Ruhr, in Wicke, Christian, Berger, Stefan and Golombek, Jana (eds.), Industrial Heritage and Regional Identity (London: Routledge, 2018), pp. 74–94.

Borsdorf, Ulrich and Grütter, Heinrich Theodor (eds.), Ruhr Museum. Natur –Kultur – Geschichte (Essen: Klartext, 2010).

Bundesministerium für Verkehr, Innovation und Technologie, https://nachhaltigwirtschaften.at/resources/hdz_pdf/events/20150831_staedtebauliche_exkursion_am_alm-_bot_ham_endbericht.pdf?m=1469661506 [accessed 28 August 2019].

Cornelissen, Christoph, Der lange Weg zur historischen Identität: Geschichtspolitik in Nordrhein-Westfalen seit 1946, in Schlemmer, Thomas and Woller, Hans (eds.), Bayern im Bund 3: Politik und Kultur im föderativen Staat, 1949-1973 (Munich: Oldenbourg, 2004), pp. 411–484.

Ebert, Wolfgang, Kathedralen der Arbeit: historische Industriearchitektur in Deutschland (Berlin: Wasmuth, 1996).

Eiringhaus, Pia, Industrie wird Natur – postindustrielle Repräsentationen von Region und Umwelt im Ruhrgebiet (Bochum: Institut für soziale Bewegungen, 2018).

Essen 2017, Ein Jahr grüne Hauptstadt Europas – Essen 2017, https://media.essen.de/media/wwwessende/aemter/0115_1/gruene_hauptstadt_5/180803_GHE_0336_Dokumentation_22x27_96dpi.pdf [accessed 28 August 2019].

Esser, Josef and Väth, Werner, Overcoming the Steel Crisis in the Federal Republic of Germany. 1975–1983, in Mény, Yves and Wright, Vincent (eds.), The Politics of Steel: Western Europe and the Steel Industry in the Crisis Years (1978–1984) (Berlin: de Gruyter, 1987), pp. 623–691.

Farrenkopf, Michael, Wiederaufstieg und Niedergang des Bergbaus in der Bundesrepublik, in Ziegler, Dieter (ed.), Geschichte des deutschen Bergbaus, Vol. 4 Rohstoffgewinnung im Strukturwandel: der deutsche Bergbau im 20. Jahrhundert (Essen: Klartext, 2013), pp. 183–280.

Flick, Holger, Sonne, Mond und Sterne. Kultur und Natur der Energie, https://www.hsozkult.de/exhibitionreview/id/rezausstellungen-79 [accessed 2 December 2018].

Goch, Stefan, Eine Region im Kampf mit dem Strukturwandel: Bewältigung von Strukturwandel und Strukturpolitik im Ruhrgebiet (Essen: Klartext, 2002).

Günther, Janne and Günther, Roland, Sprechende Straßen in Eisenheim: Konzepte und Texte sämtlicher Tafeln in der ältesten Siedlung (1846/1901) im Ruhrgebiet (Essen: Klartext, 1999).

Hartmann, Guido M., Ein Weltkulturerbe als Jobmotor, in Die Welt, 11 June 2018, https://www.welt.de/regionales/nrw/article177206390/Das-Weltkulturerbe-Zollverein-in-Essen-schafft-Jobs.html [accessed 29 August 2019].

Herberhold, Gregor, Strahlender, farbenfroher, in Westdeutsche Allgemeine Zeitung, 4 May 2010, see: https://www.waz.de/staedte/duisburg/nord/strahlender-farbenfroher-id3500184.html [accessed 2 December 2018].

Kilper, Heiderose, Die Internationale Bauausstellung Emscher Park: eine Studie zur Steuerungsproblematik komplexer Erneuerungsprozesse in einer alten Industrieregion (Wiesbaden: Springer, 1999).

Mittags, Jürgen and Oerters, Kathrin, Kreativwirtschaft und Kulturhauptstadt: Katalysatoren urbaner Entwicklung in altindustriellen Ballungsregionen, in Quenzel, Gudrun (ed.), Entwicklungsfaktor Kultur: Studien zum kulturellen und ökonomischen Potential der europäischen Stadt (Bielefeld: Transcript, 2009), pp. 61–94.

Moore, Rowan, 'The Ten Best Parks', in The Guardian, 7 August 2015, https://www.theguardian.com/culture/2015/aug/07/10-best-parks-urban-greenspaces-high-line-new-york-hampstead-london-park-guell-barcelona [accessed 28 August 2019].

Nonn, Christoph, Die Ruhrbergbaukrise: Entindustrialisierung und Politik. 1958–1969 (Göttingen: Vandenhoeck & Ruprecht, 2001).

Pachaly, Christina, Kulturhauptstadt Europas Ruhr 2010: ein Festival als Instrument der Stadtentwicklung (Berlin: Universitätsverlag der TU Berlin, 2010).

Parent, Thomas, Das Ruhrgebiet: vom 'goldenen' Mittelalter zur Industriekultur (Cologne: Dumont, 2000).

Preuβ, Frank, 8 Millionen Übernachtungen: Revier wird Touristenmagnet, in Westdeutsche Allgemeine Zeitung, 29 January 2019, https://www.waz.de/region/rhein-und-ruhr/immer-mehr-touristen-kommen-ins-ruhrgebiet-id216313599.html [accessed 29 August 2019].

Rahner, Stefan and Schmidtmann, Peter, Gasometer Oberhausen: Geschichte – Technik – Arbeit (Essen: Klartext, 2007).

Rothberg, Michael, Multi-directional Memory: Remembering the Holocaust in the Age of Decolonization (Stanford: Stanford University Press, 2009).

Schwarz, Angela, Industriekultur, Image, Identität: die Zeche Zollverein und der Wandel in den Köpfen (Essen: Klartext, 2008).

Stiftung Zollverein, 'Das UNESCO-Welterbe Zollverein', press report, May 2018, https://www.zollverein.de/app/uploads/2018/05/180504_Basis_PM_lang_deutsch.pdf [accessed 29 August 2019].

White, Hayden, The Practical Past (Evanston, IL: Northwestern Press, 2014).

Winkels, Ralf and Zieling, Günter, Landschaftspark Duisburg-Nord: vom Eisenkochtopf zum Erlebnispark (Duisburg: Mercator-Verlag, 2009).

CHAPTER 16

Reusing Former Industrial Areas in the North-West of Italy

Anna Moro

Introduction

Before describing some of the main current and past approaches, and before taking a glance at the potential future openness in the varied discussion of reusing former industrial areas in the North-West of Italy, I will clarify some of the constituents of this contribution. There are three main keywords at the center of the discourse that will be developed here. The first is the "North-West region", the area of analysis proposed in the book. This concept employs a non-administrative boundary that has been used in previous research, generally considering Piedmont, Liguria, Valle d'Aosta and Lombardy, for their leading economic role within Italy and also for the similar trend in these areas during their phase of deindustrialization. Even if we have to declare a great non-homogeneity from different perspectives, for instance, when looking at the European

A. Moro (✉)
DAStU—Politecnico di Milano, Milan, Italy
e-mail: anna.moro@polimi.it

S. Berger et al. (eds.), *Deindustrialisation in Twentieth-Century Europe*, Palgrave Studies in the History of Social Movements,
https://doi.org/10.1007/978-3-030-89631-7_16

Community Altas,[1] we found it useful to advance our reflection at this scale, considering the role of heritage within the urban regeneration. The second term is the "former industrial areas", which restrict the domain of the investigation to a very specific, yet enormous stretch of land and number of settlements. Since the focus is on heritage sites, I will try to specify the typology of heritage we are dealing with in greater detail. Is it all to be considered one coherent category or shall we make some distinctions? Through the analysis of some known cases, I will question policies and projects recently defined to both historical or architecturally qualitative-recognized heritage areas, and to more ordinary former productive landscape. Then, I will address the "reuse" of buildings or urban structures. This term, the third, is here understood as a matter of re-functionalization and rebirth, where the focus is not on the activity or the style of restoration itself, but foremost on the process of regeneration which certainly influence the meanings and values of some of the players mentioned.

The text is hence structured into three main parts. The first one focuses on the phenomenon of *deindustrialization* analyzed for its quantitative impact on the macro-region,[2] examining simultaneous trends in other economic sectors and developments in the production of services as well, whose growth is in inverse proportion to the shrinking of the manufacturing sector. The chapter provides a mapping of the phenomenon that underscores the usefulness and significance of the geographical frame and scale adopted in the book, the North-West Italian Region. The second part deals with the issues of *reuse in the macro-region*, selecting best and worst practice examples as access points to singular stories. Those stories are of course rich and articulated, my point of view is specific. It is situated at the crossroads of the comprehension of the enhanced architectural and territorial value of heritage on the one hand and its role in orienting the conception of an open and comprehensive process of urban redevelopment on the other.

The examples (the stories) span a wide range of genres. They range from complete conservation and implementation of a heritage site within the core of a local cultural and economic system, to exploitation of the

[1] Espon Atlas, *Mapping European Territorial Structures and Dynamics*, November 2014, in: https://www.espon.eu-date [accessed February 2019].

[2] In the overview of data proposed next, I limit myself to the three main areas of interest, namely Lombardy, Piedmont and Liguria.

features of industrial heritage sites in favor of a specific sector (e.g. cultural and artistic production), to short-sighted actions of redevelopment in relation to the potential of heritage and finally to no action at all in disused abandoned sites still waiting for an adequate solution.

In the conclusion, I will focus on the role that heritage could play in the future through urban regeneration and the evolving meaning it is accumulating. I will conduct my reflection focusing on two dimensions:

1. the role of the imagination and the meanings associated with heritage and heritage sites, from a design standpoint;
2. the potential cultural and embedding role of heritage for a more locally rooted process of urban regeneration of neighborhoods, of a city, of an environment.

Paths of the Deindustrialization[3]

The chapter focuses on the spatial and functional distribution and transformation of the productive industrial sites in the North-West region of Italy, in the period between 1971 and 2011 with a view to providing an outline of some paths of deindustrialization as they are characterized in this specific aggregated geographic area. The North-West region is here analyzed as the combination of data about three main regions, namely Liguria, Piedmont and Lombardy, that is to say, three different, and sometimes incoherent, units. The analysis has been carried out by combining sets of data on economic activities. This data comprises employees and activities as displayed in calculations based on data from the Industry and Services Census.[4] The census provides information on the four thresholds of 1971, 1981, 1991 and 2001, including an evolving mapping of the industrial sites. For the situation in 2011, a static picture is provided, because comparison is complicated by variation in the classification employed by the database.

[3] The sections are authored in collaboration with Fabio Manfredini, LADEC Politecnico di Milano; maps are edited by Chiara Guazzi, internship at Politecnico di Milano, under the author's responsibility and designed by Elena Acerbi.

[4] Data are collected from the National Italian Census, Istituto Nazionale di statistica (ISTAT): https://www.istat.it/it/archivio [accessed June 2019].

An interesting research form by Banca d'Italia[5] can be used as a starting point. It analyzes the recent evolution of the economies of the Italian North-West, focusing on the phenomena of deindustrialization and outsourcing economy. A delay in the economic growth of the North-West, accentuated during the 2000s, in comparison with a group of European regions definable as industrially advanced, emerges as taking place in a context of structural changes. These changes are comparable in some regards to developments in other regions, but with relevant distinctions (see chart below).

> Some specificities seem to prevail and hold back the competitiveness of the North-West, like a too slow transition towards the sectors of technology-intensive manufacturing, and to high-content services knowledge. [...] The international comparison highlights the persistence of a gap concerning important factors for growth and innovation; among these, we note the reduction of the presence of large companies, the delays in the allocation of human capital, the weakness of the economic and financial situation of companies. [...] nevertheless signs of dynamism emerge, linked to some highly competitive entrepreneurial international leaders. (AAVV, 2015, p. 7) (author's translation)

We commence analysis by observing the number of employees in manufacturing in the three regions separately and in the North-West as a sum (Fig. 16.1). Then, we compare the relative loss in employees of the three regions to verify the existence of similar trends (Fig. 16.2). In the next step, we demonstrate the outstanding role of the North-West in terms of production and the very big loss in terms of employees over time (Fig. 16.3). The results are spatialized in maps (Figs. 16.5, 16.6, 16.7) where the corresponding data is given for the municipality level. To clarify the impact of deindustrialization in comparison to other increasing production sectors, we observe the well-known inversion between the manufacturing sector and the tertiary one. The tendency seems to also fittingly represent the entire macro-region of the North-West of Italy. Considering the previous data, from the peak of employees found for the manufacturing sector in 1981, we studied the trend of employment for activities for the trade and production of services sectors from 1981 to

[5] AA.VV., 'Deindustrializzazione e terziarizzazione: trasformazioni strutturali nelle regioni del Nord Ovest', in *Questioni di Economia e Finanza* (Occasional papers), N. 282 (2015), Banca d'Italia.

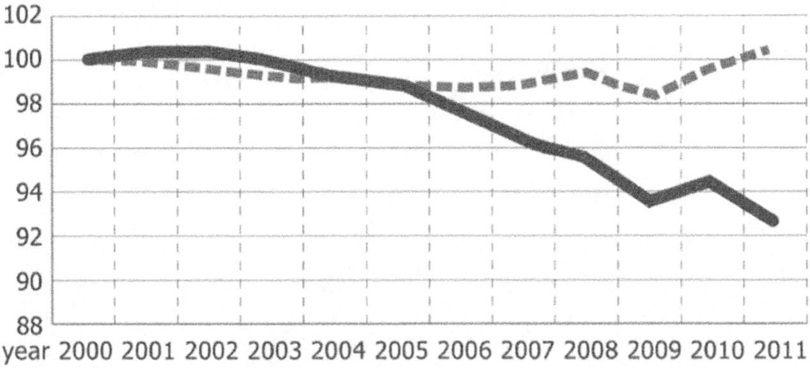

Fig. 16.1 GDP of the North-West of Italy in comparison to the average GDP of the EA12, i.e. 12 European countries (percentage values; 2000 = 100) (*Source* Eurostat Datas)[6]

2001 (Table 16.7). We can observe the growing and the declining sectors in the three different regions. Then, there will be a short comparison with 2011 data on commerce and the wider category of the "Production of Services", which indicates the same trend of growth (Table 16.8). Finally, there will be one further comparison: the decrease in manufacturing services is compared to trends in commerce and services, expressing a general trend of "substitution" of economic sectors in the North-West region. This phenomenon, however, is mostly due to the strong growth in those sectors in Lombardy. By comparison, growth is lower for Piedmont and there is a decline in manufacturing in Liguria. From 2001 to 2011, the tendency is similar, a part of Liguria is then growing, as well (see Table 16.8 again). The last map (Fig. 16.8) shows this variation in the growth of services and commerce from a geographical perspective.

The following chart shows the number of employees in manufacturing (D) in the North-West area of Italy. The decrease in the sector is compared to the growing total number of employees in all the other sectors. In *dark gray* there is the number of employees in manufacturing, in *light gray* the other areas of production are displayed (Fig. 16.2 and Tables 16.1 and 16.2).

In addition to the manufacturing sector (D), the other productive sectors considered are: Agriculture, hunting and forestry (A); Fishing

[6] The chart, extrapolated from the same source (AA.VV., 2015), p. 14, has been redrawn by the author.

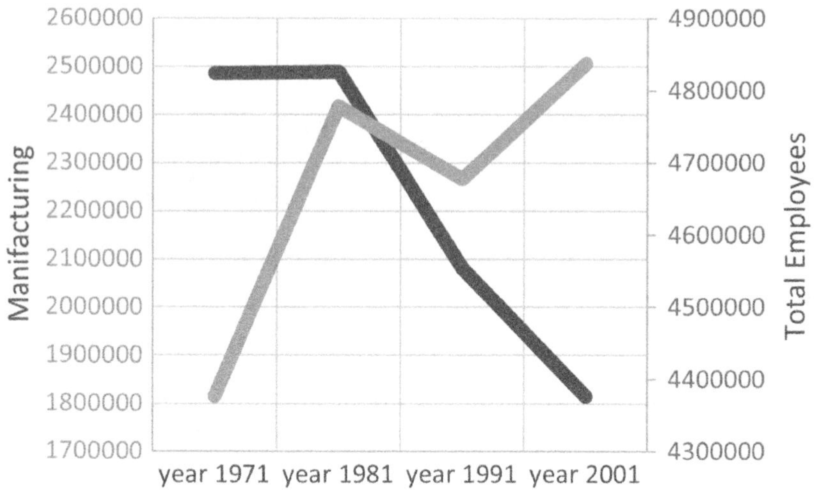

Fig. 16.2 Number of employees in the manufacturing sector and number of employees in all sectors

Table 16.1 Number of employees in manufacture (sector D)

	1971	*1981*	*1991*	*2001*	*2011**
North-West	2,485,853	2,489,268	2,081,078	1,814,332	1,405,882
Liguria	145,949	141,453	97,789	78,066	65,342
Lombardy	1,568,580	1,595,115	1,381,057	1,219,729	946,722
Piedmont	771,324	752,700	602,232	516,537	393,818
Other regions	2,615,765	3,339,194	3,131,252	3,081,546	2,481,872
Italy	5,101,618	5,828,462	5,212,330	4,895,878	3,887,754

*In 2011, the categories of the database were redefined and many sectors and subcategories were added. In this respect, the comparison between specific sectors in 2001 and 2011 can create unclear results. We can nevertheless compare the total sum of employees in the different economic sectors with due differentiation to gain an interesting overview about manufacturing, confirming the tendency from previous decades

and related services (B); Mineral extraction (C); Production and distribution of electricity, gas and water (D); Construction (E); Wholesale and retail trade (F); repair of motor vehicles, motorcycles and personal and household properties (G); Hotels and restaurants (H); Transport, storage and communications (I); Monetary and financial intermediation (J); Real estate activities, rental, IT, research, other professional and

Table 16.2 Number of employees in all sectors (A–Q)

	1971	*1981*	*1991*	*2001*	*2011**
North-West	4,376,525	4,778,451	4,676,731	4,837,238	5,309,734
Liguria	437,309	456,661	399,255	387,593	458,897
Lombardy	2,647,722	2,944,698	2,985,904	3,149,959	3,496,393
Piedmont	1,291,494	1,377,092	1,291,572	1,299,686	1,354,444
Other regions	6,701,230	8,608,440	9,073,130	9,661,119	11,114,352
Italy	11,077,755	13,386,891	13,749,861	14,498,357	16,424,086

*In 2011, the categories of the database were redefined and many sectors and subcategories were added. In this respect, the comparison between specific sectors in 2001 and 2011 can create unclear results. We can nevertheless compare the total sum of employees in the different economic sectors with due differentiation to gain an interesting overview about manufacturing, confirming the tendency from previous decades

entrepreneurial activities (K); Public administration and defense, compulsory social insurance (L); Education (M); Health and social services (N); Other public, social and personal services (O); Household services for families and cohabitation (P); Extraterritorial organizations (Q).

Here, the comparison between the three regions shows the higher relative variation in economic decrease in Liguria when compared to Piedmont and Lombardy.

The charts show the impact of the North-West overall in relation with the rest of the country (Fig. 16.4 and Tables 16.5 and 16.6).

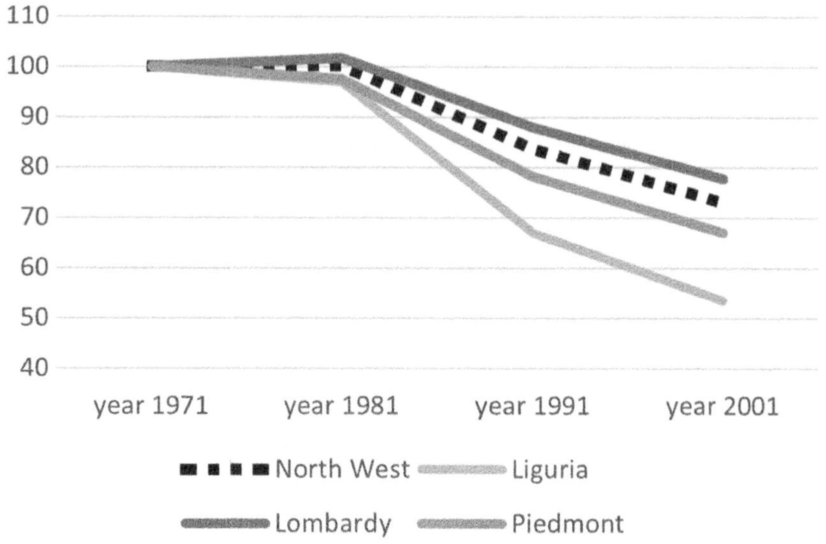

Fig. 16.3 Variation of employees in the manufacturing sector (D) and variation of employees in all sectors (the value of 1971 is made to 100)

Table 16.3 Number of employees in sector D

	1971	*1981*	*1991*	*2001*
North-West	100	1,001,373,774	8,371,685,695	7,298,629,485
Liguria	100	9,691,947,187	6,700,217,199	5,348,854,737
Lombardy	100	1,016,916,574	8,804,504,711	7,776,007,599
Piedmont	100	9,758,545,047	7,807,769,498	6,696,757,783
Other regions	100	1,276,564,982	1,197,069,309	1,178,066,837
Italy	100	1,142,473,231	102,170,135	9,596,716,179

Table 16.4 Number of employees in all sectors

	1971	*1981*	*1991*	*2001*
North-West	100	1,091,836,788	1,068,594,604	1,105,269,135
Liguria	100	1,044,252,462	9,129,814,388	8,863,137,964
Lombardy	100	1,112,162,833	1,127,725,645	1,189,686,455
Piedmont	100	1,066,278,279	1,000,060,395	1,006,343,041
Other regions	100	128,460,596	1,353,949,947	1,441,693,391
Italy	100	1,208,448,011	1,241,213,676	1,308,781,156

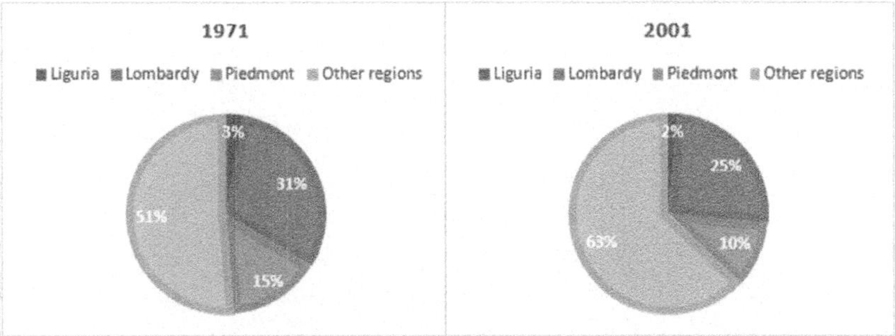

Fig. 16.4 Variation of employees in the manufacturing sector (D)

Table 16.5 Variation of employees in the manufacturing sector (D)

	1971–1981	*1981–1991*	*1991–2001*	*1971–2001*
North-West	3415	−408,190	−266,746	−671,521
Liguria	−4496	−43,664	−19,723	−67,883
Lombardy	26,535	−214,058	−161,328	−348,851
Piedmont	−18,624	−150,468	−85,695	−254,787
Other regions	723,429	−207,942	−49,706	465,781
Italy	726,844	−616,132	−316,452	−205,740

Table 16.6 Variation of employees in the manufacturing sector (D) (in %)

	1971–1981	*1981–1991*	*1991–2001*	*1971–2001*
North-West	0.14	16.40	−12.82	−27.0
Liguria	−3.08	30.87	−20.17	46.5
Lombardy	1.69	13.42	−11.68	22.2
Piedmont	−2.41	−19.99	14.23	33.0
Other regions	27.66	6.23	1.59	17.8
Italy	14.25	−10.57	6.07	4.0

Maps

Numbers of employers in the manufacturing sector in 1971 and 2001 for the three regions

The map shows the concentration in 1971 of manufacturing in the three regional capital cities. From light color (low) to dark (high) (Fig. 16.5).

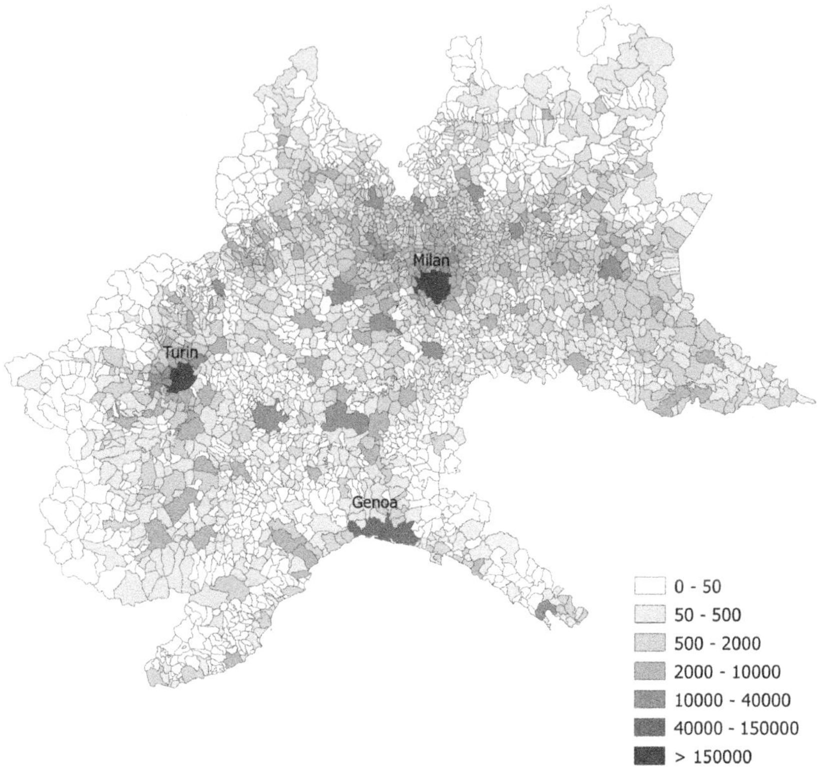

Fig. 16.5 (Map 1971)

Milan and Turin are the darkest and Genoa has the second most employees.

In 2001, the deindustrialization process produced a great loss, which was to continue throughout the next decade. The map shows the continuous leading role of the capital cities, but the urban regions around them also emerge strongly. Medium cities like Brescia are competitive, creating a more diffused and polycentric landscape (Fig. 16.6).

From light gray to dark gray, this map shows which municipalities lose the most employees, small black dots indicate gains in employees (Fig. 16.7).

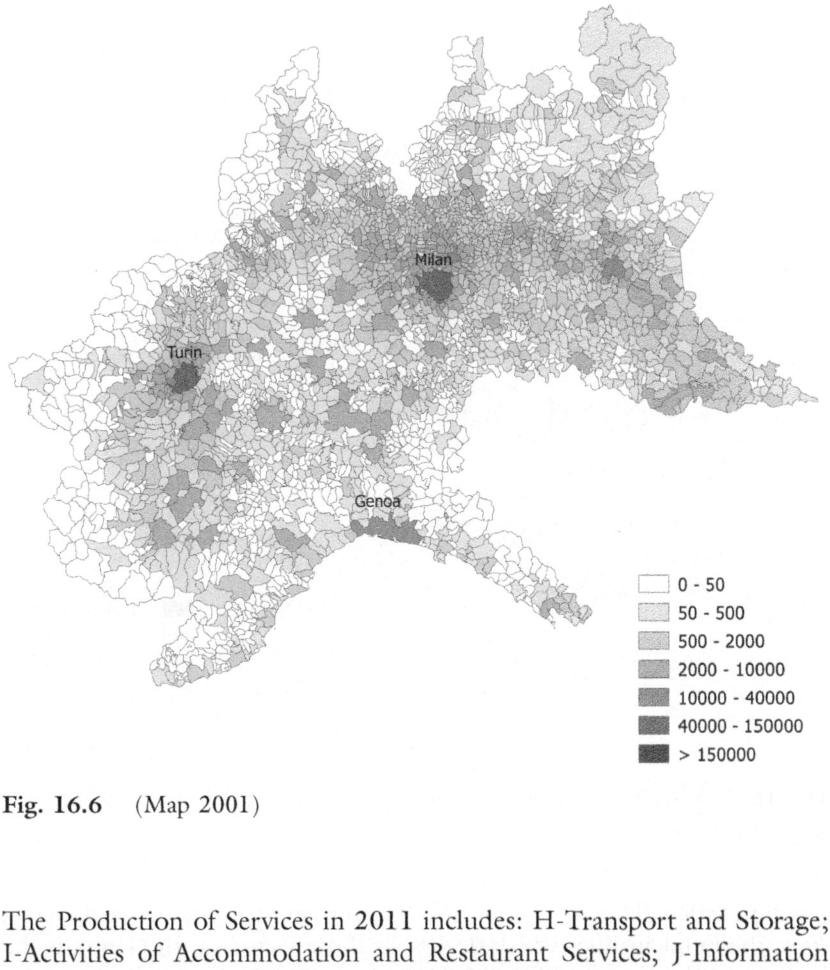

Fig. 16.6 (Map 2001)

The Production of Services in 2011 includes: H-Transport and Storage; I-Activities of Accommodation and Restaurant Services; J-Information and Communication Services; K-Financial and Insurance Activities; L-Real Estate Activities; M-Professional, Scientific and Technical Activities; N-Rental, Travel Agencies, Business Support Services; O-Public Administration and Defense, Compulsory Social Insurance; P-Education; Q-Humanity and Social Assistance; R-Artistic, Sports and Entertainment Activities; S-Other Service Activities (Table 16.8).

In *gray*, from dark to light, the strongest-growing municipalities, showing the prime position of Milan followed by Turin, but also other

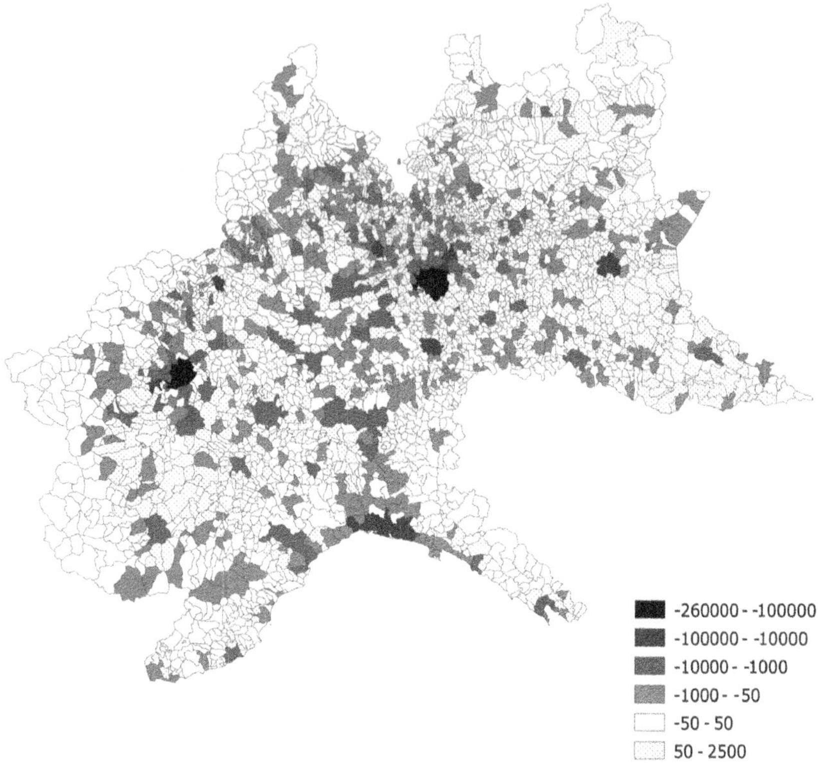

Fig. 16.7 Variation of number of employers in the manufacturing sector—for the three regions

medium cities. This map confirms the polycentric system. In *diagonal lines,* the municipalities which decline in those sectors, with Genoa as the least successful location (Fig. 16.8).

Table 16.7 Variation of employee numbers in commerce and production of services from 1981 to 2001

	Commerce	*Hotels and restaurants*	*Transport, storage and communications*	*Monetary and financial intermediation*	*Real estate activities, rental, IT, research, other professional and entrepreneurial activities*	*Education*	*Other public, social and personal services*	***Total production of services***	***Total commerce and services***
	G	*H*	*I*	*J*	*K*	*M*	*O*		
	1981–2001	*1981–2001*	*1981–2001*	*1981–2001*	*1981–2001*	*1981–2001*	*1981–2001*	***1981–2001***	***1981–2001***
North-West	15,589	52,876	20,692	50,384	475,862	−566	29,860	629,108	**644,697**
Liguria	−19,752	−1624	−23,057	4019	26,857	−57	1159	7297	**−12,455**
Lombardy	43,708	39,693	41,625	36,658	330,948	−430	24,555	473,049	**516,757**
Piedmont	−8367	14,807	2124	9707	118,057	−79	4146	148,762	**140,395**
Other regions	44,929	148,329	24,299	97,799	736,238	−866	83,304	1,089,103	**1,134,032**
Italy	60,518	201,205	44,991	148,183	1,212,100	−1432	113,164	1,718,211	**1,778,729**

Table 16.8 Employees and variation in commerce and in the production of services in 2001 and 2011

	Commerce G 2001	*Commerce G 2011*	***Variation in commerce G 2001–2011***	*Production of services 2001*	*Production of services 2011**	***Variation in production of services 2001–2011***	***Variation in commerce and services 2001–2011***
North-West	956,859	1,014,852	57,993	1,557,434	1,983,420	425,986	**483,979**
Liguria	98,179	98,124	−55	161,281	190,131	28,850	**28,795**
Lombardy	611,951	657,117	45,166	1,002,385	1,322,269	319,884	**365,050**
Piedmont	246,729	259,611	12,882	393,768	471,020	77,252	**90,134**
Other regions	2,197,676	2,431,134	233,458	3,104,383	4,060,920	956,537	**1,189,995**
Italy	3,154,535	3,445,986	291,451	4,661,817	6,044,340	1,382,523	**1,673,974**

The idea of reading the North-West region as a whole, very strongly solicited during the industrialization phase, is here solicited through a look at economic and employment data. These data verify continuity also during the deindustrialization phase (Table 16.9).

This coherence can be partially confirmed. The whole North-West region of Italy lost employers in the manufacturing sector during that phase, with a similar tendency for the entire region. That is to say that at a macroscale the phenomenon is quite similar for the three main regions considered. We can also observe a greater loss of employment for the local capital cities—Milan, Turin, Genoa—compared with other smaller cities, since they had been at the center of the local economic system (the industrial triangle) for decades.

The macro-region has followed a quite similar rhythm of deindustrialization, from 1971 to 2011. During these years, the decline was continuous (slowing around the '90s), and at the same time data is supporting the idea of a superposition of "two different types and seasons of de-industrialization" as described in Pichierri and Pacetti (2016).[7] The authors talk about a first season of deindustrialization dominating

[7] Those elements are described in the vast reflection recently made by Angelo Pichierri and Valentina Pacetti, 'Le ristrutturazioni industriali e il territorio: crisi, declino, metamorfosi?', in Emiliana Armano et al. (eds.): *Postfordismo e trasformazione urbana. Casi di recupero dei vuoti industriali e indicazioni per le politiche nel territorio torinese*, (Torino: Centro Stampa Regione Piemonte, 2016), pp. 27–43.

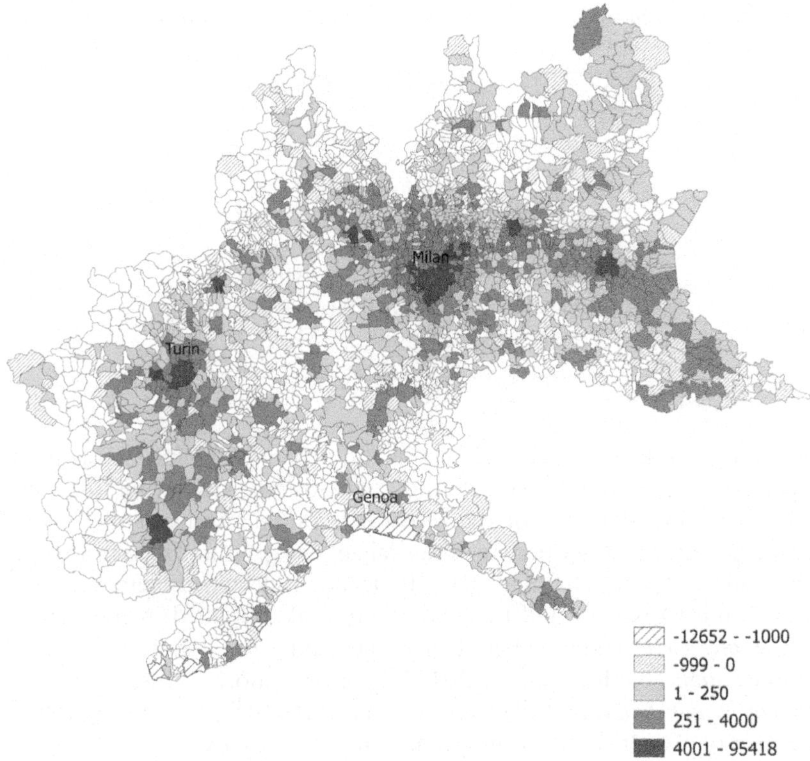

Fig. 16.8 Map—Variation of number of employers in the trade and production of services sectors—for the three regions

in the '70–'80s, when capitalism was highly industrial and deindustrialization was very selective in terms of specific products and of specific geographic areas (as had happened in the textile industry already in the '50s) and guided by policies of re-industrialization. In the second season, prevailing in the 2000s, deindustrialization was more generalized and oriented toward the transition to services and knowledge-based economy.

It has to be noted that in the whole north of Italy, from the '70s to 2000, deindustrialization was followed by a parallel decrease in urban population on the one hand, and the growth of soil urbanization on

Table 16.9 Comparison of manufacture with production of services and commerce

	Tot variation *(D)* *1981–2001*	*Tot variation* *(G) + (H − Q)* *1981–2001*
North-West	−671,521	644,697
Liguria	−67,883	−12,455
Lombardy	−348,851	516,757
Piedmont	−254,787	140,395
Other regions	465,781	1,134,032
Italy	−205,740	1,778,729

the other, producing visible effects in the urban landscape.[8] This urban expansion followed different rhythms and trends, displaying the "pluralism and diversification of the territorial configurations of the North" (ibid., p. 37) as described by the Italian Geographic Society (Società Geografica Italiana). In particular, the trends reflected the emergence of large conurbations around the capital cities, as described in the rhetoric of the *mega city region* (Hall, 1996; Hall and Pain, 1999[9]), also called *urban region* (Balducci et al., 2017[10]), or as a more diffused system of the *city-region padana* (Perulli and Picchieri, 2010[11]), all pointing toward the idea of a multicenter or polycentric urban territory.

The possibility of reading the North-West of Italy as a coherent macro-region is qualified by some relevant specificities. First, there was the

[8] The mechanisms and the outputs of this development in the Lombardy and Milan areas are analyzed from the urban and the policy-making points of view, for example in: Gabriele Pasqui and Matteo Bolocan Goldstein (eds.): *Sviluppo locale in contesti metropolitani: trasformazioni economiche e territoriali nel Milanese* (Milano: FrancoAngeli, 1988); and more recently: Andrea Arcidiacono et al., *Governare i territori della dismissione in Lombardia: caratteri, contesti, prospettive* (Santarcangelo di Romagna: Maggioli, 2015).

[9] Peter Hall, *Le città mondiali* (Milano: Il Saggiatore, 1966); Peter Hall and Kathy Pain, *The polycentric Metropolis: Learning from Mega-City Regions in Europe* (London and Sterling: EarthScan, 2006).

[10] Francesco Curci, Alessandro Balducci and Valeria Fedeli (eds.), *Post-Metropolitan Territories: Looking for a New Urbanity* (London: Routledge, 2017).

[11] Paolo Perulli and Angelo Pichierri, *La crisi italiana nel mondo globale. Economia e società nel nord* (Torino: Einaudi, 2010).

outstanding role of Milan and Lombardy during the deindustrialization phase. They saw the substitution of production with other economic sectors like an economy of services, the knowledge economy, high technology investments and mostly with the financial sector. This kind of transformation is not competitive at all with the other productive regions in Europe (Banca D'Italia, 2015), but took place, nonetheless.

The deindustrialization of Liguria is also quite outstanding. Observing the line indicating occupations in manufacturing (in chart 2 "Variation of Employees in sector Manufacturing (D) and Variation of Employees in all sectors"), we assume that the course of this line was mostly associated with the first phase of deindustrialization, with a greater loss of jobs in the '80s caused by the dismantling of very large and publicly supported enterprises. Growth in the services and tertiary sector could not offset this loss of jobs, resulting in an overall decline for the city of Genova. Piedmont and Turin are more comparable to Lombardy and Milan, but the processes of their deindustrialization are specifically interlaced with local and regional history and development.

What the above maps indicate as a specificity of the present analysis is the existence of some niches in which a productive economic landscape could be preserved. This is even the case outside the three capitals. The maps also show that some of those niches are linked to investment into production and services. This could be the case with some productive districts or some specific sites, where the industrial past merges with contemporary uses as those described in the following chapter.

Reusing Heritage

The second chapter is devoted to the reuse of former industrial sites, with a selective focus on the role of heritage in urban transformations. The analysis is not comprehensive but rather selects some main case studies, evenly distributed across the North-West area of Italy. They are representative of different typologies and scales of industrial heritage settlements, as well as of the form of reuse applied to these settlements. I propose some provisional distinctions in the approach to and in the discourse built around heritage in connection with urban regeneration. From this perspective, I was able to distinguish four main groups of cases. While the first two both deal with heritage preservation, the second two reveal a more conflicted relation between heritage and transformation of urban structures.

In the first group, I selected two main cases for which the aspect of preservation concerns large former industrial sites that are well-known and were influential. The second consists of more confined—but still quite relevant and well-known—interventions related to the re-functionalization of industrial heritage as tertiary-sector or cultural destinations. The third tries to explore a certain management approach in the reuse of former industrial sites, characterized by simplification or dissolution of varying existing value of heritage. The last group, which does not have to be considered as a category in itself but still needs to be mentioned, is a selection of the many examples of abandoned sites in the North-West. These examples provide glimpses of a much bigger phenomenon generally spread across Italy.

The identification of four groups is designed to reflect some recurring standpoints of the urban perspective toward former industrial heritage, while the real story of urban redevelopment of a site is generally a mix of the four approaches. In each of these stories, we can probably find different moments in which one of these has prevailed upon the others. So, full conservation (2.1), exploitation for innovative or cultural entrepreneurship (2.2), misidentification of heritage value and "loss of occasion" (2.3), even abandonment, partial or temporary (2.4), can be phases of one single story of the transformation of heritage sites.

Former Industrial Sites as Urban Icons

The process of deindustrialization has resulted in some very impressive and valuable sites. Most of them are the legacy of paternalistic actions by large and relevant firms operating during the last century. The reference is to the first industrial capitalistic phase in Italy, and mainly to the northern region, where the textile industry of the beginning of the century and other specific production can serve as examples of such sites. These plants were often big and relevant in their communities for a number of reasons. As a common feature, those buildings were created and developed in strong integration with the local context, this integration being strong enough to make the plant part of the overall regional history and of locals' self-identification. Here, the role of industrial production extends far beyond the factory perimeter, from a spatial and social standpoint. In such cases, in which impact on the urban settlement is strong, the owner (often a family) directed the growth of a town for personal vocation. Such an attitude generated services and housing for the workers while the industry was active. When the industries stopped operating, they were quickly transformed into cultural spaces or often into living museums displaying the machinery related to the specific production.

When heritage sites are defined (institutional) icons of past production, they are often associated to cultural tourism, with many potentially positive results for the territory and the community but also with some risks. They can stand out as untouched witnesses of past times, creating a special atmosphere, a mixture of desolation and time standing still, or rather be commercially exploited for their vernacular features. This detachment from the site's value and history can probably be seen as one of the causes of abandonment and decay. Otherwise, the process of reuse can be effectively integrated with the features of a community and the community in its turn can influence, by choices made, the development of the heritage site. It seems that whereas, at a higher level, international organizations have outlined a clear overall strategy for the role of heritage maintenance, tourism and community development,[12] the implementation of policies is then effectively only determined at the local administrative level, where municipalities, regions and private owners can make the difference, worsen negative effects or support appropriate strategies. Two relevant cases represent the category well; they are both UNESCO sites in the North-West macro-region: Olivetti in Ivrea in Piedmont, and the Crespi d'Adda Village in Lombardy.

Crespi Village[13]

The Crespi Village, declared a UNESCO World Heritage Site in 1995, is a unique case in Lombardy and a very rare one at both the national and international levels.[14] In fact, compared to similar cases, the village has maintained its urban and architectural characteristics unchanged over

[12] An important document from this perspective is the *International Cultural Tourism Charter: Managing Tourism at Places of Heritage Significance, 1999*, by the ICOMOS (International Council on Monuments and Sites), an organization linked to UNESCO.

[13] The "Crespi Village" and "Olivetti Ivrea" paragraphs are compiled through the support of Chiara Guazzi, internship at Politecnico di Milano, under the author's responsibility.

[14] For more description see: Paolo et al. (eds.), 'Governare l'evoluzione di un sistema urbano: Il sito UNESCO di Crespi d'Adda/Managing the evolution of an urban system. The UNESCO site of Crespi d'Adda', in *Techne: Journal of Technology for Architecture and Environment*, 12 (2016), pp. 52–56.

time. At the time of entering the World Heritage List, most of the inhabitants of the village were linked to the activities at the factory, which was still operating at the time. Therefore, it has to be clarified that the village has been admitted onto the list for many reasons. It represents a significant historical phase, has a special value in terms of territorial, social and industrial development and, above all, it is characterized by the ability to evolve over time, welcoming new economic cycles and new needs, always in coherence with the nature and vocations of the Crespi Village.

Some criticism is to be underlined. Today, the village does not present an emergency in terms of preservation, in the sense that the site is not abandoned or in unsafe condition but, with the loss of the perfect integration between residence and industry, the identity of the place seems to be at risk. The factories, for years in disuse, were characterized by an increasing degradation and some public buildings are currently disused. Buildings and private spaces are at risk of being changed every day by the actions with which the individual owners try to meet their needs for use, maintenance and comfort. Those critical aspects are reported by some active local associations.[15] To contribute to preservation of the characteristics of a UNESCO site, some effort has been made to draw up a management plan[16] which is meant to organize and ensure the maintenance of the sites and to open up to the community a participative process of planning that has been developed in the very recent years.[17] Also recently, a big private business company (the holding Odissea srl, owned by the Antonio Percassi Family Foundation) appears in the story of Crespi d'Adda as a new stakeholder, bringing the idea of new functions for the sites (headquarters of the company and a cultural center). The project and its application has encountered difficulties and the process slowed down many times due to conflicts with urbanistic parameters applied by the Municipality: probably the goals of the two agents are not completely

[15] One of the most active was 'Associazione Culturale Villaggio Crespi', http://www.villaggiocrespi.it/wp/salviamo-il-lavatoio/.

[16] I refer to the 'Piano di gestione del Sito Unesco di Crespi d'Adda 2014–2018', edited by Prof. Paolo Gasparoli and Stefano Della Torre, Department of Architecture Built Environment and Construction Engineering, Politecnico di Milano.

[17] The new plan for Crespi was approved in 2017, it contains the result of participatory planning oriented toward the integration of the inhabitants into the development of the site (the link to the general relation of the plan, see Chapter 2: https://www.halleyweb.com/c016051/zf/index.php/trasparenza/index/index/categoria/251/page/4 [accessed April 2019]).

Fig. 16.9 Villaggio Crespi, contemporary aeral views, Ph. Mario Donadoni

aligned yet and the process has not produced the expected results so far (Figs. 16.9 and 16.10).

Ivrea Olivetti

The second example is the Olivetti complex, an urban architectural area that already is home to the Olivetti factory located in Ivrea.[18] The first nucleus was built in 1896 by Camillo Olivetti and the subsequent extensions were carried out by his son Adriano Olivetti, who called upon architects such as Luigi Figini and Gino Pollini. The industrial city of Ivrea as we know it was built between 1930 and 1960 by Adriano Olivetti. The architectural and urban heritage is a legacy that the factory left to the city, covering 70% of the urban area with a "catalogue" of extraordinary quality residential blocks, industrial and social constructions. The city can therefore be defined as the result of multiple intellectual efforts aimed at

[18] For more details see: Patrizia Bonifazio and Paolo Scrivano, *Olivetti Builds: Modern Architecture in Ivrea* (Milan: Skira, 2001).

Fig. 16.10 Villaggio Crespi, contemporary aeral views, detail, Ph. Mario Donadoni

achieving Adriano Olivetti's socio-cultural idea, namely collecting around Ivrea the best urban planners and architects of the time to collaborate with him. Since the end of World War II, the famous welfare model designed by Olivetti, who can be defined an enlightened entrepreneur with the ambition to innovate production and to assist workers in all aspects of life, stands out for its industrial projects based on the principle that corporate profit must be reinvested for the benefit of the community. He managed to create a new factory experience, where workers lived in better conditions: higher wages, kindergartens and housing near the factory and advantages for employees. Even within the factory, the environment was different: during breaks, employees could use libraries, listen to concerts and there was no clear division between engineers and workers so that knowledge and skills could be available to everyone. The company also welcomed artists, writers, designers and poets: in the developed approach, the factory not only needed technicians but also people who could enrich work with creativity and sensitivity. The exceptional features of the site, the life inside of it and the kind of culture developed, were at the center of the candidacy as a UNESCO site. This application was begun by the Municipality and realized with a large panel of actors,[19] and accepted in 2018 by the Committee, putting Ivrea among the 54 UNESCO World Heritage sites in Italy.

> Ivrea città industriale del XX secolo' (Ivrea, industrial city of the XX century) is not a company town because it was not developed ex novo according to a univocal city-factory system, but is rather grafted on the urban fabric, by integrating it in a 30 year timeframe.

Today there is no notable issue in the conservation of the site, since the Municipality and the private owner are strongly oriented toward the preservation of the original values as defined in the Management Plan, updated in 2017, outlining a number of short and longer-term actions for protection, conservation and documentation. Nevertheless, more than 40% of the former industrial buildings "are vacant or underused, and there are short-term needs for maintenance strategies"[20] (Figs. 16.11 and 16.12).

The Contemporary Cultural Reinvention of the Heritage Site

The second category analyzed is the one represented by the transformation of large, often private, plants into cultural spaces, open to the public, or innovation oriented entrepreneurial spaces. Recursive features are the reuse of existing buildings, high architectural quality in remodeling, the presence of art and artists as relevant stakeholders in the process and the reference to innovation and sustainable development rhetoric. The origin

[19] The candidacy and the further agreement are the result of the cooperation between the Ivrea Municipality, the Guelpa Foundation, the Adriano Olivetti Foundation, the National Department of "Beni e delle attività culturali e turistiche", Piedmont Region, Provincia di Torino now "Città Metropolitana" (Metropolitan City). There was also support from the national and local association of companies (Confindustria).

[20] From the Unesco website, *Ivrea, Industrial City of the 20th Century*, 2018, http://whc.unesco.org/en/list/1538 [accessed July 2019].

Fig. 16.11 Ivrea, contemporary views of the productive buildings and services, Ph Anna Moro

of this current is older, and examples are distributed all around Europe and USA[21] with similar changes of uses in Italy.[22]

[21] Exemplary works in this direction date back to the '70s: for instance, the works for Gare D'Orsay, Paris, which was turned into a modern art museum, and the Renault sull'Île Seguin Factory in Boulogne-Billancourt, also a space for contemporary art; and, at a later stage, some well-known works in the Ruhr area described in this volume, such as the Oberhausen gasometer, the London works at Tate Gallery in 2000, etc. From Amsterdam, with the Dutch West India Company warehouses along the Oude Schans canal, to Bratislava, with its central indoor market, from Lichthaus and from Packhaus in Bremen, to Halles Saint-Géry and to the Tour et Taxi complex in Brussels, from the Assan mill and the Electric and Pyrotechnic Factory in Bucharest to the tram depot in Cracow, from the hydro-electric factory in Geneva to the old Belgian Grand-Hornu iron and steel complex in the Museum der Arbeit in Hamburg to that of Roubaix hosting Le Centre des Archives du Monde du Travail within the former Motte-Bossut spinning complex, to the Gasometer in Saint Petersburg and the former salt warehouse in Tallinn, in Estonia. These are examples of a blossoming of initiatives aimed at enhancing and renewing dismantled constructions, which are often refurbished in an exemplary manner.

[22] In Italy, some famous examples can be cited from Città di Castello, Fondazione Burri, where the former drying chambers of tropical tobacco hosts a contemporary art collection

Fig. 16.12 Ivrea, contemporary views of the residential building (Talponia), Ph Anna Moro

Here the approach to heritage has often been highly aesthetical: it appeared as principally focused on the restyling of the buildings, through a mix of conservative restoration and contemporary-style elements. This is evident in some relevant cases in which buildings assume a new skin, the structures are preserved, following the industrial archaeological principles of conservation. What changes most are the uses and functions hosted in the heritage sites: there is strong contrast between previous and contemporary functions, i.e. they are turned into homes for masterful pieces of art, while retaining the well-known fascination of heritage locations.

dedicated to the Umbrian maestro. In Rome, in the former Montemartini power plant areas, Ostiense district, there is an important museum of archaeological finds connected to the huge machines kept inside the power plant facilities. Still in Rome, we find the pertinent artistic and museum-related use of the former stables of the Peroni industries by the contemporary art Museum of Rome (MACRO), or the reuse of the former military depot in the Flaminio district, that is partially used for hosting the activities of the new MAXXI (National Museum of twenty-first century art).

This contrast between new objects or uses and spatial features of industrial buildings is the prerogative of those transformations that exploit the "non-human scale" of buildings for exceptional functions and experiences. Contemporary art installations can fit well into that kind of space, considering the large dimensions of some masterpieces and their potential dialogue with unconventional spatiality. Or the open space left can be easily divided into smaller compartments to meet the need to accommodate offices or other services. The question here is whether or not it is economically sustainable to adhere to rules laid down by law and regulations regarding remodeling of older buildings. The answer is dependent both on the conservation status of the buildings and on the available budget. I am here suggesting the existence of a kind of stylistic trend in showcasing the scale of industrial heritage sites through very light contemporary architectural highlights[23] combined with innovative uses and functions. It seems to me that the power of this mix serves to amplify the exceptionality of the site, thereby responding to the need for visibility and recognizability of what is supposed to become a new center of activity, by means of considerable financial investment.

Prada Foundation

In this sense, one example of best practice is the renewing of a distillery (SIS, Società Italiana Spiriti) dating from the beginning of the 900s, positioned in a semi-peripheral area of Milan. It is characterized by disused structures, separated from the city center by the railway and very close to the partially abandoned huge railway yard of Porta Romana. The operation was led by the Prada Foundation—a relevant actor in the cultural and artistic landscape that has created dialogue and supported international contemporary art since the '90s. The Foundation purchased the area to turn it into a big contemporary art museum, designed by one of the most provocative and well-known international architecture offices, OMA studio, with a design based on contrasts: old and new, horizontal and vertical, large and narrow, white and black, open and closed. Surely the site is very attractive to experts, and can be for a larger public as well, due to the specificity of the regeneration itself. From an urban development perspective, the operation could be intended as a trigger for

[23] i.e. the use of white painting for the black steel infrastructure.

Fig. 16.13 Ivrea, contemporary views of a public servicein the site, Ph Anna Moro

the redevelopment of the entire area, which is accessible but still separated from other areas. At the same time, it can be seen as part of a wider strategy shared by the main institutional stakeholders[24] in town. As the larger operation, for instance, of the renewal of the seven abandoned Railway Yards in Milan that are to be redeveloped (Figs. 16.13 and 16.14).

Officine Grandi Riparazioni

"Another recent example is the Officine Grandi Riparazioni (OGR) in the center of Turin, a historical site of a rail vehicle maintenance facility established at the end of the '800s shut down at the beginning of the'

[24] The main players are the Municipality of Milan for its role as planner and decision-maker. Additionally, for being one of the owners of the land, the national railway company (FS) is relevant alongside the Lombardy Region.

Fig. 16.14 Fondazione Prada, Milan: external view, Ph Anna Moro

90s, it was abandoned until 2011, when the site was used for some initiatives related to the celebration of the 150 years of Italian Unification". In 2015, it was redeveloped as a cultural and economic hub, combining art and technological research on the same site. The operation is headed by the private non-profit owner, Foundation CRT.[25] The dimension of the operation can be traced as follows.

> With Euro 90 million for the restoration and for the regeneration of the H-shape historical and impressive building (of approximately 20,000 sqm floor space times 16 metres high throughout a total area of 35,000 sqm), the OGR are the largest investment made directly by Fondazione

[25] La CRT Foundation is a private non-profit entity born from the philanthropic activity, started in 1827, of *Cassa di Risparmio di Torino*, a well-known bank in Turin. The Foundation started to operate at the beginning of the '90s based in the city center of Turin, dealing with three topics: Art and Culture, Research and Arte e Cultura, Ricerca e Istruzione, Welfare and Territory.

> CRT in one single project, in addition to being the biggest philanthropy venture project in Europe at present, aimed at the territory's economic, cultural and innovation growth and development. The impressive regeneration works have involved local undertakings and have engaged more than 100 people, for approximately 300,000 hours of work, as a whole. Once running, the OGR will create new jobs for more than 150 positions.[26]

With this kind of reuse, redevelopment of the heritage building gave space to contemporary art and other interesting initiatives. However, it seems to me that one aspect prevails in the discourse about heritage: the fascination of industrial archaeology as an economic factor for the relaunch of investments in urban redevelopment. This has a potentially positive impact on occupation and adds value to urban areas or neighborhoods. But investment in those kinds of projects seems to be a notable economic effort and only affordable if important forces are leading the process. What is overlooked is the sum of meanings ascribed to former industrial spaces by the previously concerned community (workers, associations, families, local culture in general). This part, the historical and the cultural value of the site and of the former production, is neglected here to a degree.

Other examples of integration between local value, existing communities, art programs and new businesses around the former industrial complexes are, e.g., the emblematic case of "Citta dell'arte-Fondazione Pistoletto", in Biella in the Piedmont region. It is part of the North-West region where, in 1998, artist Michelangelo Pistoletto transformed the original textile plant into a truly interdisciplinary and creative artistic laboratory where important initiatives open to the public take place.[27]

Nevertheless, often seems that, in this category of reuse, in which the quality of architecture is high and preservation issues are urgent, the complexity of the operation and the related costs necessitated investment by large private companies or a joint private–public investment. At that point, the integration of other dimensions and values depends on the owner's vision and eventual philanthropic intention. Community-based initiatives more often play a role with minor industrial heritage, sites

[26] *Source* Official presentation of the project *Il progetto delle nuove OGR: presentazione al Teatro Carignano di Torino* at http://www.ogrtorino.it/updates/presentazione-delle-nuove-ogr-al-teatro-carignano, and http://www.fondazionecrt.it/news/07.03.2017-ogr-presentazione.html [accessed June 2019].

[27] http://www.cittadellarte.it/.

certainly not eligible for UNESCO candidacy. Here, the continuity of meaning from the past to the present can be more easily preserved, even an evolution in the uses of buildings. More on ordinary heritage sites can be found in paragraph 2.4.

The Missed Opportunity

The third group of examples can be understood as a sort of prevailing of functionalist aspects and feasibility aspects in accomplishing urban transformation, mixed with short comprehension of the inherent value and meaning associated with heritage sites. It often leads to the canceling of the heritage value or to an incomplete integration of the new functions of the buildings with the place and space. Heritage sites can thus lose their potential to be a point of material and symbolic interconnection of past and contemporary life of a place, of a city. Whether or how a site is reformed certainly depends on the circumstances in which the transformation happens but, from a "cultural" (maybe ethical, maybe political...) point of view, it can probably be understood as one of the effects of an "attitude to the making", typical of northern Italy, or better, associable to a highly performing entrepreneurship model. At the same time, the denial of the heritage value of a site and the choice of an erase-and-rebuild intervention in pleace of a conservative one, can be seen as the quickest response to honest criticism. This criticism concerns complicated italian administrative authorizations and the rise of the provisional costs associated with reuse interventions. Some examples of these attitudes, with a different story and context each time, can be fruitfully understood through one single relevant case. It is that of a former industrial area in Sesto San Giovanni, on the northern border with the municipality of Milan, where the Falck steel mill and many other important productive sites developed over time, as already described in this book.

Considering all the original production sites, it might be among Italy's largest ongoing transformation projects in Italy, with its about 2 million sqm^2 (1,500,000 qm^2 as per the Ex Falck site and 700,000 sqm^2 as per the Vulcano site). Moreover, it catches our attention since the deindustrialization phase has been very long and complex, involving many political seasons, many planners and investors, for many different ideas of development. At the moment the entire process is at a significant point: (in 2019) it is partially completed, part of the land is being reclaimed and

Fig. 16.15 Fondazione Prada, Milan: interior courtyard, Ph Anna Moro

designs for the rest have been completed. I will describe three different moments within this story of reuse to make my point (Fig. 16.15).

The Vulcano Site

The first deals with the transformation of the Vulcano site in the north of the area. This part of the site was the first to shut down production and close in 1975. The buildings were demolished to build, through a long process, a new operation: the so-called "Caltacity", from the name of the developer's family, a new residential and tertiary neighborhood. But what was built in 2000 at first stage was a large commercial mall that only kept the name of Vulcano. This phase mostly corresponds to the functional, profit maximizer approach to urban redevelopment, which only exploits the positional value of the site close to metropolitan accessibility vectors.

Nevertheless, the Municipality of Sesto San Giovanni decided to preserve one of the most relevant buildings, named Decapaggio, used for pickling iron, built in the '20s as one of the first iron foundries. Contructed in two blocks—the offices on two levels and the two lateral blocks to be used as the workers' canteen and laboratories—its distinctive trait is the semi-circular shape derived from the course of Via Trento, and the treatment of the details of the façade, which corresponds to an idea of ornament typical of industrial buildings of that time. The building stands out from other common large industrial complexes for its small scale and marked stylistic features. For the symbolic value and the architectural quality, the City Council decided to restore it and transformed it into social housing for young couples,[28] that is to say a public service. Preserving the value of the building would have corresponded to giving it a public function that answers to current needs of the community. It is very recent news that the City Council has withdrawn the restricion and permitted its demolition for high costs and a lack of need for social housing.[29] A similar story can be frequently told for other sites in Italy and in the North-West region under investigation here.

The Pasini Sale and the Decay of the Constructions

Another episode of the story of the Falck site tells of unawareness and short comprehension of the potential value of the historical memory incorporated in urban fabrics and objects. Production shut down in the rest of the compound in 1995, but the renewal of use was delayed for decades. The site's property passed from one owner to another, sometimes entangled with financial difficulty, political scandals and bribes. With the Pasini family and company, in particular, while the economic failure was soon to come, the historical machinery and most of the buildings were quickly dismantled and cut into pieces to be sold. Criticism of this choice is, e.g., to be found afterward in the application for the candidacy

[28] The project for the new social housing is by MTA Studio in Milan.

[29] The declaration appears in the newspaper, in August 2018: "*We have released the restrictions because, for us, it is pointless to spend Euro 6 million, of which Euro 3 million at the Municipality's expense, to develop mini-houses that we do not need - replies Antonio Lamiranda, Town Planning Councillor -. The aim there is to generate more services and more widespread green areas*" [author's translation], in: "Aree dismesse a Sesto San Giovanni, restano i fantasmi di cemento. Dal Decappaggio al Vulcano, i piani di riconversione industriale sono di fatto fermi al palo", in *Il Giorno*, 22. August 2018, https://www.ilgiorno.it/sesto/cronaca/aree-dismesse-sesto-san-giovanni-1.4100563 [accessed June 2019].

as a UNESCO site. One of the main difficulties probably was the discontinuation of the category in which an application would have been best suited: it has been impossible to enter neither the category of "testifying memory of the productive process", since machinery no longer exist, nor that of the "architectonic value".

The Commercial Heritage Mall

More controversial and critical than the complete demolition of buildings and memories, I may argue, could be the choice of a dissonant new functionalization of heritage constructions and sites. To build an argument on this theory, I will describe some aspects of the currently approved master plan (2018) for the whole area. Designed by the Renzo Piano Building Workshop (RPBW), with the developer and owner (Bizzi & Partners) and the Municipality, the so-called *MilanoSesto* proposes an entirly new settlement, with mixed uses, a large park and a major attractive function, the so-called *Città della Salute e della Ricerca*, a large medical research center incorporating many companies existing in the Milan metropolitan region. In the certainly very complex and rich project with many positive elements, the treatment of the former industrial heritage buildings has been a blurred objective. In making the masterplan, it could have had a more explicit role in the whole design, and could have been treated with due concern and interest: an imprecise program is easily replaced. During the process, the masterplan changed a lot, mostly in terms of quality. And one of these main changes is indeed the relocation of a multifunctional commercial center that is to be displaced from the central crossing of main axes of the site (cardo and decumano) to occupy the probably most fascinating construction, the impressive structure of the "T5 pagoda" steel furnace.[30]

There is something raw in the combination of the new planned uses and the related atmosphere with this majestic steel structure. What was happening inside of it in past times, what it represents today and also the high visibility of the T5 from the large road surrounding the area and

[30] The news in the newspaper is in: 'L'area ex Falck rinasce: un nuovo centro commerciale, multisala e una stazione alle porte di Monza. Il progetto e il rendering degli interventi, in *Milano Today*, 13 March 2018, http://www.monzatoday.it/foto/cronaca/rendering-area-falck-urbanfile/#rendering-area-falck-ubranfile-1.html [accessed June 2019].

Fig. 16.16 Ex Falck area: the mall (*Source* Rendering by Urbanfile, in https://blog.urbanfile.org/2019/05/07/milano-sesto-san-giovanni-milanosesto-siglato-laccordo/)

the outlook on the future park. A fact that produces some confusion: is that structure a new one or is it old? The touch of mimesis in the new architectonic inserts, which fill the void underneath the original structure, subtracts the necessary distance for the comprehension of the spatiality of a heritage building and discourages the comprehension of the new project as well (Fig. 16.16).

All phases of the process were led by Strategic agent led all phases of the process: the site owners (who changed over time), the Municipality, the Region, private Foundations, architects and planners with reputation. But close to them, other relevant actors and actions took place. Around the middle of the '90s, openness and public objectives fulfilled the redevelopment strategy of the site, through the principle of a quite famous City Land Use Plan by Gregotti and Cagnardi. This phase of the Falck reconversion process produced some original tools[31] for cooperation and integration of various voices, which inaugurated an open reflection about future development. But unfortunately, many initiatives in this direction

[31] Such as the Falck Observatory, the Forum for Northern Milan Development and the Northern Milan Development Agency (ASNM, Agenzia di Sviluppo Nord Milano) of which several Municipalities are members, just as the Province of Milan, the Chamber of Commerce and local companies.

did not lead to any material outcomes in terms of definitions of objectives or programs. The transformation took decades to start. In this "in-between time", a cultural grassroots set of activities took place, not organized in one general program but confluent in the same objective: the openness of the site to citizens and awareness of the hidden heritage. This perspective is shared by many initiatives of a part of the Municipality of Sesto San Giovanni, also in the context of the submitted candidature as UNESCO World Heritage Sites. The actions taken in this framework, eventually solicited and inspired by associations and researchers,[32] managed to unite the Sesto community and restore cultural values and historical memories associated with the factory, from workers' and inhabitants' point of view.[33] Consequently, the cultural dimension is addressed here through initiatives that deal with the historical dimension of the site, the heritage, and future organization of the area, but also through education, managing the relationship with pupils and students at different levels and Politecnico di Milano in particular.[34]

The Abandoned Landscape

A peripheral but essential place in the discourse about urban regeneration and heritage has to be given in this overview to a large number of abandoned, non-functional sites. A noteworthy feature of the North-West region of Italy, as in the whole country, is the large number of abandoned,

[32] Some buildings were recovered and kept for public service mission. Among these, we can find the temporary reuse of the "Bulloneria Concordia" building that was turned into MAGE by the "Temporiuso" Association, a project that combines the promotion of local heritage with new services and production, placing Sesto alongside European experiments at the forefront of the renovation of former industrial sites.

[33] Examples are: "I racconti del Villaggio Falck", a dialogue between Sestopedia (Sesto's Wikipedia) and the inhabitants of Villaggio Falck; guided tours and bicycle itineraries proposed by the Sesto San Giovanni for the UNESCO team; many workshops for children around historical values of work; some projects devoted to elderly people, like "Sette No(n)ni", recovering the workers' memories.

[34] Three semi-annual workshops (2012–2013) with students of different schools of Politecnico di Milano, in cooperation with the Renzo Piano Building Workshop and Bizzi & Parteners Development were an important occasion (that I had the opportunity to co-conduct) to study the area and the planning process from a privileged point of view.

formally industrial, military and technology plants. This vast and pervasive category is not a specific phenomenon of the North-West region,[35] but here the concentration of production probably makes it more visible.

These sites can be very large and relevant for their history, economic and urban impact, dispersed and fragmented within the urban structures, or isolated and surrounded by the natural landscape. Today, whatever their shape and scale they represent one of the biggest unsolved urban questions in the region. To look briefly at the phenomenon, analyzed in many relevant pieces of research and census, I will mention three prominent examples.

The SNIA Varedo

The first is the 50 hectares of SNIA in Varedo Lombardy—the major plant of the big production system of SNIA Viscosa scattered throughout Italy, located in the heart of the province of Monza Brianza, a few km north of Milan—an enormous abandoned site now stigmatized for improper uses, like drug dealing, prostitution and toxic waste disposal.[36] The plant was founded in 1924 by the Varedo Artificial Silk Company, was then acquired by SNIA in 1927, implementing the site as the biggest in Lombardy. Initially dedicated only to the production of viscose rayon, it began to also produce "nylon 6" in post-war period, growing to as many as 6000 employees. In 1982, the production of viscose was stopped (due to the oil crisis, competition from foreign countries, as well as the introduction of new environmental regulations), while production of nylon continued until 2003, when the entire Varedo complex closed down. Since then, it has been in a state of neglect, although clean-up operations have been underway since 2008. In 2015, there were thoughts of reuse as an Expo site but the plant was quickly abandoned in favor of other sites. The urgency of an answer about its future has become a matter of public health, mostly due to its proximity to the town center.

[35] For more case-studies and general overview on the issue, see: Cristina Bianchetti (ed.), *Territorio e produzione* (Macerata: Quodlibet, 2019).

[36] In the newspaper the site is described as unsafe, see: 'Degrado e spaccio nella ex Snia a Varedo: operatori Rai accerchiati e aggrediti', *MonzaToday*, 7 June 2019, http://www.monzatoday.it/cronaca/snia-operatori-rai-aggrediti.html [accessed June 2019].

Milanese & Azzi Cement Industry

Another impressive site, set in a remarkable landscape, is the Milanese & Azzi in Piedmont, in the evocative Monferrato area (Ozzano Monferrato) (1894–1964), where the value of industrial archaeological heritage can be easily appreciated along the Valley of Rio Fontanola. Here grew an important architectural and technical plant for the production of lime and the cement industry, which prospered between the nineteenth and twentieth centuries. The preserved building, whose origins date back to 1894, consists today of only a part of the whole plant, more precisely of six vertical cement kilns made entirely of masonry. Around 1930, natural cement began to decline in favor of artificial clinker, manufactured in rotating kilns. The factory was definitively closed down in 1964 and today is in a state of abandonment, even if its structure is not statically damaged. Being one of the best-preserved natural cement plants in Italy, the national institute for heritage (Fondo Ambiente Italiano, FAI) included it in the "Census of places to remember".[37] Even if it was recently included in the proposal for a regional industrial heritage and landscape museum project, a feasible restoration and use of the site is still to be clarified, hopefully in connection with such a remarkable landscape (Figs. 16.17 and 16.18).

The third type of abandonment is related to many urban structures, affecting and damaging large geographic areas. It can be diffused and dispersed and at a microscale, e.g., in the landscape of the northern part of Lombardy. There, the productive Brianza area with its typical production-housing binomial property[38] is affected. Or it can be shaped in productive macro lots, such as those in the Cusio and Ossola areas in

[37] FAI is the "Fondo Ambiente Italiano" (Italian Environment Fund), the site is inserted within the section "I Luoghi del Cuore-Il censimento dei luoghi italiani da non dimenticare": https://www.fondoambiente.it/luoghi/ex-stabilimento-milanese-e-azzi?ldc [accessed April 2019].

[38] The production north of Milano is described in an Italian well-known publication by Stefano Boeri, Arturo Lanzani and Edoardo Marini, *Il territorio che cambia: Ambienti, paesaggi e immagini della regione milanese* (Milano: Abitare Segesta Cataloghi, 1993) and more recently described in: Arturo Lanzani, Cristina Mattioli and Giulia Setti, 'Urbanizzazione pedemontana lombarda. Un progetto di territorio', in Cristina Bianchetti (ed.), *Territorio e produzione* (Macerata: Quodlibet, 2019).

Fig. 16.17 Front view of the abandoned site of the Milanese and Azzi Cement Industry

Piedmont.[39] The kind of settlements we deal with is often characterized by low architectural quality and, spatial and ecological dysfunctionality of the surroundings. Nevertheless, within this neglected landscape, some valuable structures can be found and potential new and interesting uses could be planned.

Beyond financial statements and management reasons, the negative legacy of past industrial production, depicted as unhealthy, unsafe, dirty, impossible to live in for bad working conditions and the current state of sites result in very strong constraints for the reuse of these areas. But some attempts of re-fuctionalization of ordinary productive landscape show an interesting potentiality at the intersection with contemporary practice, still related to work or to cultural initiatives and social programs.

[39] Interesting cases for the Piedmont region and the metropolitan area of Turin, but also for other regions, are also contained in Cristina Bianchetti (ed.), *Territorio e produzione* (Macerata: Quodlibet, 2019).

Fig. 16.18 Street-view of the abandoned site of the Milanese and Azzi Cement Industry

The Sense of Heritage Valorization in Contemporary Urban Processes

As a sort of trajectory, following the role and meaning associated with heritage, the previous chapter has depicted a gradient of its enhancement. In this increase from the most safeguarded to the least, principally relevant cases were taken into account, for they are probably part of the dominant discourse about the reuse of heritage within the transformation of the city. From this perspective, I will consider a potentially more effective and just role of the heritage dimension within urban culture.[40] I will try to suggest matching some crucial elements described so far.

First, I want to refocus on the abundance of undeveloped industrial sites particularly those with potential, despite their at times advanced problematic state. For these cases, specific solutions could probably, in

[40] The framework of this reflection is close to the relation between heritage and regional or local identity as developed in: Stefan Berger, Jana Golombek and Christian Wicke (eds.), *Industrial Heritage and Regional Identities* (London: Routledge, 2018).

active contexts close to urban systems or linkable to valuable natural environments, match the need of local communities. Thinking about the difficulties in triggering redevelopment of a series of large abandoned areas, for instance, in the Milan area, together with the financial crisis and the stalling of the real estate market starting from 2008, some conditions and critical factors are recurrent. They concern the ownership of the areas, for example, an issue regarding which we observe great complexity in the range of agents involved: sometimes they are both public and private, big and small, projecting an imbalanced power and diverging objectives; or vice versa, the land is only public property and the public institutions are incapable of starting the process alone. This element, combined with the high costs related to land reclamations (in addition to the typical cost for infrastructure), raises the threshold feasibility threshold beyond difficult, if not impossible, to manage.

Moreover, from the financial and construction crisis in 2008, the attractiveness of urban sites redevelopment per se as a favorable economic investment[41] is no longer viable as it has been for decades. Former industrial areas have probably lost part of their intrinsic capacity to attract people, capital and imagination to trigger positive developments. Among the effects of this criticism, there is an overlap and continuous rewriting of forecasts and projections produced in different phases and then obsolete. For some areas (I can tell for the Milan context, but could easily expand the perspective to Turin and Genoa), this has happened so often that local authorities for some time lost part of their ability to generate new visions for the future. Such developments can considerably impact public opinion and companies' willingness to invest. Nevertheless, some big operations in the North-West region occurred recently. They can be understood as strategies of resistance of an old model supported by "the special occasion". The transformations are set into motion when an eccentric special occasion arises. Those can be for instance:

1. the entry of a foreign operator into the process of negotiating future plans, an agent that only has a financial role and objectives (think, e.g. about foreign investors as Emirates that became the sponsor

[41] The equation was based on the fact that the incomes of real estate development, controlled through density (high-rise buildings), could pay for infrastructure, services and quality.

of many urban redevelopment projects in the North-West region, financing especially large operations);
2. exceptional supra-local functions (as, e.g. the "Città della Salute e Ricerca" in Sesto San Giovanni as described in paragraph 2.3),
3. international events, primers of wider redevelopments and investments in a city or region (I am referring to the Winter Olympic Games in Turin in 2006 or the International Expo Milan 2015),
4. or finally the reduction of the impact of rules (Moro and Tosoni, 2019[42]). But this happens just in some very special cases.

A quite different, but still relevant, resource is already available to public decision-makers. Besides the scarcity of public material resources and lack of imagery, a new attitude is taking the floor. Public urban policies are learning and profitably interacting with the activism of our contemporary society, with a remarkable response in some areas of the North-West region.[43] Here, a number of smaller initiatives and proposals—dispersed over the territory analyzed so far—present other forms of remodeling heritage and unused open spaces in general. This wave of reappropriation is catching the attention of political and entrepreneurial stakeholders. It is the case of many more minor renovations and temporary activities, carried out by local civic society in associations, artists and start-ups, supported by foundations, private companies and municipalities. They have a certain lesser impact in terms of financial resources and of the caliber of the initiatives, but they are very precious because they can tell what the right function, player and atmosphere of a renewed site might be. Since they are

[42] Anna Moro and Ilaria Tosoni, 'Strategie di allineamento e micro azioni per lo spazio pubblico. Riflessioni intorno a luoghi emblematici in attesa dell'area milanese', in AA. VV., *Atti della XXI Conferenza Nazionale SIU: CONFINI, MOVIMENTI, LUOGHI. Politiche e progetti per città e territori in transizione, Firenze 6–8 giugno 2018* (Rome and Milan: Planum Publisher, 2019).

[43] Some references for new policies of cooperation can be seen in the new season of pacts and agreement on the public sphere adopted by the Municipality of Milan. Among them those for the shared gardens, cooperation alliances on public spaces ("Patto di collaborazione"), which have led to the definition of a general large agreement ("Regolamento dei Beni comuni") in 2018. Other regions and cities (Bologna as the first one in Italy) like Piedmont have collected a large number of agreements in line with the cooperation pacts, for a general overview see: 'Rapporto 2017 sull'amministrazione condivisa dei beni comuni', by Labsus, https://www.labsus.org/wp-content/themes/Labsus/media/Rapporto_Labsus_2017.pdf-date [accesses August 2019].

locally based, they have the privilege of being networked with a powerful net of relations. Since they are not moving a large amount of capital, they can further develop if conceived as experiments, tests to be repeated and perfected. Many studies on contemporary urban development are looking with interest into this set of best practices, and there are numerous public conferences and debates on them.[44]

To experiment with the role played by the renewal of heritage sites within a community, interlaced with a broader net of players, preferably conceiving the entire operation as a process of continuous co-design, could sound like part of a parallel narrative besides the one told by general renewal policies as described in the previous paragraphs. And potential alliances and agreements between significant stakeholders (foundations, companies, etc.) and local actors (new entrepreneurs) could be formed. Establishing a culture and conscience of remembrance of industrial heritage and the values inscribed into it could be central for future developments in the mentioned regions.

Some failures in large industrial site transformations are also partially ascribable to a lack of immersion into and intention to connect with the social and historical tissue. Thinking again about Sesto San Giovanni, for instance, a parallel path/process to the one of the big master plan is followed by essential initiatives (by the Municipality and associations) and should be better and bravely integrated. The issue of what a vast heritage building can host and will become in the future (for any site and so especially for the Italian Stalingrad, as Sesto San Giovanni is called) should be considered as a central factor, a driving decision that affects the entire masterplan, not one to be made afterward when occasions arise. It is something the community should pay attention to.

It is around public functions, symbols of public life, that collective values and memories could be better integrated with any future site redevelopment. And for some former industrial sites, the enhancement of heritage could add a few powerful ingredients: the link to the constructive idea of an active space dedicated to work and the link with the past, that is to say, the dimension of time, through memory. Close to those

[44] The program "Recycle Italy" (2015–2017) is a national research endeavor addressing the issue of abandonment and reuse that is widespread in the entire Italian territory, https://recycleitaly.net/- [accessed June 2019].

concepts is the one of nostalgia (as developed in Berger, 2019[45]), which may be used effectively to understand the potential role that heritage actively plays as an initiator of developments and processes. The result could be the activation of hybrid spaces in contemporary cities. Hubs, where interlacing synergies between local entrepreneurial, artistic, social and cultural activism and bigger functions and institutions could emerge as experimental new alliances.

A full Complete integration of the co-creation approach as a means of rethinking strategies for the development of urban design processes for heritage sites is a potentially rich path to follow. From this point of view, the focus on everyday life would be a minor but nonetheless significant dimension to better link redevelopment to the local context and produce effects in terms of livability and reappropriation of space. Today, it is an important aspect which does not fully fall within the definition of urban regeneration strategies. Understanding the design object and the proximity to one's daily experience (and need) allows non-experts to approach the project dimension more effectively. Therefore, a connection between redevelopment processes with the practices of use, not only for public or open spaces but also for housing, services and above all work, is crucial to the success of the regeneration effort. This means, for example, early attention to synergies with end-users of facilities and spaces, designing strategies tailored to real or potential subjects and companies.

This approach could, in the end, help manage the frequent conflict that could emerge between different stakeholders (local citizens, local economic agents, institutions, big firms, etc.) regarding the development of abandoned heritage areas, as such an approach would help display diverse objectives or scenarios. This could be a way for the two currently parallel discourses around former industrial heritage to intertwine profitably with each other.

References

Arcidiacono, Andrea et al., Governare i territori della dismissione in Lombardia: caratteri, contesti, prospettive (Santarcangelo die Romagna: Maggiolo, 2015).

[45] Stefan Berger, 'Industrial Heritage and the Ambiguities of Nostalgia for an Industrial Past in the Ruhr Valley, Germany', in *Labor: Studies in Working-Class History* 16/1 (2019).

Berger, Stefan, Industrial Heritage and the Ambiguities of Nostalgia for an Industrial Past in the Ruhr Valley, Germany, in Labor: Studies in Working-Class History 16:1 (2019), pp. 37–64

Berger, Stefan et al. (eds.), Industrial Heritage and Regional Identities (London: Routledge, 2018).

Bianchetti, Christina (ed.), Territorio e produzione (Macerata: Quodlibet, 2019).

Boeri, Stefano et al., Il territorio che cambia: Ambienti, paessagi e immagini della regione Milanese (Milano: Abitare Segesta Cataloghi, 1993).

Bonifazio, Patrizia and Scrivano, Paolo, Olivetti Builds: Modern Architecture in Ivrea (Milan: Skira, 2001).

Borgarino, Maria Paola et al., Governare l'evoluzione di un sistema urbano: Il sito UNESCO di Crespi d'Adda/Managing the evolution of an urban system, in: Techne: Journal of Technology for Architecturee and Enviroment 12 (2016), pp. 52–56.

Curci, Francesco, Balducci, Alessandro and Fedeli, Valeria (eds.), Post-metropolian Territories: Looking for an New Urbanity (London: Routledge, 2017).

Deindustrializzazione e terziarizzazione: trasformazioni strutturali nelle regioni del Nord Ovest, in Questioni di Economia e Finanza 282 (2015), pp. 21–23.

Degrado e spaccio nella ex Snia a Varedo: operatori Rai accerchiati e aggrediti', MonzaToday, 7 June 2019, http://www.monzatoday.it/cronaca/snia-operatori-rai-aggrediti.html [accessed June 2019].

Hall, Peter, Le città mondiali (Milano: Il Saggiatore, 1966).

Hall, Peter and Pain, Kathy, The Polycentric Metropolis: Learning from Mega-Ciry Regions in Europe (London and Sterling: EarthScan, 2006).

ICOMOS, International Cultural Tourism Charter: Managing Tourism at Places of Heritage Significance, 1999.

Instituto Nazionale di statistica (ISTAT), https://www.istat.it/it/archivio [accessed June 2019].

'L'area ex Falck rinasce: un nuovo centro commerciale, multisala e una stazione alle porte di Monza. Il progetto e il rendering degli interventi, in Milano Today, 13 March 2018, http://www.monzatoday.it/foto/cronaca/rendering-area-falck-urbanfile/#rendering-area-falck-ubranfile-1.html [accessed June 2019].

Labsus, Rapporto, 2017 sull'amministrazione condivisa dei beni comuni, https://www.labsus.org/wpcontent/themes/Labsus/media/Rapporto_Labsus_2017.pdf-date [accesses August 2019].

Lanzani, Arturo et al., Urbanizzazione pedemontana lombarda. Un progetto di territorio', in Bianchetti, Cristina (ed.), Territorio e produzione (Macerata: Quodlibet, 2019), pp. 48–57.

Moro, Anna and Tosoni, Ilaria, Strategie di allineamento e micro azioni per lo spazio pubblico. Riflessioni intorno a luoghi emblematici in attesa dell'area

Milanese, in AA.VV., Atti della XXI Conferenza Nazionale SIU: CONFINI, MOVIMENTI, LUOGHI. Politiche e progetti per città e territory in transizione, Firenze 6–8 giugno 2018 (Rome and Milan: Planum Publisher, 2019).

OGR Torino, Il progetto delle nuove OGR: presentazione al Teatro Carignano di Torino, https://ogrtorino.it/updates/presentazione-delle-nuove-ogr-al-teatro-carignano [accessed June 2019].

Paolo et al. (eds.), Governare l'evoluzione di un Sistema urbano: Il sito UNESCO die Crespi d'Adda/Managing the evolution of an urban system. The UNESCO site of Crespi d'Adda, in Techne: Journal of Technology for Architecture and Environment 12 (216), pp. 52–56.

Pasqui, Gabriele and Bolocan Goldstein, Matteo (eds.), Sviluppo locale in contesti metropolitani: trasformazioni economiche e territoriali nel Milanese (Milano: FrancaAngeli, 1988).

Perulli, Paolo and Pichierri, Angelo: La crisi italiana nel mondo globale. Economia esocietà nel nord (Torina: Einaudi, 2010).

Pichierri, Angelo and Pacetti, Valentina, ristrutturazioni industriali e il territorio: crisi, declino, meta- morfosi?, in Armano, Emiliana et al. (eds.), Postfordismo e trasformazione urbana. Casi di recupero dei vuoti industriali e indicazioni per le politiche nel territorio torinese (Torina: Centro Stampa Regione Piemonte, 2016), pp. 27–43.

UNESCO, Ivrea, Industrial City of the 20th Century, https://whc.unesco.org/en/list/1538 [accessed July 2019].

CHAPTER 17

Toward the Comparative and Transnational Study of Deindustrialization

Steven High

> Regions, rather than nations, might be the more useful spatial categories for historical studies of industrialization [and deindustrialization].—Christian Wicke[1]

Deindustrialization emerged as a key explanatory framework to describe the hollowing out of the industrial heartlands of North America and the United Kingdom in the 1970s and 1980s. That this idea should be popularized first in English was no coincidence given the extreme nature and rapidity of the process across the Anglo-Saxon world.[2] Mills and factories

[1] Christian Wicke, "Introduction: Industrial Heritage and Regional Identities," Christian Wicke, Stefan Berger and Jana Golombek, eds. *Industrial Heritage and Regional Identities*, (London: Routledge, 2018), 1.

[2] Marion Fontaine and Xavier Vigna. "La désindustrialisation, une histoire en cours." *20 & 21. Revue d'histoire* 4, 144 (2019): 2–17.

S. High (✉)
Montreal, QC, Canada
e-mail: steven.high@concordia.ca

S. Berger et al. (eds.), *Deindustrialisation in Twentieth-Century Europe*, Palgrave Studies in the History of Social Movements,
https://doi.org/10.1007/978-3-030-89631-7_17

were made to close as part of a wider restructuring of the international division of labor designed to drive down labor costs, crush unions, and increase profits.[3] There was none of the "social cushioning" (see the chapter by Stefan Goch) that we see in this volume. Industrial workers and their unions were almost entirely on their own. In the United States, for example, labor law worked against a political response, as unions accepted a token extension of health-care coverage or added severance from their departing employers in close-out agreements. Their silence was bought cheaply compared to Italy and pre-1989 West Germany.

Language is both a product of history and a structuring force that shapes how we understand the sweeping changes around us. That "Strukturwandel," translated here by Stefan Moitra as structural change or transformation, should emerge as the dominant descriptor of industrial decline in Germany, instead of deindustrialization, speaks to the ways that the state managed and softened industrial decline in the Ruhr Valley. Industrial closure in Italy's North-West was more brutal, but here too, the state offered wage replacement guarantees (a kind of redundancy fund) and early retirement to protect the standard of living of workers. These measures acted, in the memorable words of Marco Doria, as "social shock-absorbers." For this reason, perhaps, Gilda Zazzara finds that *deindustrializzazione* only entered common usage after the 2008 financial shock.[4] By that time, the country's social shock-absorbers had been largely dismantled in Italy. Ultimately, however, Doria concludes that: "irrespective of its actual contribution to significantly mitigating the crisis social costs, this redundancy fund failed to provide any solutions in terms

[3] There is of course a large scholarship. A number of regional (or nation within a nation) studies come immediately to mind, including Ewan Gibbs, *Coal Country: The Meaning and Memory of Deindustrialization in Postwar Scotland*, (London: University of London Press, 2021); Pascal Raggi, *La Désindustrialisation de la Lorraine du fer*, (Paris: Classiques Garnier, 2019); Gregory S. Wilson, *Communities Left Behind: The Area Redevelopment Administration*, (Knoxville: University of Tennessee Press, 2009); David Koistinen, *Confronting Decline: The Political Economy of Deindustrialization in Twentieth-Century New England*, (Gainesville: University Press of Florida, 2013); as well as Lloyd Rodwin and Hidehiko Sazanami, *Deindustrialization and Regional Economic Transformation: The Experience of the United States*, (Boston: Unwin Hyman, 1989).

[4] For more on deindustrialization in Italy see: Gilda Zazzara and Roberta Garruccio, "La rivoluzione deindustriale," in *PASSATO E PRESENTE* 34, 177–203; Gilda Zazzara, "Deindustrializzazione e industrial heritage. Approcci alla memoria del passato industriale." *Italia Contemporanea* 292 (2020), 117–143; and Roberta Garruccio, "Chiedi alla ruggine. Studi e storiografia della deindstrializzazione." *Meridiana* 85 (2016), 35–60.

of industrial reconversion and growth." Both industrial regions largely deindustrialized and the social costs were, to varying degrees, passed on to the next generation.

Much of the deindustrialization scholarship remains focused on a single locality or region in isolation. The sustained inter-regional comparison offered in this volume reminds us that deindustrialization and its politics unfolded differently across time and space. In doing so, this volume challenges the normalization of any single economic or political trajectory. To be sure, the histories of the Ruhr Valley and the industrial triangle of North-West Italy shared much in common. Both deindustrialized in large part but neither one saw the regional stigmatization experienced elsewhere. After all, America's industrial Midwest turned into the Rust Belt during these years.[5] My own work has shown how the rusting image of the US industrial heartland was part of a wider geography of rise and decline in that country. The booming US Sunbelt in the Southern United States emerged at the same time as the declining Rust Belt. Regional identities are therefore constructed relationally. "Social and spatial changes were interwoven," radical geographer Doreen Massey once explained.[6] I suspect that the Italy's South and Germany's unified East, already stigmatized, helped to bolster the reputations of the two regions in question. Gilda Zazzara makes this point in her chapter on Italian politics, as have others elsewhere. However, in both instances, some localities—and many working-class people—were left behind and their pain submerged in a regional narrative of successful transition.

But there are also important differences between the two regions. In their introduction, the editors of this volume note that Germany's history of tripartite (state-business-union) corporatism, what they call Rhenish capitalism, offered a centralized top-down framework for managing industrial decline. To some extent, structural change thus unified heretofore divergent interests between employers and employee representatives. Importantly, Stefan Moitra notes that state managed decline in coal mining did not necessarily play out the same way in other industries such as steel-making. The timing of decline and the industry's perceived

[5] Steven High, *Industrial Sunset: The Making of North America's Rust Belt*, (Toronto: University of Toronto Press, 2003), see chapter 1 especially.

[6] Doreen Massey, *Spatial Divisions of Labour: Social Structures and the Geography of Production*, (London: Macmillan, 1984).

centrality seems to be key. By comparison, there was far more political fragmentation and division in Italy, especially in Genoa where the Communist Party was particularly strong. This resulted in political accommodation rather than consensus, and even this seemed to breakdown during the 1990s.

The rich multi-layered regional comparison that unfolds in these pages offers much to the study of deindustrialization. Most importantly, perhaps, the regional scale of analysis provides middle-ground between more macro political and economic histories and more localized experiential histories. The strength of regional identity in the Ruhr, reinforced by German federalism and the "Strukturwandel" process itself, leads the German contributors to focus effortlessly on the North Rhine-Westphalia region as a whole. This was not the case in North-West Italy, a regional label that is not in popular usage and which spans three administrative provinces, each with its own history and state actors. Its artificiality leads most of the Italian contributors to opt for single-city studies of Milan, Turin and Genoa: the three urban points in this industrial triangle. One therefore gets a much better sense of how deindustrialization unfolded differently within the region than in the Ruhr. It would have been interesting to have paired Roberta Garruccio's contribution on Sesto San Giovanni with one focusing on the tough northern fringe of the Ruhr which stands outside the regional mainstream and on the margins of the regional scholarship. As the editors and contributors recognize, a region is a historical process rather than a static thing and is therefore bound-up in the economic, political, social and cultural process that is deindustrialization.

The geographic scale of the region, however, does come with some drawbacks for those of us interested in deindustrialization and its politics. For starters, the focus on industrial heartland areas risks occluding other industrial sectors that were deemed more peripheral to the national or regional economy. There were industrial lives beyond coal, steel, automanufacturing, and ship-building. That all of these industries employed male proletarians was no coincidence. As Stefano Musso notes in his contribution, the Italian textile industry had its own industrial geography and historical timeline. That it began to deindustrialize in the 1950s, unsettles the periodization of deindustrialization offered by Gilda Zazzara in another chapter. Did the history of social consensus-building and accommodation recounted here extend to female dominated industries? To what extent did the gender division of labor structure the experience and geographic pattern of deindustrialization within these two regions? The regional case study in Italy, for example, focuses on the three major cities but what of the smaller towns and cities within the triangle itself? Zazzara's chapter points to essential differences in this regard. But if we are not careful, the focus on industrial heartland areas may serve to reify longstanding processes of invisibilization within the industrial working-class.[7] Some have also argued that the experience and politics of industrial decline play out differently in areas not primarily associated with manufacturing.[8] The industrial region casts a long shadow. There is also a political danger in fixing deindustrialization only to signature regions, as it can politically contain the problem and let central governments off the hook. Historian Jim Tomlinson has therefore sought to nationalize this history in the United Kingdom, arguing that it was not just a regional problem.[9]

But, as we see so clearly in this volume, regional comparisons offer important insights into the politics of the economic transformation underway. Both the Ruhr Valley and Italy's North-West embraced the "events city" formula[10] to renew their rusting images. Genoa (2004) and Essen (2010) were declared European Capitals of Culture and Turin hosted the Winter Olympics (2006). In the case of the two Italian cities, they used this international recognition as an opportunity to pivot away from their industrial past. Several contributors, especially Marco Doria and Sergio Scamuzzi, document how local actors rebranded Genoa as a center of art and history, centered on its old port area, and those in Turin cast their city as a center of culture and innovation instead of Italy's motor city. Regional state actors in the Ruhr Valley, by contrast, embraced the area's industrial past, and integrated it into its forward-facing—but visibly

[7] For an example in France, see: Jackie Clarke, "Closing Moulinex: Thoughts on the Visibility and Invisibility of Industrial Labour in Contemporary France," *Modern & Contemporary France* 19, 4 (2011), 443–458; and Jackie Clarke, "Afterlives of a Factory: Memory, Place and Space in Alençon," in Steven High, Lachlan MacKinnon and Andrew Perchard, eds. *The Deindustrialized World: Confronting Ruination in Post-Industrial Places*, (Vancouver: University of British Columbia Press, 2017).

[8] David Nettleingham, "Beyond the Heartlands: Deindustrialisation, Naturalisation, and the Meaning of an 'Industrial' Tradition," *British Journal of Sociology* 70, 2 (2019), 617.

[9] Jim Tomlinson, "De-industrialization: Strengths and Weaknesses as a Key Concept for Understanding Post-War British History," *Urban History* 47 (2020), 199–219.

[10] See, for example, Seamus O'Hanlon, "The Events City: Sport, Culture and the Transformation of Inner Melbourne, 1977–2006," *Urban History Review* 37, 2 (2009), 30–39.

post-industrial—vision for the region. As Christa Reicher shows here, the International Building Exhibition Emscher Park, which unfolded from 1989 until 1999, saw the development of an eighty-kilometer-long landscape park. The stunning Zollverein site, whose headframe has become an iconic monument symbolizing the new Ruhr, was named a UNESCO World Heritage site in 2001, and the Ruhr was even named European Green Capital for 2017—which would have been unthinkable a generation earlier. While much of this industrial heritage landscape stages the deindustrial sublime, the Henrichshutte museum is exceptional in so far as it centers its interpretation on the process of deindustrialization and resistance of steelworkers. Likewise, as Stefan Moitra points out, the oral history work of the German Mining Museum and other heritage actors in the region has sought to integrate the voices of ordinary workers into site interpretation and, in doing so, complicate the official heritage discourse in the Ruhr.[11]

The wider industrial heritage scholarship makes clear that this consensus narrative is not exceptional to the Ruhr. Australian historian Lucy Taksa has argued that industrial heritage interpretation has focused mainly on material objects and a depoliticized birthplace of industry narrative devoid of class conflict. Heritage, she argues, is a political process: "By discarding stories of struggles to improve working conditions, and to preserve the places in which those struggles occurred, individual workers, their trade unions, and their families are excluded from public memorializing."[12] A similar point is made by US historian Jeffrey Manuel who argued in his book *Taconite Drams* that industrial heritage in Minnesota's Iron Range "played a crucial role in depoliticizing industrial decline."[13] Too often, he argued, the heritage on display

[11] For more on the value of oral history to the study of deindustrialization and industrial heritage, see the essays in Stefan Moitra and Katarzyna Nogueira (eds.), "(Post-) Industrial Memories. Oral History and Structural Change. Special issue to *BIOS. Zeitschrift für Biographieforschung, Oral History und Lebensverlaufsanalysen* BIOS, 31: 2 (2019); and, Steven High, Lachlan Mackinnon, and Andrew Perchard, eds. *The Deindustrialized World: Confronting Ruination in Post-Industrial Places*, (Vancouver: University of British Columbia Press, 2017).

[12] Lucy Taksa, "Labor History and Public History in Australia: Allies or Uneasy Bedfellows?" *International Labor and Working Class History* 76 (2009), 99.

[13] Jeffrey T. Manuel, *Taconite Dreams: The Struggle to Sustain Mining on Minnesota's Iron Range, 1915–2000*, (Minneapolis: University of Minnesota Press, 2015), xxv. For a Scottish example, see: Arthur McIvor, "Where is Red Clydeside? Industrial Heritage,

in that region deflected wider concerns about the environment, working conditions and capitalism itself. Cathy Stanton's important work on the national historic site in Lowell, Massachusetts, goes a step further and questions the politics of the historical construction of pastness itself.[14] If hard times and oppression are located in the past and not the present in site interpretation, it can far too easily reinforce notions of societal progress that renders invisible present-day injustice and inequality. My own research in Montreal has also pointed to the ways that industrial heritage can become an agent of residential displacement as part of wider gentrification processes.[15] Intentionally or not, the symbolic recognition of working-class histories—and the cultural continuity that it promises—can serve to camouflage or even politically facilitate ongoing processes of dispossession. At the very least, it is poor compensation for a lost way of life, but it is better than the physical and cultural erasure that usually accompanies deindustrialization.

In Pia Eiringhaus's contribution to this volume, we see how "ecological renewal" was coupled with industrial heritage at the Duisburg North site of a former integrated steel mill in Germany transformed into a landscape park in the 1990s under the direction of architect Peter Latz. There is nothing like the fascinating concept of "Industrienature," or industrial nature, in the English-speaking world, except perhaps the urban rewilding movement in some cities. The paired chapter on Italy, written by Egidio Dansero et al., on the greening of Turin, examines the reterritorialization process as former industrial lands are decontaminated and then revitalized for new post-industrial uses. The greening processes has proven far more controversial in North America where it is associated with gentrification. Jennifer Foster and L. Anders Sandberg, for example, co-edited a special issue of *Local Environment* on the relationship between urban greenspace and gentrification. They argued that "green sentiments have numbed the American middle-class concern over urban industrial decline, and desensitized them to the significance of industrial physical ruins, toxic legacies

Working-Class Culture and Memory in the Glasgow Region," in Stefan Berger and C. Wicke, eds. *Constructing Industrial Pasts: Industrial Heritage Making in Britain, the West and Post-Socialist Countries*, (New York: Berghahn Press, 2019).

[14] Cathy Stanton, *The Lowell Experiment: Public History in a Postindustrial City*, (Amherst: University of Massachusetts Press, 2006).

[15] Steven High, *Deindustrializing Montreal: Entangled Histories of Race, Residence and Class*, (Montreal: McGill-Queen's University Press, forthcoming).

and the deep painful history of working people who lived and worked in these environments."[16] Hence, the "staging of greenspace" is "overtly political in determining who may rightfully inhabit rediscovered urban space."[17] New York's High-Line is but one notable example. As a North American specialist, the fact that gentrification is almost never raised in these chapters surprised me. Does this absence result from the experience of the histories of the two regions, or is it a product of the historiographical divide between deindustrialization and gentrification studies? I don't have an answer to this question, but I find it difficult to believe that these two regions were somehow immune to gentrification.

Similarly, the aestheticization of deindustrial rubble into ruin has proven more controversial in North America where a heated debate has erupted over middle-class ruin-gazing and ruin porn. Detroit is the most obvious example of the deindustrial apocalypse in North America, only worsened by "fetishized scenes" of urban decline and industrial ruins.[18] Over the years, I have written extensively about the need to shift our attention from ruins to ruination: a political process that has often left working-class communities impoverished and stigmatized.[19] The beautifully staged ruins of the Ruhr Valley therefore leave me distinctly uncomfortable, but perhaps this is the point. Simply demolishing the past as we do in Canada is even worse as it erases working-class histories altogether. But we do need to ask ourselves what is being preserved and for whom?

The rise of right-wing populism in Italy's old industrial triangle has seen the toppling of former left-wing strongholds. Even red Genoa has fallen. In her chapter in this volume, Roberta Garruccio shows the political consequences of Sesto San Giovanni resident Anis Amri purposefully driving into a crowd at a Berlin Christmas market in 2016, killing

[16] Jennifer Foster and L. Anders Sandberg, "Post-Industrial Urban Greenspace: Justice, Quality of Life and Environmental Aesthetics in Rapidly Changing Urban Environments," *Local Environment* 19, 10 (2014), 1043.

[17] Ibid., 1044.

[18] Sarah Arnold, "Urban Decay Photography and Film: Fetishism and the Apocalyptic Imagination," *Journal of Urban History* 41, 2 (2015), 326; George Steinmetz, "Drive-By Shooting: Making a Documentary about Detroit," *Michigan Quarterly Review* 45 3 (2006), 491–515.

[19] See my urban exploration chapter in Steven High, *Corporate Wasteland: The Landscape and Meaning of Deindustrialization*, (Ithaca: Cornell University Press, 2007).

twelve. Here, too, the political left was ousted from a former bastion. In this rapidly changing political environment, Gilda Zazzara argues, "trade unions are often little more than custodians of the bitter-sweet memories of 'worker centrality.'" We must be careful not to fall into the same political trap, as "smokestack nostalgia" is a political dead-end.[20] The same boiling class resentments are also evident in the former East Germany, which had little of the "social cushioning" that was in place in the Ruhr, when its industries were privatized and largely closed after reunification. A surging right-wing populism has spilled over into other parts of Germany including the northern fringe of the Ruhr, yet another reminder that this area needs more historical research.[21]

Experiencing and Managing Deindustrialization is part of a wider effort to scale-up our analysis of deindustrialization from the stand-alone locality or region. The editors have been central to this historiographic trend in recent years, organizing conferences, networks, and edited volumes such as this one.[22] Cross-regional comparisons have been the foundation of this work, bridging divides within Europe and beyond. Stefan Berger's recent edited volume, for example, brings the histories of deindustrialized Europe into conversation with industrial heritage in China and Australia.[23] Alice Mah's comparison of ruined industrial cities in the United States, Canada, the UK, and Russia is another notable

[20] Jefferson Cowie and Joseph Heathcott, eds. *Beyond the Ruins: The Meaning of Deindustrialization*, (Ithaca: Cornell University Press, 2003), introduction.

[21] For an interesting study of the contestation over regional memory in a former industrial heartland, see Marion Fontaine, "From Myth to Stigma? The Political Uses of Mining Identity in the North of France," *Labor: Studies in Working Class History* 16, 1 (2019), 65–80.

[22] Stefan Berger, Jana Golombek and Christian Wicke, eds. *Industrial Heritage and Regional Identities*, (London: Routledge, 2018); Stefan Berger, Christian Wicke and Jana Golombek, eds., "Special Issue on Deindustrialization, Heritage, and Representations of Identity," *The Public Historian* 39, 4 (2017); Stefan Berger and Steven High, eds., "(De)Industrial Heritage special issue," *Labor: Studies in Working-Class History* 16, 1 (2019); and, Stefan Berger, *Constructing Industrial Pasts: Heritage, Historical Culture and Identity in Regions Undergoing Structural Economic Transformation*, (New York: Berghahn Books, 2020).

[23] Stefan Berger, *Constructing Industrial Pasts: Heritage, Historical Culture and Identity in Regions Undergoing Structural Economic Transformation*, (London: Berghahn, 2019).

example.[24] So, too, is Jefferson Cowie's classic 1999 study of RCA as it shifted television production from one US city to another until the jobs ended up in Mexico.[25] Several scholars have recently argued that the "geographical imagination" of deindustrialization studies has remained "strikingly limited" to Western Europe and North America.[26] There is more going on, they argue, in the Global South than its presumed role as a "non-descript destination" of runaway factories. Andy Pike, among others, has called on deindustrialization scholars to expand their geographic horizons and consider the ways that this process is global.[27] To that end, we would be well served in returning to the foundational work of Doreen Massey on the changing international division of labor. She concludes that "a country's internal economic geography reflects its place in the international political economy, the international division of labour."[28] No region nor country is an economic island onto itself.

References

Arnold, Sarah, Urban Decay Photography and Film: Fetishism and the Apocalypic Imagination, in: Journal of Urban History 41:2 (2015), pp. 326–339.

Berger, Stefan, Constructing Industrial Pasts: Heritage, Historical Culture and Identity in Regions Undergoing Structural Economic Transformation (New York: Berghahn Books, 2020).

Berger, Stefan, Golombek, Jana and Wicke, Christian (eds.), Industrieal Heritage and Regional Identities (London: Routledge, 2018).

Berger, Stefan and High, Steven (eds.), (De)industrial Heritage Special Issue, in Labor: Studies in Working-Class History 16:1 (2019).

[24] Alice Mah, *Industrial Ruination, Community, and Place: Landscapes and Legacies of Urban Decline*, (Toronto: University of Toronto Press, 2012).

[25] Jefferson Cowie, *Capital Moves: RCA's Seventy-Year Quest for Cheap Labor*, (Ithaca: Cornell University Press, 1999).

[26] Seth Schindler, Tom Gillespie, Nicola Banks, et al., "Deindustrialization in Cities of the Global South," *Area Development and Policy* 5, 3 (2020), 284–285.

[27] Andy Pike, "Coping with Deindustrialization in the Global North and South," *International Journal of Urban Sciences* (2020), 15. For deindustrialization in the Americas, see: Lachlan Mackinnon and Steven High. "Deindustrialization," in Olaf Kaltmeier, Anne Tittor, Daniel Hawkins, Eleonora Rohland, eds., *The Routledge Handbook to the Political Economy and Governance of the Americas*, (London: Routledge, 2020).

[28] Doreen Massey, *Spatial Divisions of Labour: Social Structures and the Geography of Production*, (London: Macmillan, 1984), 82.

Berger, Stefan, Wicke, Christian and Golombek, Jana (eds.), Special Issue on Deindustrialization, Heritage, and Representations of Identity, in The Public Historian 39:4 (2017).

Clarke, Jackie, Closing Moulinex: Thoughts on the Visibility and Invisibility of Industrial Labour in Contemporary France, in Modern Contemporary France 19:4 (2011), pp. 443–458.

Clarke, Jackie, Afterlives of a Factory: Memory, Place and Space in Alençon, in High, Steven, MacKinnon, Lachlan and Perchard, Andrew (eds.), The Deindustrialized World: Confronting Ruination in Post-industrial Places (Vancouver: University of British Columbia Press, 2017), pp. 111–125.

Cowie, Jefferson, Capital Moves: RCA's Seventy-Year Quest for Cheap Labor (Ithaca: Cornell University Press, 1999).

Cowie, Jefferson and Heathcott, Joseph, Introduction, in Cowie, Jefferson and Heathcott, Joseph (eds.), Beyond the Ruins: The Meaning of Deindustrialization (Ithaca: Cornell University Press, 2003), pp. 1–18.

Fontaine, Marion, From Myth to Stigma? The Police Uses of Mining Identity in the North of France, in Labor: Studies in Working Class History 16:1 (2019), pp. 65–80.

Fontaine, Marion and Vigna, Xavier, La désindustrialisation, une histoire en cours, in Revue d'histoire 4:144 (2019), pp. 2–17.

Forster, Jennifer and Sandberg, Andreas L., Post-industrial Urban Greenspace: Justice, Quality of Life and Environmental Aesthetics in Rapidly Xhanging Urban Environments, in Local Environment 19:10 (2014), pp. 1043–1048.

Garruccio, Roberta, Chiedi alla ruggine. Studi e storiografia della deindustrializzazione, in Meridiana 85 (2016), pp. 35–60.

Garruccio, Roberta and Zazzara, Gilda, La rivoluzione deindustriale, in Passato e Presente 34 (2018), pp. 177–203.

Gibbs, Ewan, Coal Country: The Meaning and Memory of Deindustrialization in Postwar Scotland (London: University of London Press, 2021).

High, Steven, Industrial Sunset: The Making North America's Rust Belt (Toronto: University of Toronto Press, 2003).

High, Steven, Corporate Wasteland: The Landscape and Meaning of Deindustrialization (Ithaca: Cornell University Press, 2007).

High, Steven, Deindustrializing Montreal: Entangled Histories of Race an Class (Montreal: McGill-Queen's University Press, forthcoming).

High, Steven, Mackinnon, Lachlan and Perchard, Andrew (eds.), The Deindustrialized World: Confronting Ruination in Post-industrial Places (Vancouver: University of British Columbia Press, 2017).

Koistinen, David, Confronting Decline: The Political Economy of Deindustrialization in Twentieth-Century New England (Gainesville: University Press of Florida, 2013).

Mackinnon, Lachlan and High, Steven, Deindustrializantion, in Kaltmeier, Olaf, Tittor, Anne, Hawkins, Daniel and Rohland, Eleonora (eds.), The Routledge Handbook to the Political Economy and Governance of the Americas (London: Routledge, 2020), pp. 57–67.

Mah, Alice, Industrial Ruination, Community, and Place: Landscapes and Legacies of Urban Decline (Toronto: University of Toronto Press, 2012).

Manuel, Jeffrey T., Taconite Dreams: The Struggle to Sustain Mining on Minnesota's Iron Range, 1915-2000 (Minneapolis: University of Minnesota Press, 2015).

Massey, Dorren, Spatial Divisions of Labour: Social Structures and the Geography of Production (London: Macmillan, 1984).

McIvor, Arthur, Where Is Red Clydeside? Industrial Heritage, Working Class Culture and Memory in the Glasgow Region, in Berger, Stefan and Wicke, Christian (eds.), Constructing Industrial Pasts: Industrial Heritage Making in Britain, the West and Post-socialist Countries (New York: Berghan Press, 2019), pp. 47–67.

Moitra, Stefan and Nogueira, Katarzyna (eds.), (Post-) Industrial Memories. Oral History and Structual Change, Special issue to BIOS. Zeitschrift für Biographieforschung, Oral History und Lebensverlaufanalysen BIOS 31:2, 2019.

Nettleingham, David, Beyond the Heartlands: Deindustrialisation, Naturalisation, and the Meaning of an 'Industrial' Tradition, in British Journal of Sociology 70:2 (2019), pp. 610–626.

O'Hanlon, The Events City: Sport´, Culture and the Transformation of Inner Melbourne, 1977-2006, in Urban History Review 37:2 (2009), pp. 30–39.

Pike, Andy, Coping with Deindustrializationin in the Global North and South, in International Journal of Urban Sciences (2020), pp. 1–22.

Raggi, Pascal, La Désindustrialisation de la Lorraine du fer (Paris: Classiques Garnier, 2019).

Rodwin, Lloyd and Sazanami, Hidehiko, Deindustrialization and Regional Economic Transformation: The Experience of the United States (Boston: Urwin Hyman, 1989).

Schindler, Seth, Gillespie, Tom, Banks, Nicola et al., Deindustrialization in Cities of the Global South, in Area Development and Policy 5:3 (2020), pp. 283–304.

Stanton, Cathy: The Lowell Experiment: Public History in a Postindustrial City (Amherst: University Press of Massachusetts, 2006).

Steinmetz, George, Drive-by Shooting: Making a Documentary about Detroit, in Michigan Quarterly Review 45:3 (2006), pp. 491–515.

Taksa, Lucy, Labor History and Public History in Australia: Allies or Uneasy Bedfellows?, in International Labor and Working Class History 76 (2009), pp. 82–104.

Tomlinson, Jim, De-industrialization: Strengths and Weaknesses as a Key Concept for Understanding Post-war British History, in Urban History 47 (2020), pp. 199–219.
Wicke, Christian, Introduction: Industrial Heritage and Regional Identities, in Berger, Stefan, Golombek, Jana and Wicke, Christian (eds.), Industrial Heritage and Regional Identities (London: Routledge, 2018).
Wilsonm, Gregory S., Communities Left Behind: The Area Redevelopment Administration (Knoxville: University of Tennessee Press, 2009).
Zazzara, Gilda, Deindustrializzazione e industrial heritage. Approcci alla memoria del passato industirale, in Italia Contemporanea 292 (2020), pp. 117–143.

Index

S. Berger et al. (eds.), *Deindustrialisation in Twentieth-Century Europe*, Palgrave Studies in the History of Social Movements, https://doi.org/10.1007/978-3-030-89631-7

D

H

J

N

S

The manufacturer's authorised representative in the EU is Springer Nature Customer Service Centre GmbH, Europaplatz 3, 69115 Heidelberg, Germany. If you have any concerns regarding our products, please contact ProductSafety@springernature.com

Printed and bound by CPI Group (UK) Ltd, Croydon, CR0 4YY

22/09/2026

02221050-0001